Winnie & [handwritten]

HIDDEN® Hawaii

"A bible."
—*Honolulu Advertiser*

"The perfect choice for the visitor who wants an active
vacation in the islands."
—*Travel & Leisure*

"Paints a vivid picture of each island's history, natural wonders
and unique qualities."
—*Travel Holiday*

"Explores even deeper for the hidden places at the heart of island life."
—*American Bookseller*

"A view no travel agent can offer. Riegert's adventures are crammed with
fascinating insider's advice."
—*Los Angeles Times*

"A polished, authoritative and thoroughly enjoyable handbook
for travelers."
—*Our World*

"Unlike many guides that claim to offer inside information,
this one actually delivers."
—*Vancouver Sun*

"Offers the best of all worlds to the Hawaii visitor."
—*Dallas Morning News*

HIDDEN ®

Hawaii

Ray Riegert

NINTH EDITION

Ulysses Press
BERKELEY, CALIFORNIA

Copyright © 1979, 1982, 1985, 1987, 1989, 1991, 1993, 1994, 1996 Ray Riegert. All rights reserved, including the right to reproduce this book or portions thereof in any form whatsoever, except for use by a reviewer in connection with a review.

Published by:
ULYSSES PRESS
P.O. Box 3440
Berkeley, CA 94703-3440

Library of Congress Catalog Card Number 96-60707

ISBN 1-56975-068-8

Printed in the United States by R.R. Donnelley & Sons

30 29 28 27 26 25 24 23

EDITORIAL DIRECTOR: Leslie Henriques
MANAGING EDITOR: Claire Chun
PROJECT DIRECTOR: Lee Micheaux
COPY EDITOR: David Sweet
EDITORIAL ASSOCIATES: Lily Chou, Kenya Ratcliff,
    Deema Khorsheed, Toby Bielawski, Mark Rosen
CARTOGRAPHERS: Wendy Logsdon, Phil Gardner
COVER DESIGN: Sarah Levin
INDEXER: Sayre Van Young
COVER PHOTOGRAPHY: Front: Larry Ulrich
    Circle and back: Robert Holmes
    Color insert: Robert Holmes
ILLUSTRATOR: Jen-Ann Kirchmeier

Distributed in the United States by Publishers Group West, in Canada by Raincoast Books, and in Great Britain and Europe by World Leisure Marketing

HIDDEN is a federally registered trademark of BookPack, Inc.

The author and publisher have made every effort to ensure the accuracy of information contained in *Hidden Hawaii*, but can accept no liability for any loss, injury or inconvenience sustained by any traveler as a result of information or advice contained in this guide.

To Jim Chanin,
for years of friendship

Acknowledgments

Since this book is now entering its ninth edition, there are several generations of people to thank. The person to whom I owe the deepest gratitude has been working on the project since the very beginning. I met my wife Leslie when I first arrived in the islands to write *Hidden Hawaii*. Since then she has contributed to the book as an editor, writer, researcher and innovator. Her energy and spirit have been an inspiration throughout.

The current edition results from the efforts of several people. Claire Chun skillfully shepherded the book through many stages. Lee Micheaux worked her magic as the project director. Sayre Van Young once again lent her skill as indexer; my wife Leslie, Sarah Levin and Sara Glaser devoted their talents to the cover design; Larry Ulrich and Robert Holmes provided outstanding cover photos, with Bob Holmes also contributing all the photographs inside the book. Lily Chou, Kenya Ratcliff, Deema Khorsheed, Toby Bielawski and Mark Rosen aided and abetted with research and other matters large and small. My son Keith and daughter Alice also merit a warm note of thanks for their encouraging smiles and infectious energy.

People to whom I am indebted for prior work on *Hidden Hawaii* include Carlene Scnabel, the project coordinator for the earlier editions; Jen-Ann Kirchmeier, who contributed her boundless enthusiasm as well as a collection of marvelous drawings; Marlyn Amann and Alison McDonald, who worked on the first edition; and Ed Silberstang, who offered expert assistance above and beyond the call of friendship.

To everyone, I want to extend a *mahalo nui loa*—thank you a thousand times for your *kokua*.

What's Hidden?

At different points throughout this book, you'll find special listings marked with a hidden symbol:

◀ HIDDEN

This means that you have come upon a place off the beaten tourist track, a spot that will carry you a step closer to the local people and natural environment of Hawaii.

The goal of this guide is to lead you beyond the realm of everyday tourist facilities. While we include traditional sightseeing listings and popular attractions, we also offer alternative sights and adventure activities. Instead of filling this guide with reviews of standard hotels and chain restaurants, we concentrate on one-of-a-kind places and locally owned establishments.

Our authors seek out locales that are popular with residents but usually overlooked by visitors. Some are more hidden than others (and are marked accordingly), but all the listings in this book are intended to help you discover the true nature of Hawaii and put you on the path of adventure.

Write to us!

If in your travels you discover a spot that captures the spirit of Hawaii, or if you live in the region and have a favorite place to share, or if you just feel like expressing your views, write to us and we'll pass your note along to the author.

We can't guarantee that the author will add your personal find to the next edition, but if the writer does use the suggestion, we'll acknowledge you in the credits and send you a free autographed copy of the new edition.

ULYSSES PRESS
3286 Adeline Street, Suite 1
Berkeley, CA 94703
E-mail: ulypress@aol.com

Contents

Maps

Special Features

OUTDOOR ADVENTURE SYMBOLS

The following symbols accompany national, state and regional park listings, as well as beach descriptions throughout the text.

Camping		Waterskiing	
Hiking		Windsurfing	
Biking		Canoeing or Kayaking	
Horseback Riding		Boating	
Swimming		Boat Ramps	
Snorkeling or Scuba Diving		Fishing	
Surfing			

Preface

Hawaii. What images does the word bring to mind? Crystal blue waters against a white sand beach. Palm trees swaying in a soft ocean breeze. Volcanic mountains rising in the hazy distance. Bronzed beach boys and luscious Polynesian women. Serenity. Luxury. Paradise.

To many it conjures still another dream—the perfect vacation. There is no more beautiful hideaway than this spectacular chain of tropical islands. For over a century Hawaii has been the meeting place of East and West, a select spot among savvy travelers. These adventurers are attracted not by Hawaii's famed tourist resorts—which are usually crowded and expensive—but by the opportunity to travel naturally and at low cost to an exotic locale.

As you'll find in the following pages, it is possible to tour economically through Hawaii's major sightseeing centers. It's even easier to explore the archipelago's more secluded realms. Few people realize that most of Hawaii's land is either rural or wilderness, and there's no price tag on the countryside. You can flee the multitudes and skip the expense by heading into the islands' endless backcountry. And if you venture far enough, you'll learn the secret that lies at the heart of this book: The less money you spend, the more likely you are to discover paradise.

Quite simply, that's the double-barreled purpose of *Hidden Hawaii*—to save you dollars while leading you to paradise. Whatever you're after, you should be able to find it right here. When you want to relax amid the comforts of civilization, this book will show you good restaurants, comfortable hotels, quaint shops and intriguing nightspots.

When you're ready to depart the beaten track, *Hidden Hawaii* will guide you to untouched beaches, remote campsites, underwater grottoes and legendary fishing holes. It will take you to the Pacific's greatest surfing beaches, on hiking trails across live volcanoes, into flower-choked jungles, through desert canyons and up to the top of the world's most massive mountain.

Hidden Hawaii is a handbook for living both in town and in the wild. The first chapter covers the nuts and bolts—how to get to the islands, what to bring and what to expect when you arrive. Chapter Two prepares you for outdoor life—swimming, hiking, camping, skindiving and living off the land. The third chapter, covering Hawaii's history and language, will familiarize you with the rich tropical culture.

The last six chapters describe individual islands. Each island is divided geographically. Here you'll find specific information on sightseeing, hotels, restaurants, shops, nightspots and beaches.

This book is not intended for those tourists in plastic leis who plop down on a Waikiki beach, toast for two weeks, then claim they've seen Hawaii when all they've really seen is some bizarre kind of Pacific Disneyland. No, *Hidden Hawaii* is for adventurers: people who view a vacation not as an escape from everyday routine, but rather as an extension of the most exciting aspects of their daily lives. People who travel to faraway places to learn more about their own homes. Folks like you and me who want to sit back and relax, but also seek to experience and explore.

Ray Riegert
Honolulu, 1979

Introduction

Reading *Hidden Hawaii* brought back memories of my long and frustratingly unconsummated love affair with the islands. Throughout my childhood I listened spellbound as my father and uncles swapped tales of sun-washed beaches far across the Pacific. Like millions of other sailors and GIs, they had toured distant lands courtesy of that great travel agent, Uncle Sam. Between battles they recuperated under swaying coco palms, swilling warm beer and bartering with the natives. Stale Lucky Strikes were traded for hand-forged bolo knives and intricately carved hardwood spears. And though their travels took them far beyond "Pearl," to me the atolls, jungles and magical reefs of which they spoke all spelled Hawaii.

"Hawaii Granted Statehood," the headline ran. I folded the damp newspaper, hurled it toward my customer's front porch and pedaled angrily along my paper route. *They* had done it, by a simple stroke of an administrative pen. My dream of retiring to the islands at age fifteen gave a violent lurch. Hawaii suddenly shifted from the distant edge of the unknown Orient to just another state. The Iowa of the Pacific. Offshore California. No more need for a passport or an interpreter. No gorging on exotic mahimahi and poi—the fabled Sandwich Islands would now feed me on McBurgers and cola.

I survived the disillusionment of statehood and though, two years later, I squandered my meager savings (earmarked for passage to the islands) on a battered motorbike, the dream did not fade entirely. Friends-of-friends returned from two-week Hawaiian idylls, faces and arms tanned to an improbable richness. Wilted leis would be casually draped over lampshades and mantlepieces, a not-so-subtle reminder of their brief fling in the sun. I could only wait.

Later, the islands subverted my college career. In the storm clouds gathering above the campus, I saw the foam of a turquoise wave curling around a slender surfer. Rain-washed ivy dissolved into frangipani and bougainvillea. The neo-Gothic monstrosity of the campus library became a battered volcanic grotto, rumbling with echoes of ocean rollers. My instructors, unable to see beyond the tips of their umbrellas, rewarded my visions of paradise with neat lines of zeroes.

Flunking out of college, however, almost brought me my dream. I found myself low man on the totem pole on a disabled fishing boat, drifting helplessly across the gulf of Alaska. There seemed little promise of sunburns and coco palms in those cold, relentless waves. And then the captain took a close look at the charts.

"Well, boys, if this keeps up, we'll just head for Hawaii," he muttered. It had already been two endless weeks. Given the force of wind and current, we would hail the islands' sparkling shores within a month.

But it was just another lost chance, thwarted by an annoyingly efficient Norwegian chief engineer who dreamed of cod and boiled salmon heads rather than pineapple and passion fruit. The ancient engine coughed to life and took us north, back into the Big Grey.

Like many early explorers before me, I now took the only reasonable alternative left in my unsuccessful quest for the islands: I gave up. I went south instead, to a land where coconuts and tequila create a dream of their own. I traded my vision of a Polynesian outrigger for a ticket on the Greyhound, drawn to the irresistible warmth of a Mexican sun. Hawaii receded over the horizon.

A few years later, returning north through California, land of surprises, the dream suddenly reappeared. My partner Lorena and I were invited to a birthday luau honoring King Kamehameha, father of the islands. In the shade of a redwood forest we feasted on rich, greasy barbecued pork, delicate raw fish, tropical fruits, palm hearts and that exotic beverage, Budweiser-on-tap. Frustrated Hawaiians weaving another year's dream from Maui smoke, we lay back on soft aromatic pine needles, lulled into fantasies of graceful sea canoes, the melancholy summons of conch shell trumpets, the rhythmic sweep of the paddles . . . carrying us off to the islands.

We could resist no longer; we determined to make the big break with the mainland. Having already written a travel book on Mexico, I now had the ultimate justification. We would go to Hawaii and return with knowledge and advice to pass on to others—while also earning a royalty that would guarantee a long rest on a hidden beach. Lorena was enthusiastic; between the native herbs and tropical sunsets, she could pass many many days. The final lure was thrown to us by our publisher: the promise of an advance to finance the journey. "But only when you've finished your camping book on Mexico," he warned.

• • •

"Hey, Carl, remember the book you were going to do on Hawaii?" I held the phone in a white-knuckled grip. Publishers are notorious for their twisted humor. Surely "remember" and "were going to do" were just sad attempts to cheer me toward my deadline.

"Yeah," I answered, "I have my Hawaiian shirt on right now. The one you bought me at Goodwill. *Remember?*"

There was a short, cynical laugh.

"Well, Ray Riegert just wrote it for you. Looks like it's time to play spin-the-globe again."

I slammed the phone down. Moments later I was trudging through the dusty Mexican streets, snarling at burros and stray dogs. At least my new recipe for mai tais wouldn't be wasted!

• • •

Good travel writers must constantly walk a tightrope between telling too much and not telling enough. The lazy tourist demands to be led by the nose to a comfortable yet inexpensive hotel and from there to a tasteful, quaint café. Nothing can be left to the demons of surprise and chance. Restless natives laboring over tom-toms in the middle of the night must be courtesy of the local tourist bureau, a civic contribution to amuse the traveler, rather than an inconvenient rebellion.

And with the distance between the islands and the continental U.S. reduced to nothing more than a quick lunch and a few drinks on a passenger jet, the pressures of tourism have become enormous. Hawaii's very lure is in danger of becoming its downfall.

This has created a situation in which a responsible and imaginative writer can perform a service both to adventurers and to the places they travel to see. A sensitive and aware guidebook like *Hidden Hawaii* helps educate and, in so doing, creates sensitive and aware travelers. The vast majority of guidebooks are not actually guides but consumer directories: where to spend your money with a minimum of distraction. That type of book actually steers us away from the heart of a place and an understanding of its peoples, on to nothing more than a superficial tour of the "sights." Ray Riegert shows us a Hawaii blessed with an incredible richness of cultures, history, topography and climates.

Hidden Hawaii not only points out attractive and inexpensive alternatives in meals, lodging, entertainment and shopping, but also takes us beyond Hawaii's often overdeveloped facade: where to watch whales; how to find the best parks, trails and campsites; how to live on the beach, foraging, fishing and diving; where to go shell collecting, volcano gazing . . . a variety of information as broad as the interests of travelers who want a lot out of a trip without going bankrupt. *Hidden Hawaii* demonstrates a very encouraging trend: I like guidebooks that are starting points for my own explorations, not addictive crutches. A little help can, and should, go a long way. Travel is a creative activity, one that should enhance the traveler as well as the places and people visited.

This is a book with an underlying attitude of respect and an awareness that it is more often one's attitude, rather than physical presence, that can be destructive. The hiker's motto, "Walk softly on the earth," is just as valid to the traveler strolling the streets of Lahaina as it is to the explorer on the trails of Kauai or the hidden beaches of Molokai.

It's up to *us* to keep hidden Hawaii unspoiled and enjoyable for everyone.

Carl Franz
San Miguel de Allende, 1979

No alien land in all the world has any deep, strong charm for me but that one, no other land could so longingly and so beseechingly haunt me, sleeping and waking, through half a lifetime, as that one has done. Other things leave me, but it abides; other things change, but it remains the same. . . . In my nostrils still lives the breath of flowers that perished twenty years ago.

—*Mark Twain, 1889*

ONE

The Aloha State

Hawaii is an archipelago that stretches more than 1500 miles across the North Pacific Ocean. Composed of 132 islands, it has eight major islands, clustered at the southeastern end of the chain. Together these larger islands are about the size of Connecticut and Rhode Island combined.

Each island, in a sense, is a small continent. Volcanic mountains rise in the interior, while the coastline is fringed with coral reefs and white-sand beaches. In the parlance of the Pacific, they are "high islands," very different from the low-lying atolls found elsewhere in Polynesia.

The northeastern face of each island, buffeted by trade winds, is the wet side. The contrast between this side and the island's southwestern sector is sometimes startling. Dense rainforests in the northeast are teeming with exotic tropical plants, while across the island you're liable to see cactus growing in a barren landscape!

Deciding to take a vacation in Hawaii is easy; the hard part comes when you have to choose which islands to visit. All six are remarkably beautiful places, each with unique features to offer the traveler. Eventually, you should try to tour them all, but on a single trip you'll probably choose only one, two or three. Traveling to more in the course of a typical vacation is counterproductive.

To help you decide which to see, I'll briefly describe the key features of each. For more detailed information, you can turn to the introductory notes in each of the island chapters.

My personal favorites are the Big Island and Kauai, the easternmost and westernmost islands in the chain, and I often recommend to friends unfamiliar with Hawaii that they visit these two islands. That way they manage to travel to both ends of the chain, experiencing the youngest and most rugged, and the oldest and most lush, of all the islands. The two offer a startling contrast, one that quickly shatters any illusion that all the islands are alike.

▼▼▼▼▼▼▼▼▼▼
Where to Go

Oahu, Hawaii's most populous island, is dominated by the capital city of Honolulu. Featuring the Waikiki tourist center, this is the most heavily touristed island. It's too crowded for many visitors. But Oahu *is* a prime place to mix city living with country exploring. It's also rich in history, culture and beautiful beaches.

The island of Hawaii, or the **Big Island**, is true to its nickname. Located at the southeastern end of the Hawaiian chain, and dominated by two 13,000-foot volcanoes, this giant measures more than twice the size of all the other islands combined. It's a great place to mountain climb and explore live volcanoes, to snorkel along the sun-splashed Kona Coast, or to tour orchid farms in the verdant city of Hilo.

Maui, the second largest island, is rapidly becoming Hawaii's favorite destination for young visitors. Haleakala alone, the extraordinary crater that dominates the island, makes the "Valley Isle" worth touring. The island also sports many of Hawaii's nicest beaches and provides an offshore breeding ground for rare humpback whales.

Directly to the west, lying in Maui's wind shadow, sits the smallest and most secluded island. **Lanai** is an explorer's paradise, with a network of jeep trails leading to hidden beaches and scenic mountain ridges. There are only 2000 people and about 20 miles of paved road here. If you're seeking an idyllic retreat, this is the place.

Molokai, slightly larger but nearly as remote, provides another extraordinary hideaway. With white-sand beaches, a mountainous interior and a large population of Hawaiians, the "Friendly Isle"

◆◆◆◆◆◆◆◆◆◆◆◆◆◆◆◆◆◆◆◆◆◆◆◆

retains a unique sense of old Hawaii. Here you can visit a leper colony on the windswept Kalaupapa Peninsula, a pilgrimage that could prove to be the most inspiring of all your experiences in Hawaii.

The oldest island in the chain, **Kauai** is also Hawaii's prettiest, most luxuriant island. Located at the northwestern end of the chain, it is filled with jewel-like beaches and uninhabited valleys. Along the north shore are misty cliffs that fall precipitously to the sea; from the island's center rises a mountain that receives more rainfall than any place on earth; and along Kauai's southern flank there's a startling desert region reminiscent of the Southwest.

The island of Kauai boasts the wettest spot on earth, but its southwestern flank resembles the Arizona desert!

Only seven of the major islands are inhabited: the eighth, Kahoolawe, although sacred to Hawaiians, was used for decades as a bombing range for the U.S. Navy, then was finally turned over to the state of Hawaii in 1994. The seventh island, Niihau, is inhabited but is privately owned and off-limits to the public. So in planning your trip, you'll have six islands to choose from.

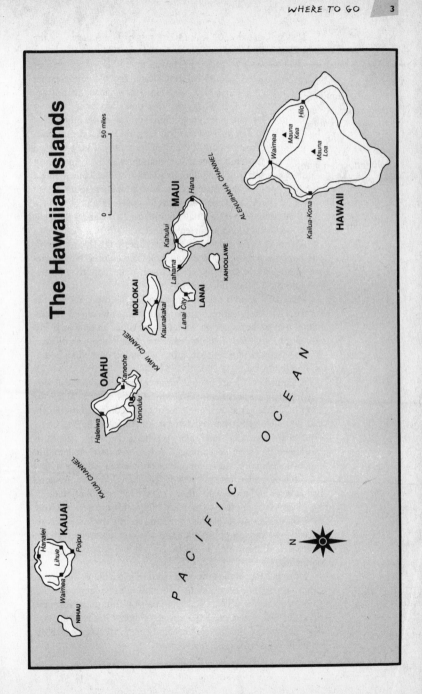

The Hawaiian Islands

50 miles

0

NIIHAU

KAUAI
Hanalei
Waimea   Lihue   Poipu

KAUAI CHANNEL

OAHU
Kaneohe
Haleiwa   Honolulu

KAIWI CHANNEL

MOLOKAI
Kaunakakai

LANAI
Lanai City

KAHOOLAWE

MAUI
Kahului   Hana
Lahaina

ALENUIHAHA CHANNEL

Waimea
Mauna Kea   Hilo
Mauna Loa

Kailua-Kona

HAWAII

PACIFIC   OCEAN

N

They're located 2500 miles southwest of Los Angeles, on the same 20th latitude as Hong Kong and Mexico City. It's two hours earlier in Hawaii than in Los Angeles, four hours before Chicago and five hours earlier than New York. Since Hawaii does not practice daylight-saving, this time difference becomes one hour greater during the summer months.

> Seeking a cooler climate? Head up to the mountains; for every thousand feet in elevation, the temperature drops about 3°. If you climb high enough on Maui or the Big Island, you might even encounter snow!

For years, sugar was king in Hawaii, the most lucrative part of the island economy. Today, tourism is number one. More than three million Americans, and over six million travelers worldwide, including a rapidly increasing contingent of Japanese tourists, visit the Aloha State every year. It's now a $10.9 billion business that expanded exponentially during the 1970s and 1980s, but has leveled off during the current decade.

With 50,729 personnel stationed in Hawaii, the U.S. military is another large industry. Concentrated on Oahu, where they control one-quarter of the land, the armed forces pour more than $3 billion into the local economy every year.

Marijuana is now Hawaii's foremost cash crop (in 1992, the Attorney General's office reported that marijuana valued at $3.4 billion was eradicated or seized, less than *half* of an estimated $10 billion industry). *Pakalolo* flourishes on Maui, Hawaii and Kauai. It's a very controversial product, one which has created an underground economy.

Of course, no Chamber of Commerce report will list the demon weed as Hawaii's prime crop. Officially, sugar is still tops. While the $245 million sugar industry is small potatoes compared to tourism and the military, Hawaii remains one of America's largest sugar-producing states. But sugar, like everything else in the islands, is threatened by urban development. A ton of water is required to produce a pound of sugar. Since the construction industry is now a 4.3 billion-dollar business, new housing developments are competing more and more with sugar cane for the precious liquid.

Pineapple is another crop that's ailing. Stiff competition from the Philippines, where labor is cheap and easily exploitable, has reduced Hawaii's pineapple plantations to a few relatively small operations. It is, however, the second leading individual crop grown on the islands.

Hawaii is one of the only places in the United States that grows coffee. The islands do a booming business in macadamia nuts, orchids, anthuriums, guava nectar and passion fruit juice. Together, these industries have created a strong economy in the 50th state. The per capita income is greater than the national average, and the standard of living is generally higher.

There are two types of seasons in Hawaii, one keyed to tourists and the other to the climate. The peak tourist seasons run from mid-December until Easter, then again from mid-June through Labor Day. Particularly around the Christmas holidays and in August, the visitors centers are crowded. Prices increase, hotel rooms and rental cars become harder to reserve, and everything moves a bit more rapidly.

If you plan to explore Hawaii during these seasons, make reservations several months in advance; actually, it's a good idea to make advance reservations whenever you visit. Without doubt, the off-season is the best time to hit the islands. Not only are hotels more readily available, but campsites and hiking trails are also less crowded.

Climatologically, the ancient Hawaiians distinguished between two seasons—*kau*, or summer, and *hooilo*, or winter. Summer extends from May to October, when the sun is overhead and the temperatures are slightly higher. Winter brings more variable winds and cooler weather.

The important rule to remember about Hawaii's beautiful weather is that it changes very little from season to season but varies dramatically from place to place. The average yearly temperature is about 75°, and during the coldest weather in January and the warmest in August, the thermometer rarely moves more than 5° or 6° in either direction. Similarly, sea water temperatures range comfortably between 74° and 80° year-round.

A key aspect to this luxurious semitropical environment is the trade wind that blows with welcome regularity from the northeast, providing a natural form of air-conditioning. When the trades stop blowing, they are sometimes replaced by *kona* winds carrying rain and humid weather from the southwest. These are most frequent in the winter, when the Hawaiian islands receive their heaviest rainfall.

While summer showers are less frequent and shorter in duration, winter storms are sometimes quite nasty. I've seen it pour for five consecutive days, until hiking trails disappeared and city streets were awash. If you visit in winter, particularly from December to March, you're risking the chance of rain.

A wonderful factor to remember through this wet weather is that if it's raining where you are, you can often simply go someplace else. And I don't mean another part of the world, or even a different island. Since the rains generally batter the northeastern sections of each island, you can usually head over to the south or west coast for warm, sunny weather.

Sometimes nasty weather engulfs the entire chain, but there's usually a sunny refuge somewhere. I once spent a strenuous period along the Kona Coast working on a suntan. Across the island near Hilo, flood warnings were up. Twenty-five inches of rain dropped in 24 hours; five feet of water fell in seven days. Toward the end of the week, when my major problem was whether the tan would peel, officials in Hilo declared a state of emergency.

CALENDAR OF EVENTS

Something else to consider in planning a visit to Hawaii is the amazing lineup of annual cultural events. For a thumbnail idea of what's happening when, check the calendar below. You might just find that special occasion to climax an already dynamic vacation.

JANUARY

During January On Maui, the Four Seasons Resort Wailea sponsors the **Celebration of Whales**, an international gathering with discussions, whale watching, entertainment and an art exhibit.

Mid-January or February The month-long **Narcissus Festival** begins with the Chinese New Year. During the weeks of festivities, there are open houses, street parties and parades in Honolulu's Chinatown.

Late January through March The Japanese community celebrates its **Cherry Blossom Festival** in Honolulu with tea ceremonies, kabuki theater presentations, martial arts demonstrations and crafts exhibits.

FEBRUARY

During February Architecture students from the University of Hawaii challenge local professionals in the annual **Sandcastle Building Contest** at Kailua Beach Park, Oahu. **Art Maui** is a month-long juried art show featuring new work by local artists.

Mid-February If weather conditions permit, the **Mauna Kea Ski Meet** is held on the 13,000-foot slopes of the Big Island volcano.

MARCH

During March On Maui, you can volunteer to help the Pacific Whale Foundation count humpbacks during the **Great Whale Count**. Athletes compete in Kauai's **Prince Kuhio Ironman/Ironwoman Canoe Race**.

Early March The **Maui Marathon** is run from the Maui Shopping Mall in Kahului to Whalers Village.

March 26 Major festivities on Kauai mark the **Prince Kuhio Festival**, commemorating the birthdate of Prince Jonah Kuhio Kalanianaole, Hawaii's first delegate to the U.S. Congress.

APRIL

Early April The **O'Neill Pro Board Windsurfing Competition** is a popular ten-day tournament that's held at Hookipa Beach Park on Maui. The weeklong **Merrie Monarch Festival** on the Big Island pays tribute to David Kalakaua, Hawaii's last king. Festivities include musical performances, pageants and a parade. Buddhist temples on all the islands mark **Buddha Day**, the luminary's birthday, with special services. Included among the events are pageants, dances and flower festivals.

During May Molokai Hula Piko marks the birth of hula on Molokai. Hula dancers, local musicians and Hawaiian craftspeople display their many talents. The **Pineapple Festival**, held in Lanai City, features contemporary Hawaiian music, pineapple cooking contests and arts and crafts. Held every weekend in May, the **50th State Fair** features agricultural exhibits, food stalls, dances, music and displays of island arts and crafts. **MAY**

May 1 Lei Day is celebrated in the islands by people wearing flower leis and colorful Hawaiian garb. In Oahu's Kapiolani Park, there are pageants and concerts.

During June In Honolulu, the music, dance and customs of more than 40 Pacific Rim areas are showcased at the annual **Festival of the Pacific**. This two-week event features performers from American Samoa, New Zealand, Guam and Hawaii. Also on Oahu, the **Hawaiian Bodysurfing Championships** are held at Point Panic on the weekend with the best surf. *Halaus* from around the world participate in Oahu's **Annual King Kamehameha Hula Competition**. On Maui, the **Kapalua Music Festival** features chamber music by internationally acclaimed artists. Staged at the Eddie Tam Center in Makawao, the **Annual Upcountry Fair** is where the 4-H crowd swings into action. Enjoy the live entertainment and local delicacies and, if you're an aspiring performer, don't miss the Star Search. **JUNE**

June 11 Kamehameha Day, honoring Hawaii's first king, is celebrated on all six islands with parades, chants, hula dances and exhibits.

June through August On Oahu and the other islands, Buddhists perform colorful **Bon Dances** every weekend to honor the dead.

During July On the Big Island, the **Hilo Orchid Society Flower Show** is a showy demonstration of tropical colors. On Maui, more than 100 different wines from California, Oregon and Washington, as well as Australia, are sampled at the **Kapalua Wine and Food Symposium**. **JULY**

Late July Hundreds of ukelele players gather at Kapiolani Park in Waikiki for the **Annual Ukelele Festival**. Akin to a county fair, the **Maui Jaycees Carnival** comes to the Maui War Memorial Sports Complex. Local entertainment, games, rides and commercial booths are part of the fun.

During August On Oahu, you can see the dramatic **Hawaii State Surfing Championships** and the **Wahine Bodyboard Champion- **AUGUST**

ships. In Honolulu, dancers six to twelve years old gather to compete in the **Queen Liliuokalani Keiki Hula Festival**. In addition to a raw onion–eating contest, **The Maui Onion Festival** features food booths, live music, a farmers market and an onion recipe contest.

August 21   Local residents celebrate **Admission Day**, the date in 1959 when Hawaii became the 50th state.

Late August   Visitors to Molokai won't want to miss the **Molokai Ranch Rodeo**, a full two-day rodeo with barbecues and live bands.

SEPTEMBER   **During September**   The six-person **Hana Relay**, a 54-mile Maui swim from Kahului to Hana, is one of autumn's more challenging events. **Maui Cycle to the Sun** is the ultimate uphill challenge: a 38-mile bike ride from the ocean to the 10,023-foot peak of Haleakala. Covering the same route is the **Haleakala Run to the Sun**.

Early September   The **Queen Liliuokalani Canoe Regatta** is staged on Oahu. Everyone keeps their eyes on Maui's **Kapalua Tennis Open Tournament**; it has Hawaii's largest tennis purse. A six-person relay across the nine-mile channel from Lanai to Kaanapali draws 50 international teams to the **Maui Channel Relay Swim**.

Mid-September   The **Hawaii County Fair** in Hilo on the Big Isle features an orchid show, steer show, lei contest, agricultural displays, plus exhibits of Hawaiian arts and crafts.

Late September and during October   The highlight of Hawaii's cultural season is the **Aloha Week** festival, a series of week-long celebrations featuring parades, street parties and pageants. Each week, a different island stages the festival and the entire sequence ends with a **Molokai-to-Oahu Canoe Race**.

OCTOBER   **During October**   The **Honolulu Orchid Society Show** in Honolulu presents thousands of orchids and other tropical plants. The **Hyatt Regency Maui Kaanapali Classic Golf Tournament** on Maui draws top stars from the PGA Tour.

Mid-October   The **Maui County Fair** features agricultural exhibits and arts-and-crafts displays; the **Iron Man Triathlon World Championship** on the Big Island tests the stamina of the world's best-conditioned athletes.

Late October   The **Lahaina Halloween Hoolaulea** is a memorable street party with a parade, food fair, music and dancing on Front Street.

Late October to Mid-November   The Big Island's **Kona Coffee Festival** celebrates the coffee harvest with a parade, international food bazaar and musical entertainment.

NOVEMBER   **Mid-November**   *Paniolos* on the Big Island turn out for the **Parker Ranch Bull and Horse Show**.

During November   Surfers and landlubbers alike gather for the Hawaiian Pro Surfing Championships on Oahu. The **Aloha Classic Windsurfing** at Hookipa Beach on Maui is a key event during the Pro Boardsailing Association World Tour.

November through December   The world's greatest surfers compete on Oahu's north shore in a series of contests including the **Pipeline Masters, World Cup of Surfing** and the **Hawaiian Pro Surfing Classic**. With 20-foot waves and prize money topping $50,000, these are spectacular events. Hawaiian and other crafts are showcased at the **Lokahi Pacific Christmas Craft Fair**, held at the War Memorial Sports Complex in Wailuku, Maui.

During December   The **Festival of Trees** at Honolulu's Amfac Plaza marks the Christmas season. Maui celebrates with arts and crafts, music and dance at the **Na Mele O Maui Festival**.

Early December   Buddha's enlightenment is commemorated on all the islands with **Bodhi Day** ceremonies and religious services.

Mid-December   Runners by the thousands turn out for the **Honolulu Marathon**.

Late December   The **Pipeline Bodysurfing Classic** takes place on Oahu's North Shore.

DECEMBER

The **Hawaii Visitors Bureau**, a state-run agency, is a valuable resource from which to obtain free information on Hawaii. With offices nationwide and branches on each of the four largest islands, the Bureau can help plan your trip and then offer advice once you reach Hawaii.

▼▼▼▼▼▼▼▼▼
Before You Go

VISITORS CENTERS

Details concerning the island offices appear in the "Addresses and Phone Numbers" section at the end of the Oahu, Hawaii, Maui and Kauai chapters. On the mainland, you can contact the **Hawaii Visitors Bureau** at 350 Fifth Avenue, Suite 1827, New York, NY 10118; 212-947-0717; 800-353-5846.

Another excellent resource is the **Hawaii State Library Service**. With a network of libraries on all the islands, this government agency provides facilities for residents and non-residents alike. The libraries are good places to find light beach-reading material as well as books on Hawaii. Visitors can check out books by simply applying for a library card with a valid identification card.

When I get ready to pack for a trip, I sit down and make a list of everything I'll need. It's a very slow, exact procedure: I look in closets, drawers and shelves, and run through in my mind the activities in which I'll participate, determining which items are required for each. After all the planning is complete and when I have the entire inventory collected in one long list, I sit for a minute or two, basking in my wisdom and forethought.

PACKING

Then I tear the hell out of the list, cut out the ridiculous items I'll never use, halve the number of spares among the necessary items, and reduce the entire contents of my suitcase to the bare essentials.

Before I developed this packing technique, I once traveled overland from London to New Delhi carrying two suitcases and a knapsack. I lugged those damned bundles onto trains, buses, jitneys, taxis and rickshaws. When I reached Turkey, I started shipping things home, but by then I was buying so many market goods that it was all I could do to keep even.

I ended up carrying so much crap that one day, when I was sardined in a crowd pushing its way onto an Indian train, someone managed to pick my pocket. When I felt the wallet slipping out, not only was I unable to chase the culprit—I was so weighted down with baggage that I couldn't even turn around to see who was robbing me!

I'll never travel that way again, and neither should you. Particularly when visiting Hawaii, where the weather is mild, you should pack very light. The airlines permit two suitcases and a carry-on bag; try to take one suitcase and maybe an accessory bag that can double as a beach bag. Dress styles are very informal in the islands, and laundromats are frequent, so you don't need a broad range of clothing items.

Remember, you're packing for a semitropical climate. Take along a sweater or light jacket for the mountains, and a poncho to protect against rain. But otherwise, all that travelers in Hawaii require are shorts, bathing suits, lightweight slacks, short-sleeved shirts and blouses, and summer dresses or muumuus. Rarely do visitors require sport jackets or formal dresses. Wash-and-wear fabrics are the most convenient.

For footwear, I suggest soft, comfortable shoes. Low-cut hiking boots or tennis shoes are preferable for hiking; for beachgoing, there's nothing as good as sandals.

There are several other items to squeeze in the corners of your suitcase—suntan lotion, sunglasses, a towel and, of course, your copy of *Hidden Hawaii*. You might also consider packing a mask, fins and snorkel, and possibly a camera.

If you plan on camping, you'll need most of the equipment required for mainland overnighting. In Hawaii, you can get along quite comfortably with a lightweight tent and sleeping bag. You'll also need a knapsack, canteen, camp stove and fuel, mess kit, first-aid kit (with insect repellent, water purification tablets and Chapstick), toilet kit, a pocket knife, hat, waterproof matches, flashlight and ground cloth.

LODGING   Accommodations in Hawaii range from funky cottages to bed-and-breakfast inns to highrise condos. You'll find inexpensive family-run hotels, middle-class tourist facilities and world-class resorts.

Whichever you choose, there are a few guidelines to help save money. Try to visit during the off-season, avoiding the high-rate periods during the summer and from Christmas to Easter. Rooms with mountain views are less expensive than ocean view accommodations. Another way to economize is by reserving a room with a kitchen. In any case, try to reserve far in advance.

To help you decide on a place to stay, I've described the accommodations not only by area but also according to price (prices listed are for double occupancy during the high season; prices may decrease in low season). *Budget* hotels are generally less than $50 per night for two people; the rooms are clean and comfortable, but lack luxury. The *moderately* priced hotels run $50 to $90, and provide larger rooms, plusher furniture and more attractive surroundings. At *deluxe*-priced accommodations you can expect to spend between $90 and $130 for a homey bed and breakfast or a double in a hotel or resort. You'll check into a spacious, well-appointed room with all modern facilities; downstairs the lobby will be a fashionable affair, and you'll usually see a restaurant, lounge and a cluster of shops. If you want to spend your time (and money) in the island's very finest hotels, try an *ultra-deluxe* facility, which will include all the amenities and price above $130.

> Generally, the farther a hotel is from the beach, the less it costs.

Bed-and-Breakfast Inns The bed-and-breakfast business in Hawaii becomes more diverse and sophisticated every year. Today there are several referral services that can find you lodging on any of the islands. Claiming to be the biggest clearinghouse in the state, **Bed & Breakfast Honolulu (Statewide)** represents over 300 properties. ~ 3242 Kaohinani Drive, Honolulu, HI 96817; 595-7533, 800-288-4666, fax 595-2030.

The original association, **Bed & Breakfast Hawaii**, claims more than 150 locations. This Kauai-based service was founded in 1976 and is well known throughout Hawaii. ~ P.O. Box 449, Kapaa, HI 96746; 822-7771, 800-733-1632, fax 822-2723.

You can also try **Affordable Accommodations**, which is based on Maui. ~ 2825 Kauhale Street, Kihei, HI 96753; 879-7865. Or call **All Islands Bed & Breakfast**, an Oahu-based reservation service that represents hundreds of bed and breakfasts. ~ 823 Kainui Drive, Kailua, HI 96734; 263-2342, 800-542-0344, fax 263-0308.

While the properties represented by these agencies range widely in price, **Hawaii's Best Bed & Breakfasts** specializes in small, upscale accommodations on all the islands. With about 100 establishments to choose from, it places guests in a variety of privately owned facilities; most are deluxe priced. ~ P.O. Box 563, Kamuela, HI 96743; 885-4550, 800-262-9912, fax 885-0559.

CONDOS

Many people visiting Hawaii, especially those traveling with families, find that condominiums are often cheaper than hotels. While some hotel rooms come with kitchenettes, few provide all the amenities of condominiums. A condo, in essence, is an apartment away from home. Designed as studio, one-, two- or three-bedroom apartments, they come equipped with full kitchen facilities and complete kitchenware collections. Many also feature washer/dryers, dishwashers, air-conditioning, color televisions, telephones, lanais and community swimming pools.

Utilizing the kitchen will save considerably on your food bill; by sharing the accommodations among several people, you'll also cut your lodging bill. While the best way to see Hawaii is obviously by hiking and camping, when you're ready to come in from the wilds, consider reserving a place that provides more than a bed and a night table.

DINING

A few guidelines will help you chart a course through Hawaii's countless dining places. Within a particular chapter, the restaurants are categorized geographically, with each restaurant entry describing the establishment as budget, moderate, deluxe or ultra-deluxe in price.

To establish a pattern for Hawaii's parade of dining places, I've described not only the cuisine but also the ambience of each establishment. Restaurants listed offer lunch and dinner unless otherwise noted.

Dinner entrées at *budget* restaurants usually cost $8 or less. The ambience is informal café style and the crowd is often a local one. *Moderately* priced restaurants range between $8 and $16 at dinner and offer pleasant surroundings, a more varied menu and a slower pace. *Deluxe* establishments tab their entrées above $16, featuring sophisticated cuisines, plush decor and more personalized service. *Ultra-deluxe* restaurants generally price above $24.

Breakfast and lunch menus vary less in price from restaurant to restaurant. Even deluxe-priced kitchens usually offer light breakfasts and lunch sandwiches, which place them within a few dollars of their budget-minded competitors. These early meals can be a good time to test expensive restaurants.

TRAVELING WITH CHILDREN

Hawaii is an ideal vacation spot for family holidays. The pace is slow, the atmosphere casual. A few guidelines will help ensure that your trip to the islands brings out the joys rather than the strains of parenting, allowing everyone to get into the *aloha* spirit.

Use a travel agent to help with arrangements; they can reserve spacious bulkhead seats on airlines and determine which flights are least crowded. They can also seek out the best deals on inexpensive condominiums, saving you money on both room and board.

Planning the trip with your kids stimulates their imagination. Books about travel, airplane rides, beaches, whales, volcanoes and

Hawaiiana help prepare even a two-year-old for an adventure. This preparation makes the "getting there" part of the trip more exciting for children of all ages.

And "getting there" means a long-distance flight. Plan to bring everything you need on board the plane—diapers, food, toys, books and extra clothing for kids and parents alike. I've found it helpful to carry a few new toys and books as treats to distract my son and daughter when they get bored. I also pack a few snacks.

Allow extra time to get places. Book reservations in advance and make sure that the hotel or condominium has the extra crib, cot or bed you require. It's smart to ask for a room at the end of the hall to cut down on noise. And when reserving a rental car, inquire to see if they provide car seats and if there is an added charge. Hawaii has a strictly enforced car seat law.

Besides the car seat you may have to bring along, also pack shorts and T-shirts, a sweater, sun hat, sundresses and waterproof sandals. A stroller with sunshade for little ones helps on sightseeing sojourns; a shovel and pail are essential for sandcastle building. Most importantly, remember to bring a good sunblock. The quickest way to ruin a family vacation is with a bad sunburn. Also plan to bring indoor activities such as books and games for evenings and rainy days.

Most towns have stores that carry diapers, food and other essentials. However, prices are much higher in Hawaii. To economize, some people take along an extra suitcase filled with diapers and wipes, baby food, peanut butter and jelly, etc. If you're staying in Waikiki, ABC stores carry a limited selection of disposables and baby food. Shopping outside Waikiki in local supermarkets will save you a considerable sum: Star Market is open from 6 a.m. to 1 a.m. ~ 2470 South King Street, Honolulu; 973-1666.

A first-aid kit is always a good idea. Also check with your pediatrician for special medicines and dosages for colds and diarrhea. If your child does become sick or injured in the Honolulu area,

KEIKI CAMP

Some resorts and hotels have daily programs for kids during the summer and holiday seasons. Hula lessons, lei making, storytelling, sandcastle building and various sports activities keep *keikis* (kids) over six happy while also giving Mom and Dad a break. As an added bonus, these resorts offer family plans, providing discounts for extra rooms or permitting children to share a room with their parents at no extra charge. Check with your travel agent.

contact **Kapiolani Medical Center** (973-8511). On the Windward Coast of Oahu, call **Castle Medical Center** (263-5500); on the North Shore, **Kahuku Hospital** (293-9221); and on the leeward side, **Wahiawa General Hospital** (621-8411). On the Big Island's east side, there's **Hilo Medical Center** (969-4111); in Kona, **Kona Hospital** (322-9311); Maui, **Maui Memorial Hospital** (242-2343); Lanai, **Lanai Community Hospital** (565-6411); Molokai, **Molokai General Hospital** (553-5331); and Kauai, **Wilcox Memorial Hospital and Health Center** (245-1100). There's also a **Poison Control Center** in Honolulu, which can be reached from the outer islands at 800-362-3585 or from Oahu at 941-4411.

Hotels often provide access to babysitters. On Oahu, a bonded babysitting agency is available: **Aloha Babysitting Service.** ~ 732-2029. In the Kaanapali area of Maui, you can try **Babysitting Services of Maui.** ~ 661-0558.

When choosing which island to visit, consider how many diversions it will take to keep your children happy. Oahu offers numerous options, from the Honolulu Zoo to theme parks to museums, while the outer islands have fewer attractions. It might be helpful to read the introductory passages to each of the island chapters before planning your vacation.

WOMEN TRAVELING ALONE

It is sad commentary on life in the United States, but women traveling alone must take precautions. It's entirely unwise to hitchhike and probably best to avoid inexpensive accommodations on the outskirts of town; the money saved does not outweigh the risk. Bed and breakfasts, youth hostels and YWCAs are generally your safest bet for lodging.

If you are hassled or threatened in some way, never be afraid to scream for assistance. It's a good idea to carry change for a phone call. Throughout the islands there are many organizations that can help you in case of emergency. On Oahu, contact the **Sex Abuse Treatment Center.** ~ 524-7273. On Hawaii, the **Sex Assault Support Service** will offer assistance. ~ 935-0677. Travelers to Maui, Lanai and Molokai can call the **Sexual Assault Hotline.** ~ 242-4357. On Maui there's **Women Helping Women**, a domestic violence shelter. ~ 579-9581. The **Rape Crisis Team** can be of help on Kauai. ~ 245-4144.

GAY & LESBIAN TRAVELERS

The **Gay & Lesbian Community Center**, specializing in support groups and community outreach, supplies Oahu visitors with gay-relevant information. Stop by during office hours to pick up lesbian and gay newspapers and brochures. Located in the YWCA, it's open Monday through Friday from noon to 3 p.m. ~ 1566 Wilder Avenue; 951-7000.

For monthly updates on the gay and lesbian scene in Hawaii, pick up a copy of *Island Lifestyle Magazine* at any local newsstand.

Along with coverage of news and entertainment, it provides a calendar of events and a listing of services. **Lifestyle Publishing** also puts out *The Pages,* an annual publication that includes everything of interest to the gay community. This handy directory can be purchased through the mail for $4. ~ Lifestyle Publishing, P.O. Box 11840, Honolulu, HI 96828; 737-6400, fax 735-8825.

The *Guide to Hawaii,* published by **Pacific Ocean Holidays,** is also helpful for gay travelers. It comes out three times a year and lists the best and hottest establishments and beaches that Hawaii has to offer. Send $5 per copy (via mail only) if ordering from the mainland. This outfit can also help book reservations. ~ P.O. Box 88245, Honolulu, HI 96830-8245; reservations only 923-2400, 800-735-6600.

Hawaiinet Tour & Travel Services Network, Inc. offers special tour packages to both gays and straights. They can help decide on hotels, condos and restaurants. This gay-owned company also delivers Hawaiian food, music and other goodies to the mainland. ~ P.O. Box 15671, Honolulu HI 96830; 545-1119, 800-992-5642, fax 524-9572, E-mail hinet@hula.net, http://www.hawaiinet.com.

For information on the gay and lesbian scene on Maui, contact **Both Sides Now**. They can provide details on lodging, upcoming events and social gatherings. ~ P.O. Box 5042, Kahului, HI 96732; 244-4566. Lesbians can also call **Contact Dykes**. ~ 879-2971.

Women can call the **Women's Events Hotline** for goings-on around the island. ~ 573-3077.

To carry you to all these places, consider **Island Pride Taxis & Tours**, a gay-owned chauffeur and tour service. ~ 732-6518, fax 923-2499.

For further information, be sure to look under "gay and lesbian travelers" in the index at the end of the book.

Hawaii is a hospitable place for senior citizens to visit. Countless museums, historic sights and even restaurants and hotels offer senior discounts that can cut a substantial chunk off vacation costs. The national park system's Golden Age Passport, which must be applied for in person, allows free admission for anyone 62 and older to the national parks in the islands.

SENIOR TRAVELERS

The **American Association of Retired Persons** (AARP) offers membership to anyone over 50. AARP's benefits include travel discounts with a number of firms. ~ 3200 East Carson Street, Lakewood, CA 90712; 310-496-2277, 800-424-3410.

Elderhostel offers reasonably priced, all-inclusive educational programs in a variety of locations throughout the year. ~ 75 Federal Street, Boston, MA 02110; 617-426-7788.

Be extra careful about health matters. Consider carrying a medical record with you—including your medical history and current medical status as well as your doctor's name, phone number and address. Make sure your insurance covers you while you are away from home.

DISABLED TRAVELERS   The **Commission on Persons with Disabilities** publishes a survey of the city, county, state and federal parks in Hawaii that are accessible to travelers with disabilities. They also provide "Aloha Guides to Accessibility," which cover Oahu, Maui, Kauai and the Big Island, and give information on various hotels, shopping centers, and restaurants that are accessible. ~ 919 Ala Moana Boulevard, Room 101, Honolulu, HI 96814; 586-8121.

The **Society for the Advancement of Travel for the Handicapped** offers information for travelers with disabilities. ~ 347 5th Avenue, #610, New York, NY, 10016; 212-447-7284. **Travelin' Talk,** a network of people and organizations, also provides assistance. ~ P.O. Box 3534, Clarksville, TN 37043; 615-552-6670.

Be sure to check in advance when making room reservations. Some hotels feature facilities for those in wheelchairs.

FOREIGN TRAVELERS   **Passports and Visas**   Most foreign visitors are required to obtain a passport and tourist visa to enter the United States. Contact your nearest United States Embassy or Consulate well in advance to obtain a visa and to check on any other entry requirements.

Customs Requirements   Foreign travelers are allowed to carry in the following: 200 cigarettes (1 carton), 50 cigars or 2 kilograms (4.4 pounds) of smoking tobacco; one liter of alcohol for personal use only (you must be 21 years of age to bring in alcohol); and US$100 worth of duty-free gifts that include an additional quantity of 100 cigars. You may bring in any amount of currency, but must fill out a form if you bring in over US$10,000. Carry any prescription drugs in clearly marked containers. (You may have to produce a written prescription or doctor's statement for the customs officer.) Meat or meat products, seeds, plants, fruits and narcotics are not allowed to be brought into the United States. Contact the **United States Customs Service** for further information. ~ 1301 Constitution Avenue NW, Washington, DC 20229; 202-927-6724.

Driving   If you plan to rent a car, an international driver's license should be obtained prior to arrival. Some rental car companies require both a foreign license and an international driver's license. Many car rental agencies require that the lessee be at least 25 years of age; all require a major credit card.

Currency   United States money is based on the dollar. Bills come in six denominations: $1, $5, $10, $20, $50 and $100. Every dollar is divided into 100 cents. Coins are the penny (1 cent), nickel (5 cents), dime (10 cents) and quarter (25 cents).

You may not use foreign currency to purchase goods and services in the United States. Consider buying traveler's checks in dollar amounts. You may also use credit cards affiliated with an American company such as Interbank, Barclay Card, VISA, Master-Card and American Express.

Electricity and Electronics   Electric outlets use currents of 110 volts, 60 cycles. For appliances made for other electrical systems, you need a transformer or adapter. Travelers who use laptop computers for telecommunication should be aware that modem configurations for U.S. telephone systems may be different from their European counterparts. Similarly, the U.S. format for videotapes is different from that in Europe; U.S. Park Service visitors centers and other stores that sell souvenir videos often have them available in European format.

When traveling around Christmas and during the summer high season, it's wise to book reservations as far in advance as possible.

Weights and Measurements   The United States uses the English system of weights and measures. American units and their metric equivalents are as follows: 1 inch = 2.5 centimeters; 1 foot (12 inches) = 0.3 meter; 1 yard (3 feet) = 0.9 meter; 1 mile (5280 feet) = 1.6 kilometers; 1 ounce = 28 grams; 1 pound (16 ounces) = 0.45 kilogram; 1 quart (liquid) = 0.9 liter.

MAIL

If you're staying in a particular establishment during your visit, you can usually have personal mail sent there. Otherwise, for cardholders, **American Express** will hold letters for no charge at its Honolulu office for 30 days, and will provide forwarding services. If you decide to use their facilities, have mail addressed to American Express, Client Mail, 2424 Kalakaua Avenue, Honolulu, HI 96815. ~ 922-4718. If you don't use this service, your only other recourse is to have mail sent to a particular post office in care of general delivery.

Transportation

GETTING TO THE ISLANDS

During the 19th century, sleek clipper ships sailed from the West Coast to Hawaii in about 11 days. Today, you'll be traveling by a less romantic but far swifter conveyance—the jet plane. Rather than days at sea, it will be about five hours in the air from California, nine hours from Chicago, or around 11 hours if you're coming from New York.

There's really nothing more rewarding than catching a plane to Hawaii. No fewer than seven major airlines—**United, Northwest, Hawaiian, Continental, American,** TWA and **Delta**—fly regular schedules to Honolulu. American and Delta also offer flights to Maui, and United flies directly to Maui as well as the Big Island. This nonstop service is particularly convenient for travelers who are interested in visiting the outer islands while bypassing Honolulu.

Whichever carrier you choose, ask for the economy or excursion fare, and try to fly during the week; weekend flights are generally higher in price. To qualify for the lower price fares, it is sometimes necessary to book your flight two weeks in advance and to stay in the islands at least one week. Generally, however, the restrictions are minimal. Children under two years of age can fly for free, but they will not have a seat of their own. Each passenger is permitted two large pieces of luggage plus a carry-on bag. Shipping a bike or surfboard will cost extra.

In planning a Hawaiian sojourn, one potential moneysaver is the package tour, which combines air transportation with a hotel room and other amenities. Generally, it is a style of travel that I avoid. However, if you can find a package that provides air transportation, a hotel or condominium accommodation and a rental car, all at one low price—it might be worth considering. Just try to avoid the packages that preplan your entire visit, dragging you around on air-conditioned tour buses. Look for the package that provides only the bare necessities, namely transportation and lodging, while allowing you the greatest freedom.

However you decide to go, be sure to consult a travel agent. They are professionals in the field, possessing the latest information on rates and facilities, and their service to you is usually free.

GETTING BETWEEN ISLANDS

Since cruise ships are the only commercial boats serving all six Hawaiian islands, most of the transportation is by plane. **Aloha Airlines** and **Hawaiian Airlines**, the state's major carriers, provide frequent inter-island jet service. If you're looking for smooth, rapid, comfortable service, this is certainly it. You'll be buckled into your seat, offered a low-cost cocktail and whisked to your destination within about 20 minutes.

Without doubt, the best service aboard any inter-island carrier is on Aloha Airlines. They have an excellent reputation for flying on time and offer a seven-day, unlimited travel pass for island-hopping travelers. I give them my top recommendation.

Now that you know how to fly quickly and comfortably, let me tell you about the most exciting way to get between islands. Several small airlines—such as **Aloha Island Air** and **Mahalo Air**—fly twin-engine propeller planes. These small airplanes travel at low altitudes and moderate speeds over the islands. Next to chartering a helicopter, they are one of the finest ways to see Hawaii from the air.

The service is very personalized; often the pilot will point out landmarks along the route, and sometimes he'll fly out of his way to show you points of particular interest. I often fly this way when I'm in the islands and highly recommend these small planes to anyone with a sense of adventure.

Let me describe a typical flight I took between Honolulu and Kona. So that I'd get a better view, the captain suggested that I sit up front in the copilot's seat. After taking off in a wide arc around Honolulu, we passed close enough to Diamond Head to gaze down into the crater, then headed across the Kaiwi Channel to Molokai. Since we had to pick up passengers at Molokai's lonely airstrip, the pilot gave us a tour of the island. We paralleled the island's rugged north face, where sharp cliffs laced with waterfalls drop thousands of feet to the sea. Then we swept in toward Maui for a view of Haleakala Crater, and continued past the Big Island's snowtipped volcanoes before touching down in Kona. All for the price of an airline ticket!

Rates for these twin-engine propeller planes are very competitive when compared with the inter-island jets. Coupled with the fact that your ticket on the smaller carriers is worth a guided tour as well as a trip between islands, you really can't do better than booking your flights on these sturdy little planes.

Hawaii's grand oceanliner tradition is carried on today by **American Hawaii Cruises**. The S.S. *Independence* cruises the inter-island waters, docking at Maui, the Big Island, Kauai and Pier 2 in Honolulu. The cruises are week-long affairs that evoke memories of the old steamship era. ~ 2 North Riverside Plaza, Chicago, IL 60606; 800-765-7000.

CAR RENTALS

Renting a car is as easy in Hawaii as anywhere. Every island supports at least several rental agencies, which compete fiercely with one another in price and quality of service. So before renting, shop around: check the listings in this book, and also look for the special temporary offers that many rental companies sometimes feature.

There are several facts to remember when renting a car. First of all, a major credit card is essential. Also, many agencies don't rent at all to people under 25. Regardless of your age, many companies charge several dollars a day extra for insurance. The insurance is optional and expensive, and in many cases, unnecessary (many credit cards provide the same coverage when a rental is charged to the card). Find out if you credit card company offers this coverage. Your personal insurance policy may also provide for rental cars and, if necessary, have a clause added that will include rental car protection. Check on this before you leave home. But remember, whether you have insurance or not, you are liable for the first several thousand dollars in accident damage.

Rates fluctuate with the season; slack tourist seasons are great times for good deals. Also, three-day, weekly and monthly rates are almost always cheaper than daily rentals; cars with standard shifts are generally less than automatics; and compacts are more economical than the larger four-door models.

Other than on the island of Lanai, I don't recommend renting a jeep. They're more expensive and less comfortable than automobiles, and won't get you to very many more interesting spots. In addition, the rental car collision insurance provided by most credit cards does not cover jeeps. Except in extremely wet weather when roads are muddy, all the places mentioned in this book, including the hidden locales, can be reached by car.

TWO

The Land
and Outdoor Adventures

GEOLOGY More than 25 million years ago a fissure opened along the Pacific floor. Beneath tons of sea water molten lava poured from the rift. This liquid basalt, oozing from a hot spot in the earth's center, created a crater along the ocean bottom. As the tectonic plate that comprises the ocean floor drifted over the earth's hot spot, numerous other craters appeared. Slowly, in the seemingly endless procession of geologic time, a chain of volcanic islands, stretching almost 2000 miles, emerged from the sea.

On the continents it was also a period of terrible upheaval. The Himalayas, Alps and Andes were rising, but these great chains would reach their peaks long before the Pacific mountains even touched sea level. Not until a few million years ago did these underwater volcanoes break the surface and become islands. By then, present-day plants and animals inhabited the earth, and apes were rapidly evolving into a new species.

For a couple of million more years, the mountains continued to grow. The forces of erosion cut into them, creating knife-edged cliffs and deep valleys. Then plants began germinating: mosses and ferns, springing from windblown spores, were probably first, followed by seed plants carried by migrating birds and on ocean currents. The steep-walled valleys provided natural greenhouses in which unique species evolved, while transoceanic winds swept insects and other life from the continents.

Some islands never survived this birth process: the ocean simply washed them away. The first islands that did endure, at the northwestern end of the Hawaiian chain, proved to be the smallest. Today these islands, with the exception of Midway, are barren uninhabited atolls. The volcanoes that rose last, far to the southeast, became the mountainous archipelago generally known as the Hawaiian Islands.

With its luxurious parks, mountain retreats and deserted beaches, Hawaii is a paradise for campers and backpackers. Because of the varied terrain and the islands' microenvironments, it's possible to experience all kinds of outdoor adventures. One day you'll hike through a steaming rainforest filled with tropical flowers; the next night you'll camp atop a volcanic crater in a stark, windblown area that resembles the moon's surface; then you'll descend to a curving white-sand beach populated only by shorebirds and tropical fish.

Paradise means more than physical beauty, however. It also involves an easy life and a bountiful food supply. The easy living is up to you; just slow down from the frantic pace of mainland life and you'll discover that island existence can be relaxing. As for wild food—you'll find it hanging from trees, swimming in the ocean and clinging to coral reefs. With the proper techniques and a respect for conservation needs, it's yours to take.

In this chapter, I'll detail some of the outdoor skills necessary to camp, hike and live naturally in Hawaii. This is certainly not a comprehensive study of how to survive on a Pacific island; I'm just passing along a few facts I've learned while exploring Hawaii. I don't advise that you plan to live entirely off the land. Hawaii's environment is too fragile to support you full-time. Anyway, living that way is a hell of a lot of work! I'll just give a few hints on how to supplement your provisions with a newly caught fish or a fresh fruit salad. That way, not only will you save on food bills, you'll also get a much fuller taste of the islands.

Obviously, none of these techniques were developed by me personally. In fact, most of them date back centuries to the early days, when Polynesian explorers applied the survival skills they had learned in Tahiti and the Marquesas to the newly discovered islands of Hawaii. So as you set out to fish along a coral reef, hunt for shellfish in tidepools or gather seaweed at low tide, give a prayerful thanks to the generations of savvy islanders who have come before you.

Flora and Fauna

FLORA

Many of the plants you'll see in Hawaii are not indigenous. In fact, much of the lush vegetation of this tropical island found its way here from locations all over the world. Sea winds, birds and seafaring settlers brought many of the seeds, plants, flowers and trees from the islands of the South Pacific, as well as from other, more distant regions. Over time, some plants adapted to Hawaii's unique ecosystem and climate, creating strange new lineages and evolving into a completely new ecosystem. This process has long interested scientists, who call the Hawaiian Islands one of the best natural labs for studies of plant evolution.

Sugar cane arrived in Hawaii with the first Polynesian settlers, who appreciated its sweet juices. By the late 1800s, it was well established as a lucrative crop. The pineapple was first planted during the same century. A member of the bromeliad family, this spiky plant is actually a collection of beautiful pink, blue and purple flowers, each of which develops into fruitlets. The pineapple is a collection of these fruitlets, grown together into a single fruit that takes 14 to 17 months to mature. Sugar cane and pineapple are still the main crops in Hawaii, although competition from other countries and environmental problems caused by pesticides have taken their toll.

Visitors to Hawaii will find the islands a perpetual flower show. Sweetly scented plumeria, deep red, shiny anthurium, exotic ginger, showy birds of paradise, small lavender crown flowers, highly fragrant gardenias and the brightly hued hibiscus run riot on the islands and add color and fragrance to the surrounding area. Scarlet and purple bougainvillea vines, and the aromatic lantana, with its dense clusters of flowers, are also found in abundance.

Each of the main islands has designated a specific bloom as its island flower. Oahu has the *ilima*, a small golden blossom, and the Big Island has the red *lehua*, a furry flower with needle petals resembling a bottlebrush plant. Maui spotlights the *lokelani*, or pink cottage rose while Kauai's pick is the *mokihana*, which is actually a light green berry. Molokai's flower of choice is the small, white *kukui* blossom and Lanai's is the vibrant airborne *kaunaoa*.

The beautiful, delicate orchid thrives in Hawaii's tropical heat and humidity. Cultivated primarily on the Big Island, the most popular orchids are the *vendrobium*, which can come in white, purple, lavender, or yellow; the *vanda*, which is lavender with white petals and often used for making leis; and the popcorn, which has small, yellow flowers. The wild *vanda*, with its white and purple petals, can be spotted along the side of the road year-round.

Hawaii's most unique plant is the silversword. Delicate looking, this silvery green plant is actually very hardy. It thrives on the moonscape of Haleakala, 6000 to 10,000 feet above sea level on Maui. Very adaptable, it can survive in extreme hot and cold tem-

FROM SURF TO SNOW

With several distinct biological regions, there's much more to the islands than lush tropics. Rainforests give way to dry forests, and to coastal habitats where the vegetation is specially suited to withstand wind and salt. Higher in altitude are the bogs, pools of standing water containing rare life forms that have been forced to adapt to a difficult environment. Highest in altitude is the alpine zone, consisting of bare volcanic surfaces scattered with clumps of low-growing herbs and shrubs. Subzero temperatures, frost and even snow help keep this region desolate.

peratures with little moisture. Its silvery hairs reflect the sun and its leaves curl inward, protecting the stalk and creating a sort of bowl where rain is collected and stored. The plant lives from five to thirty years, waiting until the right moment before sprouting a three- to nine-foot stalk composed of hundreds of small, reddish flowers—and then it dies. In the same family as the sunflower, this particular type of silversword lives only on Haleakala and has been close to extinction for many years. Now protected, it is currently making a comeback.

Another curious specimen found on the leeward slopes of Haleakala and on the Big Island is the protea. With 1500 varieties, this remarkable plant comes in a myriad of shapes, sizes and colors. Some look like pin cushions, others resemble corn cobs. Originally from South Africa and Australia, the Hawaiian plant is a hybrid.

Although many people equate the tropics with the swaying palm tree, Hawaii is home to a variety of exotic trees. The famed banyan tree, known for pillarlike aerial roots that grow vertically downward from the branches, spreads to form a natural canopy. When the roots touch the ground, they thicken, providing support for the tree's branches to continue expanding. The candlenut, or *kukui*, tree, originally brought to Hawaii from the South Pacific islands, is big, bushy and prized for its nuts, which can be used for oil or polished and strung together to make leis. With its cascades of bright yellow or pink flowers, the cassia tree earns its moniker—the shower tree. Covered with tiny pink blossoms, the canopied monkeypod tree has fernlike leaves that close up at night.

Found in a variety of shapes and sizes, the ubiquitous palm does indeed sway to the breezes on white-sand beaches, but it also comes in a short, stubby form featuring more frond than trunk. The fruit, or nuts, of these trees are prized for their oil, which can be utilized for making everything from margarine to soap. The wood (rattan for example) is often used for making furniture.

FRUITS AND VEGETABLES   There's a lot more to Hawaii's tropical wonderland than gorgeous flowers and overgrown rainforests. The islands are also teeming with edible plants. Roots, fruits, vegetables, herbs and spices grow like weeds from the shoreline to the mountains. Following is a list of some of the more commonly found edibles.

Avocado: Covered with either a tough green or purple skin, this pear-shaped fruit sometimes weighs as much as three pounds. It grows on ten- to forty-foot-high trees, and ripens from June through November.

Bamboo: The bamboo plant is actually a grass with a sweet root that is edible and a long stem frequently used for making furniture. Often exceeding eight feet in height, bamboo is green until picked, when it turns a golden brown.

Banana: Polynesians use banana trees not only for food but also for clothing, roofing, medicines, dyes and even alcohol. The fruit, which grows upside down on broad-leaved trees, can be harvested as soon as the first banana in the bunch turns yellow.

Breadfruit: This large round fruit grows on trees that reach up to 60 feet in height. Breadfruit must be boiled, baked or fried.

Coconut: The coconut tree is probably the most important plant in the entire Pacific. Every part of the towering palm is used. Most people are concerned only with the hard brown nut, which yields delicious milk as well as a tasty meat. If the coconut is still green, the meat is a succulent jellylike substance. Otherwise, it's a hard but delicious white rind.

Guava: A roundish yellow fruit that grows on a small shrub or tree, guavas are extremely abundant in the wild. They ripen between June and October.

Lychee nut: Found hanging in bunches from the lychee tree, this popular fruit is encased in red, prickly skin that peels off to reveal the sweet-tasting, translucent flesh.

Mango: Known as the king of fruits, the mango grows on tall shade trees. The oblong fruit ripens in the spring and summer.

Maui onion: Resembling an ordinary yellow onion in size and color, these bulbs are uncommonly mild. They are grown on the south side of Haleakala in rich volcanic soil, and enjoy enough sun and altitude to make them very sweet. A member of the lily family, the Maui onion is best eaten raw.

Mountain apple: This sweet fruit grows in damp, shaded valleys at an elevation of about 1800 feet. The flowers resemble fluffy crimson balls; the fruit, which ripens from July to December, is also a rich red color.

Papaya: This delicious fruit, which is picked as it begins to turn yellow, grows on unbranched trees. The sweet flesh can be bright orange or coral pink in color. Summer is the peak harvesting season.

Passion fruit: Oval in shape, this tasty yellow fruit grows to a length of about two or three inches. It's produced on a vine and ripens in summer or fall.

Taro: The tuberous root of this Hawaiian staple is pounded, then made into a grayish purple paste known as *poi*. One of the most nutritious foods, it has a rather bland taste. The plant has wide, shiny, thick leaves with reddish stems; the root is white with purple veins.

PAKALOLO For decades, Hawaii has been known for its sparkling beaches and lofty volcanoes. Agriculturally, the islands have grown famous by producing sugar cane and pineapples. But during the last several decades, the 50th state has become renowned for another crop, one which some deem a sacrament and others consider a sin.

In the islands it's commonly referred to as *pakalolo*. Mainlanders know it more familiarly by the locales in which it grows—Maui Wowie, Kona Gold, Puna Butter and Kauai Buds. Because of Hawaii's lush tropical environment, marijuana grows year-round and has become the state's number-one cash crop. Plants easily reach ten- or twelve-foot heights; colas as thick as bottle brushes drip with resin.

Now that marijuana is big business, ripoffs have become a harrowing problem in Hawaii. Growers often guard their crops with guns and booby traps. Because of this armed protection, it can be very dangerous to wander through someone's dope patch. It might be on public land far from the nearest road, but in terms of the explorer's personal safety, a marijuana plantation should be treated as the most private property imaginable. In the words of the islanders, it is strictly *kapu*.

FAUNA

In Hawaii, it seems there is more wildlife in the water and air than on land. A scuba diver's paradise, the ocean is also a promised land for many other creatures. Coral, colorful fish and migrating whales are only part of this underwater community. Sadly, many of Hawaii's coral reefs have been dying mysteriously in the last several years. No one is sure why, but many believe this is partially due to runoff from pesticides used in agriculture.

For adventure lovers, Maui, and to a lesser extent the Big Island, offer excellent opportunities for whale watching. Every year, humpback whales converge in the warm waters off the islands to give birth to their calves. Beginning their migration in Alaska, they can be spotted in Hawaiian waters from November through May. The humpback, named for its practice of showing its dorsal fin when diving, is quite easy to spy. They feed in shallow waters, usually diving for periods of no longer than 15 minutes. They often sleep on the surface and breathe fairly frequently. Quite playful, they can be seen leaping, splashing and flapping their 15-foot tails over their backs. The best time for whale-watching is from January to April.

One of the few animals to live in the Hawaiian islands before the Polynesians' arrival, the Hawaiian monk seal has been hunted for its hide to the point of extinction. Now protected as an endangered species, this tropical seal is found mostly on the outer islands, although it is occasionally spotted on Kauai, and more rarely, on Oahu. Closely related to the elephant seal, the monk seal is not as agile or as fond of land as other seals.

Green sea turtles are common on all of the Hawaiian islands, although this was not always the case. Due to the popularity of their skins, they spent many years on the endangered species list, but are now making a comeback. Measuring three to four feet in diameter, these large reptiles frolic in saltwater only, and are often visible from the shore.

Hawaii is also home to many rare and endangered birds. Like the flora, the birds on the islands are highly specialized. The state bird, the nene, or Hawaiian goose, is a cousin to the Canadian goose and mates for life. Extinct on Maui for many years, several birds were reintroduced there in the late 1950s. There's still some doubt as to whether they'll survive on their own in the wild. The only places they currently live are on the Big Island and Haleakala. The slopes of Haleakala are also home to two other endangered birds: the crested honeycreeper and the parrotbill.

On the endangered species list for many years, the Hawaiian hawk, or *io*, has had its status changed to "threatened." Existing exclusively on the Big Island, the regal *io* is found in a variety of habitats from forest to grassland, but is most often sighted on the slopes of Mauna Kea and Mauna Loa.

There *are* a few birds native to Hawaii that have thus far avoided the endangered species list. Two of the most common birds are the yellow-green *amakihi* and the red *iiwi*.

Known in Hawaiian mythology for its protective powers, the *pueo*, or Hawaiian owl, a brown-and-white-feathered bird, resides on Kauai, the Big Island and in Haleakala crater. On Oahu the Hawaiian owl is considered an endangered species.

The *koae kea*, or "tropic bird," lives on Haleakala, as well as in the Kilauea Crater, and Kauai's Waimea Canyon. Resembling a seagull in size, it has a long, thin white tail and a striking striping pattern on the back of the wings.

Another common bird is the *iwa*, or frigate, a very large creature measuring three to four feet in length, with a wing span averaging seven feet. The males are solid black, while the females have a large white patch on their chest and tail. A predatory bird, they're easy to spot raiding the nesting colonies of other birds along the offshore rocks. If you see one, be careful not to point at it; legend has it that it's bad luck. Other birds that make the islands their home are the Hawaiian stilt and the Hawaiian coot—both water birds—along with the black noddy, American plover and wedge-tailed shearwater.

Not many wild four-footed creatures roam the islands. Deer, feral goats and pigs were brought here early on and have found a home in the forests. Some good news for people fearful of snakes:

THE LEVIATHAN TOP-40

Unlike other whales, humpbacks have the ability to sing. Loud and powerful, their songs carry above and below the water for miles. The songs change every year, yet, incredibly, all the whales always seem to know the current one.

There is nary a serpent (or a sea serpent) in Hawaii, although lizards such as skinks and geckos abound.

One can only hope that with the renewed interest in Hawaiian culture, and growing environmental awareness, Hawaii's plants and animals will continue to exist as they have for centuries.

Outdoor Adventures

FISHING

While you're exploring the islands, the sea will be your prime food source. Fishing in Hawaii is good year-round, and the offshore waters are crowded with many varieties of edible fish. For deep-sea fishing you'll have to charter a boat, and freshwater angling requires a license; so I'll concentrate on surf-casting. It costs nothing to fish this way.

In the individual island chapters, you'll find information on the best spots to fish for different species; in the "Addresses" section of those chapters, you'll usually see a fishing supply store listed. For information on seasons, licenses and official regulations, check with the Aquatic Resources Division of the State Department of Land and Natural Resources. This agency has offices on most of the major islands.

The easiest, most economical way to fish is with a hand-held line. Just get a 50- to 100-foot line, and attach a hook and a ten-ounce sinker. Wind the line loosely around a smooth block of wood, then remove the wood from the center. If your coil is free from snags, you'll be able to throw-cast it easily. You can either hold the line in your hand, feeling for a strike, or tie it to the frail end of a bamboo pole.

Beaches and rocky points are generally good places to surf-cast; the best times are during the incoming and outgoing tides. Popular baits include octopus, eel, lobster, crab, frozen shrimp and sea worms.

TORCHFISHING & SPEARFISHING

The old Hawaiians also fished at night by torchlight. They fashioned torches by inserting nuts from the *kukui* tree into the hollow end of a bamboo pole, then lighting the flammable nuts. When fish swam like moths to the flame, the Hawaiians speared, clubbed or netted them.

Today, it's easier to use a lantern and spear. (In fact, it's all *too* easy and tempting to take advantage of this willing prey: Take only edible fish and only what you will eat.) It's also handy to bring a

HOOK UP WITH A FRIEND

The ancient Hawaiians used pearl shells to attract the fish, and hooks, some made from human bones, to snare them. Your friends will probably be quite content to see you angling with store-bought artificial lures.

facemask or a glass-bottomed box to aid in seeing underwater. The best time for torchfishing is a dark night when the sea is calm and the tide low.

During daylight hours, the best place to spearfish is along coral reefs and in areas where the bottom is a mixture of sand and rock. You can use a speargun or make your own spear with heavy rubber bands and a piece of metal. Then, equipped also with mask, fins and snorkel, you can explore underwater grottoes and spectacular coral formations while seeking your evening meal.

CRABBING

For the hungry adventurer, there are two important crab species in Hawaii—Kona crabs and Samoan crabs. The Kona variety are found in relatively deep water, and can usually be caught only from a boat. Samoan crabs inhabit sandy and muddy areas in bays and near river mouths. All you need to catch them is a net fastened to a round wire hoop and secured by a string. The net is lowered to the bottom; then, after a crab has gone for the bait, the entire contraption is raised to the surface.

SQUIDDING

Between June and December, squidding is another popular sport. Actually, the term is a misnomer: squid inhabit deep water and are not usually hunted. What you'll really be after are octopuses. There are two varieties in Hawaii, both of which are commonly found in water three or four feet deep: the *hee*, a greyish-brown animal that changes color like a chameleon, and the *puloa*, a red-colored mollusk with white stripes on its head.

Both are nocturnal and live in holes along coral reefs. At night by torchlight you can spot them sitting exposed on the bottom. During the day, they crawl inside the holes, covering the entrances with shells and loose coral.

The Hawaiians used to pick the octopus up, letting it cling to their chest and shoulders. When they were ready to bag their prize, they'd dispatch the creature by biting it between the eyes. You'll probably feel more comfortable spearing the beast.

SHELLFISH GATHERING

Other excellent food sources are the shellfish that inhabit coastal waters. Oysters and clams, which use their muscular feet to burrow into sand and soft mud, can be collected along the bottom of Hawaii's bays. Lobsters, though illegal to spear, can be taken with short poles to which cable leaders and baited hooks are attached. You can also gather limpets, though I don't recommend it. These tiny black shellfish, locally known as *opihi*, cling tenaciously to rocks in areas of very rough surf. The Hawaiians gather them by leaping into the water after one set of waves breaks, then jumping out before the next set arrives. Being a coward myself, I simply order them in Hawaiian restaurants.

SEAWEED GATHERING

There are still some people who don't think of seaweed as food, but it's very popular among Japanese, and it once served as an integral part of the Hawaiian diet. It's extremely nutritious, easy to gather and very plentiful.

Rocky shores are the best places to find the edible species of seaweed. Some of them float in to shore and can be picked up; other species cling stubbornly to rocks and must be freed with a knife; still others grow in sand or mud. Low tide is the best time to collect seaweed: more plants are exposed, and some can be taken without even getting wet.

OCEAN SAFETY

For swimming, surfing, snorkeling and diving, there's no place quite like Hawaii. With endless miles of white-sand beach, the islands attract aquatic enthusiasts from all over the world. They come to enjoy Hawaii's colorful coral reefs and matchless surf conditions.

Many water lovers, however, never realize how awesome the sea can be. Particularly in Hawaii, where waves can reach 30-foot heights and currents flow unobstructed for thousands of miles, the ocean is sometimes as treacherous as it is spectacular. Dozens of people drown every year in Hawaii, many others are dragged from the crushing surf with broken backs, and countless numbers sustain minor cuts and bruises.

These accidents can be entirely avoided if you approach the ocean with a respect for its power as well as an appreciation of its beauty. All you have to do is heed a few simple guidelines. First, never turn your back on the sea. Waves come in sets: one group may be small and quite harmless, but the next set could be large enough to sweep you out to sea. Never swim alone.

Don't try to surf, or even bodysurf, until you're familiar with the sports' techniques and precautionary measures. Be extremely careful when the surf is high.

If you get caught in a rip current, don't swim *against* it: swim *across* it, parallel to the shore. These currents, running from the shore out to sea, can often be spotted by their ragged-looking surface water and foamy edges.

Around coral reefs, wear something to protect your feet against coral cuts. Particularly good are the inexpensive Japanese *tabis*, or reef slippers. If you do sustain a coral cut, clean it with hydrogen peroxide, then apply an antiseptic or antibiotic substance. This is also a good procedure for octopus bites.

When stung by a Portuguese man-of-war or a jellyfish, mix unseasoned meat tenderizer with alcohol, leave it on the sting for ten or twenty minutes, then rinse it off with alcohol. The old Hawaiian remedies, which are reputedly quite effective, involve applying urine or green papaya.

The New Travel

Travel today is becoming a personal art form. A destination no longer serves as just a place to relax: It's also a point of encounter. To many, this new wave in travel customs is labeled "adventure travel" and involves trekking glaciers or sweeping along in a hang glider; to others, it connotes nothing more daring than a restful spell in a secluded resort. Actually, it's a state of mind, a willingness not only to accept but seek out the uncommon and unique.

Few places in the world are more conducive to this imaginative new travel than Hawaii. Several organizations in the islands cater specifically to people who want to add local customs and unusual adventures to their vacation itineraries.

The **Nature Conservancy of Hawaii**, a nonprofit conservation organization, conducts natural history day hikes of Oahu, Maui and Molokai. Led by expert guides, small groups explore untrammeled beaches, rainforest and an ancient bog. The tours provide a singular insight into the plant and animal life of the islands. Reservations should be made at least one month in advance. ~ P.O. Box 1716, Makawao, HI 96768; 572-7849 on Maui, 537-4508 on Oahu, and 553-5236 on Molokai.

Eye of the Whale features a ten-day tour of Kauai, Maui and the Big Island, including hiking and snorkeling. ~ P.O. Box 1269, Kapaa, HI 96755; 889-0277, 800-659-3544.

Paradise Safaris offers a sunset stargazing trip. Small groups board a four-wheel-drive wagon to the summit of Mauna Kea to enjoy a sunset view and learn about the mountaintop observatory's telescope. There's a hands-on stargazing experience at mid-mountain before returning. ~ P.O. Box 9027, Kailua-Kona, HI 96745; 322-2366.

Hike Maui leads day hiking trips all around the Valley Isle. Ranging from five to ten hours in duration, these treks can be custom-designed to your interests. ~ P.O. Box 330969, Kahului, HI 96733; 879-5270.

When you're ready to take up the challenge of this new style of free-wheeling travel, check with these outfits. Or plan your own trip. To traditional tourists, Hawaii means souvenir shops and fast-food restaurants. But for those with spirit and imagination, it's a land of untracked beaches and ancient volcanoes waiting to be explored.

If you step on the sharp, painful spines of a sea urchin, soak the affected area in very hot water for 15 to 90 minutes. Another remedy calls for applying urine or undiluted vinegar. If any of these preliminary treatments do not work, consult a doctor.

Oh, one last thing. The chances of encountering a shark are about as likely as sighting a UFO. But should you meet one of these ominous creatures, stay calm. He'll be no happier to see you than you are to confront him. Simply swim quietly to shore. By the time you make it back to terra firma, you'll have a hell of a story to tell.

CAMPING & HIKING

Camping in Hawaii usually means pitching a tent or reserving a cabin. Throughout the islands there are secluded spots and hidden beaches, plus numerous county, state and federal parks. All of these campsites, together with hiking trails, are described in the individual island chapters; it's a good idea to consult those detailed listings when planning your trip. You might also want to obtain some hiking maps; they are available from **Hawaii Geographic Maps & Books**. The camping equipment you'll require is listed in the "Packing" section of the preceding chapter. ~ P.O. Box 1698, Honolulu, HI 96806; 538-3952.

Before you set out on your camping trip, there are a few very important matters that I want to explain more fully. First, bring a campstove: firewood is scarce in most areas and soaking wet in others. It's advisable to wear long pants when hiking in order to protect your legs from rock outcroppings, insects and spiny plants. Also, if you are going to explore the Mauna Kea, Mauna Loa or Haleakala volcanoes, be sure to bring cold-weather gear; temperatures are often significantly lower than at sea level and these peaks occasionally receive snow.

Most trails you'll be hiking are composed of volcanic rock. Since this is a very crumbly substance, be extremely cautious when climbing any rock faces. In fact, you should avoid steep climbs if possible. Stay on the trails: Hawaii's dense undergrowth makes it very easy to get lost. If you get lost at night, stay where you are. Because of the low latitude, night descends rapidly here; there's practically no twilight. Once darkness falls, it can be very dangerous to move around. You should also be careful to purify all of your drinking water. And be extremely cautious near streambeds as flash-flooding sometimes occurs, particularly on the windward coasts. This is particularly true during the winter months, when heavy storms from the northeast lash the islands.

Another problem that you're actually more likely to encounter are those nasty varmints that buzz your ear just as you're falling asleep—mosquitoes. Hawaii contains neither snakes nor poison ivy, but it has plenty of these dive-bombing pests. Like me, you

probably consider that it's always open season on the little bas-
tards.

With most of the archipelago's other species, however, you'll
have to be a careful conservationist. You'll be sharing the wilderness with pigs, goats, tropical birds, deer and mongooses, as well
as a spectacular array of exotic and indigenous plants. They exist
in one of the world's most delicate ecological balances. There are
more endangered species in Hawaii than in all the rest of the
United States. So keep in mind the maxim that the Hawaiians try
to follow. *Ua mau ke ea o ka aina i ka pono:* The life of the land
is preserved in righteousness.

THREE

History and Culture

POLYNESIAN ARRIVAL The island of Hawaii, the Big Island, was the last land mass created in the dramatic geologic upheaval that formed the Hawaiian islands. But it was the first island to be inhabited by humans. Perhaps as early as the third century, Polynesians sailing from the Marquesas Islands, and then later from Tahiti, landed near Hawaii's southern tip. The boats were formidable structures, catamaran-like vessels with a cabin built on the platform between the wooden hulls. The sails were woven from coconut fibers. Some of the vessels were a hundred feet long and could do 20 knots, making the trip to Hawaii in a month.

The Polynesians had originally come from the coast of Asia about 3000 years before. They had migrated through Indonesia, then pressed inexorably eastward, leapfrogging across archipelagoes until they finally reached the last chain, the most remote—Hawaii.

These Pacific migrants were undoubtedly the greatest sailors of their day, and stand among the finest in history. When close to land they could smell it, taste it in the seawater, see it in a lagoon's turquoise reflection on the clouds above an island. They knew 150 stars. From the color of the water they determined ocean depths and current directions. They had no charts, no compasses, no sextants; sailing directions were simply recorded in legends and chants. Yet Polynesians discovered the Pacific, from Indonesia to Easter Island, from New Zealand to Hawaii. They made the Vikings and Phoenicians look like landlubbers.

CAPTAIN COOK They were high islands, rising in the northeast as the sun broke across the Pacific. First one, then a second and, finally, as the tall-masted ships drifted west, a third island loomed before them. Landfall! The British crew was ecstatic. It meant fresh water, tropical fruits, solid ground on which to set their boots and a chance to carouse with the native women. For their captain, James Cook, it was another in an amazing career of discoveries. The man whom many call history's greatest explorer was about to land in one of the last spots on earth to be discovered by the West.

He would name the place for his patron, the British earl who became famous by pressing a meal between two crusts of bread. The Sandwich Islands. Later they would be called Owhyhee, and eventually, as the Western tongue glided around the uncharted edges of a foreign language, Hawaii.

It was January 1778, a time when the British Empire was still basking in a sun that never set. The Pacific had been opened to Western powers over two centuries before, when a Portuguese sailor named Magellan crossed it. Since then, the British, French, Dutch and Spanish had tracked through in search of future colonies.

They happened upon Samoa, Fiji, Tahiti and the other islands that spread across this third of the globe, but somehow they had never sighted Hawaii. Even when Cook finally spied it, he little realized how important a find he had made. Hawaii, quite literally, was a jewel in the ocean, rich in fragrant sandalwood, ripe for agricultural exploitation and crowded with sea life. But it was the archipelago's isolation that would prove to be its greatest resource. Strategically situated between Asia and North America, it was the only place for thousands of miles to which whalers, merchants and bluejackets could repair for provisions and rest.

Cook was 49 years old when he shattered Hawaii's quiescence. The Englishman hadn't expected to find islands north of Tahiti. Quite frankly, he wasn't even trying. It was his third Pacific voyage and Cook was hunting bigger game, the fabled Northwest Passage that would link this ocean with the Atlantic.

But these mountainous islands were still an interesting find. He could see by the canoes venturing out to meet his ships that the lands were inhabited; when he finally put ashore on Kauai, Cook discovered a Polynesian society. He saw irrigated fields, domestic animals and high-towered temples. The women were bare-breasted, the men wore loincloths. As his crew bartered for pigs, fowls and bananas, he learned that the natives knew about metal and coveted iron like gold.

If iron was gold to these "Indians," then Cook was a god. He soon realized that his arrival had somehow been miraculously timed, coinciding with the Makahiki festival, a wild party celebrating the roving deity Lono whose return the Hawaiians had awaited for years. Cook was a strange white man sailing monstrous ships—obviously he was Lono. The Hawaiians gave him gifts, fell in his path and rose only at his insistence.

But even among religious crowds, fame is often fickle. After leaving Hawaii, Cook sailed north to the Arctic Sea, where he failed to discover the Northwest Passage. He returned the next year to Kealakekua Bay on the Big Island, arriving at the tail end of another exhausting Makahiki festival. By then the Hawaiians had tired of his constant demands for provisions and were suffering from a new disease that was obviously carried by Lono's archangelic crew—syphilis. This Lono was proving something of a freeloader.

Tensions ran high. The Hawaiians stole a boat. Cook retaliated with gunfire. A scuffle broke out on the beach and in a sudden violent outburst, which surprised the islanders as much as the interlopers, the Hawaiians discovered that their god could bleed. The world's finest mariner lay face down in foot-deep water, stabbed and bludgeoned to death.

Cook's end marked the beginning of an era. He had put the Pacific on the map, his map, probing its expanses and defining its fringes. In Hawaii he ended a thousand years of solitude. The archipelago's geographic isolation, which has always played a crucial role in Hawaii's development, had finally failed to protect it, and a second theme had come into play—the islands' vulnerability. Together with the region's "backwardness," these conditions would now mold Hawaii's history. All in turn would be shaped by another factor, one which James Cook had added to Hawaii's historic equation: the West.

KAMEHAMEHA AND KAAHUMANU The next man whose star would rise above Hawaii was present at Cook's death. Some say he struck the Englishman, others that he took a lock of the great leader's hair and used its residual power, its *mana*, to become king of all Hawaii.

Kamehameha was a tall, muscular, unattractive man with a furrowed face, a lesser chief on the powerful island of Hawaii. When he began his career of conquest a few years after Cook's death, he was a mere upstart, an ambitious, arrogant young chief. But he fought with a general's skill and a warrior's cunning, often plunging into the midst of a melee. He had an astute sense of technology, an intuition that these new Western metals and firearms could make him a king.

In Kamehameha's early years, the Hawaiian islands were composed of many fiefdoms. Several kings or great chiefs, continually warring among themselves, ruled individual islands. At times, a few kings would carve up one island or a lone king might seize several. Never had one monarch controlled all the islands.

But fresh players had entered the field: Westerners with ample firepower and awesome ships. During the decade following Cook, only a handful had arrived, mostly Englishmen and Americans, and they had not yet won the influence they soon would wield. However, even a few foreigners were enough to upset the balance of power. They sold weapons and hardware to the great chiefs, making several of them more powerful than any of the others had ever been. War was imminent.

Kamehameha stood in the center of the hurricane. Like any leader suddenly caught up in the terrible momentum of history, he never quite realized where he was going or how fast he was moving. And he cared little that he was being carried in part by Westerners who would eventually want something for the ride. Kamehameha was no fool. If political expedience meant Western intrusion, then so be it. He had enemies among chiefs on the other islands; he needed the guns.

When two white men came into his camp in 1790, he had the military advisers to complement a fast expanding arsenal. Within months he cannonaded Maui. In 1792, Kamehameha seized the Big Island by inviting his main rival to a peaceful parley, then slaying the hapless chief. By 1795, he had consolidated his control of Maui, grasped Molokai and Lanai, and begun reaching greedily toward Oahu. He struck rapidly, landing near Waikiki and sweeping inland, forcing his enemies to their deaths over the precipitous cliffs of the Nuuanu Pali.

The warrior had become a conqueror, controlling all the islands except Kauai, which he finally gained in 1810 by peaceful negotiation. Kamehameha proved to be as able a bureaucrat as he had been a general. He became a benevolent despot who, with the aid of an ever-increasing number of Western advisers, expanded Hawaii's commerce, brought peace to the islands and moved his people inexorably toward the modern age.

He came to be called Kamehameha the Great, and history first cast him as the George Washington of Hawaii, a wise and resolute leader who gathered a wartorn archipelago into a kingdom. Kamehameha I. But with the revisionist history of the 1960s and 1970s, as Third World people questioned both the Western version of events and the virtues of progress, Kamehameha began to resemble Benedict Arnold. He was seen as an opportunist, a megalomaniac who permitted the Western powers their initial foothold in Hawaii. He used their technology and then, in the manner of great men who depend on stronger allies, was eventually used by them.

As long a shadow as Kamehameha cast across the islands, the event that most dramatically transformed Hawaiian society occurred after his death in 1819. The kingdom had passed to Kamehameha's son Liholiho, but Kamehameha's favorite wife, Kaahumanu, usurped the power. Liholiho was a prodigal son, dissolute,

SAILORS EXTRAORDINAIRE

Centuries before Columbus happened upon the New World, and during a time when European mariners were rarely venturing outside the Mediterranean Sea, entire families of Polynesians were crossing 2500 miles of untracked ocean in hand-carved canoes.

lacking self-certainty, a drunk. Kaahumanu was a woman for all seasons, a canny politician who combined brilliance with boldness,

◆◆◆◆◆◆◆◆◆◆◆◆◆◆◆◆◆◆◆◆◆◆ the feminist of her day. She had infuriated

While British sailors were discovering Hawaii, the English army was battling a ragtag band of revolutionaries for control of the American colonies.

Kamehameha by eating forbidden foods and sleeping with other chiefs, even when he placed a taboo on her body and executed her lovers. She drank liquor, ran away, proved completely uncontrollable and won Kamehameha's love.

It was only natural that when he died, she would take his *mana*, or so she reckoned. Kaahumanu gravitated toward power with the drive of someone whom fate has unwisely denied. She carved her own destiny, announcing that Kamehameha's wish had been to give her a governmental voice. There would be a new post and she would fill it, becoming in a sense Hawaii's first prime minister.

And if the power, then the motion. Kaahumanu immediately marched against Hawaii's belief system, trying to topple the old idols. For years she had bristled under a polytheistic religion regulated by taboos, or *kapus*, which severely restricted women's rights. Now Kaahumanu urged the new king, Liholiho, to break a very strict *kapu* by sharing a meal with women.

Since the act might help consolidate Liholiho's position, it had a certain appeal to the king. Anyway, the *kapus* were weakening: these white men, coming now in ever greater numbers, defied them with impunity. Liholiho vacillated, went on a two-day drunk before gaining courage, then finally sat down to eat. It was a last supper, shattering an ancient creed and opening the way for a radically new divinity. As Kaahumanu had willed, the old order collapsed, taking away a vital part of island life and leaving the Hawaiians more exposed than ever to foreign influence.

Already Western practices were gaining hold. Commerce from Honolulu, Lahaina and other ports was booming. There was a fortune to be made dealing sandalwood to China-bound merchants, and the chiefs were forcing the common people to strip Hawaii's forests. The grueling labor might make the chiefs rich, but it gained the commoners little more than a barren landscape. Western diseases struck virulently. The Polynesians in Hawaii, who numbered 300,000 in Cook's time, were extremely susceptible. By 1866, their population had dwindled to less than 60,000. It was a difficult time for the Hawaiian people.

MISSIONARIES AND MERCHANTS   Hawaii was not long without religion. The same year that Kaahumanu shattered tradition, a group of New England missionaries boarded the brig *Thaddeus* for a voyage around Cape Horn. It was a young company—many were in their twenties or thirties—and included a doctor, a printer and several teachers. They were all strict Calvinists, fearful that the second coming was at hand and possessed of a mission. They were bound for a strange land called Hawaii, 18,000 miles away.

Hawaii, of course, was a lost paradise, a hellhole of sin and savagery where men slept with several wives and women neglected to wear dresses. To the missionaries, it mattered little that the Hawaiians had lived this way for centuries. The churchmen would save these heathens from hell's everlasting fire whether they liked it or not.

The delegation arrived in Kailua on the Big Island in 1820 and then spread out, establishing important missions in Honolulu and Lahaina. Soon they were building schools and churches, conducting services in Hawaiian and converting the natives to Christianity.

The missionaries rapidly became an integral part of Hawaii, despite the fact that they were a walking contradiction to everything Hawaiian. They were a contentious, self-righteous, fanatical people whose arrogance toward the Hawaiians blinded them to the beauty and wisdom of island lifestyles. Where the natives lived in thatch homes open to the soothing trade winds, the missionaries built airless clapboard houses with New England–style fireplaces. While the Polynesians swam and surfed frequently, the new arrivals, living near the world's finest beaches, stank from not bathing. In a region where the thermometer rarely drops much below seventy degrees, they wore long-sleeved woolens, ankle-length dresses and claw-hammer coats. At dinner they preferred salt pork to fresh beef, dried meat to fresh fish. They considered coconuts an abomination and were loath to eat bananas.

And yet the missionaries were a brave people, selfless and God-fearing. Their dangerous voyage from the Atlantic had brought them into a very alien land. Many would die from disease and overwork; most would never see their homeland again. Bigoted though they were, the Calvinists committed their lives to the Hawaiian people. They developed the Hawaiian alphabet, rendered Hawaiian into a written language and, of course, translated the Bible. Theirs was the first printing press west of the Rockies. They introduced Western medicine throughout the islands and created such an effective school system that, by the mid-19th century, 80 percent of the Hawaiian population was literate. Unlike almost all the other white people who came to Hawaii, they not only took from the islanders, they also gave.

But to a missionary, *giving* means ripping away everything repugnant to God and substituting it with Christianity. They would have to destroy Hawaiian culture in order to save it. Though instructed by their church elders not to meddle in island politics, the missionaries soon realized that heavenly wars had to be fought on earthly battlefields. Politics it would be. After all, wasn't government just another expression of God's bounty?

They allied with Kaahumanu and found it increasingly difficult to separate church from state. Kaahumanu converted to Christianity, while the missionaries became government advisers and helped pass laws protecting the sanctity of the Sabbath. Disgusting practices such as hula dancing were prohibited.

Politics can be a dangerous world for a man of the cloth. The missionaries were soon pitted against other foreigners who were quite willing to let the clerics sing hymns, but were damned opposed to permitting them a voice in government. Hawaii in the 1820s had become a favorite way station for the whaling fleet. As the sandalwood forests were decimated, the island merchants began looking for other industries. By the 1840s, when over 500 ships a year anchored in Hawaiian ports, whaling had become the islands' economic lifeblood.

Like the missionaries, the whalers were Yankees, shipping out from bustling New England ports. But they were a hell of a different cut of Yankee. These were rough, crude, boisterous men who loved rum and music, and thought a lot more of fornicating with island women than saving them. After the churchmen forced the passage of laws prohibiting prostitution, the sailors rioted along the waterfront and fired cannons at the mission homes. When the smoke cleared, the whalers still had their women.

Religion simply could not compete with commerce, and other Westerners were continuously stimulating more business in the islands. By the 1840s, as Hawaii adopted a parliamentary form of government, American and British fortune hunters were replacing missionaries as government advisers. It was a time when anyone, regardless of ability or morality, could travel to the islands and become a political powerhouse literally overnight. A consumptive American, fleeing the mainland for reasons of health, became chief justice of the Hawaiian Supreme Court while still in his twenties. Another lawyer, shadowed from the East Coast by a checkered past, became attorney general two weeks after arriving.

The situation was no different internationally. Hawaii was subject to the whims and terrors of gunboat diplomacy. The archipelago was solitary and exposed, and Western powers were beginning to eye it covetously. In 1843, a maverick British naval officer actually annexed Hawaii to the Crown, but the London government later countermanded his actions. Then, in the early 1850s, the threat of American annexation arose. Restless Californians, fresh from the gold fields and hungry for revolution, plotted unsuccessfully in Honolulu. Even the French periodically sent gunboats in to protect their small Catholic minority.

Finally, the three powers officially stated that they wanted to maintain Hawaii's national integrity. But independence seemed increasingly unlikely. European countries had already begun claiming other Pacific islands, and with the influx of Yankee missionaries and whalers, Hawaii was being steadily drawn into the American orbit.

THE SUGAR PLANTERS   There is an old Hawaiian saying that describes the 19th century: The missionaries came to do good, and they did very well. Actually the early evangelists, few of whom profited from their work, lived out only half the maxim. Their sons would give the saying its full meaning.

This second generation, quite willing to sacrifice glory for gain, fit neatly into the commercial society that had rendered their fathers irrelevant. They were shrewd, farsighted young Christians who had grown up in Hawaii and knew both the islands' pitfalls and potentials. They realized that the missionaries had never quite found Hawaii's pulse, and they watched uneasily as whaling became the lifeblood of the islands. Certainly it brought wealth, but whaling was too tenuous—there was always a threat that it might dry up entirely. A one-industry economy would never do; the mission boys wanted more. Agriculture was the obvious answer, and eventually they determined to bind their providence to a plant that grew wild in the islands—sugar cane.

During the heyday of the whaling industry, more American ships visited Hawaii than any other port in the world.

The first sugar plantation was started on Kauai in 1835, but not until the 1870s did the new industry blossom. By then, the Civil War had wreaked havoc with the whaling fleet, and a devastating winter in the Arctic whaling grounds practically destroyed it. The mission boys, who prophesied the storm, weathered it quite comfortably. They had already begun fomenting an agricultural revolution.

Agriculture, of course, means land, and in the 19th century practically all Hawaii's acreage was held by the king and the chiefs. So in 1850, the mission sons, together with other white entrepreneurs, pushed through the Great Mahele, one of the slickest real estate laws in history. Rationalizing that it would grant chiefs the liberty to sell land to Hawaiian commoners and white men, the mission sons established a western system of private property.

The Hawaiians, who had shared their chiefs' lands communally for centuries, had absolutely no concept of deeds and leases. What resulted was the old $24-worth-of-beads story. The benevolent Westerners wound up with the land, while the lucky Hawaiians got practically nothing. Large tracts were purchased for cases of whiskey; others went for the cost of a hollow promise. The entire island of Niihau, which is still owned by the same family, sold for $10,000. It was a bloodless coup, staged more than 40 years before the revolution that would topple Hawaii's monarchy. In a sense it made the 1893 uprising anticlimactic. By then Hawaii's future would already be determined: white interlopers would own four times as much land as Hawaiian commoners.

Following the Great Mahele, the mission boys, along with other businessmen, were ready to become sugar planters. The *mana* once again was passing into new hands. Obviously, there was money to be made in cane, a lot of it, and now that they had land, all they needed was labor. The Hawaiians would never do. Cook might have recognized them as industrious, hardworking people, but the sugar planters considered them shiftless. Disease was killing them off anyway, and the Hawaiians who survived seemed to lose the will to live. Many made appointments with death, stating that in a week they would die; seven days later they were dead.

Foreign labor was the only answer. In 1850, the Masters and Servants Act was passed, establishing an immigration board to import plantation workers. Cheap Asian labor would be brought over. It was a crucial decision, one that would ramify forever through Hawaiian history and change the very substance of island society. Eventually these Asian workers transformed Hawaii from a chain of Polynesian islands into one of the world's most varied and dynamic locales, a meeting place of East and West.

The Chinese were the first to come, arriving in 1852 and soon outnumbering the white population. Initially, with their long pigtails and uncommon habits, the Chinese were a joke around the islands. They were poor people from southern China whose lives were directed by clan loyalty. They built schools and worked hard so that one day they could return to their native villages in glory. They were ambitious, industrious and—ultimately—successful.

Too successful, according to the sugar planters, who found it almost impossible to keep the coolies down on the farm. The Chinese came to Hawaii under labor contracts, which forced them to work for five years. After their indentureship, rather than reenlisting as the sugar bosses had planned, the Chinese moved to the city and became merchants. Worse yet, they married Hawaiian women and were assimilated into the society.

These coolies, the planters decided, were too uppity, too ready to fill social roles that were really the business of white men. So in the 1880s, they began importing Portuguese. But the Portuguese thought they already *were* white men, while any self-respecting American or Englishman of the time knew they weren't.

The Portuguese spelled trouble, and in 1886 the sugar planters turned to Japan, with its restricted land mass and burgeoning population. The new immigrants were peasants from Japan's southern islands, raised in an authoritarian, hierarchical culture in which the father was a family dictator and the family was strictly defined by its social status. Like the Chinese, they built schools to protect their heritage and dreamed of returning home someday; but unlike their Asian neighbors, they only married other Japanese. They sent home for "picture brides," worshipped their ancestors and Emperor and paid ultimate loyalty to Japan, not Hawaii.

The Japanese, it soon became evident, were too proud to work long hours for low pay. Plantation conditions were atrocious; workers were housed in hovels and frequently beaten. The Japanese simply did not adapt. Worst of all, they not only bitched, they organized, striking in 1909.

So in 1910, the sugar planters turned to the Philippines for labor. For two decades the Filipinos arrived, seeking their fortunes and leaving their wives behind. They worked not only with sugar cane but also with pineapples, which were becoming a big business in the 20th century. They were a boisterous, fun-loving people, hated by the immigrants who preceded them and used by the whites who hired them. The Filipinos were given the most menial jobs, the worst working conditions and the shoddiest housing. In time, another side of their character began to show—a despondency, a hopeless sense of their own plight, their inability to raise passage money back home. They became the niggers of Hawaii.

> Between 1850 and 1930, 180,000 Japanese, 125,000 Filipinos, 50,000 Chinese, and 20,000 Portuguese immigrated to Hawaii.

REVOLUTIONARIES AND ROYALISTS Sugar, by the late 19th century, was king. It had become the center of island economy, the principal fact of life for most islanders. Like the earlier whaling industry, it was drawing Hawaii ever closer to the American sphere. The sugar planters were selling the bulk of their crops in California; having already signed several tariff treaties to protect their American market, they were eager to further strengthen mainland ties. Besides, many sugar planters were second-, third- and fourth-generation descendants of the New England missionaries; they had a natural affinity for the United States.

There was, however, one group that shared neither their love for sugar nor their ties to America. To the Hawaiian people, David Kalakaua was king, and America was the nemesis that had long threatened their independence. The whites might own the land, but the Hawaiians, through their monarch, still held substantial political power. During Kalakaua's rule in the 1870s and 1880s, anti-colonialism was rampant.

The sugar planters were growing impatient. Kalakaua was proving very antagonistic; his nationalist drumbeating was becoming louder in their ears. How could the sugar merchants convince the United States to annex Hawaii when all these silly Hawaiian royalists were running around pretending to be the Pacific's answer to the British Isles? They had tolerated this long enough. The Hawaiians were obviously unfit to rule, and the planters soon joined with other businessmen to form a secret revolutionary organization. Backed by a force of well-armed followers, they pushed through the "Bayonet Constitution" of 1887, a self-serving document that weakened the king and strengthened the white landowners. If Hawaii was to remain a monarchy, it would have a Magna Carta.

But Hawaii would not be a monarchy long. Once revolution is in the air, it's often difficult to clear the smoke. By 1893, Kalakaua was dead and his sister, Liliuokalani, had succeeded to the throne. She was an audacious leader, proud of her heritage, quick to defend it and prone to let immediate passions carry her onto dangerous ground. At a time when she should have hung fire, she charged, proclaiming publicly that she would abrogate the new constitution and reestablish a strong monarchy. The revolutionaries had the excuse they needed. They struck in January, seized government buildings and, with four boatloads of American marines and the support of the American minister, secured Honolulu. Liliuokalani surrendered.

Hawaii's first president was Sanford Dole, a missionary's son whose name eventually became synonymous with pineapples.

It was a highly illegal coup; legitimate government had been stolen from the Hawaiian people. But given an island chain as isolated and vulnerable as Hawaii, the revolutionaries reasoned, how much did it really matter? It would be weeks before word reached Washington of what a few Americans had done without official sanction, then several more months before a new American president, Grover Cleveland, denounced the renegade action. By then the revolutionaries would already be forming a republic.

Not even revolution could rock Hawaii into the modern age. For years, an unstable monarchy had reigned; now an oligarchy composed of the revolution's leaders would rule. Officially, Hawaii was a democracy; in truth, the Chinese and Japanese were hindered from voting, and the Hawaiians were encouraged not to bother. Hawaii, reckoned its new leaders, was simply not ready for democracy. Even when the islands were finally annexed by the United States in 1898 and granted territorial status, they remained a colony.

More than ever before, the sugar planters, alias revolutionaries, held sway. By the early 20th century, they had linked their plantations into a cartel, the Big Five. It was a tidy monopoly composed of five companies that owned not only the sugar and pineapple industries, but the docks, shipping companies and many of the stores, as well. Most of these holdings, happily, were the property of a few interlocking, intermarrying mission families—the Doles, Thurstons, Alexanders, Baldwins, Castles, Cookes and others—who had found heaven right here on earth. They golfed together and dined together, sent their daughters to Wellesley and their sons to Yale. All were proud of their roots, and as blindly paternalistic as their forefathers. It was their destiny to control Hawaii, and they made very certain, by refusing to sell land or provide services, that mainland firms did not gain a foothold in their domain.

What was good for the Big Five was good for Hawaii. Competition was obviously not good for Hawaii. Although the Chinese and Japanese were establishing successful businesses in Honolulu and some Chinese were even growing rich, they posed no immediate threat to the Big Five. And the Hawaiians had never been good at capitalism. By the early 20th century, they had become one of the world's most urbanized groups. But rather than competing with white businessmen in Honolulu, unemployed Hawaiians were forced to live in hovels and packing crates, cooking their poi on stoves fashioned from empty oil cans.

Political competition was also unhealthy. Hawaii was ruled by the Big Five, so naturally it should be run by the Republican Party. After all, the mission families were Republicans. Back on the mainland, the Democrats had always been cool to the sugar planters, and it was a Republican president, William McKinley, who eventually annexed Hawaii. The Republicans, quite simply, were good for business.

The Big Five set out very deliberately to overwhelm any political opposition. When the Hawaiians created a home-rule party around the turn of the century, the Big Five shrewdly co-opted it by running a beloved descendant of Hawaii's royal family as the Republican candidate. On the plantations they pitted one ethnic group against another to prevent the Asian workers from organizing. Then, when labor unions finally formed, the Big Five attacked them savagely. In 1924, police killed 16 strikers on Kauai. Fourteen years later, in an incident known as the "Hilo massacre," the police wounded 50 picketers.

The Big Five crushed the Democratic Party by intimidation. Polling booths were rigged. It was dangerous to vote Democratic—workers could lose their jobs, and if they were plantation workers, that meant losing their houses, as well. Conducting Democratic meetings on the plantations was about as easy as holding a hula dance in an old missionary church. The Democrats went underground.

Those were halcyon days for both the Big Five and the Republican Party. In 1900, only five percent of Hawaii's population was white. The rest was comprised of races that rarely benefitted from Republican policies. But for the next several decades, even during the Depression, the Big Five kept the Republicans in power.

While the New Deal swept the mainland, Hawaii clung to its colonial heritage. The islands were still a generation behind the rest of the United States—the Big Five enjoyed it that way. There was nothing like the status quo when you were already in power. Other factors that had long shaped Hawaii's history also played into the hands of the Big Five. The islands' vulnerability, which had always favored the rule of a small elite, permitted the Big Five to establish an awesome cartel. Hawaii's isolation, its distance from the mainland, helped protect their monopoly.

THE JAPANESE AND THE MODERN WORLD   All that ended on December 7, 1941. On what would afterwards be known as the "Day of Infamy," a flotilla of six aircraft carriers carrying over 400 planes unleashed a devastating assault on Pearl Harbor. Attacking the Pacific Fleet on a Sunday morning, when most of the American ships were unwisely anchored side by side, the Japanese sank or badly damaged six battleships, three destroyers and several other vessels. Over 2400 Americans were killed.

The Japanese bombers that attacked Pearl Harbor sent shock waves through Hawaii that are still rumbling today. World War II changed all the rules of the game, upsetting the conditions that had determined island history for centuries.

Ironically, no group in Hawaii would feel the shift more thoroughly than the Japanese. On the mainland, Japanese-Americans were rounded up and herded into relocation camps. But in Hawaii that was impossible; there were simply too many, and they comprised too large a part of the labor force.

Many were second-generation Japanese, *nisei*, who had been educated in American schools and assimilated into Western society. Unlike their immigrant parents, the *issei*, they felt few ties to Japan. Their loyalties lay with America, and when war broke out they determined to prove it. They joined the U.S. armed forces and formed a regiment, the 442nd, which became the most frequently decorated outfit of the war. The Japanese were heroes, and when the war ended many heroes came home to the United States and ran for political office. Men like Dwight Eisenhower, Daniel Inouye, John Kennedy and Spark Matsunaga began winning elections.

By the time the 442nd returned to the home front, Hawaii was changing dramatically. The Democrats were coming to power. Leftist labor unions won crucial strikes in 1941 and 1946. Jack Burns, an ex-cop who dressed in tattered clothes and drove around Honolulu in a beat-up car, was creating a new Democratic coalition.

Burns, who would eventually become governor, recognized the potential power of Hawaii's ethnic groups. Money was flowing into the islands—first military expenditures and then tourist dollars, and non-whites were rapidly becoming a new middle class. The Filipinos still constituted a large part of the plantation force, and the Hawaiians remained disenchanted, but the Japanese and Chinese were moving up fast. Together they comprised a majority of Hawaii's voters.

Burns organized them, creating a multiracial movement and thrusting the Japanese forward as candidates. By 1954, the Democrats controlled the legislature, with the Japanese filling one out of every two seats in the capital. Then, when Hawaii attained statehood five years later, the voters elected the first Japanese ever to serve in Congress. Today one of the state's U.S. senators and a congressman are Japanese. On every level of government, from municipal to federal, the Japanese predominate. They have arrived. The *mana*, that legendary power coveted by the Hawaiian chiefs and then lost to the sugar barons, has passed once again—to a people who came as immigrant farm-workers and stayed to become the leaders of the 50th state.

When Japan's Emperor declared war on the United States in 1941, 160,000 Japanese-Americans were living in Hawaii, fully one-third of the islands' population.

The Japanese and the Democrats were on the move, but in the period from World War II until the present day, everything was in motion. Hawaii was in upheaval. Jet travel and a population boom shattered the islands' solitude. While in 1939 about 500 people flew to Hawaii, now more than six million land every year. The military population escalated as Oahu became a key base not only during World War II but throughout the Cold War and the Vietnam War, as well. Hawaii's overall population exploded from about a half-million just after World War II to over one million at the present time.

No longer did the islands lag behind the mainland; they rapidly acquired the dubious quality of modernity. Hawaii became America's 50th state in 1959, Honolulu grew into a bustling highrise city, and condominiums mushroomed along Maui's beaches. Outside investors swallowed up two of the Big Five corporations, and several partners in the old monopoly began conducting most of their business outside Hawaii. Everything became too big and moved too fast for Hawaii to be entirely vulnerable to a small interest group. Now, like the rest of the world, it would be prey to multinational corporations. By the 1980s, it would also be of significant interest to investors from Japan. In a few short years they succeeded in buying up a majority of the state's luxury resorts, including every major beachfront hotel in Waikiki, sending real estate prices into an upward spiral that did not level off until the early 1990s.

One element that has not plateaued during the current decade is the Native Hawaiian movement. Nativist sentiments were spurred in January 1993 by the 100th anniversary of the American overthrow of the Hawaiian monarchy. Over 15,000 people turned out to mark the illegal coup. Later that year, President Clinton signed a statement issued by Congress formally apologizing to the Hawaiian people. Then in 1994, the United States Navy returned the island of Kahoolawe to the state of Hawaii. Long a rallying symbol for the Native Hawaiian movement, the unoccupied island had been used for decades as a naval bombing target. By 1996, efforts to clean away bomb debris and make the island habitable were well under way.

Today, with its own indigenous people's movement, average house prices over $300,000 and an inflation factor that saw prices rise over 200% in 20 years, Hawaii has finally arrived. It is so much a part of the United States that one segment of the population is advocating secession. An island chain that slept for centuries has been awakened by the forces of change and is in turn beginning to disrupt the complacency of the forces that have long kept it dormant.

Culture

Hawaii, according to Polynesian legend, was discovered by Hawaii-loa, an adventurous sailor who often disappeared on long fishing trips. On one voyage, urged along by his navigator, Hawaii-loa sailed toward the planet Jupiter. He crossed the "many-colored ocean," passed over the "deep-colored sea," and eventually came upon "flaming Hawaii," a mountainous island chain that spewed smoke and lava.

History is less romantic. The Polynesians who found Hawaii were probably driven from their home islands by war or some similar calamity. They traveled in groups, not as lone rangers, and shared their canoes with dogs, pigs and chickens, with which they planned to stock new lands. Agricultural plants such as coconuts, yams, taro, sugar cane, bananas and breadfruit were also stowed on board.

Most important, they transported their culture, an intricate system of beliefs and practices developed in the South Seas. After undergoing the stresses and demands of pioneer life, this traditional lifestyle was transformed into a new and uniquely Hawaiian culture.

It was based on a caste system that placed the *alii* or chiefs at the top and the slaves, *kauwas*, on the bottom. Between these two groups were the priests, *kahunas* and the common people or *makaainanas*. The chiefs, much like feudal lords, controlled all the land and collected taxes from the commoners who farmed it.

Life centered around the *kapu*, a complex group of regulations that dictated what was sacred or profane. For example, women were not permitted to eat pork or bananas; commoners had to prostrate themselves in the presence of a chief. These strictures were vital to Hawaiian religion; *kapu* breakers were directly violating the will of the gods and could be executed for their actions. And there were a lot of gods to watch out for, many quite vindictive. The four central gods were *Kane*, the creator; *Lono*, the god of agriculture; *Ku*, the war god; and *Kanaloa*, lord of the underworld. They had been born from the sky father and earth mother, and had in turn created many lesser gods and demigods who controlled various aspects of nature.

It was, in the uncompromising terminology of the West, a stone-age civilization. Though the Hawaiians lacked metal tools, the wheel and a writing system, they managed to include within their short inventory of cultural goods everything necessary to sustain a large population on a chain of small islands. They fashioned fish nets from coconut fibers, made hooks out of bone, shell and ivory, and raised fish in rock-bound ponds. The men used irrigation in their farming. The women made clothing by pounding mulberry bark into a soft cloth called *tapa*, dyeing elaborate patterns into the fabric. They built peak-roofed thatch huts from native *pili* grass and *lauhala* leaves. The men fought wars with spears, slings, clubs and daggers! The women used mortars and pestles to pound the roots of the taro plant into poi, the islanders' staple food.

The West labeled these early Hawaiians "noble savages." Actually, they often lacked nobility. The Hawaiians were cannibals who sometimes practiced human sacrifice and often used human bait to fish for sharks. They constantly warred among themselves and would mercilessly pursue a retreating army, murdering as many of the vanquished soldiers as possible.

But they weren't savages either. The Hawaiians developed a rich oral tradition of genealogical chants and created beautiful lilting songs to accompany their hula dancing. Their musicians mastered several instruments including the *ukeke* (a single-stringed device resembling a bow), an *ohe* or nose flute, conch shells, rattles and drums made from gourds, coconut shells or logs. Their craftsmen produced the world's finest featherwork, weaving thousands of tiny feathers into golden cloaks and ceremonial helmets. The Hawaiians helped develop the sport of surfing. They also swam, boxed, bowled and devised an intriguing game called *konane*, a cross between checkers and the Japanese game of go. They built hiking trails from coral and lava, and created an elemental art form in the images—petroglyphs—that they carved into rocks along the trails.

They also achieved something far more outstanding than their varied arts and crafts, something which the West, with its awesome knowledge and advanced technology, has never duplicated. The Hawaiians created a balance with nature. They practiced conser-

◆◆

A SLICE OF THE PIE

In ancient Hawaii, each island was divided like a pie into wedge-shaped plots, *ahupuaas*, which extended from the ocean to the mountain peaks. In that way, every chief's domain contained fishing spots, village sites, arable valleys and everything else necessary for the survival of his subjects.

vation, establishing closed seasons on certain fish species and carefully guarding their plant and animal resources. They led a simple life, without the complexities the outside world would eventually thrust upon them. It was a good life: food was plentiful, people were healthy and the population increased. For a thousand years, the Hawaiians lived in delicate harmony with the elements. It wasn't until the West entered the realm, transforming everything, that the fragile balance was destroyed. But that is another story entirely.

PEOPLE

Because of its unique history and isolated geography, Hawaii is truly a cultural melting pot. It's one of the few states in the union in which caucasians are a minority group. Whites, or haoles as they're called in the islands, comprise only about 23 percent of Hawaii's 1.1 million population. Japanese constitute 20 percent, Filipinos 10 percent, Hawaiians and part-Hawaiians account for 19 percent, Chinese about 5 percent and other racial groups 23 percent.

It's a very young, vital society. More than half the community is under thirty-five and over one-third of the people were born of racially mixed parents.

One trait characterizing many of these people is Hawaii's famous spirit of *aloha*, a genuine friendliness, an openness to strangers, a willingness to give freely. Undoubtedly, it is one of the finest qualities any people has ever demonstrated.

Three out of every four Hawaii residents live on the island of Oahu, and almost half reside in Honolulu.

Aloha originated with the Polynesians and played an important role in ancient Hawaiian civilization. When the Western colonialists arrived, however, they viewed it not as a Hawaiian form of graciousness, but rather as the naivete of a primitive culture. They turned *aloha* into a tool for exploiting the Hawaiians, taking practically everything they owned.

Today, unfortunately, the descendants of the colonialists are being repaid in kind. The *aloha* spirit is still present in the islands, but another social force has arisen—racial hatred.

Sometimes this hatred spills into ripoffs and violence. Therefore, mainland visitors must be very careful, particularly when traveling in heavily touristed areas. Try not to leave items in your car; if you absolutely must, lock them in the trunk. Don't leave valuable gear unattended in a campsite. And try not to antagonize the islands' young people.

It's exciting to meet folks, and I highly recommend that you mix with local residents, but do it with forethought and consideration. A lot of locals are eager to make new acquaintances; others can be extremely hostile. So choose the situation. If a local group looks bent on trouble, mind your own business. They don't need you, and you don't need them. For most encounters, I'd follow this general rule—be friendly, but be careful.

CUISINE

Nowhere is the influence of Hawaii's melting pot population stronger than in the kitchen. While in the islands, you'll probably eat not only with a fork, but with chopsticks and fingers, as well. You'll sample a wonderfully varied cuisine. In addition to standard American fare, hundreds of restaurants serve Hawaiian, Japanese, Chinese, Korean, Portuguese and Filipino dishes. There are also fresh fruits aplenty—pineapples, papayas, mangoes, bananas and tangerines—plus native fish such as mahimahi, marlin and snapper.

The prime Hawaiian dish is poi, made from crushed taro root and served as a pasty purple liquid. It's pretty bland fare, but it does make a good side dish with roast pork or tripe stew. You should also try *laulau*, a combination of fish, pork and taro leaves wrapped in a *ti* leaf and steamed. And don't neglect to taste baked *ulu* (breadfruit) and *opihi* (limpets). Among the other Hawaiian culinary traditions are *kalua* pig, a shredded pork dish baked in an *imu* (underground oven); *lomilomi* salmon, which is salted and mixed with onions and tomatoes; and chicken *laulau*, prepared in taro leaves and coconut milk.

A good way to try all these dishes at one sitting is to attend a luau. I've always found the tourist luaus too commercial, but you might watch the newspapers for one of the special luaus sponsored by civic organizations.

Japanese dishes include sushi, sukiyaki, teriyaki and tempura, plus an island favorite—sashimi, or raw fish. On most any menu, including McDonald's, you'll find *saimin*, a noodle soup filled with meat, vegetables and *kamaboko* (fishcake).

You can count on the Koreans for *kim chi*, a spicy salad of pickled cabbage and *kun koki*, barbecued meat prepared with soy and sesame oil. The Portuguese serve up some delicious sweets including *malasadas* (donuts minus the holes) and *pao doce*, or sweet bread. For Filipino fare, I recommend *adobo*, a pork or chicken dish spiced with garlic and vinegar, and *pochero*, a meat entrée cooked with bananas and several vegetables. In addition to a host of dinner dishes, the Chinese have contributed some less common treats such as *manapua* (a steamed bun filled with barbecued pork) and oxtail soup. They also introduced crack seed to the islands. Made from dried and preserved fruit, it provides a treat as sweet as candy.

As the Hawaiians say, *"Hele mai ai."* Come and eat!

LANGUAGE

The language common to all Hawaii is English, but because of its diverse cultural heritage, the archipelago also supports several other tongues. Foremost among these are Hawaiian and pidgin. Hawaiian, closely related to other Polynesian languages, is one of the most fluid and melodious languages in the world. It's composed of only twelve letters: five vowels—*a, e, i, o, u* and seven consonants—*h, k, l, m, n, p, w*.

At first glance, the language appears formidable: how the hell do you pronounce *humuhumunukunukuapuaa*? But actually it's quite simple. After you've mastered a few rules of pronunciation, you can take on any word in the language.

The first thing to remember is that every syllable ends with a vowel, and the next to last syllable receives the accent.

The next rule to keep in mind is that all the letters in Hawaiian are pronounced. Consonants are pronounced the same as in English (except for the *w*, which is pronounced as a *v* when it introduces the last syllable of a word—as in *ewa* or *awa*. Vowels are pronounced the same as in Latin or Spanish: *a* as in *among*, *e* as in *they*, *i* as in *machine*, *o* as in *no* and *u* as in *too*. Hawaiian has four vowel combinations or diphthongs: *au*, pronounced *ow*, *ae* and *ai*, which sound like *eye*, and *ei*, pronounced *ay*.

By now, you're probably wondering what I could possibly have meant when I said Hawaiian was simple. I think the glossary that follows will simplify everything while helping you pronounce common words and place names. Just go through the list, starting with words like aloha and luau that you already know. After you've practiced pronouncing familiar words, the rules will become second nature; you'll practically be a *kamaaina*.

Just when you start to speak with a swagger, cocky about having learned a new language, some young Hawaiian will start talking at you in a tongue that breaks all the rules you've so carefully mastered. That's pidgin. It started in the 19th century as a lingua franca among Hawaii's many races. Pidgin speakers mix English and Hawaiian with several other tongues to produce a spicy creole. It's a fascinating language with its own vocabulary, a unique syntax and a rising inflection that's hard to mimic.

Pidgin is definitely the hip way to talk in Hawaii. A lot of young Hawaiians use it among themselves as a private language. At times they may start talking pidgin to you, acting as though they don't speak English; then if they decide you're okay, they'll break into English. When that happens, you be one *da kine brah*.

So *brah*, I take *da kine* pidgin words, put 'em together with Hawaiian, make one big list. Savvy?

> *aa* (**ah**-ah)—a type of rough lava
> *ae* (eye)—yes
> *aikane* (eye-**kah**-nay)—friend
> *akamai* (ah-**kah**-my)—wise
> *alii* (ah-**lee**-ee)—chief
> *aloha* (ah-**lo**-ha)—hello; greetings; love
> *aole* (ah-**oh**-lay)—no
> *auwe* (ow-**way**)—ouch!
> *brah* (bra)—friend; brother; bro'

bumby (**bum**-bye)—after a while; by and by

dah makule guys (da mah-**kuh**-lay guys)—senior citizens

da kine (da kyne)—whatdyacallit; thingamajig; that way

diamondhead—in an easterly direction

duh uddah time (duh **uh**-duh time)—once before

ewa (**eh**-vah)—in a westerly direction

hale (**hah**-lay)—house

haole (**how**-lee)—Caucasian; white person

hapa (**hah**-pa)—half

hapa-haole (**hah**-pa **how**-lee)—half-Caucasian

heiau (hey-ee-**ow**)—temple

hele on (**hey**-lay own)—hip; with it

holo holo (**ho**-low **ho**-low)—to visit

howzit? (hows-it)—how you doing? what's happening?

hukilau (**who**-key-lau)—community fishing party

hula (**who**-la)—Hawaiian dance

imu (**ee**-moo)—underground oven

ipo (**ee**-po)—sweetheart

jag up (jag up)—drunk

kahuna (kah-**who**-nah)—priest

kai (kye)—ocean

kaka-roach (**kah**-kah roach)—ripoff; theft

kamaaina (kah-mah-**eye**-nah)—a longtime island resident

kane (**kah**-nay)—man

kapu (**kah**-poo)—taboo; forbidden

kaukau (cow-cow)—food

keiki (**kay**-key)—child

kiawe (key-**ah**-vay)—mesquite tree

kokua (ko-**coo**-ah)—help

kona winds (**ko**-nah winds)—winds that blow against the trades

lanai (lah-**nye**)—porch; also island name

lauhala (lau-**hah**-lah) or *hala* (**hah**-lah)—a tree whose leaves are used in weaving

lei (lay)—flower garland

lolo (low-low)—stupid

lomilomi (**low**-me-**low**-me)—massage; also raw salmon

luau (**loo**-ow)—feast

mahalo (mah-**hah**-low)—thank you

mahalo nui loa (mah-**ha**-low **new**-ee **low**-ah)—thank you very much

mahu (**mah**-who)—gay; homosexual

makai (mah-**kye**)—toward the sea

malihini (mah-lee-**hee**-nee)—newcomer; stranger

mauka (**mau**-kah)—toward the mountains

nani (**nah**-nee)—beautiful
ohana (oh-**hah**-nah)—family
okole (oh-**ko**-lay)—rear; ass
okolemaluna (oh-ko-lay-mah-**loo**-nah)—a toast: bottoms up!
ono (**oh**-no)—tastes good
pahoehoe (pah-**hoy**-hoy)—ropy lava
pakalolo (pah-kah-**low**-low)—marijuana
pakiki head (pah-**key**-key head)—stubborn
pali (**pah**-lee)—cliff
paniolo (pah-nee-**oh**-low)—cowboy
pau (pow)—finished; done
pilikia (pee-lee-**key**-ah)—trouble
puka (**poo**-kah)—hole
pupus (**poo**-poos)—hors d'oeuvres
shaka (**shah**-kah)—great; perfect
swell head—angry
tapa (**tap**-ah)—tree bark which is used as a fabric
wahine (wah-**hee**-nay)—woman
wikiwiki (**wee**-key-**wee**-key)—quickly; in a hurry
you get stink ear—you don't listen well

MUSIC

Music has long been an integral part of Hawaiian life. Most families keep musical instruments in their homes, gathering to play at impromptu living room or backyard jam sessions. Hawaiian folk tunes are passed down from generation to generation. In the earliest days, it was the sound of rhythm instruments and chants that filled the air. Drums were fashioned from hollowed-out gourds, coconut shells and breadfruit logs, then covered with sharkskin. Gourds and coconuts, adorned with tapa cloth and feathers, were also filled with shells or pebbles to produce a rattling sound. Other instruments included the nose flute, a piece of bamboo similar to a mouth flute, but played by exhaling through the nostril; the bamboo organ; and *puili*, pieces of bamboo split into strips, which were struck rhythmically against the body.

Western musical scales and instruments were introduced by explorers and missionaries. As ancient Hawaiian music involved a completely different musical system, Hawaiians had to completely

NO OOMPAH-PAH! MO' BETTAH BRAH!

Strangely enough, a Prussian bandmaster named Henry Berger had a major influence on contemporary Hawaiian music. Brought over in the 19th century by King Kalakaua to lead the Royal Hawaiian Band, Berger helped Hawaiians make the transition to western instruments.

re-adapt. Actually, western music caught on quickly, and the hymns brought by missionaries fostered a popular musical style—the *himeni* or Hawaiian church music.

Hawaii has been the birthplace of several different musical instruments and styles. The ukulele, modeled on a Portuguese guitar, quickly became the most popular Hawaiian instrument. Its small size made it easy to carry, and with just four strings, it was simple to play. During the early 1900s, the steel guitar was exported to the mainland. Common in country-and-western music today, it was invented by a young man who experimented by sliding a steel bar across guitar strings.

The slack-key style of guitar playing also comes from Hawaii. In tuning, the six strings are loosened and then played in a variety of ways, from plucking or slapping the strings to sliding along them. A number of different tunings exist, and many have been passed down through families for generations.

During the late 19th century, *"hapa*-haole" songs became the rage. The ukelele was instrumental in contributing to this Hawaiian fad. Written primarily in English with pseudo-Hawaiian themes, songs like "Tiny Bubbles" and "Lovely Hula Hands" were later introduced to the world via Hollywood.

The Hawaiian craze continued on the mainland with radio and television shows such as "Hawaii Calls" and "The Harry Owens Show." In the 1950s, little mainland girls donned plastic hula skirts and danced along with Hilo Hattie and Ray Kinney.

It was not until the 1970s that both the hula and music of old Hawaii made a comeback. Groups such as the Sons of Hawaii and the Makaha Sons of Niihau, along with Auntie Genoa Keawe and the late Gabby Pahinui, became popular. Before long, a new form of Hawaiian music was being heard, a combination of ancient chants and contemporary sounds, performed by such islanders as Henry Kapono, Kalapana, Olomana, the Beamer Brothers, the Peter Moon Band and the Brothers Cazimero.

Today many of these groups, along with other notables such as Hapa, the Kaau Crater Boys, Brother Nolan, Willie K. and Butch Helemano, bring both innovation to the Hawaiian music scene and contribute to the preservation of an ancient tradition.

HULA

Along with palm trees, the hula—swaying hips, grass skirts, colorful leis—is linked forever in people's minds with the Hawaiian Islands. This western idea of hula is very different from what the dance has traditionally meant to native Hawaiians.

Hula is an old dance form, its origin shrouded in mystery. The ancient hula, *kahiko*, was more concerned with religion and spirituality than entertainment. Originally performed only by men, it was used in rituals to communicate with a deity—a connection to nature and the gods. Accompanied by drums and chants, *kahiko* expressed the islands' culture, mythology and history in hand and body movements. It later evolved from a strictly religious rite to a method of communicating stories and legends. Over the years, women were allowed to study the rituals and eventually became the primary dancers.

When westerners arrived, the *kahiko* hula began another transformation. Explorers and sailors were more interested in its erotic element, ignoring the cultural significance. Missionaries simply found it scandalous and set out to destroy the tradition. They dressed Hawaiians in western garb and outlawed the *kahiko* hula.

The hula tradition was resurrected by King David Kalakaua. Known by the moniker "Merrie Monarch," Kalakaua loved music and dance. For his coronation in 1883, he called together the kingdom's best dancers to perform the chants and hulas once again. He was also instrumental in the development of the contemporary hula, the *auwana* hula, which added new steps and movements and was accompanied by ukeleles and guitars rather than drums.

By the 1920s, modern hula had been popularized by Hollywood, westernized and introduced as kitschy tropicana. Real grass skirts gave way to cellophane versions, plastic leis replaced fragrant island garlands, and exaggerated gyrations supplanted the hypnotic movements of the traditional dance.

Fortunately, with the resurgence of Hawaiian pride in recent decades, Polynesian culture has been reclaimed and *kahiko* hula and chants have made a welcome comeback.

FOUR

Oahu

Honolulu, Somerset Maugham once remarked, is the meeting place of East and West. Today, with its highrise cityscape and crowded commercial center, Hawaii's capital is more the place where Hong Kong meets Los Angeles. It's the hub of Hawaii— a city that dominates the political, cultural and economic life of the islands.

And it's the focus of Oahu as well. Honolulu has given Oahu more than its nickname, The Capital Island. The city has drawn three-fourths of Hawaii's population to this third-largest island, making Oahu both a military stronghold and a popular tourist spot.

With military installations at Pearl Harbor and outposts seemingly everywhere, the armed forces control about one-quarter of the island. Most bases are off-limits to civilians; and tourists congregate in Honolulu's famed resort area—Waikiki. Both defense and tourism are big business on Oahu, and it's an ironic fact of island life that the staid, uniformly dressed military peacefully coexist here with crowds of sun-loving, scantily clad visitors.

The tourists are attracted by one of the world's most famous beaches, an endless white-sand ribbon that has drawn sun worshipers and water lovers since the days of Hawaiian royalty. In ancient times Waikiki was a swamp; now it's a spectacular region of world-class resorts.

Indeed, Waikiki is at the center of Pacific tourism, just as Honolulu is the capital of the Pacific. Nowhere else in the world will you find a population more varied or an ambience more vital. There are times when Waikiki's Parisian-size boulevards seem ready to explode from the sheer force of the crowds. People in bikinis and wild-colored aloha shirts stroll the streets, while others flash past on mopeds.

Since the 1980s this sun-splashed destination has also become a focal point for millions of wealthy tourists from Japan. As a result, Waikiki now has money-changing shops, restaurants displaying menus in Japanese only, stores where the clerks speak no English and an entire mall filled with duty-free shops.

Today the development craze that created modern-day Waikiki is continuing on to the southwest corner of the island in an area called Koolina. Here a major tourist facility named Ihilani Resort & Spa opened near Ewa Beach and plans are afoot to create Kapolei, a "second city" of as many as 200,000 people.

So hurry. Visitors can still discover that just beyond Honolulu's bustling thoroughfares stretches a beautiful island, featuring countless beaches and two incredible mountain ranges. Since most of the tourists (and a vast majority of the island's 863,000 population) congregate in the southern regions around Honolulu, the north is rural. You can experience the color and velocity of the city, then head for the slow and enchanting country.

As you begin to explore for yourself, you'll find Oahu also has something else to offer: history. *Oahu* means "gathering place" in Hawaiian, and for centuries it has been an important commercial area and cultural center. First populated by Marquesans around 500 A.D., the island was later settled by seafaring immigrants from Tahiti. Waikiki, with its white-sand beaches and luxurious coconut groves, became a favored spot among early monarchs.

Warring chiefs long battled for control of the island. According to legend, Kamehameha I seized power in 1795 by sweeping an opposing army over the cliffs of Nuuanu Pali north of Honolulu. Several years earlier the British had "discovered" Honolulu Harbor, a natural anchorage destined to be one of the Pacific's key seaports. Over the years the harbor proved ideal first for whalers and sandalwood traders and eventually for freighters and ocean liners.

In 1850 the city, which had grown up around the shipping port and become the focus of Hawaii, became the archipelago's capital as well. Here in 1893 a band of white businessmen illegally overthrew the native monarchy. Almost a half-century later, in an ill-advised but brilliantly executed military maneuver, the Japanese drew the United States into World War II with a devastating air strike against the huge naval base at Pearl Harbor.

There are some fascinating historical monuments to tour throughout Honolulu, but I recommend you also venture outside the city to Oahu's less congested regions. Major highways lead from the capital along the east and west coasts of this 608-square-mile island, and several roads bisect the central plateau en route to the North Shore. Except for a five-mile strip in Oahu's northwest corner, you can drive completely around the island.

Closest to Honolulu is the east coast, where a spectacular seascape is paralleled by the Koolaus, a jagged and awesomely steep mountain range. This is Oahu's rain-swept Windward Coast. Here, traveling up the coast past the bedroom communities of Kailua and Kaneohe, you'll discover beautiful and relatively untouched white-sand beaches. On the North Shore are some of the world's most famous surfing spots—Waimea Bay, Sunset, the Banzai Pipeline—where winter waves 20 and 30 feet high roll in with crushing force.

The Waianae Range, rising to 4040 feet, shadows Oahu's western coast. The sands are as white here, the beaches as uncrowded, but I've always felt uncomfortable on the Leeward Coast. Racial hostility is sometimes aimed at visitors on Oahu, as evidenced by theft, vandalism and beatings. It is particularly bad along this shore.

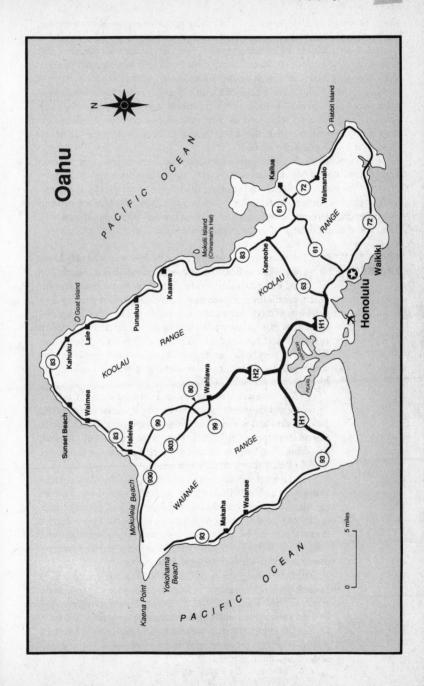

Oahu

Wherever you go on Oahu you have to be careful not to leave valuables unattended, but be particularly watchful around Waianae.

Between the Koolau and Waianae ranges, remnants of the two volcanoes that created Oahu, spreads the Leilehua Plateau. This fertile region is occupied by sugar and pineapple plantations as well as several large military bases.

Geologically, Oahu is the second-oldest island in the chain; two million years ago it was two individual islands, which eventually were joined by the Leilehua Plateau. Among its geographic features is the *pali*, an awesome wall of sheer cliffs along the windward coastline, and three famous tuff-cone volcanoes—Diamond Head, Punchbowl and Koko Head.

Hosting millions of tourists each year, Oahu has become a favorite location among travel agents. Many people can't even conceive of visiting Hawaii without going to "the gathering place," and some never venture out to any of the other islands. Oahu does have its virtues. But if, like me, you think of a vacation in terms of experiencing the crowds, and then leaving them behind—plan on fully exploring Oahu and then continuing on to the neighbor islands.

▼▼▼▼▼▼▼▼▼
Waikiki

To understand the geography of Waikiki you need only know about Waikiki Beach. And to understand Waikiki Beach, you must know two things. The first is that major hotels line the beach, practically from one end to the other, and are used as landmarks by visitors and local residents alike. The other fact to remember is that to visitors Waikiki Beach is a single sandy ribbon two miles long, but to local folks it represents many beaches in one. When you park your beach towel here, consider that every few strides will carry you into another realm of Waikiki's culture and history.

Waikiki once served as a retreat for Hawaiian kings and queens. By the turn of the century it was favored by writer-adventurers like Jack London and Robert Louis Stevenson. During World War II, GIs on leave soaked up its sun. Then in the jet age that followed, it became a highrise resort area. As a result, different sections of Waikiki Beach answer to different names.

This fabled peninsula extends two miles from the Ala Wai Yacht Harbor to Diamond Head and measures a half-mile in width from the Ala Wai Canal to the Pacific. Kalakaua Avenue, the main drag, is packed elbow to elbow with throngs of visitors. Paralleling the ocean, this broad boulevard is noisy, annoying, cosmopolitan and fascinating. Today visitors from Japan, arriving in ever-increasing numbers, add to the international atmosphere.

But the main appeal is still the district's white-sand corridor. Dotting the beach are picnic areas, restrooms, showers, concession stands and beach equipment rentals. Most of the beach is protected by coral reefs and sea walls, so the swimming is excellent, the snorkeling fair. This is also a prime area for surfing. Two- to four-foot waves, good for beginners and still challenging to experienced surfers, are common here.

The western flank of Waikiki Beach sits near the **Ilikai Hotel**. Here you will find a pretty lagoon fringed by palm trees. ~ 1777 Ala Moana Boulevard.

The curving strand nearby, fronting Hilton Hawaiian Village at 2005 Kalia Road, is called **Kahanamoku Beach**. Named for Hawaii's great surfer, Duke Kahanamoku, it features numerous facilities. Beach stands rent everything from towels, chairs and air mattresses to snorkel sets, surfboards and Hobie-cat sailboats.

Also here is Port Hilton, the pier from which the resort complex launches catamaran cruises. One of these boats will take you to what may be the only hidden attraction around Waikiki, the **Atlantis Submarine**, a 48-passenger sub located just off the coast that carries visitors to the bottom for a close-up look at an artificial reef, complete with sunken ships and airplanes, created to bring back marine life to the area. Admission. ~ 973-9811, 800-548-6262.

Fort De Russy Beach, owned by the military but open to the public, features the area's widest swath of white sand. It is also beautifully backdropped by a grove of palm trees. There are restrooms, picnic tables and barbecues, plus tennis, squash and volleyball courts.

The nearby **U.S. Army Museum of Hawaii** has every weapon from Hawaiian shark teeth blades to modern-day instruments of destruction. You can also trace the United States' unending series of military campaigns from the uniforms (ours and theirs) on exhibit here. Closed Monday. ~ Kalia Road; 438-2821.

Past Fort De Russy Beach stretches a palisade of highrise hotels. Lining the beachfront, they provide numerous facilities for thirsty sunbathers or adventuresome athletes. Continue on and you will pass the Sheraton strip, a lengthy stretch of Waikiki Beach fronted entirely by Sheraton hotels. This section marks Waikiki's center of action. The first hotel is the **Sheraton Waikiki**. A highrise structure built with two curving wings, it resembles a giant bird roosting on the beach. ~ 2255 Kalakaua Avenue.

The hotels here are so famous that the nearby strand is named **Royal-Moana Beach**. Stretching between the Royal Hawaiian and Moana hotels, it has been a sun-soaked gathering place for decades.

◆◆

CATCH A WAVE

All along Waikiki Beach, concessions offer rides on **outrigger canoes**. They are long, sleek fiberglass crafts resembling ancient Polynesian canoes. Each seats four to six passengers, plus a captain. For several dollars you can join the crew on a low-key wave-riding excursion that will have you paddling as hard and fast as you can to catch waves and ride them far into the shore.

That's because these two grand dames are Waikiki's oldest hotels. The **Royal Hawaiian Hotel** is Hawaii's "Pink Palace," a Spanish Moorish–style caravansary painted shocking pink. Built in 1927, it is a labyrinth of gardens, colonnades and balconies; the old place is certainly Waikiki's most interesting edifice. ~ 2259 Kalakaua Avenue; 923-7311.

The woodframe **Sheraton Moana Surfrider Hotel,** built in 1901, was Waikiki's first resort. Its vaulted ceilings, tree-shaded courtyard and spacious accommodations reflect the days when Hawaii was a retreat for the rich. This beach is also the site of one of Waikiki's most renowned surfing spots, Canoe's Surf. ~ 2365 Kalakaua Avenue; 922-3111.

Just beyond the Moana Hotel at 2453 Kalakaua Avenue is **Kuhio Beach Park,** which runs along Kalakaua Avenue from Kaiulani to Kapahulu avenues. In addition to a broad sandy beach, there are numerous facilities here—picnic areas, beach equipment rentals, showers, restrooms and lifeguards on duty. The shady pavilions in this public park also attract local folks who come to play cards and chess. Needless to say, this convenient beach is often quite crowded. Diners like it because of its proximity to many Waikiki budget restaurants; parents favor the beach for its protective sea wall, which provides a secure area where children can swim; and people-watchers find it an ideal place to check out the crowds of tourists and local residents.

HIDDEN ▶   The strand just beyond is called **Queen's Surf**. Here also are picnic areas, shady pavilions, restroom facilities and showers. Something of a Bohemian quarter, this pretty plot draws gays, local artists and a wide array of intriguing characters. On the weekends, conga drummers may be pounding out rhythms along the beach while other people gather to soak in the scene.

Kapiolani Park next door extends across 140 acres on both sides of Kalakaua Avenue. Hawaii's oldest park, this tree-studded playland dates back more than 100 years. Perhaps more than anything else, it has come to serve as a jogger's paradise. From dawn 'til dark, runners of all ages, colors, sizes and shapes beat a path around its perimeter. But Kapiolani offers something to just about anyone. There are tennis courts, softball and soccer fields, an archery area, and much more. To fully explore the park, you must visit each of its features in turn.

First is the **Waikiki Aquarium,** the place where you can finally discover what a *humuhumunukunukuapuaa*, that impossibly named fish, really looks like. (Don't be surprised if the name proves to be longer than the fish.) Within the aquarium's glass walls, you'll see more than 350 different species of fish originating from Hawaiian and South Pacific waters. Ranging from rainbow-hued tropical fish to blacktip reef sharks, they constitute a broad range of under-

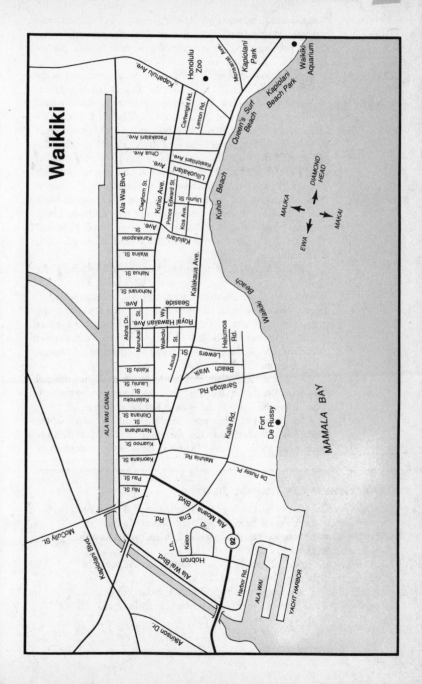

water species. Then there are Hawaiian monk seals (an endangered species) and other intriguing creatures. A biodiversity exhibit features a rotating display of creatures not native to Hawaii. Admission. ~ 2777 Kalakaua Avenue; 923-9741.

HIDDEN ►   The **Queen Kapiolani Garden** is planted across the park at the corner of Monsarrat and Paki avenues. With its colorful flowerbeds and shady pavilion, this is a pretty place to stroll and picnic.

There's one event that takes place in Kapiolani Park that has become an institution—the **Kodak Hula Show**, staged in the bleachers near the Waikiki Shell and Monsarrat Avenue. This free, hour-long presentation features ukulele music and hula dancers in ti-leaf skirts. The ukuleles plunk, the dancers sway and the tourists snap pictures (presumably using Kodak cameras and film). It is one of those attractions that is so hokey it is actually interesting. Some people come just to watch the tourists with their sunburned faces and matching aloha shirts. In any case, every Tuesday through Thursday at 10 a.m. you will encounter swarms of people lining the bleachers. ~ 627-3300.

The park's most outstanding feature is the **Honolulu Zoo.** Like city zoos everywhere, this tropical facility has a resident population of elephants, giraffes, ostriches, zebras, hippos, catacals, Sumatran tigers, black-mane lions, alligators and so on. But it also includes animals more common to the islands, creatures like the nene (a rare goose), Vietnamese pot-bellied pig and wild sheep. Perhaps most interesting of all, there is an outstanding collection of tropical birds. Admission. ~ 971-7171.

Just beyond Kapiolani Park stretches beautiful and tranquil **Sans Souci Beach,** which extends from the Natatorium to the New Otani Kaimana Beach Hotel. ~ 2863 Kalakaua Avenue.

Sans Souci is certainly not a hard place to find, as one of the world's most famous landmarks rises just behind it. More than any other place in the islands, **Diamond Head** is the trademark of

●●

✔ CHECK THESE OUT—UNIQUE SIGHTS

- Learn the hula, look into 19th-century Hawaiian history and linger beside the outrigger canoes and royal feather capes at the **Bishop Museum.** *page 96*
- Peer down from the **Nuuanu Pali Lookout** at the sharp, rugged Koolau cliffs that fall 3000 feet to a coastal shelf far below. *page 97*
- Meditate beside a placid reflecting pool or beneath a massive statue of Buddha at the **Byodo-In Temple.** *page 110*
- Cross a double-rainbow bridge en route to **Haleiwa,** a clapboard plantation town that is a haven for surfers and counter-culturalists. *page 122*

Hawaii. A 760-foot crater, it is the work of a volcano that has been dead for about 100,000 years. To the Hawaiians it was known as *Leahi*. They saw in its sloping hillsides the face of an ahi, or yellow-fin tuna. Then, in the 19th century, sailors mistook its volcanic glass rocks for rare gems and gave the promontory its present name. Formed 350,000 years ago, this natural landmark was a sacred place to the ancient Hawaiians. A *heiau* once graced its slopes and King Kamehameha is said to have worshiped here, offering a human sacrifice to the Polynesian war god.

It is possible to drive into the gaping maw of this old dragon. Just take Kalakaua Avenue until it meets Diamond Head Road, then follow the latter around to the inland site of the crater. From there a tunnel leads inside. Once within, there is a three-quarter-mile trail climbing to the rim of the crater. From here you can gaze along Oahu's southeast corner and back across the splendid little quarter called Waikiki.

LODGING

While it may no longer be the simple country retreat it was at the century's turn, Waikiki does have one advantage: believe it or not, it's a great place to find low-rent hotels. A lot of the cozy old hostelries have been torn down and replaced with highrises, but a few have escaped the urban assault. Some of those skyscrapers, too, are cheaper than you might think. So let's take a look at some of the better bargains Waikiki has to offer.

The **Malihini Hotel** will give you a feel for Honolulu's earlier, lowrise era. An attractive complex that spreads out instead of up, this 30-unit hotel is just a short stroll from the beach. Though pretty on the outside, its sparse furnishings, scant decoration and cinderblock walls give a vacant feel to the place. But the studios are spacious and come equipped with kitchenettes. The one-bedroom apartments have air conditioning and will sleep up to five people. ~ 217 Saratoga Road; 923-9644. BUDGET.

Rising higher from the ground, while still keeping costs low, is the **Royal Grove Hotel**, a six-story, 87-unit establishment. If you can get past the garish pink exterior here, you'll find the rooms more tastefully designed. All are carpeted and comfortably furnished, and some are decorated in simple but appealing styles. There are televisions and telephones in many of the higher-priced rooms upstairs, plus an almond-shaped pool and spacious lobby downstairs. Rents vary according to which wing of this sprawling building your bags are parked in. Some rooms even have kitchenettes and air conditioning, so it's hard to go wrong here. ~ 151 Uluniu Avenue; 923-7691, fax 922-7508. BUDGET TO MODERATE.

If you'd like to stay directly across the street from the beach, check into the **Waikiki Circle Hotel**. This 14-story hotel-in-the-round has air-conditioned rooms at reasonable rates. Many have an ocean view, which is the main advantage here. ~ 2464 Kalakaua Avenue; 923-1571, 800-922-7866, fax 926-8024. DELUXE.

An inexpensive place for both men and women in Waikiki is the YMCA Central Branch. It's handily situated across the street from Ala Moana Center and a block from the beach. And you're welcome to use the gym, pool, saunas, television room and coffee shop. You can also expect the usual Y ambience—long sterile hallways leading to an endless series of identical, cramped, uncarpeted rooms. You will pay several dollars more for a private bathroom, but low prices help make up for the lack of amenities. ~ 401 Atkinson Drive; 941-3344, fax 941-8821. BUDGET.

Interclub Waikiki is a sparkling clean hostel close to the beach, featuring dormitory and private rooms alike. Numbering 140 beds, it features a TV lounge complete with checkerboard, dart board and plenty of plump furniture. There is a laundry but no kitchen facilities. ~ 2413 Kuhio Avenue; 924-2636, fax 922-3993. BUDGET.

The walls are still cinderblock, but some recent remodeling should perk up the Waikiki Prince Hotel. Many of the rooms are equipped with kitchenettes. ~ 2431 Prince Edward Street; 922-1544, fax 924-3712. BUDGET.

Budget travelers should also consider a stay at Hostelling International—Waikiki. This helpful facility features dormitory-style accommodations and private studio units available for couples. The latter are plain cinder block rooms with private baths and mini-refrigerators. Open to both men and women, the hostel provides bedding, a common kitchen and creates a family-style atmosphere conducive to meeting other travelers. ~ 2417 Prince Edward Street; 926-8313, fax 922-3798. BUDGET.

There are two places in the moderate-price category that I particularly recommend. All are small, intimate and close to the beach. First is the Hale Pua Nui, a congenial home away from home. There are 22 studio apartments here, each spacious, well-furnished and cross-ventilated. The rooms are quaintly decorated, carpeted and equipped with kitchenettes, cable television and air conditioning. The personalized service you receive from the management makes the Hale Pua Nui an ideal vacation spot. ~ 228 Beach Walk; 923-9693, fax 923-9678. MODERATE.

The second is Kai Aloha Apartment Hotel, just around the corner. Here intimacy is combined with modern convenience; each room has air conditioning, an all-electric kitchen, radio, telephone with voice mail, cable television and carpeting. Studio apartments have lovely rattan furniture and are attractively decorated with old drawings and paintings. The one-bedroom apartments will comfortably sleep four people. Daily maid service. ~ 235 Saratoga Road; 923-6723, fax 922-7592. MODERATE.

A lowrise hotel tucked away in the shadow of vaulting condominiums, **The Breakers** is truly a find. Dating to the 1950s, this ◄ *HIDDEN* Waikiki original consists of 66 rooms and 15 suites surrounding a pool and landscaped patio. Shoji doors add to the ambience while kitchenettes in every room and a location one block from the beach round out the features. ~ 250 Beach Walk; 923-3181, 800-426-0494, fax 923-7174. DELUXE.

Beach Walk is one street in Waikiki that specializes in hotel bargains. In addition to the Hale Pua Nui and The Breakers, you'll find the **Hawaiiana Hotel**. Another intimate, low-slung facility, it offers a garden courtyard arrangement with rooms surrounding either of the hotel's two pools. Many of the rooms have a private lanai; all have wicker armoires, a full kitchen and pastel decor. ~ 260 Beach Walk; 923-3811, 800-535-0085, fax 926-5728. MODERATE TO DELUXE.

If you're willing to sacrifice intimacy, you may find that the **Outrigger Coral Seas Hotel** is the best deal in Waikiki. This seven-story hostelry is located just a hundred yards from the beach. They are appealing accommodations with air conditioning, telephones, wall-to-wall carpeting and small lanais. In some units you can add a mini-kitchenette to the list of extras. There's a pool at another Outrigger hotel next door that guests may use. If you want, just for the hell of it, to directly experience the Waikiki tourist scene, this is the place. The Outrigger Coral Seas Hotel is at the heart of the action. ~ 250 Lewers Street; 923-3881, 800-462-6262, fax 800-622-4852. MODERATE.

Also in the center of Waikiki is the nearby **Edgewater Hotel**. Located a stone's skip from the beach, this 184-unit colossus offers excellent accommodations at low prices. Each room comes with

✔ **CHECK THESE OUT—UNIQUE LODGING**

- *Budget:* Check in to a restored plantation house across the street from the beach at the North Shore's **Plantation Village**. *page 124*
- *Moderate:* Avoid Waikiki's high room rates and highrise hotels at **The Breakers**, a cozy resting place just one block from the beach. *page 67*
- *Deluxe:* Step back to the Victorian era and relax out on the veranda of the **Manoa Valley Inn**. *page 98*
- *Ultra-deluxe:* Discover why local residents call the **Royal Hawaiian** (a French provincial fantasy right on Waikiki Beach) "The Pink Palace." *page 70*

Budget: under $50 Moderate: $50–$90 Deluxe: $90–$120 Ultra-deluxe: over $120

carpeting, telephone, TV, cable movies, refrigerator and shared lanai; many rooms also have a kitchenette. The decor is bland but the furniture comfy. Downstairs is an open-air lobby with adjoining restaurant and pool. ~ 2168 Kalia Road; 922-6424, 800-462-6262, fax 922-8509. MODERATE TO DELUXE.

The **Honolulu Prince Hotel** was once a college dormitory. Today it's a ten-story hotel with a comfortable lobby. The standard rooms are small and blandly decorated; some are equipped with full kitchens. Located near the beach, this hotel also has one- and two-bedroom apartments available. ~ 415 Nahua Street; 922-1616, 800-922-7866, fax 922-6223. MODERATE TO DELUXE.

Tourists are relative newcomers to Hawaii: Not a single hotel in Waikiki was built before the 20th century.

White Sands Waikiki Resort is more expensive but also more fashionable. This is a modern, attractive complex of three low-slung buildings surrounding a garden and swimming pool. The rooms come with all-electric kitchenette, telephone, color TV and air conditioning. ~ 431 Nohonani Street; 923-7336, 800-634-6981, fax 733-0941. DELUXE.

Dominating the mid-range hotel scene in Waikiki are the Outrigger hotels. It seems like everywhere you turn in this tourist enclave another one looms above: There are almost two dozen. While prices range across the entire spectrum, one facility that offers a special value is the **Outrigger Village**. Located on a busy street a block from the beach, it offers rooms with or without kitchenettes at reasonable cost. You can expect street noise, and the lobby caters more to vendors than guests, but there is a pool. ~ 240 Lewers Street; 923-3881, 800-462-6262, fax 922-2330. MODERATE.

The **Coconut Plaza**, a ten-story highrise, has some accommodations with kitchenettes; all guest rooms have refrigerators and microwaves. Decorated in Mexican tile and furnished with wicker, the rooms are attractively appointed. The lobby adds elements of elegance in the form of an open-air lounge and pool. Breakfast included. ~ 450 Lewers Street; 923-8828, 800-882-9696, fax 923-3473. DELUXE.

The **Ewa Hotel** has 90 rooms. Tucked away on a back street one block from the beach, this pastel-and-rattan establishment has a spiffy 1980s aura about it. Close to Kapiolani Park and offering kitchenettes in many rooms, it is particularly convenient for families. ~ 2555 Cartwright Road; 922-1677, 800-359-8639, fax 923-8538. MODERATE.

About the same size is the **Waikiki Hana Hotel**, a 73-room place that offers a restaurant and small lobby. Quiet (for Waikiki), friendly and comfortable, its rooms are brightly decorated and trimly appointed with air conditioning and color televisions. Some have kitchenettes and lanais. ~ 2424 Koa Avenue; 926-8841, 800-367-5004, fax 533-0472. MODERATE TO DELUXE.

One of the island's few gay-run hotels, **Hotel Honolulu** rests on a quiet side street just off Kuhio Avenue. It's a three-story deco post-modern structure that has been beautifully landscaped and finely decorated. Guest rooms are bright, carpeted wall-to-wall and equipped with tile bathrooms, stall showers and kitchen facilities. Each is decorated along a different theme: Japanese, English, Chinese, Hollywood, Safari and so on. There's also a rooftop garden sundeck to round off this well-run facility. ~ 376 Kaiolu Street; 926-2766, 800-426-2766, fax 922-3326. MODERATE TO DELUXE.

If the **Outrigger Waikiki Surf Hotel** has no space in its central facility, they can probably fit you into one of their two other buildings. All are located in central Waikiki. The guest rooms are adequately, if unimaginatively, decorated and come with television, air conditioning, telephone and lanai. ~ 2200 Kuhio Avenue; 923-7671, 800-462-6262, fax 921-4959. MODERATE.

Holiday Inn Waikiki, another good bargain, is easy walking distance from both Ala Moana Center and the beach. For the price, accommodations at this 17-story caravansary are relatively plush. Each room has air conditioning, television, telephone, decorations, carpeting, a shower-tub combination, a small refrigerator, in-room coffee and an in-room safe. The room I saw was quite spacious and contained a king-size bed. ~ 1830 Ala Moana Boulevard; 955-1111, 800-465-4329, fax 947-1799. MODERATE TO DELUXE.

Also consider the **Mark Waikiki Grand Hotel**, across the street from lush Kapiolani Park. The standard rooms in this ten-story building are comfortable, pleasant places to park your bags. Downstairs there's a windswept lobby. ~ 134 Kapahulu Avenue; 923-1511, 800-533-0385, fax 923-4708. DELUXE.

Also in the Mark Waikiki Grand Hotel is the **Polynesian Hostel Beach Club**. Bunks are set up in former hotel rooms which means that each room has its own refrigerator and bathroom and only sleeps four to five people. Laundry facilities and a full kitchen are available for guests, but the real highlight is the top-floor sundeck with its view of Kapiolani Park, Diamond Head and the beach. ~ 134 Kapahulu Avenue; 922-1340, fax 955-4470. BUDGET.

If you'd prefer to go native and stay in a private home, contact one of the bed and breakfast referral numbers. These include **Bed and Breakfast Honolulu** (595-7533, 800-288-4666, fax 595-2030), **Pacific Hawaii Bed and Breakfast** (phone/fax 486-8838, 800-999-6026) or **Bed and Breakfast Hawaii** (822-7771, 800-733-1632, fax 822-2723). They offer accommodations on all islands, priced in the moderate to deluxe range.

The **Queen Kapiolani Hotel** is a 314-room facility that rises 19 stories above nearby Kapiolani Park. There's a spacious lobby, three floors of public rooms, several shops and a swimming pool here. The guest rooms are plainly decorated and modest in size.

Located one block from the beach. ~ 150 Kapahulu Avenue; 922-1941, 800-367-5004, fax 596-0158. DELUXE.

There are also two attractive facilities on the edge of Waikiki that are removed from the crowds. The **New Otani Kaimana Beach Hotel** rests beside beautiful Sans Souci Beach in the shadow of Diamond Head. Its two restaurants and oceanside bar lend the feel of a big hotel, but the friendly staff and standard rooms create a family atmosphere. ~ 2863 Kalakaua Avenue; 923-1555, 800-356-8264, fax 922-9404. DELUXE TO ULTRA-DELUXE.

HIDDEN ▶ Another hotel, equally secluded, has been nicely refurbished. Located even closer to the fabled crater, the **Diamond Head Beach Hotel** is an ultra-contemporary establishment. The rooms are done in soft pastel tones and adorned with quilted beds and potted plants. Located on the ocean, this 13-story facility is one of the most chic resting places around. Continental breakfast is served to the guests and some rooms come with a kitchen. ~ 2947 Kalakaua Avenue; 922-1928, 800-923-1928, fax 924-8980. ULTRA-DELUXE.

There are two hotels right on the beach at Waikiki that capture the sense of old Hawaii. Waikiki was little more than a thatch-hut village when its first deluxe hotel went up in 1901. Today the **Sheraton Moana Surfrider Hotel** retains the aura of those early days in its Colonial architecture and Victorian decor. Insist on a room in the main building with its traditional appointments and turn-of-the-century ambience. Downstairs are restaurants, bars, a lobby filled with wicker furniture, and an ancient banyan tree beneath which Robert Louis Stevenson once wrote. ~ 2365 Kalakaua Avenue; 922-3111, 800-325-3535, fax 923-0308. ULTRA-DELUXE.

Just down the beach resides the grand dame of Hawaiian hotels. Built in 1927 and affectionately known as "The Pink Palace," the **Royal Hawaiian** is an elegant, Spanish Moorish–style building complete with colonnaded walkways and manicured grounds. This castle away from home is decorated in French provincial fashion and features a fabulous lobby bedecked with chandeliers. Adjacent to the original building is a 17-story tower that brings the room count to 675. Worth visiting even if you never check in. ~ 2259 Kalakaua Avenue; 923-7311, 800-325-3535, fax 924-7098. ULTRA-DELUXE.

CONDOS The **Royal Kuhio**, a good bet for families, is a 389-unit highrise two blocks from Waikiki Beach. One-bedroom units feature fully equipped kitchens and balconies with ocean or mountain views. Prices start at $95. ~ 2240 Kuhio Avenue; 923-0555, 800-927-0555, fax 923-0720.

Kaulana Kai Resort at Waikiki has 90 comfortable units with kitchenettes and private lanais. The suites, which include a full living room, are a good value for families. Studios run $99 to $120 and suites begin at $140. ~ 2425 Kuhio Avenue; 922-7777, 800-367-5666, fax 922-9473.

At the **Aston Waikiki Beach Tower** all 90 suites and penthouses feature contemporary furniture, wetbars, kitchens and beautiful lanais. The kids will enjoy the game room, pool and paddle tennis court. One-bedroom units begin at $335. Suites for up to six guests start at $445. This is Waikiki's finest condominium. ~ 2470 Kalakaua Avenue; 926-6400, 800-922-7866, fax 926-7380.

At **Patrick Winston's Hawaiian King Rentals**, one-bedroom apartments rent for $59 to $129 for one to four people. All suites are comfortably furnished with rattan furniture and feature lanais and full and complete kitchens. Eight of the eleven units have washers and dryers. One block from the beach. ~ 417 Nohonani Street; 924-3332 phone/fax, 800-545-1948.

Aston Waikiki Shore offers 90 studios as well as one- and two-bedroom units. These condos feature complete kitchens, washer/dryers and great views. Studios run $150 to $165. One bedroom units are $210 to $235. Two-bedroom units accommodating up to six cost $295 to $335. ~ 2161 Kalia Road; 926-4733, 800-367-2353, fax 922-2902.

Waikiki Lanais is located on a quiet street near the Ala Wai Canal and has 160 one- and two-bedroom units, each with a good-sized living room and kitchen. One-bedroom accommodations start at $159. Two-bedroom condos, sleeping up to six, begin at $199. ~ 2452 Tusitala Street; 923-0994, 800-535-0085, fax 922-2421.

The **Pacific Monarch** has studio apartments from $120 to $160 offering kitchenettes and balconies, and one-bedroom units are $150 to $200 for up to four. There is a rooftop pool, jacuzzi and sauna, and the beach is just two blocks away. ~ 142 Uluniu Avenue; 923-9805, 800-922-7866, fax 924-3220.

At **Waikiki Banyan** one-bedroom units are $145 to $200 for one to four people. These highrise ocean and mountain view units have full kitchens, rattan furniture and lanais. One block from the beach. ~ 201 Ohua Avenue; 922-0555, 800-366-7765, fax 922-0906.

◆◆◆

STAY AT SOMEBODY ELSE'S PLACE!

If you're planning on staying in Honolulu for a week or more and would like to do so in the comfort of someone else's fully furnished apartment, **Waikiki Vacation Rentals** offers studios as well as one- and two-bedroom condos. The months of December, January and February are often booked two to three months in advance, so call ahead for availability. ~ 1860 Ala Moana Boulevard #108; 946-9371, 800-543-5663, fax 922-9418. BUDGET TO ULTRA-DELUXE.

What better combination can you ask for than a place that is both a hotel *and* a hostel? At the **Island Hostel/Hotel**, located inside the Hawaiian Colony building, you can book a room with private bath or join fellow travelers in a coed dorm room. Both include kitchen privileges. ~ 1946 Ala Moana Boulevard; phone/fax 942-8748. BUDGET.

Several services rent condominiums on Oahu. They include **Condo Rentals of Waikiki** at 413 Seaside Avenue (923-0555, 800-927-0555, fax 922-0720) and **Marc Resorts** at 2155 Kalakaua Avenue (926-5900, 800-535-0085, fax 922-9421).

DINING

This tourist mecca is crowded with restaurants. Since the competition is so stiff, the cafés here are cheaper than anywhere else on the islands. There are numerous American restaurants serving moderately good food at modest prices, so diners looking for standard fare will have no problem. But as you're probably seeking something more exotic, I'll also list some interesting Asian, Hawaiian, health food and other offbeat restaurants.

To find an affordable meal on Kalakaua Avenue, the ocean-front strip, try the bottom floor of the **Waikiki Shopping Plaza**. Here about a dozen ethnic and American restaurants offer takeout food as well as full course sitdown dinners. ~ 2250 Kalakaua Avenue. BUDGET.

Near the center of the action on busy Lewers Street, about 50 macadam-paved yards from the beach, is **J. R.s**. This glorified takeout stand has balcony seating overlooking the street. Downstairs you place your order for incredibly cheap breakfast specials, sandwiches and plate lunches, and dinners. ~ 226 Lewers Street; 971-3593. BUDGET.

Jungle Waikiki is a hot nightclub later on, but at lunch and dinner, it's a well-regarded, excellently priced restaurant. Using all fresh ingredients, they prepare chicken dijon, skewered shrimp, fettuccine primavera, penne with meat sauce and fresh fish. ~ 311 Lewers Street; 922-7808. BUDGET.

Up on the third floor of the Royal Hawaiian Shopping Center you'll happen upon **Spaghetti! Spaghetti!**. At lunch or dinner there's an all-you-can-eat spaghetti buffet and salad bar. The spread includes several different types of pastas as well as an array of sauces. A great place to pack away those carbohydrates. ~ 2201 Kalakaua Avenue, Suite A-313; 922-7724. BUDGET TO MODERATE.

On a balcony in the International Market Place, **Coconut Willy's Bar & Grill** has a dinner menu that includes a teriyaki steak and shrimp platter, fish and chips, and mahimahi. There are also hamburgers, sandwiches and salads. Set beside the banyan tree that dominates the market, the place has a funky appeal. ~ 2330 Kalakaua Avenue; 923-9454. MODERATE.

Regent Hotel, 2552 Kalakaua Avenue; 924-0123. MODERATE TO DELUXE.

It's not surprising that Waikiki's most fashionable hotel, the Halekulani, contains one of the district's finest restaurants. Situated on an open-air balcony overlooking the ocean, **La Mer** has a reputation for elegant dining in intimate surroundings. French-inspired dishes include rack of lamb marinated in thyme and garlic and filet of Barbary duck crusted with goat cheese. Add the filigree woodwork and sumptuous surroundings and La Mer is one of the island's most attractive waterfront dining rooms. Dinner only. ~ 2199 Kalia Road; 923-2311. ULTRA-DELUXE.

> During the last decade, Waikiki has changed from a ticky tacky shopping enclave to an upscale international marketplace.

Downstairs from La Mer is **Orchids**, serving a mix of Hawaiian and Continental cuisine like roasted duckling with wild rice and lamb Provençal. Orchids is open for breakfast, lunch and dinner. ~ 2199 Kalia Road; 923-2311. DELUXE TO ULTRA-DELUXE.

GROCERIES

The best grocery store in Waikiki is also the biggest. Prices at **The Food Pantry** are inflated, but not as much as elsewhere in this tourist enclave. ~ 2370 Kuhio Avenue; 923-9831.

ABC Discount Stores, a chain of sundry shops with branches all around Waikiki, are convenient, but have a very limited stock and even higher prices.

If you are willing and able to shop outside Waikiki, you'll generally fare much better price-wise. Try the **Foodland** supermarket in the Ala Moana Center just outside Waikiki. Cheaper than Waikiki groceries, it's still more expensive than Greater Honolulu stores. ~ 1450 Ala Moana Boulevard; 949-5044.

Also in the Ala Moana Center, **Vim and Vigor** has a standard stock of food items, as well as a juice bar and lunch counter. ~ 1450 Ala Moana Boulevard; 955-3600.

SHOPPING

This tourist mecca is a great place to look but not to buy. Browsing the busy shops is like studying a catalog of Hawaiian handicrafts. It's all here. You'll find everything but bargains. With a few noteworthy exceptions, the prices include the unofficial tourist surcharges that merchants worldwide levy against visitors. Windowshop Waikiki, but plan on spending your shopping dollars elsewhere.

One Waikiki shopping area I do recommend is **Duke's Lane**. This alleyway, running from Kalakaua Avenue to Kuhio Avenue near the International Market Place, may be the best place in all Hawaii to buy jade jewelry. Either side of the lane is flanked by mobile stands selling rings, necklaces, earrings, stick pins, bracelets and more. It's a prime place to barter for tiger's eyes, opals and mother-of-pearl pieces.

The main shopping scene is in the malls. **Waikiki Shopping Plaza** has six floors of stores and restaurants. ~ 2250 Kalakaua Avenue. Here are jewelers, sundries and boutiques, plus specialty shops like **Waldenbooks**, with an excellent line of magazines as well as paperbacks and bestsellers. ~ 922-4154.

The nearby **Royal Hawaiian Shopping Center** spans Kalakaua Avenue from Lewers Street all the way to the Royal Hawaiian Hotel. Along this four-tiered marathon course, you can purchase jewelry, cameras or ice cream. There are boutiques, sporting-goods stores, surf shops, art galleries, craft shops and practically everything else conceivable—all at the very center of Waikiki. ~ Kalakaua Avenue.

Then there's **King's Village**, a mock Victorian town that suggests how Britain might have looked had the 19th-century English invented polyethylene. The motif may be trying to appear antiquated, but the prices are unfortunately quite contemporary. ~ 131 Kaiulani Avenue at Kalakaua Avenue.

International Market Place is my favorite browsing spot. With tiny shops and vending stands spotted around the sprawling grounds, it's a relief from the claustrophobic shopping complexes. There's an old banyan spreading across the market, plus thatched treehouses, a carp pond, brick sidewalks and woodfront stores. You won't find many bargains, but the sightseeing is priceless. ~ 2330 Kalakaua Avenue.

The **Waikiki Trade Center** is another strikingly attractive mall. With an air of Milanese splendor about it, this glass-and-steel complex is a maze of mirrors. In addition to the stained-glass windows and twinkling lights, there are several worthwhile shops. The **Waldenbooks** (924-8330) outlet here is an excellent resource for books on Hawaii as well as general trade titles. ~ Kuhio and Seaside avenues.

Some of Hawaii's smartest shops are located in the **Atrium Shops** at the Hyatt Regency Waikiki. This triple-tiered arcade is *the* place to look when you are seeking the very best. Glamour and style are passwords around here. There are fine-art shops, designer apparel stores, gem shops and much more. ~ 2424 Kalakaua Avenue.

Hilton Hawaiian Village contains the **Rainbow Bazaar**, an array of shops spread around the grounds of Hawaii's largest resort complex. This plaza contains a number of stores specializing in island fashions, plus gift shops and import emporia. The shopping center has been designed in Oriental style, with curving tile roofs and brilliantly painted roof beams. You can stroll along an Asian arcade, past lofty banyan trees and flowering gardens, to stores filled with rare art and Far Eastern antiquities. ~ 2005 Kalia Road.

Actually it's the other 20 percent that predominates at **80% Straight Inc.** This gay men's shop has cards, clothes, videos and gift items. Located on the 2100 block of Kuhio Avenue, it's in the heart of Waikiki's gay district. ~ 2139 Kuhio Avenue; 923-9996.

Just a couple doors down, **Down Under Honolulu** has the widest array of men's underwear in creation (or at least in Honolulu). ~ 2139-F Kuhio Avenue; 922-9229.

Following a similar theme but covering the rest of the body is **Physique**. This men's clothing store has T-shirts, slacks and a limited assortment of other apparel items. ~ 2139-A Kuhio Avenue; 921-7297.

Extending from Kuhio Avenue to Kalaimoku Street, **Old Waikiki Market** is an open-air, low-rent "mall." Here vendors sell souvenirs, T-shirts and assorted gewgaws from thatch-roofed kiosks. ~ 2139 Kuhio Avenue.

Looking for a vintage silk shirt? Those famous Hawaiian styles, like the one Montgomery Clift sported in *From Here to Eternity*, are among the alluring items at **Bailey's Antiques and Aloha Shirts**. ◄ HIDDEN If an original silky is beyond your means, they also have a collection of reproductions. ~ 517 Kapahulu Avenue; 734-7628.

Hawaii has a strong musical tradition, kept alive by excellent **NIGHTLIFE** groups performing their own compositions as well as old Polynesian songs. I'm not talking about the "Blue Hawaii"–"Tiny Bubbles"–"Beyond the Reef" medleys that draw tourists in droves, but *real* Hawaiian music as performed by Hapa, the Brothers Cazimero, Keola and Kapono Beamer, Marlene Sai, Melveen Leed and others.

If you spend any time in Honolulu, don't neglect to check out such authentic sounds. One or more of these musicians will probably be playing at a local club. Consult the daily newspapers, or, if you want to hear these groups before paying to see them, listen to KCCN at 1420 on the radio dial. This all-Hawaiian station is the home of island soul.

The posh **Monarch Room** features varying entertainment; check with the hotel concierge to get a schedule. ~ Royal Hawaiian Hotel, 2259 Kalakaua Avenue; 923-7311.

Over at **Nick's Fishmarket**, the hot sounds of a contemporary band draw flocks of locals and visitors alike Wednesday through Saturday, while a solo guitarist strums Sunday through Tuesday. ~ 2070 Kalakaua Avenue; 955-6333.

On weekends a contemporary Hawaiian duo stars at the **Paradise Lounge**. Choose between table or lounge seating in this carpeted club, which is decorated with Hawaiian landscapes painted by local artists. ~ 2005 Kalia Road; 949-4321.

The **Esprit Nightclub** is a congenial spot. Situated right on Waikiki Beach, this cozy club features live oldie rock-and-roll shows and spectacular ocean views every night of the week. ~ Sheraton Waikiki Hotel, 2255 Kalakaua Avenue; 922-4422.

Tired of the old nine-to-five grind? For a change of pace try **Scruples,** where the schedule is eight to four. 8 p.m. to 4 a.m. that is. Promising "dance and romance," this popular night spot features dancing to Top-40 tunes. Cover and minimum. ~ 2310 Kuhio Avenue; 923-9530.

The **Maharaja Restaurant,** an establishment as formal and upscale as its name implies, offers dancing to Top-40 deejay music. Cover and dress code. ~ Waikiki Trade Center, 2255 Kuhio Avenue; 922-3030.

The **Cellar** specializes in dancing, with Top-40 tunes spun by a deejay Wednesday through Sunday. It's a top spot for a hot night. Cover. ~ 205 Lewers Street; 923-9952.

Lewers St. Annex has dancing nightly to Top-40 tunes. The sound here is a deejay mix and the atmosphere is quintessential bar scene. ~ Holiday Isle Hotel, 270 Lewers Street; 971-1002.

At the other end of the street, **Waikiki Broiler** has live entertainment in the form of a band. ~ 200 Lewers Street at Kalia Road; 923-8836.

The light show and sound system at **Jungle Waikiki** are cutting edge. You'll hear the pulsing sounds of house, trance and techno. There's dancing nightly to a deejay. Cover. ~ 311 Lewers Street; 922-7808.

Eurasia Night Club and Sports Bar pulses with house, industrial and alternative sounds one night and classic and alternative rock-and-roll another. Call for the daily musical menu. There's a light show, dancefloor and dartboards. Live bands Thursday and Friday, deejay music other nights. Cover nightly. ~ Hawaiian Regent Hotel, 2552 Kalakaua Avenue; 921-5335.

Acqua offers live contemporary music nightly in a plush setting. With an ocean view and relaxing ambience, this lounge in the Hawaiian Regent Hotel is part of a light, airy, Mediterranean restaurant. ~ 2552 Kalakaua Avenue; 924-0123.

Coconut Willy's Bar & Grill, situated on a balcony in the International Market Place, has a live band that starts in the afternoon and continues on into the night. It may be local music or country. Attractive setting. ~ 2330 Kalakaua Avenue; 923-9454.

HIDDEN ▶

Locals head for **Duke's Canoe Club** to hear Hawaiian and contemporary musicians perform nightly. You'll hear slack-key and steel guitars on a balcony overlooking the Pacific. ~ 2335 Kalakaua Avenue; 922-2268.

For live sounds, cruise into **Wave Waikiki** and catch the progressive rock bands that perform nightly (except on Monday, when the house rocks to a double-deejay hip-hop dance contest). Cover after 10 p.m. ~ 1877 Kalakaua Avenue; 941-0424.

With room for 300 of your closest friends, **Moose McGilly-cuddy's Pub and Café** is a prime place to dance to live bands.

Known for its weird pictures, this establishment is easily spotted. Just look for the only building on Lewers Street sporting a stuffed moose head. Weekend cover. ~ 310 Lewers Street; 923-0751.

The sound is a mix of '80s alternative, funk classics and industrial dance music at **Rendezvous**. This place is billed as Honolulu's "hot mod dance party." But remember, no baseball caps and no sagging pants. ~ 478 Ena Road; 942-5282.

GAY SCENE The gay scene centers around several clubs on Waikiki's Kuhio Avenue. **Treats** is a U-shaped bar with a side patio. With recorded music and television, it's a major spot for drinking and carousing. Formerly known as Hamburger Mary's, it has been drawing crowds for years. ~ 2109 Kuhio Avenue; 923-0669. Together with **Hula's Bar and Lei Stand** next door, it forms an unbeatable duo. ~ Hula's, a disco complete with strobe-lit dancefloor and videos, rocks nightly until 2 a.m. ~ 2103 Kuhio Avenue; 923-0669.

Next door, **Trixx** is a patio-style bar with deejay music and dancing nightly. On Thursday through Saturday night from 11 p.m. to 1 a.m., they feature dancers. Together with Treats and Hula's, which are actually part of the same complex, it is the capital of gay nightlife not only in Waikiki, but throughout Hawaii. Cover. ~ 2109 Kuhio Avenue; 923-0669.

Fusion Waikiki is another gay club open until 4 a.m. This three-floor hot spot features dancing to progressive deejay music. There are male strip shows four nights a week. Cover. ~ 2260 Kuhio Avenue; 924-2422.

Eaton Square, a little hideaway mall off Ala Moana Boulevard, houses **Windows**. Stylish yet casual in its decor, this gay bar, popular with men and women, is adorned with sensual prints. The featured entertainment consists of darts, pool and relaxation. ~ 444 Hobron Lane; 946-4442.

For a historical and cultural tour of Hawaii's state capital, simply head toward Downtown Honolulu. A financial center for the entire Pacific Rim, Honolulu's importance to both North America and Asia is manifest in the highrise cityscape. The historical significance of this port city is evident from the 19th-century buildings that lead to the financial district in the heart of the city.

▼▼▼▼▼▼▼▼▼▼▼▼▼
Downtown Honolulu

A fitting place to begin your tour is among the oldest homes in the islands. The buildings at the **Mission Houses Museum** seem to be borrowed from a New England landscape, and in a sense they were. The Frame House, a trim white wooden structure, was cut on the East Coast and shipped around the Horn to Hawaii. That was back in 1821, when this Yankee-style building was used to house missionary families.

SIGHTS

Like the nearby Chamberlain Depository and other structures here, the Frame House represents one of the missionaries' earliest centers in Hawaii. It was in 1819 that Congregationalists arrived in the islands; they immediately set out to build and proselytize. In 1831, they constructed the Chamberlain Depository from coral and used it as a storehouse. The neighborhood's Coral House, built of the same durable material ten years later, was used by the first press ever to print in the Hawaiian language. The Mission Houses complex tells much about the missionaries, who converted Hawaiian into a written language, then proceeded to rewrite the entire history of the islands. The museum is run by the Hawaiian Mission Children's Society. Closed Sunday and Monday. Admission. ~ 553 South King Street; 531-0481.

Opposite, at South King and Punchbowl streets, is the **Kawaihao Church**. This imposing edifice required 14,000 coral blocks for its construction. Completed in 1842, it has been called the Westminster Abbey of Hawaii, because coronations and funerals for Hawaiian kings and queens were once conducted here. Services are still performed in Hawaiian and English every Sunday at 10:30 a.m.; attending them is not only a way to view the church interior, but also provides a unique cultural perspective on contemporary Hawaiian life. Also note that the tomb of King Lunalilo rises in front of the church, and behind the church lies the cemetery where early missionaries and converted Hawaiians were buried.

Across South King Street, that brick structure with the stately white pillars is the **Mission Memorial Building**, constructed in 1916 to honor those same early church leaders. The nearby Renaissance-style building with the tile roof is **Honolulu Hale**, the City Hall. You might want to venture into the central courtyard, an open-air plaza surrounded by stone columns.

As you continue along South King Street in a westerly direction toward the center of Honolulu, **Iolani Palace** will appear on your right. Built for King Kalakaua in 1882, this stunning Renaissance-style mansion served as a royal residence until Queen Liliuokalani was overthrown in 1893. Later the ill-starred monarch was imprisoned here; eventually, after Hawaii became a territory of the United States, the palace was used as the capitol building. Today it represents the only royal palace in the United States. Guided tours lead you along the *koa* staircases and past the magnificent chandeliers and Corinthian columns that lend a touch of European grandeur to this splendid building. Admission.

Also located on the palace grounds are the **Iolani Barracks**, where the Royal Household Guards were stationed, and the **Coronation Pavilion** upon which the "Champagne King" was crowned. You can tour the palace grounds for free, but there is an admission charge for the building. Reservations are strongly advised; children

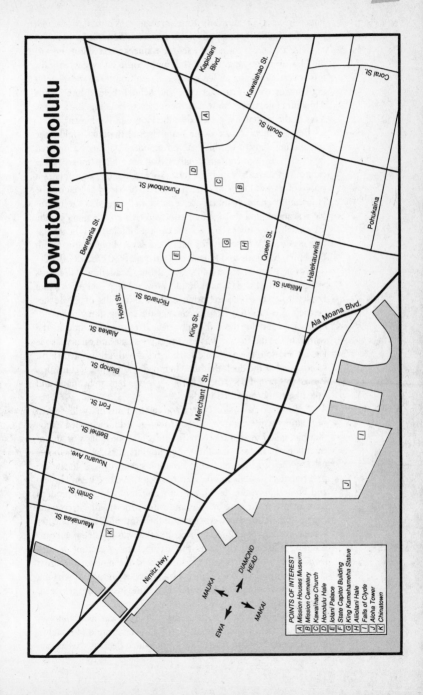

Downtown Honolulu

POINTS OF INTEREST
A Mission Houses Museum
B Mission Cemetery
C Kawaiahao Church
D Honolulu Hale
E Iolani Palace
F State Capitol Building
G King Kamehameha Statue
H Aliiolani Hale
I Falls of Clyde
J Aloha Tower
K Chinatown

MAUKA
DIAMOND HEAD
EWA
MAKAI

Kapiolani Blvd.
Kawaiahao St.
Coral St.
South St.
Punchbowl St.
Beretania St.
Queen St.
Halekauwila
Pohukaina
Miililani St.
Ala Moana Blvd.
Hotel St.
Richards St.
King St.
Alakea St.
Bishop St.
Merchant St.
Fort St.
Bethel St.
Nuuanu Ave.
Smith St.
Maunakea St.
Nimitz Hwy.

under five are ot allowed. Tours are given Wednesday through Saturday. ~ South King and Richards streets; 522-0832.

Directly across the street rises the **Kamehameha Statue**, honoring Hawaii's first king. A huge gilt-and-bronze figure cast in Italy, it is covered with flower leis on special occasions. The spear-carrying warrior wears a feather cape and helmet. Behind him stands **Aliiolani Hale**, better known as the Judiciary Building. Back in the days of the monarchy, it served as the House of Parliament.

Behind Iolani Palace is the **State Capitol Building**. Unlike the surrounding structures, this is an ultramodern building, completed in 1969. Encircled by flared pillars that resemble palm trees, the capitol represents a variety of themes. Near the entrance there's a statue of Father Damien, the leper martyr of Molokai Island. The House and Senate chambers are designed in a cone shape to resemble volcanoes, and the open-air courtyard is a commentary on the state's balmy weather. Tours of the capitol building and the legislature are given Wednesday through Saturday. ~ Bounded by South Beretania, Richards and Punchbowl streets; 586-0178, 587-0790.

For a tour of Honolulu's waterfront, head down Richards Street from the State Capitol Building toward Pier 7 on Ala Moana Boulevard, where the imposing and historic **Falls of Clyde** lies berthed. A completely restored century-old sailing ship, the *Falls of Clyde* is reputedly the only fully rigged four-masted ship in the world. In the old days it was used to carry sugar and oil across the Pacific. Honolulu was then a harbor filled with tall-masted ships, so crowded at the dock that they bumped one another's gunwales. Part of this proud fleet, the *Falls of Clyde* was built in Scotland and sailed halfway round the world.

For a single admission charge you can tour this marvelous piece of floating history and view the *Hokulea*, a double-hulled canoe that has sailed several times to Tahiti. A 60-foot replica of an ancient Polynesian craft, it follows the traditional designs of the boats used by the early Tahitians. On several historic voyages during the past two decades this fragile craft has been sailed between Hawaii and French Polynesia by Hawaiian navigators. Using no modern instruments, navigating by stars and wave patterns, they traced the course of their ancestors. Also part of this **Hawaii Maritime Center** is the Kalakaua Boathouse (adjacent to the *Falls of Clyde*), an outstanding museum that traces the archipelago's maritime history from the era of Polynesian exploration to the days of the great ocean liners and beyond. Other displays focus on the old whaling trade, the invention of surfing and the natural history of the ocean. Admission. ~ Pier 7; 536-6373.

It's also fun to wander the nearby wharves, catching glimpses of the shops and pleasure boats that still tie up around Honolulu's historic port. You can take in the city's fishing fleet, as well as several tour boats, at **Kewalo Boat Basin**, also known as Fisherman's Wharf, midway between Waikiki and Downtown Honolulu. ~ Ala Moana Boulevard and Ward Avenue.

From the Hawaii Maritime Center, follow the roadway along the water to **Aloha Tower** at Pier 9. You'll see it nearby, rising like a spire along the water's edge. Earlier in the century, when many visitors arrived in luxurious ocean liners, this slender structure was Hawaii's answer to the Statue of Liberty. It greeted guests when they arrived and bade them farewell upon departure. Now dwarfed by the skyscrapers of Downtown Honolulu, proud Aloha Tower still commands an unusual view of the harbor and ocean. Any day between 9 a.m. and 9 p.m. you can ride an elevator to the tenth floor observation deck for a crow's nest view. ~ For ship arrival and departure information, call 537-9260.

Today, **American Hawaii Cruises** carries on the ocean-liner tradition in part. They operate the SS *Independence* and the SS *Constitution*, which ply the waters between the islands regularly, docking at Kauai, Maui and the Big Island, and in Honolulu near Aloha Tower. ~ For information on their week-long cruises around the Hawaiian islands, call 800-765-7000.

After years of painstaking restoration, the **Hawaii Theatre** is again a study in neoclassical architecture. With gilded decor, Corinthian columns and striking mosaics, it has been elevated again to the grand status it enjoyed when the theater first opened in 1922. In 1929, it was the first movie theater in the islands to show movies with sound. Tours are available at this nationally registered historic place. Admission. ~ 1130 Bethel Street; 528-0506.

It's not far to **Fort Street Mall**, a seven-block stretch of Downtown Honolulu that has been refurbished and converted into an attractive pedestrian thoroughfare. There are restaurants galore here. The mall is also a good place to spend a little time shopping. Located miles from the Waikiki tourist beat, the stores here cater to local people, so you'll be able to discover objects unobtainable in kitschier quarters.

THE MERRY MONARCH

The king who commissioned the Iolani Palace, David Kalakaua, was a world traveler with a taste for the good life. Known as the Merry Monarch, he planned for his coronation the greatest party Hawaii had ever seen. He liked to spend money with abandon and managed to amass in his lifetime a remarkable collection of material goods, not the least of which was his palace.

Fort Street Mall leads to **Merchant Street**, center of the old downtown section of Honolulu. The 19th- and early-20th-century buildings in this neighborhood re-create the days before Hawaii became the 50th state, when the islands were almost totally controlled by "The Big Five," an interlocking group of powerful corporations. Today the brick-rococo district remains much the same on the outside. But the interiors of the buildings have changed markedly. They now house boutiques and gourmet restaurants downstairs and multinational corporations on the upper floors.

After proceeding away from the waterfront all the way to the end of Merchant Street, take a right on Nuuanu Avenue, then a left on Hotel Street. As you walk along this thoroughfare, which seems to change its identity every block or two, you will pass from Honolulu's conservative financial district into one of its most intriguing ethnic neighborhoods, **Chinatown**.

HIDDEN ▶

The Chinese first arrived in Hawaii in 1852, imported as plantation workers. They quickly moved to urban areas, however, became merchants and proved very successful. Many settled right here in this weather-beaten district, which has long been a center of controversy and an integral part of Honolulu's history. When bubonic plague savaged the Chinese community in 1900, the Caucasian-led government tried to contain the pestilence by burning down afflicted homes. The bumbling white fathers managed to raze most of Chinatown, destroying businesses as well as houses.

Today Hotel Street, the spine of Chinatown, is undergoing a major renovation. Many buildings have already been restored and newly refurbished shops now stand cheek-by-jowl with quaint, time-worn stores. Even here, however, you can still encounter the other side of Chinatown, the seedy, late-night face of the neighborhood. Strung like a neon ganglion along the thoroughfare are porno movie places, flophouses, barrooms and pool halls. This was once a booming red-light district, the haunt of sailors and ragged characters.

The ultimate emblem of Chinatown's revitalization is **Maunakea Marketplace**. This Amerasian shopping mall, with a statue of Confucius overlooking a brick courtyard, houses an Oriental an-

HEART OF A NEIGHBORHOOD

Some of Chinatown's woodframe buildings still suggest the old days and traditions. Wander down side streets like Maunakea Street and you will encounter import stores, Chinese groceries and noodle factories. You might also pop into one of the medicinal herb shops, which feature strange potions and healing powders. There are chop suey joints, acupuncturists and outdoor markets galore, all lending a priceless flavor of the Orient.

tique shop and a Chinese art store. The most interesting feature is the produce market, a series of traditional hanging-ducks-and-live-fish stalls inside an air-conditioned building. ~ Hotel and Mauna-kea streets.

The best way to visit this neighborhood is on one of the **China-** ◄ *HIDDEN* **town Walking Tours** sponsored by the Chinese Chamber of Commerce. Chinatown today is an eclectic community, containing not only Chinese, but Filipinos, Hawaiians, and recent arrivals from Vietnam and Laos. To fully understand Hawaii's melting-pot population, it's important to visit this vibrant district. The walking tour is given on Tuesday mornings, and will carry you past temples and other spots all around the neighborhood. Fee. ~ 42 North King Street; 533-3181.

Continuing north along Hotel Street across Nuuanu Stream, turn right on College Walk and follow it a short distance upstream. You'll pass the **Izumo Taishakyo Mission**, a Shinto Shrine.

Proceed farther and you will arrive at **Foster Botanical Garden**. This 14-acre plot is planted with orchids, palms, coffee trees, poisonous plants and numerous other exotic specimens. There are about 4000 species in all, dotted around a garden that was first planted over 125 years ago. You can meditate under a bo tree or wander through a "prehistoric glen," a riot of ancient ferns and unusual palms. Or you can stroll through and marvel at the universe of color crowded into this small urban garden. Admission. ~ 50 North Vineyard Boulevard; 522-7065.

On the way back to Chinatown, walk along the other side of Nuuanu Stream and stop at the **Cultural Plaza**. This Asian-style shopping mall is bounded by Kukui, Maunakea and Beretania streets, and by the stream. You'll find porcelain, Chinese jewelry, spices and perhaps even acupuncture supplies.

Another important cultural point in the downtown district is the **Honolulu Academy of Arts**. This outstanding museum often displays author James Michener's collection of woodblocks from Japan. There are also works by European, Asian and American masters, as well as important art by local painters and sculptors. Several elegantly landscaped courtyards add to the beauty here. Closed Monday. Admission. ~ 900 South Beretania Street; 532-8700.

Farther afield lies **Dole Cannery Square**, once the site of Hawaii's largest pineapple cannery. The 195-foot-high pineapple tower is currently down for repairs, but when it's standing, the factory is one of Honolulu's most recognizable landmarks. Visitors can watch a slideshow on the history of the pineapple industry and enjoy fresh pineapple juice. ~ 650 Iwilei Road; 548-6600.

Centrally located between Waikiki and Downtown Honolulu is the **LODGING** **Nakamura Hotel**. It's a pleasant place, but the only reason I can conceive for staying here is the locale. The hotel itself is adequate;

the rooms are neatly furnished, carpeted and equipped with private telephones for guests (though phone service is cut off at night). I'd ask for accommodations on the *mauka* side, since the other side fronts noisy King Street. ~ 1140 South King Street; 593-9951. BUDGET.

You'll discover in Downtown Honolulu that in the course of a few short blocks you have passed from Hong Kong into Tokyo.

The **Pagoda Hotel** is sufficiently removed from the crowds but still only a ten-minute drive from the beach. Spacious studio and one-bedroom units put the accent on rattan furniture. The carpeted rooms feature views of the hotel garden or distant mountains. Two-bedroom units in the adjoining Pagoda Terrace offer kitchens. ~ 1525 Rycroft Street; 941-6611, 800-472-4632, fax 955-5067. MODERATE TO DELUXE.

On the outskirts of Chinatown is the **Town Inn**. This is an excellent spot to capture the local color of Honolulu's Chinese section, though the hotel itself is rather nondescript. The rooms are clean, carpeted and sparsely furnished—some even have air conditioning—and all are practically devoid of decoration. ~ 250 North Beretania Street; 536-2377. BUDGET.

DINING

Rather than list the city's restaurants according to price, I'll group them by area. As you get away from Waikiki you'll be dining with a more local crowd and tasting foods more representative of island cuisine, so I would certainly advise checking out some of Honolulu's eating places.

HIDDEN ▶

Right next to Waikiki, in Ala Moana Center, there are numerous ethnic takeout restaurants that share a large dining pavilion called **Makai Market**. Best of all is **Patti's Chinese Kitchen** (946-5002), a crowded and noisy gathering place. At Patti's you can choose two or more main dishes plus a side order of fried rice, or *chow fun*. The courses include almond duck, lemon-sauce chicken, tofu, beef tomato, sweet-and-sour pork, barbecued ribs, pigs' feet and shrimp with vegetables. It's quite simply the best place near Waikiki for a low-cost meal. There's also the **Poi Bowl** (949-8444), a takeout stand serving Hawaiian dishes. **Lyn's Delicatessen** (941-3388) features a full line of deli sandwiches as well as chicken baskets and plate lunches. BUDGET.

Or you can ride the escalator to the upper level of Ala Moana Center. Here **Shirokiya**, a massive Asian department store, features an informal Japanese restaurant and deli. ~ 973-9111. MODERATE.

Hawaiian regional cuisine accented by island fruits is featured at the **Prince Court**. The Hawaii Prince Hotel's harborside restaurant, this dining room is known for dishes like sea scallops, Kahuku shrimp, lobster and mahi salad niçoise. A big wine list is another plus at this Polynesian-style dining room appointed with floral bouquets. ~ 100 Holomoana Street; 956-1111. MODERATE TO DELUXE.

Ward Centre, midway between Waikiki and Downtown Honolulu, is a focus for gourmet dining. A warren of wood-paneled restaurants, it features several outstanding eateries. Particularly recommended for the price is **Scoozee's**, a "pasta, pizza, pizzazz" restaurant that has nothing on its menu above $10. ~ 1200 Ala Moana Boulevard; 597-1777. BUDGET.

Also consider **Compadres**, upstairs in the same complex. This attractive Mexican restaurant, with oak bar and patio dining area, prepares a host of dishes from south of the border as well as sandwiches, salads, steaks and seafood. It specializes in tropical ambience, good food and fishbowl-size margaritas. ~ 1200 Ala Moana Boulevard; 591-8307. MODERATE.

Located in the ultra-contemporary Restaurant Row shopping mall, **Sunset Grill** is a minimalist's delight. Track lights, exposed pipes, raw wood and poured concrete establish a kind of early-21st-century motif. The only area devoted to excess is the kitchen, which serves up a lavish array of *kiawe*-grilled dishes, such as smoke-infused marinated salmon. ~ 500 Ala Moana Boulevard, #1-A; 521-4409. MODERATE TO DELUXE.

Also in this complex, **Cafe Athena** specializes in Mediterranean cuisine with the accent on Greek cooking. We're talking informal atmosphere—oilcloth on the tables and a gyros-falafel-kabob menu. ~ 500 Ala Moana Boulevard; 553-0665. MODERATE.

Fresh *ono*, mahimahi, *opakapaka* and ahi highlight the vast seafood menu at **John Dominus**. A sprawling establishment midway between Waikiki and Downtown Honolulu, it features huge pools filled with hundreds of live lobsters. The wood-paneled dining room overlooks the water and the chefs know as much about preparing seafood as the original Polynesians. For landlubbers, steak and veal are also on the menu. ~ 43 Ahui Street; 523-0955. DELUXE TO ULTRA-DELUXE.

For sushi, sukiyaki, tempura and other Japanese specialties, try the **Pagoda Floating Restaurant**. This restaurant-in-the-round sits above a pond populated with gaily colored koi fish. Several cascades and a fountain feed the pond. The surrounding grounds have been carefully landscaped. This dining room, which offers a lunch and dinner buffet, also serves steaks, scampi and other Western dishes. ~ 1525 Rycroft Street; 941-6611. MODERATE.

Honolulu has numerous seafood restaurants. Some of them, fittingly enough, are located right on the water. But for an authentic seafront feel, it's nice to be where the fishing boats actually come in. **Fisherman's Wharf** provides just such an atmosphere. This sprawling facility is festooned with nautical gear. The "Seafood Grotto" topside has a shoalful of seafood selections ranging from live Maine lobster to Dungeness crab. ~ 1009 Ala Moana Boulevard; 538-3808. MODERATE TO DELUXE.

Up on the second level of the Aloha Tower Marketplace, toward the back overlooking the water, there's the **Kau Kau Corner Food Lanai**. This cluster of food stands ranges from Villa Pizza to Belinda's Aloha Kitchen to the Pacific Vegetarian Cafe and beyond. There's comfortable seating in an attractive setting, all at economical prices. ~ Aloha Tower Marketplace, Pier 8; 528-5700. BUDGET.

There are several other dining spots situated along interior streets away from the water that I particularly like. These are also located between Waikiki and Downtown Honolulu. For Italian-style seafood, **Philip Paolo's** is highly recommended by local residents. Set in a trim woodframe house, it features shrimp scampi, *frutti di mare* (seafood combination) and a host of pasta dishes. The interior is very fashionably done. ~ 2312 South Beretania Street; 946-1163. MODERATE.

In the same part of town sits one of Honolulu's best budget-priced Chinese restaurants. The decor at **King Tsin Restaurant** is rather bland, but the Mandarin cuisine adds plenty of spice. You can order Szechuan dishes like shredded pork or a Mongolian beef dish. These are plenty hot; you might also want to try the milder seafood, pork, vegetable, fowl and beef dishes. ~ 1110 McCully Street; 946-3273. BUDGET.

Auntie Pasto's is a popular Italian restaurant with oilcloth on the tables and a map of the mother country tacked to the wall. Pasta is served with any of a dozen different sauces—meat sauce, clams and broccoli, creamy pesto, carbonara and seafood. There are salads aplenty plus an assortment of entrées that includes veal marsala, chicken cacciatore and calamari steak. ~ 1099 South Beretania Street; 523-8855. BUDGET TO MODERATE.

For Southeast Asian cuisine, try the **Thai Taste**. At this modest café you can savor *kang som* (hot-and-sour fish soup), fried pork with garlic and pepper, or a tasty garlic prawn dish. ~ 1246 South King Street; 596-8106. BUDGET.

HIDDEN ► In Downtown Honolulu, near the city's financial center, there's a modest restaurant that I particularly like. **People's Café** has been serving Hawaiian food for over 60 years. The place is owned by a Japanese family, which helps explain the teriyaki dishes on the menu. But primarily the food is Polynesian: This is a splendid spot to order poi, *lomi* salmon, *kalua* pig and other island favorites. *Ono, ono!* ~ 1310 Pali Highway; 536-5789. BUDGET TO MODERATE.

For Chinese food, try **Yong Sing Restaurant**. This high-ceilinged establishment, catering to local businesspeople, has some delicious dishes. I thought the oyster sauce chicken particularly tasty. With its daily lunch specials, Yong Sing is a perfect stopoff when you're shopping or sightseeing downtown. ~ 1055 Alakea Street; 531-1367. BUDGET TO MODERATE.

But for the true flavor of China, head over to Chinatown, just a few blocks from the financial district. Amid the tumbledown buildings and jumble of shops, you'll happen upon **Double Eight Restaurant**. Although the service is forgettable and the decor non-existent, they do know how to cook up Hong Kong–style delicacies. One fortuitous sign of quality is that few of the employees speak any English. Good luck and bon appetit! ~ 1113 Maunakea Street; 526-3887. BUDGET.

There's **A Little Bit of Saigon** right in the heart of Chinatown. Small it may be, but this café represents a triple threat to the competition—attractive decor, good prices and excellent food. Little wonder it has gained such a strong reputation among the local gentry. The menu covers the spectrum of Vietnamese dishes, and the interior, lined with tropical paintings, is easy on the eyes. ~ 1160 Maunakea Street; 528-3663. BUDGET TO MODERATE.

◀ HIDDEN

And there's a little bit of every other ethnic cuisine at the food stalls in **Maunakea Marketplace**. Here you'll find vendors dispensing steaming plates of Thai, Chinese, Japanese, Hawaiian, Filipino, Korean, Vietnamese and Italian food. Italian? Small tables are provided. ~ Hotel and Maunakea streets. BUDGET.

By way of Filipino food, **Mabuhay Cafe** comes recommended by several readers. It's a plainly adorned place on the edge of Chinatown that serves a largely local clientele. The menu is extensive, covering the full spectrum of Filipino dishes. ~ 1049 River Street; 545-1956. BUDGET.

For upscale dining in Chinatown, the address is **Indigo**. This Eurasian dining room casts an aura of the Orient with its dark wicker chairs, ornamental gong and intaglio-carved furnishings. Expect more than a dozen dim sum dishes plus "Peking pizzettas." The soups and salads include tea-smoked chicken jook and grilled goat cheese in lotus leaf. Among the entrées, they offer peppered Mongolian beef, a "Buddhist vegetable" medley and seven-spice duck confit. What an adventure! No lunch on Sunday. ~ 1121 Nuuanu Avenue; 521-2900. MODERATE.

◆◆

✔ CHECK THESE OUT—UNIQUE DINING

- *Budget:* Dig in to a platter of poi and *kalua* pig while rubbing elbows with local folks at **Ono Hawaiian Foods**. *page 100*
- *Moderate:* Tuck yourself into a wicker chair, listen for the ornamental gong and order the seven-spice duck confit at **Indigo**. *page 89*
- *Deluxe:* Join the savvy diners enjoying Hawaii regional cuisine and ultra-chic surroundings at **Roy's Restaurant**. *page 107*
- *Ultra-deluxe:* Sit out on a balcony overlooking the ocean at **La Mer** and order fresh seafood that's prepared with a French touch. *page 75*

Budget: under $8   Moderate: $8–$16   Deluxe: $16–$24   Ultra-deluxe: over $24

GROCERIES Midway between Waikiki and Downtown Honolulu there's a **Times Supermarket**. ~ 1290 South Beretania Street; 524-5711. Nearby is a **Safeway** store. ~ 1121 South Beretania Street; 538-7315. There's another **Safeway** in Downtown Honolulu. ~ 1360 Pali Highway; 538-3953.

Also look for **The Carrot Patch** with its health and diet products. ~ 700 Bishop Street; 531-4037.

You might want to browse around the mom-and-pop grocery stores spotted throughout Chinatown. They're marvelous places to pick up Chinese foodstuffs and to capture the local color.

HIDDEN ▶ Don't miss the **Open Market** in Chinatown. It's a great place to shop for fresh foods. There are numerous stands selling fish, produce, poultry, meat, baked goods and island fruits, all at low-overhead prices. ~ Along North King Street between River and Kekaulike streets.

SHOPPING **Ala Moana Center**, on the outskirts of Waikiki, is the state's largest shopping center. This multi-tiered complex has practically everything. Where most self-respecting malls have two department stores, Ala Moana has four: **Sears** (947-0211), **JC Penney** (946-8068), Hawaii's own **Liberty House** (941-2345) and a Japanese emporium called **Shirokiya** (973-9111). There's also a **Woolworth's** (973-2235) and **Longs Drug Store** (941-4433), both good places to buy inexpensive Hawaiian curios. For contemporary fashion there is **United Colors of Benetton** (973-2670), among numerous other shops. You'll also find an assortment of stores selling liquor, antiques, tennis and golf supplies, stationery, leather goods, cameras, shoes, art, tobacco, etc. ~ 1450 Ala Moana Boulevard.

And, in a paragraph by itself, there's the **Honolulu Book Shop**. Together with its sister store downtown at 1001 Bishop Street, this is Hawaii's finest bookstore. Both branches contain excellent selections of Hawaiian books, bestsellers, paperbacks, calendars, magazines and out-of-town newspapers. ~ Ala Moana Center; 941-2274.

One of Honolulu's sleeker shopping malls is **Ward Centre**, an ultramodern facility at 1200 Ala Moana Boulevard. Streamlined and stylized, it's an elite enclave filled with designer shops and spiffy restaurants. In addition to boutiques and children's shops, there's a bookstore and a gourmet grocery, **R. Field Wine Co.** (596-9463). Adorned with blond-wood facades, brick walkways and brass-rail restaurants, the shopping complex provides a touch of Beverly Hills.

Anchoring Ward Centre at the far end is **Borders Books & Music** (591-8995), a superstore that is chockablock with everything for your reading and listening pleasure. They have two floors of paperbacks, hardbacks, audiotapes and CDs.

Just down the walkway in Ward Centre, you can home in on **Sedona**, the self-proclaimed "unique place to find yourself." If you're looking for aromatherapy oils, visionary music, inspirational gifts or a personal psychic reading, you have discovered the place. ~ 591-8115.

Ala Moana may be the biggest, but **Ward Warehouse**, located on Ala Moana Boulevard between Waikiki and Downtown Honolulu, is another very interesting shopping center. It features stores such as **Mamo Howell** (592-0616), which stocks original Hawaiian wear—aloha shirts and dressy muumuus. **Out of Africa** (591-6260) is a gallery with art, masks and jewelry from all over the world.

Honolulu's newest shopping complex is a California-style affair complete with white stucco walls and curved tile roof. **Aloha Tower Marketplace** is on the waterfront overlooking Honolulu Harbor. With its flagstone walkways and open-air courtyards, it's worth visiting even if buying something is the last thing on your mind. Among the over 100 shops and restaurants are about 25 devoted to apparel, a handful of galleries and perhaps three dozen specialty shops. There are also inexpensive food stands and several full-service restaurants. Tucked between the Hawaii Maritime Museum and Aloha Tower, it's set near one of the busiest parts of the harbor. ~ Pier 8; 528-5700.

If you're seeking Oriental items, then Chinatown is the place. Spotted throughout this refurbished neighborhood are small shops selling statuettes, pottery, woodcrafts and other curios. It's also worthwhile wandering through the **Cultural Plaza**, on the corner of Beretania and Maunakea streets. This mall is filled with Asian jewelers, bookstores and knickknack shops. ~ 521-4934.

If you love those claustrophobic antique stores that have keepsakes stacked to the rafters and spilling into the aisles, then the 900 block of Maunakea Street is calling. Here **Aloha Antique & Collectibles** extends for three storefronts with everything imaginable in the priceless-to-worthless range. ~ 930 Maunakea Street; 536-6187.

At the edge of Chinatown along Nuuanu Avenue are several galleries and shops worthy of a visit. The **Pegge Hopper Gallery** is here, displaying line drawings and the female portraits for which she is renowned. ~ 1164 Nuuanu Avenue; 524-1160.

NIGHTLIFE

The first thing you'll see upon entering the Prince Kuhio Hotel is **Cupid's Lobby Bar**. The lounge area features tropical palms, tapestries, rock walls and a small mirrored bar. Order drinks and *pupus* while enjoying light piano music and vocalists. An outdoor garden is adjacent. ~ 2500 Kuhio Avenue; 922-0811.

At **Rumours**, theme nights are the spice of life. Ballroom dancing, college night and karaoke are all featured, along with dancing to Top-40 music provided by deejays. Located in the Ala Moana Hotel, this club is decorated with artwork and neon fixtures. Weekend cover. ~ 410 Atkinson Drive; 955-4811.

A harbor view and Hawaiian/contemporary music played on weekends by an acoustic guitarist make **Kincaid's** a good choice for a relaxing evening. This lounge is part of a popular Honolulu restaurant. ~ 1050 Ala Moana Boulevard; 591-2005.

Located east of Waikiki, the **Hard Rock Cafe** is always a kick. Decorated with tons of rock-and-roll memorabilia, this restaurant/bar is a popular nightspot for those who like loud music and a big crowd. ~ 1837 Kapiolani Boulevard; 955-7383.

Near Downtown Honolulu, the ultra-contemporary Restaurant Row, offers several nightspots including **Studebaker's Hawaii**, where a deejay plays '50s through '90s tunes. Cover. ~ 500 Ala Moana Boulevard; 526-9888.

Also on Restaurant Row, there's dancing and billiards at the **World Cafe.** ~ 500 Ala Moana Boulevard; 599-4450.

For something more refined and classical, consider **Chamber Music Hawaii,** which presents 20 to 25 concerts annually at several different locations around the city. ~ 947-1975.

The **Hawaii Theatre** offers the best in Broadway performances, dance troupes, classical music and much more. The Hawaii International Film Festival is held here every November. ~ 1130 Bethel Street; 528-0506.

The **Honolulu Symphony**, with a season that runs from September to May, provides a delightful schedule of programs. ~ 524-0815.

At the **Hawaii Opera Theater**, you can see works like Saint-Saens' *Samson and Delilah*, Puccini's *Madame Butterfly* and *Die Fledermaus* by Strauss. This regional company features stars from the international opera scene. ~ Neal Blaisdell Concert Hall, Ward Avenue and King Street; 596-7372, box office 596-7858.

A variety of youth- and family-oriented productions are performed by the **Honolulu Theater for Youth**, at a number of venues throughout Oahu. The company also tours the neighbor islands twice a year. ~ 2846 Ualena Street; 839-9885.

At the other end of the cultural spectrum (and at the other end of town), the Honolulu red-light scene centers around Hotel Street in Chinatown. This partially refurbished, partially run-down strip is lined with hostess bars and adult bookstores. Prostitutes, straight and gay, are on the street regularly.

BEACHES & PARKS

HIDDEN ►

ALA MOANA REGIONAL PARK This 119-acre park is a favorite with Hawaii residents. On weekends every type of outdoor enthusiast imaginable turns out to swim, snorkel, fish (common catches are *papio*, bonefish, goatfish and *moano*), jog, fly model airplanes, sail model boats and so on. It's also a good place to surf; there are three separate breaks here: "Concessions," "Tennis Courts" and "Baby Haleiwa" all have summer waves.

There's a curving length of beach, a grassy park area, a helluva lot of local color and facilities that include a picnic area, restrooms, showers, concession stands, tennis courts, a recreation building, a bowling green and lifeguards. Markets and restaurants are nearby. ~ On Ala Moana Boulevard at the west end of Waikiki, across from Ala Moana Center.

SAND ISLAND STATE RECREATION AREA 🏊 ⛵ This 140-acre ◄ HIDDEN park wraps around the south and east shores of Sand Island, with sections fronting both Honolulu Harbor and the open sea. Despite the name, there's only a small sandy beach here, and jet traffic from nearby Honolulu International might disturb your snoozing. But there is a great view of Honolulu. While the swimming and snorkeling are poor here, there are good surf breaks in summer and fishing is usually rewarding. Bonefish, goatfish, *papio* and *moano* are the prime catches. Facilities include restrooms and a picnic area. Markets and restaurants are nearby. ~ From Waikiki, take Ala Moana Boulevard and Nimitz Highway several miles west to Sand Island Access Road.

▲ State permit required for tent camping in the grassy area facing the ocean.

▼▼▼▼▼▼▼▼▼▼▼▼

Greater Honolulu

Framed by the Waianae Range in the west and the Koolau Range to the east, Honolulu is a nonstop drama presented within a natural amphitheater. Honolulu Harbor sets the stage to the south; at the center lie Waikiki and Downtown Honolulu. Wrapped around these tourist and business centers is a rainbow-shaped congeries of sights and places that for lack of a better name constitutes "Greater Honolulu."

It extends from navy-gray Pearl Harbor to the turquoise waters of the prestigious Kahala district and holds in its ambit some of the city's prettiest territory. These points of interest are dotted all across the city, and to see them you must ride buses or taxis or rent a car. But all are well worth the extra effort. Many are visited more by local residents than tourists and offer a singular perspective on island life and culture. Others contain an interesting mix of local folk and out-of-towners. In any case, be sure to visit a few of these outlying spots.

NUUANU AVENUE The first district is actually within walking   **SIGHTS** distance of Downtown Honolulu, but it's a relatively long walk, so transportation is generally advised. Nuuanu Avenue begins downtown and travels uphill in a northeasterly direction past several intriguing points. First stop is **Soto Mission of Hawaii**, home of a meditative Zen sect. Modeled after a temple in India where the Buddha gave his first sermon, this building is marked by dramatic towers, and beautiful Japanese bonsai plants decorate the landscape. ~ 1708 Nuuanu Avenue. Here and at nearby **Honolulu Myohoji Temple** the city seems like a distant memory. The latter building, placidly situated along a small stream, is capped by a peace tower. ~ 2003 Nuuanu Avenue.

Uphill from this Buddhist shrine lies **Honolulu Memorial Park**. There is an ancestral monument here, bordered on three sides by a pond of flashing carp and a striking three-tiered pagoda. ~ 22 Craigside Place. This entire area is a center of simple yet beautiful Asian places of worship. For instance, **Tenrikyo Mission** is a wood-frame temple that was moved here all the way from Japan. One intriguing fact about this fragile structure is that large sections were built without nails. ~ 2236 Nuuanu Avenue.

HIDDEN ► The Hawaiian people also have an important center here. The **Royal Mausoleum** is situated across the street from the Tenrikyo Mission. This was the final resting place for two of Hawaii's royal families, the Kamehameha and Kalakaua clans. Together they ruled 19th-century Hawaii. Today the area is landscaped with palms, ginger, plumeria and other beautiful plants and flowers. ~ 2261 Nuuanu Avenue.

PUNCHBOWL AND TANTALUS   It is a few miles from Downtown Honolulu to **Punchbowl**, the circular center of an extinct volcano. You'll find it northeast of town, at the end of Ward Avenue and just off Prospect Drive, which circles the crater. A youngster in geologic terms, the volcano is a mere 150,000 years old. From the lip of the crater, there is a marvelous vista sweeping down to Diamond Head, across Honolulu and all the way out to the Waianae Range.

The most important feature here, however, is the **National Memorial Cemetery**, where over 25,000 war dead have been interred. Victims of both World Wars, as well as the Korean, Spanish-American and Vietnam wars, are buried here. There is also an impressive monument to the "Courts of the Missing," which lists the names of soldiers missing in action. Ironically, of all the people buried here, the most famous was not a soldier but a journalist— Ernie Pyle, whose World War II stories about the average GI were eagerly followed by an entire nation. Near his grave you will also find the burial site of Hawaii's first astronaut, Ellison Onizuka, who died in the *Challenger* space shuttle disaster. Guided walking tours are offered by the American Legion. Fee. ~ 946-6383.

HIDDEN ► You can explore the heights by following Tantalus Drive as it winds up the side of **Tantalus**, a 2013-foot mountain. Together with Round Top Drive, Tantalus Drive forms a loop that circles through the residential areas hidden within this rainforest. There are spectacular views all along the route, as well as hiking trails that lead from the road into verdant hilltop regions. Here you'll encounter guava, banana, eucalyptus and ginger trees as well as wild-

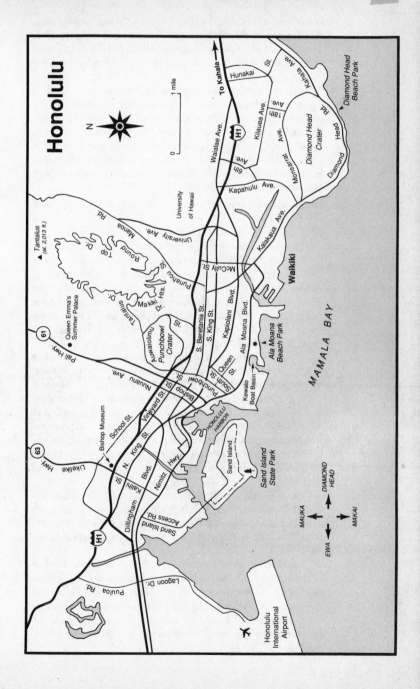

Honolulu

N

▲ Tantalus (el. 2,013 ft.)

To Kahala

Hunakai St.

Diamond Head Beach Park

Kahala Ave.

18th Ave

Kilauea Ave.

Diamond Head Crater

Rd

Diamond Head

Monsarrat Ave.

Diamond

Waialae Ave.

6th Ave

Kapahulu Ave.

H1

Kalakaua Ave.

University of Hawaii

Manoa Rd.

University Ave.

Top Dr.

Round Dr.

Punahou St.

McCully St.

Waikiki

Tantalus Dr.

Makiki Dr. Hts.

Queen Emma's Summer Palace

61

Pali Hwy.

Auwaiolimu St.

Punchbowl Crater

S. Beretania St.

S. King St.

Kapiolani Blvd.

Ala Moana Blvd.

Nuuanu Ave.

Punchbowl St.

South St.

Queen St.

Ala Moana Beach Park

Bishop St.

Kewalo Boat Basin

MAMALA BAY

Vineyard St.

School St.

Bishop Museum

N. King St.

HONOLULU HARBOR

63

Likelike Hwy

Kalihi St.

Nimitz Hwy.

Sand Island

Sand Island State Park

Dillingham Blvd.

Sand Island Access Rd.

H1

MAUKA

DIAMOND HEAD

EWA

MAKAI

Puuloa Rd.

Lagoon Dr.

Honolulu International Airport

0 1 mile

flowers and an occasional wild pig. One of the best views of all is found at **Puu Ualakaa Park**, a lovely retreat located along the drive. The vista here extends from Diamond Head west to Pearl Harbor, encompassing in its course a giant swath of Honolulu and the Pacific.

En route stop by the **Contemporary Museum**. In addition to changing exhibitions of contemporary art, the museum features the works of several well-known artists in its sculpture garden including David Hockney, Robert Arneson, Charles Arnoldi and Tom Wasselman. Boasting five galleries, an inspired gift shop and a gourmet café, the museum is nevertheless upstaged by its magnificently landscaped grounds. Closed Monday. Admission. ~ 2411 Makiki Heights Drive; 526-1322.

CROSS-ISLAND EXPRESS   Along the outskirts of Honolulu, there are several more points of interest. The best way to tour them is while traveling along the two highways that cut across the Koolaus, connecting Honolulu directly with the island's Windward Coast.

The Likelike Highway, Route 63, can be reached from Route H-1, the superhighway that serves Honolulu. Before heading up into the mountains, you will encounter the **Bishop Museum** near the intersection of Routes 63 and H-1. Built around the turn of the century, it houses an excellent collection of Hawaiian and Pacific artifacts.

Of all the exhibits at the Bishop Museum, the most spectacular are cloaks worn by Hawaiian kings and fashioned from tens of thousands of tiny feathers.

Here you'll find outrigger canoes, thrones, primitive artworks, royal feather capes and fascinating natural-history exhibits. There are plaited mats woven from pandanus, drums made with shark skin, 19th-century surfboards, and helmets decorated with dog teeth and pearl shells. The 19th-century whaling trade is represented with menacing harpoons and yellowing photographs of the oil-laden ships. There are displays capturing the Japanese, Chinese and Filipino heritage in Hawaii and a hall devoted to other cultures of the Pacific.

The museum also offers a planetarium, a Hall of Discovery with children's activities, and classes in quilting, hula dancing, lei-making and weaving. The Bishop is truly one of the finest museums of its kind in the world. Admission. ~ 1525 Bernice Street; 847-3511.

The other, more scenic road across the mountains is the Pali Highway, Route 61. As it ascends, it passes **Queen Emma's Summer Palace**. Constructed in 1848, the palace was originally used by King Kamehameha IV and his wife, Queen Emma. Today the gracious white-pillared house is a museum. Here you can view the Queen's personal artifacts, as well as various other period pieces. Admission. ~ 595-3167.

You can also walk the tree-shaded grounds of **Nuuanu Pali Drive** ◀ HIDDEN
and follow until it rejoins the highway. This residential boulevard,
with its natural canopy and park-like atmosphere, is one of Honolulu's many idyllic hideaways.

Farther along Pali Highway, there is a turnoff to **Nuuanu Pali
Lookout**. It is a point that must not be missed, and is without
doubt Oahu's finest view. Gaze down the sheer, rugged face of the
Koolau cliffs as they drop 3000 feet to a softly rolling coastal shelf.
Your view will extend from Makapuu Point to the distant reaches
of Kaneohe Bay, and from the lip of the cliff far out to sea. It was
from these heights, according to legend, that a vanquished army
was forced to plunge when Kamehameha I captured Oahu in 1795.

PEARL HARBOR   Many people consider a trip to Pearl Harbor a
pilgrimage. It was here on a sleepy Sunday morning, December 7,
1941, that the Japanese launched a sneak attack on the United
States naval fleet anchored in the port, immediately plunging the
nation into World War II. As Japanese planes bombed the harbor,
over 2400 Americans lost their lives. Eighteen ships sank that day
in the country's greatest military disaster.

The battleship USS *Arizona* was hit so savagely by aerial bombs
and torpedoes that it plunged to the bottom, entombing over 1100
sailors within its hulk; today they remain in that watery grave. A
special **USS Arizona Memorial** was built to honor them; it's a museum constructed directly above the ship, right in the middle of
Pearl Harbor. In addition to the museum displays, the memorial
includes a shrine with the name of each sailor who died aboard the
ship carved in marble. Gazing at this too, too long list of names,
and peering over the side at the shadowy hull of the ship, it's hard
not to be overcome by the tragic history of the place. Daily from 8
a.m. to 3 p.m., the United States Navy sponsors free boat tours out
to this fascinating memorial. Before boarding, be sure to remember, no bathing suits, bare feet or children under 45 inches are permitted. Pearl Harbor, several miles northwest of Downtown Honolulu, can be reached by car or bus. ~ 422-0561.

Anchored nearby the *Arizona* visitors center is the **USS Bow-
fin/Pacific Submarine Museum**. This World War II–era submarine
is a window into life beneath the waves. It provides an excellent
opportunity to tour the claustrophobic quarters in which 80 men
spent months at a time. The accompanying museum, filled with
submarine-related artifacts, will help provide an even fuller perspective. Admission. ~ 423-1341.

MANOA VALLEY   Residents of a different sort are found in the city's
beautiful Manoa Valley, a couple of miles northeast of Waikiki.
Among the elegant homes decorating the region are some owned by
the New England families that settled in Hawaii in the 19th century.

The **University of Hawaii** has its main campus here; almost 20,000 students and 2000 faculty members attend classes and teach on these grounds, which are set amid rolling lawns and backdropped by the Koolau Mountains. ~ 2540 Dole Street; 956-8111.

HIDDEN ▶

On campus is the **East-West Center**, a private research facility. Designed by noted architect I. M. Pei, the center is devoted to the study of Asian and American cultures. The center also contains a number of priceless Asian artworks, well worth viewing. ~ 1777 East-West Road; 944-7111.

From here you can head deeper into Manoa Valley along Oahu Avenue and Manoa Road. You'll pass the **Waioli Tea Room**, a cozy dining room tucked into a garden setting (closed at the present time). ~ 2950 Manoa Road; 988-9488. Here also is the **Little Grass Shack** that was once occupied by novelist Robert Louis Stevenson (or so the story goes), and a small chapel replete with stained-glass windows.

Adjacent to the park is **Lyon Arboretum**, a magnificent 194-acre garden with over 8000 plant species, research greenhouses, hiking trails and perhaps the world's largest collection of palm trees. The arboretum also offers a variety of one-day classes on topics such as horticulture and lei-making. Closed Sunday. ~ 3860 Manoa Road; 988-3177.

KAHALA On the far side of Diamond Head, along a string of narrow beaches, lie many of Honolulu's most admired addresses. To reach this residential promised land follow Diamond Head Road.

Diamond Head Beach Park, a twisting ribbon of white sand, nestles directly below the famous crater. Whenever the wind and waves are good, you'll see windsurfers and surfers galore sweeping in toward the shoreline. The coral reef here makes for good skin-diving, too. It's a pretty beach, backdropped by the Kuilei cliffs and watched over by the **Diamond Head Lighthouse**.

From Diamond Head, continue east along Diamond Head Road and Kahala Avenue. These will lead through the Kahala District, home to the island's elite. Bordered by the ocean and the exclusive Waialae Country Club is a golden string of spectacular oceanfront homes with carefully manicured lawns.

LODGING

The **Nuuanu** YMCA has inexpensive accommodations for men. Complete athletic facilities are available. ~ 1441 Pali Highway; 536-3556. BUDGET.

HIDDEN ▶

Hawaii's foremost bed-and-breakfast inn rests in a magnificent old mansion near the University of Hawaii campus. Set in the lush Manoa Valley, the **Manoa Valley Inn** is a 1915 cream-colored Victorian featuring seven guest rooms and an adjacent cottage. Decorated with patterned wallpaper and old-style artworks, the rooms are furnished in plump antique armchairs. Guests enjoy a sunroom and parlor, as well as a spacious veranda and lawn. For luxury and privacy, this historic jewel is one of the island's finest spots. Continental breakfast and evening wine and cheese are included. ~ 2001 Vancouver Drive; 947-6019, 800-634-5115, fax 946-6168. DELUXE TO ULTRA-DELUXE.

Also in Manoa Valley, the **Fernhurst YWCA** is an appealing three-story lowrise that provides a residence for women. Rooms are single or double occupancy with connecting baths. Among the facilities are microwaves, refrigerators, laundry, dining room, swimming pool and lounge. Rates include breakfast and dinner Monday through Friday. ~ 1566 Wilder Avenue; 941-2231. BUDGET.

The **Atherton YWCA** is a coed facility with accommodations for men and women. Across the street from the University of Hawaii campus, it's open year-round to full-time students (of any institution, but you have to show registration and student ID) and during the summer to the general public. There's a nonrefundable application fee and a refundable deposit. Facilities include laundry, lounge and a microwave. Reservations must be booked at least two weeks in advance and the facility is closed weekends and holidays, so plan accordingly. ~ 1810 University Avenue; 946-0253, fax 941-7802. BUDGET.

The **Honolulu International Youth Hostel** is a dormitory-style crash pad with separate living quarters for men and women. Shared kitchen facilities, television lounge, garden patio and laundry are available. ~ 2323-A Sea View Avenue; 946-0591, fax 946-5904. BUDGET.

With two rooms and a cottage, **Bed & Breakfast Manoa** offers cozy surroundings as well as spectacular views of Diamond Head. Light pastels and a southern-style decor add to the homey aura, and those mild Hawaiian nights make it possible to sleep outdoors. ~ 2651 Terrace Drive; 988-6333, fax 988-5240. MODERATE TO DELUXE.

◄ HIDDEN

With its breezy corner rooms and strict nonsmoking policy, **The Mango House** caters entirely to women. There are two rooms and a cottage, each comfortably furnished and decorated with local artwork. One of the rooms includes a hot tub, which is almost as appealing as the homemade mango jam that is served for breakfast. Set in a residential neighborhood, The Mango House enjoys panoramic views of Honolulu. Three-night minimum stay. ~ 2087 Iholina Street; phone/fax 595-6682, 800-776-2646, E-mail mango@pixi.com. MODERATE TO DELUXE.

Liliha Seafood Restaurant, a neighborhood café out past Downtown Honolulu, comes highly recommended by local folks. This could very well be the only Hawaiian dining spot that offers sweet-and-sour sea bass, squid with sour mustard cabbage and fried

DINING

◄ HIDDEN

squid with *ong choy*. In addition to two dozen seafood dishes, they have a host of chicken, pork, vegetable and noodle selections. ~ 1408 Liliha Street; 536-2663. BUDGET.

One of the ethnic restaurants most popular with local folks is **Keo's Thai Cuisine**. Fulfilling to all the senses, this intimate place is decorated with fresh flowers and tropical plants. The cuisine includes such Southeast Asian dishes as the "evil jungle prince," a sliced beef, shrimp or chicken entrée in hot sauce. You can choose from dozens of fish, shellfish, fowl and meat dishes. The food is very, very spicy, and highly recommended. Dinner only. ~ 625 Kapahulu Avenue; 737-8240. MODERATE TO DELUXE.

HIDDEN ►

For Japanese dining, one of my favorites is **Irifune**, a charming place with a warm and friendly ambience. There are tasty curry, teriyaki and tempura dishes, plus several other Asian delectables. Closed Monday. ~ 563 Kapahulu Avenue; 737-1141. MODERATE.

Quantity and quality don't usually come together, particularly where gourmet restaurants are concerned. But at **Sam Choy** you can count on platter-size portions of macadamia-crushed *ono*, Oriental lamb chops, oven-roasted duck or tofu lasagna. Considered one of the top Hawaiian cuisine restaurants on the island, it sits with unassuming grace on the second floor of a strip mall. Eat heartily (and well)! Dinner and Sunday brunch. ~ 449 Kapahulu Avenue, Suite 201; 732-8645. DELUXE TO ULTRA-DELUXE.

For local-style plate lunches, cruise in to **Rainbow Drive-In**. Popular with *kamaainas* and tourists alike, the menu includes hamburger steak, beef curry, chili and fried chicken served with two scoops of rice and macaroni salad. ~ 3308 Kanaina Avenue; 737-0177. BUDGET.

Ono Hawaiian Foods is a must for all true Hawaii lovers. It's a hole-in-da-wall eatery on a busy street. But if you're lucky enough to get one of the few tables, you can feast on *laulau, kalua* pig, *pipikaula,* poi and *haupia*. The walls are papered with signed photographs of local notables and the place is packed with locals, notable and otherwise. Closed Sunday. ~ 726 Kapahulu Avenue; 737-2275. BUDGET.

Near the University of Hawaii campus, there are pizzas, hero sandwiches, spaghetti and a salad bar at **Mama Mia**. Open for lunch on weekends and dinner every day, it's a great place to snack or stop for a cold beer. ~ Puck's Alley, 1015 University Avenue; 947-5233. MODERATE.

Or you can check out **Anna Banana's**, a combination bar and Mexican restaurant that draws a swinging crowd. Located a half-mile from campus, this dim eatery serves burritos, enchiladas and other south-of-the-border favorites. Decorated in slapdash fashion with propellers, antlers, surfboards, boxing gloves and trophies, Anna's is the local center for slumming. ~ 2440 South Beretania Street; 946-5190. BUDGET.

Waialae Avenue, a neighborhood strip several miles outside Waikiki, has developed into a gourmet ghetto. **Azteca Mexican Restaurant** is a vinyl-booth-and-plastic-panel eatery that serves a delicious array of Mexican food. ~ 3617 Waialae Avenue; 735-2492. BUDGET TO MODERATE.

For spicy and delicious Asian dishes, it is hard to find a more appealing place than **Hale Vietnam**. A family restaurant that draws a local crowd, it features traditional Vietnamese soup and a host of excellent entrées. ~ 1140 12th Avenue; 734-7581. MODERATE.

◄ HIDDEN

A good place to shop near the University of Hawaii's Manoa campus is at **Star Market**. ~ 2470 South King Street; 973-1666.

GROCERIES

The best place in Honolulu to buy health foods is at **Down To Earth Natural Foods**. ~ 2525 South King Street; 947-7678. **Kokua Market** is another excellent choice. ~ 2643 South King Street; 941-1922.

Scattered around town are several shops that I recommend you check out. At **Lanakila Crafts** most of the goods are made by the disabled, and the craftsmanship is superb. There are shell necklaces, woven handbags, monkeypod bowls and homemade dolls. You'll probably see these items in other stores around the islands, with much higher price tags than here at the "factory." ~ 1809 Bachelot Street; 531-0555.

SHOPPING

Out at the Bishop Museum be sure to stop by **Shop Pacifica**, which offers a fine selection of Hawaiiana. There are books on island history and geography, an assortment of instruments that include nose flutes and gourds, plus cards, souvenirs and wooden bowls. ~ 1525 Bernice Street, near the intersection of Routes 63 and H-1; 848-4158.

One of Honolulu's most upscale shopping centers is **Kahala Mall**, where you'll find designer shops galore. This attractive complex also hosts an array of moderately priced stores. ~ 4211 Waialae Avenue; 732-7736.

Barnes & Noble has a superstore here. In addition to a comprehensive line of books, they sell tapes and CDs and feature a café on the premises. ~ Kahala Mall, 4211 Waialae Avenue; 737-3323.

◆◆

SWAP 'EM, BRAH

For secondhand items, try the **Kam Super Swap Meet**. It's a great place to barter for bargains, meet local folks and find items you'll never see in stores. It's open on Wednesday, Saturday, Sunday and some holidays. ~ 98-850 Moanalua Road; 483-5933.

NIGHTLIFE Outside Honolulu there are a couple of prime spots to hear Hawaiian music. **Jubilation**, past Downtown Honolulu, has live bands every night. ~ 1007 Dillingham Boulevard; 845-1568.

Over by the University of Hawaii's Manoa campus, there's **Anna Banana's**. A popular hangout for years, this wildly decorated spot has live entertainment several nights a week. There's likely to be a local band cranking it up and a local crowd headed for the dancefloor. Cover. ~ 2440 South Beretania Street; 946-5190.

Up at the **Bishop Museum**, you'll be serenaded by the Brothers Cazimero, one of the island's very finest musical groups. Their two-man show, which performs Wednesday, Thursday and Sunday, has been an integral part of the Honolulu scene for years. The admission price is hefty but includes a tour of the museum before the show. I recommend going for the show only and skipping the dinner. ~ 1525 Bernice Street; 847-6353.

BEACHES & PARKS **KEAIWA HEIAU STATE RECREATION AREA** 🏃 Amazing as it sounds, this is a wooded retreat within easy driving distance of Honolulu. Situated in the Koolau foothills overlooking Pearl Harbor, it contains the remains of a *heiau*, a temple once used by Hawaiian healers. There's an arboretum of medicinal plants, a forest extending to the far reaches of the mountains and a network of hiking trails. Facilities include picnic area, showers and restrooms. Markets and restaurants several miles away. ~ Located in Aiea Heights. To get there from Honolulu, take Route 90 west to Aiea, then follow Aiea Heights Drive to the park.

HIDDEN ►

▲ Tents only. State permit required.

HIDDEN ► **DIAMOND HEAD BEACH PARK** 🏄 ⛵ 🎣 🏊 A heaven to windsurfers, this twisting ribbon of white sand sits directly below the crater. It's close enough to Waikiki for convenient access but far enough to shake most of the crowds. The Kuilei cliffs, covered with scrub growth, loom behind the beach. Snorkeling is good here as a coral reef extends offshore through this area. There's also a good year-round surf break called "Lighthouse." And for the anglers, your chances are good to reel in *ulua*, *papio* or *mamao*. A shower is the sole facility. Markets and restaurants in Waikiki are about two miles away. ~ Located just beyond Waikiki along Diamond Head Road at the foot of Diamond Head; watch for parked cars.

KUILEI CLIFFS BEACH PARK AND KAALAWAI BEACH 🏄 ⛵ 🎣 🏊 Extending east from Diamond Head Beach Park, these sandy corridors are also flanked by sharp sea cliffs. Together they extend from Diamond Head Lighthouse to Black Point. The aquatic attractions are the same as at Diamond Head Beach Park and both beaches can be reached from it (or from cliff trails leading down from Diamond Head Road). A protecting reef makes for good swimming at Kaalawai Beach (which can also be reached via a public accessway off Kulumanu Place).

WAIALAE BEACH PARK 🐚 🦀 🎣 Smack in the middle of Honolulu's prestigious Kahala district, where a million dollars buys a modest house, sits this tidy beach. Its white sand neatly groomed, its spacious lawn shaded by palms, Waialae is a true find. It has good swimming and fishing. There are bathhouse facilities, beachside picnic tables and a footbridge arching across the stream that divides the property. (Groceries are several miles away in Waikiki or along Waialae Avenue.) To the west of the park lies **Kahala Beach**, a long, thin swath of sand that extends all the way to Black Point. There's good snorkeling near the Kahala Hilton. ~ Located on the 4900 block of Kahala Avenue in Kahala.

▼▼▼▼▼▼▼▼▼▼▼▼

Southeast Oahu

Out past Honolulu, beyond the lights of Waikiki and the gilded neighborhoods of Kahala, the pace slackens, the vistas open and Oahu begins to look more like a tropical island. As the sunny south shore gives way to the windward side of the island, you'll encounter volcanic craters, famous body-surfing beaches and a dramatic blowhole. A major road, Route 72—the Kalanianaole Highway—leads from Honolulu along this southeastern coast.

SIGHTS

This thoroughfare streams through Hawaii Kai and other residential areas, then ascends the slopes of an extinct volcano, 642-foot **Koko Head**. Here Madame Pele is reputed to have dug a hole for the last time in search of fiery volcanic matter. **Koko Crater**, the second hump on the horizon, rises to over 1200 feet. This fire-pit, according to Hawaiian legend, is the vagina of Pele's sister. It seems that Pele, goddess of volcanoes, was being pursued by a handsome demigod. Her sister, trying to distract the hot suitor from Pele, spread her legs across the landscape.

From the top of Koko Head, a well-marked sideroad and trail lead down to **Hanauma Bay**, one of the prettiest beaches in all Hawaii. This breathtaking place is a marine preserve filled with multicolored coral and teeming with underwater life. The word *hanauma* means "the curved bay," and you will clearly see that this inlet was once a circular volcano, one wall of which was breached by the sea. Little wonder that Hollywood chose this spot as the prime location for Elvis Presley's movie, *Blue Hawaii*. Elvis' grass shack was right here, and the strand was also a setting in the classic film *From Here to Eternity*.

The swimming and snorkeling are unmatched anywhere and the mazework of coral formations along the bottom adds to the snorkeling adventure. Or you can stroll along the rock ledges that fringe the bay and explore **Toilet Bowl**, a tidepool that "flushes" as the waves wash through it. The best time to come is early morning before other swimmers stir up the waters. Hanauma Bay is an extremely popular picnic spot among local folks, so it is also advisable to visit on a weekday rather than face bucking the crowds on Saturday and Sunday.

Hanauma Bay is located about 12 miles east of Waikiki. From here the highway corkscrews along the coast. Among the remarkable scenes you'll enjoy en route are views of Lanai and Molokai, two of Oahu's sister islands. On a clear, clear day you can also see Maui, an island that requires no introduction.

At an overlook you will encounter **Halona Blowhole**, a lava tube through which geysers of seawater blast. During high tide and when the sea is turbulent, these gushers reach dramatic heights. *Halona* means "peering place," and that is exactly what everyone seems to do here. You can't miss the spot, since the roadside parking lot is inevitably crowded with tourists. Between December and April this vista is also a prime whale-watching spot.

Just beyond spreads **Sandy Beach**, one of Hawaii's most renowned bodysurfing spots. It's a long, wide beach piled with fluffy sand and complete with picnic areas and showers. Inexperienced bodysurfers are better off enjoying the excellent sunbathing here, since the dramatic shorebreak that makes the beach so popular among bodysurfers can overwhelm beginners.

HIDDEN ►   Across from the beach a side road leads up to **Koko Crater Botanical Gardens**, a 200-acre collection of cacti, plumeria and other flowering plants. ~ 408 Kealahou Street, next to the Koko Crater Stables; 522-7060.

Past this pretty spot, Route 72 rounds Oahu's southeastern corner and sets a course along the eastern shoreline. It also climbs to a scenic point from which you can take your first view of the Windward Coast. You will be standing on **Makapuu Point**. Above you rise sharp lava cliffs, while below are rolling sand dunes and open ocean. The slope-faced islet just offshore is **Rabbit Island**. The distant headland is Makapuu Peninsula, toward which you are bound.

From this perfect perch you can also spy a complex of buildings. That's **Sea Life Park**, a marine-world attraction comparable to those in California and Florida. Among the many features at this park is the "Hawaiian Reef," a 300,000-gallon oceanarium inhabited by about 4000 sea creatures. To see it you wind through a spiral viewing area that descends three fathoms along the tank's glass perimeter. At times a scuba diver will be hand-feeding the fish. Swimming about this underwater world are sharks, stingrays and a variety of lesser-known species. The park also features a touch pool, turtle lagoon, penguin habitat and the only known *wholphin* (half whale, half dolphin) living in captivity.

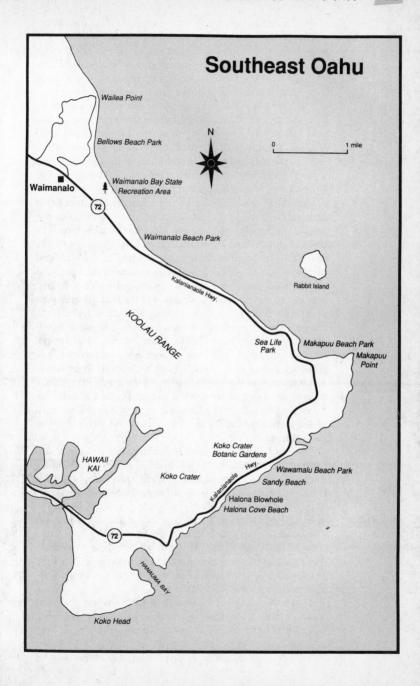

Southeast Oahu

Wailea Point

Bellows Beach Park

■ **Waimanalo**

Waimanalo Bay State Recreation Area

(72)

Waimanalo Beach Park

Kalanianaole Hwy.

KOOLAU RANGE

Rabbit Island

Sea Life Park

Makapuu Beach Park

Makapuu Point

Koko Crater Botanic Gardens

Koko Crater

HAWAII KAI

Kalanianaole Hwy.

Wawamalu Beach Park

Sandy Beach

Halona Blowhole

Halona Cove Beach

(72)

HANAUMA BAY

Koko Head

N

0   1 mile

At the Ocean Science Theatre, trained dolphins, false killer whales, penguins and sea lions perform regularly. The whales star in an aquatic pageant, while the other entertainers leap and gambol through sophisticated routines. You can feed the sea animals if you wish, or wander over to the *Essex*, a 70-foot replica of a whaling ship that lies anchored in the park's lagoon. Since whalers played such an important part in Hawaii's 19th-century history, this is a particularly interesting feature, as is the **Pacific Whaling Museum**, where Hawaii's harpoon heyday is re-created through displays of artifacts and scrimshaw artistry. Admission. ~ Makapuu Point; 942-3100.

Rabbit Island, located off Makapuu Point, resembles a bunny's head, but was actually named for a former rabbit-raising farm there.

Across the road from Sea Life Park spreads **Makapuu Beach Park**, another fabled but daunting bodysurfing spot that is set in a particularly pretty location. Nearby black lava cliffs are topped by a white lighthouse and **Rabbit Island** is anchored just offshore. The beach itself is a short, wide rectangle of white sand. It's an ideal place to picnic, but when the surf is up, beware of the waves.

The road continues along the shoreline between soft sand beaches and rugged mountain peaks. For the next 30 miles your attention will be drawn back continually to those rocky crags. They are part of the **Koolau Range**, a wall of precipitous mountains that vault up from Oahu's placid interior. Their spires, minarets and fluted towers are softened here and there by lush, green valleys, but never enough to detract from the sheer beauty and magnitude of the heights. Light and shade play games along their moss-covered surfaces, while rainbows hang suspended between the peaks. If wind and weather permit, you will see hang gliders dusting the cliffs as they sail from the mountains down to the distant beach.

The road continues through **Waimanalo**, an old ranching area that today has been turned to fruit and flower cultivation. Outside town you will see **Olomana Peak**. Favored by rock climbers, it is a double-barreled peak that seems to belong in the Swiss Alps.

DINING

Spotted along Oahu's southeastern shore are a number of moderately priced restaurants (and a couple of expensive but worthy ones) that may prove handy if you're beachcombing or camping. Most are located on or near Route 72 (Kalanianaole Highway). For the sake of convenience, I'll list the restaurants as they will appear when you travel east and north.

You're bound to feel Eurocentric at the **Swiss Inn**, where the menu includes wienerschnitzel, veal with a cream mushroom sauce and cheese fondue. There's also a beef fondue with 24-hour advance notice. On the dessert menu you'll find Swiss chocolate mousse, peach melba and fresh fruit tarts. The wood-paneled Old

World look features pictures of villages that make you yearn for the Matterhorn. ~ Niu Valley Shopping Center, 5730 Kalanianaole Highway; 377-5447. DELUXE.

Tucked away in unassuming fashion in a business park is one of the area's top dining spots. You'll have to travel all the way to Hawaii Kai, several miles east of Waikiki, to find **Roy's Restaurant**. It's small, intimate and ultracontemporary, from the magazine clips framed on the walls to the cylindrical fish tank near the door. One of the most innovative of Hawaii's "Nouvelle Pacific" cuisine dining rooms, it specializes in fresh local ingredients. The main complaints you hear about this wildly popular restaurant are that it's too crowded and too noisy. ~ 6600 Kalanianaole Highway; 396-7697. DELUXE TO ULTRA-DELUXE.

Waimanalo Bar-B-Q has breakfasts, plate lunches and sandwiches at greasy-spoon prices. No gourmet's delight, this tiny eatery is well placed for people enjoying Waimanalo's beaches. ~ 41-857 Kalanianaole Highway, Waimanalo; no phone. BUDGET.

A few doors down is one of Hawaii's great Mexican restaurants. **Bueno Nalo** may be short on looks, but it's definitely long on taste. ~ 41-865 Kalanianaole Highway, Waimanalo; 259-7186. BUDGET.

◄ HIDDEN

GROCERIES

A convenient place to shop in Oahu's southeast corner is at the Koko Marina Shopping Center's **Foodland**. ~ 7192 Kalanianaole Highway, Hawaii Kai; 395-3131. Proceeding north along the coast, there's **Mel's Market**, a small store in Waimanalo. ~ 41-1029 Kalanianaole Highway, Waimanalo; 259-7550.

BEACHES & PARKS

HANAUMA BAY NATURE PARK One of Oahu's prettiest and most popular beaches, this curving swath of white sand extends for almost a half-mile. The bottom of the bay is a maze of coral reef, and the entire area has been designated a marine preserve; fishing is strictly prohibited. As a result, the skindiving is unmatched and the fish are tame enough to eat from your hand. (Just beware of "Witches Brew," a turbulent area on the bay's right side, and the "Molokai Express," a wicked current sweeping across the mouth of the bay.) You can also hike along rock ledges fringing the bay and explore some mind-boggling tidepools. Crowded though it is, this is one strand that should not be bypassed. Get here early—the beach closes at 7 p.m. every day. Facilities include a picnic area, restrooms, showers, a snack bar, snorkeling equipment rentals and lifeguards. It's one mile to restaurants and markets at Koko Marina Shopping Center. ~ Located about nine miles east of Waikiki. Take Kalanianaole Highway (Route 72) to Koko Head, then turn onto the side road near the top of the promontory. This leads to a parking lot; leave your vehicle and walk the several hundred yards down the path to the beach.

HIDDEN ► **HALONA COVE BEACH** 🏊 🐟 ⚓ This is the closest you'll find to a hidden beach near Honolulu. It's a patch of white sand wedged between Halona Point and the Halona Blowhole lookout. Located directly below Kalanianaole Highway (Route 72), this is not exactly a wilderness area. But you can still escape the crowds massed on the nearby beaches. Swimming and snorkeling are good when the sea is gentle but extremely dangerous if it's rough. Prime catches are *ulua*, *papio* and *mamao*. There are no facilities; the closest markets and restaurants are two miles away in Koko Marina Shopping Center. ~ Stop at the Halona Blowhole parking lot on Kalanianaole Highway (Route 72), about ten miles east of Waikiki. Follow the path from the right side of the lot down to the beach.

SANDY BEACH 🏊 🏄 ⚓ This long, wide beach is a favorite among Oahu's youth. The shorebreak makes it one of the finest, and most dangerous, bodysurfing beaches in the islands. Surfing is good and very popular but beware of rip currents. Lifeguards are on duty. It's a pleasant place to sunbathe, but if you go swimming, plan to negotiate a pounding shoreline. Anglers try for *ulua*, *papio* and *mamao*. There are picnic areas, restrooms and showers; it's three miles to the restaurants and markets in Koko Marina Shopping Center. Should you want to avoid the crowds, head over to **Wawamalu Beach Park** next door to the east. ~ Head out on Kalanianaole Highway (Route 72) about 12 miles east of Waikiki.

People come from all over the world to body surf Sandy Beach and Makapuu Beach Park.

MAKAPUU BEACH PARK 🏊 ⚓ It's set in a very pretty spot with lava cliffs in the background and Rabbit Island just offshore. This short, wide rectangle of white sand is Hawaii's most famous bodysurfing beach. With no protecting reef and a precipitous shoreline, Makapuu is inundated by awesome swells that send wave riders crashing onto shore. Necks and backs are broken with frightening regularity here, so if the waves are large and you're inexperienced—play the spectator. If you take the plunge, prepare for a battering! Snorkeling is usually poor and surfing is not permitted here. Common catches are *ulua*, *papio* and *mamao*. The only facilities are restrooms and a lifeguard. There's a restaurant across the road in Sea Life Park. ~ Located on Kalanianaole Highway (Route 72) about 13 miles east of Waikiki.

▲ Currently not permitted, but it will probably reopen to the public so it's worth checking out.

WAIMANALO BEACH PARK AND WAIMANALO BAY STATE RECREATION AREA 🏊 🐟 ⚓ Located at the southeast end of Waimanalo's three-and-a-half-mile-long beach, this is a spacious 38-acre park. It's studded with ironwood trees and equipped with numerous recreation facilities including a playground, a basketball court and a baseball field. Waimanalo Beach Park and Waimanalo Bay State Recreation Area, a mile farther north, are both excellent spots for picnicking, swimming, snorkeling and sunbathing. The latter is farther removed from the highway in a grove of ironwood trees known to local residents as "Sherwood Forest." Waimanalo is a good place to fish for *papio*, bonefish, milkfish and goatfish. There are picnic areas, restrooms and showers at both. ~ Waimanalo Beach Park is located at 41-471 Kalanianaole Highway (Route 72) about 15 miles east of Waikiki. Waimanalo Bay State Recreation Area is on Oloiloi Street a mile farther north.

▲ A county permit required at both of the parks for tent and trailer camping.

BELLOWS BEACH PARK 🏊 🏄 🎣 🛶 This is one of Oahu's prettiest parks. There's a broad white-sand beach bordered by ironwood trees, with a marvelous view of the Koolau mountains. It's a great place for swimming and snorkeling. It's also a good surf spot for beginners and fishing usually rewards with *papio*, bonefish, milkfish and goatfish. Sounds great, huh? The catch is that Bellows Park is situated on a military base and is open to visitors only from Friday noon until 8 a.m. Monday. Facilities include a picnic area, showers, a restroom and a lifeguard; restaurants and markets are about a mile away in Waimanalo. ~ Turn off Kalanianaole Highway (Route 72) toward Bellows Air Force Station. The park is located near Waimanalo, about 17 miles east of Waikiki.

◀ HIDDEN

▲ County permit required.

Windward Coast

Named for the trade winds that blow with soothing predictability from the northeast, this sand-rimmed shoreline lies on the far side of the *pali* from Honolulu. Between these fluted emerald cliffs and the turquoise ocean are the bedroom communities of Kailua and Kaneohe and the agricultural regions of the Waiahole and Waikane valleys. As suburbs give way to small farms, this florid region provides a relaxing transition between the busy boulevards of Honolulu and the wild surf of the North Shore.

From the southeastern corner of the island, the Kalanianaole Highway flows into Kailua, where it intersects with Route 61, or Kailua Road. If you go right for a quarter of a mile along this road you will encounter **Ulupo Heiau** (it's behind the YMCA). According to Hawaiian legend, this temple (which stands 30 feet high and measures 150 feet in length) was built by *Menehunes*, who passed the building stones across a six-mile-long bucket brigade in a one-night construction project. The *Menehunes*, in case you haven't been introduced, were tiny Hobbit-like creatures who inhabited Hawaii even before the Polynesians arrived. They were reputed to be su-

SIGHTS

◀ HIDDEN

perhumanly strong and would work all night to build dams, temples and other structures. Several mysterious manmade objects in the islands that archaeologists have trouble placing chronologically are claimed by mythmakers to be *Menehune* creations.

Heading back to the main highway, you will find that Route 72 immediately merges into Route 61, which then continues for two miles to Route 83, the Kahekili Highway. Above this thoroughfare, spreading across 400 acres at the foot of the *pali* is **Hoomaluhia Botanical Garden,** a botanic garden and nature conservancy. With sheer cliffs rising on one side and a panoramic ocean view opening in the distance, it is a special place indeed. There is a 32-acre lake as well as a visitors center and hiking trails. The fruits, flowers and trees include hundreds of species native to Hawaii. ~ Off Route 83 at the end of Luluku Road, Kaneohe; 233-7323.

HIDDEN ►

The Kahekili Highway will also carry you to the graceful **Haiku Gardens,** located just outside Kailua. Formerly a private estate, the gardens rest in a lovely spot with a lofty rockface backdrop. Within this preserve are acres of exotic plant life, including an enchanting lily pond as well as numerous species of flowers. Hawaii specializes in beautiful gardens; the frequent rains and lush terrain make for luxuriant growing conditions. This happens to be one of the prettiest gardens of all. ~ 46-336 Haiku Road; 247-6671.

Farther along you'll encounter the "Valley of the Temples," a verdant chasm folded between the mountains and the sea. Part of the valley has been consecrated as a cemetery honoring the Japanese. Highlighting the region is the **Byodo-In Temple.** Rimmed by 2000-foot cliffs, this Buddhist shrine is a replica of a 900-year-old temple in Kyoto, Japan. It was constructed in 1968 in memory of the first Japanese immigrants to settle in Hawaii. The simple architecture is enhanced by a bronze bell weighing seven tons that visitors are permitted to ring. A statue of Buddha dominates the site. Walk along the placid reflecting pool with its swans, ducks and multihued carp and you will be drawn a million miles away from the bustle of Honolulu. Admission. ~ 47-200 Kahekili Highway, Kaneohe; 239-8811.

An alternate route through Kailua and Kaneohe will carry you near the water, though the only really pretty views of Kaneohe Bay come near the end. Simply follow North Kalaheo Avenue through Kailua, then pick up Kaneohe Bay Drive, and turn right on Route 836, which curves for miles before linking with Route 83. At Heeia Kea Boat Harbor you can take an hour-long glass bottom boat ride aboard the **Coral Queen.** ~ 235-2888.

Kaneohe Bay is renowned for its coral formations and schools of tropical fish that are as brilliantly colored as the coral. This expansive body of water possesses the only barrier reef in Hawaii. Along its shores are ancient Hawaiian fish ponds, rock-bound en-

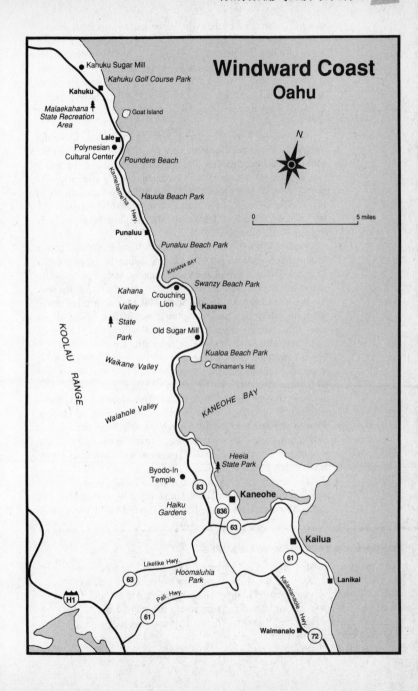

Windward Coast
Oahu

Kahuku Sugar Mill
Kahuku Golf Course Park
Kahuku
Malaekahana State Recreation Area
Goat Island
Laie
Polynesian Cultural Center
Pounders Beach
Hauula Beach Park
Punaluu
Punaluu Beach Park
KAHANA BAY
Swanzy Beach Park
Crouching Lion
Kaaawa
Kahana Valley State Park
Old Sugar Mill
Kualoa Beach Park
Chinaman's Hat
Waikane Valley
Waiahole Valley
KANEOHE BAY
Heeia State Park
Byodo-In Temple
83
Kaneohe
Haiku Gardens
836
63
Kailua
61
Likelike Hwy.
Hoomaluhia Park
63
Lanikai
Kamehameha Hwy.
KOOLAU RANGE
Kalanianaole Hwy.
H1
Pali Hwy.
61
Waimanalo
72

N

0   5 miles

closures constructed by the early Polynesians to raise fresh seafood. Though they once lined the shores of Oahu, today only five remain; four rest along this Windward Coast. As a matter of fact, the largest of all is located at **Heeia State Park**. It's an impressive engineering feat that measures 500 feet in length and once contained an 88-acre fish farm. The stone walls in places are 12 feet thick. ~ Located along Route 836 a few hundred yards before it merges with Route 83.

High above Kaneohe, gazing down upon the bay, is **Senator Fong's Plantation and Gardens**. Here you can take a narrated tram tour of 725 acres of gardens and orchards. This luxurious preserve was donated by one of Hawaii's most famous U.S. senators, so be prepared to venture from Eisenhower Valley to Kennedy Valley (sugar cane) to the Johnson Plateau (fruit orchards) to Nixon Valley (gardens) to the Ford Plateau (pine trees)! Admission. ~ 47-285 Pulama Road, Kaneohe; 239-6775.

Route 83 soon becomes known as the Kamehameha Highway as it courses past taro patches and lazy fishing boats, then enters Waiahole Valley and **Waikane Valley**, some of the last places on the island where Hawaiian farmers grow crops in the traditional way.

Just down the road, the **Old Sugar Mill**, Oahu's first, lies in ruin along the side of the road. Built during the 1860s, it fell into disuse soon after completion and has since served only as a local curiosity.

Three miles later you will arrive at a rock profile that resembles a **Crouching Lion**. To the ancient Hawaiians, who had never experienced the king of the jungle, the stone face was, in fact, that of Kauhi, a demigod from the island of Tahiti.

Next is coral-studded **Kahana Bay**. Then the road, still crowding the coastline, traverses the tiny towns of Punaluu and Hauula. The old **Hauula Door of Faith Church**, a small chapel of clapboard design, is surrounded by palms. Not far from here is another aging woodframe sanctuary, **Hauula Congregational Christian Church**, built of wood and coral back in 1862.

The nearby town of Laie is populated by Mormons. The Hawaii campus of **Brigham Young University** is located here, as well as the **Mormon Temple**. The Mormons settled here back in 1864;

◆◆◆

RORSCHACH TEST, HAWAIIAN STYLE

That cone-shaped island offshore is **Chinaman's Hat**. It was named for its resemblance to a coolie cap, though the Hawaiians had another name for it long before the Chinese arrived in the islands. They called it Mokolii Island, or "little dragon," and claimed it represented the tail of a beast that resided under the water. Watch for frigate birds and delicate Hawaiian stilts flying overhead.

today there are about 25,000 in Hawaii. The courtyards and grounds of the temple are open to the public, but only Mormons are permitted to enter the temple sanctuary.

The Mormons also own Oahu's most popular tourist attraction, the **Polynesian Cultural Center**. Set right on Kamehameha Highway in Laie, it represents one of the foremost theme parks in the entire Pacific, a 42-acre attempt to re-create ancient Polynesia. As you wander about the grounds you'll encounter ersatz villages portraying life in the Marquesas, Tahiti, Fiji, Tonga, New Zealand and old Hawaii. Step over to the Tahitian hamlet and you will experience the rocking *tamure* dance. Or wander onto the islands of Samoa where the local inhabitants demonstrate how to climb coconut trees. In Tonga a native will be beating tapa cloth from mulberry bark, while the Fijians are pounding rhythms with poles of bamboo. These mock villages are linked by waterways and can be visited in canoes. The boats will carry you past craftsmen preparing poi by mashing taro roots and others husking coconuts.

The most popular shows are the "Pageant of the Long Canoes," in which the boats head up a lagoon amid a flurry of singing and dancing, and "Horizons." The latter is an evening show similar to Waikiki's Polynesian revues, though generally considered more elaborate. Most of the entertainers and other employees at this Hawaiian-style Disneyland are Mormon students attending the local university. Closed Sunday. Admission. ~ Kamehameha Highway, Laie; 293-3000.

Be sure to take in the town's natural wonder, **Laie Point**. This headland provides extraordinary ocean views sweeping for miles along the shoreline. Since the breezes and surf are wilder here than elsewhere on the Windward Coast, you'll often encounter waves lashing at the two offshore islets with amazing force. ~ Anemoku Street, off Kamehameha Highway.

Then the main road goes to Kahuku, past the **Kahuku Sugar Mill**, a turn-of-the-century plant. In an effort to refurbish the old mill several years ago, gears and crushers were painted tropical hues and the entire complex was turned into an entertaining museum-cum-shopping mall. You'll find a few restaurants and gift shops, and the machinery of the old mill.

LODGING

Out in the suburban town of Kailua, where trim houses front a beautiful white-sand beach, you'll discover **Kailua Beachside Cottages**. Overlooking Kailua Beach Park and about 100 yards from the beach sits a cluster of woodframe cottages. Each is equipped with a full kitchen, cable television and a telephone. Some of the furniture is nicked, but these duplex units are clean and cozy. They sit in a yard shaded with *hala*, coconut and breadfruit trees and provide an excellent value. ~ 204 South Kalaheo Avenue, Kailua; 262-4128, 261-1653, fax 261-0893. MODERATE TO DELUXE.

HIDDEN ▶

You can't get much closer to the water than **Schrader's Windward Marine Resort**. With about 50 units for rent, this unusual resting place consists of several woodframe buildings right on the edge of Kaneohe Bay. There are picnic tables, barbecue grills, a pool and a spa on the two-acre property, as well as a tour boat that can take you snorkeling, kayaking or sightseeing on the bay. The guest rooms are cottage style with kitchenettes; many have lanais and bay views. Prices include continental breakfast. ~ 47-039 Lihikai Drive, Kaneohe; 239-5711, 800-735-5711, fax 239-6658. MODERATE.

The **Windward Bed & Breakfast** offers two rooms with private baths. The Victorian room features antiques and vintage paintings, while the Circus room has large circus posters, many of them originals, from around the world. This contemporary Hawaiian home has a shake roof and is furnished in antiques and Persian rugs. A full breakfast is served poolside every morning. ~ 46-251 Ikiiki Street, Kaneohe; phone/fax 235-1124, 800-235-1151. BUDGET TO MODERATE.

If you don't mind funky living, check out the **Countryside Cabins** in Punaluu. These old clapboard structures, complete with fading paint and linoleum floors, are set in beautiful garden surroundings across the street from the ocean. Depending on your taste, you'll find the one-room cottages either claustrophobic or quaint. But no one will find fault with the low prices on these units and the two-bedroom cottages, or with Margaret Naai, the charming Asian woman who runs this unique establishment. ~ 53-224 Kamehameha Highway, Punaluu; 237-8169. BUDGET

The **Roadway Inn Hukilau Resort** is a low-slung motel with two floors of rooms surrounding a swimming pool. This is a standard Coke-machine-in-the-courtyard facility located next to the Polynesian Cultural Center. Weekly rates available. ~ 55-109 Laniloa Street, Laie; 293-9282, 800-526-4562, fax 293-8115. MODERATE.

DINING

Kailua is a bedroom community with little to offer the adventurer. But since you might find yourself nearby at lunchtime or when returning from the beach, I'll briefly describe a few restaurants. You can try **Times Coffee Shop** for fried rice, hamburger steaks or sandwiches. ~ 43-3 Oneawa Street, Kailua; 262-7122. BUDGET.

Saeng's Thai Cuisine is a freshly decorated ethnic restaurant with a hardwood bar and potted plants all around. Located in a strip mall, it nevertheless conveys a sense of elegance. The menu focuses on vegetarian, seafood and curry dishes. ~ 315 Hahani Street, Kailua; 263-9727. BUDGET.

Old World Bistro is a Continental restaurant that serves up fresh fish, steak and veal in an informal atmosphere. Closed Monday. ~ 20 Kainehe Street, Kailua; 261-1987. MODERATE TO DELUXE.

HIDDEN ▶

Known for years as a prime breakfast and lunch place, **Cinnamon's Restaurant** eventually added dinner on Thursday and Friday nights. It draws a local crowd, which sits beneath the dining room gazebo or out on the patio. The menu is best described as Hawaiian-American as it's a traditional cuisine with a local spin— barbecued pork ribs, poached mahimahi, hamburger steak. My advice? Dinner is good but breakfast is best. ~ Kailua Square Shopping Center, 315 Uluniu Street, Kailua; 261-8724. MODERATE.

What sets **The Chart House at Haiku Gardens** apart is its idyllic setting. A terraced dining area overlooks sharp cliffs and peaceful flower beds, making this a choice stop for dinner (brunch is served on Sunday). Even though the atmosphere aries from the average Chart House, the menu remains the same: steak, seafood and prime rib. ~ 46-336 Haiku Road, Kailua; 247-6671. DELUXE.

In Kaneohe you might like **Koa Omelette House**. It's a tastefully appointed restaurant with a breakfast bill of fare that includes pancakes and crêpes suzette and a lunch menu with salads, sandwiches, teriyaki chicken and seafood. ~ 46-126 Kahuhipa Street, Kaneohe; 235-5772. BUDGET.

Or, if you want to take a snack to the beach, check out **Fuji Delicatessen and Restaurant** with its inexpensive sandwiches and Japanese plates. ~ 45-270 William Henry Road, Kaneohe; 235-3690. BUDGET.

The **Crouching Lion Inn**, set in a vintage 1927 wood-shingle house, serves sandwiches and hamburgers, mahimahi and teriyaki steak for lunch. At dinner there's a surf-and-turf menu. Enjoying a beautiful ocean view, this attractive complex is popular with tour buses, so try to arrive at an off-hour. ~ 51-666 Kamehameha Highway, Kaaawa; 237-8511. MODERATE TO DELUXE.

Paniolo is Hawaiian for cowboy and the decor at the **Paniolo Café** is a literal translation. Wagon wheels and longhorns set the scene at this steak-and-seafood roadhouse. There's beef brisket (that "melts in your mouth") and beef ribs ("da kine!!"); among the seafood selections—mahimahi, scallops and shrimp brochette. ~ 53-146 Kamehameha Highway, Punaluu; 237-8020. MODERATE.

Appropriately enough, you'll find the **Old Plantation Restaurant & Bar** in the old Kahuku Sugar Mill. The menu includes steak, shrimp and fresh fish. The dining room, with woodpaneled walls and ceiling fans, is located inside the sugar mill: Gaze past the glass lamps and it's all cogs and gears, conveyors and chains. ~ Kahuku; 293-7427. MODERATE.

GROCERIES

In Kailua and Kaneohe, you'll encounter large supermarkets. In the Kailua Shopping Center there's **Times Supermarket**. ~ Kailua Road, Kailua; 262-2366. **Foodland** is in the Windward City Shopping Center. ~ At Kamehameha Highway and Kaneohe Bay Drive, Kaneohe; 247-3357.

For health food, you might try the **Vim and Vigor** store. ~ 345 Hahani Street, Kailua; 261-4036.

These are good places to stock up, since the next large supermarket is **Lindy's Food**. ~ Hauula Kai Center on Kamehameha Highway, Hauula; 293-9722.

All along the Kamehameha Highway in Waiahole and Waikane valleys, there are small stands selling fresh fruit grown right in this lush area.

Between these major shopping complexes there are smaller facilities such as the **7-11**. ~ 51-484 Kamehameha Highway, Kaaawa; 237-8810. You can get fresh fish at **Masa and Joyce Fish Market** in the Temple Valley Shopping Center. ~ Kahekili Highway (Route 83), just north of Kaneohe; 239-6966.

There's a large **Foodland** grocery store in the Laie Village Shopping Center. ~ Kamehameha Highway, Laie; 293-4443.

SHOPPING   **Kailua Shopping Center** offers a wide range of services at 40 stores. ~ Kailua Road, Kailua; 947-2618. **Kaneohe Shopping Center** also serves the region with 26 stores. ~ 94050 Farrington Highway, Kaneohe; 537-4519. These malls represent the prime shopping opportunities on this side of the island and provide a full assortment of shops.

HIDDEN ►   Up in Punaluu, the **Punaluu Art Gallery** features batik work, calabash bowls, pottery, oil paintings, photography, blown glass, hand-carved candles and unusual pieces like landscapes made from banana leaves, all by local artists. Closed Tuesday and Wednesday. ~ 53-352 Kamehameha Highway, Punaluu; 237-8221.

Calling itself **The Only Show In Town** is a slight (very slight) exaggeration, but claiming to be "Kahuku's largest antique and vintage collectible shop" is definitely warranted. Some store specialties include Japanese glass fishing floats, ivory and Coca-Cola memorabilia. Fittingly, this wonderful antique store is located in the old Tanaka Plantation Store, an early 20th-century woodframe building. ~ 56-901 Kamehameha Highway, Kahuku; 293-1295.

NIGHTLIFE   At **Fast Eddie's** you can dance to disco music in the lounge or listen to recorded music and watch games in the sports bar. There's also karaoke for anyone with the nerve to sing along. Weekend cover. ~ 52 Oneawa Street, Kailua; 261-8561.

Paniolo Café, a get-down, western-style saloon, draws hordes of Windward Coast regulars on Friday, Saturday and Sunday night. That's when live bands are highlighted; the rest of the week it's jukebox city. ~ 53-146 Kamehameha Highway, Punaluu; 237-8020.

BEACHES & PARKS   **KAILUA BEACH** ➤ 🏊 🛶 Stretching for two miles with white sand all the way and tiny islands offshore, this is one of the prettiest beaches around. It's in the suburban town of Kailua, so you'll trade seclusion for excellent beach facilities. The center of activity is Kailua Beach Park at the end of Kailua Road near the south end of the beach. This 30-acre facility has a grassy expanse shaded by ironwood and coconut trees and perfect for picnicking. There are restrooms and a pavilion with a snack bar. You can also access the beach farther north via side streets off Kalaheo Avenue. Kalama Beach County Park, a small park with restrooms in the middle of Kailua Beach, is located at 250 North Kalaheo Avenue and is less crowded. Swimming, surfing and bodysurfing are good all along the strand and windsurfing is excellent; but exercise caution.

LANIKAI BEACH Everyone's dream house is on the beach at Lanikai. This sandy stretch, varying from 20 to 100 feet in width, extends for over a mile. The "Twin Islands," tiny bird sanctuaries, rest offshore. The entire beach in this residential community is lined with those houses everybody wants. The water is the color of cobalt and the protecting reef offshore makes the entire beach safe for swimming. The nearest facilities are at Kailua Beach. ~ The strand parallels Mokulua Drive in Lanikai, which in turn is reached by driving south along the beachfront roads in Kailua.

KUALOA BEACH PARK You could search the entire Pacific for a setting as lovely as this one. Just 500 yards offshore lies the islet of Mokolii, better known as Chinaman's Hat. Behind the beach the *pali* creates a startling background of fluted cliffs and tropical forest. The beach is a long and narrow strip of sand paralleled by a wide swath of grass parkland. Little wonder this is one of the Windward Coast's most popular picnic areas. It's also a favorite for swimming, snorkeling and fishing (common catches are *papio*, bonefish, milkfish and goatfish). Facilities include picnic areas, restrooms and showers. ~ Located along Kamehameha Highway (Route 83) about ten miles north of Kaneohe.

▲ Tent camping permitted. County permit required.

SWANZY BEACH PARK, PUNALUU BEACH PARK AND HAUULA BEACH PARK These three county facilities lie along Kamehameha Highway (Route 83) within seven miles of each other. Swimming is generally good at each. Along this coast the most abundant fish is *papio*, followed by bonefish, milkfish and goatfish. Camping is allowed at all except Punaluu, but none compare aesthetically with other beaches to the north and south. Swanzy is located on the highway but lacks a sandy beach. However, it has the best diving. It's surf break "Crouching Lion," is for experts only; Punaluu, though possessing a pretty palm-fringed beach, is cramped; and Hauula, a spacious park with a beach and a winter surf break for beginners, is visited periodically by tour buses. So put these beach parks near the bottom of your list, and bring them up only if the other beaches are too crowded. All three beaches have picnic areas and restrooms; all are within a few miles of markets and restaurants. ~ These parks are all located along

Kamehameha Highway (Route 83). Swanzy lies about 12 miles north of Kaneohe, Punaluu is about four miles north of Swanzy, and Hauula is about three miles beyond that.

▲ Tent and trailer camping allowed at Hauula Beach Park as well as at Swanzy Beach Park on weekends. County permit required.

KAHANA VALLEY STATE PARK 🏃 🏊 🎣 This 5228-acre paradise, set on a white-sand beach, offers something for every adventurer. You can pick fruit in a lush forest, picnic in a coconut grove and sightsee the ancient Huilua Fishpond. You can also fish for *papio*, bonefish, milkfish and goatfish. Swimming is generally good. Surfing is a possibility but is mediocre at best. There are picnic areas and restrooms; markets and restaurants are nearby. ~ Located along Kamehameha Highway (Route 83) about 14 miles north of Kaneohe.

> Follow Kahana Valley State Park's five-mile trail up into the lush valley and you'll pass a succession of old Hawaiian farms.

▲ There's camping across the street at Kahana Beach Park. State permit required.

KOKOLOLIO BEACH PARK 🏊 🏃 🎣 Here's one of the prettiest beaches on the Windward Coast. With trees and a lawn that extends toward the white-sand beach, it's a highly recommended spot for day-tripping. It's also a good beach for swimming and bodysurfing and in winter there are breaks up to six feet, with right and left slide. Common catches include *papio*, bonefish, goatfish and milkfish. There are picnic areas and restrooms; markets and restaurants are nearby. ~ Located at 55-051 Kamehameha Highway (Route 83) in Laie about 20 miles north of Kaneohe.

POUNDERS BEACH 🏊 🎣 Named for the crushing shorebreak that makes it a popular bodysurfing beach, this quarter-mile-long strand features a corridor of white sand and a sandy bottom. Swimming is good near old landing at the western end of the beach. Anglers try for *ono*, *moi* and *papio*. There are no facilities here but restaurants and markets are nearby. ~ It's along Kamehameha Highway north of Kakela Beach.

HUKILAU BEACH 🏊 🎣 🏃 🎣 This privately owned facility fronts a beautiful white-sand beach that winds for more than a mile. Part of the beach is lined with homes, but much of it is undeveloped. Several small islands lie anchored offshore, and the park contains a lovely stand of ironwood trees. All in all this enchanting beach is one of the finest on this side of the island. Swimming is good; bodysurfing is also recommended. Snorkeling is usually fair and there are small surfable waves with left and right slides. The principal catch is *papio*; milkfish, bonefish and goatfish are also caught. There are no facilities here, but you'll find both markets and restaurants are nearby. ~ Located on Kamehameha Highway (Route 83) in Laie about 22 miles north of Kaneohe.

MALAEKAHANA STATE RECREATION AREA AND GOAT ISLAND   ◀ HIDDEN

This is a rare combination. The Malaekahana facility is one of the island's prettiest parks. It's a tropical wonderland filled with palm, *hala* and ironwood trees, and graced with a curving, white-sand beach. And then there's Goat Island, just offshore. Simply put, if you visit Oahu and don't explore Goat Island, you'll be missing an extraordinary experience. I hope you'll make an extra effort to get here. It's a small, low-lying island covered with scrub growth and scattered ironwood trees. On the windward side is a coral beach; to leeward lies a crescent-shaped white-sand beach that seems drawn from a South Seas dream and is the best place on the island to swim because it is shallow and well-protected. There are also good places for snorkeling and in winter you can paddle out to a break with a left slide. Feel like fishing? You may well reel in *papio*, the most abundant fish along here; goatfish, milkfish and bonefish are also caught. Goat Island (which no longer contains goats) is now a state bird refuge, so you might see wedge-tailed shearwaters nesting. Whatever activity you choose, make sure you don't disturb the birds. Goat Island will return the favor—there'll be nothing here to disturb you either. Facilities include showers, bathrooms, barbecue pits and electricity in the cabins. ~ Located on Kamehameha Highway (Route 83) in Laie about 23 miles north of Kaneohe.

▲ Tent camping allowed. State permit required. There are also very rustic cabins available a mile down the road at Malaekahana Beach Park. These beachfront units rent from $35 per night (one-bedroom tent cabin) to $250 per night (six-room cabin). Tent sites are $5 for a single person, or $4.50 per person for a group per night. Bring your own bedding and cooking gear and be prepared for funky accommodations. For information, call 293-1736.

KAHUKU GOLF COURSE PARK   Other than Goat Island, this is about the closest you'll come to a hidden beach on the Windward Coast. Granted, there's a golf course paralleling the strand, but sand dunes hide you from the duffers. The beach is long, wide and sandy white. Swimming is fair, but exercise caution. In winter, surfers work the "Seventh Hole" breaks, which reach up to eight feet and have a right and left slide. *Papio*, bonefish, goatfish and milkfish are common catches. There are restrooms at the golf course; a restaurant and market are nearby. ~ In Kahuku, about 25 miles north of Kaneohe, turn off Kamehameha Highway (Route 83) toward the ocean. Park at the golf course, then walk the gated road to the beach.

▲ Unofficial camping perhaps.

▼▼▼▼▼▼▼▼▼
North Shore

Wide, wide beaches heaped with white, white sand roll for miles along the North Shore. Some of them have become famous throughout the world. Not, however, for their size or their sand, but rather because of their waves. If you have ever owned a surfboard, or even a Beach Boys album, you know Waimea Bay and Sunset Beach. The names are synonymous with surfing. They number among the most challenging and dangerous surf spots anywhere. During the winter 15- to 20-foot waves are as common as blond hair and beach buggies. The infamous "Banzai Pipeline," where surfers risk limb and longevity as thunderous waves pass over a shallow reef, is here as well.

Curving in a bowl shape from Kahuku Point in the east to Kaena Point in the west, the coast is backdropped by both Oahu mountain ranges. Most dramatic are the Waianaes, dominated by 4025-foot Mt. Kaala, the island's highest peak.

While the aquatic oriented zero in on the international surfing competitions that occur annually, many other residents work the small farms and ranches that checkerboard the tableland between the mountains and sea. All of them look to Haleiwa, a refurbished plantation town, as their primary gathering place.

SIGHTS

Stretching for two miles and averaging 200 feet in width, **Sunset Beach** (Kamehameha Highway) is one of Hawaii's largest strands. When the surf is up you can watch world-class athletes shoot the curl. When it's not, Sunset becomes a great place to swim. The best place to go is **Ehukai Beach Park,** just off Kamehameha Highway about seven miles northeast of Haleiwa. Just 100 yards to the west sits the **Banzai Pipeline** (Ke Nui Road), where a shallow coral shelf creates tubular waves so powerful and perfect they resemble pipes. First surfed in 1957, it lays claim to cracked skulls, lacerated legs and some of the sport's greatest feats.

HIDDEN ►

On a plateau between Sunset Beach and Waimea Bay is **Puu o Makuha Heiau,** Oahu's oldest temple. A split-level structure built of stone, it once was used for human sacrifices. Today you will encounter nothing more menacing than a spectacular view and perhaps a gentle breeze from the ocean. To get there from Kamehameha Highway, turn left near the Sunset Beach Fire Station onto Pupukea Road, then follow the Hawaii Visitors & Convention Bureau signs.

At **Waimea Valley** you can wander through a tropical preserve stretching across 1800 acres. Once a Hawaiian village, it is an amazingly luxurious area crisscrossed with hiking trails and filled with archaeological ruins. A tram carries visitors to the famous **Waimea Falls,** where you can swim or picnic. The arboretum in the park features tropical and subtropical trees from around the world. There are also beautiful botanical gardens, including a particularly fascinating one featuring local Hawaiian species. Then there are

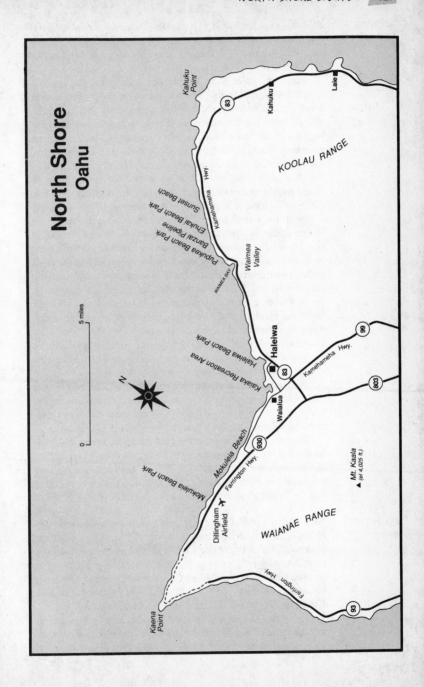

North Shore
Oahu

the birds, caged and wild, that populate the complex; since this nature park serves as a bird sanctuary, it attracts a magnificent assortment. Admission. ~ Kamehameha Highway, five miles northeast of Haleiwa; 638-8511.

Across the street looms **Waimea Bay**, another fabled place that sports the largest surfable waves in the world. When surf's up in winter, the monster waves that roll in are so big they make the ground tremble when they break. Salt spray reaches as far as the highway. Thirty-foot waves are not uncommon. Fifty-foot giants have been recorded; though unsurfable, these are not tidal waves, just swells rising along the incredible North Shore. In summer Waimea is a pretty blue bay with a white-sand beach. The water is placid and the area perfect for picnicking and sunbathing. So when you visit Waimea, remember: swim in summer, sunbathe in winter.

Next, the Kamehameha Highway crosses a double rainbow—shaped bridge en route to **Haleiwa**, an old plantation town with a new facelift. Fortunately, the designers who performed the surgery on this village had an eye for antiquity. They planned it so the modern shopping centers and other facilities blend comfortably into the rural landscape. The community that has grown up around the new town reflects a rare combination of past and future. The old Japanese, Filipinos and Hawaiians have been joined by blond-mopped surfers and laidback counterculturalists. As a result, this clapboard town with wooden sidewalks has established itself as the "in" spot on the North Shore. Its stylish nonchalance has also proved popular among canny travelers.

From here, head west and pick up Farrington Highway (Route 930). This country road parallels miles of unpopulated beachfront, and arrives at Dillingham Airfield, where you can take **The Original Glider Ride** along the Waianae Mountains. ~ 677-3404.

Beyond this landing strip, the road continues for several miles between ocean and mountains before turning into a very rugged dirt track. Along this unpaved portion of roadway you can hike out about ten miles to **Kaena Point** on Oahu's northwest corner (see the "Hiking" section at the end of this chapter).

LODGING   For a resort experience in a rustic setting, consider the **Turtle Bay Hilton**. This rural retreat sprawls across 808 acres on a dramatic peninsula. With a broad beach at the doorstep and mountains out back, it's an overwhelming spot. Add to that riding paths, two golf courses, tennis courts and a pair of swimming pools. Every room features a sea view. ~ 57-091 Kamehameha Highway, Kahuku; 293-8811, 800-445-8667, fax 293-9147. ULTRA-DELUXE.

Turtle Bay Condos has one-, two- and three-bedroom units with kitchen facilities and private lanais that overlook an 9-hole golf course. Studios run $85 to $105; one-bedrooms units with a loft

How to Beat
the Heat with
a Sweet Treat

Since the early days of Hawaiian royalty, people have complained about Honolulu's shirt-sticking weather. Come summer, temperatures rise and the trade winds stop blowing. Visitors seeking a golden tan discover they're baking without browning. And residents begin to think that their city, renowned as a cultural melting pot, is actually a pressure cooker.

With the ocean all around, relief is never far away. But a lot of folks, when not heading for the beaches, have found another way to cool off: shave ice. Known as ice frappes among the Japanese originators and snow cones back on the mainland, these frozen treats are Hawaii's answer to the Good Humor man.

They're made with ice that's been shaved from a block into thin slivers, packed into a cone-shaped cup and covered with sweet syrup. Health-minded people eat the ice plain or with a low-calorie or sugar-free syrup, and some folks ask for a scoop of ice cream or sweet black beans (*azuki* beans) underneath the shavings. Most people just order it with their favorite syrup flavors—grape, root beer, cola, cherry, orange, lemon-lime, vanilla, fruit punch, banana, strawberry or whatever.

Whichever you choose, you'll find it only costs about a buck at the many stands sprinkled around town. You might try **Island Snow Hawaii**, which has a second location on the Windward coast at 130 Kailua Road in Kailua. ~ 2201 Kalakaua Avenue. Watch for stands up on the North Shore, too. No doubt you'll see a long line outside Oahu's most famous shave ice store, **Matsumoto's**. ~ 66-087 Kamehameha Highway, Haleiwa.

As a matter of fact, anyplace where the sun blazes overhead you're liable to find someone trying to beat the heat by slurping up a "snow cone" before it melts into mush.

sleeping up to four guests are $130 to $145. ~ 56-565 Kamehameha Highway, Kahuku; 293-2800, fax 293-2169.

Surfers, scuba divers and budget-minded travelers will find two ideal addresses along Oahu's vaunted North Shore. Managed by the same folks, and within walking distance of each other are **Vacation Inn** and **Plantation Village**. The first consists of a central building that provides hostel-style rooms and features a TV lounge and kitchen. There's also a back house with private rooms that share a kitchen and bath. Like the hostel it's budget-priced. Across the street, and directly on the beach, there's a house with private apartments that include their own kitchen and bathroom and are moderately priced. Plantation Village consists of nine restored plantation houses with shared kitchens and baths. Set on a landscaped acre, the accommodations are moderate-to-deluxe in price, but budget-priced hostel facilities are also available. Both the Vacation Inn and Plantation Village have laundry facilities and barbecue areas for guests. They also sponsor daily activities and provide excellent opportunities for meeting other travelers. ~ 59-788 Kamehameha Highway, Haleiwa; 638-7838, fax 638-7515. BUDGET TO DELUXE.

Offering houses right on the beach, **Ke Iki Hale** is located between the Banzai Pipeline and Waimea Bay. Here you'll find moderate- and deluxe-priced duplexes and an ultra-deluxe-priced cottage on an acre-and-a-half of palm-shaded property. They are basic woodframe buildings with plain furnishings. The complex includes barbecue facilities and a volleyball court. ~ 59-579 Ke Iki Road, Haleiwa; 638-8229, 800-377-4030. MODERATE TO ULTRA-DELUXE.

DINING

The Turtle Bay Hilton features two good restaurants. At the **Palm Terrace**, overlooking the hotel's lovely grounds, you'll encounter moderate-priced dining in an attractive environment. The restaurant, serving three meals, offers everything from burgers to *saimin* and teriyaki to linguine. Or, for a splurge meal, try **The Cove**. This gourmet establishment serves lobster, lamb chops, filet mignon, a seafood gumbo dish and a host of other delights. Reservations are required at The Cove. ~ 57-091 Kamehameha Highway, Kahuku; 293-8811. MODERATE TO DELUXE.

When you're around Sunset Beach, **D'Amico's** is quite convenient. It's a roadside restaurant serving pizzas, pasta, sandwiches and other surfer fare. ~ 59-026 Kamehameha Highway, Haleiwa; 638-9611. BUDGET.

Otherwise, the best place to chow down is in Haleiwa, the main town on the North Shore. For a fashionable spot overlooking the ocean, try **Jameson's By The Sea**. This split-level establishment features a patio downstairs and a formal dining room upstairs. For lunch there are sandwiches, chowders and fresh fish dishes; at dinner they specialize in seafood. ~ 62-540 Kamehameha Highway, Haleiwa; 637-4336. MODERATE TO DELUXE.

Haleiwa Beach Grill, a small café in the center of Haleiwa, is as colorful as coral. Matter of fact, the tropic-hued walls are adorned with a wide range of vintage albums from the '60s and '70s. Read the menu and you'll discover fried chicken, grilled sandwiches, burritos and "islander plates." There are *kalbi* ribs, teriyaki chicken and a mixed grill dish that includes mahimahi. ~ 66-079 Kamehameha Highway, Haleiwa; 637-3394. BUDGET.

At Café Haleiwa surfers swear by the huevos rancheros, pancakes and "the Barrel"—a blend of eggs, potatoes, green salsa and cheese wrapped in a tortilla. Located in a century-old building featuring local artwork, surfboards and surfing memorabilia, this local favorite also serves an excellent quesadilla. ~ 66-460 Kamehameha Highway, Haleiwa; 637-5516. BUDGET.

Paradise Found has a juice bar and vegetarian restaurant serving sandwiches, soups and salads. ~ Inside Celestial Natural Foods, 66-443 Kamehameha Highway, Haleiwa; 637-4540. BUDGET.

Meg's Country Drive-In is a small eatery serving local-style plate lunches and daily specials such as fried noodles with teriyaki beef. You can take your meal to-go or dine on the adjoining lanai. No dinner. ~ 66-200 Kamehameha Highway, Haleiwa; 637-9122. BUDGET.

Years ago Haleiwa was home to Da Cuppa Kope, a great café and gathering place. Today it has been supplanted by an even better coffeehouse, the Coffee Gallery. In addition to the best cappuccino on the island, this homespun restaurant, decorated with coffee sacks, serves pastries, waffles, bagels, pasta, pizza and a variety of sandwiches. ~ North Shore Marketplace, 66-250 Kamehameha Highway, Haleiwa; 637-5571. BUDGET.

◄ HIDDEN

Mexican restaurants in Hawaii are different from their counterparts elsewhere in one respect—fish tacos. True to the islands, Rosie's Cantina offers them. They also have a menu filled with the culinary features found in every south-of-the-border eatery. In the case of Rosie's, you also get a steam-pipe-and-raw-wood interior complete with colored lights. ~ Haleiwa Shopping Plaza, Kina Kamehameha Highway, Haleiwa; 637-3538. MODERATE.

Appropriately enough, Portofino captures an air of the Mediterranean with its cream-colored pastel walls, blond-wood furniture, overhead fans and breezy ambience. This Italian restaurant prepares rosemary chicken, penne capricciosa (with eggplant and

KUA AINA IS DA KINE

Surfers pour into Kua Aina Sandwich, where they order hamburgers, fries and mahimahi sandwiches at the counter, then kick back at one of the roadside tables. Great for light meals, the place is a scene and a half. ~ 66-214 Kamehameha Highway, Haleiwa; 637-6067. BUDGET.

shrimp) and a catch-of-the-day dish. So sink onto one of the upholstered banquettes or sidle over to the granite bar. ~ 66-250 Kamehameha Highway, Haleiwa; 638-8731. MODERATE.

GROCERIES   **Haleiwa Supermarket,** one of the few large markets on the entire North Shore, is the best place to shop. ~ 66-197 Kamehameha Highway, Haleiwa; 637-5004. Out by Sunset Beach you'll find a **Foodland Super Market.** ~ 59-720 Kamehameha Highway, Haleiwa; 638-8081. There's also **Sunset Beach Store,** which has a small stock but is also conveniently located near Sunset Beach. ~ 59-026 Kamehameha Highway, Haleiwa; 638-8207.

Celestial Natural Foods has an ample supply of health foods and fresh produce. ~ 66-443 Kamehameha Highway, Haleiwa; 637-6729.

SHOPPING   Trendy shoppers head for the burgeoning town of Haleiwa. During the past several years boutiques and galleries have mushroomed throughout this once somnolent town. Now there is a modern shopping center and an array of shops. Since Haleiwa is a center for surfers, it's a good place to buy sportswear and aquatic equipment.

Iwa Gallery features a unique collection of artwork by a number of local island artists. ~ 66-119 Kamehameha Highway, Haleiwa; 637-4865.

Sunset Hawaii Clothing carries Hawaiian wear for the whole family. Bathing suits, accessories, handmade books, dolls, toys and stuffed animals round out their inventory. ~ 66-226 Kamehameha Highway, Haleiwa; 637-4782.

Oceania offers women's wear and jewelry. ~ 66-218 Kamehameha Highway, Haleiwa; 637-1516.

Silver Moon Emporium offers women's wear and jewelry. ~ 66-250 Kamehameha Highway, in the North Shore Marketplace, Haleiwa; 637-7710.

For an excellent selection of women's clothing and accessories, head to **Pomegranates In The Sun.** ~ North Shore Marketplace, 66-250 Kamehameha Highway, Haleiwa; 637-9260.

Strong Current stocks everything imaginable that's related to surfing. They even have a small "surfing museum," consisting of memorabilia from the sport's early days. Then there are the books, videos, posters, boards and other appurtenances, all relating to a single theme. ~ North Shore Marketplace, 66-250 Kamehameha Highway, Haleiwa; 637-3406.

NIGHTLIFE   Entertainment is a rare commodity on the North Shore, but you will find contemporary Hawaiian music at the **Bay View** at the Turtle Bay Hilton; on Friday and Saturday they feature disco music. ~ 57-091 Kamehameha Highway, Kahuku; 293-8811.

To mix with the locals, head to the **Sugarbar**, where you'll find live rock, rhythm-and-blues or Hawaiian music Wednesday through Sunday. ~ 67-069 Kealohani Street, Waialua; 637-6989.

SUNSET BEACH 🏊 🏄 ⚓ While Sunset Beach is actually only a single surfing spot, the name has become synonymous with a two-mile-long corridor that includes Banzai Beach and the adjacent Pipeline. As far as surfing goes, this is the place! I think the best way to do Sunset is by starting from **Ehukai Beach Park**. From here you can go left to the "Banzai Pipeline," where crushing waves build along a shallow coral reef to create tube-like formations. To the right lies "Sunset," with equally spectacular surfing waves. Throughout the area the swimming is fair in summer; however, in winter it is extremely dangerous. From September to April, high waves and strong currents prevail. Be careful! Snorkeling here is poor; but some of the island's best snorkeling is at Pupukea Beach Park, a marine reserve on Kamehameha Highway six miles northeast of Haleiwa. This 80-acre park, fringed by rocky shoreline, divides into several section. Foremost is "Shark's Cove," located on the north side of the fire station, which contains spectacular tidepools and dive sites. Game fish caught around Sunset include *papio*, *menpachi* and *ulua*. Ehukai Beach Park has picnic areas, restrooms and shower; nearby there are also markets and restaurants. ~ Ehukai Beach Park is off Kamehameha Highway (Route 83) about seven miles northeast of Haleiwa.

WAIMEA BAY BEACH PARK 🏊 🤿 🏄 ⚓ If Sunset is *one* of the most famous surfing spots in the world, Waimea is *the* most famous. The biggest surfable waves in the world roll into this pretty blue bay. There's a wide white-sand beach and a pleasant park with a tree-studded lawn. It's a marvelous place for picnicking and sunbathing. During the winter crowds often line the beach watching top-notch surfers challenge the curl; in summer the sea is flat and safe for swimming; you can also bodysurf in the shorebreak and snorkel when the bay is calm. *Papio*, *menpachi* and *ulua* are common catches. Facilities include a picnic area, restrooms, showers and a lifeguard; restaurants and markets are about a mile away near Sunset Beach. ~ On Kamehameha Highway (Route 83) about five miles northeast of Haleiwa.

HALEIWA BEACH PARK 🏊 🤿 ⚓ This is an excellent refuge from the North Shore's pounding surf. Set in Waialua Bay, the beach is safe for swimming almost all year. You can snorkel, although it's only fair. Surfing in not possible here but "Haleiwa" breaks are located across Waialua Bay at Alii Beach Park. Facilities include a picnic area, restrooms, showers, a snack bar, a ball field, a basketball court, volleyball courts and a playground. The primary catches at Haleiwa are *papio*, *menpachi* and *ulua*. ~ On Kamehameha Highway (Route 83) in Haleiwa.

KAIAKA RECREATION AREA 🏊 🎣 🛶 The setting at this park is beautiful. There is a secluded area with a tree-shaded lawn and a short strip of sandy beach. A rocky shoreline borders most of this peninsular park, so I'd recommend it more for picnics than water sports. You *can* swim and snorkel but there's a rocky bottom. Fishing is good for *papio*, *menpachi* and *ulua*. The only facilities are a picnic area and restrooms; restaurants and markets are nearby in Haleiwa. ~ Located on Haleiwa Road just outside Haleiwa.

▲ Permitted; a county permit is required.

HIDDEN ► **MOKULEIA BEACH PARK AND MOKULEIA BEACH** 🏊 🎣 🛶 The 12-acre park contains a sandy beach and large un-shaded lawn. An exposed coral reef detracts from the swimming, but on either side of the park lie beaches with sandy ocean bottoms. If you do swim, exercise caution, especially in winter months; there's no lifeguard. There's good snorkeling and in winter the surf breaks up to ten feet near Dillingham Airfield. Anglers try for *papio*, *menpachi* and *ulua*. Whatever your activity of choice, you'll have to contend with the noise of small planes from nearby Dillingham Airfield. The park is also an excellent starting point for exploring the unpopulated sections of Mokuleia Beach. Facilities include picnic areas, restrooms and showers; markets and restaurants are in Haleiwa. ~ On Farrington Highway (Route 930) about seven miles west of Haleiwa. To the west of the park, this beach stretches for miles along a secluded coast. You can hike down the beach or reach its hidden realms by driving farther west along Farrington Highway (Route 930), then turning off onto any of the numerous dirt side roads.

At Mokuleia, watch for skydivers and hang gliders, who often use the beach for their landings.

▲ Tent and trailer camping are allowed with a county permit. Unofficial camping along the undeveloped beachfront is common.

Central Oahu

The 1000-foot-high Leilehua Plateau, a bountiful agricultural region planted with sugar and pineapple, extends from the North Shore to the southern reaches of Oahu. Situated in the middle of the island between the Waianae and Koolau ranges, this tableland has become a vital military headquarters. Wheeler Air Force Base, Schofield Barracks and several other installations occupy large plots of land here.

Wahiawa, a small, grimy city, is the region's commercial hub. Somehow, between the agriculture and the armed forces, I've never found much in this part of Oahu. I usually pass quickly through this area on my way north or south. But there are a few places you might find worth touring.

From Haleiwa south to Wahiawa you can take Route 803, Kau-koahuna Road, a pretty thoroughfare with excellent views of the Waianaes, or follow Route 99, the Kamehameha Highway, which passes through verdant pineapple fields. The **Dole Pineapple Plantation**, often crowded with tourists, sells (who would have guessed) pineapple products. ~ 64-1550 Kamehameha Highway, Wahiawa; 621-8408. And the **Pineapple Variety Garden** displays many different types of the fruit in a garden museum. ~ Kamehameha Highway and Kamananui Road, Wahiawa.

The highway also passes near **Kukaniloho**, a cluster of sacred stones marking the place where Hawaiian royalty gave birth to the accompaniment of chants, drums and offerings. Studded with eucalyptus trees, this spot has held an important place in Hawaiian mythology and religion for centuries. ~ Follow the dirt road across from Whitmore Avenue just north of Wahiawa.

◄ HIDDEN

For a scenic and historic detour from Route 99, pull up to the sentry station at Schofield Barracks and ask directions to **Kolekole Pass**. On that "day of infamy," December 7, 1941, Japanese bombers buzzed through this notch in the Waianae Range.

You'll be directed through Schofield up into the Waianaes. When you reach Kolekole Pass, there's another sentry gate. Ask the guard to let you continue a short distance farther to the observation point. From here the Waianaes fall away precipitously to a plain that rolls gently to the sea. There's an astonishing view of Oahu's west coast. If you are denied permission to pass the sentry point, then take the footpath that begins just before the gate, leading up the hill. From near the cross at the top, you will have a partial view of both the Waianaes' western face and the central plateau region.

Wahiawa Botanical Gardens, spreading across 27 acres, offers a handsome retreat studded with tropical vegetation. There are plants from Africa and Australia, Asian camphor trees and gum trees from New Guinea. ~ 1396 California Avenue, Wahiawa; 621-7321.

From Wahiawa, Route H-2 provides the fastest means back to Honolulu; the most interesting course is along Route 750, Kunia Road, which skirts the Waianaes, passing sugar cane fields and stands of pine.

Along the way you can take in the **Hawaiian Plantation Village**, a partially re-created and partially restored village that spreads across three acres of Waipahu Cultural Park in Waipahu. Comprised of over two dozen buildings, it includes a Japanese Shinto shrine, company store and a Chinese Society building. Hawaii's many ethnic groups are represented in the houses, which span several architectural periods of the 19th and 20th centuries. Together they provide visitors with a window into traditional life on a plantation. Closed Sunday. ~ 94-695 Waipahu Street, Waipahu; 676-6727.

▼▼▼▼▼▼▼▼▼▼▼
Leeward Coast

Out along the west coast of Oahu, less than 30 miles from the sands of Waikiki, Hawaiian culture is making a last stand. Here on the tableland that separates the Waianae Range from the ocean, the old ways still prevail. Unlike the cool rainforests of the Windward Coast or the rain-spattered area around Honolulu, this is a region of stark beauty, resembling the American Southwest, with rocky crags and cactus-studded hills.

Hawaiian and Samoan farmers populate the place. Since much of the rest of Oahu has been developed, the Leeward Coast has become the keeper of the old ways. Residents here jealously guard the customs and traditions that they see slipping away in the rest of Hawaii.

Few tourists pass this way and few tourist amenities line the roadway. The scenery consists of farmyards with chicken-wire pens, dusty houses and sunblasted churches. Sideroads off the main highway often turn to dirt and climb past truck farms and old homesteads. For entertainment there are family luaus, cockfights and slack-key guitarists.

Travelers who do venture out here have sometimes been hassled by local residents seeking to keep the *malihinis* in Honolulu. But if you are considerate and careful, you should do just fine. This is one of those places that really should be seen, and seen soon, for it, too, is falling to the forces of change. The new Ihilani Resort & Spa in the Koolina area is only the beginning of the inevitable encroachment along this side of the island.

SIGHTS

From Honolulu you can visit the region by traveling west on Route H-1 or Route 90. If you want to tour a prime sugar-growing area, take Route 90 past Pearl Harbor, then turn left on Fort Weaver Road (Route 760). This country lane leads to the plantation town of **Ewa**. With its busy sugar mill and trim houses, Ewa is an enchanting throwback to the days when sugar was king. This town is a slow, simple place, perfect for wandering and exploring.

Near Oahu's southwest corner, Routes H-1 and 90 converge to become the Farrington Highway (Route 93). If you turn up Mailiilii Street in **Waianae**, you'll pass placid Hawaiian homesteads and farmlands. This side road also provides sweeping views of the Waianae Range.

Makaha Beach, one of Hawaii's most famous surfing spots, is the site of an international surfing championship every year. The Makaha Valley, extending from the ocean up into the Waianaes, is home to the **Kaneaki Heiau**, a 17th-century temple dedicated to the god Lono and used as a site for human sacrifices. You can wander past prayer towers, grass huts and the altar used for the gruesome ritual. ~ 695-8174.

The highway continues along the coastline past several beaches and parks. Across from Kaena Point State Park you'll come upon

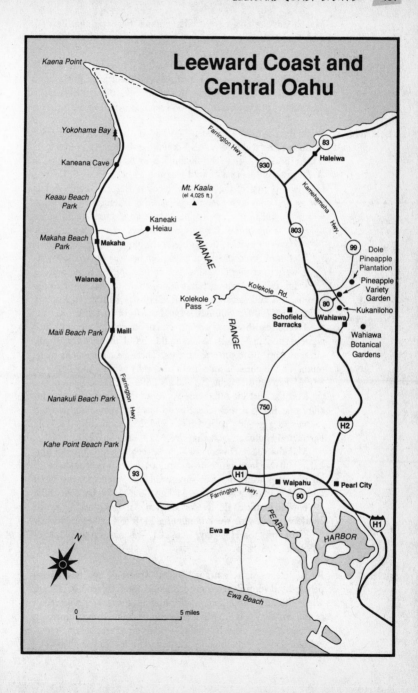

Leeward Coast and Central Oahu

Kaena Point

Yokohama Bay

Kaneana Cave

Keaau Beach Park

Makaha Beach Park — Makaha

Waianae

Maili Beach Park — Maili

Nanakuli Beach Park

Kahe Point Beach Park

Farrington Hwy.

930

803

750

H1

93

Mt. Kaala
(el 4,025 ft.)

Kaneaki Heiau

WAIANAE

Kolekole Pass

Kolekole Rd.

RANGE

Schofield Barracks

Farrington Hwy.

Waipahu

90

Ewa

PEARL

HARBOR

Ewa Beach

83

Haleiwa

Kamehameha Hwy.

99

80

Dole Pineapple Plantation

Pineapple Variety Garden

Kukaniloho

Wahiawa

Wahiawa Botanical Gardens

H2

Pearl City

H1

N

0   5 miles

Makua Cave, a lava cavern large enough for exploring. Beyond that, where the road turns to dirt, lies Yokohama Bay, with its curving sand beach and inviting turquoise waters.

The road past Yokohama is partially passable by auto, but it's very rough. If you want to explore Kaena Point from this side of the island, you'll have to hike. It's about two miles to the northwest corner of Oahu, past tidepools teeming with marine life.

LODGING   While the premise of "hidden Hawaii" is that you'll save money by uncovering secluded places, sometimes the remote comes with a hefty price tag. Take the Ihilani Resort & Spa. Backed by the Waianaes and facing a curved expanse of ocean, this 387-room hideaway is part of the 640-acre Koolina Resort. There's a golf course, six tennis courts, four restaurants and a sophisticated spa facility. More important, you'll find a string of four lagoons, each with a crescent beach and a cluster of islets that protects the mouth of the lagoon. All this material and natural splendor lies way out in the southwestern corner of Oahu. The entire complex is quite beautiful, from the trim green grounds to the atrium lobby to the spacious and elegant rooms. ~ 92-1001 Olani Street, Koolina Resort; 679-0079, 800-626-4446, fax 679-0080. ULTRA-DELUXE.

Kaena Point Satellite Tracking Station sits atop the Waianae Range.

There are also several oceanfront condominiums along Oahu's western shore in Makaha. Makaha Beach Cabanas has very small, attractive one-bedroom apartments. There is a four-night minimum. This highrise condo fronts a pretty white-sand beach. ~ 84-965 Farrington Highway, Makaha; 696-2166. MODERATE.

Makaha Surfside offers one-bedroom units in a sprawling facility that fronts a rocky beach and has two swimming pools, a sauna and a jogging path. Units are $625 per month. ~ 85-175 Farrington Highway, Makaha; 696-6325, fax 696-7871.

Makaha Valley Towers is a highrise set along the slopes of Makaha Valley. Units range from studios to two-bedrooms, with nightly, weekly and monthly stays available. Studios for one week cost $550. ~ End of Kili Drive, Makaha; 696-4499, fax 696-1805.

Hawaii Hatfields Realty Corporation manages privately owned condominiums. One-week minimum; $450 to $1200 per week. ~ 85-833 Farrington Highway, Suite 201, Waianae, HI 96792; 696-4499, fax 696-1805.

DINING   By way of resort restaurants, Ihilani Resort & Spa has several deluxe- and ultra-deluxe-priced dining rooms. Foremost is Azul, where the lamb chops come with couscous, the lobster is served in *pistou* and the ideas are Mediterranean. Ushiotei is the ultimate in Japanese cuisine. And Naupaka, a poolside terrace serving cross-cultural dishes, is the Ihilani's answer to informality and easy ele-

gance. ~ 92-1001 Olani Street, Koolina Resort; 679-0079. DELUXE
TO ULTRA-DELUXE.

This sparsely populated strip of shoreline has several other dining spots. All are located on Farrington Highway, the main road,
and most are in the town of Waianae. **Cathay's Inn Chop Suey** is a
good choice for Chinese food. ~ 86-088 Farrington Highway, Waianae; 696-9477.

Close by is **Hannara Restaurant** offering Korean and Hawaiian
cuisines. ~ 85-888 Farrington Highway, Waianae; 696-6137. BUD-
GET TO MODERATE.

Nearby **E. J.'s** offers homestyle cooking in a casual, country-
style atmosphere. Breakfast favorites include burritos, banana pancakes and home fries. Burgers, salads and sandwiches are prepared
for lunch. Dinner entrées may include filet mignon, vegetarian
lasagna or baked mahimahi. ~ 85-773 Farrington Highway, Waianae; 696-9676. BUDGET TO MODERATE.

The Anchorage By the Sea sports an ocean view and a mixed
local/tourist clientele. Serving breakfast, lunch and dinner, this
eatery offers up pasta, steak and seafood dishes. For decoration
there are TV sets (TV sets?) and potted plants. ~ 87-064 Farrington
Highway, Waianae; 696-6121. MODERATE TO DELUXE.

Out at the Sheraton Makaha Resort Golf Course there is the
19th Hole, an open-air café overlooking the golf course, serves
scrambled eggs in the morning and *saimin*, hot dogs, sandwiches
and plate lunches at lunchtime. ~ 84-626 Makaha Valley Road,
Makaha; 695-9511. BUDGET.

GROCERIES

Sack 'n Save Foods is the prime market in this area. ~ 87-2070
Farrington Highway, Nanakuli; 668-1277.

NIGHTLIFE

The **Lobby Lounge** features nightly live entertainment. The Ililani
is also home to the **Hokulea**, a nightspot that often has live music.
~ Ililani Resort & Spa, 92-1001 Olani Street, Koolina Resort;
679-0079.

**BEACHES
& PARKS**

HAWAIIAN ELECTRIC BEACH PARK ⚓ 🏄 🏊 🛶 This once
privately owned park, across the highway from a monstrous power
plant, is now run by the county. There's a rolling lawn with palm
and *kiawe* trees, plus a white-sand beach and coral reef. You can
swim, snorkel, surf year-round and fish for *papio, ulua, moano* and
menpachi. The drawbacks are the lack of facilities (there are restrooms and a picnic area) and the park's proximity to the electric
company. ~ The park is located on Farrington Highway (Route 93)
about seven miles south of Waianae.

▲ Not allowed here; but tent and trailer camping are okay at
nearby Kahe Point Beach Park, with a county permit.

NANAKULI BEACH PARK 🏊 🎣 ⛷ ⛵ This park is so large that a housing tract divides it into two parts. The main section features a white-sand beach, *kiawe*-studded camping area and a recreation complex. It's simply a park with everything, unfortunately including weekend crowds. Needless to say, the swimming and snorkeling are good. There are winter breaks with right and left slides. Fishing often rewards with *papio, ulua, moano* and *menpachi*. Facilities include picnic areas, restrooms, showers, a ball field, a basketball court and a playground. ~ Located on Farrington Highway (Route 93) about five miles south of Waianae; 668-1137.

▲ Tent and trailer camping are allowed, but a county permit is required.

MAILI BEACH PARK 🏊 🎣 ⛷ ⛵ A long winding stretch of white sand is the high point of this otherwise unimpressive facility. The swimming is good; snorkeling is only fair. There are winter surf breaks with a right slide. The principal game fish caught here are *papio, ulua, menpachi* and *moano*. The park contains shade trees and a spotty lawn. There are restrooms and showers; a market and restaurant are nearby. ~ Located on Farrington Highway (Route 93) in Maili a few miles south of Waianae.

▲ Not permitted here, but tent camping, with a county permit, is allowed in the summer at nearby **Lualualei Beach Park**.

MAKAHA BEACH PARK 🏊 🎣 ⛷ ⛵ Some of the finest surfing in the world takes place right offshore here. This is the site of international competitions, drawing championship surfers from all across the Pacific. For more relaxed sports, there's a white-sand beach to sunbathe on and some good places to skindive. Swimming and snorkeling are both good when the sea is calm; otherwise, exercise extreme caution. Anglers try for *papio, ulua, moano* and *menpachi*. The precipitous Waianae Mountains loom behind the park. There are picnic tables, restrooms and showers; a market and restaurant are nearby. ~ Located on Farrington Highway (Route 93) in Makaha, two miles north of Waianae.

KEAUU BEACH PARK 🏊 🎣 ⛷ ⛵ Except for the absence of a sandy beach, this is the prettiest park on the west coast. It's a long, narrow grassy plot spotted with trees and backdropped by the Waianaes. Sunsets are spectacular here, and on a clear day you can see all the way to Kauai. There's a sandy beach just west of the park. Unfortunately, a coral reef rises right to the water's edge, making entry into the water difficult. But once you're in there's great snorkeling, swimming and bodysurfing. In summer there are good surf breaks with a left slide. People fish for *papio, ulua, moano* and *menpachi*. There are picnic areas, restrooms and showers; markets and restaurants are several miles away in Waianae. ~ Located on Farrington Highway (Route 93) about five miles north of Waianae.

▲ Tent and trailer allowed. County permit required.

KAENA POINT STATE PARK (YOKOHAMA BAY)   ⟨icons⟩   ◄ HIDDEN

This curving stretch of white sand is the last beach along Oahu's northwest coast. With the Waianae Range in the background and coral reefs offshore, it's a particularly lovely spot. Though officially a state park, the area is largely undeveloped. You can walk from Yokohama Bay past miles of tidepools to Oahu's northwest corner at Kaena Point, the legendary home of Nanue the Shark Man. Keep an eye out for porpoises. Yokohama Bay is a prime region for beach lovers and explorers both. When the sea is calm the swimming is good and the snorkeling is excellent but exercise extreme caution if the surf is up. There are summer breaks up to 15 feet over a shallow reef (left slide). Fish caught in this area include *papio*, *ulua*, *moano* and *menpachi*. Restrooms and showers are the only facilities. ~ Located at the end of the paved section of Farrington Highway (Route 93), about nine miles north of the town of Waianae.

▼▼▼▼▼▼▼▼▼▼▼▼▼
Outdoor Adventures

CAMPING

Along with its traffic and crowds, Oahu has numerous parks. Unfortunately, these disparate elements overlap, and you may sometimes find you've escaped from Honolulu's urban jungle and landed in a swamp of weekend beachgoers. So it's best to plan outdoor adventures far in advance and to schedule them for weekdays if possible.

Camping at **county parks** requires a permit. Tent camping is permitted every night except Wednesday and Thursday; there are no trailer hookups. The free permits can be obtained from the Department of Parks and Recreation. ~ Honolulu Municipal Building, 650 South King Street, Honolulu, HI 96813; 587-0300. They are also available at any of the "satellite city halls" around the island.

State parks allow camping for five days and work on a first-come, first-served basis. The Division of State Parks issues the free permits. ~ 1151 Punchbowl Street, Room 310, Honolulu, HI 96813; 587-0300. You can also write in advance for permits.

Remember when planning your trip, rainfall is heaviest on the Windward Coast, a little lighter on the North Shore and lightest of all on the Leeward Coast.

For camping equipment in Honolulu check with **Omar The Tent Man**. Omar rents and sells supplies. Closed Sunday. ~ 650-A Kakoi Street; 836-8785. **The Bike Shop** rents backpacks and two-person tents and has for sale a comprehensive line of camping equipment, from clothing and sleeping bags to tents and stoves. ~ 1149 South King Street; 596-0588. **McCully Bicycle and Sporting Goods** is another place to purchase camping equipment. ~ 2124 South King Street; 955-6329.

DIVING

One of the great myths about Hawaii is that you need to go far off the beaten track to discover its secret treasures. The fact is that within half an hour of Waikiki are excellent snorkeling and diving opportunities. Only an hour away are excellent reefs easily reached by dive boats. From popular Hanauma Bay, just a short ride from the heart of Honolulu, to Kahe Point on the Leeward Coast, there are snorkeling and diving opportunities for beginners and certified pros alike. Because conditions vary, I strongly recommend seeking instruction and advice from local diving experts before setting out.

Depending on the season, the **Haleiwa Surf Center** teaches such sports as snorkeling, surfing, swimming, lifesaving, windsurfing and sailing. This county agency is also an excellent source of information on island water sports and facilities. ~ Haleiwa-Alii Beach Park, Haleiwa; 637-5051.

In addition, many shops rent and sell diving equipment and offer underwater tours. **South Seas Aquatics** features dives off a custom 38-foot dive boat. ~ 870 Kapahulu Avenue #109, Honolulu; 735-0437. **Aloha Dive Shop** runs courses for certified divers and students at Maunalua Bay in the southeast corner of the island. ~ Koko Marina Shopping Center, 7192 Kalanianaole Highway, Hawaii Kai; 395-5922. **Hawaii Sea Adventures** heads to the west side of Oahu and dives the *Mahi* shipwreck. They feature lessons as well as half- and full-day trips and charters. ~ 98-718 Moanalua Road, Pearl City; 487-7515. **Windward Dive Center** offers classes and does a few trips. ~ 789 Kailua Road, Kailua; 263-2311.

At **Aaron's Dive Shop** you can choose between beach and boat dives, as well as special night trips. ~ 602 Kailua Road, Kailua; 261-1211. Up in the North Shore town of Haleiwa, check out **Surf 'n Sea**. They offer beach dives on the North Shore and Leeward Coast including the *Mahi* shipwreck. ~ 62-595 Kamehameha Highway; 637-9887.

SURFING & WIND-SURFING

Surfing, a sport pioneered centuries ago by Hawaiian royalty, is synonymous with Oahu. Stars bring their boards from all over the world to join international competitions that take advantage of ideal surf and wind conditions. From the 30-foot winter rollers on the North Shore to beginner lessons off Waikiki, this is beach boy and girl territory. Windsurfing is equally popular in areas like Kailua Bay and along the North Shore.

If you'd like to surf Waikiki, you can rent a board from **Prime Time Rentals** on Fort De Russy Beach. ~ 949-8952. At the **Aloha Beach Service** you can take lessons and rent a long board. ~ In front of the Sheraton Moana Surfrider Hotel; 922-3111.

Kailua Sailboard and Kayak Company will teach you the tricks of the trade or help you brush up on your technique. Rentals are also available here. ~ 130 Kailua Road; 262-2555. In the same area, **Naish Hawaii** offers lessons and rentals. This company manufactures its own boards and also operates a shop filled with the latest in sailboarding apparel and accessories. ~ 155-A Hamakua Drive; 261-6067.

A good way to catch marlin, mahimahi, *ahi* and *ono* is to head out 20 to 30 miles off the Leeward Coast. There are also prime fishing grounds off the south coast of Oahu.

A resource for both the participatory and spectator aspects of surfing and windsurfing is the **Haleiwa Surf Center**. Surf lessons normally run September through early May and windsurfing is taught from May through early September. ~ Haleiwa-Alii Beach Park, Haleiwa; 637-5051. In the same area surfing lessons and rentals are also available from **Surf and Sea**. ~ 62-595 Kamehameha Highway, Haleiwa; 637-9887.

A number of stores located in different parts of the island also rent boards and sails. Near downtown go to **Local Motion**. ~ 1714 Kapiolani Boulevard, Honolulu; 955-7873. In the Diamond Head area there's **Downing Hawaii**. ~ 3021 Waialae Avenue, Honolulu; 737-9696. On the Windward Coast try **Windsurfing Hawaii**. ~ 155-A Hamakua Drive, Kailua; 261-3539.

FISHING

From deep sea-fishing to trolling for freshwater bass, Oahu offers challenges to suit any angler. You can try game fishing out in the Pacific, head down to the beach for surf casting or try one of the island's popular lakes.

Most of the island's fishing fleet dock at Kewalo Basin (Fisherman's Wharf) on Ala Moana Drive between Waikiki and downtown Honolulu.

Among the outfits you'll find **Kono Sports Fishing**, which fishes the Leeward Coast and the waters off Molokai. ~ Kewalo Basin, Honolulu; 536-7472. Departing on similar trips from Kewalo Basin is **Island Charters**. ~ 536-1555. Or consider **Sport Fishing**, which also ties up in Kewalo Basin. ~ 521-2087.

For freshwater angling head up into the Koolau Mountains to fish the **Nuuanu Reservoir** (open to the public one Sunday a month). Another possibility is the **Wahiawa Public Fishing Area**. Both of these reservoirs are good places to catch Chinese catfish.

SAILING

One of the best ways to enjoy Oahu is aboard a sailboat. From brief cruises off Honolulu to a day-long charter along the North Shore, this is the perfect antidote to the tourist crowds. It's also surprisingly affordable.

Honolulu Sailing Company and the beach stands in front of Hilton Hawaiian Village in Waikiki sponsor cruises, whale-watching trips and interisland sailing. ~ 47-335 Lulani Street; 239-3900. **Above Heaven's Gate** operates charter group cruises to the Diamond Head reef area aboard a 56-foot teakwood pirate ship. You can also take a guided Hobie-cat tour off the Windward Coast to undiscovered islands most tourists miss (by appointment only). Along the way you'll enjoy Waimanalo, Lanikai and Kailua Bay. You can also learn how to sail this swift 16-foot craft. ~ 41-1010 Laumilo Street, Waimanalo Bay; 259-5429, 800-800-2933, fax 259-5653, E-mail ahg@aloha.net.

If you're eager to charter your own yacht, contact **The Yacht Connection**. The company charters all sizes of vessels ranging from fishing boats to luxury yachts. ~ 1750 Kalakaua Avenue, Suite 3138, Honolulu; 523-1383.

KAYAKING

A sport well suited for Oahu, kayaking is an ideal way to explore the island's protected bays, islands and inland rivers. For kayak rentals contact **Kailua Sailboard Company**. ~ 130 Kailua Road, Kailua; 262-2555. **Twogood Kayak Hawaii** also rents kayaks. ~ 171-B Hamakua Drive, Kailua; 262-5656

To rent or purchase kayaks and equipment, or to sign up for lessons and tours, consider **Go Bananas** just outside Waikiki. ~ 732 Kapahulu Avenue; 737-9514.

RIDING STABLES

Located on the Windward Coast across from Chinaman's Hat, **Kualoa Ranch** leads one- and two-hour weekend rides in Kaaawa Valley. A longer, four-and-a-half-hour trip includes a visit to a hidden beach near an ancient Hawaiian fish pond (offered during the week). Don't forget your swimsuit. ~ 49-560 Kamehameha Highway, Kaaawa; 237-8515.

The **Turtle Bay Hilton** on the North Shore has riding programs for guests and the general public. ~ 293-8811.

GOLF

For a round of golf in Honolulu, try the **Ala Wai Golf Course**, Hawaii's first municipal course. ~ 404 Kapahulu Avenue; 296-4653. **Hawaii Kai Golf Course** is a popular spot with both tourists and *kamaainas*. ~ 8902 Kalanianaole Highway; 395-2358.

Over on the Windward Coast, the lush **Olomana Golf Links** has an 18-hole course. ~ 41-1801 Kalanianaole Highway, Waimanalo; 259-7926. For a cheap round of golf visit the **Bay View Golf Links**. ~ 45-285 Kaneohe Bay Drive, Kaneohe; 247-0451. Located below the Nuuanu Pali Lookout, the **Pali Golf Course** affords sweeping views of the rugged Koolaus and the windward coastline. ~ 45-050 Kamehameha Highway, Kaneohe; 261-9784. If you want to play a casual game, try the nine-hole **Kahuku Golf Course**. ~ Kahuku; 293-5842.

On the North Shore, two courses—an 18-hole and a 9-hole course that can be played twice—are open to the public at the **Turtle Bay Hilton**. ~ Kahuku; 293-8811. The 18-hole course was designed by golf professional Arnold Palmer.

Not all of Oahu's beaches are crowded. Leave Waikiki and within a few miles you'll discover places like Halona Cove Beach.

Top: Horseback trails above Hanalei offer stunning views of the Hanalei Valley.

Above left: Kayakers navigate Kauai's lovely Hanalei Bay.

Above right: Cyclists cruise by the Big Island's Parker Ranch, one of the world's largest independently owned cattle ranches.

Right: Ocean breezes at Diamond Head Beach Park provide perfect conditions for Oahu windsurfers.

Set amid fields of sugarcane and pineapple along the Leilehua Plateau in the center of Oahu, the **Hawaii Country Club** is a bit run-down, but offers some challenging holes. ~ 94-1211 Kunia Road, Wahiawa; 622-1744. The **Mililani Golf Club**, though not particularly demanding, provides lovely views of the Koolau and Waianae ranges. ~ 95-176 Kuahelani Avenue, Mililani; 623-2254. The flat **Ted Makalena Golf Course** is not well maintained, but is still popular with local golfers. ~ 93-059 Waipio Point Access Road, Waipahu; 296-7888.

Out toward the Leeward Coast, a series of lakes, brooks and waterfalls meanders through the 18 holes at **Koolina Golf Club**. ~ 92-1220 Aliinui Drive, Kapolei; 676-5309. Bounded by the Waianae Range, the beautiful **Sheraton Makaha West Golf Course** is among Oahu's foremost courses. ~ 84-626 Makaha Valley Road, Makaha; 695-9544.

Many of Oahu resorts offer complete tennis facilities. But don't despair if your hotel lacks nets. There are dozens of public tennis courts located around the island.

TENNIS

In the Waikiki area, try **Kapiolani Park**. ~ Kalakaua Avenue. **Diamond Head Tennis Center** is another option in the area. ~ Paki Avenue. There are courts across from Ala Moana Center at **Ala Moana Regional Park**. ~ Ala Moana Boulevard. In Greater Honolulu you can serve and volley at **Keehi Lagoon**. ~ Off the Nimitz Highway, Honolulu. Or opt for a set in the lush Manoa Valley at **Manoa Valley District Park**. ~ 2721 Kaaipu Avenue, Manoa.

For your tennis needs on the Windward Coast, try **Kailua District Park**. ~ 21 South Kainalu Drive, Kailua. Or visit **Kaneohe District Park**. ~ 45-660 Keaahala Road, Kaneohe. **Sunset Beach Neighborhood Park**, with two lighted courts, is an option on the North Shore. ~ 59-360 Kamehameha Highway, Haleiwa. Lighted courts are also available at **Waianae District Park** on the Leeward Coast. ~ 85-601 Farrington Highway, Waianae.

◆◆

✔ CHECK THESE OUT—UNIQUE OUTDOOR ADVENTURES

- Enjoy the green grass, white-sand beach and local color at **Ala Moana Regional Park**, the best spot in all Hawaii for a Sunday picnic. *page 92*
- Surf the largest waves in the world, or safely sit back and enjoy the sun, at **Waimea Bay**. *page 122*
- Set out from Yokohama Bay past miles of tidepools to **Kaena Point**, legendary home of Nanue the Shark Man. *page 135*
- Soar past mountains, sugar-cane fields and roaring surf while exploring the North Shore on a **glider ride**. *page 122*

Call the County Department of Parks and Recreation for more information on public courts. ~ 971-7150. The Hawaii Visitors & Convention Bureau has information on private courts. ~ 923-1811.

BIKING

Oahu is blessed with excellent roads, well-paved and usually flat, and cursed with heavy traffic. About three-quarters of Hawaii's population lives here, and it sometimes seems like every person owns a car.

Honolulu can be a cyclist's nightmare, but outside the city the traffic is somewhat lighter. And Oahu drivers, accustomed to tourists driving mopeds, are relatively conscious of bicyclists.

Keep in mind that the Windward Coast is the wet side, the North Shore is slightly drier and the south and west coasts are the driest of all. And remember, rip-offs are a frequent fact of life on Oahu. Leaving your bike unlocked is asking for a long walk back.

If you'd like a little two-wheeled company, check out the **Hawaii Bicycling League**, which regularly sponsors bike rides. ~ Box 4403, Honolulu, HI 96812; phone/fax 735-5756.

Bike Rentals   In Waikiki, **Coconut Cruisers** rents beach cruisers and mountain bikes. ~ 2301 Kalakaua Avenue; 924-1644. Also in Waikiki, **Adventure Rentals** rents mountain bikes. ~ 1705 Kalakaua Avenue #1; 941-2222. **Blue Sky Rentals** has mountain, road and tandem. bikes. ~ 1920 Ala Moana Boulevard; 947-0101.

Bike Repairs   In addition to doing repair work, **Eki Cyclery** sells accessories and mountain bikes. ~ 1603 Dillingham Boulevard, Honolulu; 847-2005. With mountain, road and triathlon bikes for sale, **The Bike Shop** also does repair work. ~ 1149 South King Street, Honolulu; 596-0588. In central Oahu, try **Waipahu Bicycle** for repairs or to purchase a new bike. ~ 94-320 Waipahu Depot Street, Waipahu; 671-4091.

HIKING

There are numerous hiking trails within easy driving distance of Honolulu. I have listed these as well as trails in the Windward Coast and North Shore areas. Unfortunately, many Oahu treks require special permission from the state, the armed services or private owners. But you should find that the hikes suggested here, none of which require official sanction, will provide ample adventure.

To hike with a group or to obtain further information on hiking Oahu, contact the **Sierra Club**. ~ 233 Merchant Street; 538-6616, fax 537-9019. Another agency that also sponsors regular weekend hikes is the **Hawaii Trail and Mountain Club**. ~ 262-2845, 488-1161. The **Hawaii Nature Center** offers guided hikes every Saturday morning. Call ahead to make a reservation. ~ 2131 Makiki Heights Drive; 955-0100.

GREATER HONOLULU   If you're staying in Waikiki, the most easily accessible hike is the short jaunt up **Diamond Head** crater.

There's a sweeping view of Honolulu from atop this famous land-mark. The trail begins inside the crater, so take Diamond Head Road around to the inland side of Diamond Head, then follow the tunnel leading into the crater.

In the Koolau Mountains above Diamond Head there is a trail that climbs almost 2000 feet and affords excellent panoramas of the Windward Coast. To get to the **Lanipo Trail** (3 miles), take Waialae Avenue off of Route H-1. Then turn up Wilhelmina Road and follow until it reaches Maunalani Circle and the trailhead.

For spectacular vistas overlooking the lush Palolo and Manoa Valleys, you can hike **Waahila Ridge Trail** (2 miles). To get there, take St. Louis Heights Drive (near the University of Hawaii cam-pus) and then follow connecting roads up to Waahila Ridge State Recreation Area.

The following trails can be combined for longer hikes. Contact the **Hawaii Nature Center** for free maps and trail information. ~ 2131 Makiki Heights Drive, Honolulu; 955-0100. **Manoa Falls Trail** (0.8 mile) goes through Manoa Valley. This is a pleasant jaunt that follows Waihi Stream through a densely vegetated area to a charming waterfall. **Manoa Cliffs Trail** (3 miles) a pleasant family hike, follows a precipice along the west side of Manoa Valley. And **Puu Ohia Trail** (2 miles), which crosses Manoa Cliffs Trail, provides splendid views of the Manoa and Nuuanu valleys. Both trails begin from Tantalus Drive in the hills above Honolulu. **Makiki Valley Trail** (1.1 miles) begins near Tantalus Drive. Composed of three in-terlinking trails, this loop passes stands of eucalyptus and bamboo trees and offers some postcard views of Honolulu. Another loop trail, **Judd Memorial** (1.3 miles), crosses Nuuanu Stream and tra-verses bamboo, eucalyptus and Norfolk pine groves en route to the Jackass Ginger Pool. To get there, take the Pali Highway (Route 61) several miles north from Honolulu. Turn onto Nuuanu Pali Drive and follow it about a mile to Reservoir Number Two spillway.

Another hike located in this general area, along **Waimano Trail** (7 miles), climbs 1600 feet to an astonishing vista point above Oahu's Windward Coast. There are swimming holes en route to the vista point. To get there, take Kamehameha Highway (Route 90) west to Waimano Home Road (Route 730). Turn right and go two-and-a-half miles to a point along the road where you'll see a building on the right and an irrigation ditch on the left. The trail follows the ditch.

SOUTHEAST OAHU   There are several excellent hikes along this shore. The first few are within ten miles of Waikiki, near **Hanauma Bay**. From the beach at Hanauma you can hike two miles along the coast and cliffs to the Halona Blowhole. This trek passes the Toilet Bowl, a unique tidepool with a hole in the bottom that causes it to fill and then flush with the wave action. Waves sometimes wash the rocks along this path, so be prepared to get wet (and be careful!).

At the intersection where the short road leading down toward Hanauma Bay branches from Kalanianaole Highway (Route 72), there are two other trails. **Koko Head Trail**, a one-mile hike to the top of a volcanic cone, starts on the ocean side of the highway. This trek features some startling views of Hanauma Bay, Diamond Head and the Koolau Range. Another one-mile hike, along **Koko Crater Trail**, leads from the highway up to a 1208-foot peak. The views from this crow's nest are equally spectacular.

WINDWARD COAST   There are several other particularly pretty hikes much farther north, near the village of Hauula. **Sacred Falls Trail** (2.2 miles) gently ascends through a canyon and arrives at a waterfall and swimming hole. The trailhead for this popular trek is near Kamehameha Highway (Route 83) just south of Hauula.

Then, in Hauula, if you turn off of Kamehameha Highway and head inland for about a quarter-mile up Hauula Homestead Road, you'll come to Maakua Road. Walk up Maakua Road, which leads into the woods. About 300 yards after entering the woods, the road forks. Maakua Gulch Trail branches to the left. If you continue straight ahead you'll be on Hauula Trail, but if you veer left onto Maakua Gulch Trail, you'll encounter yet another trail branching off to the left in about 150 yards. This is Papali Trail (also known as Maakua Trail).

Maakua Gulch Trail (3 miles), en route to a small waterfall, traverses a rugged canyon with extremely steep walls. Part of the trail lies along the stream bed, so be ready to get wet. **Hauula Trail** (2.5 miles) ascends along two ridges and provides fine vistas of the Koolau Range and the Windward Coast. **Papali Trail** (2.5 miles) drops into Papali Gulch, then climbs high along a ridge from which you can view the surrounding countryside.

NORTH SHORE AND LEEWARD COAST   In the mountains above Pearl Harbor, at Keaiwa Heiau State Park, you will find the **Aiea Loop Trail** (4.8 miles). Set in a heavily forested area, this hike passes the wreckage of a World War II cargo plane. It provides an excellent chance to see some of the native Hawaiian trees—*lehua*, *ohia* and *koa*—used by local woodworkers. (For directions to Keaiwa Heiau State Park, see the "Leeward Coast" section in this chapter.)

You can approach the trail to **Kaena Point** either from the North Shore or the Leeward Coast. It's a dry, rock-strewn path that leads to Oahu's northwest tip. There are tidepools and swimming spots en route, plus spectacular views of a rugged, uninhabited coastline. To get to the trailhead, just drive to the end of the paved portion of Route 930 on the North Shore or Route 93 on the Leeward Coast. Then follow the jeep trail out to Kaena Point. Either way, it's about a two-mile trek.

There's one airport on Oahu and it's a behemoth. **Honolulu International Airport** is a Pacific crossroads, an essential link between North America and Asia. Most visitors arriving from the mainland land here first, and find it a convenient jumping-off point for venturing farther to the various neighbor islands. Aloha Airlines and Hawaiian Airlines provide regular jet service to the outer islands, while smaller outfits like Aloha Island Air and Mahalo Air fly prop planes.

Honolulu International includes all the comforts of a major airport. You can check your bags or rent a locker; fuel up at a restaurant, coffee shop or cocktail lounge; shop at several stores; or shower.

If you have spare time, stop by the **Pacific Aerospace Museum**, a technology exhibition devoted to aviation and the islands. In one exhibit a six-inch-tall "holovision" pilot guides you around a 1930s-era prop plane, explaining how it flies. Or you can design your own plane, using a computer-assisted design monitor. Then take the flight simulator controls and "land" a jet at Honolulu International. There are also two theaters that recapture the dramatic history of aviation. Admission. ~ Honolulu International Airport, second floor; 839-0777.

To cover the eight or so miles into Waikiki, it's possible to hire a cab for approximately $20, plus a small charge for each bag. For $7, **Hawaii Airport Transportation Services** will take you to your Waikiki hotel or condominium. ~ 566-7333, 800-533-8765. And city bus #19 or #20 travels through Downtown Honolulu and Waikiki. This is the cheapest transportation, but you're only allowed to carry on baggage that fits on your lap. So, unless you're traveling very light, you'll have to use another conveyance.

Of all the islands, Oahu offers the most rental agencies. At the airport, **Avis Rent A Car** (834-5536, 800-331-2212), **Budget Rent A Car** (836-1700, 800-527-0700), **Dollar Rent A Car** (831-2330, 800-800-4000), **National Interrent** (831-3800, 800-227-7368) and **Hertz Rent A Car** (831-3500, 800-654-3011) all have booths. Their convenient location helps to save time while minimizing the problem of picking up your car.

Though not at the airport, **Alamo Rent A Car** (833-4585, 800-327-9633) provides airport pick-up service.

There are many other Honolulu-based companies offering very low rates but providing limited pick-up service at the airport. I've never found the inconvenience worth the savings. There you are—newly arrived from the mainland, uncertain about your environment, anxious to check in at the hotel—and you're immediately confronted with the Catch-22 of getting to your car. Do you rent a vehicle in which to pick up your rental car? Take a bus? Hitchhike? What do you do with your bags meanwhile?

If your budget is important, consider one of the following cheaper but less convenient outfits: **Sears Rent A Car** (599-2205) or **VIP Car Rental** (922-4605).

If you prefer to go in high style, rent a Rolls Royce from **Cloud Nine** (524-7999, 800-524-7999) or a vintage car at **Cruisin' Classics Car Rentals** (923-6446, fax 800-722-3785).

JEEP RENTALS

Adventure Rentals (941-2222), **Dollar Rent A Car** (831-2330) and **VIP Car Rental** (922-4605) provide jeeps.

MOPED RENTALS

In Waikiki, **Adventure Rentals** rents mopeds and motorcycles. ~ 1705 Kalakaua Avenue #1; 941-2222. You can also try **Blue Sky Rentals**, located on the ground floor of the Inn On The Park Hotel. ~ 1920 Ala Moana Boulevard; 947-0101.

PUBLIC TRANSIT

Oahu has an excellent bus system that runs regularly to points all over the island and provides convenient service throughout Honolulu. Many of the beaches, hotels, restaurants and points of interest mentioned in this chapter are just a bus ride away. It's even possible to pop your money in the fare box and ride around the entire island.

TheBus carries more than 250,000 people daily, loading them into any of 700 vehicles that rumble along city streets and country roads from 4:50 a.m. until midnight. There are also express buses traveling major highways. Most buses are handicapped accessible and many have bike racks.

If you stay in Waikiki you'll inevitably be sardined into a #19 or #20 bus for the ride through Honolulu's tourist mecca. Many bus drivers are Hawaiian; I saw some hysterical scenes on this line when tourists waited anxiously for their stop to be called, only to realize they couldn't understand the driver's pidgin. Hysterical, that is, after those early days when *I* was the visitor with the furrowed brow.

But you're surely more interested in meeting local people than tourists, and you can easily do it on any of the buses outside Waikiki. They're less crowded and a lot more fun for people-watching.

For information on bus routes call **TheBus** at 848-5555. And remember, the only carry-on luggage permitted is baggage small enough to fit on your lap.

HITCHING

Thumbing is not as popular on Oahu as one might think, so the competition for rides is not too great. The heavy traffic also increases your chances considerably. Officially, you're supposed to hitch from bus stops only. While I've seen people hitching in many different spots, I'd still recommend standing at a bus stop. Not only will you be within the law, but you'll also be able to catch a bus if you can't hitch a ride.

The quickest way to see all Oahu has to offer is by taking to the air. In minutes you can experience the island's hidden waterfalls, secluded beaches and volcanic landmarks. Tranquil gliders and hovering whirlybirds all fly low and slow to make sure you see what you missed on the trip over from the mainland. You can also take extended flights that include the outer islands.

AERIAL TOURS

Rainbow Pacific Helicopters Ltd. offers tours of Waikiki and Honolulu, Hanauma Bay, the Koolau Mountains, Chinaman's Hat and Sacred Falls. ~ 1108 Kapalulu Place, Honolulu; 834-1111.

To enjoy a one- or two-passenger glider trip, head out to **The Original Glider Rides** and talk to Mr. Bill. On your 20-minute trip you're likely to see fields of sugar cane, marine mammals, surfers working the North Shore and neighboring Kauai. You'll also enjoy peace and quiet while working your way down from 3000 feet. A videotape of the ride and your reactions makes a memorable souvenir. ~ Dillingham Airfield, Mokuleia; 677-3404.

What better way to stroll through the past than with a company called **TimeWalks**. Based in Honolulu and featuring master storyteller Glen Grant, they offer a number of walking tours. One guided walk takes you to the sinful saloons of Old Honolulu, another focuses on Mark Twain's favorite spots, and one of the most popular visits the haunted places (including Iolani Palace!) of Honolulu. ~ 943-0371.

WALKING TOURS

With all the highrise hotels and plate-glass condominiums, Waikiki appears to have no history at all. But behind all that steel and brass beats an ancient heart. To help you discover its pulse, an outfit called **Passport Hawaii** conducts "A Journey to Old Waikiki." ~ 2634 South King Street; 943-0371.

The best way to visit Chinatown is on one of the walking tours sponsored by the **Chinese Chamber of Commerce**. The walking tour will carry you past temples, specialty stores and other intriguing spots around this diverse neighborhood. Fee. ~ 533-3181.

▼▼▼▼▼▼▼▼▼▼▼▼▼▼▼▼▼▼▼▼
Addresses & Phone Numbers

OAHU ISLAND

County Department of Parks and Recreation ~ Honolulu Municipal Building, 650 South King Street, Honolulu; 523-4525

Division of State Parks ~ 1151 Punchbowl Street, Room 310, Honolulu; 587-0300

Hawaii Visitors & Convention Bureau ~ 2270 Kalakaua Avenue, Room 801, Honolulu; 923-1811

Weather Report ~ 973-4380 for Honolulu; 973-4381 for entire island; 973-4383 for surfing weather

HONOLULU

Ambulance ~ 911

Books ~ Honolulu Book Shops, Ala Moana Center or 1001 Bishop Street; 941-2274 or 537-6224

Fire Department ~ 911

Fishing Supplies ~ K. Kaya Fishing Supplies, 901 Kekaulike; 538-1578

Hardware ~ Kaimuki Ace Hardware, 3367 Waialae Avenue; 732-2888

Hospital ~ Queen's Medical Center, 1301 Punchbowl; 538-9011

Laundromat ~ Waikiki Ena Road Laundry, 478-A Ena Road; 942-3451

Library ~ 478 South King Street; 586-3500

Pharmacy ~ Longs Drugs, Ala Moana Center, 1450 Ala Moana Boulevard; 941-4433

Photo Supply ~ Francis Camera Shop, Ala Moana Center, 1450 Ala Moana Boulevard; 973-4480

Police Department ~ 801 South Beretania Street; 529-3111 or 911 for emergencies

Post Office ~ 330 Saratoga Road; 423-3990

WINDWARD COAST

Ambulance ~ 911

Fire Department ~ 911

Laundromat ~ Kailua Laundromat, Aulike Street, Kailua; 261-9201

Police Department ~ 801 South Beretania Street; 529-3111 or 911 for emergencies

NORTH SHORE

Ambulance ~ 911

Fire Department ~ 911

Police Department ~ 911

LEEWARD COAST

Ambulance ~ 911

Fire Department ~ 911

Laundromat ~ Waianae Speed Wash, 85-802 Farrington Highway; 696-9115

Police Department ~ 911

FIVE

Hawaii

The Big Island, they call it, and even that is an understatement. Hawaii, all 4030 square miles, is almost twice as large as all the other Hawaiian islands combined. Its twin volcanic peaks, Mauna Kea and Mauna Loa, dwarf most mountains. Mauna Kea, rising 13,796 feet, is the largest island-based mountain in the world. Mauna Loa, the world's largest active volcano, which last erupted in 1950, looms 13,677 feet above sea level. This is actually 32,000 feet from the ocean floor, making it, by one system of reckoning, the tallest mountain on earth, grander even than Everest. And in bulk it is the world's largest. The entire Sierra Nevada chain could fit within this single peak.

Kilauea, a third volcano whose seething firepit has been erupting with startling frequency, is one of the world's most active craters. Since its most recent series of eruptions began in 1983, the volcano has swallowed almost 200 houses. In 1990 it completely destroyed the town of Kalapana, burying a once lively village beneath tons of black lava; then in 1992 it destroyed the ancient Hawaiian village of Kamoamoa. There is little doubt that the Big Island is a place of geologic superlatives.

But size alone does not convey the Big Island's greatness. Its industry, too, is expansive. Despite the lava wasteland that covers large parts of its surface, and the volcanic gases that create a layer of "vog" during volcanic eruptions, the Big Island is the state's greatest producer of sugar, papayas, vegetables, anthuriums, macadamia nuts and cattle. Its orchid industry, based in rain-drenched Hilo, is the world's largest. Over 22,000 varieties grow in the nurseries here.

Across the island in sun-soaked Kona, one of the nation's only coffee industries operates. Just off this spectacular western coast lie some of the finest deep-sea fishing grounds in the world. Between Hilo and Kona, and surrounding Waimea, sits the Parker Ranch. Sprawling across 225,000 acres, it is one of the world's largest independently owned cattle ranches.

Yet many of these measurements are taken against island standards. Compared to the mainland, the Big Island is a tiny speck in the sea. Across its broadest reach it measures a scant 93 miles long and 76 miles wide, smaller than Connecticut. The road around the island, totals only 300 miles, and can be driven in a day, though I'd recommend taking at least five. The island's 135,500 population comprises a mere seven percent of the state's citizens. Its lone city, Hilo, has a population of only 46,100.

But large or small, numbers cannot fully describe the Big Island, for there is a magic about the place that transcends statistics. Hawaii, also nicknamed the Orchid Island and Volcano Island, is the home of Pele, the goddess of volcanoes. Perhaps her fiery spirit is what infuses the Big Island with an unquantifiable quality. Or maybe the island's comparative youth (still growing in size from two active volcanoes, it is geologically the youngest spot on earth, one million years old) is what makes the elements seem nearer, more alluring and strangely threatening here. Whatever it might be, the Big Island has always been where I feel closest to the Polynesian spirit. Of all the Hawaiian islands, this one I love the most.

It was here, possibly as early as 400 A.D., that Polynesian explorers first landed when they discovered the island chain. Until the advent of the white man, it was generally the most important island, supporting a large population and occupying a vital place in Hawaii's rich mythology. Little wonder then that Kamehameha the Great, the chief who would become Hawaii's first king, was born here in 1753. He established the archipelago's first capital in Kailua and ruled there until his death in 1819.

Within a year of the great leader's passing, two events occurred in Kailua that jolted the entire chain far more than any earthquake. First the king's heir, Liholiho, uprooted the centuries-old taboo system upon which ancient Polynesian religion rested. Then, in the spring of 1820, the first American missionaries dropped anchor off the coast of Kailua-Kona. It was also near here that Captain James Cook, history's greatest discoverer, was slain in 1779 by the same people who had earlier welcomed him as a god. Across the island another deity, Pele, was defied in 1824 when the high chieftess Kapiolani, a Christian, ate *kapu* (forbidden) fruit on the rim of Kilauea crater.

As stirring as the Big Island's story might be, much of its drama still awaits the visitor. For the land—the volcanoes, beaches and valleys—is as vital and intriguing today as in the days of demigods and kings. This is a place for the adventurer to spend a lifetime.

On the east coast, buffeted by trade winds, lies Hilo, a lush tropical town that soaks up 140 inches of rain annually. Here anthuriums and orchids are cultivated in a number of spectacular nurseries. Just to the south—smoking, heaving and sometimes erupting—sits Hawaii Volcanoes National Park.

The Puna District that straddles the coast between the volcanoes and Hilo has been the site of dramatic eruptions during the past decade. This lush rainforest is also the scene of a major political debate that has pitted environmentalists against developers of a geothermal power plant.

In the north, from the Hamakua Coast to the Kohala Peninsula, heavy erosion has cut through jutting cliffs to form spectacular canyons such as the Waipio Valley.

Hawaii

N

Upolu Point
Hawi
KOHALA MOUNTAIN
HAMAKUA COAST
WAIPIO VALLEY
Kawaihae
Honokaa
Waimea
19
Waikoloa
Mauna Kea
(el 13,796 ft.)
190
Puuanahulu
Mauna Kea
State Park
Hualalai
(el 8,271 ft.)
Saddle   Rd.
19
Kailua-Kona
200
Hilo
Keaau
130
Captain Cook
Hawaii Volcanoes
National Park
Pahoa
Honaunau
Mauna Loa
(el 13,680 ft.)
Hawaii   Volcanoes
National   Park
11
KAU DESERT
Milolii
Punaluu
PACIFIC OCEAN
11
Naalehu

South Point

0   20 miles

All along the Hamakua plateau, sugar plantations, fed by waters from Mauna Kea, stretch from the mountains to the surf.

In startling contrast to these verdant mountains is the desert-like Kau district at the southern tip of the island (and, for that matter, the southernmost point in the United States). Along the west coast stretches the Kona district, a vacationer's paradise. Suntan weather, sandy beaches and coral reefs teeming with tropical fish make this an ideal area to just kick back and enjoy. The island's central tourist area is located here in Kailua-Kona, where Hawaiian royalty settled in the 19th century.

And for something unique to the Big Island, there's Waimea with its rolling grasslands, range animals and *paniolos*, or Hawaiian-style cowboys. In fact, one of the biggest Hereford cattle herds is located here in the center of the island.

It's an island I don't think you should miss, an island that's beginning to change rapidly with the creation of a string of resorts along the Kohala coast, but one that still retains its original charm. To geologists the Big Island is a natural laboratory in which the mysteries of volcanic activity are a fact of everyday life; to many Hawaiians it is the most sacred of all the islands. To everyone who visits it, Hawaii is a place of startling contrasts and unspeakable beauty, an alluring and exotic tropical island.

Hilo

▼▼▼▼▼▼▼▼▼

There's one thing you'll rarely miss in this tropical city—rain. Hilo gets about 140 inches a year. The Chamber of Commerce will claim it rains mostly at night, but don't be deceived. It's almost as likely to be dark and wet at midday. There is a good side to all this bothersome moisture—it transforms Hilo into an exotic city crowded with tropical foliage, the orchid capital of the United States.

Hilo is the closest you will approach in all Hawaii to a Somerset Maugham–style South Seas port town. With its turn-of-the-century stores, many badly needing a paint job, and old Chinese shops, it's a throwback to an era when tourists were few and Hawaii was a territory. Sections of town, especially around Waianuenue Avenue, have been refurbished and dabbed with 1990s flash, but much of the downtown is still a collection of ethnic eateries, swap shops and Japanese groceries. The gutters are rusty, the rain awnings have sagged, and an enduring sense of character overhangs the place with the certainty and finality of the next downpour.

SIGHTS

Hilo is a tropical wonderland, a rainforest with hotels, shops and great places to visit. A visit to one of the city's many flower nurseries is an absolute must. These gardens grow orchids, anthuriums and countless other flowers. There are three that I highly recommend. **Orchids of Hawaii** specializes in *vanda* orchids, birds of paradise and anthurium leis and corsages. Closed Saturday and Sunday. ~ 2801 Kilauea Avenue; 959-3581. **Nani Mau Gardens** is a 20-acre visual feast that houses a wide variety of tropical flowers and plants. It has a gift shop, a botanical museum and a restaurant that serves lunch only. Admission. ~ Several miles south of Hilo near

Route 11 at 421 Makalika; 959-3541. Another beatiful nursery is **Big Island Tropical Gardens** which has over 900 different varieties of plants and flowers. ~ 1477 Kalanianaole Avenue; 961-6621.

Banyan Drive is another green thumb's delight. Sweeping past Hilo's nicest hotels, this waterfront road is shaded with rows of giant banyan trees. Next to this verdant arcade are the **Liliuokalani Gardens**, 19 acres exploding with color. These Japanese gardens, featuring both Hawaiian and Asian trees, are dotted with pagodas and arched bridges.

From Banyan Drive, a short footbridge crosses to **Coconut Island**, a palm-studded islet in Hilo Bay. This old Hawaiian sanctuary presents a dramatic view of Hilo Bay and, on a clear day, of Mauna Kea and Mauna Loa as well.

A stone's skip across from the island, at **Suisan Fish Market**, fishing boats land their catches. Try to get there around 8 in the morning for a lively fish auction and a dose of local color. ~ Banyan Drive and Lihiwai Street; 935-9349.

◄ HIDDEN

It's not far to **Wailoa River State Park**, where grassy picnic areas surround beautiful **Waiakea Fishpond**. Across one of the pond's arching bridges, at Wailoa Visitors Center, there are cultural exhibits and an information desk. ~ Off Kamehameha Avenue; 933-4360.

In downtown Hilo, the **Lyman Mission House** is a fascinating example of a 19th-century missionary home. Built in 1839, the house is furnished with elegant period pieces that create a sense of this bygone era (the house is open to guided tours only). Also on the property is a Hawaiian history museum focusing on Hawaiian culture and the islands' many ethnic groups, an excellent collection of rocks and minerals, and an exhibit on the islands' indigenous flora and fauna. Admission. ~ 276 Haili Street; 935-5021.

The **East Hawaii Cultural Center Gallery** displays the work of local artists in a series of ever-changing exhibits. The building it-

---

✔ CHECK THESE OUT—UNIQUE SIGHTS

- Explore the rainforest primeval, **Akaka Falls State Park**—home to giant philodendrons and bamboo groves—en route to a sheer 420-foot waterfall. *page 160*
- Wander **Kona coffee country** past tinroof general stores, sagging coffee shacks and miles of shimmering java plantations. *page 192*
- Discover Hawaii's Great Wall, a 17-foot-thick lava barricade at **Puuhonua o Honaunau** that protected an ancient city of refuge. *page 193*
- Test your belief in miracles at **Cape Kumukahi Lighthouse**, saved when a wall of molten lava flowed all around it. *page 211*

self, an old police station that has achieved historic landmark status, is a work of art. Closed Sunday. ~ 141 Kalakaua Street; 961-5711. Fronting the library on nearby Waianuenue Avenue are the **Naha** and **Pinao Stones**. According to legend, whoever moved the massive Naha Stone would rule all the islands. Kamehameha overturned the boulder while still a youth, then grew to become Hawaii's first king.

Continue up Waianuenue Avenue to **Rainbow Falls**, a foaming cascade in Wailuku River State Park. Here, particularly in the morning, spray from the falls shimmers in spectral hues. It's another two miles to **Boiling Pots**, where a series of falls pours turbulently into circular lava pools. The rushing water, spilling down from Mauna Kea, bubbles up through the lava and boils over into the next pool.

Kaumana Drive, branching off Waianuenue Avenue, leads five miles out of town to **Kaumana Caves**. A stone stairway leads from the roadside down to two fern-choked lava tubes, formed during Mauna Loa's devastating 1881 eruption. Explore the lower tube, but avoid the other—it's dangerous.

HIDDEN ▶   Also be sure to visit the **Panaewa Rainforest Zoo**. Located in a lush region that receives over 125 inches of rain annually, this modest facility houses numerous rainforest animals as well as other species. There are water buffaloes and tigers, plus an array of exotic birds that include crowned cranes, macaws, parrots, Hawaiian coots, laysan ducks and nenes. ~ One mile off the Mamalahoa Highway several miles south of town; 959-7224.

LODGING   The main hotel district in this rain-plagued city sits astride the bay along Banyan Drive. Most hotels offer moderately priced accommodations, while a few are designed to fit the contours of a more slender purse.

Near the far end of beautiful Banyan Drive lies the **Hilo Seaside Hotel**. This charming place is actually on a side street fronting Reed's Bay, an arm of Hilo Bay. Owned by the Kimis, a Hawaiian family, it has the same friendly ambience that pervades their other hotels. There's a large lobby decorated with tile, *koa* wood and bamboo. A carp pond complete with footbridges dominates the grounds. The rooms are small and plainly decorated. Most are wallpapered and equipped with telephone, television and a combination shower-tub (perfect for soaking away a rainy day). The lanais overlook lush gardens and the hotel swimming pool. All in all, for friendly ambience and a lovely setting, the Seaside is a prime choice. ~ 126 Banyan Way; 935-0821, 800-367-7000, fax 922-0052. MODERATE TO DELUXE.

Hilo Bay Hotel is another economical oceanfront establishment. The theme here is Polynesian, and proprietor "Uncle Billy" carries it off with flair: wicker furniture, thatch and *tapa* in the lobby, a

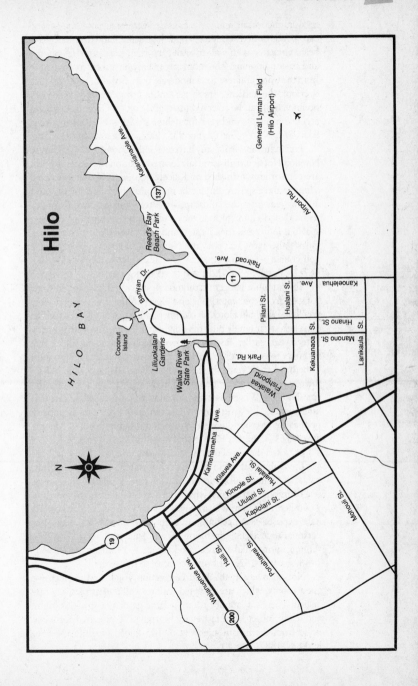

Hilo

restaurant/cocktail lounge, a bayside swimming pool and several carp ponds dotted about the tropical gardens. Standard rooms have been renovated with wall-to-wall carpeting, televisions, telephones and air-conditioning. The rooms are plainly furnished, located away from the water and rent for a moderate price. Superior rooms (which overlook the gardens, are larger, more attractive and come with ocean views) can be reserved for slightly more. Oceanfront rooms are also available and rent for deluxe prices. ~ 87 Banyan Drive; 935-0861, 800-367-5102, fax 935-7903. MODERATE TO DELUXE.

For luxurious living my favorite Hilo hostelry is the **Hawaii Naniloa Hotel**, a highrise affair located right on the water. Rooms are comfortably furnished and nicely adorned. Restaurants, bars, a lounge and a spa are among the many amenities here, but the most alluring feature is the landscape—the tree-studded lawn is fringed with tidepools and volcanic rock. Add outdoor swimming pools, a spacious lobby and friendly staff and you have Hilo's premier hotel. Guests also have access to the Naniloa Country Club's nine-hole golf course across the street. ~ 93 Banyan Drive; 969-3333, 800-367-5360, fax 969-6622. DELUXE TO ULTRA-DELUXE.

To find more budget accommodations, you'll have to tote your bags up from the waterfront and closer to the town center. Here you'll find the **Hilo Hotel**, an oldtimer dating back to 1888 when the Spreckels sugar family built the original ten-room, two-bath hostelry. Fifteen years earlier, Princess Ruth reputedly planted the rubber tree that once towered more than 100 feet above the hotel's lush grounds. Time has left no trace on the hotel's older Kalakaua wing, where the rooms are tastefully decorated, most with TVs. The newer, quieter Niolopa Wing has two-bedroom wood-paneled suites with kitchenettes. Guests in both wings can enjoy the hotel swimming pool as well as the adjoining lounge and restaurant. ~ 142 Kinoole Street; 961-3733, fax 935-7836. BUDGET TO MODERATE.

On a tree-lined residential street just across the Wailuku River sits the **Dolphin Bay Hotel**. This comfortable two-story establishment has 18 units, all equipped with kitchenettes. There are studios, one bedroom apartments, which can accommodate up to four, and a two-bedroom unit, which houses as many as six. Rooms upstairs have exposed-beam ceilings; all units have cinderblock walls, but personal touches like fresh flowers and fruit, and a garden with a running spring, make this a good choice. ~ 333 Iliahi Street; 935-1466, fax 935-1523. BUDGET TO MODERATE.

Not far away at the **Wild Ginger Inn** you'll find inexpensive guest rooms, which are carpeted wall-to-wall and attractively furnished. There's a laundry room, a large garden, a spacious lobby and a full buffet breakfast every morning. Be prepared for some noise from the nearby highway. ~ 100 Puueo Street; 935-5556, 800-882-1887. BUDGET.

Arnott's Lodge is a clean, bright attractive hostel. Just one block from the waterfront, it is on the outskirts of Hilo in a low-key residential area. There are dormitory rooms available as well as private singles and doubles. Group activities such as hiking and snorkeling trips are frequently arranged, and there is a communal barbecue Wednesday and Saturday nights. With low-cost prices, and full kitchen and laundry facilities provided, it's one of the area's best bargains. ~ 98 Apapane Road; 969-7097, 800-368-8752, fax 961-9638. BUDGET.

Scattered throughout Hilo are numerous cafés, lunch counters and chain restaurants serving low-cost meals.

DINING

Try the lunch menu at **Restaurant Kiku**, near the edge of hotel row, which consists of sandwiches (many at low, low cost) as well as Asian and American platters. The menu's limited and the atmosphere nonexistent, but Gwen's place isn't bad for a quick lunch or breakfast. ~ 96 Kalanianaole Avenue; 961-2044. BUDGET.

Ken's House of Pancakes has to top the list for all-American fare. If you've ever been to a Denny's or Howard Johnson's, you've been in Ken's. Endless rows of naugahyde booths, a long counter next to the kitchen, uniformed waitresses—the classic roadside America motif. The cuisine is on a par with the decorative taste: hamburgers and roast beef, mediocre in quality. But when all else is closed, it's a good late-night option. ~ 1730 Kamehameha Avenue; 935-8711. MODERATE.

> Forget five-star restaurants and gourmet cuisine; Hilo is *the* place for ethnic eating on a budget.

Another mediocre spot is **Hukilau Restaurant**, adjacent to the popular Hilo Seaside Hotel. Decorated in tiled walls and *koa* paneling, the Hukilau features a fresh seafood menu complemented with meat 'n' potato favorites like pork chops, steak and fried chicken. Dinners come with salad bar, soup, dessert and beverage. For lunch, they offer sandwiches and other mid-day fare; also open at breakfast time. ~ 136 Banyan Way; 935-4222. MODERATE.

Uncle Billy's at the nearby Hilo Bay Hotel sports a Hawaiian decor. In addition to its rattan furnishings, this cozy club hosts Polynesian dinner shows nightly. The menu is filled with surf-and-turf dishes priced comfortably. There's no lunch here, but they do offer breakfast daily. ~ 87 Banyan Drive; 935-0861. BUDGET TO MODERATE.

A local favorite that specializes in fresh, nutritious food is **Broke the Mouth**. Their plate lunches include pesto pasta, taro and Hawaiian salads. Don't expect more than a takeout counter and a few picnic tables. Breakfast and lunch served. ~ 55 Mamo Street; 934-7670. BUDGET.

Elsie's Fountain should be listed under sightseeing attractions. A classic soda fountain complete with red swivel seats and formica

◀ *HIDDEN*

counter, it hasn't changed since the 1950s. Even the signs picturing the food are period pieces. Hamburgers cost $1.15! Tuna sandwiches are $.95! But a root beer float will set you back $1.50. I am not making this up. Stop by and see for yourself. No dinner served, sorry. ~ 339 Keawe Street; 935-8681. BUDGET.

You can dine or take out at **Café Pesto**, an appealing eatery located in the historic S. Hata Building. This downtown Hilo gathering place serves wood-fired pizza, calzone, risotto dishes and salads. ~ 308 Kamehameha Avenue; 969-6640. MODERATE.

It's hard to say whether **Lehua's Bar & Grill** is retro or ultramodern: There are elements of both in the decor. Located in the historic heart of Hilo, the dining room is decorated with old photos—memorabilia from the Hawaii of yore, and modern art. One thing is certain, the menu is as up-to-date as you'll find anywhere: The fresh fish and steak dishes are charbroiled and the house specialties include linguine with charbroiled chicken in a cilantro pesto sauce, stir-fried vegetables and Cajun fish burger. ~ 90 Kamehameha Avenue; 935-8055. MODERATE.

In Hilo you'll find many more good Asian restaurants than appealing American restaurants. For example, **Sachi's Gourmet**, a small café downtown, serves Japanese meals. Sachi cooks several *donburi*, *udon* and tempura dishes as well as several special seafood dishes. Open for breakfast, lunch and dinner. Closed Sunday morning and Monday evening. ~ 250 Keawe Street; 935-6255. MODERATE.

For Chinese food, **Mun Cheong Lau Chop Suey Restaurant** is the Orient's answer to the greasy spoon (greasy chopstick?) café. The place is as big as a barn and gaudily decorated with magenta walls and plastic lanterns. If you can get past the interior devastation, there's an ample menu listing numerous seafood, fowl, pork and rice dishes at chop suey prices. And in case of late-evening munchie attacks, Mun Cheong stays open until 10 p.m. Closed Tuesday. ~ 172 Kilauea Avenue; 935-3040. MODERATE.

Thailand and the Philippines are represented by **Reychel's**. Serving *phad thai* and traditional curries, it's open for lunch and dinner. Closed Sunday. ~ Hilo Shopping Center, Kilauea Street; 934-7426. BUDGET TO MODERATE.

At **K. K. Tei Restaurant** you can enjoy lunch or dinner while overlooking a lovely bonsai garden. The dining room offers a selection of traditional Japanese dishes. In addition to sukiyaki and tempura plates, the chefs prepare salmon, scallops and shrimp. After dining, stroll past the pagodas and arched bridges that ornament K. K.'s Japanese Garden. No lunch on Saturday and Sunday. ~ 1550 Kamehameha Avenue; 961-3791. MODERATE TO DELUXE.

Hilo boasts a very fine Japanese restaurant that combines excellent cooking with private dining. At **Restaurant Fuji** in the Hilo

Hotel, you can dine at the poolside lanai on delicious *teppanyaki* dishes or pass indoors to an attractive dining room. In addition to *wafu* steak, *dotenabe* and tempura dishes, there are several *teishoku* (complete dinner) choices served with chicken salad, vegetables and soup. Closed Monday. ~ 1550 Kamehameha Avenue; 961-3791. MODERATE TO DELUXE.

> Scene of a lively auction every morning, **Suisan Company Limited** is a great place to buy fresh fish. ~ 93 Lihiwai Street; 935-9349.

One of the island's finest restaurants is found, surprisingly enough, in an old bank building in downtown Hilo. **Roussel's** is the creation of two brothers who replaced fluorescent lights with brass chandeliers and linoleum with hardwood floors, then converted the vault into a dining area. Painted in contemporary pastel hues, Roussel's specializes in French/Creole cuisine, offering up soft-shell crab, shrimp and oyster gumbo, blackened mahimahi and trout amandine. No lunch on Saturday and Sunday. ~ 60 Keawe Street; 935-5111. MODERATE TO DELUXE.

Hilo's foremost steak-and-seafood restaurant is **Harrington's**, a waterfront dining room that is particularly popular with locals. Here you can dine in a congenial atmosphere to the strains of Hawaiian music in the background. Harrington's also has a lively bar scene and can be counted on for good food and a good time. ~ 135 Kalanianaole Street; 961-4966. MODERATE TO DELUXE.

GROCERIES

The island's largest city, Hilo has several supermarkets. Foremost are **Sure Save** in the Kaikoo Mall on Kilauea Avenue and **Sack-N-Save** at 2100 Kanoelehua Avenue in the Puainako Shopping Center.

Hilo hosts an excellent natural food outlet—**Abundant Life Natural Foods**. It contains healthy supplies of vitamins and juices, as well as a deli and fresh organic fruits and vegetables. ~ 292 Kamehameha Avenue; 935-7411.

Holsum/Oroweat Bakery Thrift Store offers fresh and day-old baked goods at unbeatable prices. Closed Sunday. ~ 302 Kamehameha Avenue; 935-2164.

SHOPPING

The most convenient way to shop in Hilo is at **Prince Kuhio Plaza**, a full-facility complex featuring everything from small crafts shops to swank boutiques to a sprawling department store. The Big Island's largest mall, it's a gathering place for local shoppers and a convenient spot for visitors. ~ Route 11 just outside town. But bargains and locally crafted products are probably what you're after. So it's a good idea to window-shop through the centers, checking out products and prices, then do your buying at smaller shops. For woodwork, just head across the street from Kaikoo Mall to **Dan DeLuz Woods**. The beautiful pieces are fashioned from banyan, sandalwood, *koa* and *milo*, all priced reasonably. The **DeLuz**, the craftspeople who own the shop, do all their carving in a back-room workshop. If you'd like a description of how the bowls are made, they're happy to provide an informal tour. ~ 760 Kilauea Avenue; 935-5587.

The Most Irresistible Shop in Hilo doesn't quite live up to its bold name but does create a strong attraction with jewelry, ceramics, books, toys and piñatas. ~ 110 Keawe Street; 935-9644.

For beach-reading materials, try **The Book Gallery**. This well-stocked shop has many popular titles. ~ 111 East Puainko Street, Prince Kuhio Plaza; 959-7744. If maps, guidebooks and volumes on Hawaiiana sound more inviting, **Basically Books** is an excellent choice. ~ 46 Waianuenue Avenue; 961-0144.

Mauna Kea Galleries specializes in Hawaiian and Polynesian art, antiques and artifacts. They have a selective but fascinating collection of ceramics, hula dolls, graphics and quilts. ~ 276 Keawe Street; 969-1184.

Following a similar theme, **Hana Hou** is a tiny shop filled with "vintage island treasures." Among those keepsakes are old Hawaiian song sheets, Matson menus and aloha shirts. ~ 38 Kalakaua Street; 935-4555.

Specializing in "distinct island wearables, bedding and gifts," **Sig Zane Designs** has its own designer line of island dresses and aloha shirts. ~ 122 Kamehameha Avenue; 935-7077.

If it's fine *koa* wood pieces you're after, **Big Island Woodworks Gallery** is waiting for you. They have a finely honed collection of bowls and decorative pices. ~ 308 Kamehameha Avenue #112; 961-0400.

NIGHTLIFE   The main scene centers around the big hotels along Banyan Drive. By far the best place is the Hawaii Naniloa Hotel. This luxury hotel has a nicely appointed nightclub, **The Crown Room**. The lounge usually books local groups, but every once in a while it imports a mainland band for special events. There's a cover charge and two-drink minimum. Then there is **Joli's Lounge**, which has nightly piano tunes. ~ 46 Waianuenue Avenue; 961-0144.

Harrington's hosts a Hawaiian guitarist on weekends. ~ 135 Kalanianaole Avenue; 961-4966.

The **Waioli Lounge** at the Hilo Hawaiian Hotel has live music nightly. Usually it's a contemporary duo. ~ 71 Banyan Drive; 935-9361.

Lehua's Bar & Grill features dancing to a live band on selected weekends. The sounds are contemporary rhythm and blues. ~ 90 Kamehameha Avenue; 935-8055.

BEACHES & PARKS   **KALAKAUA PARK** Located on the corner of busy Kinoole Street and Waianuenue Avenue, this pretty little park has a grand old banyan tree and a pleasant picnic area.

REED'S BAY BEACH PARK 🏊 Reed's Bay, a banyan-lined cove is a marvelous picnic spot. The bay is actually an arm of Hilo Bay, but unlike the larger body of water, Reed's Bay offers excellent swimming in smooth water (though an underwater spring keeps the water cold). ~ Located at the end of Banyan Drive.

ONEKAHAKAHA, KEALOHA AND LELEIWI COUNTY PARKS 🏊 None of these three parks have sand beaches, but all possess lava pools or other shallow places for swimming. They also have grassy plots and picnic areas, plus restrooms and showers. If you fish along these shores, chances are good you'll net *papio*, threadfin, mountain bass, mullet, big-eyed scad, mackerel scad, milkfish, bonefish, or goatfish. Kealoha Park offers good snorkeling, surfing, spear-fishing and throw-netting. ~ All three parks are located within five miles of Hilo, east along Kalanianaole Avenue.

RICHARDSON'S OCEAN PARK 🏊 This black-sand ◀ **HIDDEN** beach, south of Hilo Bay, is without doubt the finest beach in the area. From there you can see Mauna Kea hulking in the background. Coconut palms and ironwood trees fringe the beach, while a lava outcropping somewhat protects swimmers. The protected areas also make for good snorkeling. This is one of the best spots around Hilo for surfing as well as bodysurfing and bodyboarding. Winter break with right slides. Mornings and evenings are the prime times, but at all times beware of currents and riptides. Anglers try for *papio*, mountain bass, mullet, big-eyed scad, mackerel scad, milkfish, bonefish and goatfish. Facilities here include restrooms and showers; it's five miles to Hilo restaurants and markets. ~ Take Kalanianaole Street to within a quarter-mile of where the paved road ends; watch for the sign to Richardson Ocean Park. The beach is behind and to the right of the center; 935-3830.

▼▼▼▼▼▼▼▼▼▼▼
Hamakua Coast

Route 19, the Mamalahoa Highway, leads north from Hilo along the rainy, windswept Hamakua Coast. Planted in sugar and teeming with exotic plant life, this elevated coastline is as lushly overgrown as Hilo.

A softly rolling plateau that edges from the slopes of Mauna Kea to the sea, the region is cut by sharp canyons and deep gulches. Waterfalls cascade down emerald walls and tumbling streams lead to lava-rock beaches. Beautiful is too tame a term for this enchanting countryside. There are stands of eucalyptus, shadowy forests and misty fields of sugar cane. Plantation towns, filled with pastel-painted houses and adorned with flower gardens, lie along the route.

Several miles outside Hilo, follow the signs to the **Scenic Drive.** **SIGHTS** This old coast road winds past cane fields and shantytowns before rejoining the main highway. Alexander palms line the road. Watch for Onomea Bay: There you'll see a V-shaped rock formation where a sea arch collapsed in 1956.

You can also take in **Hawaii Tropical Botanical Garden**, an exotic nature preserve with streams, waterfalls, rugged coastline and over 2000 plant species. This jungle garden, edged by the Pacific and inhabited by shore birds and giant sea turtles, is a place of uncommon beauty. Closed Saturday and Sunday. Admission. ~ Five-mile marker on Scenic Drive, 964-5233.

Back on the main road, you'll soon come to a turnoff heading inland to **Akaka Falls State Park**. Don't bypass it! A short nature trail leads past bamboo groves, ferns, ti and orchids to Akaka Falls, which slide 420 feet down a sheer cliff face, and Kahuna Falls, 400 feet high. This 66-acre preserve is covered in a canopy of rainforest vegetation. There are birds of paradise, azaleas and giant philodendrons whose leaves measure as much as two feet.

Countless gulches ribbon the landscape between Hilo and Honokaa. For a unique tour, take the road from Hakalau that **HIDDEN ►** winds down to **Hakalau Gulch**. Literally choked with vegetation, this gorge extends to a small beach. Towering above the gulch is the highway bridge.

Another side road several miles north corkscrews down to **Laupahoehoe Point**, a hauntingly beautiful peninsula from which 24 students and teachers were swept by the 1946 tidal wave. Here gently curving palm trees and spreading lawns contrast with the lash of the surf.

The plantation town of **Paauilo** offers a glimpse of vintage Hawaii: decaying storefronts and tinroof cottages. Then it's on to Honokaa, the world center of macadamia nut growing. The **Hawaiian Holiday Macadamia Nut Factory** is open, but don't anticipate a wildly informative visit. This establishment concentrates more on selling macadamia products to tourists. ~ 775-7743.

HIDDEN ► I'd bypass the place and head out Route 240 to **Waipio Valley**, the islands's largest valley. One mile wide and six miles long, this luxurious canyon, sparsely populated today, once supported thousands of Hawaiians. Agriculturally bountiful, Waipio is also rich in history. Here in 1780 Kamehameha the Great acknowledged the war god who would propel him to victory. At that time the valley, which has been inhabited for over 1000 years, supported a population of about 4000 Hawaiians. It also looms large in island mythology. Wakea, the Zeus of Hawaii, loved the valley, as did two other members of the Polynesian pantheon, Kane and Kanaloa. The god Lono came here seeking a wife and Maui himself is said to have died in the Waipio Valley.

Taro patches and tumbledown cottages still dot the valley. From the lookout point at road's end, a jeep trail drops sharply into Waipio. Explorers can hike down or take an hour-and-a-half four-

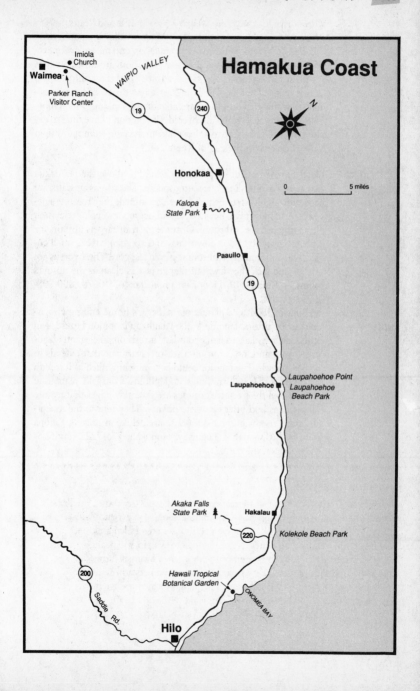

Hamakua Coast

Imiola Church

WAIPIO VALLEY

Waimea

Parker Ranch Visitor Center

(19)

(240)

N

0   5 miles

Honokaa

Kalopa State Park

Paauilo

(19)

Laupahoehoe Point
Laupahoehoe Beach Park

Laupahoehoe

Akaka Falls State Park   **Hakalau**

(220)   *Kolekole Beach Park*

(200)

Hawaii Tropical Botanical Garden

ONOMEA BAY

Saddle Rd.

Hilo

wheel-drive tour with the **Waipio Valley Shuttle and Tours**. ~ 775-7121. Another agency with tours is **Waipio Valley Wagon Tour**. ~ 775-9518. Both tours travel several miles up into the valley for eye-boggling views of 1200-foot Hiilawe Falls. Both are closed Sunday.

Eden for explorers, the valley territory and the rainforest is a riot of tropical colors. The homes of a few dozen dedicated residents dot the area and there are abandoned buildings, swimming holes and cascades to be discovered. (If you don't have time to explore the valley, be sure to at least take in the vista from the **Waipio Valley Lookout** at the end of Route 240.)

LODGING   **Hotel Honokaa Club**, perched on a hillside above the Hamakua Coast, has a boardinghouse atmosphere. The rooms upstairs are kept thoroughly scrubbed and freshly painted; they're quite adequate. A modest price buys a splendid ocean view, color television plus a tiny private bathroom. Or trade the trim carpets upstairs for a plain hardwood floor downstairs and you can have a small cubicle with community bathroom at even less cost. These rooms are smaller and lack the view, but they're just as clean as the upstairs rooms. ~ Route 240, Honokaa; phone/fax 775-0678, 800-808-0678. BUDGET.

HIDDEN ►   Built in 1921 as a plantation manager's house and now registered as an historic landmark, the **Paauhau Plantation House** is an extraordinary place to hang your hat. It rests on an elegantly landscaped plot and looks out on a sea of sugar cane that extends to the ocean itself. The interior could be a museum, filled as it is with fine antiques, *koa* furnishings and photos from old plantation days. Within the five-acre grounds are several cottages that feature full kitchens and offer complete privacy. They rent in the moderate range; rooms in the main house are deluxe in price. ~ Kalopa Road, off Mamalahoa Highway, Honokaa; 775-7222, fax 775-7223. MODERATE TO DELUXE.

HIGHRISE HOTEL

The **Waipio Treehouse Waterfall Retreat** really does have a treehouse. Smaller than the two cottages on the property, this unique lodging experience will take you 30 feet off the ground. All three guesthouses are nestled amid the lush foliage and undulating waterfalls of the remote Waipio Valley and enjoy spectacular views. Each is equipped with kitchen facilities (bring your own food, this retreat is *very* secluded). Guests immerse themselves in Japanese hot tubs and then fall prey to the hands of the massage therapist. Guided hiking and horseback eco-tours add to the adventure. ~ P.O. Box 5086, Honokaa; phone/fax 775-7160. ULTRA-DELUXE.

One of the most primitive, secluded and unusual lodgings any-where in the islands is Tom Araki's five-room **Waipio Hotel**. Set ◀ HIDDEN deep in the luxurious Waipio Valley, this idyllic retreat is sur-rounded by waterfalls, sharp cliffs and a black-sand beach. Don't expect too many amenities here in Eden—gas, electricity and meal service are unheard of and the rooms are small and simple. But there are two kitchens available as well as a landscape filled with orchards. Accessible only by four-wheel drive or shuttle, it's the only commercial facility in an isolated and extraordinarily beauti-ful valley. The price of admission to paradise? A pittance. ~ For reservations write to 25 Malana Place, Hilo, HI 96720 or call 775-0368. BUDGET.

Honokaa offers a convenient stop for those making a day-trip be- **DINING** tween Hilo and Kona. The **Hotel Honokaa Club** has a banquet-sized dining room that's large enough to play hockey on. The last time I was there, on a wet and miserable day, it was cold enough inside to do just that. So don't expect a cozy hideaway. At least the food is hot, and priced well, too. The menu is an interesting mix of Japanese and American food. ~ Route 240, Honokaa; 775-0678. MODERATE.

Jolene's Kau Kau Korner has plate lunches, burgers and sand-wiches during daylight hours. At dinner, they move on to mahi-mahi, shrimp and vegetable tempura, stir-fry beef and grilled chicken with pineapple. It's a simple café but reasonably priced. ~ 45-3625 Mamane Street, Honokaa; 775-9498. BUDGET.

Your best chance is **Ishigo's General Store**. Located in Honomu on **GROCERIES** the road to Akaka Falls, Ishigo's has a limited stock, but you may find what you need. ~ 963-6128. If not, try **Earl's Mini Mart** on Route 240 in Honokaa. ~ 775-9330.

Several small shops between Hilo and Waimea are worth a visit. **SHOPPING** The **Akaka Falls Flea Market**, on the road to Akaka Falls, is set in an old plantation store. In addition to aloha wear, it features shell jewelry as well as books and calendars. ~ 963-6171.

A little farther up that same road in Honomu, you'll happen upon **Hawaii's Artist Ohana**. Here is a wide array of work by local artists and craftspeople. Of particular note are photographs of a volcano erupting on the Big Island. ~ 963-5467.

Kamaaina Woods, in Honokaa on Lehua Street (the road to the macadamia nut factory) has a splendid assortment of handmade bowls and decorations. With items fashioned from *milo*, mango and *koa*, this shop is practically a museum. And if you are inter-ested in learning more about these woods, you can view the fac-tory through the window. ~ 775-7722.

The falsefront town of Honokaa also has a **Hawaiian Shop**, which is positively packed with Polynesian chatchkas. ~ Mamane Street.

Right next door is **Poi Pounder**, equally as crowded with hand-carved museum replicas—Maori statuary, masks from New Guinea and Western-style mermaids. ~ Mamane Street.

The **Waipio Valley Artworks**, located near the Waipio Valley Lookout, is also cluttered with woodcarvings. Made from several different woods, some of these creations are extremely beautiful. This shop also features paintings, ceramics and other locally crafted items. ~ Route 240; 775-0958.

BEACHES & PARKS

KOLEKOLE BEACH PARK 🏖️ 🏕️ Located at the mouth of a wide gulch lush with tropical vegetation, this comfortable park has a large and pleasant grassy area. A stream and waterfall tumble through the park down to the rocky, surf-torn shore. The sandy beach and natural beauty of the place make it very popular among local residents. You can swim in the stream but the ocean here is forbiddingly rough. Threadfin, *menpachi*, *papio* and *ulua* are the common catches. Facilities consist of a picnic area, restrooms and electrical hookups; there is no drinking water. It's one mile to markets and restaurants in Honomu. ~ Located just off Mamalahoa Highway (Route 19) about 12 miles northwest of Hilo.

▲ Tent and trailer; $1 per night. County permit required.

LAUPAHOEHOE BEACH PARK 🏖️ 🎣 🏊 🏕️ Set on a low-lying peninsula that was inundated by the 1946 tidal wave, this hauntingly beautiful park is still lashed by heavy surf. A precipitous *pali* and lava-strewn shoreline surround the area. Swimming, snorkeling and surfing are good at times, but usually very dangerous. You can fish for *ulua*, *papio*, *menpachi* and *moi*. Facilities include a picnic area, restrooms, showers and electrical hookups. It's at least 15 miles to restaurants or markets in Honokaa, so bring a lunch. ~ One mile off Route 19 down a well-marked twisting road, about 27 miles northwest of Hilo.

▲ Tent and trailer camping permitted; $1 per night. County permit required.

KALOPA STATE PARK 🚶 A wooded retreat set in the mountains above the Hamakua Coast, this 615-acre park has both untouched expanses ripe for exploring and several beautifully landscaped acres. Ranging from 2000 to 2500 feet elevation, it's a great place for hiking or just for escaping. There are picnic areas, restrooms, showers and cabins; it's about five miles to markets and restaurants in Honokaa. ~ Take Route 19 southeast from Honokaa for about three miles. A well-marked paved road leads from the highway another two miles to the park.

▲ Tent camping is permitted and cabins are also available; call 933-4200 for reservations.

Just 15 miles from the tablelands of Honokaa and ten miles from the Kohala Coast, at an elevation of 2670 feet, sits Waimea. Covered with rolling grassland and bounded by towering mountains, Waimea (also called Kamuela) is cowboy country. Here *paniolos*, Hawaiian cowboys, ride the range on one of the world's largest independently owned cattle ranches. Founded by John Palmer Parker, an adventurous sailor who jumped ship in 1809, the Parker Ranch extends from sea level to over 9000 feet.

This cool rustic countryside, rare in a tropical retreat like Hawaii, is dotted with carpenter's Gothic houses and adorned with stables and picket fences. There are Victorian buildings and deep green trees, cattle grazing in the meadows and horses edging along the fence line.

SIGHTS

The museum at **Parker Ranch Visitors Center** presents a history of the Parker family that will carry you back 140 years with its displays of Victorian-era furniture and clothing. In addition to the artifacts and family momentos, there is a movie that tells the story of the Parker family from its earliest days to the present. Admission. ~ 885-7655.

And at the **Historic Parker Ranch Homes** you can view the family's original 1840s-era ranch house and an adjoining century-old home (which doubles as a museum filled with extraordinary French Impressionist artwork). While the original home was built of *koa* and contains a collection of antique calabashes, the latter-day estate boasts lofty ceilings, glass chandeliers and walls decorated with Renoirs, Chagalls and Pissarros. ~ Mamalahoa Highway, one-half mile west of town.

Another fine display is at the **Kamuela Museum**. Founded by J. P. Parker's great-great-granddaughter, this private collection of everything from Royal Hawaiian artifacts to moon-flight relics is fascinating, if poorly organized. Admission. ~ Junction of Kawaihae Road and Kohala Mountain Road; 885-4724.

For a splendid example of *koa* woodworking, visit **Imiola Congregational Church** on the east side of town. Built in 1857, this clapboard church has an interior fashioned entirely from the native timber. ~ Mamalahoa Highway; 885-4987.

LODGING

Set amid the Kohala Mountains in the cowboy town of Waimea are two hotels, both within walking distance of local markets and restaurants. **Waimea Country Lodge**, a modern multi-unit motel, is owned by John Parker's son. Guest rooms are large, carpeted and equipped with telephones, shower-tub combinations and color televisions; some have small kitchenettes. The ceilings are exposed beam; the furniture is knotty pine. ~ 65-1210 Lindsey Road, Waimea; 885-4100, 800-272-5275, fax 885-6711. MODERATE.

Kamuela Inn, a neighbor just down the street, has modest one- and two-room units, and suites in the new wing. These are clean and bright with private baths. Many of the 31 units are equipped with a TV and some have refrigerators. Guests are served a continental breakfast. ~ Kawaihae Road, Waimea; 885-4243, fax 885-8857. MODERATE TO DELUXE.

Combining style with personalized service, **Hawaii's Best Bed & Breakfasts** specializes in small, upscale bed-and-breakfast accommodations on all the islands. With more than 100 places to choose from, it places guests in a variety of privately owned facilities; most are deluxe in price. The unit I saw was a woodframe cottage that shared over an acre of land with the owner's house. Set in Waimea beside a stream and surrounded by trees and lofty green hills, it included a kitchen and sitting area. ~ P.O. Box 563, Kamuela 96743; 885-4550, 800-262-9912.

More than 55,000 cattle roam Parker Ranch's sprawling 225,000-acre domain.

DINING

Waimea is short on short-order restaurants. With all the fine-dining possibilities here there is not much in the way of inexpensive ethnic restaurants. You will find two in Waimea Center (Mamalahoa Highway): **Great Wall Chopsui** has steam-tray Chinese food. Closed Wednesday. ~ 885-7252. BUDGET. **Yong's Kalbi** serves Korean dishes. Closed Monday. ~ 885-8440. BUDGET.

There's a booth that seats 14 people at **Hawaiian Style Cafe**, but you'll probably be more comfortable at the U-shaped counter or a small table. You can settle in for a hearty island breakfast or a lunch that varies from sautéed mahimahi to tripe stew. There are hamburgers and sandwiches plus a few Asian dishes like *kalbi* and teriyaki steak. No dinner. Closed Saturday. ~ Kawaihae Road; 885-4295. BUDGET.

HIDDEN ▶ **Mean Cuisine** is where you'll find local folks, not tourists. It's a comfortable place offering home-style cooking. At lunch there are soups and sandwiches plus entrées like vegetarian lasagna, curry dishes and prime rib. At dinner, the ever-changing menu might feature pasta with clam sauce, chicken creole, vegetable enchiladas, or roast turkey and gravy. No dinner on Sunday. ~ Opelo Plaza, Kawaihae Road; 885-6325. MODERATE.

If you're hankering for a steak up here in cowboy country, then ride on in to **Paniolo Country Inn**. There are branding irons on the walls and sirloins on the skillet. The booths are made of knotty pine and dishes have names like "Lone Ranger" and "bucking bronco." You can order barbecued chicken, baby back ribs or a "south of the border" special. ~ Kawaihae Road; 885-4377. MODERATE.

One of my favorite Waimea dining spots is the **Edelweiss** restaurant, a cozy club with a knockout interior design. The entire place was fashioned by a master carpenter who inlaid *sugi* pine, *koa* and silver oak with the precision of a stonemason. Run by a German chef who gained his knowledge at prestigious addresses like Maui's plush Kapalua Bay Hotel, Edelweiss is a gourmet's delight. The dinner menu includes wienerschnitzel, roast duck, roast pork with sauerkraut and a house specialty—sautéed veal, lamb, beef and bacon with *pfifferling*. For lunch there is bratwurst and sauerkraut, turkey sandwiches, sautéed chicken breast and club sandwiches. Closed Sunday and Monday and closed during September. ~ Kawaihae Road; 885-6800. MODERATE TO DELUXE.

Waimea's contribution to Hawaii regional cuisine is **Merriman's**, a very highly regarded restaurant that has received national attention. The interior follows a colorful neo-tropical theme and the menu is tailored to what is fresh and local. Since the locale is not simply Hawaii, but upcountry Hawaii, the cuisine combines the seashore and the cattle ranch. You might find fresh fish with spicy *lilikoi* sauce, wok-charred *ahi*, steak with *kiawe*-smoked tomato sauce or veal sautéed with macadamia nuts. Highly recommended. No lunch Saturday and Sunday. ~ Opelo Plaza, Kawaihae Road; 885-6822. DELUXE.

Island Bistro creates a casual atmosphere with blond wood furniture and overhead fan. It also promises Hawaii regional cuisine and delivers in the form of wok-seared tenderloin of beef, Thai marinated chicken and *nori* sautéed salmon. My first choice in this category is Merriman's, to which there is no comparison. But if Merriman's is booked, or should the spirit move you . . . Lunch Monday through Friday. ~ Kawaihae Road; 885-1222. DELUXE.

GROCERIES

Sure Save Super Market, located in Waimea at the Parker Ranch Shopping Center, is one of only two large supermarkets along this route. Open Monday through Saturday 7 a.m. to 9 p.m. and Sunday 7 a.m. to 8 p.m. ~ 885-7345. The other one is **K.T.A. Super Store,** open daily from 7 a.m. to 11 p.m. ~ Mamalahoa Highway, Waimea; 885-8866.

Kona Healthways has a large supply of vitamins, baked goods, spices, cosmetics and so on. ~ Waimea Center, Waimea; 885-6775.

If you're looking for meat products, definitely check out the **Kamuela Meat Market.** The butchers sell delicious beef fresh from the ranch, and at good prices. Closed Sunday. ~ Parker Ranch Center; 885-4601.

SHOPPING

Parker Ranch Center and **Waimea Center** are *the* shopping complexes in Waimea's cattle country. These modern centers feature sporting goods stores, boutiques, book shops and more. If you're like me and enjoy browsing through stores in order to capture the flavor of a place, you'll find both malls located in the center of Waimea.

Most-favored-store status in Parker Ranch Center goes to **Collectibles**. Small as it is, this shop has Asian art, batik dresses and fine Hawaiian *koa* pieces. They also offer photographs, oil paintings and pen-and-ink drawings of the islands. ~ 885-0536.

Parker Square (Waimea) specializes in "distinguished shops." Particularly recommended here is the **Gallery of Great Things**, a store that fulfills the promise of its name. ~ 885-7706.

In keeping with Waimea's *paniolo* culture, **Kamuela Traders** supplies boots, shirts, hats and even belt buckles to genuine cowboys and wannabe buckaroos alike. It's a far cry from what you'll see in the shops at the oceanfront resorts. ~ Kawaihae Road; 885-2767.

NIGHTLIFE   Pop in at the **Bree Garden** on a weekend and you might just find guests belting out their favorite karaoke hits or dancing to a live band. ~ Route 19, behind the Texaco gas station; 885-8849.

The 480-seat **Kahilu Theatre** offers dance performances, concerts, plays and current movies. ~ Parker Ranch Center; 885-6017.

▼▼▼▼▼▼▼▼▼
Kohala Coast

Stretching from the northern boundary of Kona to the northwestern tip of the Big Island are the districts of South and North Kohala. During the past two decades South Kohala, which includes some of the island's prettiest beaches, has seen the building of one deluxe resort after another. Farther north, where Kohala Mountain forms a 5000-foot-high spine, the territory remains much as it has for decades.

As the Kaahumanu Highway (Route 19) gives way to the northerly Akoni Pule Highway (Route 270), the landscape eventually changes from dry and barren to tropical and luxurious.

All along the Kaahumanu Highway, there's a type of graffiti unique to the Big Island. Setting white coral atop black lava, and vice versa, ingenious residents have spelled out their names and messages.

Geologically, this was the section of the island that first rose from the sea. Later, as the volcanoes that formed Kohala Mountain became extinct, the region evolved into a center of historical importance.

Kamehameha I was born and raised along this wind-blasted coastline and it was here that he initially consolidated his power base. The region is filled with ancient *heiaus* as well as more recent cemeteries that date to the era when sugar plantations dominated the local economy.

Exploring this region from Kailua-Kona you will find that Kaahumanu Highway cuts across a broad swath of lava-crusted country. There are views of Maui to the north, Mauna Kea to the east and Hualalai to the south.

SIGHTS   For evidence of Kohala's historic significance you need look no further than Waikoloa. While the area is now heavily developed with tourist resorts, it is also the site of the **Waikoloa Petroglyph Field**.

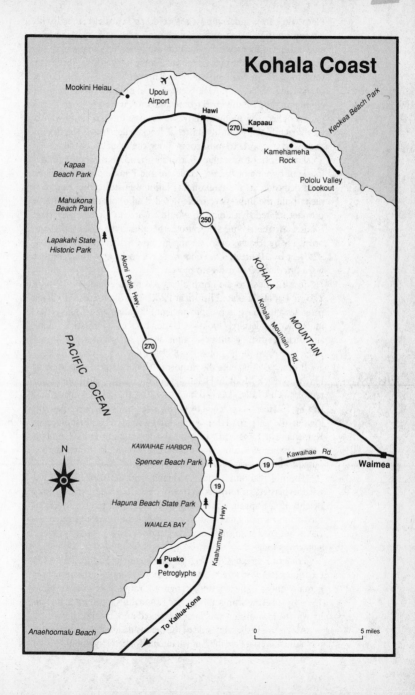

Kohala Coast

Mookini Heiau

Upolu Airport

Hawi

Kapaau 270

Keokea Beach Park

Kamehameha Rock

Kapaa Beach Park

Pololu Valley Lookout

Mahukona Beach Park

250

Lapakahi State Historic Park

KOHALA MOUNTAIN

Akoni Pule Hwy.

Kohala Mountain Rd.

PACIFIC OCEAN

270

N

KAWAIHAE HARBOR

Kawaihae Rd.

Spencer Beach Park

19

Waimea

19

Hapuna Beach State Park

WAIALEA BAY

Kaahumanu Hwy.

Puako

Petroglyphs

Anaehoomalu Beach

To Kailua-Kona

0   5 miles

Here you can wander amidst a forbidding lava field etched with ancient symbols. The contrast, with a modern golf course on one side and primitive rock carvings on the other, is ironic to say the least. The path to the petroglyphs is .3-mile in length and begins at the Kings' Shops Mall in Waikoloa. This rough lava course is part of the King's Trail, a mid-19th century trail built for horseback riders making the 32-mile trip from Kailua to Puako.

From here, the highway moves north past the luxurious Mauna Kea Beach Hotel. Built by Laurence Rockefeller, it was the first of the five-star resorts to mushroom along the Kohala coastline.

The harbor of Kawaihae, one of the island's busiest ports, is the locale of two major *heiaus*, Mailekini and Puukohola, which have been dedicated as the **Puukohola National Historic Site**. Kamehameha built the impressive triple-tiered Puukohola in 1791 after a prophet related that doing so would ensure his victory over rival islands. At the temple dedication, the ambitious chief aided the prophecy by treacherously slaying his principal enemy. Measuring 224 feet by 100 feet, it was built of lava rocks and boulders that were fitted together using no mortar.

Just 12 miles to the north along Akoni Pule Highway (Route 270) is **Lapakahi State Historical Park**, where a preserved village provides a unique glimpse into ancient Hawaiian ways. This is definitely worth a leisurely look-see. Dating back 600 years, this unique site includes fishing shrines, canoe sheds, house sites and burial plots (not open to the public). ~ 889-5566.

If time permits, take the turnoff to Upolu Airport (just west of Hawi) to reach **Mookini Heiau**, one of the island's most important temples. This holy place—dating to 480 A.D. and measuring 250 feet by 130 feet—is reached by taking a left at the airport, then following the dirt road for a mile-and-a-half. The **Birthplace of Kamehameha I**, marked with a plaque, lies one-third mile (and two gates) farther west along the same road. The boulders here are reputed to be the original birthstones.

HIDDEN ▶

The old plantation town of **Hawi**, with its trim houses and weatherblasted storefronts, harkens back to an earlier era. Like neighboring **Kapaau**, it is showing a few signs of refurbishment in the form of small galleries and local shops. Both are charming enclaves adorned with small churches and relics from the days when sugar was king.

Pride of Kapaau is the original **Kamehameha Statue**, a nine-ton creation cast in bronze. The more famous Honolulu monument is actually only a replica of this gilt figure. Crafted in Florence around 1879 by an American sculptor, the original disappeared at sea on its way to Hawaii but was later recovered and installed here.

Along this lush, rainy side of the peninsula are taro patches and pandanus forests. Past the **Kamehameha Rock** (a large boulder that the mighty conqueror reputedly carried from the sea), the road ends at **Pololu Valley Lookout**. The view here overlooking Pololu Valley extends along the monumental cliffs that guard Hawaii's north coast.

From this cul-de-sac you must backtrack to Hawi, where you can climb the back of **Kohala Mountain** along Route 250 (Kohala Mountain Road), completing a loop tour of North Kohala. Rising to 3564 feet, the road rolls through cactus-studded range country and offers startling views down steep volcanic slopes to the sea. En route are cattle ranches, stands of Norfolk pine and eucalyptus, and curving countryside covered with sweet grasses and wildflowers.

LODGING

In the small rustic town of Hawi near Hawaii's northwestern tip, the **Kohala Village Inn** and an adjacent restaurant are the hottest spots around. But there's still privacy and quiet aplenty out back in the sleeping quarters. Rooms in this refurbished establishment feature tinroofs and handsome hardwood floors, and face a small courtyard. The place is tidy, if less than elegant. There are also rooms in an adjacent building. ~ 889-0419. BUDGET.

You might try your luck down the road in Kapaau at the **Kohala Club Hotel**. I hope you fare better than I did. All I could discover was that the landlady rents rooms in these tinroof clapboard buildings mostly to local folks and doesn't talk to travel writers. ~ Route 270, Kapaau; 889-6793. MODERATE.

Waikoloa Village is a collection of townhouse-style condos on the lower slopes of Mauna Kea. Located inland from the South Kohala coast, Waikoloa is a self-contained village with store, post office, pool, restaurant, tennis courts, golf course and riding stables. ~ For condominium rentals, call 329-5300, 800-929-7667 or fax 329-8102. MODERATE TO DELUXE.

✔ CHECK THESE OUT—UNIQUE LODGING

- *Budget:* Unwind at **Kalani Honua Culture Center**, a New Age retreat that rests on 20 acres above a black-sand beach. *page 212*
- *Moderate:* Check in to the **Keauhou Beach Hotel**, then check out the grounds, which include archaeological sites, tidepools and an ancient *heiau. page 184*
- *Deluxe:* Stay near the the volcano at **Kilauea Lodge**, where the quilts and fireplace make your mountain abode cozy and snug. *page 208*
- *Ultra-deluxe:* Settle into a thatch-roof *hale* on a remote beach at the exclusive **Kona Village Resort**. *page 184*

Budget: under $50 Moderate: $50–$90 Deluxe: $90–$120 Ultra-deluxe: over $120

For years the Kohala district was a placid region strewn with lava and dotted by several pearly beaches. A single resort stood along its virgin coastline. Today it's one of the fastest developing spots in Hawaii. The **Royal Waikoloan**, a sprawling 550-unit resort, now stands along Anaehoomalu Beach. ~ Kaahumanu Highway, Waikoloa; 885-6789, 800-462-6262, fax 885-7852. DELUXE TO ULTRA-DELUXE.

Several miles north, the **Mauna Lani Bay Hotel**, a 3200-acre resort, rests on another white-sand beach. Designed in the shape of an arrowhead and boasting 354 rooms, this luxurious facility offers two golf courses, ten tennis courts and seven restaurants, several of which are award-winners. With brilliant green gardens set against black lava, the landscape combines curving lawns and palm-ringed fishponds. Each guest room is spaciously laid out and designed in a pastel motif. ~ 68-1400 Mauna Lani Drive, Kawaihae; 885-6622, 800-367-2323, fax 885-1484. ULTRA-DELUXE.

The sprawling **Hapuna Beach Prince Hotel** is the sister resort of the illustrious Mauna Kea Beach Hotel. The posh Hapuna features the same beautifully landscaped grounds and also offers two golf courses, tennis courts and its own white-sand beach. The 350 rooms are decorated in soothing shades of peach and beige, and all have large lanais and ocean views. ~ 62-100 Kaunaoa Drive, Kawaihae; 880-1111, 800-882-6060, fax 880-4162. ULTRA-DELUXE.

DINING

Outside the expensive resorts, you'll find very few restaurants along Hawaii's northwestern shore. Sailors say that any port is good in a storm, and on such a sparsely settled coast any restaurant is probably worth heading for.

If you cast anchor in the town of Kawaihae, consider Café Pesto. Pizza is the specialty at this simple café. But you'll also find linguini marinara, fettuccine al pesto, fresh fish and even a Cajun shrimp dish. ~ Kawaihae Center; 882-1071. BUDGET.

The food is Mexican but the theme is surfing at **Tres Hombres Beach Grill**, located in the same complex. There is a great display of surfing memorabilia and some of the bar counters are even fashioned from surfboards. ~ 882-1031. MODERATE.

For very inexpensive food, try the **Blue Dolphin Restaurant**. This takeout stand has a small dining pavilion in back. There are plate lunches and sandwiches and full dinners. Closed Sunday. ~ Across from Kawaihae Harbor; 882-7771. BUDGET TO MODERATE.

Up near Kohala's northern tip, in the timeworn town of Hawi, is the **Bamboo Restaurant**. Located in the 80-year-old general store, this restaurant is decorated with tropical plants and deep wicker chairs. The menu offers a mix of Pacific regional and "local style" cuisine and includes such items as coconut clam chowder, Thai broiled prawns and grilled fresh island fish with a variety of Thai sauces. All meats and produce served are locally grown. Closed Monday. ~ Akoni Pule Highway; 889-5555. BUDGET TO MODERATE.

For a taste of funky, traditional Hawaii there's **The Soda Fountain**. Set in a tinroof plantation building with bare walls and plastic tablecloths, it serves breakfast, lunch and dinner at super low prices. ~ Just off Akoni Pule Highway about one mile east of Hawi; 889-0208. BUDGET.   ◄ HIDDEN

A little farther along, you'll find **Tropical Dreams Ice Cream**, where the owners create homemade exotic flavored ice creams like mango and lychee. ~ Akoni Pule Highway, Kapaau; 889-0077.

Nearby, across the street from the King Kamehameha statue, is **Don's Family Deli**. It serves homemade soups, quiches, sandwiches, vegetarian dishes, fresh fruit smoothies and cappuccinos until 6 p.m. ~ Akoni Pule Highway, Kapaau; 889-5822. BUDGET.

Generally, in outlying areas like the Kohala Peninsula, you'll find that although the restaurants are few and simple, they have a homey atmosphere about them that can never be captured in crowded urban areas. As I'm sure you're well aware, this fact sometimes makes dining in the outback almost as grand an adventure as hiking or camping.

With all the development that's been occurring along the Kohala Coast, it seems inevitable that gourmet restaurants would become an important part of the landscape. Thus far few independent dining rooms have opened; most are connected with one of the several resorts now dotting the shoreline.

For the ultimate luncheon buffet, try **The Terrace** at the Mauna Kea Beach Hotel. This hotel, built on the Kohala coast by Laurence Rockefeller, is famous for its fabulous feasts. Every afternoon the staff spreads out assorted cold cuts and salads, plus steaming dishes such as hot sausages with sauerkraut and chicken paella, and a dessert table that resembles the window of a Parisian *patisserie*. The tab will be high, but this bounteous meal could be all you eat for the entire day. In fact, you may want to skip breakfast if you plan on lunching here. ~ Kaahumanu Highway, Kawaihae; 882-7222. DELUXE.

The Mauna Lani Bay Hotel (68-1400 Mauna Lani Drive, Kawaihae) hosts some well-known, formal and very expensive restaurants. The **Bay Terrace**, serving three meals a day, features an everchanging dinner menu. The offerings may include fresh grilled salmon in an asparagus sauce or mahimahi with feta cheese. Beef dishes include prime rib with a spicy horseradish sauce and Black Angus steak. ~ 885-6622. ULTRA-DELUXE.

Also located at the Mauna Lani Bay Hotel is the **Canoe House**, one of the Big Island's most highly regarded dining rooms. Specializing in Pacific Rim cuisine and offering spectacular sunsets as an appetizer, it delivers fine food and a fine time. The menu, which changes frequently, is a creative mix of island and Asian dishes. Dinner only. ~ 885-6622. ULTRA-DELUXE.

At the Royal Waikoloan (Kaahumanu Highway, Waikoloa; 885-6789) you have two choices in dining. The wood-paneled **Tiara Room** serves French-Polynesian cuisine. Closed Sunday and Wednesday. ~ DELUXE. The **Royal Terrace** features an island-style menu. ~ MODERATE.

GROCERIES   On the western side of the island, there are several stores on the Kohala peninsula. Between Kawaihae and Kailua is one store in Puako, **Puako General Store**, with a small collection of groceries and dry goods. ~ 7 Puako Beach Drive; 882-7500.

K. Takata Store is an old market with an ample stock of groceries. It's the best place to shop north of Kailua. Closed Sunday afternoon. ~ Route 27, between Hawi and Kapaau; 889-5261.

A. Arakaki Store is conveniently located for campers and picnickers headed out to Pololu Valley. ~ Route 270, Halaula; 889-5262.

SHOPPING   Shopping in Kohala was once a matter of uncovering family-owned crafts shops in tiny towns. Now that it has become a major resort area, you can also browse at designer stores in several top-flight hotels. Simply drive along Akoni Pule Highway between Kailua and the Kohala Peninsula; you'll encounter, from south to north, the **Royal Waikoloan**, **Hilton Waikoloa Village**, **Mauna Lani Bay Hotel** and the **Mauna Kea Beach Hotel**. Each of these large resort complexes features an array of boutiques, knickknack shops, jewelers, sundries and other outlets.

Also consider the **Kings' Shops** in Waikoloa. Set on the road leading in to the Waikoloa resort complex, this mall contains clothing stores, a sundries shop and several other promising enterprises.

The diminutive town of Hawi, another of the island's clapboard plantation towns, hosts several artist shops. **Hawaiian Moon** has a marvelous little collection of island clothes, keepsakes and knickknacks. ~ Akoni Pule Highway; 889-0880. Another lunar landing place just down the road, **Sugar Moon** is a ceramics shop with beautifully crafted works in clay. ~ Akoni Pule Highway; 889-0994.

Farther along Akoni Pule Highway, in the falsefront town of Kapaau, you'll find **Ackerman Galleries**. Divided into two different stores on opposite sides of the street, Ackerman's features fine art in one location and crafts items in the other. ~ 889-5971.

NIGHTLIFE   Night owls along the Kohala Coast roost at one of four resort hotels. The Mauna Kea Beach Hotel has a Hawaiian band at **The Terrace** and features popular dance music in the **Batik Room**. ~ Kaahumanu Highway, Kawaihae; 882-7222.

The **Honu Bar** at the Mauna Lani Bay Hotel (68-1400 Mauna Lani Drive, Kawaihae) swings to life each night with a live jazz band. Guests may choose to dance the night away in this elegant establishment or engage in pleasant conversation over a drink or two. Some guests, however, may prefer a game of chess, pool or backgammon. ~ 885-6622.

Also at the Mauna Lani Bay Hotel there's a sleek rendezvous called "**the bar,**" which hosts a jazz band nightly. At other places in this spacious resort, you can also dance, listen to Hawaiian music or imbibe in a lovely, open-air setting. ~ 885-6622.

Up in Kawaihae, there is the **Tres Hombres Beach Grill**, where you can enjoy the original collection of surfing memorabilia that decorates the place. ~ Kawaihae Center, Kawaihae; 882-1031.

The night scene at the **Royal Waikoloan** centers around several watering holes that offer a variety of diversions ranging from ocean views to live bands to Polynesian revues. ~ Kaahumanu Highway, Waikoloa; 885-6789.

At the Hilton-Waikoloa Village, the **Second Floor** features dancing to deejay music every night of the week. ~ 69-425 Waikoloa Beach Drive, Kamuela; 885-1234.

The **Lobby Lounge** at the Orchid at Mauna Lani hosts a classic guitarist Tuesday through Thursday, and a pianist Friday through Saturday. ~ 1 North Kaniku Drive; 885-2000.

For Hawaiian music, try the **Bamboo Restaurant** on Friday and Saturday nights. They also have karaoke on Thursday. ~ Akoni Pule Highway, Hawi; 889-5555.

ANAEHOOMALU BEACH An enchanting area, this is one of the island's most beautiful beaches. There are palm trees, a luxurious lagoon and a long crescent of white sand. Turn from the sea and take in the gorgeous mountain scenery. Or explore the nearby petroglyph field and archaeological ruins. This beach is very popular and often crowded since it's fronted by a major resort complex. Swimming is excellent along this partially protected shore. Snorkeling is good for beginners but it lacks the scenic diversity elsewhere. Mullet, threadfin, big-eyed scad, bonefish and *papio* are among the usual catches here. Facilities include picnic tables, restrooms and showers; there are restaurants in the adjacent Royal Waikoloan. ~ Located a half-mile off Kaahumanu Highway, about 25 miles north of Kailua near the 76-mile marker.

BEACHES & PARKS

"69" BEACH OR WAIALEA BAY No, it's not what you might think. This lovely beach is named for a nearby highway marker rather than for licentious beach parties. The white-sand shoreline extends several hundred yards along a rocky cove. Despite houses nearby, the spot is fairly secluded; fallen *kiawe* trees

◄ *HIDDEN*

Text continued on page 178.

Snorkeling and Scuba Diving the Gold Coast

Simply stated, Hawaii's Kona Coast offers some of the world's most spectacular diving. All along this western shoreline lie magnificent submerged caves, lava flows, cliffs and colorful coral reefs. Protected from prevailing trade winds by Mauna Kea and Mauna Loa, Kona enjoys the gentlest conditions. Usually the weather is sunny, the surf mild and the water clear (visibility is usually in the 100-foot range). Locals claim they get about 345 ideal diving days a year. It's small wonder, then, that adventurers travel from all over the world to explore Kona's underwater world.

What will you see if you join them? The Kona Coast has over 650 species of reef fish including the brightly colored yellow tang, the aptly named raccoon butterflyfish, the trumpetfish, the coronetfish, the cow-eyed porcupine pufferfish, and the graceful black, yellow and white moorish idol. Large marine animals abound as well, including green sea turtles, hawksbill turtles, manta rays, spotted eagle rays, pilot whales, pygmy killer whales and humpback whales.

When looking for marine life, swim over the coral, looking in, under and around all the corners, caves and crevices. Many spectacular sea creatures await discovery in these hiding spots. Keep in mind that while coral looks like rock, it is a living creature that can be easily killed. Standing on it, touching it, kicking it with your fin or even kicking sand onto it from the ocean floor can damage the coral. So gently drift over the reef and you will be rewarded with new discoveries and close encounters with beautiful tropical fish.

Following are brief descriptions of the best snorkeling and diving spots, as well as shops that provide equipment and tours. For specific information on a particular dive sight, drop by one of these shops. I also recommend you buy a waterproof fish identification cards. You can take it right into the water with you and use it to identify these magnificently colored fish.

KOHALA COAST SPOTS **Anaehoomalu Beach** is good for beginners, but it lacks the scenic diversity of other areas. There's good diving at the end of the road leading to **Puako**, but it's rocky. **"69" Beach** (or **Waialea Bay**) features good underwater opportunities when the surf is mild. **Hapuna Beach State Park** has an area that abounds in coral and fish near the rocks and cliffs at the end of the beach. **Spencer Beach Park** is filled with coral and suits beginners and experts alike.

Mahukona Beach Park is an old shipping area littered with underwater refuse which makes for great exploring. **Kapaa Beach Park** offers good diving, but it has a rocky entrance and tricky currents. **Keokea Beach Park**, an excellent spearfishing area, is often plagued by wind and high surf.

KAILUA-KONA AREA SPOTS **Kamakahonu Beach**, the sand patch next to Kailua's King Kamehameha Kona Beach Hotel, is a crowded but conveniently located dive site. There are corals and many species of fish here, but watch out for heavy boat traffic along the nearby wharf. **Hale Halawai**, an ocean-front park in Kailua, has good snorkeling off its rocky beach.

Old Airport Beach, just a stone's skip north of town, affords excellent diving all along its length. The entry is rocky, but once in, you'll find the waters spectacular. Some glass-bottom boats tour this area.

Honokohau Beach has some good spots south of the small-boat harbor. Stay away from the harbor itself, though; sharks are frequent.

Kahaluu Beach Park, with its easy entry to the water and complete beach services including restrooms, lifeguard, picnic tables and showers, is a good spot for beginners. The waters here are a too shallow for great scuba diving, which means they're all the better for snorkeling.

There's also good diving off the **Kona Surf Hotel** at the south end of Alii Drive, but the currents can be very dangerous here so caution is advised.

SOUTH KONA SPOTS **Napoopoo Beach Park** is an excellent diving spot—so good, in fact, that it draws diving tours and glass-bottom boats. The best diving is across Kealakekua Bay near the Captain Cook Monument.

Keei Beach features a lot of coral and, reportedly, a sea grotto. At **Puuhonua o Honaunau Park**, also known as the City of Refuge, there are two natural steps carved into the rocky shoreline that allow for easy entry directly into swarms of reef fish. Because of the abundance of colorful marine life, the accessible location, the easy entry and the variety of depths, this is one of the coast's best spots for snorkelers and scuba divers alike. **Hookena Beach Park** offers some good dive spots near the cliffs south of the beach. **Milolii** has some excellent diving areas as well as fascinating tidepools.

DIVING TOURS AND EQUIPMENT **Jack's Diving Locker** has detailed information and complete equipment rentals. They also have two dive boats and offer guided trips fo snorkelers and scuba divers to offshore reefs. Jack's Diving Locker is a PADI 5 Star facility, a NAUI Dream Resort as well as a SSI Resort Member. ~ Coconut Grove Market Place, 75-5819 Alii Drive, Kailua; 329-7585.

Fair Wind offers guided snorkeling and Scuba expeditions and supplies you with all the necessary equipment. The doubledecker *Fairwind II* picks up divers at Keauhou Bay and goes out to Kealakekua Bay. The speedy *Thrillcraft* takes divers on a four-hour exploration to sea cave and lava tube exploration. This four-hour excursion stops at Kealakekua Bay and Honaunau Bay. ~ 78-7130 Kaleopapa Road, Keauhou Bay; 322-2788.

along the beachfront provide tiny hideaways. It's a good place to swim but exercise caution. When the water is calm it's also a good spot for snorkeling. Surfers paddle out to the breaks near the southwest end of the bay and off the northwest point. There are no facilities here. ~ Located near the entrance to Hapuna Beach Park, three miles south of Kawaihae. From Kaahumanu Highway, turn into the park entrance. Then take the paved road that runs southwest from the park (between the beach and the A-frames). Go about six-tenths of a mile on this road and then turn right on a dirt road (the road at the very bottom of the hill). When the road forks, after about one-tenth mile, go left. Follow this road another one-tenth mile around to the beach.

HAPUNA BEACH STATE PARK Here's one of the state's prettiest parks. A well-tended lawn—studded with *hala*, coconut and *kiawe* trees—rolls down to a wide corridor of white sand that extends for one-half mile, with points of lava at either end. Maui's Haleakala crater looms across the water. This is a popular and generally very crowded place. Unfortunately, a major resort hotel was recently built at one end of the beach. Swimming is excellent at the north end of the beach but beware of dangerous currents when the surf is high. Snorkelers enjoy the coral and fish near the rocks and cliffs at the end of the beach. *Papio*, red bigeye, mullet, threadfin and *menpachi* are often caught here. Facilities include picnic areas, restrooms and showers. It's three miles to market and restaurants in Kawaihae. ~ Located on Kaahumanu Highway, three miles south of Kawaihae; 882-7995.

▲ No tent or trailer camping is allowed. However, screened A-frame shelters, located on a rise above the beach, can be rented. These cottages, which cost $20 per night, are equipped with a table, sleeping platforms and electricity; they sleep up to four people. Bring your own bedding and cooking utensils. Toilet and kitchen facilities are shared among all six A-frames. For reservations, contact Hawaii State Parks. ~ 933-4200.

SPENCER BEACH PARK Lacking the uncommon beauty of Anaehoomalu or Hapuna, this spacious park is still lovely. There's a wide swath of white sand, backed by a lawn and edged with *kiawe* and coconut trees. Swimming is excellent here and snorkeling will satisfy beginners and experts alike. Anglers try for *papio*, red bigeye, mullet, threadfin and *menpachi*. There are plenty of facilities: picnic area, restrooms, showers, a large pavilion, volleyball and basketball courts and electrical hookups. A market and restaurants are located less than a mile away in Kawaihae. ~ The park is located off Akoni Pule Highway about one mile south of Kawaihae.

▲ Bath...   ...ing are allowed; $1 per night.
...ired. This has been a very
...now limits the number of

...▲ This now-abandoned
...along a rocky, windswept
...e trees;

The good news: The Kohala Coast is home to the island's best beaches. The bad news: Since the 1980s, they've all been developed.

...areas lie
...from the
...The rocks
...t snorkeling
...adfin, mullet,
...lities include a
...ookups. There's
...ants and markets
...oni Pule Highway

County permit required.

K...   esides a spectacular view of M... ...as little to offer. It does have a n... ...trees, but lacks any sand, whi... ...beach. Swimming is difficult beca... ...od diving but the entrance is rocky ...the currents are tricky. Fishing is probably your best bet here since you can stand on the rocks and try for threadfin, mullet, red bigeye, *papio* and *menpachi*. Picnic areas and restrooms are the only facilities. There's no drinking water. The closest markets and restaurants are in Kawaihae. ~ Located off Akoni Pule Highway about 14 miles north of Kawaihae.

▲ Tents and trailers are allowed, but the terrain is very rocky for tent camping; $1 per night. County permit required.

KEOKEA BEACH PARK ▲ Seclusion is the password to this beautiful little park with its cliff-rimmed cove and tiered lawn fringed by *hala* and palm trees. Set way out on the Kohala peninsula, this retreat receives very heavy rainfall. You can swim here but only with extreme caution. It's an excellent area for spearfishing but is often plagued by high wind and high surf. Mullet, *papio*, red bigeye, threadfin and *menpachi* are the main catches here. There are picnic areas, restrooms and showers. The closest restaurants and markets are in Hawi. ~ Take Akoni Pule Highway about six miles past Hawi. Turn at the sign and follow the winding road one mile.

▲ Tent and trailer; $1 per night. County permit required.

HAWAII VOLCANOES NATIONAL PARK

GOOD 7 DAYS
NON TRANSFERABLE
NON REFUNDABLE

04/09/97   10:41AM
001#8582   A

REG PASS $10.00

CASH $10.00

▼▼▼▼▼▼▼▼▼▼▼▼▼
Kailua-Kona Area

At the center of the tourist scene on the Kona Coast is the contemporary town of Kailua. Here, extending for five miles along Alii Drive from the King Kamehameha Hotel to Keauhou Bay, is a string of hotels, restaurants, condominiums and shopping malls. Like a little Waikiki, Kailua-Kona is the commercial focus for this entire side of the island.

SIGHTS

Despite the tinsel and tourist trappings, this old fishing village and former haunt of Hawaiian royalty still retains some of its charm. If you tour **Kailua wharf** around 4 p.m., the fishing boats may be hauling freshly caught marlin onto the docks. Some of the finest marlin grounds in the world lie off this shoreline and the region is renowned for other deep-sea fish. The wharf itself is a departure point not only for fishing charters but for snorkeling tours and glass-bottom boat cruises as well. It's also a favorite place for viewing Kona's fabled sunsets. ~ Alii Drive.

On the grounds of the nearby King Kamehameha Hotel rests **Ahuena Heiau**, an important historical site that has been partially reconstructed and combined, in truly tacky fashion, with a hotel luau facility. This compound represents the royal grounds used by Kamehameha I for several years during the early 19th century. Tours of the hotel grounds are offered Monday through Thursday at 1:30 p.m. ~ 75-5660 Palani Road; 329-2911.

Hulihee Palace, a small but elegant estate built in 1838, sits on Alii Drive in the middle of town. Today it's a museum housing royal Hawaiian relics. It seems that this two-story estate was built by the brother-in-law of Kamehameha I and later used by King Kalakaua as a summer palace during the 1880s. Among the fine furnishings are many handcrafted from native *koa*. Admission. ~ Alii Drive; 329-1877.

Mokuaikaua Church, directly across the street, is the oldest church in the islands. The first missionaries anchored offshore in 1820 after sailing over 18,000 miles around Cape Horn from Boston. They built the imposing lava-and-coral structure in 1836. By the way, that churchyard tree with the weird salami-shaped fruit is a sausage tree from West Africa.

Contrasting with these venerable sites is the **Atlantis Submarine**, an 80-ton craft parked just offshore. Diving to depths of 100 feet, this 46-passenger sub explores tropical reefs. During the hour-long voyage, passengers view the underwater world through large viewing ports. Admission. ~ 329-6626.

Almost everything in Kailua sits astride Alii Drive, the waterfront street that extends south from town to Keauhou Bay. Several miles from Kailua, this road passes **Disappearing Sands Beach** (or Magic Sands Beach). The lovely white sand here is often washed away by heavy winter surf and then redeposited when the big waves subside.

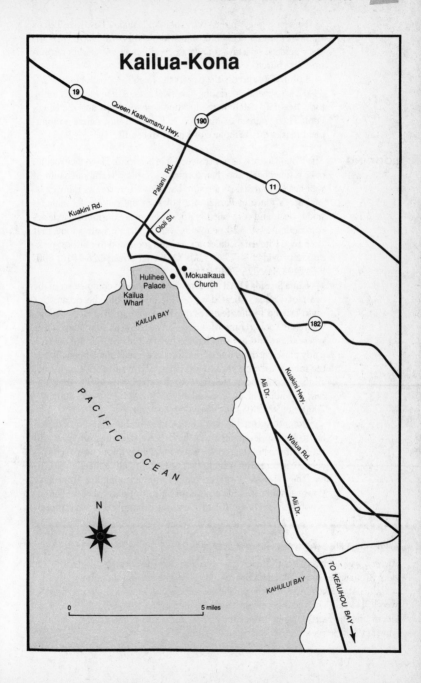

Kailua-Kona

19

Queen Kaahumanu Hwy.

190

11

Palani Rd.

Kuakini Rd.

Ololi St.

Hulihee
Palace   Mokuaikaua
Church

Kailua
Wharf

KAILUA BAY

182

PACIFIC

OCEAN

Alii Dr.

Kuakini Hwy.

Wailua Rd.

Alii Dr.

N

KAHULUI BAY

0   5 miles

TO KEAUHOU BAY

Farther along, on the rocky shore of Kahaluu Bay, is **St. Peter's Catholic Church**. This blue-and-white clapboard chapel, precariously perched on a lava foundation, is reputedly the world's second-smallest church.

Located just across the bay, at the Keauhou Beach Hotel (322-3441), are several interesting historical sites. Ask in the hotel lobby for a free map detailing the location of two *heiaus* and the **King's Pool**. Then you can continue on to Keauhou Bay, where a monument marks the **Birthplace of Kamehameha III**.

LODGING   The Kona Coast is as expensive as it is beautiful. Hawaiian royalty once resided here, and their former playground is still the haunt of well-heeled tourists. As a result, bargains are as rare as rainy days.

Patey's Place in Paradise, a hostel in the center of Kailua, is small, clean and conveniently priced. There are dormitory-style accommodations for 20 people as well as three private rooms that sleep two. Kitchen facilities, a television room and free airport pickup are provided. ~ 75-195 Ala Ona Ona Street; 326-7018, 800-972-7408, fax 326-7640. BUDGET.

Kona Seaside Hotel is a sprawling 225-room complex set in the heart of Kailua. Located across the street from the ocean, this multi-faceted facility features the Tower Wing; the Garden Wing, where the rooms come with mini-kitchenettes; and the Pool Wing, where the rooms are smaller and less fashionable but are conveniently placed around one of the hotel's two swimming pools. While the more expensive rooms add lanais and wall-to-wall carpeting, all the accommodations are tastefully done. A lounge and restaurant are adjacent. ~ 75-5646 Palani Road; 329-2455, 800-367-7000, fax 922-0052. MODERATE TO DELUXE.

Kona Bay Hotel is part of the old Kona Inn, the rest of which fell to Kailua developers, who have perversely transformed it into yet another shopping mall. What remains is a four-story semicircular structure with a pool, bar, restaurant and lounge in the center. The rooms are large, tastefully furnished and quiet. Some have lava walls that provide a pleasant backdrop plus excellent soundproofing. The staff is friendly, and the atmosphere is very appeal-

◆◆

A TIP OF THE HAT TO THE *CHALLENGER*

You can pay your respects to the crew of the space shuttle *Challenger* at the **Astronaut Ellison S. Onizuka Space Center**. Located eight miles north of Kailua at Keahole Airport, this pavilion is a tribute to Onizuka, who lived in Hawaii, and the other astronauts who died in the 1986 tragedy. Videos and interactive displays trace the astronauts' lives and the development of the space program. Admission. ~ 329-3441.

ing. I once spent a relaxing month here and highly recommend the place. ~ 75-5739 Alii Drive; 329-1393, 800-367-5102, fax 935-7903. MODERATE.

Kona Islander Inn occupies several three-story buildings spread across a lush swath of land. Set between Alii Drive and Route 11 on Kailua's outskirts, this chain hotel has a large lobby and an oval pool flanked by MacArthur palms. All rooms have small lanais, cable televisions, refrigerators, carpets and air-conditioning. Tastefully appointed, but lacking a good ocean view. ~ 75-5776 Kuakini Highway; 329-3181, 800-922-7866, fax 326-9339. DELUXE.

Kona Tiki Hotel, a mile down the road, is a quaint hotel neatly situated on the ocean. The rooms are bright and clean. Despite the contrasting decorative themes and the noise from Alii Drive, I recommend this 15-unit establishment for its oceanview lanais, oceanfront pool, barbecue, garden and complimentary continental breakfast. The rooms are equipped with mini-kitchenettes (sink, refrigerator and two-burner stove crowded into one unit). ~ 75-5968 Alii Drive; 329-1425, fax 327-9402. MODERATE.

A better bargain still are the rooms at **Kona White Sands Apartment Hotel**. Located just across the street from Disappearing Sands Beach (the nicest beach along Alii Drive), this ten-unit hotel offers one-bedroom apartments. Each comes with kitchenette and ceiling fans. The cinderblock and plasterboard walls are pretty plain, but who needs fancy interior decoration with that knockout ocean view? Rooms are cross-ventilated, and the cooling breeze will probably bring along noise from cars and sun revelers. That's the extra price for living this close to the Kona Coast. Many people are willing to pay it, so you'll have to reserve a room far in advance. ~ 77-6467 Alii Drive. Contact the Hawaii Resorts Management for reservations, 75-5776 Kuakini Highway, Suite 105-C, Kailua-Kona, HI 96740; 329-9393, 800-553-5035, fax 326-4137. MODERATE.

Anchoring one end of Kailua Bay is the town's most historic hotel. The **King Kamehameha Kona Beach Hotel**, priced higher than its young neighbors, is nonetheless deserving of note. The lobby alone is worth the price of admission: It's a wood-paneled affair along which you can trace the history of ancient Hawaii. For its guests, the "King Kam" has a pool, tennis courts and jacuzzi, plus a host of other amenities ranging from an activities desk to room service. The rooms themselves are quite spacious, fashionably decorated and equipped with positively everything. You'll find plush carpeting, color televisions, air-conditioning, refrigerators and lanais with spectacular views of the ocean or mountains. ~ 75-5660 Palani Road; 329-2911, 800-367-2111, fax 329-4602. DELUXE TO ULTRA-DELUXE.

Situated on a lava-rock beach just outside Kailua is the **Kailua Plantation House**. This contemporary two-story, plantation-style bed and breakfast has five rooms, all with private baths and lanais.

Three of the rooms also feature oceanfront views. There's a jacuzzi and tiny pool along the oceanfront and a comfortable sitting room for guests. The entire place, painted white with oak trim, is light, bright and airy. Island art adorns the walls and a sense of easy elegance pervades the place. ~ 75-5948 Alii Drive; 329-3727. DELUXE TO ULTRA-DELUXE.

Keauhou Beach Hotel is a true sleeper. A large, blocky, seven-story hotel, it hardly seems on the outside to possess the Hawaiian spirit. But the grounds include an ancient *heiau* and other archaeological sites and the waterfront location boasts magnificent tidepools that extend for acres. The complex includes an oceanfront swimming pool, restaurant and a cozy waterfront bar and room service is available. ~ 78-6740 Alii Drive; 322-3441, 800-367-6025, fax 322-6586. MODERATE TO DELUXE.

Architecturally, one of the region's most intriguing spots is the **Kona Surf Resort**, a 530-room hotel. Situated on 14 acres along a peninsula that juts into Keauhou Bay, the facility fans out into four wings. At the center of the configuration is a lobby area complete with restaurants, lounges and shops. It lacks a sand beach, but there's a freshwater as well as a saltwater pool and the snorkeling in the bay is good; adjacent to tennis and golf. ~ 78-128 Ehukai Street; 322-3411, 800-367-8011, fax 322-3245. DELUXE TO ULTRA-DELUXE.

HIDDEN ▶ Of course, when money is no object the place to stay is **Kona Village Resort**, a very plush, very private colony located 12 miles north of Kailua. Favored by movie stars and other celebrities seeking escape from autograph hounds and aggressive agents, this regal retreat is set along a white-sand cove in an ancient Hawaiian fishing village. The individual guest cottages are thatched-roof structures (*hales*), variously designed to represent the traditional houses of Hawaiian, Tahitian, Fijian, Samoan and other Polynesian groups. There are no TVs, telephones, radios, clocks or air-conditioners in the rooms, but you will find serenity, solitude and a well-heeled version of hidden Hawaii, not to mention tennis courts, sailboats, outrigger canoes and glass-bottom excursion boats. Prices are in the stratosphere and are based on the American plan. ~ P.O. Box 1299, Kaupulehu-Kona, HI 96745; 325-5555, 800-367-5290, fax 325-5124. ULTRA-DELUXE.

CONDOS   One-bedroom, two-bath apartments at **Kona Alii** run from $119 double (and from $99 during the off-season, April 1 to December 15). This seven-story building is just across the street from the ocean. ~ 75-5782 Alii Drive; 329-9393.

The Sea Village offers one-bedroom garden view units starting at $90 single or double; two bedrooms, two baths are $130 for one to four people. Prices increase from mid-December to mid-April. There's a jacuzzi, swimming pool and tennis courts. Oceanfront, but no beach. ~ 75-6002 Alii Drive, about one mile south of Kailua; 329-1000, 800-367-5205, fax 533-4621.

Kona Riviera Villa is a relatively small condo on a lava-rock beach outside Kailua. It's attractively landscaped, has a pool and rents one-bedroom units for $75 to $100 ($60 to $90 from April 15 to December 14). ~ 75-6124 Alii Drive; 329-1996. For reservations, contact Knutson and Associates, 75-6082 Alii Drive, Suite 80, Kailua-Kona, HI 96740; 800-800-6202, fax 326-2178.

Studio apartments at **Kona Bali Hai** are $120, and one-bedroom apartments with mountain views go for $140 for one to four people. One and two bedrooms on the ocean start at $170 ($200 peak). Amenities include a jacuzzi and pool. It's just one mile from Disappearing Sands Beach. ~ 76-6246 Alii Drive; 329-9381, 800-777-1700, fax 326-6056.

Kona Magic Sands has a studio apartment renting for $70 ($80 peak) single or double. It's located on the ocean, next to Disappearing Sands Beach. Three-night minimum. ~ 77-6452 Alii Drive; 329-6488, 800-367-5168, fax 329-5480.

Aston Kona By The Sea is a large, trimly landscaped complex on a lava-rock beach. The suites are one- and two-bedroom; all have two baths and a lanai; there's a pool and jacuzzi. Rates start at $215 ($195 from April 1 to December 21). ~ 75-6106 Alii Drive; 327-2300, 800-922-7866, fax 327-2333.

For anyone on a tight budget, Kailua would seem an unlikely place to find a decent meal. Most restaurants along the Gold Coast cater to gilded tourists and wealthy residents. If you work at it, though, you'll locate a few low-cost eating places.

DINING

Kona Coast Shopping Center, located at 74-5588 Palani Road, houses several short-order joints. **Betty's Chinese Kitchen** serves tasty, nutritious, inexpensive meals at its cafeteria-style emporium. ~ 329-3770. BUDGET. **Poquito Más** is a Mexican food stand two doors down. You can dine on burritos, enchiladas or tostadas in the adjacent patio area. Of special interest are the fish tacos and the San Felipe–style shrimp tacos. ~ 329-3528. BUDGET.

If this doesn't intrigue you, head downhill to the North Kona Shopping Center. **Kuakini Café** is not as bad as all that. Matter of fact, some people find the plate lunches and hamburgers downright *ono*. Closed Sunday. ~ 329-1166. BUDGET.

In the King Kamehameha Mall, between the King Kamehameha Hotel and the Kona Industrial Area, is **Ocean Seafood Chinese Restaurant**. In traditional Chinese-restaurant style, the menu is divided into 13 sections ("A" through "M") with about 15 dishes for each category. So I won't even begin to tell you what they have. Suffice it to say that it's all there. ~ 75-5626 Kuakini Highway; 329-3055. BUDGET TO MODERATE.

Sibu Café prepares a host of Indonesian dishes daily for lunch and dinner. Among the tangy favorites at this outdoor café are beef saté, tofu and vegetable stir-fry and Balinese chicken (which is marinated, cooked over an open flame, then served with peanut sauce). ~ Banyan Court, Alii Drive; 329-1112. BUDGET TO MODERATE.

Tolkien fans should stop by **Tom Bombadil's** quaint little place near Alii Drive. The murals decorating this small café represent scenes from the *Lord of the Rings* trilogy. In addition to pizza, Tom serves sandwiches straight from Goldberry's pantry. But take heed: In these parts a roast beef sandwich translates as "The Pride of Gondor," turkey is a "Withywindle," and for ham and cheese read "Rivendell." Tom also serves fish and chicken dishes as well as salads. ~ 75-5864 Walua Road; 329-1292. BUDGET TO MODERATE.

The **Oceanview Inn**, a large, informal dining room opposite Kailua Bay, has a voluminous menu. Chinese, American, Hawaiian, fresh fish and meat dishes, served all day, comprise only part of the selection. You can try local fish, caught several miles offshore in some of the world's finest fishing grounds. There's also a complete breakfast menu. Closed Monday. ~ Alii Drive; 329-9998. BUDGET TO MODERATE.

Next door is **Stan's Restaurant**, where you can order from a unique menu that lists dinners by price. Here you'll find numerous steak, seafood and chicken concoctions. This open-air establishment overlooking Kailua Bay offers significantly more atmosphere than the Oceanview. There are rattan-style furnishings and a windswept waiting area. Lunch isn't served, but breakfast features papaya, pineapple or banana hotcakes. ~ 75-5687 Alii Drive; 329-4500. MODERATE.

Kona Amigos, on the same waterfront drive, specializes in south-of-the-border cuisine. Here you'll dine out on a lanai overlooking Kailua Bay or in one of several rooms attractively paneled in *lauhala* and bamboo. This American-Mexican restaurant offers crab enchiladas, fajitas, steak sandwiches and fresh fish dishes. ~ 75-5669 Alii Drive; 326-2840. MODERATE.

Guiseppe's Italian Café, a hole-in-the-wall bistro punched into a corner of the Kailua Bay Inn Shopping Plaza, has reasonably priced Italian food. The menu is pretty standard as is the red-checkered oilcloth interior. No lunch on Sunday. ~ 75-5699 Alii Drive; 329-8836. MODERATE.

You not only can dine inexpensively at **Aki's Cafe**, you can dine under an umbrella overlooking the water. They may not live up to their motto of "fine Japanese and American food," but the cuisine is passable. They offer hamburgers, fish and chips and spaghetti on the American side of the menu, with sushi, stir-fry, yakitori and curry dishes on the other. For dinner, there's steak, chicken teriyaki and fish *misoyaki*. ~ 75-5699 Alii Drive; 329-0090. BUDGET TO MODERATE.

If you care for Mediterranean, **Cassandra's Greek Tavern** has tables out on the patio as well as in a cozy little dining room. Souvlaki, kebobs, moussaka and dolmas dominate the menu, but they also prepare steak and seafood dishes. No lunch on Sunday. ~ 75-5719 Alii Drive; 334-1066. MODERATE.

Aesthetically speaking, **Kona Ranch House** swings both ways. One section of the trimly appointed restaurant features informal dining in an understated and comfortable environment. In the adjoining Plantation Lanai facility you can treat yourself to a candle-light-and-linen-tablecloth experience. The menu is the same for both sections of this switch-hitting establishment. Drop in for lunch or dinner and you'll find an inventory of entrées ranging from ribs to chicken and from New York steak to fresh fish. There are also inexpensive sandwiches and appetizer dishes. At breakfast Kona Ranch House offers an array of egg dishes. So take your pick of locales, easy or elegant, and enjoy good food at modest prices. ~ 75-5653 Ololi Street; 329-7061. MODERATE.

The commemorative sign at the **Kona Inn** tells the tale of the old inn—how it was built back in the steamship era when Kona was gaining fame as a marlin fishing ground. The bad news is that the original hotel was razed and replaced with a mall—of which this contemporary namesake is a part. The good news is that the restaurant is quite attractive—an open-air, oceanfront affair with two separate dining facilities. The Kona Inn Café Grill serves grilled appetizers and sandwiches. The dining room serves several fresh fish dishes daily as well as prime rib and Hawaiian-style chicken. Dinner only. ~ 75-5744 Alii Drive; 329-4455. MODERATE TO DELUXE.

Set on a second-story terrace overlooking the ocean, **Palm Café** is one of Kailua's most romantic addresses. You can lean against the marble bar or sink into an upholstered booth, then order from a Pacific Rim menu. There's marinated mahimahi with lobster

✔ **CHECK THESE OUT—UNIQUE DINING**

- *Budget:* Enjoy Pacific Rim dishes at plebeian prices while relaxing in an upholstered booth or beside the marble bar at **Under the Palm**. *page 188*
- *Moderate:* Order the roast duck or wienerschnitzel at one of the state's finest German restaurants, **Edelweiss**. *page 166*
- *Deluxe:* Discover that Hawaii regional cuisine means everything from wok-charred ahi to veal with macadamia nuts at **Merriman's**. *page 167*
- *Ultra-deluxe:* Order a spectacular sunset as an appetizer at the oceanfront **Canoe House**, then finish up with an Asian-style entrée. *page 173*

Budget: under $8 Moderate: $8–$16 Deluxe: $16–$24 Ultra-deluxe: over $24

sauce, black sesame crust ono and beef tenderloin with Thai curry sauce. Highly acclaimed by the critics. Dinner only. ~ 75-5819 Alii Drive; 329-7765. DELUXE TO ULTRA-DELUXE.

There's a less expensive alternative right **Under the Palm**. Located just downstairs, with the same management, it's a patio-style café with sandwiches, salads, light appetizers and several pasta dishes. Among the last mentioned you'll find linguine with pancetta and artichoke hearts, bow tie pasta with fricassee of wild mushroom, and wok-fried Asian vegetables. Not bad for an inexpensive café! ~ 75-5819 Alii Drive; 329-7765. BUDGET.

Jameson's By The Sea is a lovely waterfront restaurant with an emphasis on fresh local seafood dishes. Tucked unpretentiously into the corner of a large condominium, Jameson's conveys a modest sense of elegance: bentwood furniture, potted palms, a seascape from the lanai or through plate-glass windows and good service. Choose from an enticing menu of fresh local catches, steaks, veal, chicken dishes and other gourmet delights. Lunch and dinner weekdays, dinner only on weekends. ~ 77-6452 Alii Drive near Disappearing Sands Beach; 329-3195. DELUXE.

For Continental cuisine in a fashionable setting, consider **La Bourgogne French Restaurant**. This French country dining room features New York steak with peppercorn sauce, roast saddle of lamb, veal sweetbreads with Madeira sauce, coquilles St. Jacques and fresh fish selections. For appetizers there are escargots, truffled mousse and steak tartar. Round off the meal with cherries jubilee or chocolate mousse and you have a French feast right here in tropical Hawaii. Reservations are highly recommended. Dinner only. Closed Sunday. ~ Kuakini Plaza on Kuakini Highway, four miles south of Kailua; 329-6711. DELUXE.

GROCERIES　The best place to shop anywhere along the Kona Coast is in the town of Kailua. This commercial center features several supermarkets as well as a number of specialty shops. One of the first choices among supermarkets is **Sack 'n Save** in the center of Kailua. It has everything you could possibly need. ~ 75-5595 Palani Road; 326-2729.

◆◆

MEXICAN STANDOFF

For Mexican food along Alii Drive, you can choose based on price or view. At **Rico's** you'll get a good, filling Mexican meal in a plain café. ~ Alii Sunset Plaza, 75-5799 Alii Drive; 326-7655. BUDGET. On the other hand, if you're seeking a tropical drink and a tropical sunset over the water, then **Pancho & Lefty's Cantina & Restaurante** is the place. Similar food, different price. ~ 75-5719 Alii Drive; 326-2171. MODERATE.

If you'd prefer another supermarket with a similar selection, try **K.T.A. Super Store**. It's open every day from 6 a.m. to midnight, and is another of the Kailua-Kona area's most convenient and accessible shopping facilities. ~ Kona Coast Shopping Center; 329-1677.

Kona Healthways has an ample stock of vitamins, bathing supplies, grains, fruits and vegetables. By the simple fact that it is the only store of its kind in the area, it wins my recommendation. ~ Kona Coast Shopping Center; 329-2296.

SHOPPING

You might remember that song about how "L.A. is a great big freeway." Well, the Hawaiian version could easily be "Kailua is a great big mall." I've never seen so many shopping arcades squeezed into so small a space. Here are goldsmiths, boutiques, jewelers galore, travel agencies, sundries, knickknack shops, sandal-makers, T-shirt shops and much, much more, all crowded onto Alii Drive.

Personally, I think most of the items sold along this strip are tacky or overpriced, and in some cases, both. You may find something worth buying, but you'll probably discover it's best to browse here and buy outside town. One place I do recommend is **Middle Earth Bookshoppe**. Here you'll find a good selection of Hawaiian books, as well as paperbacks and current bestsellers. ~ Kona Plaza Shopping Arcade, 75-5719 Alii Drive; 329-2123.

The **Kona Inn Shopping Village**, which parallels the waterfront, features dozens of shops. Because of its convenient location and variety of stores, it is the center of the visitor shopping scene. ~ Alii Drive.

While here be sure to stop by **Hula Heaven**. This retro Hawaiian shop has old movie posters, antique ukeleles, hula girl knickknacks and reproduction dresses and aloha shirts. ~ 75-5744 Alii Drive; 329-7885.

Kona Marketplace across the street is another prime tourist destination. Within the Marketplace is **B. T. Pottery**, a husband-and-wife craft shop that features pottery inlaid with black sand as well as an array of handmade jewelry. ~ Alii Drive; 326-4989.

One of the newer and more tastefully designed malls is **Waterfront Row**, a raw-wood-and-plank-floor shopping complex with perhaps a dozen stores and restaurants. ~ 75-5770 Alii Drive.

The **Hulihee Palace Gift Shop**, a small store located behind the palace, specializes in Hawaiian handicrafts and literature. ~ Alii Drive; 329-1877.

In addition to the centers located along Alii Drive, there are two large shopping malls a couple blocks up from the water. **Kona Coast Shopping Center** and **Lanihau Center** sit on either side of Palani Road near the Kaahumanu Highway intersection. The latter contains one of the town's few bookstores, a **Waldenbooks**. ~ Palani Road; 329-0015.

The **King Kamehameha Kona Beach Hotel** has a cluster of shops. Several decades back, before the luxury hotels mushroomed along the Kohala Coast, this hotel was a prime stop for shoppers and sojourners alike. Today its glory has faded, but it still sports several interesting stores. ~ 75-5660 Palani Road; 329-2911.

Right next door, between the hotel and the Kona Industrial Area, is the **King Kamehameha Mall**, a small, modern complex with perhaps a dozen shops. ~ 75-5626 Kuakini Highway.

Kailua Village Farmers Market, where local growers gather under plastic tarps to sell their wares, is a good place to pick up home-grown fruits and vegetables. ~ Alii Drive, just south of Hualalai Road.

Out toward the end of Alii Drive, several miles south of Kailua, stands the **Keauhou Shopping Center**. With several dozen stores, it is one of the largest complexes on the island (though granted, *Big* Island does not mean big shopping malls). ~ Alii Highway and Kamehameha III Road.

Fisherman's Landing in the Kona Inn Shopping Village is a restaurant/ lounge with a Hawaiian soloist and knockout sunset views nightly. ~ 75-5744 Alii Drive; 326-2555.

NIGHTLIFE   What action there is here is near the shorefront on Alii Drive. Both of the following places have stunning ocean views and are usually packed to the gills. **Huggo's** features karaoke and various live bands every evening. ~ Alii Drive and Kakakai Road; 329-1493. Hawaiian contemporary bands play Friday and Saturday at **Jolly Roger**. ~ 75-5776 Alii Drive; 329-1344.

The **Billfish Bar**, located poolside at the King Kamehameha Kona Beach Hotel, has live country-and-western music on weekends. ~ 75-5660 Palani Road; 329-2911.

For an evening of slow rhythms and dancing cheek-to-cheek, there's the **Windjammer Lounge** at the Royal Kona Resort. When I went by recently, the band was playing Hawaiian sounds. ~ 75-5852 Alii Drive; 329-3111.

There's dancing to live Hawaiian and rock music Wednesday, Thursday and Sunday at the **Eclipse Nightclub**. On Friday and Saturday, you can dance to deejay music. Closed Monday and Tuesday. Cover. ~ 75-5711 Kuakini Highway; 329-4686.

Another good bet is the **Kona Surf Resort**, which sports the Puka Bar. They feature karaoke most nights. ~ 78-128 Ehukai Street, Keauhou; 322-3411.

Catering to both a gay and straight clientele, **The Other Side** offers pool tables, dart boards and recorded sounds. ~ 74-5484 Kaiwi Street; 329-7226.

BEACHES & PARKS   **HALE HALAWAI** This small oceanfront park, fringed with coconut trees, has an activities pavilion but no beach. Its central location in Kailua does make the park a perfect place to watch the sunset, though. ~ Located near the intersection of Alii Drive and Hualalai Road in Kailua.

OLD KONA AIRPORT STATE RECREATION AREA   ◄ *HIDDEN*
This white-sand beach parallels Kailua's former landing strip, extending for a half-mile along a lava-crusted shore. Very popular with Kailuans, this is a conveniently located spot for catching some rays. The water is shallow, with a rocky bottom. There are a few sand channels for entering the water; and there is a sandy inlet good for kids just north of the lighthouse. This area offers excellent diving. Principal catches are threadfin, big-eyed scad, bonefish, *papio* and especially mullet. Facilities include a picnic area, restrooms and showers; you can walk to the Kailua markets and restaurants less than a half-mile away. ~ Located about one-half mile northwest of the King Kamehameha Kona Beach Hotel on Kuakini Highway in Kailua. The park gate is closed every evening at 8 p.m.

HONOKOHAU BEACH   This is Kailua's nude beach.   ◄ *HIDDEN*
Folks come for miles to soak up the sun on this long narrow strand. Bordered by a lagoon, backdropped by distant mountains, protected by a shallow reef and highly recommended for the adventurous. Since the water is well protected, it's good for swimming, although a bit shallow. There are recommended spots for skindiving south of the small-boat harbor but stay away from the harbor itself since sharks are frequent. Surfers enjoy Honokohau's waves. Rather than fish here try Kaloko Pond about one-half mile north. There are no facilities here. The closest markets and restaurants are in Kailua. ~ Take Kaahumanu Highway a couple miles north from Kailua. Turn onto the road to Honokohau Small Boat Harbor. From the north side of the harbor, walk about 600 yards farther north to the beach.

KONA COAST STATE PARK   Set at the end of a bumpy lava-bed road, this beach park is certainly secluded. You'll drive in a mile-and-a-half from the highway to a sand-and-coral beach that is bordered by a small lagoon and young palm trees. You can swim, although the bottom is rocky and the surf is often high—that's when the surfers come out. Anglers also frequent this beach. The only facilities are picnic tables and portable toilets. The closest markets and restaurants are located in Kailua. ~ Located one and one-half miles off Kaahumanu Highway, about ten miles north of Kailua near the 91-mile marker.

DISAPPEARING SANDS BEACH   A small strand studded with volcanic rocks, this spot is also called Magic Sands. It seems that the white sand periodically washes away, exposing a lava shoreline. When still carpeted with sand, this is a very popular and crowded place. This is a favorite area for swimming and bodysurfing. Kona's best surfing spot is just north of here at

"Banyans," with breaks year-round over a shallow reef. There are right and left slides. The major catches include mullet, threadfin, big-eyed scad, bonefish and *papio*. Restrooms and showers are the only facilities. ~ Located on Alii Drive four miles south of Kailua.

KAHALUU BEACH PARK Set along the south shore of Kahaluu Bay, this county park is fringed with palm trees. The salt-and-pepper beach is small and often crowded. Swimming is excellent here since the cove is partially protected by outlying rocks. Tropical fish abound, making this a recommended place for snorkeling, especially for beginners. Surfing is good near the reef during periods of high surf. Anglers fish for mullet, threadfin, big-eyed scad, bonefish and *papio*. The bay is also a good spot for throw-netting and surround-netting. Facilities include picnic areas, pavilions, showers and restrooms. A small market and restaurant are next door at the Keauhou Beach Hotel. ~ Located on Alii Drive five miles south of Kailua.

Kona/Kau District

One element that comes as a visual shock to many first-time visitors to the Kona Coast is the endless stretch of black lava that blankets this dry terrain. Backdropped by 8271-foot Hualalai and standing in the wind-shadow of both Mauna Loa and Mauna Kea, Kailua and the entire Kona region project the bald unreality of a moonscape.

SIGHTS

But the ragged shoreline has been trimmed with stands of palm trees and sections along the roadways are splashed with bougainvillea. Even in this land of lava you don't need to venture far to discover soft foliage and tropical colors. Along the lower slopes of Hualalai just above Kailua lies **Kona coffee country**. This 20-mile-long belt, located between the 1000- and 2000-foot elevation and reaching south to Honaunau, is an unending succession of plantations glistening with the shiny green leaves and red berries of coffee orchards. If you prefer your vegetation decaffeinated, there are mango trees, banana fronds, macadamia nut orchards and sunbursts of wildflowers. To make sure you remember that even amid all the black lava you *are* still in the tropics, old coffee shacks and tinroof general stores dot the countryside.

So rather than heading directly south from Kailua, make sure you take in the full sweep of Kona's coffee country. Just take Palani Road (Route 190) uphill from Kailua, then turn right onto Route 180. This winding road cuts through old Kona in the heart of the growing region—watch for orchards of the small trees. Before the coast road was built, this was the main route. Today it's somewhat off the beaten track, passing through funky old country towns like Holualoa before joining the Mamalahoa Highway (Route 11) in Honalo.

Once on this latter highway, you'll encounter the old Greenwell Store, a stone building that dates to 1867, and a perfect place to combine shopping with museum browsing. The **Kona Historical Society Museum** has taken over this former general store. Today it's filled with artifacts from Kona's early days plus contemporary postcards, calendars and other items. Of particular interest are the marvelous collections of photos and antique bottles. Closed Saturday and Sunday. ~ Mamalahoa Highway, Kealakekua; 323-3222.

This main route continues south along the western slopes of **Hualalai**. Near the town of Captain Cook, Napoopoo Road leads down to Kealakekua Bay. First it passes the **Royal Aloha Coffee Mill & Museum**. I don't know about you, but I'm a confirmed "caffiend," happily addicted to java for years. So it was mighty interesting to watch how the potent stuff goes from berry to bean to bag, with a few stops between. If you haven't tried Kona coffee, one of the few brews grown in the United States, this is the time. ~ 160 Napoopoo Road; 566-2269.

At the **Fuku-Bonsai Center** on the southern outskirts of Holualoa, you can take a self-guided tour through a series of nine bonsai gardens. Among the most fascinating miniatures are the banyans. There is also a fine gift shop on the premises. Admission. ~ 78-6767 Mamalahoa Highway; 322-9222.

Kealakekua Bay is a marine reserve with technicolor coral reefs and an array of tropical fish species. Spinner dolphins swim close to shore in this area. Here you can also check out the reconstructed temple, **Hikiau Heiau**, where Captain James Cook once performed a Christian burial service for one of his crewmen. Captain Cook himself had little time left to live. Shortly after the ceremony, he was killed and possibly eaten by natives who had originally welcomed him as a god. A white obelisk, the **Captain Cook Monument**, rises across the bay where the famous mariner fell in 1779.

Puuhonua o Honaunau National Historical Park sits four miles south of Kealakekua Bay on Route 160. This ancient holy ground, also known as the City of Refuge, was one of the few places to which *kapu* breakers and refugees could flee for sanctuary. Once inside the Great Wall, a lava barricade ten feet high and 17 feet wide, they were safe from pursuers. Free booklets are available for self-guided tours to the palace, *heiaus* and menacing wooden idols that made this beachfront refuge one of Hawaii's most sacred spots. The *heiaus*, dating back to the 16th and 17th centuries, are among the finest examples of ancient architecture on the Big Island. Also explore the house models, built to traditional specifications, the royal fishpond and the displays of ancient arts and crafts. Admission. ~ 328-2288.

St. Benedict's, my favorite church in all the islands, lies just up the hill. An imaginative Belgian priest, hoping to add color and imagery to the mass, transformed this rickety wooden chapel into a **Painted Church** by covering the interior walls with murals. He depicted several religious scenes and painted a vaulted nave behind the altar to give this tiny church the appearance of a great European cathedral. The exterior, equally charming, is carpenter's Gothic in style with a dramatic spire. Stop by and take a look, then proceed back to Mamalahoa Highway in Captain Cook. ~ 328-2227.

The cliffs looming behind the Captain Cook marker are honeycombed with **Hawaiian burial caves.**

At **Bay View Farm** you can tour a mill that produces Kona coffee. The trees here, like those you'll see along the roadside, grow to six or eight feet. Each will produce about 12 pounds of berries, which, after being picked by hand, will eventually produce two pounds of beans. Like peas in a pod, there are two beans per berry. A pulping machine squeezes them out of the berry skin. Next, the beans are dried for up to a week and are turned every hour, 24 hours a day. Finally, the skin layers are removed and the beans are graded and bagged for shipping. ~ Located on the same road as Painted Church, Honaunau; 328-8693.

HIDDEN ▶

Located on an ancient Hawaiian agricultural site, the **Amy B. H. Greenwell Ethnobotanical Garden** spreads across 12 acres of upland countryside. The land is divided into four vegetation zones, varying from seaside plants to mountain forests, and is planted with hundreds of Polynesian and native Hawaiian species. On a self-guided tour, you can wander through fields cleared by Hawaiians in pre-contact days and view the plants that were vital to early island civilizations. Closed Saturday and Sunday, but guided tours are offered the second Saturday of every month at 10 a.m. ~ Off Mamalahoa Highway, Captain Cook; 323-3318.

There is little except you, dark lava and the black macadam of the Mamalahoa Highway as you proceed toward the southern extremities of the Big Island. Here along the lower slopes of Mauna Loa, lifeless lava fingers cut across lush areas teeming with tropical colors. The contrast is overwhelming: Rounding a bend, the road travels from an overgrown land of poinsettias and blossoming trees to a bleak area torn by upheaval, resembling the moon's surface. Once past the lava flows that have ravaged the countryside, you'll discover a terrain that, though dry and windblown, is planted with macadamia nut orchards and fields of cattle-range grasses.

About 30 miles south of Kailua, take the turnoff to the quaint Hawaiian fishing village at **Milolii** (see the "Beaches & Parks" section below). This is a vintage South Seas scene that should not be missed.

Continuing south, the highway passes **James Stewart's Hoomau Ranch** (87-mile marker), then a sprawling **macadamia nut orchard.**

Eventually, the road arrives at the **South Point** turnoff. South Point Road leads through 11 miles of rolling grassland to the na-

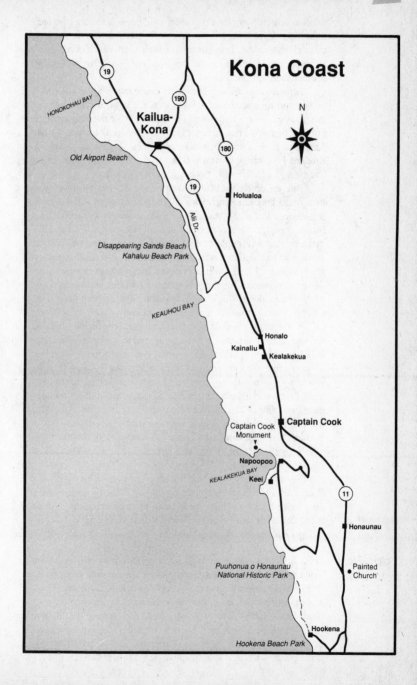

Kona Coast

tion's southernmost point. En route you'll pass a cluster of windmills that draw energy from the trades that blow with ferocity through this region. Fishermen have built **platforms** along the sea cliff here to haul their catches up from the boats that troll these prime fishing grounds.

There are also **ancient Hawaiian canoe moorings** in the rocks below, and the remains of a *heiau* near the light tower. Some archaeologists believe that South Point was one of the places where Polynesian discoverers first settled. Another local feature, **Green Sand Beach**, is a two-mile hike along the waterfront from the Kaulana boat ramp. Olivine eroding from an adjacent cinder cone has created a beach with a decidedly greenish hue.

Continue on to **Naalehu**, the nation's southernmost town, and then on to **Punaluu Beach Park**. With its palm trees and enchanting lagoon, Punaluu's black-sand beach is simply gorgeous. The tourist complex detracts from the natural beauty, but to escape the madding mobs the explorer need wander only a couple of hundred yards east to the rocky remains of **Kaneeleele Heiau**. Or venture about one-third mile south to **Ninole Cove**. Though there's a condominium complex nearby, this spot is a bit more secluded. Many of the stones along Ninole's pebbly beach are filled with holes containing "baby" stones that are said to multiply.

From Punaluu to Volcanoes National Park, the highway passes through largely uninhabited grassland and sugar cane areas. **Pahala**, the only town along this stretch, is a plantation colony. For *HIDDEN* ▶ an interesting side trip, go through Pahala to **Wood Valley Temple**, where a Tibetan Buddhist monk and his followers have taken over an old Japanese temple. Situated on 25 acres, the temple was dedicated in 1980 by the Dalai Lama. A tranquil but dynamic place, it is painted in floral colors and adorned with a gilded statue of the Buddha. Since the small staff here has many responsibilities, call ahead for permission to visit and directions to the temple. ~ P.O. Box 250, Pahala, HI 96777; 928-8539.

To see the valley for which the temple is named, go right onto Pikake Street at the first stop sign in Pahala. When it forks after a little more than four miles, go left and proceed along the road as *HIDDEN* ▶ it continues up into luxuriant **Wood Valley**, the scene of a devastating 1868 earthquake and mudslide.

LODGING   For a funky country place high in the mountains overlooking the Kona Coast, try the **Kona Hotel**. Catering primarily to workers, this 11-unit hotel remains a real sleeper. It might be difficult to book a room during the week, but on weekends, the lunchpail crowd heads home and you can rent a small place at an unbelievably low rate. Shared bathroom facilities. It's five miles to the beaches and action around Kailua, but if you're after an inexpensive retreat, this is the place. ~ Route 180, Holualoa; 324-1155. BUDGET.

Down the road, **Teshima's Inn** has small, cozy rooms at similar rates. These are set in an L-shaped structure fronting a Japanese garden. The rooms have linoleum floors and wood-paneled walls decorated with Japanese art. Here you're 1300 feet above sea level and seven miles from Kailua. This charming inn is run by Mrs. Teshima, a delightful Japanese woman who has operated the establishment for years. ~ Mamalahoa Highway, Honalo; 322-9140. BUDGET.

Buddhist services are performed in Tibetan every morning and evening at Wood Valley Temple.

One of the more unique places to stay on the Big Island is **The Dragonfly Ranch**. Spread across two acres, several hideaways and a main house comprise this "tropical fantasy lodging." The grounds are as thick and luxurious as a well-tended jungle and the atmosphere is decidedly New Age. The "honeymoon suite" has an outdoor waterbed complete with canopy and mosquito netting. Each of the four units have partial kitchen facilities. Don't expect telephones and air-conditioning, but do prepare yourself for an experience. ~ Route 160, Honaunau; 328-2159, 800-487-2159, fax 328-9570. MODERATE TO ULTRA-DELUXE.

At **H. Manago Hotel**, you'll have a varied choice of accommodations. Rooms in the creaky old section have communal baths. The battered furniture, torn linoleum floors and annoying street noise make for rather funky living here. Rooms in the new section rise in price as you ascend the stairs. First-floor accommodations are the least expensive and rooms on the ethereal third floor are the most expensive, but all reside in the budget range. The only advantage for the extra cost is a better view. All these rooms are small and tastelessly furnished—somehow orange carpets don't make it with naugahyde chairs. But you'll find visual relief in the marvelous views of mountain and sea from the tiny lanais. There's also a restaurant and television room in the old section. ~ Mamalahoa Highway, Captain Cook; 323-2642, fax 323-3451. BUDGET.

Shirakawa Motel, the country's southernmost hotel, sits on stunningly beautiful grounds. There's a fruit farm out back and poinsettias lining the driveway. Once when I stopped by, a rainbow lay arched across the landscape and birds were loudly rioting in the nearby hills. Located 1000 feet above sea level, this corrugated-roof, 12-room hostelry offers quaint rooms with faded furniture and functional kitchenettes. Without cooking facilities, the bill is even less. ~ Mamalahoa Highway, Waiohinu; 929-7462. Write P.O. Box 467, Naalehu, HI 96772 for reservations. BUDGET.

◄ HIDDEN

Wood Valley Temple, a Buddhist retreat, has dormitory-style and private rooms. Set on 25 landscaped acres, it provides a serene resting place. The guest rooms are pretty basic but have been pleasantly decorated and are quite comfortable. Baths are shared and guests have access to the ample kitchen facilities. Call for reservations; two-night minimum. ~ Four miles outside Pahala; 928-8539, fax 928-6271. BUDGET.

Sea Mountain at Punaluu is a welcome contradiction in terms—a secluded condominium. Situated in the arid Kau District south of Hawaii Volcanoes National Park, it rests between volcanic headlands and a spectacular black-sand beach. A green oasis surrounded by lava rock and desert vegetation, the complex contains a golf course, pool, tennis courts and jacuzzi. The several dozen condos are multi-unit cottages (moderate to deluxe). The condos are well decorated and include a bedroom, sitting room, kitchenette and lanai; larger units available (deluxe to ultra-deluxe). ~ Off Mamalahoa Highway, Punaluu; 928-8301, 800-488-8301, fax 928-8008. MODERATE TO ULTRA-DELUXE.

GAY LODGING Spanning the entire Hawaiian chain, the Big Island–based **Black Bamboo Guest Services** unearths the best dwellings for gay and straight travelers to stay at: cottages, apartments and houses. This service also arranges hiking tours, birdwatching trips and other sporting activities for its guests. ~ P.O. Box 211, Kealakekua; 328-9607, 800-527-7789.

With manicured grounds leading to a tiled-roof villa, **Kealakekua Bay Bed and Breakfast** combines picture-perfect views of Kealakekua Bay with equally impeccable accommodations. Three light and airy suites are available, with the Alii suite taking up the entire second floor. The Alii includes a jacuzzi tub to relax in, but all rooms flaunt private entrances, private baths and refrigerators. Contemporary wallhangings, wicker furniture and ceiling fans adorn each room, including the lounge and dining room. ~ P.O. Box 1412, Kealakekua; 328-8150, 800-328-8150. DELUXE TO ULTRA-DELUXE.

Looking like a Southern plantation relocated in a tropical setting, **R.B.R. Farms** is actually a coffee and macadamia nut plantation. With ocean views and serenity included in the price of admission, guests don't mind staying a minimum of two nights in this four-room, one-cottage dwelling. The cottage is located next to the swimming pool and boasts rattan furniture and a private lanai. The other rooms in this predominantly gay bed and breakfast are furnished just as comfortably and all have access to the hot tub. ~ P.O. Box 930, Captain Cook; 328-9212, 800-328-9212. MODERATE TO ULTRA-DELUXE.

DINING From Kailua south, the Mamalahoa Highway heads up *mauka* into the mountains above the Kona Coast. There are numerous restaurants in the little towns that dot the first 15 miles. All sit right on the highway.

Teshima's is a pleasant restaurant modestly decorated with lanterns and Oriental paintings. It's a good place to enjoy a Japanese meal or a drink in the lounge. This café is very busy at lunch. Dinner features several Japanese and American delicacies. Breakfast is also served. ~ Mamalahoa Highway, Honalo; 322-9140. MODERATE.

There's a different mood entirely at the **Aloha Theatre Café**. Here in the lobby of the town's capacious movie house, a young crew serves delicious breakfasts as well as sandwiches and Mexican dishes during lunch and dinner. So if for some bizarre reason you've always longed to dine in the lobby of a movie theater . . . . If not, you can eat out on the oceanview lanai. ~ Kainaliu; 322-3383. MODERATE.

H. Manago Hotel has a full-size dining room. Primarily intended for the hotel guests, the menu is limited and the hours restricted to "meal times" (7 to 9 a.m., 11 a.m. to 2 p.m., and 5 to 7:30 p.m. Tuesday through Thursday). Lunch and dinner platters consist of a few daily specials. Sandwiches are also available. Closed Monday. ~ Mamalahoa Highway, Captain Cook; 323-2642. MODERATE.

In Kealakekua Ranch Center, a shopping center on Mamalahoa Highway in Captain Cook, there are two low-priced eateries. **Real Mexican Food** is a takeout stand. ~ 323-3036. **Hong Kong Chop Suey** is one of those Chinese restaurants that have (literally) about 100 items on the menu. ~ 323-3373. BUDGET.

Canaan Deli comes recommended by several readers, who like the hoagies and the pastrami sandwiches. They also have pizzas and hamburgers at this friendly stopping place, as well as a breakfast menu. Personally, I go for the bagels with cream cheese and lox. ~ Mamalahoa Highway, Kealakekua; 323-2577. BUDGET.

On the road down to Puuhonua O Honaunau, there's a great lunch stop—**Wakefield Gardens & Restaurant**. You can wander the tropical preserve, then dine on a papaya boat, homemade soup, fresh garden salad, braised tofu or a "healthy burger" (made with natural grains). Lunch only. ~ Route 160, Honaunau; 328-9930. BUDGET.

In the Kau district, the **Ohana Drive-Inn** has breakfast items, sandwiches and hot platters. Fancy it's not, just a counter for ordering and a few tables. BUDGET. ~ 78-mile marker, Mamalahoa Highway; 929-7679.

For something more comfortable, try the **South Point Bar & Restaurant**. At this small dining room, the menu includes steak, prawns and teriyaki chicken. In an area lacking in full-service dining facilities, this restaurant is a welcome oasis. ~ 76-mile marker, Mamalahoa Highway; 929-9343. MODERATE TO DELUXE.

Down in Naalehu, the nation's southernmost town, you'll find the **Naalehu Coffee Shop**. Some people like the place. I was completely put off by all the tourist trappings: books, slides, knick-knacks—even the wall decorations are for sale. But the banana bread is good and the menu is varied. There are full-course breakfasts; at lunch they serve sandwiches with salad; the dinner menu has beef, seafood and chicken dishes. Closed Sunday. ~ Naalehu Spur Road, Naalehu; 929-7238. BUDGET TO MODERATE.

Along the lengthy stretch from Naalehu to Hawaii Volcanoes National Park, one of the few dining spots you'll encounter is the **Seamountain Golf Course & Lounge** in Punaluu. Situated a short distance from the black-sand beach, this restaurant serves a lunch consisting of cold sandwiches only. Topping the cuisine are the views, which range across the links out to the distant volcanic slopes. ~ Punaluu; 928-6222. BUDGET.

GROCERIES   Strung along Mamalahoa Highway south of Kailua is a series of small towns that contain tiny markets. The only real supermarket en route is **Sure Save**. ~ At the Kealakekua Ranch Center, Captain Cook; 323-2695.

Sea Fresh Hawaii, about ten miles south of Kailua, has fresh seafood. ~ Mamalahoa Highway, Captain Cook; 323-3040.

Down the road, **Ohana O Ka Aina Cooperative** has a similar inventory, plus an herb shop and deli. ~ Mamalahoa Highway, Kainaliu; 322-2425.

Kahuku Mini-Mart, in the Kau district, has an ample inventory of groceries and drugstore items. ~ 78-mile marker, Mamalahoa Highway; 929-9011.

Down at the southern end of the island, the **Naalehu Island Market** is the prime place to stock up. ~ Mamalahoa Highway, Naalehu. ~ 929-7527.

SHOPPING   After escaping the tourist traps in Kailua, you can start seriously shopping in South Kona. Since numerous shops dot the Mamalahoa Highway as it travels south, I'll list the most interesting ones in the order they appear.

For hats and baskets woven from pandanus and bamboo, and sold at phenomenally low prices, turn off the main road onto Route 18 and check out **Kimura Lauhala Shop**. ~ Holualoa; 324-0053.

Blue Ginger Gallery displays an impressive array of crafts items produced by local artisans. There are ceramics, custom glass pieces,

STILL LIFE WITH GALLERIES

Holualoa is a center for artists and art galleries. Within the ambit of this one-street town you'll find the **Kona Arts Center**, housed in an old church on Route 18, plus several privately owned galleries nearby. Among the most noteworthy is **Studio 7 Gallery**, a beautifully designed multi-room showplace that displays pottery, paintings and prints. ~ 324-1335.

woodwork and hand-painted silk scarves. ~ Mamalahoa Highway, Kainaliu; 322-3898.

Another recommended store is **Paradise Found**, which features contemporary and Hawaiian-style clothes. ~ Mamalahoa Highway, Kainaliu; 322-2111. **Big Island Antiques** is the place for things old and aging. ~ Mamalahoa Highway, Kealakekua; 323-2890.

Kakanahou Hawaiian Foundation, an apprentice school teach-   ◄ *HIDDEN*
ing Hawaiians native arts, sells hand-wrought hula drums and other instruments, as well as masks and other crafts. It also serves as an introduction to Hawaiian music as you view bamboo nose flutes, musical bows, dancing sticks and ceremonial drums. Call ahead for weekend visits. ~ Mamalahoa Highway, Kealakekua; 322-3901.

My favorite shop is **Kealakekua's Grass Shack**. This place is crowded with Hawaiiana, not just from native Polynesians, but from the island's late arrivals as well—Americans, Chinese, Japanese, Portuguese. As owner John Jens explains, "We go all the way from poi to tofu." There are *milo* and *koa* wood pieces, handwoven baskets and much more. Most interesting of all, to me at least, are the antique tools and handicrafts that Jens has gathered. This transplanted Dutchman is something of an authority on Hawaiian history and culture, combining a scholar's knowledge with a native's love for the islands. Ask him for a tour of his mini-museum. It'll be an education in things Hawaiian. ~ Mamalahoa Highway, Kealakekua; 323-2877.

Not to be bypassed is **Wood Works**, a shop specializing in *koa* and other exotic hardwoods. The shop was born when three local woodworkers, alienated by the high prices demanded for their pieces by galleries, decided to go into business for themselves. The result is a shop where the work is not only exquisite but also accessible to the common person. Among the many items, you'll find bowls, boxes, cutting boards and salad spoons as well as larger, more elaborate creations. ~ 82-6156 Mamalahoa Highway, Captain Cook; 323-2247.

Cottage Gallery is an artists' cooperative displaying the work—paintings, ceramics, jewelry, clothing, sculpture—of many local artists. ~ Mamalahoa Highway, Honaunau; 328-2650.

The **Aloha Theater**, home to the Aloha Performing Arts Center,   **NIGHTLIFE**
features an ongoing series of theatrical performances. In addition to plays, it periodically schedules concerts. ~ Mamalahoa Highway, Kainaliu; 322-9924.

Way out where you'd least expect it, with little but lava for miles around, is the **South Point Bar & Restaurant**. There's a live band rocking out here every Friday night; otherwise expect standard bar music. ~ 76-mile marker, Mamalahoa Highway; 929-9343.

BEACHES & PARKS

NAPOOPOO BEACH PARK 🏊 🎣 🏕 ⚓ Many small boats moor at this black-rock beach on Kealakekua Bay. Set amidst cliffs that rim the harbor, it's a charming spot. Unfortunately, it draws caravans of tour buses on their way to the nearby Hikiau Heiau and Captain Cook Monument. Kealakekua Bay, one mile wide and filled with marine life, is an underwater preserve that attracts snorkelers and glass-bottom boats. In the bay there are good-sized summer breaks. Just north, at "Ins and Outs," the surf breaks year-round. Mullet, *moi*, bonefish, *papio* and big-eyed scad are the common catches. A picnic area and restrooms are the only facilities. There's a soda stand just up from the beach; the closest markets and restaurants are in Captain Cook. ~ In the town of Captain Cook, take Napoopoo Road, which leads two miles down to Kealakekua Bay.

HIDDEN ▶ **KEEI BEACH** 🏊 🎣 ⚓ This salt-and-pepper beach extends for a quarter-mile along a lava-studded shoreline. Situated next to the creaky village of Keei, this otherwise mediocre beach offers marvelous views of Kealakekua Bay. It is far enough from the tourist area, however, that you'll probably encounter only local people along this hidden beach. What a pity—no white shoes and polyester here! The very shallow water makes swimming safe, but limited. Try the north end. Plenty of coral makes for good snorkeling. Mullet, threadfin, bonefish, *papio* and big-eyed scad are common catches here. There are no facilities. Both markets and restaurants will be found several miles away in the town of Captain Cook. ~ Take the Mamalahoa Highway to Captain Cook, then follow Napoopoo Road down to Kealakekua Bay. At the bottom of the hill, go left toward the Puuhonua o Honaunau National Historical Park. Take this road a half-mile, then turn right onto a lava-bed road. Now follow this road another half-mile to the beach.

▲ You could pitch a tent, but only with difficulty along this narrow strand.

HOOKENA BEACH PARK 🏊 🎣 ⚓ Popular with adventurous travelers, this is a wide, black-sand beach, bordered by sheer rock

◆◆

SUNBATHE IN THE SHADOW OF HISTORY

Puuhonua o Honaunau Park, part of the Puuhonua o Honaunau National Historical Park (City of Refuge), is an excellent picnic spot when you're sightseeing. Besides the picnic tables and other facilities, enjoy the sandy sunbathing area. There's no beach, but the tidepools along the lava shoreline are fascinating. ~ Off Route 160 just south of the National Historical Park displays.

walls. Coconut trees abound along this lovely strand, and there's a great view of the South Kona coast. This is a recommended beach for swimming and bodysurfing. Near the cliffs south of the beach are some good dive spots. Mullet, threadfin, bonefish, *papio* and big-eyed scad are among the most common catches. A picnic area and restrooms are the only facilities. There is no drinking water. A small market is four miles away in Kealia. ~ Take the Mamalahoa Highway south from Kailua for about 21 miles to Hookena. Turn onto the paved road at the marker and follow it four miles to the park.

▲ Tent camping is allowed; county permit required.

MILOLII BEACH PARK ⟵ Even if you don't feel like a character from Somerset Maugham, you may think you're amid the setting for one of his tropical stories. This still-thriving fishing village is vintage South Seas, from tumbledown shacks to fishing nets drying in the sun. Unfortunately, however, new houses have been springing up in the last few years. There are patches of beach near the village, but the most splendid resources are the tidepools, some of the most beautiful I've ever seen. This area is fringed with reefs that create safe but shallow areas for swimming, and great spots for snorkeling. Exercise extreme caution if you go beyond the reefs. This beach is a prime area for mullet, bonefish, *papio*, thread-fin and big-eyed scad. Facilities include restrooms, picnic area and a volleyball court. There's no running water. There's a small market up the street in town. ~ Take the Mamalahoa Highway south from Kailua for about 33 miles. Turn off onto a well-marked macadam road leading five miles down to the village.

◄ HIDDEN

▲ Permitted only in the seaside parking lot. Get there early and you can park a tent beneath the ironwood trees with the sea washing in just below. County permit required.

MANUKA STATE PARK This lovely botanic park, almost 2000 feet above sea level, has a beautiful ocean view. The rolling terrain is planted with both native and imported trees and carpeted with grass. The only facilities are restrooms and a picnic area. ~ On Mamalahoa Highway 41 miles south of Kailua.

▲ No tent and trailers allowed, but you can park your sleeping bag in the pavilion. A state permit is required.

WHITTINGTON BEACH PARK ⟵ This pretty little park features a small patch of lawn dotted with coconut, *hala* and ironwood trees. It's set on a lava-rimmed shoreline near the cement skeleton of a former sugar wharf. There are some marvelous tidepools here. Access to the water over the sharp lava rocks is pretty rough on the feet. But once you're in the snorkeling is very good and there's a good surf break in summer with a left slide. Mullet, *menpachi*, red bigeye, *ulua* and *papio* are the most frequent species caught. Facilities consist of picnic area, restrooms, showers and electrical hookups. It's three miles to the markets and restaurants in Naalehu. ~ Across from the abandoned sugar mill on Mamalahoa Highway, three miles north of Naalehu.

▲ Tent and trailer camping allowed; county permit required.

PUNALUU BEACH PARK A black-sand beach fringed with palms and bordered by a breathtaking lagoon, this area, unfortunately, is regularly assaulted by tour buses. Still, it's a place of awesome beauty, one I would not recommend bypassing. For more privacy, you can always check out **Ninole Cove**, a short walk from Punaluu. This attractive area has a tiny beach, grassy area and lagoon, which is a good swimming spot for children. Exercise caution when swimming outside the lagoon. Facilities include a picnic area, restrooms, showers and electrical hookups. The snorkeling is only mediocre. Surfers attempt the short ride over a shallow reef (right slide). Principal catches are red bigeye, *menpachi*, *ulua* and *papio*. There's a restaurant nearby, with a museum and tourist complex on the premises. ~ Located about a mile off Mamalahoa Highway, eight miles north of Naalehu.

▲ Tents and trailers are allowed; county permit required.

Hawaii Volcanoes National Park

Covering 344 square miles and extending from 13,677-foot Mauna Loa to 4090-foot Kilauea to the Puna shoreline, this incredible park (admission) is deservedly the most popular feature on the Big Island. Its two live volcanoes, among the most active in the world, make the region as elemental and unpredictable as the next eruption.

Unlike Washington's Mt. St. Helens and Mt. Pinatubo in the Philippines, eruptions here are not explosive. So even Kilauea, which has destroyed several hundred homes and devoured an entire town during the last decade, has gained a reputation as a "drive-in volcano" where you can stand shoulder to shoulder with geologists and journalists watching Madame Pele vent her wrath.

SIGHTS

Also contained within this singular park are rainforests, black-sand beaches, rare species of flora and fauna, and jungles of ferns. If you approach the park from the southwest, traveling up the Mamalahoa Highway (Route 11), the points of interest begin within a mile of the park boundary. Here at the trailhead for **Footprints Trail**, you can follow a two-mile-long path that leads to the area where Halemaumau's hellish eruption overwhelmed a Hawaiian army in 1790. The troops, off to battle Kamehameha for control of the island, left the impressions of their dying steps in molten lava. Many tracks have eroded, but two centuries later some still remain imprinted on the ground.

Continuing along the highway, turn up Mauna Loa Strip Road to the **Tree Molds**. Lava flowing through an *ohia* forest created

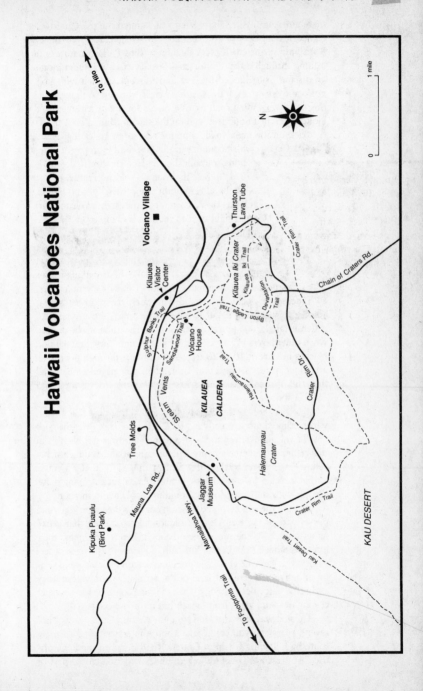

these amazing fossils. The molten rock ignited the trees and then
cooled, leaving deep pits in the shape of the incinerated tree trunks.
It's a little farther to **Kipuka Puaulu** or **Bird Park**, a nature trail
leading through a densely forested bird sanctuary. *Kipuka* means
an "island" surrounded by lava and this one is filled with koa,
kolea and *ohia* trees. If the weather's clear, you can continue along
this narrow, winding road by foot or car for about ten miles to a
lookout perched 6662 feet high on the side of Mauna Loa.

Back on the main road, continue east a few miles to **Kilauea
Visitors Center**, which contains a museum, a film on recent eruptions, souvenir shop and information desk. ~ 967-
7311. Across the road at **Volcano House**, there's
a hotel and restaurant. An earlier Volcano House,
built in 1877, currently houses the **Volcano Art
Center**, right next to the visitor complex.

During the last two cen-
turies, Big Island volca-
noes have covered
200,000 acres with
black lava, destroying
almost everything in
their path.

From here you can pick up Crater Rim Drive, one of
the islands' most spectacular scenic routes. This 11-mile
loop passes lava flows and steam vents in its circuit
around **Kilauea Caldera**. It also takes in everything from a
rainforest to a desert and provides views of several craters.

Proceeding clockwise around the crater, the road leads near
Thurston Lava Tube, a 450-foot tunnel set amid "the fern jungle,"
a dense tangle of luxurious vegetation. The tube itself, created
when outer layers of lava cooled while the inner flow drained out,
reaches heights of 10 to 20 feet. You can hike through the tunnel
and along nearby **Devastation Trail**, a half-mile paved asphalt trail
that cuts through a skeletal forest of *ohia* trees devastated in a
1959 eruption.

Another short path leads to **Halemaumau Crater**. This firepit,
which erupted most recently in 1982, is the home of Pele, the goddess of volcanoes. Even today steam and sulfurous gas blast from
this hellhole, filling the air with a pungent odor and adding a sickly
yellow-green luster to the cliffs. Halemaumau is actually a crater
within a crater, its entire bulk contained in Kilauea's gaping maw.
(People with sulfur sensitivity should probably avoid this site.)

Around the southern and western edges of the crater, the road
passes part of the **Kau Desert**, a landscape so barren that astronauts bound for the moon were brought here to train for their
lunar landing. At the **Jaggar Museum**, adjacent to the park observatory, you can catch an eagle-eye glimpse into Halemaumau Crater and take in a series of state-of-the-art displays on volcanology
and Hawaiian volcano myths. Then the road continues on to a succession of steam vents from which hot mists rise continually.

The highway zips into Hilo from the Kilauea Crater area. Until
several years ago you could take a more interesting and leisurely
route by following **Chain of Craters Road** down to the Puna district. At present a lava flow several miles wide has closed part of

the road. The 20-mile-long section that is still open skirts several volcanic craters and recent lava flows and dips toward the sea, arriving on the coast near **Puuloa,** where a two-mile trail leads to an excellent collection of petroglyphs.

The road continues to hug the shoreline, but stops before the ancient Hawaiian village of **Lae Apuki,** which was destroyed by the 1995 lava flow. This dead end is an excellent vantage point for following volcanic activity.

The town of Wahaula currently lies about five miles in from the end of the road. Behind the charred remains of the visitors center lies **Wahaula Heiau,** one of the islands' oldest temples. Built about 1250 A.D., this was the last *heiau* where priests practiced human sacrifice. Unfortunately, this temple is now inaccessible to the public.

LODGING

Volcano House, a 42-room hotel, perches 4000 feet above sea level on the rim of Kilauea Crater. Situated near the entrance to Hawaii Volcanoes National Park, this hotel provides a unique resting place. You can watch the steam rise from Halemaumau Crater or study the rugged contours of slumbering Kilauea. Standard rooms are unfortunately located in a separate building behind the main hotel. For a view of Kilauea, ask for a superior or deluxe room on the volcano side. The rooms are small and decorated in an ever tidy and cozy fashion. There's wall-to-wall carpeting but no TV or radio. And you certainly won't need an air-conditioner at these breathless heights. ~ Near the entrance to Hawaii Volcanoes National Park; 967-7321, fax 967-8429. MODERATE TO DELUXE.

Kilauea Lodge does not rest on the lip of the crater, but that doesn't prevent it from being the finest place in the area to stay. Set on tropically wooded grounds, this hideaway nevertheless conveys a mountain atmosphere. Some guest rooms have fireplaces and quilts; all have private baths. This coziness carries over into an inviting common room shared by guests and furnished with rocking chairs and a tile fireplace. The lodge, built in 1938 as a boys' camp, rests at the 3700-foot elevation and combines the best features of a Hawaiian plantation house and an alpine ski lodge. It also provides a memorable contrast to the ocean-oriented places that you'll probably be staying in during the rest of your visit. ~ Old Volcano Road, Volcano Village; 967-7366, fax 967-7367. DELUXE.

There are also a number of small, privately run bed-and-breakfast inns around the volcano area. For information, contact **Volcano Accommodations,** a central agency that can help book reservations. ~ 967-8662, 800-733-3839.

DINING

If you're looking for a vista, **Volcano House Restaurant**—perched on the rim of Kilauea Crater—affords extraordinary views. Located at the 4000-foot elevation in Hawaii Volcanoes National Park, this spacious dining room looks out on sheer lava walls and angry steam vents. If you can tear yourself away from the stunning scenery, there's buffet-style breakfast and lunch, and an ample dinner menu highlighted by mahimahi, prime rib, chicken and a variety of seafood dishes. ~ 967-7321. DELUXE.

For quick, inexpensive meals you can't top the **Alii Bakery & Drive Inn**. Adjacent to the only grocery hereabouts, this takeout stand with tables has sandwiches and plate lunches. ~ Old Volcano Road, Volcano Village; 967-7103. BUDGET.

And for those languorous evenings when time is irrelevant and budgets forgotten, there is **Kilauea Lodge**. You can sit beside a grand fireplace in an atmosphere that mixes tropical artwork with alpine sensibility. The exposed-beam ceiling and elegant hardwood tables comfortably contrast with a menu that features "prawns Mauna Loa," catch of the day and chicken Milanese. Dinner only. ~ Old Volcano Road, Volcano Village; 967-7366. DELUXE.

GROCERIES   The **Volcano Store**, located just outside the National Park, has a limited stock of groceries and dry goods. ~ Old Volcano Road, Volcano Village; 967-7210.

BEACHES & PARKS   **KIPUKA NENE** Easily accessible by paved road, this windswept campsite nevertheless offers considerable privacy. Tourists use the road less than most other thoroughfares in Hawaii Volcanoes National Park, and the park remains relatively secluded. It's surrounded by a dry forest and backdropped by Mauna Loa. The park may be closed for months at a time when the nenes are nesting. Call the Volcano National Park Headquarters in advance at 967-7311. The only facilities are a picnic area, water tank and pit toilets. A restaurant and information booth are in the park center. ~ Once in Hawaii Volcanoes National Park, take Chain of Craters Road south from Crater Rim Drive. Turn right onto Hilina Pali Road and follow it for five miles until Kipuka Nene appears on the left.

▲ Tent and trailer camping. No permit is required, but there is a seven-day limit.

NAMAKANI PAIO Situated in a lovely eucalyptus grove at the southern end of Volcanoes National Park, this campground offers both outdoor and cabin camping. There is a picnic area and restrooms, and a restaurant and information booth in the park center. ~ On Mamalahoa Highway (Route 11) about three miles west of park headquarters and 31 miles southwest of Hilo.

▲ Tent and trailer camping. No permit required, but, as always, campers should note that there is a seven-day limit. Cabins are rented from the Volcano House (967-7321). Each cabin has one double and two single beds, plus an outdoor grill. No firewood

The Volcano Update, a 24-hour recorded message, provides information on the latest eruptions. ~ 967-7977.

or cooking utensils are provided. The units rent for $32 a day for two people, $6 for each additional person up to four. Sheets, blankets and towels are provided, but it's recommended that you bring a sleeping bag. Showers are not available for campers.

This alternate route across the island climbs from Hilo to an elevation of over 6500 feet (bring a sweater!). While the eastern section is heavily wooded with *ohia* and fern forests, most of the later roadway passes through the lava wasteland that divides Mauna Kea and Mauna Loa. You cross lava flows from 1855 and 1935 while gaining elevation that will provide you with the finest view of these mountains anywhere on the island.

▼▼▼▼▼▼▼▼
Saddle Road

SIGHTS

Near the 27-mile marker, the road to Mauna Kea leads 13 miles up to the 13,796-foot summit. The first six miles are passable by passenger car and take in a lookout and the **Onizuka Center for International Astronomy.** ~ 961-2180.

Beyond this point you will need a four-wheel drive vehicle. Be sure to call ahead since the visitor station at the center sponsors tours of the summit and star-gazing opportunities. At the summit you'll find the Mauna Kea Observatory complex, one of the finest observatories in the world. You'll also be treated to some of the most otherworldly views in the world. For a four-wheel-drive tour of the summit, you can also contact **Waipio Valley Shuttle and Tours.** ~ 775-7121.

Mauna Kea State Park, with cabins and recreation area, lies about midway along the Saddle Road. The road continues past a United States military base, then descends through stands of eucalyptus into Waimea cattle country. Here you can pick up the Mamalahoa Highway (Route 190) southwest to Kailua. Passing through sparsely populated range country over 2000 feet in elevation, this road has sensational views of the Kona Coast and Maui. Near the rustic village of **Puuanahulu** stands **Puu Waawaa**, the island's largest cinder cone.

It's only 87 miles from Hilo to Kailua by way of this interior shortcut. Before setting out, pack warm clothing and check your gas gauge—there are no service stations or stores en route. And consult your car rental agency: Some do not permit driving on Saddle Road.

PARKS

MAUNA KEA STATE PARK   Situated on the tableland between Mauna Kea and Mauna Loa at 6500-feet elevation, this is an excellent base camp for climbing either mountain. The cabins here are also convenient for skiers headed up to Mauna Kea. With its stunning mountain views, sparse vegetation and chilly weather, this rarefied playground hardly seems like Hawaii. For remoteness and seclusion, you can't choose a better spot. To be sure you fully enjoy it, dress warmly. A picnic area and restrooms are the only facilities. You'll need to travel roughly 35 miles to the restaurants and markets of Hilo if you need supplies, so plan ahead. ~ On the Saddle Road about 35 miles west of Hilo.

▲ No tents or trailers allowed. The cabins can be rented from the Division of State Parks, 75 Aupuni Street, Hilo, Hawaii, HI 96721; 933-4200. The individual cabins, each accommodating up to six people, have two bedrooms, bath, kitchenette and an electric heater. Cabins have loads of cooking utensils and sufficient bedding. Rates are $45 for four people and $5 for each additional person. There are also four-plex cabinettes that rent for $55 for eight people and $5 or each additional person. These aren't nearly as nice as the individual cabins. They are one-bedroom units crowded with eight bunks; cooking is done in a community dining and recreation area next door.

▼▼▼▼▼▼▼▼▼▼
Puna District

That bulging triangle in the southeast corner of the Big Island is the Puna District, a kind of living geology lab where lush rainforest is cut by frequent lava flows. Here at the state's easternmost point, black-sand beaches, formed when hot lava meets the ocean and explodes into crystals, combine with anthurium farms and papaya orchards to create a region both luxurious and unpredictable. There are lava tubes, arches and caves galore, all formed by the lava that flows inexorably down from the rift zones of Kilauea.

SIGHTS

Now that Chain of Craters Road is covered in a layer of black lava, the only way to visit the area is by following Route 130, which will carry you through the tumbledown plantation town of **Keaau** and near the artistic little community of **Pahoa**, or along Route 137, an enchanting country road that hugs the coast.

In 1990, **lava flows** poured through Kalapana, severing Routes 130 and 137 (which have since been reconnected) and covering many houses. Kalapana, once home to more than 400 people, was largely destroyed. Today, a few isolated houses form oases in a desert of black lava. Just above the town, where the roadway comes to an abrupt halt, you can see how the lava crossed the road and gain an excellent view of any current activity. In fact, for the past several years this has been the best vantage point on the island to watch for volcanic action.

What you will not see here is the original black-sand beach at Kaimu, which was covered by lava. The ancient canoe ramp is also buried beneath black rock and the **Star of the Sea Painted Church**—a tiny 1920s-era chapel painted in imaginative fashion to make it resemble a grand cathedral—has been moved to a temporary location near the end of Route 130.

After exploring the area of recent volcanic action, you can backtrack along the coast via Route 137, which proceeds northeast through jungly undergrowth and past dazzling seascapes to the tiny villages of **Opihikao** and **Pohoiki**.

At the intersection of Route 137 and Route 132, take a right onto the dirt road and follow it seaward toward the site of a truly eerie occurrence. When the 1960 lava flow swept down to destroy this entire region, it spared the **Cape Kumukahi Lighthouse** on the state's easternmost point. Today you can see where the wall of lava parted, flowed around the beacon, then closed again as it contin-

◄ *HIDDEN*

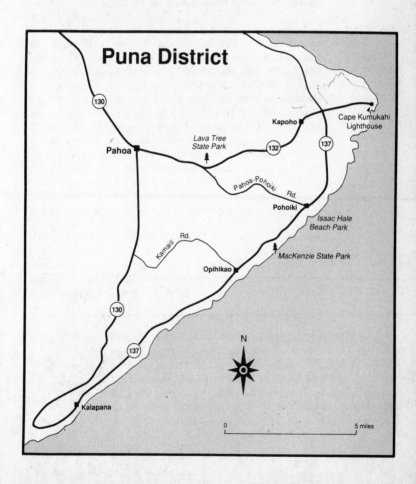

ued to the sea. In the process, it added about 500 yards of land to the point—an awesome demonstration of how young this Big Island really is.

Now return to Route 132 and head west back toward Pahoa. The road passes more of the **1960 lava flow**, which covered almost 2000 acres and totally leveled the small village of Kapoho.

An earlier eruption, circa 1790, caused the grotesque formations down the road at **Lava Tree State Park**. Here the molten rock swamped a grove of *ohia* trees, then hardened around the skeletons to create a fossil forest. When fissures in the earth drained the molten lava, these petrified trees were left as a lonely legacy. In strange and exotic fashion, these giant skeletons, mixed with fresh growth, loom above huge cracks in the landscape.

LODGING

HIDDEN ►

In the beautiful Puna District, a volcanic region fringed with black-sand beaches, there's a marvelous place called the **Kalani Honua Culture Center and Retreat**. Situated on Route 137, 20 minutes from Pahoa, it sits just above the ocean on 20 acres. In addition to lodging, this New Age resort provides a lifestyle. There are occasional classes in hula, weaving and lei making; lectures on the history and culture of Hawaii; plus programs in modern dance, aerobics and yoga. The facilities include a Japanese health spa with jacuzzi and sauna, a swimming pool, tennis court and volleyball courts. Guests stay in multi-unit lodges, sharing a spacious living room and kitchen. Sleeping accommodations are basic but appealing, with pine walls; the room decorations are crafted at the center. There are guest rooms with shared or private bath that sleep one or two and private cottages. Campsites are available at budget prices. Meals are $26 a day per person, or you can cook for yourself. ~ RR 2, Box 4500, Pahoa, HI 96778; 965-7828, 800-800-6886. MODERATE.

An enterprising family has converted the manager's residence of the old Puna Sugar Plantation into the **Banyan House Bed and Breakfast**. Set on ten tropical acres, the 1898 vintage home is sur-

BLACK HEAT

Since the latest series of volcanic eruptions began on the Big Island in 1983, the Puna District has been in constant turmoil. During one phase, an average of 650,000 tons of lava a day was spewing from the earth. In all, it has covered 40 square miles of the Big Island, creating new land masses along the ocean, destroying about 200 houses and fashioning several new black-sand beaches.

rounded by rolling lawns, orchards, flowerbeds and jungle. The two guest rooms are decorated differently, one with plantation wicker, the other with antiques, and they share a bath. The public rooms are very spacious and there are ocean views from several parts of the house. It provides a unique opportunity to experience turn-of-the-century Hawaii. ~ Route 130 about one mile southeast of Keaau; 966-8598. MODERATE.

GAY LODGING After a long day traversing the dense growth of tropical flowers and macadamia and fruit trees, women guests are grateful for a soak in a hot tub, a stint in the steam house or a minute with the masseuse. All this and more are obtainable at the **Butterfly Inn**, an all-women bed and breakfast located between Hilo and the village of Volcano. Rooms are cozily decorated, and in the morning a breakfast of assorted fruits, juices and breads may be taken onto the enclosed deck. ~ P.O. Box 6010, Kurtistown, HI 96760; 966-7936, 800-546-2442. MODERATE.

Exotic influences abound at **Huliaulea**. One guest room is furnished in Hawaiian antiques; another tips its hat to Japan, Thailand and China. The Pacific Rim–styled room includes its own entrance, private deck and all-bamboo furniture. Differences aside, all the luxurious accommodations include breakfast in the dining area, which is enclosed in glass to provide better views of Huliaulea's 22 acres of forest. A two-night-minimum stay is required. The clientele is predominantly gay. ~ P.O. Box 1030, Pahoa; 965-9175. MODERATE.

In the rustic town of Pahoa, there's **Luquin's Mexican Restaurant**, a friendly Mexican eatery serving a variety of dishes from south of the border. ~ Old Government Road, Pahoa; 965-9990. BUDGET.

DINING

◄ HIDDEN

Paradise West, a local café also located on the main drag in Pahoa, serves three hearty meals a day. Breakfast includes wholegrain pancakes and eggs with the catch of the day; lunch consists of hamburgers, sandwiches and soup. At dinner, there's steak and seafood. "Everything here is homemade." How can you go wrong? ~ Old Government Road, Pahoa; 965-9733. MODERATE.

The Banyan House Restaurant and Lounge offers dining on the veranda or indoors amidst the antiques. Both dining areas have ocean views. The menu features dishes such as prime rib with giant potatoes, shrimp curry, stuffed herbed chicken or homemade clam chowder. ~ Route 130 about one mile southeast of Keaau; 966-8598. MODERATE TO DELUXE.

In Pahoa, people often set up stands along the roadside. These freelance operations are great places to purchase fresh fish and homegrown fruits and vegetables. There are a few small markets. In

GROCERIES

Keaau, try the **Wiki Wiki Mart**. ~ Old Pahoa Highway; 966-8588.
In Pahoa, there's **Da Store**. ~ Route 130; 965-9411. For health
foods, consider **Pahoa Natural Groceries**. ~ Puna Road off Route
130, Pahoa; 965-8322.

SHOPPING   Out in the volcano region, on the road down to the Puna District,
you'll pass through the tiny town of **Pahoa**. Either side of Route
130, the main drag, is lined with falsefront buildings. Each one
seems to contain yet another ingenious craft shop run by a local
resident.

BEACHES   **ISAAC HALE BEACH PARK** 🏖 🏊 ↙ This small park on the
& PARKS   Puna coast is pretty but run-down. There's a patch of black sand
here and some hot springs nearby. A boat landing ramp makes this
a popular park with local people. Swimming is okay when the sea
is calm. There are both summer and winter breaks in the center of
the bay. The most common catches here are *papio*, *moi*, mountain
bass, *menpachi*, red bigeye, *ulua* and goatfish. A picnic area and
restrooms are the only facilities. Groceries are several miles away
in Pahoa. ~ On Route 137 about two miles northeast of MacKenzie State Park.
  ▲ Tent and trailer camping. County permit required. I much
prefer nearby MacKenzie State Park for overnighting.

MACKENZIE STATE PARK ↙ This beautiful 13-acre park lies in
an ironwood grove along a rocky coastline. King's Highway, an ancient Hawaiian trail, bisects the area. There is no swimming, snorkeling or surfing because a sea cliff borders the park. However,
there's good shore fishing from rock ledges. Picnic area and pit toilets are the only facilities. There's no drinking water. It's several
miles away from groceries in Pahoa. ~ On Route 137 near the village of Opihikao.
  ▲ Tent camping; a state permit is required.

▼▼▼▼▼▼▼▼▼▼▼▼▼▼   There are few activities on the Big Island more
Outdoor Adventures   pleasurable than camping. Beautiful state and
county parks dot the island, while enticing hiking
CAMPING   trails lead to remote mountain and coastal areas.
  No matter what you plan to do on the island, keep in mind that
the Kona side is generally dry, while the Hilo side receives considerable rain. Also remember that the mountains can be quite cold
and usually call for extra clothing and gear.
  Camping at **county parks** requires a permit. These cost $1 per
person per day (50¢ for children age 13 through 17). Pick up permits from the County Department of Parks and Recreation. ~ 25
Aupuni Street, Hilo, Hawaii, HI 96720; 961-8311. Permits are also
available at the Kona Recreation Office. ~ P.O. Box 314, Captain

Cook, Hawaii, HI 96740; 323-3060. County permits are issued for both tent and trailer camping, and can be obtained for up to two weeks at each park (one week during the summer).

Free **state parks** permits can be obtained through the State Department of Land and Natural Resources, Division of State Parks. ~ 75 Aupuni Street, Hilo, Hawaii, HI 96721; 933-4200. Maximum stay at each park is five days. For information on cabin rentals and camping in Volcanoes National Park, see the individual listings in the "Beaches & Parks" sections in this chapter.

Hilo Hawaii Sales and Surplus rents and sells sleeping bags, backpacks, tents, stoves and the like. ~ 148 Mamo Street, Hilo; 935-6398. Another place to buy camping equipment is **Honsport**. ~ 111 East Puainako, Hilo; 959-5816. **Pacific Rent-All** rents tents, backpacks, sleeping bags, stoves, coolers and other camping equipment. ~ 1080 Kilauea Avenue, Hilo; 935-2974.

DIVING

The Big Island's coastal waters offer some of the most enticing dive sites in Hawaii. Good visibility, lava and coral formations and, of course, an intriguing variety of marine life assure plenty of fun. Whether you choose a beach or boat dive, you'll find the waters relatively uncrowded. Snorkelers will be attracted to beautiful Kealakekua Bay where Captain Cook met his maker.

Nautilus Dive Center operates one- and two-tank shore dives off the Hilo coast. You'll see a variety of marine life, including sea turtles, as well as coral formations and caves. Closed Sunday. ~ 382 Kamehameha Avenue, Hilo; 935-6939.

Navatrek Explorer offers four-hour snorkeling cruises. ~ 75-5669 Alii Drive, Kailua; 329-6411.

Sandwich Isle Divers arranges dive trips to Turtle Pinnacles, Pine Trees, Golden Arches, Kaiwi Point and Kaloko Arches along the Kona Coast. ~ Kona Marketplace, Kailua; 329-9188. **King Kamehameha and Hawaiian Divers** offers daytime and night dives off the Kona Coast. For beginners, there's expert instruction offered.

◆◆

SLEEP UNDER THE BIG TOP

If camping is your idea of vacation fun, check out **Margo's Corner**. Margo's guests are generally bicyclists looking for refuge from high-rise hotels and staid inns. Hot showers and meals are provided, and sleeping quarters consist of a number of tents situated in a large yard filled with pine trees and gardens. Some visitors sleep out in the open under the canopy of trees. Also on the premises are a sweat lodge and a community room filled with books and maps. ~ P.O. Box 447; Naalehu; phone/fax 929-9614. Donations requested.

Experienced divers will enjoy exploring caves and archaeological sites. ~ King Kamehameha Hotel, Kailua; 329-5662, 800-525-7234.

Sea Paradise Scuba leads trips to lava tubes, caverns, caves and other fascinating formations at 25 locations south of Kailua. ~ 71-7128 Kaleopapa Street, Keauhou; 322-2500. **Big Island Dives** offers daytime and night dives along the Kona Coast. ~ 75-5467 Kaiwi Street, in the Kahamanu Plaza, Kailua; 329-6068.

Kohala Divers is a full-service diving center providing scuba and snorkeling lessons as well as gear rental. Closed Monday. ~ Kawaihae Shopping Center, Kawaihae; 882-7774.

(Also see the "Snorkeling and Scuba Diving the Gold Coast" section in this chapter.)

SURFING & WIND-SURFING

For surfing U.S.A., consider the dynamic Kona Coast as well as Hilo Bay. Winter is peak season for surfing popular spots such as Lyman's, Banyan's and Hunnels south of Kailua. Also popular is Pohiki in the Puna area near the Kilauea volcano. Windsurfing is good year-round. Try Anaehoomalu Beach on the Kona Coast or the South Point area.

Ocean Sports Hawaii rents sailboards and offers lessons. ~ Royal Waikoloan, Waikoloa; 885-5555. At the Kona Inn Shopping Village, **Hobie Sports Kona** also rents surfboards and boogie-boards and recommends the best locations. ~ 75-5744 Alii Drive; 329-1001.

FISHING

The waters off the Kona Coast are among the Pacific's finest fishing grounds, particularly for marlin. Many charter boats operate out of Kailua; check the phone book for names or simply walk along the pier and inquire.

Kona Charter Skippers' Association represents one of the larger outfits. They sponsor daily charters for marlin, yellowfin tuna, skipjack, *ono* and mahimahi. Using boats 26 to 50 feet in length, they charge $109 per person for a half day or $149 for a full day. ~ 75-5663 Palani Road, Kailua; 329-3600.

Head up to the tuna tower to survey the fishing scene aboard **Pamela**, a 40-foot vessel that focuses on marlin, short-nosed spearfish, mahimahi, yellowfin and wahoo. ~ Honokohau Harbor; 329-1525.

Another company offering similar service is **Kona Fuel and Marine**. ~ Honokohau Harbor, Kailua; 329-7529.

Jack's Kona Charters offers full- and half-day charters as well as overnight trips. ~ Honokohau Harbor, Kailua; 325-7558.

SAILING & PARA-SAILING

One of the authentic pleasures of a Big Island visit is a sail along the Kona or Kohala coast. Choose from a pleasure sail or take an adventure trip that includes a snorkeling excursion.

Among the popular operators is **Kamanu Charters**, which offers half-day trips with snorkeling at Pawai Bay. ~ Gentry's Complex in the Honokohau Harbor, Kailua; 329-2021. **Hawaii Sailing Company** operates half-day, full-day and overnight trips. The short four-hour sail includes snorkeling. ~ Honokohau Harbor; 326-1986. **The Maile Charters** is a 50-foot gulfstar sailboat available for a variety of trips around the Big Island. ~ Kawaihae Harbor; 326-5174.

Another popular sport in Hawaii is parasailing, in which you're strapped to a parachute that is towed aloft by a motorboat. For information, contact UFO **Parasail**. ~ Kailua; 325-5836.

Kona Kai-Yak offers beginner lessons as well full-day excursions. Kayak trips depart from boat ramps and secluded beaches up and down the Kona Coast. You can explore secluded spots like Kukio Bay and Kua Bay. Kayak rentals are also available here. Closed Sunday. ~ 74-425 Kealakehe Parkway, Honokohau Harbor, Kailua; 326-2922.

KAYAKING

Between November and May, when about 400 humpback whales inhabit Hawaiian waters, a popular spectator sport is spotting whales in the channels around the islands.

WHALE WATCHING & BOAT TOURS

Captain Zodiac leads four-hour daily trips along the Kona Coast. You may see whales, dolphins, sea turtles and other marine life as you journey along the coast and head into sea caves. There's a stop at Kealakekua Bay for snorkeling. ~ Honokohau Harbor; 329-3199.

Captain Dan McSweeney's Whale Watching Adventures operates three-hour cruises. If you don't see whales, the company will give you another trip at no charge. ~ Honokohau Harbor, Kailua; 322-0028.

✔ **CHECK THESE OUT—UNIQUE OUTDOOR ADVENTURES**

- Climb aboard the **Waipio Valley Wagon Tour** and explore a lush canyon filled with taro patches, tumbledown cottages and a 1200-foot waterfall. *page 162*
- Point your compass toward **South Point** and discover ancient canoe moorings and a beach where the sand is green. *page 194*
- Cast your fate to the fishing gods aboard a charter boat on the **Kona Coast,** one of the world's richest marlin grounds. *page 216*
- Circle Kilauea Caldera while passing steam vents, a fern forest and the Kau Desert on **Crater Rim Trail**. *page 220*

GOLF

Some of the best golfing in the country is found on the Big Island. From the stunning links on the Kohala Coast to community courses in the Hilo area, this island has everything you need for a golf-oriented vacation. Sunny conditions on the Kona side mean you generally don't need to worry about taking a rain check. Throw in views of the lava landscape, verdant shorelines and swaying banyan trees, and you've created a duffer's view of paradise.

Naniloa Country Club is a nine-hole, par-35 course overlooking Hilo Bay. This narrow course may look easy but don't be deceived: Water hazards and trees along the fairways create plenty of challenges. ~ 120 Banyan Drive, Hilo; 935-3000.

Hilo Municipal Golf Course is one of the best bargains on the islands. This 18-hole course has great views of the water and the mountains. Be sure to reserve tee times on the weekends. You can sharpen your skills on the driving range and practice greens. ~ 340 Haihai Street, Hilo; 959-7711.

Hamakua Country Club is another inexpensive choice. Located on the north shore about 40 miles from Hilo, this nine-hole course bans power carts. While it lacks the amenities of the resort links, Hamakua has a nice neighborhood feel. ~ Honokaa; 775-7244.

Paradise Safaris' Sunset Stargazing Trips takes you to the Mauna Kea summit for a telescopic adventure with astronomer Pat Wright. ~ Kailua; 322-2366.

Creating a great golf course is easy if you just dip into Laurence Rockefeller's deep pockets, hire Robert Trent Jones Sr. and buy some lava-strewn oceanfront terrain. What you'll end up with is the 18-hole **Mauna Kea Beach Golf Course**. ~ Kawaihae; 882-7222. Quite a challenge, the original links have been complemented by the new 18-hole **Hapuna Golf Course** created by Arnold Palmer. ~ 882-1035.

Waikoloa Village Golf Course is an 18-hole, par-72 layout that also includes a driving range and practice greens. This windy course, designed by Robert Trent Jones Jr., has great views of Mauna Kea and Mauna Loa. ~ Waikoloa; 883-9621. Nearby the **Waikoloa Beach Resort Golf Course** was also designed by Robert Trent Jones Jr. ~ Waikoloa; 885-6789. The adjacent **Waikoloa Kings' Golf Club** has another popular course. ~ Waikoloa; 885-4647. Convenient to the Hyatt Regency Waikoloa and the Royal Waikoloan, each course has unique features. The beach course heads through petroglyph fields while the Kings Golf Club also has beautiful lava hazards.

Mauna Lani Golf Course has two 18-hole links built across rugged lava beds. If you miss the fairway, don't expect to find your ball out there in the volcanic landscape. There's also a driving range and practice greens. ~ Kohala Coast; 885-6655.

At the **Kona Country Club**, a pair of 18-hole golf courses are ideal for those who want to bunker down. Bring along your camera to capture memorable views of the ocean course. Or head uphill to fully enjoy the challenging Mauka course. If you're looking for over-water holes and hidden hazards, you've come to the right place. ~ 78-7000 Alii Drive, Kailua; 322-2595.

Volcano Golf and Country Club is the only course I know located in the vicinity of an erupting volcano. The high elevation (4200 feet) will give your ball an extra lift on this 18-hole course. ~ Volcanoes National Park; 967-7331. **Sea Mountain Golf Course** is a popular 18-hole course located south of Kilauea volcano. It's beautifully landscaped with coconut and banyan trees. ~ Punaluu; 928-6222.

Public tennis courts are convenient to all of the Big Island's popular resort destinations. In Hilo, you can play at the courts at Kalanikoa and Piilani streets or Kilauea and Ponahawai streets.

TENNIS

In Waimea, try Waimea Park on Lindsey Road off Route 19. In the Kailua area head for Kailua Park (Old Airport Road), Higashihara Park (Mamalahoa Highway, Keauhou), or the courts at the intersection of Palani and Kuakini roads.

Call the **County Department of Parks and Recreation** for information on public courts. ~ 961-8311. Contact the **Hawaii Visitors & Convention Bureau** for information concerning private courts. ~ 961-5797, 329-7787.

Hawaii offers very good roads and many unpopulated stretches that make it ideal for cyclers. Much of the island is mountainous with some fairly steep grades in the interior. Saddle Road, the roads to Waimea, and the road from Hilo up to Volcanoes National Park will all make a heavy breather of you, but the coast roads are generally flat or gently rolling. Most roads have shoulders and light traffic.

BIKING

Keep in mind that the northeast side of the island receives heavy rainfall, while the Kona side is almost always sunny. But wet side or dry, the scenery is spectacular throughout.

Bike Rentals   In Kailua, try **Dave's Bike and Triathlon Shop**. They rent 10-speed, 12-speed and mountain bikes and do repairs. ~ 75-5669 Alii Drive, 329-4522. **B & L Bike & Sports** rents top-of-the-line Cannondales. ~ 75-5699 Kopiko Place, Kailua-Kona; 329-3309. Rentals are also available at **Hawaiian Pedals**. ~ Kona Inn Shopping Village, Kailua; 329-2294.

Bike Repairs   Ninety percent of the business at **The Bike Shop** is repairs, but they also sell mountain bikes. ~ 258 Kamehameha Avenue, Hilo; 935-7588. The folks at **Mid-Pacific Wheels** will do repair work for you or will cheerfully sell you any bike accessories. Closed Sunday. ~ 1133-C Manono Street, Hilo; 935-6211. **B & L Bike & Sports** also does repairs. Closed Sunday. ~ 75-5699 Kopiko Place, Kailua-Kona; 329-3309.

RIDING STABLES   If you're looking to enter the amazing, dwarfing world of the rainforests, **Rainforest Trail Rides** provides one- and two-hour guided tours through the rainforest on horseback. Lunch, by the way, is included with the two-hour tour. ~ Keahoumauka; 322-6609, 800-545-5662, fax 322-6507.

HIKING   Of all the islands in the chain, Hawaii has the finest hiking trails. The reason? Quite simply, it's the Big Island's size. Larger than all the other islands combined and boasting the highest peaks, Hawaii offers the greatest diversity to explorers.

Mauna Loa and Mauna Kea, each rising over 13,000 feet, provide rugged mountain climbing. To the north, the Kohala Mountains feature trails through dense tropical terrain and along awesome cliffs. In Volcanoes National Park, hikers can experience the challenge of walking through a lava wasteland and into the belly of an active volcano.

Along Hawaii's shoreline lie the remains of the Makahiki trail, a series of paths that once circled the entire island. Also known as the William Ellis trail, this ancient Hawaiian track was named after the Makahiki gods and then renamed for Ellis, the bold missionary who explored it in 1823. Today, sections of the trail can still be walked, though much of it is destroyed. Of the remaining portions, some cross private land and others are unmarked. But with a topographic map and a pair of sturdy boots you can still follow in the tracks of the gods, and, for that matter, in the tracks of William Ellis.

Hawaii's official hiking trails run through four areas: Volcanoes National Park, Kau Desert, Mauna Kea and the Kohala Mountains. These are popular and well-defined trails, many of which are described below.

VOLCANOES NATIONAL PARK   The most interesting and easily accessible trails lead through the **Kilauea Caldera** area. The caldera, three miles long and 4000 feet above sea level, can be explored either by hiking along one extended trail or over several shorter connecting trails.

Crater Rim Trail (11.6 miles long) begins near the park headquarters and encircles Kilauea Caldera. An excellent introduction to the volcanoes, this lengthy loop trail passes steam vents, the Kau Desert, the fractured Southwest Rift area and a fascinating fern forest. The views from along the rim are spectacular.

Sulphur Banks Trail (0.3 mile) begins at park headquarters and parallels Crater Rim Road past steam vents and sulphur deposits.

Halemaumau Trail (3.2 miles) starts near Volcano House, then descends into Kilauea Caldera. The trail crosses the crater floor and affords astonishing views down into steaming Halemaumau

Ski

Hawaii

During your island tour you'll inevitably pull up behind some joker with a bumper sticker reading "Think Snow." Around you trade winds may be bending the palm trees, sunbronzed crowds will be heading to the beach, and the thermometer will be approaching 80°. Snow will be the furthest thing from your mind.

But up on the 13,796-foot slopes of Mauna Kea, you're liable to see a bikini-clad skier schussing across a mantle of newly fallen snow! Any time from December until April or May, there may be enough dry snow to create ski runs several miles long and fill bowls a half-mile wide and almost a mile long. The slopes range from beginner to expert: Some have a vertical drop of over 5000 feet.

Situated above the clouds about 80 percent of the time, this snow lover's oasis is baked by a tropical sun many times more powerful than at the beach. So it's easy to tan and easier yet to burn. Combined with the thin air and winds up to 100 miles per hour, Hawaii's ski slopes are not for the faint-hearted or fair-skinned. But if you're seeking an incredible adventure and want a view of the Hawaiian islands from a 13,000-foot crow's nest, the heights of Mauna Kea await.

Ski Guides Hawaii offers all-day downhill skiing tours on Mauna Kea and cross-country skiing on Mauna Loa. The ski season lasts from December until April or May. ~ Waimea; 885-4188.

crater, then climbs back up to join Crater Rim Trail. This has got to be one of the park's finest hikes.

Kilauea Iki Trail (4 miles) loops from the Thurston Lava Tube parking lot down into Kilauea Iki crater and returns via Crater Rim Trail. Crossing the crater floor, the trail passes over a lava crust beneath which lies a pool of molten rock. Step lightly.

Sandalwood Trail (1.5 miles) loops from near the Volcano House past sandalwood and *ohia* trees and then along the side of Kilauea Caldera.

Byron Ledge Trail (2.5 miles) branches off Halemaumau Trail, crosses the Kilauea caldera floor, and then climbs along Byron Ledge before rejoining Halemaumau. This makes an excellent connecting trail.

Starting within the Kapapala Forest Reserve at 5650 feet, the **Ainapo Trail** (2.7 miles) takes hikers on a moderately challenging trek past mesic *koa* and *ohia* trees. On the way up to the Ainapo Trail Shelter at Halewai, you'll catch sight of mountain goats and sheep. More experienced hikers can climb the rest of the fog-covered trail (7.5 miles) and will be rewarded with views from the rim of the Mokuaweoweo Crater in Hawaii Volcanoes National Park. The trailhead begins at the cattleguard between the 40- and 41-mile markers on the Mamalahoa Highway between Volcano and Pahala.

Volcanoes National Park's premier hike is along **Mauna Loa Trail**. This tough 19-mile trek, requiring at least three days, leads to the top of the world's largest shield volcano. Cold-weather equipment and a sturdy constitution are absolute necessities for this challenging adventure. Permits are required for this hike.

Climbers usually hike seven miles the first day from the trailhead at the end of Mauna Loa Strip Road up to Red Hill. At this 10,035-foot way station, there is a rudimentary cabin with no provisions. A hearty 11-mile trek the second day leads to the rim of Mauna Loa's summit crater, and to the Mokuaweoweo cabin (located on the rim). The return trip takes one or two days, depending on how fast you want to come down.

Beware of altitude sickness and hypothermia, and be sure to register for a permit at park headquarters before and after hiking. Purification tablets for the water and white gas for the stoves are also essential. Don't treat this as a casual jaunt; it's a real trek. Good planning will ensure your safety and enjoyment.

A single-lane paved road climbs from Saddle Road to an area near Mauna Loa summit. This alternative hiking route lacks the adventure but reduces the time needed to ascend Mauna Loa. This road is not open to rental cars.

KAU AREA From Volcanoes National Park's southern section several trails lead into the hot, arid Kau Desert. All are long, dusty trails offering solitude to the adventurous hiker.

Kau Desert Trail (18.9 miles) branches off Crater Rim Trail and drops 2000 feet en route to the lookout at the end of Hilina Pali Road. The shelter along the way, at Kipuka Pepeiau, provides a welcome resting place on this lengthy trek.

Mauna Iki Trail (8.8 miles) leads from Mamalahoa Highway (Route 11) to Hilina Pali Road. The trail passes near Footprints Trail, where a sudden volcanic eruption in 1790 engulfed a Hawaiian army at war with Kamehameha.

Halape Trail (7.2 miles) begins at Kipuka Nene campground on Hilina Pali Road and rapidly drops 3000 feet to a sand beach at Halape. There is also a shelter at Halape. (Note that Kipuka Nene can be closed for months at a time when the endangered nene are in residence.)

MAUNA KEA This hike is not nearly as rigorous as the trek up Mauna Loa, but the scenery is just as stunning. A road leads off Saddle Road for nine miles to the trailhead at Kilohana. From this 9620-foot elevation, it is six miles to the 13,796-foot summit. Atop the state's highest peak, you'll have a spectacular view of Maui's Haleakala crater. Begin early and plan to make the hike in one day since no camping is permitted along the way.

In addition to vistas as breathtaking as the altitude, Mauna Kea features the state's highest body of water, Lake Waiau, at 13,020 feet.

KOHALA MOUNTAIN Stretching along Kohala peninsula's northeast coast is a series of sheer cliffs and wide valleys rivaling Kauai's Na Pali Coast in beauty. At either end of this rainswept *pali* are lush, still valleys that can only be reached by hiking trails.

Pololu Valley Trail (0.5 mile) descends from the Pololu Valley lookout at the end of Akoni Pule Highway to the valley floor 300 feet below. From here, a series of trails leading through the Kohala Mountains begins. Unfortunately, these trails are controlled by Chalon International of Hawaii, Inc. and are closed to hikers.

Waipio Valley Trail begins from Waipio Valley lookout at the end of Route 24. Waipio is comparable to Kauai's Kalalau Valley: a broad, lush, awesomely beautiful valley ribboned with waterfalls and rich in history. From the trailhead, a jeep trail drops steeply for one mile to the valley floor. Here the trail joins one road leading up into the valley and another heading to the beach. The high road goes toward 1200-foot Hiilawe Falls and to a now-abandoned Peace Corps training camp.

Waipio Valley is ripe for exploring, but if you want to leave civilization completely behind, continue instead along the **Waimanu Valley Trail**. This seven-mile track begins at the base of the cliff that marks Waipio's northwest border. It climbs sharply up the 1200-foot rock face in a series of switchbacks, then continues up and down across numerous gulches, and finally descends into Waimanu Valley. This exotic place, half the size of Waipio Valley, is equally as lush. Here, in addition to wild pigs, mountain apple trees and ancient ruins, you'll find naturally running water (requiring purification) and great spots for beachfront picnics. You may never want to leave.

▼▼▼▼▼▼▼▼▼▼▼
Transportation

AIR

Four airports serve the Big Island—Hilo International Airport (General Lyman Field) near Hilo, Keahole–Kona International Airport, Upolu Airport on the Kohala peninsula, and Kamuela Airport near Waimea.

The main landing facility is **Keahole–Kona International Airport**. Many mainland visitors fly here rather than to Honolulu to avoid Oahu's crowds. United Airlines, which provides the most frequent service to Hawaii, is the only carrier flying from the mainland directly to Kailua-Kona. United provides two flights daily to this airport.

This windswept facility has snack bars, cocktail lounges, duty-free shops, a restaurant and souvenir shops, but no lockers or bus service. A nine-mile cab ride into town costs about $20.

Passengers flying between the islands use Aloha Airlines, Hawaiian Airlines and Mahalo Air. The first two provide frequent jet service from Oahu and the other islands, while the other flies prop planes. Personally I prefer Aloha Airlines because of their punctuality and excellent service record.

Hilo International Airport (General Lyman Field), once the island's main jetport, is now more like a small city airport. It is served by the same inter-island carriers as Keahole Airport. Here you'll find a cafeteria-style restaurant, cocktail lounge, gift shop, newsstand and lockers, but no bus service. Covering the two miles into town means renting a car, hailing a cab, hitching or hoofing.

Upolu Airport is a desolate landing strip on the Kohala peninsula along the island's northwest coast. There are no facilities whatever and only prop planes land here.

Kamuela Airport, two miles outside the cowboy town of Waimea, is served by TransAir. There are waiting rooms, but no shops of any kind here. Airline offices are often closed unless a flight is scheduled, so it's best to make all reservations in advance.

CAR RENTALS

Big Island rental agencies generally charge slightly more than is charged on the other islands because of the longer distances traveled. Also, they often charge a fee ($40 or so) for cars rented in Hilo or Kona and dropped off in the other locale.

When choosing a rental agency, check whether they permit driving on the Saddle Road across the island and on South Point Road, both good paved roads with few potholes and many points of interest. I think it's quite unfair, even irrational, that some rental companies revoke insurance coverage if you drive these thorough-fares. But my protests will be of little benefit in case of an accident. So check first or be prepared to take your chances! It's wise to re-member that you will be driving farther on Hawaii, sometimes through quite rural areas; it may sound obvious, but remember to watch your gas gauge.

That said, my favorite car rental operations are the smaller companies. Like the nationally known firms, they generally have booths either in Hilo or Kona, or both. (The first local phone num-ber listed here is for Hilo, the second for Kona.) Generally, the lesser-known outfits tend to be easier on the purse than nationally acclaimed companies. I have always found Hawaii's small, inde-pendent car rental agencies provide comparable service, and there-fore I generally recommend them. So with your budget in mind, consider **Harper Car & Truck Rentals of Hawaii**, which rents everything from compact cars to 4x4s to vans. ~ 1690 Kameha-meha Avenue, Hilo; 969-1478, 800-852-9993.

Several other companies have franchises at the Hilo and Kailua-Kona airports. Among these are **Avis** (935-1290, 327-3001, 800-331-1212), **Budget Rent A Car** (935-6878, 329-8511, 800-527-0700), **Dollar Rent A Car** (961-6059, 329-2744, 800-800-4000), **Hertz Rent A Car** (935-2896, 329-3566, 800-654-3011) and **Na-tional Interrent** (935-0891, 329-1674, 800-227-7368).

Many outfits located outside the Hilo International Airport and Keahole Airport feature competitive rates and free service to and from the airport.

(See Chapter One for a complete explanation of car rentals in the islands.)

Budget Rent A Car rents four-wheel drives. ~ 935-6878, 329-8511, 800-527-0700.

JEEP RENTALS

The Kailua-Kona location of **Harper Car & Truck Rentals of Hawaii** doesn't rent cars but has everything else—4x4s, trucks, vans and jeeps. ~ 75-578 Kuakini Highway; 329-6688, 800-852-9993.

Motorcycles and scooters are available for rent at **DJ's Rentals**, with two locations to serve you. ~ 75-5663-A Palani Road, Kailua-Kona; 329-1700. In the Waikoloa Resort Area, check the Kings' Shops. ~ 885-7368.

MOPED RENTALS

The **Hele-On Bus** provides cross-island service Monday through Saturday between Hilo and Kailua-Kona. There are also limited intra-city buses serving Hilo. Other buses drive to the Kona and Kau coasts. The Hele-On runs Monday through Saturday; fares

PUBLIC TRANSIT

range from 75¢ for short rides to $6 for the Hilo–Kailua cross-island run. ~ 961-8343.

The Hilo bus terminal is on Kamehameha Avenue at Mamo Street. You'll see few bus stops indicated on the island. The official stops are generally unmarked, and you can hail a bus anywhere along its route. Just wave your hand. When it's time to get off, the driver will stop anywhere you wish.

For information and schedules, phone the **County Hawaiian Transit**. ~ 935-8241, 961-8343.

HITCHING

Thumbing is very popular in Hawaii. Like any place, your luck will vary here, depending on your location, looks, the time, the tides, whatever. Generally, populated areas and tourist attractions are good spots for a ride. If you venture from these beaten paths, remember that the Big Island has long stretches with nothing but macadam and lava. Be sure to bring along water with you.

Check the Hele-On bus schedule before setting out just in case you get stranded. If your luck fails, you can hail a bus from anywhere along the roadside.

AERIAL TOURS

Thanks to the Kilauea eruption, the Big Island offers a wide variety of flightseeing options. In addition to the lava flows, you'll see remote coastlines, the slopes of Mauna Kea and coffee plantations. Bring your camera because the lava flow is one of Hawaii's greatest sightseeing opportunities.

Safari Helicopters offers three tours on the Big Island that fly passengers past volcanoes and waterfalls. ~ Hilo International Airport; 969-1259.

Volcano Helitours offers a narrated 45-minute tour of all active eruptions. ~ mile marker 30, Mamalahoa Highway, Volcano; 967-7578.

At **Mauna Kea Helicopters** you have a choice of three flights lasting up to two hours. Passengers view the valleys and waterfalls on the island's northern end, as well as volcanic activity at Kilauea. ~ Mamalahoa Highway at the Waimea Airport, Waimea; 885-6400.

Big Island Air takes passengers on a circle island tour featuring Kilauea and the north end valleys and waterfalls. Flights last about 1 hour and 45 minutes. ~ Keahole Airport; 329-4868.

Papillon Helicopters offers flights from both sides of the island featuring Kilauea, the Kohala Coast, Waipio Valley, waterfalls and the rainforest. Trips last 35 minutes to two hours. ~ Waikoloa Heliport and Hilo International Airport; 606-5661. Similar tours are offered by **Kenai Helicopters**. ~Waikoloa Beach Drive, Waikoloa; 885-5833.

▼▼▼▼▼▼▼▼▼▼▼▼▼▼▼▼▼▼▼▼▼▼

Addresses & Phone Numbers

HAWAII ISLAND

County Department of Parks and Recreation ~ 25 Aupuni Street, Hilo; 961-8311.

Hawaii Visitors & Convention Bureau ~ 250 Keawe Street, Hilo; 961-5797, and Kona Plaza Shopping Arcade, Alii Drive, Kailua; 329-7787.

State Department of Land and Natural Resources ~ 75 Aupuni Street, Hilo; 933-4200.

Volcanoes National Park Headquarters ~ 967-7311.

Weather Report ~ 935-8555 for Hilo; 961-5582 for entire island.

HILO

Ambulance ~ 911 or 961-9677.

Barber Shop ~ Faye's Barber Shop, 710 Kilauea Avenue. ~ 935-4990.

Books ~ Book Gallery, Prince Kuhio Plaza; 959-7744.

Fire Department ~ 961-8336.

Fishing Supplies ~ S. Tokunaga Store, 26 Hoku Street; 935-6965.

Hardware ~ Garden Exchange, 300 Keawe Street; 961-2875.

Hospital ~ Hilo Medical Center, 1190 Waianuenue Avenue; 969-4111.

Library ~ 300 Waianuenue Avenue; 933-4650.

Liquor ~ Kadota Liquor, 194 Hualalai Street; 935-1802.

Pharmacy ~ Longs Drugs, 555 Kilauea Avenue; 935-3357.

Photo Supply ~ Hawaii Photo Supply, 250 Keawe Street; 935-6995.

Police Department ~ 349 Kapiolani Street; 935-3311.

Post Office ~ Hilo International Airport; 933-7090, and 154 Waianuenue Avenue; 933-7095.

KAILUA-KONA

Ambulance ~ 911 or 961-9677.

Barber Shop ~ The New Wave, Kona Surf Resort; 322-3335.

Books ~ Middle Earth Bookshoppe, 75-5719 Alii Drive; 329-2123.

Fire Department ~ 961-8297

Fishing Supplies ~ Yama's Specialty Shop, 75-5943 Alii Drive; 329-1712.

Hardware ~ Trojan Lumber Company, 74-5488 Kaiwi Street; 329-3536.

Hospital ~ Kona Community Hospital, Kealakekua town; 322-9311.

Laundromat ~ Hele Mai Laundromat, North Kona Shopping Center; 329-3494.

Library ~ Hualalai Road; 327-3077.

Pharmacy ~ Longs Drugs, Lanihau Shopping Center, Palani Road; 329-1380.

Photo Supply ~ Zac's Photo, Lanihau Shopping Center, Palani Road; 329-0006.

Police Department ~ 326-4201

Post Office ~ Palani Road; 329-1927

SIX

Maui

Residents of Maui, Hawaii's second-largest island, proudly describe their Valley Isle by explaining that "Maui *no ka oi*." Maui is the greatest. During the last decade, few of the island's visitors have disputed the claim. They return each year, lured by the enchantment of a place possessing 33 miles of public beaches, one of the world's largest dormant volcanoes, beautiful people, a breeding ground for rare humpback whales and a climate that varies from subtropic to subarctic.

Named after one of the most important demigods in the Polynesian pantheon, Maui has retained its mythic aura. The island is famous as a chic retreat and jet-set landing ground. To many people, Maui *is* Hawaii.

But to others, who have watched the rapid changes during the past two decades, Maui is no longer the greatest. They point to the 2.4 million tourists (second only to Oahu) who visited during a recent year, to the condominiums and resort hotels mushrooming along the prettiest beaches and to the increasing traffic over once-rural roads. And they have a new slogan. "Maui is *pau*." Maui is finished. Over-touristed. Overpopulated. Overdeveloped.

Today, among the island's 102,000 population, it seems like every other person is in the real estate business. On a land mass measuring 729 square miles, just half the size of Long Island, their goods are in short supply. During the 1970s and 1980s, land prices shot up faster than practically anywhere else in the country.

Yet over 75 percent of the island remains unpopulated. Despite pressures from land speculation and a mondo-condo mentality, Maui still offers exotic, untouched expanses for the explorer. Most development is concentrated along the south and west coasts in Kihei, Wailea and Kaanapali. The rest of the island, though more populated than neighboring islands, is an adventurer's oasis.

The second-youngest island in the chain, Maui was created between one and two million years ago by two volcanoes. Haleakala, the larger, rises over 10,000 feet, and offers excellent hiking and camping within its valley. The earlier of the two firepits created the West Maui Mountains, 5788 feet at their highest elevation. Because of their relative age, and the fact they receive 400 inches of rainfall a year, they are more heavily eroded than the smooth surfaces of Haleakala. Between the two heights lies Central Maui, an isthmus formed when the volcanoes flowed together.

The twin cities of Kahului and Wailuku, Maui's commercial and civic centers, respectively, sit in this saddle. Most of the isthmus is planted in sugar, which became king in Maui after the decline of whaling in the 1860s. A road through the cane fields leads south to the sunsplashed resorts and beaches of Kihei and Wailea.

Another road loops around the West Maui Mountains. It passes prime whale-watching areas along the south coast and bisects Lahaina, an old whaling town that is now the island's sightseeing capital. Next to this timeworn harbor stretches the town of Kaanapali with its limitless beaches and endless condominiums. Past these glass-and-steel palisades, near the island's northwest tip, lie hidden beaches, overhanging cliffs and spectacular vistas.

The road girdling Haleakala's lower slopes passes equally beautiful areas. Along the rainswept northeast coast are sheer rock faces ribboned with waterfalls and gorges choked with tropic vegetation. The lush, somnolent town of Hana gives way along the southeast shore to a dry, unpopulated expanse that is always ripe for exploration.

On the middle slopes of Haleakala, in Maui's Upcountry region, small farms dot the landscape. Here, in addition to guavas, avocados and lichee nuts, grow the sweet Kula onions for which the Valley Isle is famous.

Back in the days of California's gold rush, Maui found its own underground nuggets in potatoes: Countless bushels were grown in this area and shipped to a hungry San Francisco market. Today the crop is used to prepare Maui potato chips.

Because of its strategic location between Oahu and Hawaii, Maui has played a vital role in Hawaiian history. Kahekili, Maui's last king, gained control of all the islands except Hawaii before being overwhelmed by Kamehameha in 1790. Lahaina, long a vacation spot for island rulers, became a political center under Hawaii's first three kings and an important commercial center soon after Captain Cook sighted the island in 1778. It served as a supply depot for ships, then as a port for sandalwood exports. By the 1840s, Lahaina was the world capital of whaling. Now, together with the other equally beautiful sections of the Valley Isle, it is a mecca for vacationers.

Maui's magic has cast a spell upon travelers all over the world, making the island a vacation paradise. Like most modern paradises, it is being steadily gilded in plastic and concrete. Yet much of the old charm remains. Some people even claim that the sun shines longer on the Valley Isle than any other place on earth. They point to the legend of the demigod Maui who created his own daylight savings by weaving a rope from his sister's pubic hair and lassoing the sun by its genitals. And many hope he has one last trick to perform, one that will slow the course of development just as he slowed the track of the sun.

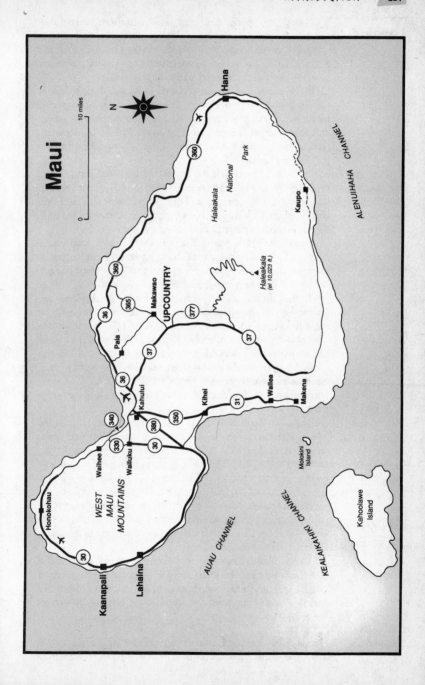

▼▼▼▼▼▼▼▼▼

Lahaina

Maui's top tourist destination is a waterfront enclave that stretches for over two miles along a natural harbor, but measures only a couple of blocks deep. Simultaneously chic and funky, Lahaina has gained an international reputation for its art galleries, falsefront stores and waterfront restaurants.

It also happens to be one of Hawaii's most historic towns. A royal seat since the 16th century, Lahaina was long a playground for the *alii*. The royal surfing grounds lay just south of today's town center, and in 1802, Kamehameha I established his headquarters here, taking up residence in the Brick Palace, the first Western-style building in Hawaii.

It was in Lahaina that the first high school and first printing press west of the Rockies were established in 1831. From Lahaina, Kamehameha III promulgated Hawaii's first constitution in 1840, and established a legislative body that met in town until the capital was eventually moved to Honolulu.

During the 1820s, this quaint port also became a vital watering place for whaling ships and evolved into the whaling capital of the world. At its peak in the mid-1840s, the whaling trade brought over 400 ships a year into the harbor.

To the raffish sailors who favored it for its superb anchorage, grog shops and uninhibited women, Lahaina was heaven itself. To the stiff-collared missionaries who arrived in 1823, the town was a hellhole—a place of sin, abomination and vile degradation. Some of Lahaina's most colorful history was written when the Congregationalists prevented naked women from swimming out to meet the whalers. Their belligerent brethren anchored in the harbor replied by cannonballing mission homes and rioting along the waterfront.

The town declined with the loss of the whaling trade in the 1860s, and was transformed into a quiet sugar plantation town, serving the Pioneer Sugar Mill that opened during the same decade. Not until developers began building resorts in nearby Kaanapali a century later did it fully revive. During the 1960s, Lahaina was designated a national historic landmark and restoration of many important sites was begun. By the 1970s, the place was a gathering spot not only for the jet set but the ultra hip as well. Clubs like the Blue Max made Lahaina a hot nightspot where famous musicians came to vacation and jam

Today Lahaina retains much of its old charm in the ramshackle storefronts that line the water along Front Street. Most points of interest lie within a half-mile of the old sea wall that protects this narrow thoroughfare from the ocean, so the best way to explore the town is on foot.

SIGHTS

Start at **Lahaina Harbor**, located on Wharf Street, and take a stroll along the docks. In addition to tour boats, pleasure craft from around the world put in here or cast anchor in the Lahaina Roads just offshore. During the heyday of the whaling industry in the 1840s, the Auau Channel between Lahaina and Lanai was a forest of masts.

Carthaginian II, the steel-hulled brig at dock's end, preserves those days in a shipboard museum. Actually a turn-of-the-century brig that was converted into a replica of an old square-rigged sailing ship, this floating display case features videotapes on whales and intriguing artifacts from days of yore. Admission. ~ 661-3262.

Across Wharf Street sits the **Pioneer Inn**, a rambling hostelry built in 1901. With its second-story veranda and landscaped garden, this aging woodframe hotel is a great place to bend an elbow and breathe in the salt air. ~ 658 Wharf Street; 661-3636.

Just north of here a Hawaii Visitors Bureau sign points out the chair-shaped **Hauola Stone**, a source of healing power for ancient Hawaiians, who sat in the natural formation and let the waves wash over them.

There is nothing left of the **Brick Palace**, the two-story structure commissioned in 1798 by Kamehameha I. Located just inshore from the Hauola Stone and built by an English convict, the palace was used by the king in 1802 and 1803 (although some say he preferred to stay in his grass shack next door). Today the original foundation has been outlined with brick paving.

To the south, a 120-year-old **banyan tree**, among the oldest and largest in the islands, extends its rooting branches across almost an entire acre. Planted in 1873 to mark the advent of Protestant missionaries in Maui 50 years earlier, this shady canopy is a resting place for tourists and mynah birds alike. ~ Front and Hotel streets.

The sprawling giant presses right to the **Old Courthouse** door. Built in 1859 from the remains of the palace of King Kamehameha III, the building was fashioned from coral blocks. The **Lahaina Visitors Center** (667-9175) is located in the courthouse. Here you can pick up maps and brochures. The **Old Jail** in the basement now

◆◆

✔ CHECK THESE OUT—UNIQUE SIGHTS

- Stand watch at **McGregor Point** for the foaming eruption of one of the 2000 humpback whales that visit Maui annually. *page 284*
- Catch a wave and check out the scene at **Makena Beach**, where rock stars jammed during the hippie days of the late '60s. *page 264*
- Climb from the oceanside into the rainforest while exploring rock-bound pools fed by waterfalls in **Oheo Gulch**. *page 289*
- Perch yourself at the 10,000-foot summit of **Haleakala** (particularly at sunrise) and peer into the mouth of a dormant volcano. *page 307*

incongruously houses **The Lahaina Art Society** (661-0111), a non-profit association of local artists. Exhibits at the gallery here are rotating collections of member artists.

Those stone ruins on either side of the courthouse are the remains of the **Old Fort**, built during the 1830s to protect Lahaina from the sins and cannonballs of lawless sailors. The original structure was torn down two decades later to build a jail, but during its heyday the fortress guarded the waterfront with 47 cannons.

Across Front Street you'll find the **Baldwin Home**, Lahaina's oldest building. Constructed of coral and stone in the early 1830s, the place sheltered the family of Reverend Dwight Baldwin, a medical missionary. Today the house contains period pieces and family heirlooms, including some of the good doctor's rather fiendish-looking medical implements. Beneath the hand-hewn ceiling beams rests the Baldwin's Steinway piano; the dining room includes the family's china, a fragile cargo that made the voyage around Cape Horn; and in the master bedroom stands a four-poster bed fashioned from native *koa*. Admission. ~ 661-3262.

The **Master's Reading Room** next door, an 1834 storehouse and library, is home to the Lahaina Restoration Foundation and not open to the public.

The **Wo Hing Temple**, a Chinese gathering place that dates to 1912, has been lovingly restored. While the temple has been converted into a small museum, the old cookhouse adjacent is used to show films of the islands made by Thomas Edison in 1898 and 1906 during the early days of motion pictures. Admission. ~ 858 Front Street; 661-3262.

The **Holy Innocents Episcopal Church** is a small structure dating from 1927. Very simple in design, the sanctuary is filled with beautiful paintings. The Hawaiian madonna on the altar and the tropical themes of the paintings are noteworthy features. ~ 561 Front Street; 661-4202.

Several other historic spots lie along Wainee Street, which parallels Front Street. **Waiola Cemetery**, with its overgrown lawn and eroded tombstones, contains graves dating to 1829. Queen Keopuolani, the wife of Kamehameha I and the mother of Hawaii's next two kings, is buried here. So is her daughter, Princess Nahienaena, and Governor Hoapali, who ruled Hawaii from 1823 to 1840. Surrounded by blossoming plumeria trees, there are also the graves of early missionaries and Hawaiian commoners.

Maui's first Christian services were performed in 1823 on the grounds of **Waiola Church** next door. Today's chapel, built in 1953, occupies the spot where Wainee Church was constructed in 1832. The earlier structure, Hawaii's first stone church, seated 3000 parishioners and played a vital role in the conversion of the local population to Christianity and Western ways. ~ 661-4349.

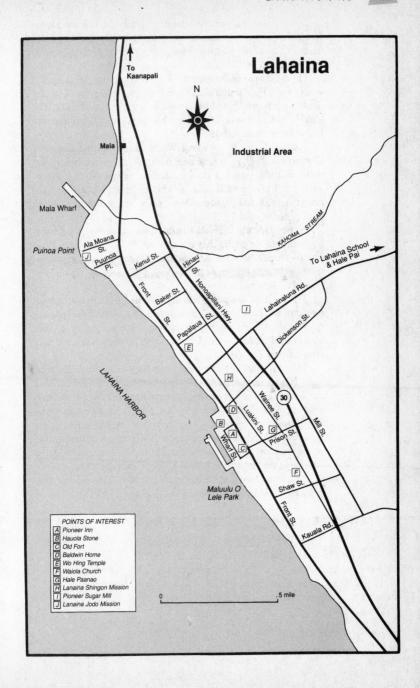

Lahaina

To
Kaanapali

N

Industrial Area

Mala

Mala Wharf

Puinoa Point

KAHOMA STREAM

To Lahaina School
& Hale Pai

Ala Moana St.
J
Puunoa Pl.

Kenui St.

Hinau St.

Front St.

Baker St.

Honoapiilani Hwy.

Papalaua St.

I

Lahainaluna Rd.

Dickenson St.

E

LAHAINA HARBOR

H

D

B

A

C

Wharf St.

Luakini St.

Wainee St.

30

G

Prison St.

Mill St.

F

Maluulu O
Lele Park

Shaw St.

Front St.

Kauala Rd.

POINTS OF INTEREST
A Pioneer Inn
B Hauola Stone
C Old Fort
D Baldwin Home
E Wo Hing Temple
F Waiola Church
G Hale Paanao
H Lanaina Shingon Mission
I Pioneer Sugar Mill
J Lanaina Jodo Mission

0   .5 mile

A little farther north on Wainee Street sits the **Lahaina Hong-wanji Temple** with its three distinctive turrets. The building dates from 1927, but the Buddhist Hongwanji sect has been meeting at this site since 1910.

On the corner of Prison and Wainee streets rise the menacing walls of old **Hale Paahao**, a prison built by convicts in 1854 and used to house rowdy sailors as well as more hardened types. The coral blocks used to build this local hoosegow were taken from the Old Fort on Front Street.

Just north of the jail along Wainee Street sits the **Episcopal Cemetery** and **Hale Aloha**. Walter Murray Gibson, a controversial figure in 19th-century Hawaii politics who eventually became an adviser to King David Kalakaua, is buried here. Hale Aloha, completed in 1858 and restored several years ago, served as a church meetinghouse.

Nearby is **Maria Lanakila Church**, a lovely white-washed building with interior pillars that was built in 1928 to replace a 19th-century chapel. Adjacent is the **Seamen's Cemetery**, a poorly maintained ground where early sailors were laid to rest. ~ Wainee and Dickenson streets.

The **Lahaina Shingon Mission**, a simple plantation-era structure with an ornately gilded altar, was built in 1902 by a Japanese monk and his followers. It now represents another gathering place for Maui's Buddhists. ~ 682 Luakini Street between Hale and Dickenson streets; 661-0466.

The proverbial kids-from-eight-to-eighty set will love the **Sugar Cane Train**, a reconstructed 1890-era steam train. Operating around the West Maui resort area, the Lahaina–Kaanapali & Pacific Railroad engine and passenger cars chug along a six-mile route midway between the mountains and ocean. Various package tours are available with the train rides, including a ride on a semisubmersible vessel in Lahaina, admission to three of Lahaina's museums, and a viewing of the film *Hawaii: Islands of the Gods*, shown on the 180-degree screen at the Omni Theatre. Admission. ~ The main station is off Hinau Street in Lahaina; 661-0089.

◆◆

ROYAL HAWAIIAN HOLIDAYS

Although the Hawaiian capital moved to Honolulu in 1850, Lahaina remained a favorite vacation spot for several kings, including Kamehameha III, IV and V, and Queen Liliuokalani. All had second homes in the area and returned often to indulge in those favorite Hawaiian pastimes, rest and relaxation.

Oceanic adventurers should take an opportunity to stop in at **Atlantis Submarines** and reserve an underwater tour. The voyage takes you aboard a 46-passenger submersible down to depths of 150 feet. En route you may see close-up views of technicolor coral reefs and outlandish lava formations. A trip to the depths requires deep pockets; these two-hour excursions aren't cheap. If the tour doesn't interest you, there is a small museum adjacent to the Atlantis office that chronicles submarine history. ~ 665 Front Street, in the Pioneer Inn; 667-2224.

And don't miss **Lahaina Jodo Mission**, a Buddhist enclave one-half mile north of Lahaina on Ala Moana Street. There's a temple and a three-tiered pagoda here, as well as the largest ceremonial bell in Hawaii. The giant bronze Buddha, with the West Maui Mountains in the background, is a sight to behold. It rests amid stone walkways and flowering oleander bushes in a park-like setting. ~ 12 Ala Moana Street; 661-4304.

For a splendid view of Lahaina, head uphill along Lahainaluna Road to **Lahainaluna School**. Established by missionaries in 1831, it is one of the country's oldest high schools. Today this historic facility serves as a public high school for the Lahaina area. On the way uphill you will pass **Pioneer Sugar Mill**, a sugar company tracing back to 1860.

◄ HIDDEN

Hale Pai, a printing house dating to 1836, is located nearby. Here early textbooks and Hawaii's first newspaper were printed. Having played a key role in the development of Hawaiian as a written language, Hale Pai is now a fascinating museum devoted to printing. Open Monday through Friday.

To fully capture the spirit of Lahaina, there's only one place to stay—the **Pioneer Inn**. Located smack on Lahaina's waterfront, this wooden hostelry is the center of the area's action. On one side, sloops, ketches and glass-bottom boats are berthed; on the other side lies bustling Front Street with its falsefront shops. The Inn is noisy, vibrant and crowded with tenants and tourists. On the ground floor, you can hunker down over a glass of grog at the saloon, or stroll through the Inn's lushly planted courtyard. You can no longer book a room above the bar, but there are accommodations in the renovated section overlooking the courtyard. These are small and plainly decorated, with telephones, overhead fans and lanais. ~ 658 Wharf Street; 661-3636, 800-457-5457, fax 667-5708. DELUXE.

LODGING

While the building is actually quite modern, the **Plantation Inn** possesses the look and ambience of a turn-of-the-century hostelry. Modeled after the plantation architecture of an earlier era, it features 19 rooms individually decorated in period furniture. Each is adorned with either poster, brass or canopy bed, stained-glass windows and tile bathrooms. Combining the atmosphere of the past with the amenities of the present, guest rooms also feature televisions, refrigerators and air conditioning, as well as VCRs on request. There's a pool with a shaded pavilion and jacuzzi on the premises. Continental breakfast. ~ 174 Lahainaluna Road; 667-9225, 800-433-6815, fax 667-9293. DELUXE.

The Oscar for most original inn goes to the **Lahaina Hotel**. Constructed earlier this century, this 12-room beauty was fully restored and appointed in Gay Nineties finery. Each room is wall to ceiling with gorgeous antiques—leaded glass lamps, mirrored armoires, original oil paintings, cast-iron beds and brass locks. Attention to detail is a way of life: the place simply exudes the aura of another era. If you don't stay here, stop by and visit. ~ 127 Lahainaluna Road; 661-0577, 800-669-3444, fax 667-9480. DELUXE.

The **Maui Islander Hotel** is a warren of woodframe buildings spread across lushly landscaped grounds. The ambience is an odd combination of tropical retreat and motel atmosphere. It features 358 trimly decorated rooms, some of which are small studios (with kitchens) and one-bedroom efficiencies. Swimming pool, laundry, tennis court, picnic area. ~ 660 Wainee Street; 667-9766, 800-367-5226, fax 661-3733. DELUXE.

CONDOS

HIDDEN ►

Perhaps the nicest place to stay on this side of the island is **Puamana**, a 28-acre retreat about a mile southeast of Lahaina. This townhouse complex, a 1920s-era sugar plantation, rests along a rock-strewn beach. The oceanfront clubhouse, open to guests, was once the plantation manager's house, and the landscaped grounds are still given over to mango, plumeria and torch ginger trees. Guests stay in low-slung plantation-style buildings that sport shake-shingle roofs and house from two to six units. Prices begin in the deluxe range for one-bedroom facilities that contain kitchens and sleep up to four people, and end in the ultra-deluxe range for two- and three-bedroom efficiencies that sleep up to six and eight, respectively. To round out the amenities there are three pools and a tennis court. Three-night minimum that increases to seven nights during the Christmas season. ~ 34 Pualima Place; 667-2551, 800-628-6731, fax 661-5875. DELUXE TO ULTRA-DELUXE.

Though it's more expensive than many others, **Lahaina Shores Hotel** has the advantage of a beachfront location in Lahaina. This sprawling condominium complex offers studio apartments beginning at $110, while one-bedroom units start at $175. With a swimming pool, jacuzzi and the nearby beach, it's quite convenient. ~ 475 Front Street; 661-4835, 800-628-6699, fax 661-1025. DELUXE TO ULTRA-DELUXE.

DINING

In keeping with the old hostelry upstairs, the **Pioneer Inn Restaurant** brings back the Lahaina of old. The main dining room is a cozy anchorage dotted with nautical fixtures and specializing in regional fare. The emphasis is on the "bounty of Hawaii"; in other words, fresh fish, upcountry produce and local ◆◆◆◆◆◆◆◆◆◆◆◆◆◆◆◆◆◆◆◆ herbs. Select one of the day's fresh fish specials and you can't go wrong. ~ 658 Wharf Street; 661-3636. DELUXE.

Hawaii's first phone line was installed from Lahaina to Haiku in 1877.

Across the lobby from the Pioneer Inn Restaurant, the **Pioneer Grill and Bar** offers similar but less formal fare and boasts a view of Lahaina Harbor. Portuguese bean soup is a specialty of both eateries and both fire their dishes on a *kiawe* grill. ~ 658 Wharf Street; 661-3636. MODERATE TO DELUXE.

I can't say much for the nomenclature, but the prices are worth note at **Cheeseburgers in Paradise.** This is a rare catch indeed—an inexpensive restaurant smack on the Lahaina waterfront. Granted, you won't find much on the menu other than hamburgers, salads and sandwiches. But if some couples can live on love, why can't the rest of us live on ocean views? ~ 811 Front Street; 661-4855. BUDGET TO MODERATE.

Oceanfront dining was never so cheap as at **Aloha Cantina Maui.** The menu spans the spectrum from ceviche and fajitas to chile rellenos and fish tacos. The margaritas are icy and the salsa is hot. Dining is on two decks overlooking the water. ~ 839 Front Street; 661-8788. BUDGET.

For a taste of the Orient, I'd head to the **Golden Palace Chinese Restaurant.** Boldly decorated with Chinese reliefs, this dimly lit establishment has an extensive Cantonese menu. There are beef, fowl, pork and seafood dishes, as well as chop suey. In the afternoon, the Palace combines sweet-and-sour ribs, roast pork and shrimp and rice chow mein. ~ Lahaina Shopping Center, Wainee Street between Papalua Street and Lahainaluna Road; 661-3126. BUDGET TO MODERATE.

Nearby, also in the Lahaina Shopping Center, is **Yakiniku Tropicana.** Specializing in Japanese and Korean food, it has a sushi bar and table seating. ~ Wainee Street between Papalua Street and Lahaina Road; 667-4646. MODERATE TO DELUXE.

Offering a partial view of the water is **Il Bucaniere,** an open-air trattoria. Although this balcony restaurant is on the wrong side of Front Street, it does provide an easy, you-can-sit-at-the-bar-or-take-a-table atmosphere. Wherever you rest your *okole,* you can dine on linguine primavera, chicken with rosemary, Italian baked pork chops or penne with gorgonzola cheese sauce. They also offer pizzas and salads. ~ 666 Front Street; 661-3966. MODERATE.

If you've seen one **Hard Rock Café,** you know about the line for the T-shirt window, the line for a table and the line for the bar. What a formula: just get yourself a show car from the '50s, a few surfboards, guitars and Buddy Holly posters, throw in an exposed-beam ceiling and circular bar and you've got the Maui branch of this popular empire. The menu runs from beef, turkey and veggie burgers to lime barbecue chicken, marinated top sirloin and fajitas. ~ 900 Front Street; 667-7400. MODERATE.

Light, bright and airy, **Compadres** is a great place to sip a margarita or enjoy a Mexican meal with an island flair. The tropical ambience is as appealing as the steaming dishes served here. Especially popular are the fajitas and pork carnitas, but the menu also offers burgers, salads and vegetarian dishes. ~ Lahaina Cannery Mall, Front and Kapunakea streets; 661-7189. MODERATE.

The preferred style of dining in Lahaina is steak and seafood at one of the waterfront restaurants along Front Street. And the common denominator is the ever-popular, usually crowded **Kimo's**, where you can enjoy all the tropical amenities while dining on seafood fettuccine, lobster or prime rib. ~ 845 Front Street; 661-4811. MODERATE TO DELUXE.

At **Lahaina Broiler** you can experience the same open-air atmosphere, though lately the place has looked slightly run down. There's always a fresh fish special, as well as an assortment of beef and chicken entrées. ~ 889 Front Street; 661-3111. MODERATE TO DELUXE.

Slightly (I said *slightly*) off the tourist track but still offering a classic Lahaina-dinner-on-the-water-with-sunset-view experience is the **Old Lahaina Café and Luau**. Overhead fans, oceanfront location, nautical feel—it's all here. The menu matches the occasion with fresh island fish, jumbo prawns (prepared five different ways) and a special Hawaiian sampler. Also open for breakfast and lunch. ~ 505 Front Street; 661-3303. MODERATE TO DELUXE.

At **Longhi's**, a European-style café that specializes in Italian dishes, informality is the password. The menu changes daily and is never written down; the waiter simply tells you the day's offerings. Usually there'll be several pasta dishes, sautéed vegetables, salads, a shellfish creation, steak, a wine-soaked chicken or veal dish and perhaps eggplant parmigiana. Longhi's prepares all of its own bread and pasta, buys Maui-grown produce and imports many cheeses from New York. The dinners reflect this diligence. Breakfasts and lunches are cooked with the same care. Definitely recommended, especially for vegetarians, who can choose from many of the dishes offered. ~ 888 Front Street; 667-2288. DELUXE TO ULTRA-DELUXE.

Hawaiian regional cuisine is the order of the day at **Avalon Restaurant & Bar**, an open-air establishment in Mariner's Alley. Adorned with the work of local artists, it is owned by Mark and Judy Ellman. Mark is the master chef—preparing wok-fried *opakapaka* in black bean sauce, Chinese duck with plum sauce and other delectables—while Judy greets the folks out front. ~ 844 Front Street; 667-5559. DELUXE.

David Paul's Lahaina Grill, headlining New American cuisine (with a Southwestern accent), is an intimate dining room with a personalized touch. According to owner/chef David Paul, the menu represents "a gathering of technique, flavors and skills from around the world, utilizing local ingredients to translate each dish into an exceptional dining experience." Order the tequila shrimp and fire cracker rice, soft-shell crabs, Kona coffee–roasted rack of lamb or macadamia-smoked tenderloin and decide for yourself whether he carries it off. ~ 127 Lahainaluna Road; 667-5117. DELUXE TO ULTRA-DELUXE.

A defining experience in Lahaina dining is **Gerard's Restaurant.** Here you'll encounter a French restaurant in a colonial setting with tropical surroundings. Housed in the Plantation Inn, a bed and breakfast reminiscent of early New Orleans, Gerard's provides a chandelier-and-pattern-wallpaper dining room as well as a veranda complete with overhead fans and whitewashed balustrade. The chef prepares fresh fish, rack of lamb, calf veal liver, *confit* of duck and puff pastry with shiitake mushrooms. Of course, that is after having started off with ahi steak tartar or crab bisque. ~ 174 Lahaina-luna Road; 661-8939. ULTRA-DELUXE.

◄ HIDDEN

Near the top of the cognoscenti's list of gourmet establishments is an unlikely looking French restaurant in Olowalu called **Chez Paul.** The place is several miles outside Lahaina in a renovated building that also houses Olowalu's funky general store. But for years this little hideaway has had a reputation far transcending its surroundings. You'll probably drive right past the place at first, but when you do find it, you'll discover a menu featuring such delicacies as *tournedos*, duck *à l'orange*, veal prepared with apples, scampi and several other tempting entrées. While the tab is ethereal, the rave reviews this prim dining room receives make it worth every franc. Closed Sunday in summer. ~ Honoapiilani Highway; 661-3843. ULTRA-DELUXE.

GROCERIES

Lahaina features two supermarkets. **Foodland** is open daily from 6 a.m. to midnight. ~ Lahaina Square Shopping Center, Wainee Street; 661-0975. You can shop at **Nagasako Supermarket** from 7 a.m. until 9 p.m. every day except Sunday (until 8 p.m.). ~ Lahaina Shopping Center, Wainee Street; 661-0985.

For health-food items, stop by **Westside Natural Food.** Open from 7:30 a.m. to 9 p.m. Monday to Saturday and 8:30 a.m. to 8 p.m. on Sunday. ~ 193 Lahainaluna Road; 667-2855.

South of Lahaina, the **Olowalu General Store** has a limited supply of grocery items. ~ Honoapiilani Highway, Olowalu; 661-3774.

SHOPPING

Lahaina's a great place to combine shopping with sightseeing. Most shops are right on Front Street in the historic wooden buildings facing the water. For a walking tour of the stores and water-front, start from the Pioneer Inn at the south end of the strip and walk north on the *makai* or ocean side. Then come back along the *mauka*, or mountain, side of the street.

One of the first shops you will encounter on this consumer's tour of Lahaina will be **Sgt. Leisure Resort Patrol**, which has an array of imaginative T-shirts. ~ 701 Front Street; 667-0661.

The Gecko Store, the only shop I've seen with a sand floor, also stocks inexpensive beachwear, as well as T-shirts and toys. ~ 703 Front Street; 661-1078.

The **Endangered Species Store**, which features a multitude of conservation-minded items such as oils and lotions from the rainforest, is a worthy stop. You will also find chimes, statues and a healthy supply of T-shirts and stuffed animals. ~ 707 Front Street; 661-0208.

Past the sea wall, in an overgrown cottage set back from the street, lie several shops including **Pacific Vision**, with its hand-etched glass and crystal pieces. ~ 819 Front Street; 661-0188.

There are just a few more street numbers before this shopper's promenade ends. Then if you cross the road and walk back in the opposite direction, with the sea to your right, you'll pass **South Seas Trading Post**, where you can barter greenbacks for Nepali wedding necklaces, Chinese porcelain opium pillows or New Guinea masks. ~ 780 Front Street; 661-3168.

> The oldest American school west of the Rockies is Lahainaluna, founded by missionaries in Lahaina in 1831.

Lahaina Galleries is of special note not only for the contemporary artworks but also because of the imaginative ways in which they're displayed. Even if you're not just dying to write that five-figure check, stop by for a viewing. ~ 728 Front Street; 667-2152.

The Gallery has jade and pearl pieces among its inventory of exotic jewelry. You'll also find Asian antiques, artwork and a ship model gallery at this unusual shop. ~ 716 Front Street; 661-0696.

Nearby at **The Wharf Cinema Center** mall, there's a maze of stores. One shop worth a look is **Seegerpeople**. Essentially a portrait studio, this store adds a twist to an otherwise traditional craft. Instead of being framed, the pictures are mounted on quarter-inch-thick Lucite, cut out in the shape of the subject and placed on a base. The result is a freestanding "photosculpture" and humorous keepsake. ~ 658 Front Street; 661-1084.

Village Gallery features paintings by modern Hawaiian artists. Amid the tourist schlock is some brilliant artwork. ~ 120 Dickenson Street; 661-4402.

Also stop in at the Lahaina Art Society's **Banyan Tree Gallery**. This is a great place if you're in the market for local artwork; on display are pieces by a number of Maui artists. ~ 649 Wharf Street, first floor of the Old Courthouse; 661-0111.

The **Lahaina Cannery Mall**, a massive complex of stores housed in an old canning factory, is the area's most ambitious project. **Lahaina Printsellers** (667-7843), one of my favorite Maui shops, has an astounding collection of ancient maps and engravings from Polynesia and other parts of the world. **Kite Fantasy** (661-4766) is the place to pick up stunt and sport kites including diamond, box and bird designs. Here you'll also find wind socks, mobiles, boomerangs, kaleidoscopes, games and a wide array of toys. Complete flying instructions, including tips on where to launch your kite, are provided by the helpful staff. ~ 1221 Honoapiilani Highway.

Those are just a couple ideas to provide you with a jump start. Propel yourself through this place and you'll find a dozen more reasons that make it a favorite among Lahaina residents. Like the **Guy Buffet Collection**, a shop specializing in the work of one of Hawaii's finest (and funniest) folk artists. ~ Lahaina Cannery Mall; 661-1119.

On the corner of Front and Papalana streets, **Lahaina Center** is another shopping mall, a sprawling complex of theaters, stores and restaurants. ~ 900 Front Street.

Among the shops here is one where everything is **Made in Hawaii**. That includes historic photographs, jewelry, featherwork, T-shirts and ceramics. They also have two larger but equally homegrown establishments, **Liberty House** (661-4451), the Hawaiian department store, and **Hilo Hattie Fashion Center** (667-7911), specializing in the tackiest alohawear imaginable. ~ Lahaina Center; 661-5883.

Built to resemble a New England fishing village, **505 Front Street** is an attractive woodframe mall. Situated south of central Lahaina at 505 Front Street, it is home to almost two dozen shops, including galleries, boutiques and jewelry stores.

Most glamorous of all the stores here is **New York–Paris Gallery**, a trendy showcase for the artistic work of several musicians, including John Lennon, Miles Davis and the Rolling Stones' Ronnie Wood. They also have album cover art and pieces signed by the Beatles and the Stones. ~ 505 Front Street; 667-0727.

Front Street's the strip in Lahaina—a dilapidated row of buildings from which stream some of the freshest sounds around.

NIGHTLIFE

At the **Pioneer Bar and Grill**, there is nightly piano music. Tucked into a corner of the Pioneer Inn, this spot features a seagoing motif complete with harpoons, figureheads and other historical nautical decor. Usually packed to the bulkheads with a lively crew, it's a great place to enjoy a tall cold one. ~ 658 Wharf Street; 661-3636.

Moose McGillycuddy's is a hot club offering a large dancefloor and a variety of live music acts. The house is congenial and the drinks imaginatively mixed; for contemporary sounds with dinner, arrive before 10 p.m. Cover. ~ 844 Front Street; 667-7758.

There's always an ocean view at **Aloha Cantina Maui**. And on Thursday, Friday and Sunday nights, add to that live music. The sound is contemporary and the source is generally a solo performer or a duo. ~ 839 Front Street; 661-8788.

Better yet, check out **World Café**, where they have pool tables and live bands. There's something going on every night, whether it be free pool for ladies, drink specials or a local band wailing away. Cover. ~ 900 Front Street; 661-1515.

At **Il Bucaniere**, an open-air dining room overlooking the Front Street action, there's a guitarist nightly. ~ 666 Front Street; 661-3966.

Lahaina's favorite pastime is watching the sun set over the ocean while sipping a tropical concoction at a waterfront watering place. A prime place for this very rewarding activity is **Kimo's**, which also features a range of live music. ~ 845 Front Street; 661-4811.

Or try the **Lahaina Broiler**. After the sun finishes performing, the Lahaina Broiler features do-it-yourself karaoke entertainment. ~ 889 Front Street; 661-3111.

Blue Tropix is one of Maui's most popular nightclubs, featuring a musical showcase that starts the evening with big band tunes and then accelerates through the decades to the 1990s. This high-tech Los Angeles–style club is done in basic black and chrome and features two circular bars and a planetarium ceiling. If that's not enough, you'll also find a huge dancefloor and 11 video screens. Most of the music emanates from a deejay, but live rock bands appear on some nights. Come check out the in crowd. Closed Tuesday and Wednesday. Cover after 9 p.m. ~ 900 Front Street; 667-5309.

For an awe-inspiring glimpse into Hawaii's past, watch the 40-minute film at the **Omni Theatre/Hawaii Experience**. Offering a three-dimensional perspective of the state's cultural and natural history, this film is shown on a huge domed 180-degree screen. Admission. ~ 824 Front Street; 661-8314.

If it's Friday, you can browse the art galleries of Lahaina, which sponsor a special Art Night every week.

BEACHES & PARKS

PAPALAUA WAYSIDE PARK *Kiawe* trees and scrub vegetation spread right to the shoreline along Papalaua Wayside Park. There are sandy patches between the trees large enough to spread a towel, but I prefer sunbathing at beaches closer to Lahaina. Bounded on one side by Honoapiilani Highway, this narrow beach extends for a mile to join a nicer, lawn-fringed park; then it stretches on toward Olowalu for several more miles. If you want to be alone, just head down the shore. Swimming is good, snorkeling is okay out past the surf break and surfing is excellent at Thousand Peaks breaks and also very good several miles east in

Maalaea Bay. There's an outhouse and picnic area at the state wayside and picnic facilities at the grassy park. ~ About ten miles south of Lahaina on Honoapiilani Highway.

OLOWALU BEACHES To the north and south of Olowalu General Store lie narrow corridors of white sand. This is an excellent area to hunt for Maui diamonds. Swimming is very good, and south of the general store, where road and water meet, you'll find an excellent coral reef for snorkeling. There is also a growing green sea turtle population that can be seen by snorkelers at the 14-mile marker. Surfers will find good breaks with right and left slides about a half-mile north of the general store. *Ulua* are often caught from Olowalu landing. There are no facilities, but there is a market nearby. ~ Go south from Lahaina on Honoapiilani Highway for about six miles.

LAUNIUPOKO WAYSIDE PARK There is a seaside lawn shaded by palm trees and a sandy beach. A rock seawall slopes gently for entering swimmers, but offers little to sunbathers. It's located near the West Maui Mountains, with great views of Kahoolawe and Lanai. When the tide is high, it's a good place to take children to swim safely and comfortably in the tidal pool on the other side of the seawall. Otherwise, swimming and snorkeling are mediocre. There is good surf-casting from the seawall and south for three miles. The park has a picnic area, restrooms and showers. ~ Three miles south of Lahaina on Honoapiilani Highway.

PUAMANA STATE WAYSIDE PARK A narrow beach and grass-covered strip wedged between Honoapiilani Highway and the ocean, Puamana Park is dotted with ironwood trees. The excellent views make this a choice spot for an enjoyable picnic. ~ About two miles south of Lahaina on Honoapiilani Highway.

ARMORY PARK The one thing going for this park is its convenient location in Lahaina. Otherwise, it's heavily littered, shadowed by a mall and sometimes crowded. If you do stop by, try to forget all that and concentrate on the sandy beach, lawn and truly startling view of Lanai directly across the Auau Channel. Swimming is okay, snorkeling good past the reef and, for surfing, there are breaks in the summer near the seawall in Lahaina Harbor. This surfing spot is not for beginners! Threadfin and *ulua* are common catches here. Restrooms and tennis courts are across the street at Maluuluolele Park near the playing field. ~ Front Street next to the 505 Front Street mall.

BABY BEACH This curving stretch of white sand is the best beach in Lahaina. It lacks privacy but certainly not beauty. From here you can look back to Lahaina town and the West Maui Mountains or out over the ocean to Kahoolawe, Lanai and Molokai. Or just close your eyes and soak up the sun. Swimming is good and well protected, if shallow. Snorkeling is only fair. In summer there are breaks nearby at Mala Wharf; left slide. Threadfin is often caught. There are restrooms and showers at the beach. ~ Take Front Street north from Lahaina for about a half-mile. Turn left on Puunoa Place and follow it to the beach.

WAHIKULI WAYSIDE PARK This narrow stretch of beach and lawn, just off the road between Lahaina and Kaanapali, faces Lanai and Molokai. There are facilities aplenty, which might be why this pretty spot is so popular and crowded. Swimming is very good, but snorkeling is only fair. (There's a better spot just north of here near the Lahaina Canoe Club.) The most common catches here are *ulua* and threadfin. Facilities include picnic areas and restrooms; there are tennis courts up the street at the Civic Center. ~ Located between Lahaina and Kaanapali on Honoapiilani Highway.

HANAKAOO BEACH PARK Conveniently located beside Kaanapali Beach Resort, this long and narrow park features a white-sand beach and grassy picnic ground, and is referred to by locals as Canoe Beach. On Saturday during the summer season, this is the place to watch Hawaiian canoe racing. The road is nearby, but the views of Lanai are outstanding. Swimming is good, snorkeling fair, but surfing poor. Common catches include *ulua* and threadfin. There are picnic areas, restrooms and showers. ~ Between Lahaina and Kaanapali on Honoapiilani Highway.

▼▼▼▼▼▼▼▼▼▼▼▼▼▼▼▼▼▼
Kaanapali–Kapalua Area

Even in the case of Maui's notorious land developers, there is method to the madness. The stretch of coastline extending for six miles along Maui's western shore, crowded to the extreme with hotels and condominiums, is anchored by two planned resorts. Like handsome bookends supporting an uneven array of dog-eared paperbacks, Kaanapali and Kapalua add class to the arrangement.

SIGHTS

Supporting the south end, **Kaanapali** is a 500-acre enclave that extends along three miles of sandy beach and includes six hotels, a half-dozen condominiums, two golf courses and an attractive shopping mall. Back in the 19th century it was a dry and barren segment of the sugar plantation that operated from Lahaina. Raw sugar was hauled by train from the mill out to Black Rock, a dramatic outcropping along Kaanapali Beach, where the produce was loaded onto waiting ships.

In 1963, Kaanapali's first resort opened near Black Rock and development soon spread in both directions. Important to developers, who built the Sheraton Maui hotel around it, **Black Rock**

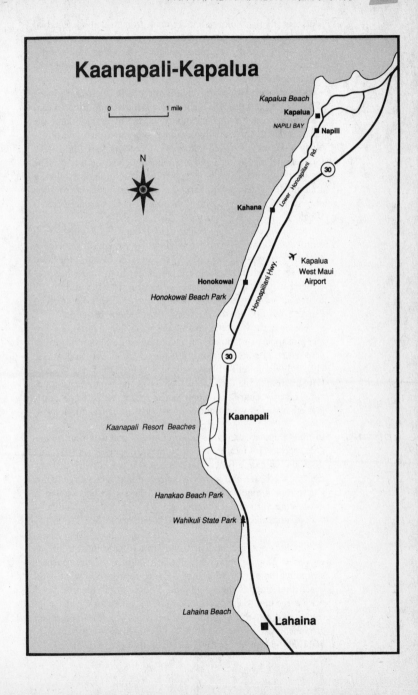

Kaanapali-Kapalua

0   1 mile

N

Kapalua Beach

Kapalua ■

NAPILI BAY   **Napili** ■

30

Lower Honoapiilani Rd.

Kahana ■

Honoapiilani Hwy.

✈ Kapalua
West Maui
Airport

Honokowai ■

Honokowai Beach Park

30

Kaanapali ■

Kaanapali Resort Beaches

Hanakao Beach Park

Wahikuli State Park

Lahaina Beach

■ **Lahaina**

(Puu Kekaa) is a volcanic cinder cone from which ancient Hawaiians believed that the dead departed the earth in their journey to the spirit world. According to legend, the great 18th-century Maui chief Kahekili proved his bravery by leaping from the rock to the ocean below.

Kaanapali's modern-day contribution to Pacific culture is the **Whalers Village Museum**. A three-part facility comprising an outdoor pavilion and two buildings connected by a sky-bridge, the museum details Lahaina's history of whaling and explains the physiology of Hawaii's beloved humpback. Outdoors, you'll find a 30-foot-long whale skeleton and a whaling longboat on display. The "golden era of whaling" is also portrayed in scrimshaw exhibits, a scale model whaling ship, harpoons and other artifacts from the days when Lahaina was one of the world's great whaling ports. ~ Whalers Village, 2435 Kaanapali Parkway; 661-5992.

An earlier chief, Piilani, built a road through the area in the 16th century and gave his name to modern-day Route 30, the Honoapiilani Highway. Translated as "the bays of Piilani," the road passes several inlets located north of Kaanapali that have been developed in haphazard fashion. Honokowai, Kahana and Napili form a continuous wall of condominiums that sprawls north to Kapalua Bay and offers West Maui's best lodging bargains.

Kapalua, the bookend holding the north side in place, is a former pineapple plantation that was converted into a luxurious 1500-acre resort. Here two major hotels, three golf courses and several villa-style communities blanket the hillside from the white sands of Kapalua Bay to the deep green foothills of the West Maui Mountains. Like the entire strip along Maui's western flank, Kapalua enjoys otherworldly sunsets and dramatic views of Lanai and Molokai.

LODGING

In the Kaanapali area the modestly priced hotel is not an endangered species, it's totally extinct! So prepare yourself for steep tariffs. The **Kaanapali Beach Hotel** is a 430-room hostelry that sits right on the beach and sports many restaurants and a large lobby. Guest rooms enjoy private lanais and guests lounge around a grassy courtyard and a swimming pool. ~ 2525 Kaanapali Parkway, Kaanapali; 661-0011, 800-262-8450, fax 667-5978. ULTRA-DELUXE.

Or check out, and check in to, the **Royal Lahaina Resort**. Spreading across 27 acres, it encompasses 542 rooms, 11 tennis courts, 3 swimming pools, 2 restaurants, a coffee shop and a white-sand beach that extends for a half-mile. Rooms in the highrise hotel price in the ultra-deluxe category, while the prices for the nicest accommodations, the multiplex cottages that dot the landscaped grounds, head for the sky. ~ 2780 Kekaa Drive, Kaanapali; 661-3611, 800-447-6925, fax 661-6150. ULTRA-DELUXE.

In the realm of luxury hotels, the **Hyatt Regency Maui** is one of the better addresses in Hawaii. Built in 1980, its atrium lobby, Asian artwork and freeform swimming pool have set the standard for resorts ever since. Unlike more recent hotels, in which the size of guest rooms is sacrificed for the sake of lavish grounds, the Hyatt Regency maintains an ideal balance between public and private areas. If you're seeking beautiful surroundings, friendly service and beachfront location, this 812-room extravaganza is the ticket. ~ 200 Nohea Kai Drive, Kaanapali; 661-1234, 800-233-1234, fax 667-4499. ULTRA-DELUXE.

A subtle architectural style gives the **Kapalua Bay Hotel** a low profile. But don't be misled. Part of a 23,000-acre plantation, this relatively small hotel, with 194 rooms and suites, is the hub of one of Maui's most appealing and romantic resorts. A hillside setting overlooking a white-sand crescent beach means that nearly all the rooms have spectacular ocean views. The accommodations are luxurious and tasteful and include rattan- and wicker-furnished sitting areas, marble baths with sunken tubs, and vanity areas. Floor-to-ceiling french doors open onto spacious lanais. Rock-lined ponds, tropical gardens, three golf courses, restaurants, shops and a tennis facility add to Kapalua's charm. ~ 1 Bay Drive, Kapalua; 669-5656, 800-367-8000, fax 669-4690. ULTRA-DELUXE.

CONDOS

Most condominiums in this area are on the beach or just across the road from it. They are ideally situated for swimming or sunbathing; the major drawback, ironically, is that there are so many other condos around.

Kaanapali Alii ranks as one of Maui's better buys. Here the immense 1500- to 1900-square-foot suites can easily be shared by two couples or a family. All 210 condo units have large living and

---

✔ **CHECK THESE OUT—UNIQUE LODGING**

- *Budget:* Rent a cabin at **Waianapanapa State Park** and wander out your front door past sea arches and lava tubes. *page 297*
- *Moderate:* Book reservations for one of the eight cozy accommodations at **Nona Lani Cottages** and explore a nearby beach that extends for miles. *page 264*
- *Deluxe:* Retreat to **Puamana**, a 1920s-era sugar plantation with tasteful condominium units spread across 28 oceanfront acres. *page 238*
- *Ultra-deluxe:* Stroll from your cottage down to the beach or out along the rolling lawns of the **Hotel Hana Maui**. *page 292*

Budget: under $50 Moderate: $50–$90 Deluxe: $90–$120 Ultra-deluxe: over $120

dining rooms, full kitchens, sitting areas and two baths. Fully carpeted and furnished with rattan, contemporary artwork and potted palms, these units start at $235 and top out at $475. The contemporary highrise facility rests along the beach and has a pool and tennis court. ~ 50 Nohea Kai Drive, Kaanapali; 667-1400, 800-642-6284, fax 661-1025.

Aston Kaanapali Shores has hotel room–style accommodations for $119 including refrigerator and microwave; studios from $169 double ($129 from April 1 to December 21) with a balcony and full kitchen; and one-bedroom units with a garden view and full kitchen for $205. ~ 3445 Lower Honoapiilani Road, Honokowai; 667-2211, 800-922-7866, fax 661-0836.

The lava rock–walled units at **Papakea Oceanfront Resort** provide a pleasant retreat. Ranging from $125 studios to $255 two-bedroom units, all 120 condominiums come with spacious lanais. ~ 3543 Lower Honoapiilani Road, Honokowai; 669-4848, 800-367-7052, fax 669-0061.

One-bedroom apartments at **Maui Sands** begin at $80 single or double; two bedrooms run $100 for one to four people. There is a seven-night minimum. Beachfront. ~ 3600 Lower Honoapiilani Road, Honokowai; 669-1902, 800-367-5037, fax 669-8790.

Paki Maui has one-bedroom apartments starting at $159, depending on the view, and sleep one to four people; two-bedroom units start at $219, accommodating up to six people. Swimming pool with jet spa. Oceanfront. ~ 3615 Lower Honoapiilani Road, Honokowai; 669-8235, 800-535-0085, fax 669-7987.

Located across the street from the beach, **Aston Maui Park** has studios from $89 ($79 from April 1 to December 21). ~ 3626 Lower Honoapiilani Road, Honokowai; 669-6622, 800-922-7866, fax 669-9647.

The one-bedroom apartments at **Honokowai Palms** have a lanai and ocean view; they run $65 double and sleep up to four people. Two-bedroom units without lanai are $75 for one to six people. It's located right across the street from the ocean. ~ 3666 Lower Honoapiilani Road, Honokowai; 669-6130, 800-669-6284, fax 661-5875.

Hale Maui has one-bedroom condos for $65 double. On the waterfront; no pool. ~ 3711 Lower Honoapiilani Road, Honokowai; 669-6312, fax 669-1302.

The one-bedroom apartments at **Kaleialoha** are $90 double; $7.50 each additional person. Oceanfront. ~ 3785 Lower Honoapiilani Road, Honokowai; 669-8197, 800-222-8688, fax 669-2502.

Hale Ono Loa offers one-bedroom units from $85 to $95 for up to four people. The condos are oceanfront but there's no beach. ~ 3823 Lower Honoapiilani Road, Honokowai; 669-9680, 800-367-5637, fax 669-0751.

Polynesian Shores has one-bedroom apartments that start at $95 double; two-bedroom units, $120 double; three-bedroom apartments, $160 double. All units have ocean view. ~ 3975 Lower Honoapiilani Road, Honokowai; 669-6065, 800-433-6284, fax 669-0909.

Mahina Surf features one-bedroom units that start at $110 double ($85 from April 15 to December 14); two-bedroom accommodations are $130 and $105, respectively. Oceanfront on a lava-rock beach. ~ 4057 Lower Honoapiilani Road, Kahana; 669-6068, 800-367-6086, fax 669-4534.

Kahana Reef has studio apartments, $85 single or double; one-bedroom apartments are $95 single or double; $15 more from December 19 to Easter. All units are oceanfront and have daily maid service. ~ 4471 Lower Honoapiilani Road, Kahana; 669-6491, 800-253-3773, fax 669-2192.

One-bedroom condos at **Napili Point Resort** are $164 for up to four people ($144 from April 20 to December 21). Here sliding doors lead out to ocean-view patios. Located on a lava rock beach, the resort is a short walk from sandy Napili Bay beach. ~ 5295 Lower Honoapiilani Road, Napili; 669-9222, 800-669-6252, fax 669-7984.

Outrigger's Napili Shores is a beautifully landscaped low-rise resort with studios and one-bedrooms running from $135 to $185. The units are appointed with rattan and oak pieces and the complex is graced by gardens of plumeria and hibiscus. The pool and beach areas are idyllic. ~ 5315 Lower Honoapiilani Road, Napili; 669-8061, 800-688-7444, fax 669-5407.

Studio apartments at **The Napili Bay** are $75 double for garden views, $85 for partial ocean views and $95 for oceanfront. ~ 33 Hui Road, Napili; 661-5200.

The **Napili Kai Beach Club** has 162 units—studios, one-bedroom and two-bedroom affairs—that range in price from $155 to $450. Most come with kitchens. All are fully carpeted and have private lanais, rattan furniture, picture windows and direct access to an impressive beach. ~ 5900 Honoapiilani Road, Napili; 669-6271, 800-367-5030, fax 669-5740.

DINING

Luigi's Pasta & Pizzeria is located near the entrance to Kaanapali Beach Resort. A patio restaurant overlooking a golf course, it's a pretty place to dine on pizza, pasta and other Italian favorites. The restaurant features a menu that includes veal marsala, chicken parmesan and shrimp scampi. Dinner only. ~ 2991 Kaanapali Parkway; 661-3160. MODERATE.

The **Kaanapali Beach Hotel Koffee Shop** serves an all-you-can-eat buffet at a price that is surprisingly out of place for this expensive hotel. But don't expect too much for so little. The menu is limited to scrambled eggs, pancakes, French toast and some side dishes at breakfast, sandwiches and a few entrées for lunch and dinner. ~ Kaanapali Beach Hotel, 2525 Kaanapali Parkway; 661-0011. BUDGET TO MODERATE.

Another way to eat at a reasonable price is by stopping at the takeout stands on the lower level of Whalers Village. There are tables inside or out in the courtyard. **Yakiniku Hahn** has Korean dishes. ~ 661-9798. At **Pizza Paradiso** they serve an assortment of pies (including by the slice) plus spaghetti and meatballs and salads. ~ 667-0333. **Kawara Sobe Takase Restaurant** has noodle dishes, *onigiri* (rice balls wrapped with seaweed) and tempura. ~ 2435 Kaanapali Parkway. BUDGET.

Peter Merriman, the chef extraordinaire who earned his reputation with a restaurant on the Big Island, transported his brand of Hawaii regional cuisine across the Alenuihaha Channel to open **Hula Grill** on the beach in Kaanapali. Specializing in seafood, this 1930s-era beach house has wok-charred ahi, seafood dim sum dishes and an array of entrées that includes Hawaiian seafood gumbo, *opakapaka* in parchment, firecracker mahimahi and teriyaki ahi. For landlubbers there's New York steak, Thai beef curry and goat cheese pizza. ~ Whalers Village; 667-6636. DELUXE.

Chico's Cantina is one of those tacky theme restaurants that prove either entertaining or annoying, depending on your disposition and mood. There is a car in the middle of the restaurant with surfboards on top of it, piñatas on the walls—that sort of thing. If you manage to get as far as the food, you'll find fajitas, chimichangas, burritos and other Mexican dishes. ~ Whalers Village; 667-2777. BUDGET TO MODERATE.

You can dine by the water at **Leilani's On The Beach**. The sunsets are otherworldly at this breezy veranda-style dining room. Trimmed in dark woods and lava rock, it's dominated by an outrigger canoe that hangs suspended from the ceiling. On the menu you'll find Malaysian shrimp, spinach and cheese ravioli, Cajun-style fresh fish, ginger chicken and teriyaki steak. Touristy but appealing. ~ Whalers Village; 661-4495. MODERATE TO DELUXE.

Beachcomber, a dinner-only dining room at the Royal Lahaina Resort, has a menu that covers the entire Pacific Rim. You'll find wicker chairs, shell lamps, decorative fans and dragons' heads providing the atmosphere. This is one of Kaanapali's better values. ~ 2780 Kekaa Drive, Kaanapali; 661-3611. MODERATE.

Located in the Maui Marriott, **Nikko** is a traditional Japanese restaurant that is decorated with woodblock prints and features tableside *teppanyaki* cooking. Specialties are filet mignon, chicken, shrimp, lobster and a vegetarian stir-fry. You can also enjoy sushi and tempura dishes for appetizers. ~ 100 Nohea Kai Drive, Kaanapali; 667-1200. DELUXE.

From the ship's rigging, captain's chairs and marlin trophies, you could never guess what they serve at **Erik's Seafood Grotto**. What a surprise to discover a menu filled with crabmeat-stuffed prawns, lobster-stuffed chicken breast, Hawaiian salmon and wahoo. Early-bird specials. ~ 4242 Lower Honoapiilani Road, Kahana; 669-4806. MODERATE TO DELUXE.

Dollie's Pub and Café offers lasagna, fettuccine alfredo, chicken parmesan, pizza and sandwiches. This is a sports-on-the-television bar with a small kitchen and dining room adjacent. During football season there is an omelette bar on Sunday mornings. ~ 4310 Lower Honoapiilani Road, Kahana; 669-0266. BUDGET TO MODERATE.

There's not much of an ocean view at **Kahana Keyes Restaurant**, but the wood-trimmed dining room is attractive. The bill of fare is pretty standard—steak and seafood; and the decor is comforting if uninspired. Check out the early-bird specials from 5 to 7 p.m. ~ 4327 Lower Honoapiilani Road, Kahana; 669-8071. MODERATE.

One of Maui's leading restaurants, **Roy's Kahana Bar and Grill** eschews the waterfalls, swans, tinkling pianists and other accoutrements of the island's top dining rooms. Instead, this spacious second-story establishment looks like a gallery with its exposed-beam ceiling, track lighting and paintings. The open kitchen serves up such creations as fresh seared lemongrass *shutome* with Thai basil peanut sauce, island-style roasted banana pork loin with Chinese black bean *hoisin* sauce, *sake* soy grilled chicken with Asian honey-mustard sauce and blackened ahi with soy-mustard butter. Reservations are a must! ~ Kahana Gateway Shopping Center, 4405 Honoapiilani Highway, Kahana; 669-6999. DELUXE TO ULTRA-DELUXE.

For Mongolian beef, Peking duck or hot Szechuan bean curd, try **China Boat**. At this family-style restaurant, you can ease into a lacquered seat and take in the Japanese *ukiyoe* prints that adorn the place. Adding to the ambience are lava walls that showcase beautiful Chinese ceramic pieces. Patio dining is also available. ~ 4474 Lower Honoapiilani Road, Kahana; 669-5089. MODERATE.

◆◆

ABOVE MAUI

High atop the Hyatt Regency Maui's Lahaina Tower, a 16-inch reflecting telescope probes deep space five nights a week, taking tourists on a trip through the planets and galaxies. The Tour of the Stars is a one-hour program managed by the hotel's director of astronomy and designed for the public. It allows guests to look through stationary eyepieces while the computer-driven telescope searches the heavens. Reservations are required. Admission ~ 200 Nohea Kai Drive, Kaanapali; 661-1234.

In addition to its namesake, **Maui Tacos** has chimichangas, tostadas, burritos, quesadillas and enchiladas. Nothing fancy, just a few formica booths and tables with molded plastic chairs. But the salsa's fresh daily, the beans are prepared without lard and the chips are made with cholesterol-free vegetable oil. ~ Napili Plaza, Napilihau Street, Napili; 665-0222. BUDGET.

At the **Orient Express**, they feature a variety of Thai and Chinese dishes including shrimp saté, clay-pot seafood dishes, sour shrimp soup, red-curry beef and Thai noodles stir-fried with pork, egg and crushed peanuts. Part of the Napili Shores Resort, this lava-walled restaurant has a shocking-pink-and-purple color scheme. ~ 5315 Lower Honoapiilani Road, Napili; 669-8077. MODERATE.

Maui aficionados agree that **The Plantation House Restaurant** is among the island's best. Capturing their accolades is a spacious establishment with panoramic views of the Kapalua region and a decor that mixes mahogany and wicker with orchids and a roaring fire. Not to be upstaged by the surroundings, the chef prepares fresh island fish five different ways. The most popular is the "taste of the rich forest"—the fish is pressed with wild mushrooms and roasted, then served on spinach with garlic mashed potatoes and Maui onion meunière sauce. For lighter appetites there are salads, pastas, honey guava scallops, and for lunch a wide range of soups and sandwiches. ~ 2000 Plantation Club Drive, Kapalua; 669-6299. DELUXE TO ULTRA-DELUXE.

There's little doubt that Hawaii's finest sunsets occur off the southwest coast of Maui. One of the best spots to catch the spectacle is **The Bay Club** at the Kapalua Bay Hotel, an oceanfront dining room that looks out on Molokai and Lanai. More than just a feast for the eyes, this open-air restaurant offers a gourmet menu at lunch and dinner. You can watch the sky melt from deep blue to flaming red while dining on bouillabaisse, seared sea scallops, Pacific lobster tail, rack of lamb or filet mignon with Maui onion rings. A rough life indeed. Dress code: no shorts, jeans, open-toed shoes or T-shirts. ~ 1 Bay Drive, Kapalua; 669-5656. ULTRA-DELUXE.

For something less expensive, consider **The Market Café**. It's located in the Kapalua Shops adjacent to the Kapalua Bay Hotel. Comfortably equipped with wooden booths and bentwood chairs, the dining area presents fresh fish, steak teriyaki, chicken tetrazzini and several other Italian specialties. ~ 115 Bay Drive, Kapalua; 669-4888. MODERATE.

GROCERIES   Out in the Kaanapali area, the best place to shop is **The Food Pantry**, a small supermarket that's open from 6:30 a.m. to 11 p.m. every day. ~ Lower Honoapiilani Road, Honokowai; 669-6208.

Toward Kapalua, try the **Napili Market**, a well-stocked supermarket that's open from 6:30 a.m. to 11 p.m. every day. ~ Napili Plaza, 5095 Napilihau Street, Napili; 669-1600

Worthy of mention is **Whalers Village** in the Kaanapali Beach   **SHOPPING**
Resort. This sprawling complex combines a shopping mall with an
outdoor museum. Numbered among the stores you'll find gift emporia featuring coral and shells, a shirt store with wild island designs, other stores offering fine men's and women's fashions.

Several shops in this split-level complex should not be missed.
Lahaina Printsellers Ltd. (667-7617) purveys "fine antique maps
and prints." At **Blue Ginger Designs** (667-5793) original styles in
women's and children's clothing are featured. For women's and children's swimwear and sportswear, head to **Maui Waterwear** (661-
3916). Another store worth visiting here is **Endangered Species** (661-
1139), a preservationist shop selling photos, sculptures and paintings
of sharks, whales and rainforests. Through the sales of these products it also helps support many environmental causes. The **Ka Honu
Gift Gallery** (661-0173) showcases locally produced goods including ornaments, dolls, lotions, soaps and jewelry. Handcrafted
Hawaiian coral jewelry is the specialty of **Maui Divers of Hawaii**
(661-1097). ~ 2435 Kaanapali Parkway.

With the continuing influx of Japanese tourists who arrive with
a yen for shopping and a strong yen in their purses, the upper tier
of Whalers Village has gone stratospheric. Among the shops representing this shift to the chic is **Chanel Boutique** (661-1555),
which displays fine jewelry and designer threads. Chanel also has
a line of purses guaranteed to put a hole in your wallet. ~ 2435
Kaanapali Parkway.

And then, to help make shopping the grand adventure it should
be, there are the displays. Within this mazework mall you'll discover blunderbusses, intricate scrimshaw pieces, the skeletal remains of leviathans and whaling boats with iron harpoons splayed
from the bow. Practically everything, in fact, that a whaler (or a
cruising shopper) could desire.

SCRIMSHAW TREASURES

Perhaps the best place in Whaler's Village to discover the whaling tradition
is **Lahaina Scrimshaw**. During their long journeys, sailors once whiled
away the hours by etching and engraving on ivory, creating beautiful
articles of scrimshaw. The sale of ivory from animals taken by hunters
is banned, but the fossilized remains of ancient mammoths and
walruses have kept this art alive. Using ivory that is thousands of
years old, artists create a wide array of functional and decorative
pieces, many of which are traded by aficionados of this art form.
~ 661-4034.

La Bareda is an excellent place to find inexpensive Hawaiian souvenirs such as sarongs, straw hats, jewelry and T-shirts. This shop in the Maui Marriott hotel is also knee-deep in key chains, pennants and ceramic pineapples. ~ 100 Nohea Kai Drive, Kaanapali; 667-8226.

For serious shoppers, ready to spend money or be damned, there is nothing to compare with the neighboring hotels. Set like gems within this tourist cluster are several world-class hotels, each hosting numerous elegant shops.

Foremost is the **Hyatt Regency Maui**, along whose wood-paneled lobby are stores that might well be deemed mini-museums. One, called **Elephant Walk**, displays koa wood furniture, baskets and Niihau shell jewelry. There are art galleries, a fabric shop, clothing stores, jewelry stores and more—set in an open-air lobby that is filled with rare statuary and exotic birds. ~ 210 Nohea Kai Drive, Kaanapali; 667-2848.

Another favorite Hyatt Regency shop is **Rhonda's Quilts**, where you'll find wallhangings, Thai silk pillows and needlepoint supplies as well as an array of quilts. Many of the quilts are designed by local artists. ~ 210 Nohea Kai Drive, Kaanapali; 661-1234.

The **Kapalua Bay Hotel** sports another upscale shopping annex. Among the temptations is **Mandalay** (669-6170), specializing in silks and cottons from Asia. There are blouses and jackets for women as well as a small collection of artfully crafted jewelry. Also stop by **South Seas of Kapalua** (669-1249), which has native masks from New Guinea and other artwork from Oceania. If you're traveling with young ones or looking for a souvenir for those you left behind, stop by **Kapalua Kids** (669-0033). Here you can buy children's books on Hawaii as well as soft toys and an array of clothing. ~ 1 Bay Drive.

◆◆

PUEONE O HONOKAHUA

The Kapalua area includes one of Maui's most important cultural zones, Pueone o Honokahua. This 14-acre preserve, near the Ritz-Carlton Kapalua, was the site of fishing shrines and *heiaus* where the ancient Hawaiians worshipped their gods and made astronomical observations. Today you can see a burial ground dating back to 950 A.D. and portions of the King's Highway, a 16th-century stone road around Maui. Also extant are the outlines of terraced taro patches farmed by early inhabitants. Although this land has been claimed in turn by King Kamehameha III, the sugar king, H. P. Baldwin, and lastly the Maui Land and Pineapple Company, the state now protects and preserves it as a native Hawaiian sanctuary.

At the **Plantation Course Golf Shop** you'll find an impressive collection of jackets, shirts, sweaters, sweatshirts and shorts, many with a tropical flair. This is also a good place to look for the work of signature designers. ~ 300 Plantation Club Drive, Kapalua; 669-8877.

Possibly the prettiest place in these parts to enjoy a drink 'neath the tropic moon is the bar at **Hula Grill**. Located in the Whalers Village mall, this beach house–style gathering place is decorated with original Hawaiian outrigger canoes. It features Hawaiian music and hula nightly until nine o'clock. The place is located right on the water, so you can listen to a slow set, then stroll the beach. ~ 2435 Kaanapali Parkway; 667-6636.

NIGHTLIFE

A solo pianist performs nightly at the Hyatt Regency Maui in the elegant waterfront **Swan Court**. For contemporary Hawaiian and guitar music, head over to the **Weeping Banyan**, an open-air lounge. ~ 200 Nohea Kai Drive; 661-1234.

There's music and Hawaiian entertainment at the Westin Maui in the **Villa Restaurant**. At the hotel's **Sound of the Falls**, a classical pianist plays nightly, except Sunday. ~ 2365 Kaanapali Parkway; 667-2525.

At the Maui Marriott, the **Makai Bar** cooks every night with a solo or duo performing Hawaiian and pop numbers. If you'd rather get up there and perform yourself, you can join the hostess in a karaoke-style sing-along at the **Lobby Bar** on Thursday, Friday or Saturday. On Sunday night a standup comedian will take your place. ~ 100 Nohea Kai Drive; 667-1200.

The Sheraton Maui is a prime nightspot both early and later in the evening. Just before sunset you can watch the torchlighting and cliff-diving ceremony from the **Sundowner Bar**. Then adjourn to **On The Rocks** for karaoke. (The Sheraton Maui is closed for renovation until November 1996.) ~ Kaanapali Parkway; 661-0031.

There's Hawaiian-style entertainment nightly at the **Royal Ocean Terrace Lounge**, a beachfront watering hole on the grounds of the Royal Lahaina Resort. Arrive early and you can watch the sunset between Lanai and Molokai followed by the ubiquitous torchlighting ceremony. ~ 2780 Kekaa Drive; 661-3611.

For soft entertainment in a relaxed setting, try the **Bay Club** at the Kapalua Bay Hotel. This open-air lounge with nightly pianist is set in a lovely restaurant overlooking the water. The melodies are as serene and relaxing as the views of neighboring Molokai. ~ 1 Bay Drive; 669-8008.

At **The Bay Lounge**, in the lobby of the Kapalua Bay Hotel, you can enjoy live Hawaiian music and a nightly hula show over cocktails and great views of the Pacific. ~ 1 Bay Drive; 367-8000.

A Hawaiian duo plays in the evenings at **The Lobby Lounge and Library** at the Ritz-Carlton Kapalua. At the **Anuenue Lounge** you can enjoy a pianist. ~ 1 Ritz-Carlton Drive, Kapalua; 669-6200.

BEACHES & PARKS

KAANAPALI RESORT BEACHES 🏊 🤽 The sprawling complex of Kaanapali hotels sits astride a beautiful white-sand beach that extends for three miles. Looking out on Lanai and Molokai, this is a classic palm-fringed strand. The entire area is heavily developed and crowded with tourists glistening in coconut oil. But it is an extraordinarily fine beach where the swimming is very good and the skindiving excellent around Black Rock at the Sheraton Maui. The beach has no facilities, but there are restaurants nearby. ~ Take the public right-of-way to the beach from any of the Kaanapali resort hotels.

HONOKOWAI BEACH PARK 🏊 🤽 🎣 Compared to the beaches fronting Kaanapali's nearby resorts, this is a bit disappointing. The large lawn is pleasant enough, but the beach itself is small, with a reef that projects right to the shoreline. On the other hand, the view of Molokai is awesome. In the shallow reef waters the swimming and snorkeling are fair; surfing is nonexistent. *Ulua* and threadfin are among the most frequent catches. Picnic tables, restrooms and showers are available and directly across the street is a supermarket. ~ North of Kaanapali in Honokowai on Lower Honoapiilani Road (which is the oceanfront section of Route 30).

NAPILI BAY 🏊 🤽 🎣 You'll find wall-to-wall condominiums along the small cove. There's a crowded but beautiful white-sand beach studded with palm trees and looking out on Molokai. Swimming and snorkeling are delightful and the surfing here is particularly good for beginners. ~ Several miles north of Kaanapali, with rights-of-way to the beach from Lower Honoapiilani Road via Napili Place or Hui Drive.

KAPALUA BEACH 🏊 🤽 This is the next cove over from Napili Bay. It's equally beautiful, but not as heavily developed. The crescent of white sand that lines Kapalua Bay is bounded on either end by rocky points and backdropped by a line of coconut trees and the Kapalua Bay Hotel. Swimming and snorkeling are excellent. ~ There's a right-of-way to the beach from Lower Honoapiilani Road near the Napili Kai Beach Club.

D. T. FLEMING PARK 🏊 🤽 🚣 One of Maui's nicest beach parks, D. T. Fleming has a spacious white-sand beach and a rolling lawn shaded with palm and ironwood trees. Unfortunately, a major resort resides just uphill from the beach. Sometimes windy, the park is plagued by rough and dangerous surf during the winter. Use caution! There's a nice view of Molokai's rugged East End. You'll find good swimming and bodysurfing and fair snorkeling. There are also good breaks nearby at Little Makaha, named after the famous Oahu beach. For anglers the prime catches are *ulua* and *papio*. There are restrooms, a picnic area and showers. ~ About seven miles north of Kaanapali just off Honoapiilani Highway.

To escape from the crowds and commotion of the Kaanapali–Kapalua area and travel north on the Honoapiilani Highway is to journey from the ridiculous to the sublime. As you curve along the edge of the West Maui Mountains, en route around the side of the island to Kahului and Wailuku, you'll pass several hidden beaches that lie along an exotic and undeveloped shore. This is a region of the Valley Isle rarely ever seen by visitors.

Northwest Maui

SIGHTS

Near the rocky beach and lush valley at **Honokohau Bay**, the Honoapiilani Highway (Route 30) becomes the Kahekili Highway (Route 340). This macadam track snakes high above the ocean, hugging the coastline. From the highway rises a series of multihued **sandstone cliffs** that seems alien to this volcanic region and creates a picturesque backdrop to the rocky shore.

As the road continues, the scenery is some of the most magnificent on Maui. Down a dirt side road sits the rustic village of **Kahakuloa**. Nestled in an overgrown valley beside a deep blue bay, the community is protected by a solitary headland rising directly from the sea. Woodframe houses and churches, which appear ready to fall to the next gusting wind, are spotted throughout this enchanting area. Kahakuloa is cattle country, and you'll find that the villagers live and farm much as their forefathers did back when most of Maui was unclaimed terrain.

◄ HIDDEN

The road ascends again outside Kahakuloa. Opening below you, one valley after another falls seaward in a series of spine-backed ridges. Above the road, the mountain range rises toward its 5788-foot summit at Puu Kukui.

Six miles beyond Kahakuloa, you'll stumble upon **Aina Anuhea Tropical Gardens,** which in this heavenly environment represents a further ascent into the ethereal. Its six acres of curving paths lead along a mountain stream, through a Japanese garden, past a waterfall and up to a solitary gazebo perched high above the world. Along the way you can take in the ginger and heliconia, the maile and lokelani. Admission. ~ Kahekili Highway, between Kahakuloa and Waihee; 244-0689.

It was from the shoreline near Kahakuloa that the Polynesian canoe *Hokulea* left on its famous voyage.

There are lush gulches farther along as the road descends into the plantation town of **Waihee.** Here cane fields, dotted with small farm houses, slope from the roadside up to the foothills of the West Maui Mountains.

You're still on the Kahekili Highway, but now once again it really is a highway, a well-traveled road that leads toward Kahului. Located just northwest of town, a side road leads to two sacred spots. The first, **Halekii Heiau,** overlooking Kahului Bay and Iao Stream, dates from the 1700s. Today this temple, once as large as a football field, is little more than a stone heap. **Pihana Kalani Heiau,** a short distance away, was once a sacrificial temple.

Before driving this route, as well as the back road from Hana to Ulupalakua, remember that the car rental agencies will not insure you over these winding tracks. Many cover the roads anyway, and I highly recommend that you explore them both if weather permits.

BEACHES & PARKS

HIDDEN ▶

MOKULEIA BEACH OR SLAUGHTERHOUSE BEACH 🏄 🎣 🏃 This lovely patch of white sand is bounded by cliffs and looks out on Molokai. Set at the end of a shallow cove, the beach is partially protected. Swimming, snorkeling and surfing are all good. This is part of a marine sanctuary so fishing is not permitted. There are no facilities here. ~ Take Honoapiilani Highway for exactly eight-tenths of a mile past D. T. Fleming Park. Park on the highway and take the steep path down about 100 yards to the beach.

HIDDEN ▶

HONOLUA BAY 🏄 🎣 🏃 ⚓ A rocky beach makes this cliff-rimmed bay unappealing for sunbathers, but there are rich coral deposits offshore and beautiful trees growing near the water. In winter you're likely to find crowds along the top of the cliff watching surfers work some of the finest breaks in all Hawaii: perfect tubes up to 15 feet. Swimming is good, but the bottom is rocky. Snorkeling is excellent, particularly on the west side of the bay. No fishing is allowed; this is part of a marine sanctuary. There are no facilities (and usually very few people) here. ~ About one-and-a-third miles north of D. T. Fleming Park on Honoapiilani Highway. The dirt road to the beach is open only to cars with boats in tow. Park with the other cars along the highway and follow the paths to the beach.

HIDDEN ▶

PUNALAU OR WINDMILL BEACH 🏄 🎣 🏃 ⚓ A white-sand beach studded with rocks, Punalau is surrounded by cliffs and intriguing rock formations. Very secluded. The swimming is okay and when the water is calm snorkeling is excellent. A fascinating reef extends along the coast all through this area. Surfing is fine, peaking in winter; left and right slides. Leatherback, *papio,* milkfish, *moano* and big-eyed scad are the primary catches for anglers. ~ Three-and-a-half miles north of D. T. Fleming Park on Honoapiilani Highway. Turn left onto the dirt road and follow it a short distance to the beach.

▲ There is a three-day limit and a $5 day-use fee, but no facilities. A permit is required from Maui Pineapple Co., Honolua Division, 4900 Honoapiilani Highway, Lahaina (669-6201) and must be obtained in person.

HONOKOHAU BAY 🏄 🎣 🏃 ⚓ This rocky beach is surrounded by cliffs. To the interior, a lush valley rises steadily into

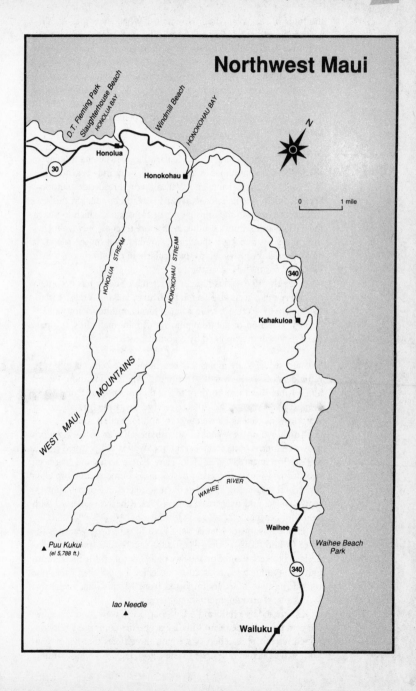

Northwest Maui

D.T. Fleming Park
Slaughterhouse Beach
HONOLUA BAY
Windmill Beach
HONOKOHAU BAY

N

30

Honolua

Honokohau

0   1 mile

HONOLUA STREAM

HONOKOHAU STREAM

340

Kahakuloa

WEST MAUI MOUNTAINS

WAIHEE RIVER

▲ Puu Kukui
(el 5,788 ft.)

Waihee

Waihee Beach
Park

340

▲ Iao Needle

Wailuku

the folds of the West Maui Mountains. When the water is calm, swimming and snorkeling are good. The surf offers rugged, two- to twelve-foot breaks. Keep in mind the changeable nature of this wave action, since it can vary quickly from the gentle to the dangerous. Milkfish, *papio*, leatherback, *moano* and big-eyed scad are the principal species caught in these waters. ~ About six miles north of D. T. Fleming Park on Honoapiilani Highway.

▲ Camping is allowed here, but the place is very rocky, and there are no facilities.

▼▼▼▼▼▼▼▼▼▼▼▼▼
Kihei–Wailea Area

Stretching from Maalaea Bay to Makena is a nearly continuous succession of beautiful beaches that make Kihei and Wailea favored resort destinations. Second only to the Lahaina–Kaanapali area in popularity, this seaside enclave rests in the rainshadow of Haleakala, which looms in the background. Maui's southeastern shore receives only ten inches of rain a year, making it the driest, sunniest spot on the island. It also experiences heavy winds, particularly in the afternoon, which sweep across the island's isthmus.

Since the 1970s, this long, lean stretch of coast has become a developer's playground. Kihei in particular, lacking a master plan, has grown by accretion from a small local community into a haphazard collection of condominiums and mini-malls. It's an unattractive, six-mile strip lined by a golden beach.

SIGHTS

HIDDEN ►

Situated strategically along this beachfront are cement **pillboxes**, reminders of World War II's threatened Japanese invasion. Placed along Kihei Road just north of town, they are not far from **Kealia Pond Bird Sanctuary**, a 300-acre reserve frequented by migratory waterfowl as well as Hawaiian stilts and Hawaiian coots.

To the south lies Wailea, an urbane answer to the random growth patterns of its scruffy neighbor. Wailea is a planned resort, all 1450 manicured acres of it. Here *kiawe* scrubland has been transformed into a flowering oasis that is home to five top-class hotels and six condos, as well as the required retinue of golf courses, tennis courts and overpriced shops. Like Kihei, it is blessed with beautiful beaches.

Home to some of Maui's most luxurious resorts, Wailea is the place to find Picasso originals, 50,000-square-foot spas and villas designed to keep a smile on the face of a high roller. Mediterranean- and plantation-style architecture, accented by polished limestone tile and granite boulders imported from Mount Fuji, make this swank resort area an international retreat.

Connected by a mile-and-a-half-long ocean walk, and lining five crescent beaches, the resort's luxury properties comprise a self-contained retreat. Spread across a region three times the size of Waikiki, Wailea is the Valley Isle's fastest growing resort destination.

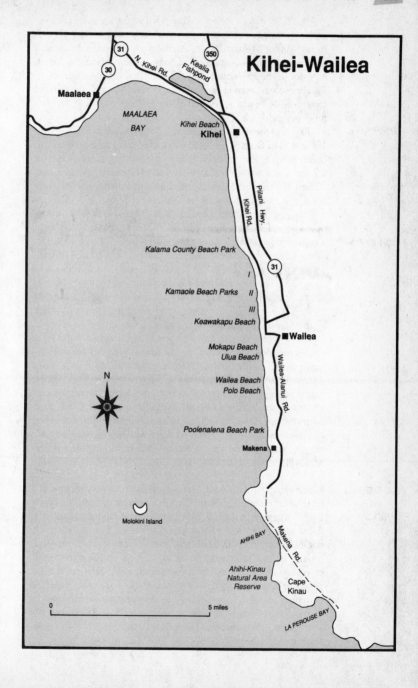

Kihei-Wailea

31
30
N. Kihei Rd.
350
Kealia
Fishpond

Maalaea ■

MAALAEA
BAY

Kihei Beach
Kihei ■

Piilani Hwy.

Kihei Rd.

Kalama County Beach Park

I
Kamaole Beach Parks II
III

Keawakapu Beach

31

■ **Wailea**

Mokapu Beach
Ulua Beach

Wailea-Alanui Rd.

Wailea Beach
Polo Beach

Poolenalena Beach Park

Makena ■

N

Makena Rd.

Molokini Island

AHIHI BAY

Ahihi-Kinau
Natural Area
Reserve

Cape
Kinau

0   5 miles

LA PEROUSE BAY

You'll have to go well past Wailea, to where the coast road becomes narrower, to escape the tourist complexes. I highly recommend visiting **Makena Beach.** Although development has struck here, too, Makena is still one of Maui's finest strands. A hippie hangout in the 1960s and early 1970s, it still retains a freewheeling atmosphere, especially at nearby "Little Makena," Maui's most famous nude beach. ~ Located along Makena Alanui about four miles beyond Wailea

HIDDEN ►

Past here the road gets rough as it presses south to **Ahihi–Kinau Natural Area Reserve.** Encompassing over 2000 acres of land and ocean bottom, this preserve harbors an amazing array of marine life and contains the remains of an early Hawaiian fishing village. Almost 100 larval fish species and about two dozen species of stony coral have been found in this ecologically rich reserve.

HIDDEN ►

The road continues on, bisecting the **1790 lava flow,** which resulted from Haleakala's last eruption. The flow created Cape Kinau, a thumb-shaped peninsula dividing Ahihi Bay and **La Perouse Bay.** When I drove this route recently in a compact rental car, I reached La Perouse Bay before being forced by poor road conditions to turn back. The bay is named for the ill-starred French navigator, Jean-François de la Pérouse, who anchored here in 1786, the first Westerner to visit Maui. After a brief sojourn in this enchanting spot, he sailed off and was later lost at sea.

Anywhere along this coastline you can gaze out at **Molokini,** a crescent-shaped islet that is a favorite spot among snorkelers. Resting in the Alalakeihi Channel three miles west of Maui, it measures a scant 19 acres in area and rises 165 feet above sea level. The island is actually a tuff cone created by volcanic eruptions deep underwater that solidified into a hard substance called tuff. Black coral divers harvested the surrounding waters until the 1970s. According to Hawaiian legend, Molokini was created when the volcano goddess Pele cut a rival lover—a lizard—in two, turning the tail into Molokini and the head into the cinder cone near Makena Beach.

LODGING

HIDDEN ►

Like Kaanapali, this oceanfront strip features condominiums, but there are a couple of hotels that I would recommend. The **Nona Lani Cottages** tops the list, with eight quaint wooden cottages situated across busy Kihei Road from a white-sand beach. Each is a one-bedroom unit with lanai, all-electric kitchen and a living room capable of housing one or two extra sleepers. There's wall-to-wall carpeting and a shower-tub combination, plus television, but no phone or air conditioner. Like most cottages in Hawaii, these are extremely popular, so you'll need to reserve them far in advance. There is a four-night minimum from April 1 to December 15; seven-night minimum from December 16 to April 1. ~ 455 South Kihei Road, Kihei; 879-2497, 800-733-2688. MODERATE.

Spread across 28 acres, the **Aston Maui Lu Resort** is tropically landscaped with palm trees and flowering plants. Within the grounds, which are across the street from a beach, you'll find a pool and two tennis courts. The guest rooms are furnished in standard fashion and located in a series of interconnecting buildings with some accommodations on the beach. ~ 575 South Kihei Road, Kihei; 879-5881, 800-922-7866, fax 879-4627. DELUXE.

Hotels are rare in Kihei. And in Wailea, a hotel in anything less than an ultra-deluxe price range is a contradiction in terms. So the **Maui Coast Hotel**, a 260-room facility across the street from the beach, provides a little (very little, I grant you) relief. It's light, airy, modern and has a pool, tennis courts and cluster of nearby restaurants. ~ 2259 South Kihei Road, Kihei; 874-6284, 800-426-0670, fax 875-4731. DELUXE TO ULTRA-DELUXE.

Down the road at the **Maui Oceanfront Hotel** you'll find a series of six buildings designed in mock-Hawaiian style and sandwiched between the highway and a white-sand beach. The rooms are tiny but attractively decorated with carpeting, air conditioning, television and refrigerator. ~ 2980 South Kihei Road, Kihei; 879-7744, 800-367-5004, fax 800-477-2329. MODERATE TO DELUXE.

Kihei is home to **Hale O'Wahine,** a women-only bed and breakfast that consists of four units, one right on Sugar Beach. ~ 2777 South Kihei Road B-105, Kihei; 874-5148, fax 572-0403. MODERATE TO DELUXE.

Also here is **Triple Lei,** an exclusively gay and lesbian bed and breakfast. This tropical contemporary home offers three rooms (with shared bath) and a 700-square-foot suite complete with a dry sauna and a private bath. There's a pool on the grounds but Little Makena beach is only five minutes away. ~ P.O. Box 959, Kihei, HI 96753; phone/fax 874-8645. MODERATE TO DELUXE.

The lushly landscaped **Four Seasons Resort Maui at Wailea** is the ultimate among ultimate destinations. The only Maui resort we know to feature a trompe l'oeil artwork in the lobby, it's a windswept, Hawaiian palace–style complex set on a luxurious beach. Furnished with wicker and rattan, most of the 380 plantation-style guest rooms offer ocean views. Casablanca fans, tropical plants and marbletop vanities add to the comfort. Louvered doors open onto spacious lanais. Reflecting pools, waterfalls and fountains give the public areas an elegant tropical air. ~ 3900 Wailea Alanui, Wailea; 874-8000, 800-334-6284, fax 874-2222. ULTRA-DELUXE.

Its remote location makes the **Makena Resort Maui Prince Hotel** an unusual find. Built around a courtyard adorned with lush tropical gardens and lily ponds, the 304-room establishment rewards those willing to drive a few extra minutes to Maui's southernmost retreat. Here you're likely to be lulled to sleep by the sound of the surf. Decorated with heliconia and bougainvillea, the rooms and suites open onto lanais. This V-shaped hotel is next door to two of Maui's top golf courses. ~ 5400 Makena Alanui, Makena; 874-1111, 800-321-6284, fax 879-8763. ULTRA-DELUXE.

CONDOS

Leilani Kai is a cozy nine-unit apartment hotel is located right on the beach. Studio apartments are $75 double ($60 during the off-season, May 1 to November 30); one-bedroom units are $100 double ($75 off-season); two bedrooms will run you $125 for one to four people ($90 off-season). ~ 1226 Uluniu Street, Kihei; 879-2606, 800-367-5234, fax 242-1845.

Oceanside one-bedroom apartments at **Kihei Kai**. are $85 to $105 double ($75 to $90 from mid-April to mid-December). Each has television, full kitchen and lanai. ~ 61 North Kihei Road, Kihei; 879-2357, 800-735-2357.

Sunseeker Resort is a small, personalized place where studios with kitchenettes go for $60 double and one-bedrooms for $70 double. Add $6 for each additional person. ~ 551 South Kihei Road, Kihei; 879-1261, 800-532-6284, fax 874-3877.

A highrise condo, **Mana Kai Maui Resort** has "hotel units" that consist of the extra bedroom and bath from a two-bedroom apartment, renting for $100 ($115 from December 17 through April 15). One-bedroom units with kitchens start at $155 ($185 in winter). The condo has a beachfront location, plus an adjoining restaurant and bar. ~ 2960 South Kihei Road, Kihei; 879-1561, 800-525-2025, fax 874-5042.

Lihi Kai has nine beach cottages with full kitchens, all renting for $59 single or double. Rates are lower for a seven-night stay. To be sure of getting a cottage, you'd best make reservations far in advance. There is a three-night minimum. ~ 2121 Iliili Road, Kihei; 879-2335, 800-544-4524.

Across the street from a beach park, **Kamaole Beach Royale** is a six-story condo with one-bedroom apartments for $65 double; two-bedroom units, $75 double. From December to April, the rates increase to $90 and $100, respectively. ~ 2385 South Kihei Road, Kihei; 879-3131, 800-421-3661, fax 879-9163.

Kapulanikai can be described as a cozy place with only 12 apartments, all of which overlook the ocean and a grassy, park-like setting. One-bedroom apartments rent for $80 single or double ($65 from April to mid-December). ~ 73 Kapu Place, Kihei; 879-1607, fax 879-3329.

DINING

Now that condominiums have mushroomed from its white sands, Kihei is no longer a poor person's paradise. Yet there are still several short-order griddles like **Suda's Store and Snack Shop**. ~ 61 South Kihei Road, Kihei; 879-2668. BUDGET.

You'll find another takeout window at **Azeka's Market Snack Shop** in nearby Azeka Place Shopping Center. For atmosphere there's a parking lot, but for food there's a fair choice, with hamburgers and plate lunches priced low. ~ 1278 South Kihei Road, Kihei; 879-0611. BUDGET.

Surfside Spirits and Deli has a takeout delicatessen serving sandwiches, salads and slaw. ~ 1993 South Kihei Road, Kihei; 879-1385. BUDGET.

At **Canton Chef**, on the other hand, the cuisine ranges from roast duck to beef with oyster sauce. This traditional Chinese restaurant offers almost 100 different choices including a selection of spicy Szechuan dishes. ~ 2463 South Kihei Road, Kihei; 879-1988. BUDGET TO MODERATE.

Margarita's Beach Cantina is one of those big brassy Mexican restaurants that are ever more present along the beaches. The kind that have live sports on big-screen television and a buzzing night scene. What sells this place is the oceanside dining and happy-hour margarita specials. The menu covers lunch and dinner, featuring carnitas, tacos and chimichangas, as well as hamburgers, chicken sandwiches, peel-and-eat shrimp and oyster shooters. ~ 101 North Kihei Road, Kihei; 879-5311. MODERATE.

For inexpensive Korean food, there's **The Kal Bi House**. Squeezed into a corner of Kihei Center and furnished with molded-plastic seats, it's not much on atmosphere. But it's hard to beat their cheap barbecued ribs, grilled chicken and beef marinated in Korean sauce, *katsu* chicken or Korean soups. A good place for a takeout meal. ~ 1215 South Kihei Road, Kihei; 874-8454. BUDGET.

Parked in the same complex is **Stella Blues Café & Delicatessen**. Here you can dine indoors or outside beneath a sidewalk umbrella. The bill of fare includes vegetarian dishes, pastas and sandwiches. ~ 1215 South Kihei Road, Kihei; 874-3779. MODERATE.

Speaking of pasta, that's the specialty at **La Pastaria**, a contemporary restaurant that features dinner shows on Wednesday night. On any evening you can order gourmet pizza, calzone, baked lasagna or spaghetti, or just sit back and enjoy a cappuccino. ~ Lipoa Center, 41 East Lipoa Street, Kihei; 879-9001. MODERATE.

There are inexpensive Japanese dishes a few doors down at **Kaipuni Restaurant**. You can order sushi, *donburi*, tempura or noodles at the counter and sit at one of the tables placed indoors and outside. Closed Sunday. ~ Lipoa Center, 41 East Lipoa Street, Kihei; 879-3854. BUDGET.

If you prefer something from Southeast Asia, **Royal Thai Cuisine** sits across the street in yet another shopping mall. Here the chairs are wood, the menu includes *dozens* of selections, such as crab legs, chili shrimp, cashew chicken or seafood combinations. ~ Azeka Place Shopping Center, 1280 South Kihei Road, Kihei; 874-0813. BUDGET TO MODERATE.

Did you say Greek? No problem. Just a few malls away (this one is called Kai Nani Village) is the **Greek Bistro** with a full selection of Mediterranean dishes such as gyros, moussaka, souvlaki, lamb kebabs and dolmas. ~ 2511 South Kihei Road, Kihei; 879-9330. MODERATE.

Or forget the ethnic food and head next door to the **Kihei Prime Rib and Seafood House**. A reliable if undistinguished dining room, it offers a good salad bar and numerous beef and fresh fish dishes. There are views across the road overlooking the ocean. Early-bird specials. ~ 2511 South Kihei Road, Kihei; 879-1954. DELUXE TO ULTRA-DELUXE.

The tab at **A Pacific Café Maui** will fluctuate dramatically depending on whether you order an inexpensive pizza or one of the dishes specially prepared on the wood-burning grill. A sister to the famous gourmet restaurant on Kauai, the Maui sibling is beautifully designed with a bolted-beam ceiling, bright pastel walls and a heart-shaped bar. From that smoky grill they serve up ahi steak, Chilean sea bass and Mongolian rack of lamb. Or how about roast duck with garlic mashed potatoes or scallops in polenta crust? ~ Azeka II, 1279 South Kihei Road, Kihei; 879-0069. DELUXE.

Why do celebrities such as Richard Dreyfuss, Harry Hamlin and Debra Winger book reservations at **Carelli's On The Beach**? Perhaps it's the imaginative Italian menu at this Keawakapu Beach establishment. Specialties include steamed clams in garlic, interesting pastas and fire-roasted rack of lamb. The open-air dining room, with its murals of Venice and the chic Mangia bar, adds to the allure. ~ 2980 South Kihei Road, Kihei; 875-0001. DELUXE.

Billed as "Wailea's alternative to high-priced dining," **Sandcastle at Wailea** is a welcome change. Bentwood chairs, brass fixtures and plastic tablecloths create a comfortable although uncreative atmosphere. The menu consists of middle-of-the-road American entrées with pizzas and pastas to round things off. ~ Wailea Shopping Village, Wailea; 879-0606. MODERATE.

◆◆◆

✔ CHECK THESE OUT—UNIQUE DINING

- *Budget:* Join the upcountry folk for tacos and tamales at **Polli's Mexican Restaurant**, a sombreros-on-the-wall eatery. *page 302*
- *Moderate:* Watch them blend their own coffee, bake the bread and grind their own sausages at **Marco's Grill and Deli.** *page 279*
- *Deluxe:* Order the tequila shrimp and fire cracker rice in the relaxed and personalized dining room at **David Paul's Lahaina Grill**. *page 241*
- *Ultra-deluxe:* Curve into a leather chair, inhale the ocean breeze and order fresh fish prepared by the master chef at **Seasons**. *page 269*

Budget: under $8   Moderate: $8–$16   Deluxe: $16–$24   Ultra-deluxe: over $24

All those *Travel/Holiday Magazine* awards at the entrance to **Raffles** signify that this is Renaissance Wailea Beach Resort's signature restaurant and one of the most highly respected dining rooms on the island. The ambience is elegant Singapore-style. The cuisine, however, is island classic: rack of lamb with papaya chutney, crisp whole fish with coconut curry, broiled filet of beef with shiitake mushrooms and daily fresh fish selections. Dinner only. Closed Sunday and Monday. ~ 3550 Wailea Alanui, Wailea; 879-4900. ULTRA-DELUXE.

From the day his ship docked in 1924 until his death four decades later, the writer Don Blanding lured visitors to the islands with more than a dozen books. An exhibition of this haole poet laureate's work is found at the Aston Wailea Resort restaurant named for one of his best-known volumes, **Hula Moons**. The open-air establishment is like a small museum appointed with art pieces, ceramic plates and aloha shirts that Blanding designed, as well as his books, poems and sheet music. The menu includes Szechuan roasted New Zealand lamb chops, South Pacific shellfish bouillabaisse and vegetarian entrées. Fresh berries in wine sauce with ice cream highlight the dessert list. ~ 3700 Wailea Alanui, Wailea; 879-1922. DELUXE TO ULTRA-DELUXE.

At **Hana Gion** you can choose between tableside *teppanyaki* cooking or a private booth. Built in Japan, broken down and shipped to Maui for reassembly, this beautiful restaurant in the Renaissance Wailea Beach Resort was created with the guidance of one of Kyoto's leading restaurant-owning families. Specialties such as tempura, *yosenabe, shabu-shabu*, sukiyaki and chicken *mizutaki* are served by kimono-clad waitresses. There's also a popular sushi bar on the premises. ~ 3550 Wailea Alanui, Wailea; 879-4900. DELUXE TO ULTRA-DELUXE.

Seasons, the signature restaurant at the Four Seasons Resort Wailea, gained a vaunted reputation soon after it opened in 1990. Marble trim, chairs upholstered in leather and knockout ocean views create the suitable ambience that is accented with a dancefloor. But it's the cuisine for which the dining room is particularly known. Specializing in fresh fish and locally grown produce prepared in a contemporary American style, it's one of Maui's top restaurants. ~ 3900 Wailea Alanui, Wailea; 874-8000. ULTRA-DELUXE.

Consider the *kiawe*-grilled hamburgers, the giant onion rings or the salads at the Kea Lani Hotel's **Polo Beach Grille and Bar**. This poolside dining spot is also a great place for a cool drink. ~ 4100 Wailea Alanui, Wailea; 808-875-4100. MODERATE TO DELUXE.

Hakone is the kind of restaurant you'd expect to find at any self-respecting Japanese-owned resort. The shoji screens, Japanese fans and a sushi bar are authentic; the ocean views are entirely Hawaiian. Start with tempura or miso soup. Entrées include sashimi, *sukiyaki* and New York steak with mushrooms and Kula onions. ~ Maui Prince Hotel, 5400 Makena Alanui, Makena; 874-111. ULTRA-DELUXE.

GROCERIES   **Foodland** is a large supermarket open 24 hours a day. ~ Kihei Town Center, South Kihei Road; 879-9350.

Star Market, also open 24 hours a day, has a large selection of groceries. ~ 1310 South Kihei Road; 879-5871.

Azeka's Market up the road is often price-competitive, though. Open Monday through Saturday, from 7:30 a.m. to 5 p.m. ~ 1278 South Kihei Road; 879-0611.

For healthful items, try **Hawaiian Moons Natural Foods**. Open 8 a.m. to 8 p.m. Monday through Saturday and 8 a.m. to 6 p.m. on Sunday. ~ 2411 South Kihei Road, Kihei; 875-4356.

If you're camping at Makena, you'll find **Whaler's General Store** in Wailea fairly convenient, but I'm afraid you'll pay for the convenience. This small store, situated in the posh Wailea Shopping Village, is painfully overpriced. Open every day from 7:30 a.m. to 9:30 p.m. ~ 3750 Wailea Alanui; 879-3044.

SHOPPING   Shopping in Kihei is centered in the malls and doesn't hold a lot of promise. You'll find swimwear shops and an assortment of other clothing outlets, but nothing with style and panache. Foremost among the malls is **Azeka Place Shopping Center**, which stretches along the 1200 South block of Kihei Road.

Kukui Mall just down the road has that most wonderful of inventions—a bookstore: a **Waldenbooks** bookstore to be exact. ~ 1819 South Kihei Road, Kihei; 874-3688.

Kihei Kalama Village, an open-air market with about 20 vendors, is a funky counterpoint to Kihei's other shopping spots. Here you'll find T-shirts, jewelry and souvenirs sold at cut-rate prices by local people. ~ 1941 South Kihei Road, Kihei.

If you don't find what you're searching for at any of these addresses, there are countless other strip malls along Kihei Road.

Or, if you prefer more sophisticated shops, continue on to Wailea. The elite counterpart to Kihei, this resort complex features two dozen different stores in **Wailea Shopping Village**.

Tropicana sells pearls and custom accessories made by leading Maui artisans. In the Aston Wailea Resort, this shop is a good place to find original designs in rings, necklaces and pendants. ~ 3700 Wailea Alanui, Wailea; 879-1922.

Much of the $30 million art collection in the Grand Wailea Resort and Spa comes from the personal holdings of the owner, Takeshi Sekiguchi. At the hotel's **Napua Gallery**, you can see some of his best Picasso lithographs, including *Les Deux Femmes Nues.* This series focuses on Picasso's longtime companion, Françoise Gilot, and demonstrates the artist's personal evolution. Also available for purchase are paintings, mixed media works and sculpture by leading contemporary artists. ~ 3850 Wailea Alanui, Wailea; 875-1234.

The **Dolphin Gallery** in the same hotel is the place to look for sculpture, art and jewelry with an emphasis on marine mammals. ~ 3850 Wailea Alanui, Wailea; 875-1234.

> Morning is the best time to go to the beach in Wailea and especially in Kihei. Later in the day, the wind picks up.

In an imaginative blend of local and European fashion designs, antique aloha shirts, Balinese sarongs, hippie dresses and Panama hats are just some of the attractions at the Kea Lani Hotel's **Mango Club**. ~ 4100 Wailea Alanui, Wailea; 875-4100.

At **Mandalay Imports** you'll find Thai silk, designer dresses, lacquer chests, Chinese opera coats, beaded belts and Balinese art. This shop in the Four Seasons Resort Wailea also sells innovative necklaces and ceramic vases. ~ 3900 Wailea Alanui, Wailea; 874-5111.

NIGHTLIFE

The Maui Lu Resort's **Ukulele Grill** features Hawaiian contemporary music nightly. They also stage special concert events in their spacious facility. ~ 575 South Kihei Road, Kihei; 879-5881.

Down the road apiece, there's a piano bar at **La Pastaria**, an Italian restaurant that also features dinner theater. ~ Lipoa Center, 41 East Lipoa Street, Kihei; 879-9001.

The **Sunset Terrace Lounge** is a pleasant spot to see live Hawaiian entertainment as day turns to night. It's located at the Renaissance Wailea Beach Resort, where you can also enjoy a quiet drink to the sound of a piano at Raffles. ~ 3550 Wailea Alanui, Wailea; 879-4900.

Live Hawaiian entertainment is a nightly feature at the Aston Wailea Resort in **Hula Moons**. Come for dinner or have a drink as you enjoy an appealing island show. ~ 3700 Wailea Alanui, Wailea; 879-1922.

Leave it to the Grand Wailea Resort Hotel and Spa—the accent's on Grand—to have Maui's most elaborate high-tech nightclub. **Tsunami** cost $4 million to build and has 20 video monitors and a 14-foot-wide karaoke screen. Cover on the weekend. ~ 3850 Wailea Alanui, Wailea; 875-1234.

A trio plays contemporary classics on the terrace of **Seasons**. A second venue here at the Four Seasons Resort Wailea is the **Cabana Café**, where live Hawaiian music and dancing is perfectly timed for a sunset drink. ~ 3900 Wailea Alanui, Wailea; 874-8000.

There is Hawaiian entertainment nightly at the **Molokini Lounge**. ~ Maui Prince Hotel, 5400 Makena Alanui, Makena; 874-1111.

BEACHES & PARKS

KIHEI BEACH This narrow, palm-fringed beach that runs from Maalaea Bay to Kihei can be seen from several points along Kihei Road and is accessible from the highway. The entire stretch is dotted with small parks and picnic areas and doesn't actually go by a specific name. There are buildings and numerous condominiums along this strip, but few large crowds on the beach. Beach joggers take note: You can run for miles along this unbroken strand, but watch for heavy winds in the afternoon. Shallow weed-ridden waters make for poor swimming and only fair snorkeling (you'll find better at Kamaole beaches). For those anglers in the crowd, bonefish, *papio*, mullet, goatfish, *ulua*, *moano* and mountain bass are all caught here. There are picnic tables and restrooms at Kihei Memorial Park, which is midway along the beach.

KALAMA COUNTY BEACH PARK This is a long, broad park that has an ample lawn but very little beach. Rather than lapping along the sand, waves wash up against a stone seawall. Backdropped by Haleakala, Kalama has stunning views of West Maui, Lanai and Kahoolawe. This is an excellent place for a picnic but, before you pack your lunch, remember that the park, like all Kihei's beaches, is swept by afternoon winds. For surfers there are summer breaks over a coral reef; left and right slides. Snorkeling and fishing are fair; swimming is poor. There are picnic areas, restrooms, a shower and tennis courts. ~ Located on South Kihei Road, across from Kihei Town Center.

KAMAOLE BEACH PARKS (I, II AND III) Strung like beads along the Kihei shore are these three beautiful beaches. Their white sands are fringed with grass and studded with trees. With Haleakala in the background, they all offer magnificent views of the West Maui Mountains, Lanai and Kahoolawe—and all are windswept in the afternoon. Each has picnic areas, restrooms, lifeguard and showers. Kamaole III also has a playground. Swimming is very good on all three beaches. The best snorkeling is near the rocks ringing Kamaole III. Goatfish is the main catch. ~ On South Kihei Road near Kihei Town Center.

KEAWAKAPU BEACH Ho hum, yet another beautiful white-sand beach . . . Like other nearby parks, Keawakapu has marvelous views of the West Maui Mountains and Lanai, but is plagued by afternoon winds. The half-mile-long beach is bordered on both ends by lava points. The swimming is good, but Keawakapu is not as well protected as the Kamaole beaches. Snorkelers explore the area around the rocks. The fishing is excellent. There are no facilities except showers, but it is only a short distance to the markets and restaurants of Kihei and Wailea. ~ Located on South Kihei Road between Kihei and Wailea.

MOKAPU AND ULUA These are two crescent-shaped beaches fringed with palms and looking out toward Lanai and Kahoolawe. Much of their natural beauty has been spoiled by

Shell Hunting

With over 1500 varieties of shells washing up on its beaches, Hawaii has some of the world's finest shelling. The miles of sandy beach along Maui's south shore are a prime area for handpicking free souvenirs. Along the shores are countless shell specimens with names like horned helmet, Hebrew cone, Hawaiian olive and Episcopal miter. Or you might find glass balls from Japan and sunbleached driftwood.

Beachcombing is the easiest method of shell gathering. Take along a small container and stroll through the backwash of the waves, watching for ripples from shells lying under the sand. You can also dive in shallow water where the ocean's surge will uncover shells.

It's tempting to walk along the top of coral reefs seeking shells and other marine souvenirs, but these living formations maintain a delicate ecological balance. Reefs in Hawaii and all over the planet are dying because of such plunder. In order to protect this underwater world, collect only shells and souvenirs that are adrift on the beach and no longer necessary to the marine ecology.

The best shelling spots along Maui's south shore are Makena, Kihei beaches, Maalaea Bay, Olowalu, the sandy stretch from Kaanapali to Napili Bay, D. T. Fleming Park and Honolua Bay. On the north coast, the stretch from Waiehu to Waihee (west of Kahului) and the beaches around Hana are the choicest hunting grounds.

After heavy rainfall, watch near stream mouths for Hawaiian olivines and in stream beds for Maui diamonds. Olivines are small, semiprecious stones of an olive hue. Maui diamonds are quartz stones and make beautiful jewelry. The best places to go diamond hunting are near the Kahului Bay hotel strip and in Olowalu Stream.

the nearby hotels and condominiums The beaches have landscaped miniparks and are popular with bodysurfers. Swimming and snorkeling are both good; restrooms and a shower are available. ~ Follow the signs near Renaissance Wailea Beach Resort.

WAILEA BEACH Another lovely white-sand strip, once fringed with *kiawe* trees, is now dominated by two very large, very upscale resorts, part of the ultramodern Wailea development here. Swimming is good (the beach is popular with bodysurfers) and so is snorkeling. Restrooms and showers are available. ~ Adjacent to the Four Seasons Wailea Resort just a half-mile south of Wailea Shopping Village.

POLO BEACH Though not quite as attractive as Wailea Beach, it still has a lot to offer. There's a bountiful stretch of white sand and great views of Kahoolawe and Molokini. The beach, popular with bodysurfers, has a landscaped minipark with picnic tables, restrooms and showers. Swimming is also good here and the snorkeling is excellent. ~ About one mile south of Wailea Shopping Village.

POOLENALENA (OR PAIPU) BEACH PARK Also known by locals as Chang's Beach, this is a lovely white-sand beach that has been transformed into an attractive little facility frequented by people from throughout the area. After Makena, it is the prettiest beach in the Kihei–Wailea region. The beach has no permanent facilities, but there are portable toilets and it is only two miles from the market in Wailea. Swimming is good, snorkeling fair and fishing very good—many species are caught here. ~ On Makena Alanui about one-and-one-half miles south of Wailea Shopping Village.

▲ There is unofficial tent camping here under the *kiawe* trees that front the beach but it is illegal and you can be arrested.

HIDDEN ► **BLACK SANDS BEACH OR ONEULI BEACH** This is a long, narrow, salt-and-pepper beach located just north of Red Hill,

MAKENA LANDING

Now a peaceful cove, Makena Landing was once a port as busy as Lahaina. During the California gold rush, prevailing winds prompted many San Francisco–bound ships coming up from Cape Horn to resupply here. Fresh fruits and vegetables, badly needed by the would-be miners, were traded in abundance. Later local ranchers delivered their cattle to market by tethering them to longboats and swimming the animals out to steamers waiting just offshore from Makena Landing.

a shoreline cinder cone. Fringed with *kiawe* trees, this stretch of beach is less attractive but more secluded than Makena. Facilities are nonexistent and it's four miles to the market in Wailea. Swimming and snorkeling are both fair, but the fishing is very good, many species being caught here. ~ Follow Makena Alanui south from Wailea Shopping Village for three-and-three-quarters miles. Turn right on the dirt road at the north end of Red Hill, then bear right to the beach.

▲ There is unofficial camping but, again, it is illegal and not recommended.

MAKENA (OR ONELOA) BEACH 🦀🏊 Much more than a beach, Makena is an institution. For over a decade, it's been a counter-cultural gathering place. There are even stories about rock stars jamming here during Makena's heyday in the early 1970s. Once a hideaway for hippies, the beach today is increasingly popular with mainstream tourists. So far this long, wide corridor of white sand curving south from Red Hill is still the most beautiful beach on Maui, but it is slated for mondo-condo development. ~ From Wailea Shopping Village, go about four-and-one-half miles south on Makena Alanui. Turn right into the parking lot.

LITTLE BEACH (PUU OLAI BEACH) 🦀🐟🏊 This pretty ◄ HIDDEN stretch of white sand next to Makena Beach, just across Red Hill, is a nude beach. It's also popular with the island's gay crowd. But if you go nude here or at Makena, watch out for police; they regularly bust nudists. Swimming is good (bodysurfing is especially good at Little Makena) and you can snorkel near the rocks at the north end of the beach. The fishing is fair. There are no facilities. ~ Follow Makena Alanui for about four-and-one-half miles south from Wailea Shopping Village. Watch for Red Hill, the large cinder cone on your right. Just past Red Hill, turn right into the parking lot for Makena Beach. From here a path leads over Red Hill to Little Beach.

▲ Camping, though unofficial, is very popular here, but beware of thieves.

▼▼▼▼▼▼▼▼▼▼▼▼▼▼

Kahului–Wailuku Area

The island's commercial and civic centers, as well as the greatest concentration of Maui residents, are located in the adjoining cities of Kahului and Wailuku. With no clear dividing place, these two municipalities seem at first glance to be "twin towns." They drift into one another as you climb uphill from Kahului Harbor toward the mountains. Kahului is significantly younger than its neighbor, however, and focuses its daily life around commerce. Maui's main airport is here, together with a skein of shopping malls and a few hotels lining a blue-collar waterfront. Wailuku presents a more rolling terrain and is the seat of government for Maui County.

SIGHTS

Kahului, with its bustling harbor and busy shopping complexes, offers little to the sightseer. The piers along the waterfront, lined with container-cargo ships and weekly cruise ships, are the embarkation point for Maui's sugar and pineapple crops. Established as a sugar town more than a century ago, Kahului has a commercial feel about it.

Coming from the airport along Kaahumanu Avenue (Route 32), you can wander through **Kanaha Pond Wildlife Sanctuary.** Once a royal fishpond, this is now an important bird refuge, especially for the rare Hawaiian stilt and Hawaiian coot.

The highway leads uphill to **Wailuku,** Maui's administrative center. Older and more interesting than Kahului, Wailuku sits astride the foothills of the West Maui Mountains. A mix of woodframe plantation houses and suburban homes, it even boasts a multistory civic building. For a short tour of the aging woodfront quarter, take a right on Market Street and follow it several blocks to **Happy Valley.** This former red-light district still retains the charm, if not the action, of a bygone era. Here you'll discover narrow streets and tinroof houses framed by the sharply rising, deeply creased face of the West Maui Mountains.

The county government buildings reside along High Street. Just across the road rests picturesque **Kaahumanu Church.** Queen Kaahumanu attended services here in 1832 when the church was a grass shack, and requested that the first permanent church be named after her. Now Maui's oldest church, this grand stone-and-plaster structure was constructed in 1876, and has been kept in excellent condition for its many visitors. With a lofty white spire, it is the area's most dramatic manmade landmark. ~ 244-5189.

Nearby you'll find the **Bailey House Museum,** run by the Maui Historical Society Museum. Housed in the home of a former missionary, the displays include 19th-century Hawaiian artifacts, remnants from the early sugar cane industry and period pieces from the missionary years. This stone-and-plaster house (completed in 1850) has walls 20 inches thick and beams fashioned from hand-hewn sandalwood. Together with an adjoining seminary building, it harkens back to Wailuku's days as an early center of western culture. Admission. ~ 2375-A Main Street; 244-3326.

Bounded on both sides by the sharp walls of Iao Valley, **Tropical Gardens of Maui** encompasses four densely planted acres of fruit trees, orchids and flowering plants. Iao Stream rushes through the property, which offers garden paths and a lily pond. Admission. ~ 244-3085.

Up the road at **Kepaniwai County Park,** there's an outdoor cultural showcase to discover. Backdropped by Iao Valley's adze-like peaks, this adult playground features lovely Japanese and Chinese monuments as well as a taro patch. There are arched bridges, a

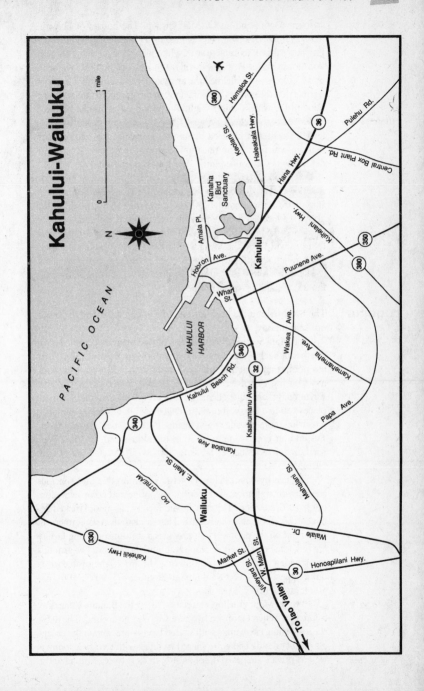

swimming pool and an Oriental garden. The houses of Hawaii's many cultural groups are represented by a Hawaiian grass hut, New England saltbox (complete with white picket fence), Filipino bamboo house and a Portuguese villa. On this site in 1790 Kamehameha's forces overwhelmed the army of a Maui chief in a battle so terrible that the corpses blocking Iao Stream gave Kepaniwai ("damming of the waters") and Wailuku ("bloody river") their names.

HIDDEN ► Uphill at the **John F. Kennedy Profile** you'll see Hawaii's answer to Mt. Rushmore, chiseled by nature. Ironically, this geologic formation, which bears an uncanny resemblance to the former president, was never noticed until after his assassination.

Iao Valley State Monument, surrounded by those same mossmantled cliffs, provides an excellent view of **Iao Needle**, a single spire that rises to a point 1200 feet above the valley (and 2250 feet above sea level). With the possible exception of Haleakala Crater, this awesome peak is Maui's most famous landmark. A basalt core that has withstood the ravages of erosion, the "Needle" and mistfilled valley have long been a place of pilgrimage for Hawaiians. (Be sure to explore the paths from the parking lot that lead across Iao Stream and up to a vista point.)

LODGING

The hotel strip in the harbor town of Kahului lies along the beach on Kahului Bay.

The **Maui Seaside Hotel** consists of two separate complexes sitting beside each other along Kaahumanu Avenue (Route 32). There is a pool, restaurant and lounge. Rooms in the older poolside wing are a bit less expensive: Clean, but lacking in decorative flair, the surroundings are quite adequate. Just a few well-spent dollars more places you in a larger, more attractive room in the newer complex, which has more upscale appointments. Both facilities feature phones, TVs and air conditioning. Some include kitchenettes. ~ 100 West Kaahumanu Avenue; 877-3311, 800-367-7000, fax 922-0052. MODERATE TO DELUXE.

The nearby **Maui Palms Hotel** has comfortable and spacious rooms with wall-to-wall carpeting, telephone and color television, but lacks decoration. This beachfront facility has a pool tucked between the lobby and the rooms. There's also an Asian-American restaurant on the premises that provides a convenient dining facility for folks staying anywhere along Kahului's hotel row. The grounds are studded with palms; considering the price, the ambience is quite appealing. ~ 170 Kaahumanu Avenue; 877-0071, 800-367-5004, fax 871-5797. MODERATE.

HIDDEN ► Even by Maui's mellow standards, life at the **Banana Bungalow** is *low* key. When I stopped by there was no one around. The guest rooms—plain, clean units with shared baths—are among the cheapest on the island. There are shared facilities with two to a room as well as private singles and doubles. A cross between a hotel and a hostel, you'll find Banana Bungalow has an ambience unlike any place else on Maui. Free coffee and tea are available in the morning at the neighboring restaurant. There are a television lounge, laundry facilities and a jacuzzi. ~ 310 North Market Street, Wailuku; 244-5090, 800-846-7835, fax 243-2219. BUDGET.

Northshore Inn is another clean, trim hostel-cum-hotel with shared rooms and private singles or doubles. The lobby/television room is decorated with surfboards, flags and modern art, and the place has an easy, windswept air about it. There are laundry and kitchen facilities; baths are shared. Every room has a refrigerator and overhead fan. ~ 2080 Vineyard Street, Wailuku; 242-8999, fax 244-5004. BUDGET.

Kahului, then Maui's largest town, was deliberately destroyed by fire in 1890 to kill rats that were spreading an epidemic of bubonic plague.

DINING

The best place in Kahului for a quick, inexpensive meal is at one of several shopping arcades along Kaahumanu Avenue (Route 32). For common fare, head over to the Maui Mall. Here you can drop in at **Restaurant Matsu** (871-0822), a short-order eatery that features such Japanese selections as tempura, yakitori, sushi and *saimin*. Next door at **Siu's Chinese Kitchen** (871-0828), they serve dim sum and other Chinese specialties. To round off the calorie count, you can try a cup of *guri guri* sherbet at **Tasaka Guri Guri Shop** (871-4513). ~ Maui Mall. BUDGET.

For good, inexpensive Chinese food, join the locals at **Ming Yen**. The decor is functional and plain, but the Cantonese and Szechuan selections make up for it. Favorite Szechuan dishes include crispy duck with fragrant sauce, mu shu pork and spicy Szechuan eggplant. On the milder side are Cantonese standbys such as lemon chicken and sweet and sour pork. ~ 162 Alamaha Street, Kahului; 871-7787. BUDGET TO MODERATE.

The white booths and black-tile tables are an appealing touch at **Marco's Grill & Deli**. So is the attention to detail at this family-operated Italian restaurant. They blend their own coffee, bake the breads, even grind their own meat for sausages and meatballs. The result is a menu that ranges from chocolate cinnamon French toast at breakfast to submarine sandwiches and vodka rigatoni later in the day. In addition to pasta entrées, they serve several seafood dishes. ~ 444 Hana Highway, Kahului; 877-4446. MODERATE.

◄ HIDDEN

If you're staying at one of Kahului's bayfront hotels, you might try **Vi's Restaurant** in the Maui Seaside Hotel. This open-air Polynesian-style establishment has seafood and other assorted dinners. The ambience here is quite pleasant, and the staff congenial, but in the past the service has sometimes been slow. Vi doesn't serve lunch, but at breakfast time (6:45 to 9 a.m.) the daily specials might include T-bone steak and eggs or banana hot cakes. ~ 100 West Kaahumanu Avenue; 871-6494. MODERATE.

The **East-West Dining Room** lies along Kaahumanu Avenue in the Maui Palms Hotel. This spacious open-air restaurant looks past the hotel lawn out over Kahului Bay. True to its name, East-West serves a Japanese buffet at dinner, and at lunch features American cuisine. Both the lunch and evening buffets are comfortably priced. The latter includes shrimp tempura, scallops, mixed vegetables, yakitori chicken, teriyaki steak, many different types of Japanese salad and a host of other dishes. ~ 170 Kaahumanu Avenue; 877-0071. MODERATE.

At **The Chart House** you can lean back in a captain's chair and gaze past the woodwork and candlelight out over Kahului Bay. There's a lavish salad-bar-in-the-round centered in the main dining room, an open grill just to the side and a cozy bar off in the wings. The menu offers a surf-and-turf selection with many dishes. ~ 500 North Puunene Avenue, Kahului; 877-2476. DELUXE.

HIDDEN ►

Up the road apiece in Wailuku there are numerous ethnic restaurants guaranteed to please both the palate and the purse. **Sam Sato's** features Japanese and American cuisine. Open for breakfast and lunch, it specializes in *manju* (a bean cake pastry), dry *mein* (a noodle dish) and the ubiquitous *saimin*. ~ 1750 Wili Pa Loop; 244-7124. BUDGET.

The nearby **Fujiya** stirs up some similar money belt–tightening Japanese meals. Well worth a visit. ~ 133 Market Street; 244-0206. BUDGET.

Siam Thai Cuisine is always a good choice for Southeast Asian fare. Attractively decorated with posters and artwork from Thailand, this restaurant features a complete menu that includes dozens of delicious dishes. Try the chicken-coconut soup, *tom-yum goong*, Siam chicken, or the *pod-pet*, beef or pork or chicken sautéed with ginger and bamboo shoots. This is a local favorite. No lunch on Sunday. ~ 123 North Market Street, Wailuku; 244-3817. BUDGET.

Local, affordable and attractively decorated—what more can you ask? Well, **Chums** will go one more and add tasty food. Settle

MAUI'S FAMOUS POTATO CHIPS

Always a favorite with locals, Maui potato chips have now become a worldwide phenomenon. One of the most popular brands is "Kitch'n Cook'd," made at the family-owned and operated **Maui Potato Chip Factory**. This place has been around since the 1950s, annually increasing in popularity, and it now brings in orders from around the globe. These chips are hard to find in mainland stores, but you can stock up on them here where they're freshly made! Closed Sunday. ~ 295 Lalo Place, off the Hana Highway, Kahului; 877-3652.

into a hardwood booth and order from an island-style menu that includes *saimin*, won ton soup, curry stew, teriyaki pork and mahi-mahi. Or stay middle-of-the-road with a sandwich or salad. ~ 1900 Main Street, Wailuku; 244-1000. BUDGET.

Saeng's Thai Cuisine sits in a beautifully designed building embellished with fine woodwork and adorned with Asian accoutrements. The menu, which lists six pages of dishes from Thailand, is like an encyclopedia of fine dining. Meals, served in the dining room or out on a windswept veranda, begin with *sateh* and spring rolls, venture on to dishes like the "evil prince" and "tofu delight," and end over tea and tapioca pudding. ~ 2119 Vineyard Street, Wailuku; 244-1567. BUDGET TO MODERATE.

Wailuku is becoming more hip by the month, and the center of "hipdom" is an espresso house with a hand-painted floor, upstairs dining room with ocean views and a pizza/quesadilla/salad/pasta menu. At **Café Kup a Kuppa** you can order scrambled eggs or bagel with lox and cream cheese for breakfast; lunch includes chicken, turkey, vegetable or tuna sandwiches, and daily specials like quiche. No dinner. Closed Saturday and Sunday. ~ 79 Church Street; 244-0500. BUDGET.

As well as being a Maui institution, **Hamburger Mary's** is a center for gays. Imaginatively decorated with surfboards and antique posters, it attracts a mixed clientele with an appealing menu of hamburgers (who would have guessed?), sandwiches, salads and steaks. There's also a hearty breakfast menu. Closed Sunday. ~ 2010 Main Street, Wailuku; 244-7776. MODERATE.

Ramon's is the region's entry in the Mexican food category. Half of this split-level eatery is decorated with sombreros and piñatas; the other part is given over to floral prints. The menu has a single theme, however, and it is spelled out with tacos, tamales and chile rellenos. ~ 2102 Vineyard Street, Wailuku; 244-7243. BUDGET.

Wailuku's low-rent district lies along Lower Main Street, where ethnic restaurants cater almost exclusively to locals. These are informal, family-owned, formica-and-naugahyde-chair cafés that serve good food at down-to-earth prices. You'll find Japanese food at **Tokyo Tei**. ~ 1063 Lower Main Street; 242-9630. BUDGET.

◄ HIDDEN

Southeast Asia is represented by **A Touch of Saigon**. On the menu you'll find stir-fried vegetables, curried chicken rice plates, shrimp in clay pot and beef noodle dishes. ~ 1246 Lower Main Street; 244-7845. BUDGET.

Kahului features two sprawling supermarkets. **Foodland** is open daily from 6 a.m. to 11 p.m. ~ Kaahumanu Center, Kaahumanu Avenue; 877-2808. **Star Super Market** is open daily from 6 a.m. to 10 p.m. ~ Maui Mall, Kaahumanu Avenue; 877-3441.

GROCERIES

Down to Earth Natural Foods in Wailuku has a complete line of health food items and fresh produce. Add to that a healthy stock of herbs and you have what amounts to a natural food supermarket. This gets my dollar for being the best place on Maui to shop for natural foods. Open every day. ~ 1910 Vineyard Street; 242-6821.

There are also stores in two of the shopping centers lining Kaahumanu Avenue: **Ah Fook's Super Market** (877-3308) in Kahului Shopping Center and **Maui Natural Foods** (877-3018) in the Maui Mall. Both open every day.

Wakamatsu Fish Market in Wailuku has fresh fish daily. ~ 145 Market Street; 244-4111.

Love's Bakery Thrift Shop sells day-old baked goods at old-fashioned prices. ~ 344 Ano Street, Kahului; 877-3160. In Wailuku, **Holsum/Orowheat Thrift Shop** is another place for baked goods. ~ 1380 Lower Main Street; 242-9155.

SHOPPING   For everyday shopping needs, you should find the Kahului malls very convenient. Three sprawling centers are strung along Kaahumanu Avenue (Route 32).

Kaahumanu Center is Maui's finest and most contemporary shopping mall, with **Liberty House** (877-3361) and **Sears** (877-2221), a photo studio, **Waldenbooks** (871-6112), boutiques, shoe stores, candy stores, a sundries shop and a jeweler. For Japanese gourmet foods, try **Shirokiya** (877-5551).

Nearby **Maui Mall** has a smaller inventory of shops. **Stanton's of Maui** (877-3711) stocks a connoisseur's selection of tobaccos and coffees, and even has a coffee bar and vegetarian deli. ~ Kaahumanu Avenue.

You might also try **Kahului Shopping Center**, though I prefer the other, more convenient malls. ~ Kaahumanu Avenue.

Up in Wailuku, a tumbledown town with a friendly face, you'll find the little shops and solicitous merchants that we have come to associate with small-town America. Along North Market Street are several imaginative shops operated by low-key entrepreneurs. There's **Traders of the Lost Art**, with ancestral carvings and art from Africa, Asia and the Pacific, as well as aloha shirts, Oriental rugs, jewelry and antiques. ~ 62 North Market Street; 242-7753.

Memory Lane features antiques and unusual collectibles. ~ 130 North Market Street; 244-4196.

Brown & Kobayashi, another nearby antique store, specializes in rare pieces from the Orient. ~ 160-A North Market Street, Wailuku; 242-0804.

While in the neighborhood, you might as well stop in at **Alii Antiques** and round out your visit to this falsefront antique row. ~ 158 North Market Street, Wailuku; 244-8012.

Wailuku Gallery specializes in works by Maui artists. ~ 28 North Market Street; 244-4544.

Some of the island's most reasonably priced souvenirs are found at the **Maui Historical Society Museum Gift Shop**. Here you'll find an outstanding collection of local history books and art prints. Quilts and *koa* bookmarks are also popular. ~ 2375-A Main Street, Wailuku; 244-3326.

NIGHTLIFE

If Kahului can be said to have an entertainment strip, Kaahumanu Avenue (Route 32) is the place. Here you can enjoy a live band and dancing at the **Maui Palms Hotel** on Saturday and karaoke on Thursday and Friday. ~ 170 Kaahumanu Avenue; 877-0071.

Up in Wailuku, **Aki's** entertains a local crowd almost every night around its bar. Located in Wailuku's Happy Valley section, it's a good place to meet people, or just to sit back and enjoy a tall, cool drink. ~ 309 North Market Street; 244-8122.

The gay nightspot on Maui is **Hamburger Mary's,** an attractive watering hole with overhead fans and a collection of antique wall-hangings worthy of a museum. There's music and dancing nightly. Attracting both gay men and women, Hamburger Mary's also draws a straight crowd, especially on nights when the cruise ship that travels around the island chain is in port. ~ 2010 Main Street, Wailuku; 244-7776.

BEACHES & PARKS

HOALOHA PARK Located next to the Kahului hotels, this is Kahului's only beach, but unfortunately the nearby harbor facilities detract from the natural beauty of its white sands. What with heavy boat traffic on one side and several hotels on the other, the place is not recommended. There are much better beaches in other areas of the island. Swimming and snorkeling are poor; surfers will find good breaks (two to six feet, with a left slide) off the jetty mouth near the north shore of Kahului Harbor. It is, however, a good spot to beachcomb, particularly for Maui diamonds. Picnic tables are available. Goatfish, *papio* and triggerfish can be hooked from the pier; *ulua* and *papio* are often caught along the shore. ~ On Kaahumanu Avenue (Route 32).

KEPANIWAI COUNTY PARK This beautiful park is carefully landscaped and surrounded by sheer cliffs. You'll discover paths over arched bridges and through gardens, plus pagodas, a thatch-roofed hut, a taro patch and banana, papaya and coconut trees. An ideal and romantic spot for picnicking, it has picnic pavilions, restrooms and a swimming pool. ~ In Wailuku on the road to Iao Valley.

WAIHEE BEACH PARK This park is used almost exclusively by local residents. Bordered by a golf course and shaded with ironwood trees and *naupaka* bushes, it has a sandy beach and one of Maui's longest and widest reefs. There's a grassy area perfect for picnicking, established picnic areas and restrooms with showers. Beachcombing, *limu* gathering, fishing, swimming and snorkeling are all good. ~ Outside Wailuku on the rural road that circles the West Maui Mountains. To get there from Route 340 in Waiehu, turn right on Halewaiu Road and then take the beach access road from Waiehu Golf Course.

▼▼▼▼▼▼▼▼▼▼
Central Maui

Central Maui is defined not by what it is but by what lies to the east and west of it. On one side Haleakala lifts into the clouds; on the other hand loom the West Maui mountains, a folded landscape over 5000 feet in elevation. Between them, at the center of the island, sits an isthmus planted in sugar cane and pineapple. Never rising more than a few hundred feet above sea level, it houses Kahului along its northern edge and serves as the gateway to both the Lahaina–Kaanapali and Kihei–Wailea areas.

Three highways cross the isthmus separating West Maui from the slopes of Haleakala. From Kahului, Mokulele Highway (Route 350) tracks south to Kihei through this rich agricultural area. The Kuihelani Highway (Route 380), running diagonally across sugar cane plantations, joins the Honoapiilani Highway (Route 30) in its course from Wailuku along the West Maui Mountains. The low-lying area that supports this network of roadways was formed by lava flows from Haleakala and the West Maui Mountains.

SIGHTS

The **Alexander & Baldwin Sugar Museum**, situated on the grounds of a working plantation, provides a brief introduction to Hawaii's main crop. Tracing the history of sugar cultivation in the islands, its displays portray everything from early life in the cane fields to contemporary methods for producing refined sugar. Closed on Sunday except in July and August. Admission. ~ Puunene Avenue and Hansen Road, Puunene; 871-8058.

The **Maui Tropical Plantation** is a 120-acre enclave complete with orchards and groves displaying dozens of island fruit plants. Here you'll see avocados, papayas, bananas, pineapples, mangoes and macadamia nuts growing in lush profusion. There's a tropical nursery and a tram that will carry you through this ersatz plantation. Ask about the plantation's Hawaiian country barbecue. On Tuesday, Wednesday and Thursday evenings you can enjoy a guided tour, cocktails, cookout dinner and a Hawaiian-style musical revue for one all-inclusive price. Admission for the tram. ~ 1670 Honoapiilani Highway; 244-7643.

Then, as you pass the small boat harbor at **Maalaea Bay**, the highway hugs the southwest coast. There are excellent lookout points along this elevated roadway, especially near the lighthouse at **McGregor Point**. During whale season you might spy a leviathan from this landlocked crow's nest. Just offshore there are prime whale breeding areas.

Down the road from McGregor Point, you'll see three islands anchored offshore. As you look seaward, the portside islet is **Molokini**, the crescent-shaped remains of a volcanic crater.

Kahoolawe, a barren, desiccated island once used for naval target practice, sits in the center. Located seven miles off Maui's south coast, it is a bald, windblasted place, hot, arid and home to feral goats. Hawaiian activists long demanded an end to the bombing of this sacred isle by the U.S. Navy. After years of demonstrations, their demands were finally acknowledged in 1994 when the island was turned over to the state of Hawaii.

The first sugar plantation laborers on Maui began to arrive from China in 1852.

The humpbacked island to starboard is **Lanai**. Lying eight miles across the Kealaikahiki Channel, it is a pear-shaped island boasting a 3370-foot peak and a population of about 2000 people.

As you continue toward Kaanapali, **Molokai** sails into view. Known as the "Friendly Isle," it covers 260 square miles and contains the highest per capita concentration of native Hawaiians of any of the main islands. With a population of 6700 people, it's a sleepy destination ideal for a Maui getaway excursion.

Hana Highway

The Hana Highway (Route 360), a bumpy, tortuous road running between Kahului and Hana, is one of the most beautiful drives in all Hawaii. Following the path of an ancient Hawaiian trail, it may in fact be one of the prettiest drives in the world. The road courses through a rainforest, a luxurious jungle crowded with ferns and African tulip trees, and leads to black sand beaches and rain-drenched hamlets. The vegetation is so thick it seems to be spilling out from the mountainside in a cascade of greenery. You'll be traveling the windward side of Haleakala, hugging its lower slopes en route to a small Hawaiian town that receives 70 inches of rain a year.

There are over 600 twists and turns and 56 one-lane bridges along this adequately maintained paved road. It'll take at least three hours to drive the 51 miles to Hana. To make the entire circuit around the south coast, plan to sleep in Hana or to leave very early and drive all day. If you can, take your time—there's a lot to see.

SIGHTS

About seven miles east of Kahului, you'll pass the quaint, weatherbeaten town of **Paia**. This old sugar plantation town, now a burgeoning artist colony and windsurfing mecca, has been painted in nursery colors. Along either of Paia's two streets, falsefront buildings have been freshly refurbished.

On the eastern side of town is the **Mantokuji Buddhist Temple**, which celebrates the sunrise and sunset every day by sounding its huge gong 18 times.

Hookipa Beach Park, one of the world's premier windsurfing spots, lies about three miles east of town. Brilliantly colored sails race along the horizon as windsurfers perform amazing acrobatic stunts, cartwheeling across the waves.

Within the next ten miles the roadway is transformed, as your slow, winding adventure begins. You'll drive past sugar cane fields, across verdant gorges, through valleys dotted with tumbledown cottages and along fern-cloaked hillsides.

Route 36 becomes Route 360, beginning a new series of mileage markers that are helpful in locating sites along the way. Near the two-mile marker, a short trail leads to an idyllic swimming hole at **Twin Falls** (the path begins from the west side of the Hoolawa Stream bridge on the right side of the road).

Nearby Huelo, a tiny "rooster town" (so named because nothing ever seems to be stirring except the roosters), is known for the **Kaulanapueo Church**. A coral chapel built in 1853, this New England–style sanctuary strikes a dramatic pose with the sea as a backdrop.

Farther along, on **Waikamoi Ridge**, you'll see picnic areas and a nature trail. Here you can visit a bamboo forest, learn about native vegetation and explore the countryside.

Another picnic area, at **Puohokamoa Falls** (11-mile marker), nestles beside a waterfall and large pool. If you packed a lunch, this is a perfect place to enjoy it. Trails above and below the main pool lead to other waterfalls.

A few zigzags farther, at **Kaumahina State Wayside** (12-mile marker), a tree-studded park overlooks Honomanu Gulch and Keanae Peninsula. From here the road descends the gulch, where a side road leads left to **Honomanu Bay** (14-mile marker) and its black sand beach.

Above Keanae Peninsula, you'll pass the **Keanae Arboretum** (16-mile marker). You can stroll freely through paved trails in these splendid tropical gardens, which feature many native Hawaiian plants including several dozen varieties of taro. Another section of the gardens is devoted to exotic tropical plants and there is a mile-long trail that leads into a natural rainforest.

HIDDEN ▶

Just past the arboretum, turn left onto the road to the **Keanae Peninsula** (17-mile marker). This rocky, windswept point offers stunning views of Haleakala. You'll pass rustic houses, a patchwork of garden plots and a coral-and-stone church built around 1860. A picture of serenity and rural perfection, Keanae is inhabited by native Hawaiians who still grow taro and pound poi. Their home is a lush rainforest—a quiltwork of taro plots, banana trees, palms—that runs to the rim of a ragged coastline.

Another side road descends to **Wailua** (18-mile marker), a Hawaiian agricultural and fishing village. Here is another luxurious checkerboard where taro gardens alternate with banana patches and the landscape is adorned with clapboard houses. The town is known for **St. Gabriel's Church**, a simple structure made completely of sand and coral, dating from 1870.

Back on the main road, there's yet another picnic area and waterfall at **Puaakaa State Wayside** (22-mile marker). The cascade tumbles into a natural pool in a setting framed by eucalyptus and banana trees.

Past here, another side road bumps three miles through picturesque **Nahiku** (25-mile marker) to a bluff overlooking the sea. The view spreads across three bays all the way back to Wailua.

◄ HIDDEN

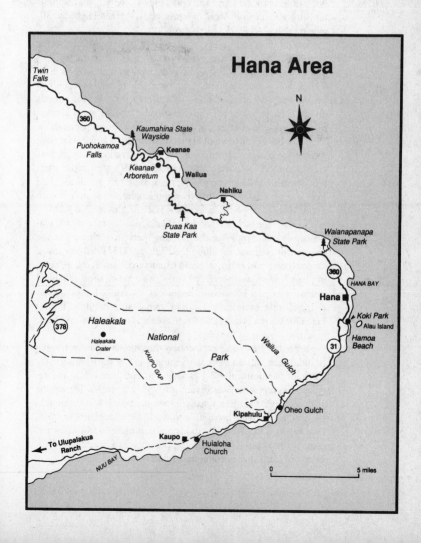

Hana Area

Twin Falls

360

Kaumahina State Wayside

Puohokamoa Falls

Keanae

Keanae Arboretum

Wailua

Nahiku

Puaa Kaa State Park

Waianapanapa State Park

360

HANA BAY

Hana

Koki Park

Alau Island

Haleakala

National

Park

Haleakala Crater

378

KAUPO GAP

Wailua Gulch

Hamoa Beach

31

Kipahulu

Oheo Gulch

To Ulupalakua Ranch

Kaupo

Huialoha Church

NUU BAY

0   5 miles

N

Directly below, the ocean pounds against rock outcroppings, spraying salt mist across a stunning vista. Set in one of the wettest spots along the entire coast, Nahiku village is inundated by rainforest and graced by yet another 19th-century church.

America's first domestic rubber plantation opened in Nahiku in 1905. You can still see a few remaining rubber plants in the area.

For a close-up of the exquisite plant life you've been passing on the Hana Highway, stop by **Hana Gardenland**. This five-acre preserve has winding paths that curve past a variety of tropical plants and trees. Here are orchids, anthuriums, heliconia and ginger as well as papaya and mango trees. This lush enclave also offers a gallery filled with local arts and crafts plus a café with an emphasis on (surprise, surprise) locally grown foods. ~ Hana Highway, 30-mile marker; 248-8975.

Several miles before Hana, be sure to stop at **Waianapanapa State Park**. Here you'll find a black-sand beach and two lava tubes, **Waianapanapa** and **Waiomao caves**. Hawaiian mythology tells of a Hawaiian princess who hid from her cruel husband here, only to be discovered by him and slain. Now every spring the waters hereabouts are said to run red with her blood. Offshore you'll also see several sea arches and nearby a blowhole that spouts periodically.

Right before the town of Hana, on the right, is **Helani Gardens**, a sprawling oasis of tropical plant life. Only a section of the gardens are currently open to the public, but it's worth a stop as they contain a wealth of flowering plants, trees and vines. You'll also find fruit trees, baobab trees, papyrus, ginger plants and even a carp pond. Visits by appointment only. ~ Hana Highway; 248-8274.

To reach the secluded hamlet of **Hana**, you can take the old Hawaiian shoreline trail (see the "Hiking" section at the end of the chapter) or continue on along the highway. This Eden-like town, carpeted with pandanus, taro and banana trees, sits above an inviting bay. Known as "heavenly Hana," it's a ranch town inhabited primarily by part-Hawaiians. Because of its remote location it has changed little over the years. The rain that continually buffets Hana makes it a prime agricultural area and adds to the luxuriant, unsettling beauty of the place.

Because of its strategic location directly across from the Big Island, Hana was an early battleground in the wars between the chiefs of Maui and the Big Island, who conquered, lost and regained the region in a succession of bloody struggles. During the 19th century it became a sugar plantation, employing different ethnic groups who were brought in to work the fields. Then, in 1946, Paul Fagan, a San Francisco industrialist, bought 14,000 acres and created the Hana Ranch, turning the area into grazing land for Hereford cattle and opening the exclusive Hotel Hana Maui.

Head down to **Hana Bay**. Here you can stroll the beach, explore the wharf and take a short path along the water to a plaque that marks the **Birthplace of Kaahumanu**, King Kamehameha I's favorite wife and a key player in the 1819 overthrow of the ancestral Hawaiian religious system. To reach this sacred spot, pick up the trail leading from the boat landing on the right side of the bay. It leads along the base of **Kauiki Hill**, a cinder cone covered with ironwood trees that was the scene of fierce battles between Kahekili, the renowned Maui chief, and the Big Island chief Kalaniopuu.

◄ HIDDEN

Near the Hotel Hana Maui (where you can request a key to open the gate), you can drive or hike up a short road to **Mount Lyons** (that camel-humped hill with the cross on top). From this aerie, a memorial to Paul Fagan, there's a fine view of Hana Bay and the surrounding coastline.

The **Hana Cultural Center**, an enticing little museum, displays such artifacts from Hana's past as primitive stone tools, rare shells and Hawaiian games. There are antique photographs and elaborately stitched quilts. ~ 4974 Uakea Street; 248-8622.

Also on the grounds, the old **Court House**, built in 1871, is a modest but appealing structure containing five small benches and the original desk for the judge.

Wananalua Church, a lovely chapel built from coral blocks during the mid-19th century, has been beautifully refurbished. Today, services are conducted in English and Hawaiian. Located atop an ancient *heiau*, stately and imposing in appearance, it is a perfect expression of the days when Christianity was crushing the old Hawaiian beliefs. ~ Hauoli Street and Hana Highway.

FROM HANA TO ULUPALAKUA   The backroad from Hana around the southeast side of Maui is one of the island's great adventures. It leads along the side of Haleakala past dense rainforest and tumbling waterfalls to an arid expanse covered by lava flows, and then opens onto Maui's vaunted Upcountry region. Since a five-mile stretch is unpaved and other sections are punctuated with potholes, car rental companies generally do not permit driving on parts of this route; so check with them in advance or be prepared to take your chances. Also check on road conditions: The road is sometimes closed during periods of heavy rain.

Past Hana, the road, now designated the Piilani Highway and renumbered as Route 31 (with mileage markers that descend in sequence), worsens as it winds toward an overgrown ravine where **Wailua Falls** (45-mile marker) and another waterfall pour down sharp cliff faces.

At **Oheo Gulch** in the Kipahulu District of the Haleakala National Park (42-mile marker), a series of waterfalls tumbles into two dozen pools before reaching the sea. The pools are rock-bound, some are bordered by cliffs, and several provide excellent swimming holes. This is an eerie and beautiful place from which you can see up and down the rugged coastline. Used centuries ago by early Hawaiians, they still offer a cool, refreshing experience.

HIDDEN ▶   Another special spot, **Charles Lindbergh's grave** (41-mile marker), rests on a promontory overlooking the ocean. The great aviator spent his last days here and lies buried beside Palapala Hoomau Church. The whitewashed chapel and surrounding shade trees create a place of serenity and remarkable beauty. (To find the grave, continue 1.2 miles past Oheo Gulch. Watch for the church through the trees on the left. Turn left onto an unpaved road and drive several hundred yards, paralleling a stone fence. Turn left into the churchyard.)

Not far from here, in **Kipahulu**, the paved road gives way to dirt. It's five miles to the nearest pavement, so your car should have good shock absorbers; sometimes the weather makes it impassable. The road rises along seaside cliffs, some of which are so steep they jut out to overhang the road. This is wild, uninhabited country, ripe for exploration.

HIDDEN ▶   **Huialoha Church**, built in 1859, rests below the road on a wind-wracked peninsula. The last time I visited this aging worship hall, horses were grazing in the churchyard. Nearby you'll encounter the tinroof town of **Kaupo**, with its funky general store. Located directly above the town is **Kaupo Gap**, through which billowing clouds pour into Haleakala Crater.

The road bumps inland, then returns seaward to **Nuu Bay's** rocky beach. From here the rustic route climbs into a desolate area scarred by lava and inhabited with scrub vegetation. The sea views are magnificent as the road bisects the **1790 lava flow**. This was the last volcanic eruption on Maui; it left its mark in a torn and terrible landscape that slopes for miles to the sea.

It's several miles farther until you reach **Ulupalakua Ranch**, a lush counterpoint to the lava wasteland behind. With its grassy acres and curving rangeland, the ranch provides a perfect introduction to Maui's Upcountry region.

NOTHING IS SACRED

Every tourist to Maui dreams of visiting the "Seven Sacred Pools" at Oheo Gulch in Hana. In fact, says Mark Tanaka-Sanders, a ranger who helps manage a coastal section of Haleakala National Park, "there are 24 pools in the area." Who's responsible for the miscount? "Blame it on the tourist industry," he says. "It's also important to know that the Hawaiian people do not consider these pools sacred." They refer to them as the pools at Oheo.

Along the Hana Highway out in Paia, about seven miles from Kahului, sits **Nalu Kai Lodge**. Tucked behind the Kihata Restaurant
near the town hub, this eight-unit resting place is a real sleeper. The
last time I was by, only three rooms were available; the others were
accommodating permanent residents. If you snag one of the vacant
rooms, you'll check into a small, plain cubicle with no carpeting
and little decoration. Sound unappealing? Well, even bare walls
sometimes look good at the right price. ~ Hana Highway; 579-
8009. BUDGET.

A very convenient accommodation located on the Hana Highway in Keanae is the Maui YMCA's **Camp Keanae**. For just $10 a
night, both men and women are welcome to roll out their sleeping
bags on bunks in the dormitory. Set in a spacious wooden house
overlooking the sea, this crash pad comes with hot showers, full-
size gym, kitchen and outdoor cooking area. Sorry, the maximum
stay here is five nights. ~ Hana Highway; 242-9007. BUDGET.

Aloha Cottages, perched on a hillside above Hana Bay, has two-
bedroom cottages that are situated among banana trees and fea-   ◄ HIDDEN
ture hardwood floors and walls fashioned from redwood. The
decor is simple, the kitchens are all-electric and many of the furnishings are rattan. Representing one of Hana's best bargains, the
cottages have been recommended many times over the years by
readers and friends. There are only five units at this small complex,
so advance reservations are a good idea. ~ 73 Keawa Place; 248-
8420. MODERATE.

You can also consider heading down toward the water to the
Hana Kai Maui Resort. Located smack on a rocky beach, these
two twin-story buildings sit amid lush surroundings. The ornamental pool is a freshwater affair fed by toe-dipping spring water. The
location and exotic grounds rate a big plus. Both studio apartments
and one-bedroom condominiums are available. ~ 1533 Ukea Road;
248-8426, 800-346-2772, fax 248-7482. DELUXE.

Speaking of scenery, **Heavenly Hana Inn** is blessed indeed.
Located about two miles outside Hana, this hostelry offers three
suites and is entered through a Japanese gate. On either side, stone
lions guard a luxuriant garden. The interior mirrors this elegance.
Each two-bedroom suite is decorated in a Japanese style with futon
beds, shoji screens and tiled bathrooms with sunken tubs. Continental breakfast provided. ~ Hana Highway; phone/fax 248-8442.
ULTRA-DELUXE.

Hana Plantation Houses has everything from homes to cottages
to studios. Scattered throughout the Hana area, there are homes
with either mountain or ocean views; each unit is fully equipped
with kitchens and hot tubs. The wood-paneled accommodations,
decorated with tapa-cloth designs and Hawaiian paintings, include
a wraparound lanai and interior garden. Most are cooled with ceiling fans and all have outdoor grills perfect for a private luau. En-

vironmentalists will want to check out the solar-powered Waika-loa Beach House. Some facilities are within walking distance of the beach and ancient Hawaiian fishponds. ~ Locations throughout Hana; 248-7868, 800-228-4262, fax 248-8240. MODERATE TO ULTRA-DELUXE.

Hana Alii Holidays offers a similar selection of accommodations—including studios and homes—in several price ranges. Here you can settle into a place on Hana Bay or on an idyllic hillside. Some units sit atop lava-rock bluffs overlooking the ocean, others are found in secluded five-acre settings. All accommodations come with lanais and outdoor barbecues; some have full kitchens. Picture windows, *koa*-wood detailing, ceiling fans and decks add to the ambience. ~ 103 Keawa Place; 248-7742, 800-548-0478. MODERATE TO ULTRA-DELUXE.

One of Hawaii's finest resting places is the **Hotel Hana Maui**, a luxurious retreat on a hillside above the bay. From ocean views to tropical landscape to rolling lawn, this friendly inn is a unique, world-class resort. Spread across the 66-acre grounds are 94 cottages, all elegantly designed and devoid of clocks, radios and televisions. The hotel's health and fitness complex sponsors a variety of hiking excursions and nature walks. The adjacent 25-meter pool, landscaped with lava walls and monkeypod trees, enjoys a spectacular setting. The staff has been here for generations, lending a sense of home to an enchanting locale. Rates for this getaway of getaways are stratospheric, but I highly recommend the Hotel Hana Maui. ~ Hana Highway; 248-8211, 800-321-4262, fax 248-7202. ULTRA-DELUXE.

Hana's three police officers report that the region's number one crime is driving without a seatbelt.

Don't forget the cabins at **Waianapanapa State Park** (for information, refer to the "Beaches & Parks" section later in this chapter).

The road to Hana is also home to several bed and breakfasts that cater to a gay, lesbian and straight clientele. **Golden Bamboo Ranch** has three suites and a cottage amid seven acres of gardens. There are views of the ocean through a horse pasture. ~ 1205 Kaupakalua Road, Haiku; 572-7824. **Halfway to Hana House** is a studio with a mini-kitchen overlooking the ocean. ~ P.O. Box 675, Haiku, HI 96708; 572-1176, fax 572-3609. BUDGET TO MODERATE.

Also serving a similar clientele, **Huelo Point Lookout** is set on two acres and bounded by the ocean on three sides. There's lodging in two cottages and a lookout house suite, each with full kitchen. Hot tub; pool. ~ P.O. Box 117, Paia, HI 96779; phone/fax 573-0914. MODERATE. **Napulani O'Hana** offers spacious but bland accommodations within a few miles of Hana. It's a ranch-style house set on four acres. ~ P.O. Box 118, Hana, HI 96713; 248-8935. DELUXE TO ULTRA-DELUXE.

Paia, an artsy little town located just a few miles out on the Hana Highway, has several restaurants to choose from. If you don't select any of them, however, be forewarned—there are no pit stops between here and Hana.

Wunderbar is an uneasy cross between a European dining room and an American bar and grill. You can order a beer at the bar or select from a nouvelle cuisine menu that includes German selections, fresh fish and pasta dishes. They also have full, American-style breakfast and lunch menus. ~ 89 Hana Highway, Paia; 579-8808. MODERATE TO DELUXE.

If you're craving a tasty fish sandwich, the **Paia Fish Market** is the place to go. When you're not in the mood for seafood, this eatery also offers burgers, pasta and Mexican dishes such as fajitas. It's is a casual place with plenty of greenery, and prints of water sports on the walls. ~ Corner of Baldwin Avenue and Hana Highway; 579-8030. BUDGET TO MODERATE.

For box lunches, drop in at **Picnics**. Open for breakfast, lunch and dinner, this light and airy café serves a variety of items including spinach-nut burger and mahimahi sandwiches. The menu also offers patrons basic breakfast selections, deli sandwiches and plain old burgers. ~ 30 Baldwin Avenue, Paia; 579-8021. BUDGET.

The Vegan Restaurant is the prime address hereabouts for vegetarian food. Place your order at the counter—there are salads, sandwiches and hot entrées that include Thai specialties. Closed Monday. ~ 115 Baldwin Avenue, Paia; 579-9144. BUDGET.

Bangkok Cuisine promises "authentic Thai food." They certainly sport an authentically attractive look with a dining room decorated with tiles and pastel walls. There's also a patio where you can dine alfresco beneath an umbrella of palm trees. Oh, and the menu—Cornish game hen in a sauce of garlic and black pepper, eggplant beef, evil prince shrimp and crab legs in bean sauce. ~ 120 Hana Highway, Paia; 579-8979. BUDGET TO MODERATE.

Just down the street you'll find **Kihata Restaurant**. This old-style restaurant, with bamboo partitions and a screen door that slams, is another favorite watering place for Paia residents. There's a glistening formica counter up front, and a cluster of tables in back. Dining in this local hangout is definitely casual. And the menu is ethnic: In addition to sushi bar specialties, it includes Japanese noodle dishes, *tonkatsu* (deep-fried pork), teriyaki and tempura. Closed Monday. ~ 115 Hana Highway, Paia; 579-9035. BUDGET.

Or, for masterfully prepared food without the sophisticated trappings, try **Mama's Fish House** outside Paia. Unlike most well-heeled restaurants, this oceanfront nook is simply decorated: shell leis, an old Hawaiian photo here, a painting there, plus potted plants. Elegant simplicity. During lunch, there is a varied menu that includes California cuisine–style dishes and ever-changing specialties. Other than a few steak and poultry dishes, the dinner menu is entirely seafood. The evening entrées include bouillabaisse, scampi and fresh Hawaiian lobster. Another of Mama's treats is fresh fish: There are always at least four varieties, prepared ten different ways. ~ Hana Highway; 579-8488. DELUXE TO ULTRA-DELUXE.

If you plan to stay in Hana for any length of time, pack some groceries in with the raingear. You'll find only four restaurants along the entire eastern stretch of the island. Luckily, they cover the gamut from budget to ultra-deluxe.

HIDDEN ▶   **Tutu's At Hana Bay**, located within whistling distance of the water, whips up sandwiches, hamburgers and teriyaki chicken for breakfast and lunch. ~ Hana Bay; 248-8224. BUDGET.

Open for breakfast and lunch, **Hana Gardenland Café** offers patio dining overlooking a tropical nursery. The menu includes such items as quiche, pastas, salads and the restaurant has Hana's only complete espresso bar. If you're headed out on a hike, stop here to pick up a picnic lunch. ~ Hana Highway at Kalo Road; 248-7340. BUDGET.

Hana Ranch Restaurant is a small, spiffy establishment decorated with blond wood and offering great ocean views. There's a flagstone lanai for outdoor dining. Open daily for lunch, they serve dinner every Monday, Friday and Saturday. On Wednesday night they serve pizza. Lunch is buffet style; in the evening they offer fresh fish, chops, steak and baby back ribs. ~ Hana Highway; 248-8255. DELUXE TO ULTRA-DELUXE.

There's also a **takeout stand** serving breakfast and lunch, with picnic tables overlooking the ocean. ~ Hana Bay. BUDGET.

Hana's premier restaurant is the dining room of the **Hotel Hana Maui**. This extraordinary resort, perched on a hillside overlooking the ocean, serves gourmet meals to its guests and the public alike. For lunch the bill of fare includes a variety of salads served in tortilla bowls, fresh fish, hibachi chicken and sashimi. The evening menu features pan-seared veal chops, bamboo-steamed seafood *lau lau* and baked Hunan-style lamb. The menu changes seasonally. ~ Hana Highway; 248-8211. ULTRA-DELUXE.

GROCERIES   You'd better stock up before coming if you plan to stay very long in this remote region. There are few restaurants and even fewer stores.

Over on the Hana Highway in Paia, **Nagata Store** has a small supply of groceries. It's open Monday through Friday 6 a.m. to 7 p.m., Saturday from 6 a.m. to 6 p.m., and Sunday from 6 a.m. to 1 p.m. ~ 579-9252.

If you can't find what you need here, check the **H&P Market & Seafood**. Open Monday through Friday 7 a.m. to 7 p.m., Saturday 7 a.m. to 6 p.m., and Sunday 7 a.m. to 1 p.m. ~ In the Nagata Store, Hana Highway (579-9640). You can also try the **Paia General Store**. Open from 6 a.m. to 9 p.m. during the week, opens at 7 a.m. on weekends. ~ Hana Highway, Paia; 579-9514.

Mana Foods has a complete stock of health foods and organic produce. Open from 8 a.m. to 8 p.m. every day. ~ 49 Baldwin Avenue, Paia; 579-8078.

With a limited stock of grocery items are **Hana Ranch Store**, open daily from 7 a.m. to 7 p.m. ~ Mill Street, Hana; 248-8261; and **Hasegawa General Store**, open Monday through Saturday from 8 a.m. to 5:30 p.m., and Sunday from 9 a.m. to 4:30 p.m. ~ Hana Highway, Hana; 248-8231.

Along the back road from Hana, there's a sleeper called **Kaupo General Store** that's usually open in the afternoon. You'll find it tucked away in the southeast corner of the island. Selling a limited range of food, drinks and wares, this 70-year-old store fills the gaps on the shelves with curios from its illustrious history. ~ 248-8054.

◄ HIDDEN

Paia, an artist colony seven miles outside Kahului, is my favorite place to shop on Maui. Many fine artisans live in the Upcountry area and come down to sell their wares at the small shops lining the Hana Highway. The town itself is a work of art, with old wooden buildings that provide a welcome respite from the crowded shores of Kaanapali and Kihei. I'll mention just the shops I like most. Browse through town to see for yourself. If you discover places I missed, please let me know.

SHOPPING

On display at the **Maui Crafts Guild** is a range of handmade items all by local artists. Here you'll find anything from pressed hibiscus flowers to bamboo furniture. There are also fabrics, ceramics, jewelry, baskets and other Maui-made items. ~ 43 Hana Highway; 579-9697.

Paia Trading Company has a few interesting antiques and a lot of junk. Among the more noteworthy items: turquoise and silver

SPRING TRAINING, HANA STYLE

In 1946, Hana hosted the only mainland American baseball team ever to conduct spring training in Hawaii. That was the year that financier Paul Fagan brought the Pacific Coast League's San Francisco Seals to the islands. Arriving with the players was a squadron of sportswriters who sent back glowing dispatches on "Heavenly Hana," helping to promote the destination and the Hotel Hana Maui, owned of course by Paul Fagan.

jewelry, wooden washboards, apothecary jars and antique glass-ware. ~ 106 Hana Highway; 579-9472.

Eddie Flotte Watercolors features original artworks by an original character. Flotte's paintings capture the down-home lifestyles of Upcountry residents. ~ 83 Hana Highway, Paia; 579-9641.

Summerhouse Boutique might be called a chic dress shop. But they sell everything from jewelry and post-cards to porcelain dolls and natural fiber garments. ~ 83 Hana Highway, Paia; 579-9201.

> The honor system is alive and well at the untended self-serve coconut stand near Hana Highway's 48-mile marker.

Around the corner on Baldwin Avenue lies another shop worth browsing. **Maui Girl and Co.** features a fine selection of women's fashions, including designer clothing, manufactured designs and locally made styles. They also have '30s and '40s aloha shirts for men, as well as informal beachwear. ~ 12 Baldwin Avenue, Paia; 579-9266.

One of my favorite shops in Hana is the **Hana Coast Gallery** in the Hotel Hana Maui. It features native Hawaiian art and artifacts and fine paintings by Maui artists, as well as pieces by the novelist Henry Miller. Also here are beautiful serigraphs, model racing canoes in *koa*, ceremonial objects, feathered leis, fiber collages and painted tapa cloth. ~ Hana Highway; 248-8636.

Also on the grounds of Hotel Hana Maui is **Susan Marie**, a shop specializing in sportswear, embroidered shirts and accessories with a tropical flair. ~ Hana Highway; 248-8211.

For everything you could possibly want or need, drop by the **Hasegawa General Store**. This store stocks everything from groceries, clothing and hardware to placemats, movie rentals, film and gas. The original Hasegawa's burned down years ago, but the name is still famous. ~ 5165 Hana Highway; 248-8231.

Hana Gardenland is a five-acre landscape nursery that seconds as an art gallery. All the orchids, bromeliads and cut flowers can be shipped home. Or you can shop in the gallery for Hawaiian crafts, including a number by artists from the Hana area. ~ Hana Highway at Kalo Road; 248-8975.

NIGHTLIFE

Wunderbar usually has live bands on Wednesday through Saturday nights as well as Sunday afternoons. This local bar often draws an Upcountry crowd. Cover. ~ 89 Hana Highway, Paia; 579-8808.

In the early evening, you can enjoy a duo singing Hawaiian music at the Hotel Hana Maui's **Paniolo Bar**. As relaxed as Hana itself, this low-key establishment is always inviting. ~ Hana Highway; 248-8211.

BEACHES & PARKS

H. A. BALDWIN PARK 🏖️ 🪁 🏊 This spacious county park is bordered by a playing field on one side and a crescent-shaped beach on the other. Palm and ironwood trees dot the half-mile-long beach. There's good shell collecting and a great view of West Maui. The swimming is good, as is the bodysurfing, but beware of currents; the snorkeling cannot be recommended. For surfing there are winter breaks, with a right slide. Fishing for threadfin, mountain bass, goatfish and *ulua* is good. Facilities include a picnic area with large pavilion, showers and restrooms. ~ About seven miles east of Kahului on the Hana Highway.

▲ Tent camping is allowed on a quarter-acre meadow; a county permit is required.

HOOKIPA BEACH PARK 🏄 🏊 For surfers and windsurfers this is one of the best spots on Maui. The beach itself is little more than a narrow rectangle of sand paralleled by a rocky shelf. Offshore, top-ranked windsurfers may be performing airborne stunts. On any day you're likely to see a hundred sails with boards attached skimming the whitecaps. The swimming is good only when the surf is low. There are picnic areas, restrooms and showers. ~ On the Hana Highway about three miles east of Paia.

HONOMANU BAY 🏊 A tranquil black-sand-and-rock beach surrounded by pandanus-covered hills and bisected by a stream, Honomanu Bay is a beautiful and secluded spot. There are no facilities, and the water is often too rough for swimming, but it's a favorite with surfers. ~ Off of the Hana Highway, about 30 miles east of Kahului. Turn off onto the dirt road located east of Kaumahina State Wayside; follow it to the beach.   ◄ HIDDEN

WAIANAPANAPA STATE PARK 🏄 🎣 🛶 Set in a heavenly seaside locale, this park is one of Hawaii's prettiest public facilities and is a very popular spot. The entire area is lush with tropical foliage and especially palmy pandanus trees. There's a black-sand beach, sea arches, a blowhole and two legendary caves. But pack your parkas; wind and rain are frequent. Swimming and snorkeling are good—when the water is calm—and the fishing is good. Facilities here include a picnic area, restrooms and showers. ~ Just off the Hana Highway about four miles north of the town of Hana.

▲ There are campsites for up to 60 people on a grass-covered bluff overlooking the sea. These are plain but attractive accommodations renting on a sliding scale (starting at $10 single and $14 double up to $30 for six people). Each one contains a small bedroom with two bunk beds, plus a living room that can double as an extra bedroom. All cabins are equipped with bedding and complete kitchen facilities, and some have ocean views. A state permit is required. The cabins are rented through the Division of State Parks. ~ 54 South High Street, Wailuku, Maui, HI 96793; 243-5354.

HANA BEACH PARK 🏄 🎣 🏊 🛶 Tucked into a well-protected corner of Hana Bay, this park has a large pavilion and a curving stretch of sandy beach. It's a great place to meet local people. Swimming is fine; snorkeling is good near the lighthouse; and surfers will find both summer and winter breaks on the north side of the bay (left slide). Bonefish, *ulua* and *papio* are routinely taken here and *moilii* run in the months of June and July. As well as the picnic area, there are restrooms and showers and there is a snack bar across the street. ~ Off the Hana Highway at Hana Bay.

HIDDEN ▶   **RED SAND BEACH** 🏃 🚣 🎣 🛶 Known to the Hawaiians as Kaihalulu ("roaring sea") Beach, this is one of the most exotic and truly secluded beaches in all Hawaii. It is protected by lofty cliffs and can be reached only over a precarious trail. A volcanic cinder beach, the sand is reddish in hue and coarse underfoot. Most dramatic of all is the lava barrier that crosses the mouth of this natural amphitheater, protecting the beach and creating an inshore pool. This is another beach popular with nudists. Swimming, snorkeling and fishing are all good. There are no facilities. ~ This is one place where getting to the beach becomes a grand adventure. It is located on the far side of Kauiki Hill in Hana. Follow Uakea Road to its southern terminus. There is a grassy plot on the left between Hana School and the parking lot for the Hotel Hana Maui's sea ranch cottages. Here you will find a trail leading into the undergrowth. It traverses an overgrown Japanese cemetery and curves around Kauiki Hill, then descends precipitously to the beach. Be careful!

HAMOA BEACH 🚣 🏊 Located at the head of Mokae Cove, this stretch of salt-and-pepper sand with rock outcroppings at each end is a pretty place. Unfortunately, the Hotel Hana Maui uses the beach as a semiprivate preserve. There are restrooms for guests and separate facilities for everybody else and a dining pavilion that is available only to guests, so a sense of segregation pervades the beach. ~ Follow the Hana Highway south from Hana for a little over a mile. Turn left on Haneoo Road and follow it for a mile to Hamoa.

KOKI BEACH PARK 🚣 A sandy plot paralleled by a grassy park, this beach is more welcoming than Hamoa. Backdropped by lofty red cinder cliffs, Koki can be very windy and is plagued by currents. With a small island and sea arch offshore, it is also very pretty. Swimming is good, but exercise caution. ~ Half a mile back up the Haenoo Road toward the highway.

OHEO GULCH 🚣 The stream that tumbles down Haleakala through the Oheo Gulch forms several large pools and numerous small ones. The main pools descend from above the Hana Highway to the sea. This is a truly enchanting area swept by frequent wind and rain, and shadowed by Haleakala. It overlooks Maui's rugged eastern shore. You can swim in the chilly waters and camp nearby. There are picnic facilities and outhouses; bring your own drinking water. ~ In the National Park's Kipahulu section (about ten miles south of Hana).

▲ Primitive, meadow-style camping is available on a bluff above the sea. No permit is required and there are no restrictions on the number of occupants but there is a three-day limit.

▼▼▼▼▼▼▼▼

Upcountry

Maui's Upcountry is a verdant mountainous belt that encircles Haleakala along its middle slopes. Situated between coastline and crater rim, it's a region of ample rainfall and sparse population that is ideal for camping, hiking or just wandering. Here the flat fields of sugar cane and pineapples that blanket central Maui give way to open ranchland where curving hills are filled with grazing horses.

Farmers plant tomatoes, cabbages, carrots and the region's famous Maui onions. Proteas, those delicate flowers native to Australia and South Africa, grow in colorful profusion. Hibiscus, jacarandas and other wildflowers sweep along the hillsides like a rainstorm. And on the region's two ranches—20,000-acre Haleakala Ranch and 20,000-acre Ulupalakua Ranch—Angus and Hereford cattle complete a picture far removed from Hawaii's tropical beaches.

SIGHTS

Home to *paniolos*, Hawaii's version of the Western cowboy, the Upcountry region lies along the highways that lead to the crest of Haleakala. Route 37, Haleakala Highway, becomes the Kula Highway as it ascends to the Kula uplands. The **Church of the Holy Ghost** (12-mile marker), a unique octagonal chapel, was built here in 1897 for Portuguese immigrants working on Maui's ranches and farms.

This roadway angles southwest through Ulupalakua Ranch to the ruins of the **Makee Sugar Mill**, a once flourishing enterprise built in 1878. A currently flourishing business, **Tedeschi Winery**, sits just across the road. Producing a pineapple wine called Maui Blanc, the winery rests in an old jailhouse built of lava and coral in 1857. Here at Hawaii's first winery you can stop for a taster's tour. ~ 878-6058.

You can also turn up Route 377 to **Kula Botanical Gardens**. An excellent place for picnicking, the landscaped slopes contain an aviary, pond, "Taboo Garden" with poisonous plants and over 40 varieties of protea, the flowering shrub that grows so beautifully in this region. Admission. ~ Kula; 878-1715.

Several farms, including **Sunrise Protea Farm**, devoted primarily to proteas, are located nearby. ~ Haleakala Crater Road; 876-0200.

Another intriguing place is the tiny town of **Makawao**, where battered buildings and falsefront stores create an Old West atmosphere. This is the capital of Maui's cowboy country, similar to Waimea on the Big Island, with a rodeo every Fourth of July.

HIDDEN ▶ From Makawao the possibilities for exploring the Upcountry area are many. There are two **loop tours** I particularly recommend. The first climbs from town along Olinda Road (Route 390) past **Pookela Church**, a coral sanctuary built in 1843.

It continues through a frequently rain-drenched region to the **Tree Growth Research Area**, jointly sponsored by state and federal forestry services. You can circle back down toward Makawao on Piiholo Road past the **University of Hawaii Agricultural Station**, where you will see more of the area's richly planted acreage.

The second loop leads down Route 365 to the Hana Highway. Turn left on the highway for several miles to Haiku Road, then head left along this country lane, which leads into overgrown areas, across one-lane bridges, past banana patches and through the tin-roof town of **Haiku**.

LODGING   A mountain lodge on the road to the summit of Haleakala offers a cold-air retreat that is well-situated for anyone who wants to catch the sunrise over the valley. For years, **Kula Lodge** has rented Swiss chalets complete with fireplaces, sleeping lofts and sweeping views. The individual chalets are carpeted wall-to-wall and trimmed with stained-wood paneling. The central lodge features a cheery restaurant, bar and stone fireplace. An appealing mountain hideaway. ~ 878-1535, 800-233-1535, fax 878-2518. DELUXE TO ULTRA-DELUXE.

What more could an urban cowpoke ask for than a bed and breakfast with trail rides that begin in the front yard? That's the
HIDDEN ▶ scene up at **Silver Cloud Ranch**, a nine-acre spread located at 3000-feet elevation on the slopes of Haleakala. In addition to a broad swath of cattle country, the ranch looks out over several neighboring islands. Accommodations include six bedrooms in a big ranch house, a bunkhouse with five studio units and a private cottage. Full breakfast, pardner. R.R. 2, Box 201, Kula, HI 96790; 878-6101, fax 878-2132. MODERATE.

One of Maui's premier gay retreats is **Camp Kula**, a spacious five-bedroom house that rests on seven acres where "HIV-positive guests are *always* welcome!" Located on the side of Haleakala at the 3000-foot level, it caters exclusively to gay men and women. Guests have full access to the kitchen, living room and other features of the house. ~ Kula; phone/fax 878-2528. BUDGET TO MODERATE.

Among other gay retreats, **Kailua Maui Gardens**, a gay-owned, mixed-clientele bed and breakfast has everything from a one-room cottage to a three-bedroom house. It's set in a tropical garden with shaded paths and bridges plus a pool and spa. ~ S.R. Box 9, Haiku, HI 96708; 572-9726, 800-258-8588. MODERATE TO DELUXE.

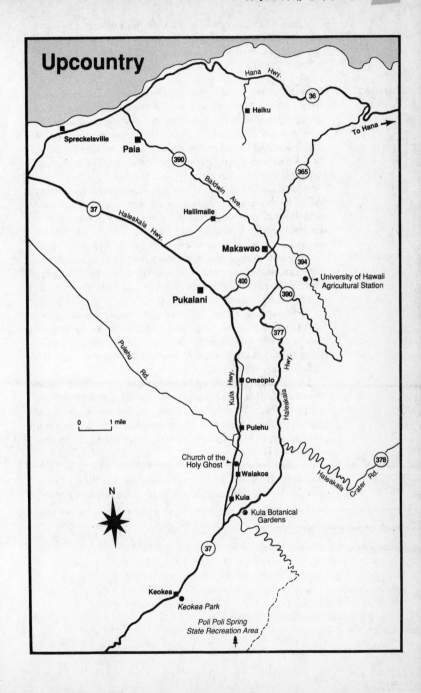

Upcountry

Hana Hwy.

36

■ Haiku

To Hana →

■ Spreckelsville

Paia ■

390

Baldwin Ave.

365

37

Haleakala Hwy.

Halimaile ■

Makawao ■

394

● University of Hawaii
Agricultural Station

400

390

Pukalani ■

377

Pulehu Rd.

Kula Hwy.

■ Omaopio

Haleakala Hwy.

0   1 mile

■ Pulehu

Church of the
Holy Ghost →

378

■ Waiakoa

Haleakala Crater Rd.

N

■ Kula

● Kula Botanical
Gardens

37

● Keokea

Keokea Park

*Poli Poli Spring
State Recreation Area*

Also with a mixed clientele is **Waipio Bay Lookout**, a two-acre spread in Huelo on a cliff above the ocean. There's a pool, jacuzzi and sundeck at this three-unit facility. ~ P.O. Box 1095, Haiku, HI 96708; 572-4530. MODERATE TO DELUXE.

DINING

There are several good dining spots in Pukalani Terrace Center. Among them is **Nick's Place**, a breakfast-and-lunch-only cafeteria serving Japanese-Chinese-American fare. Choose from such à la carte items as *chow fun*, tempura, Portuguese sausage, stew or corned-beef hash; together they make a hearty meal. At breakfast, try the eggs with Portuguese sausage. ~ Pukalani Terrace Center, Haleakala Highway, Pukalani; 572-8258. BUDGET.

A good local restaurant for breakfast or lunch is the **Up Country Café**. The theme here is bovine all the way, with the restaurant decked out in everything from cow bells to cow salt-and-pepper shakers. Breakfast is pretty predictable; lunch includes a half-dozen entrées such as prime rib and New York steak, as well as such non-bovine fare as chicken curry with fresh country vegetables, sautéed mahimahi and vegetarian lasagna. Also open for dinner Thursday through Saturday. ~ Haleakala Highway and Aewa Place, Pukalani; 572-2395. BUDGET TO MODERATE.

For something a step more upscale, consider the **Makawao Steak House.** Knotty pine walls and a comfortable lounge lend the place an air of refined rusticity. The menu, popular among the Upcountry gentry, is a mix of surf-and-turf dishes. Dinner only. ~ 3612 Baldwin Avenue, Makawao; 572-8711. DELUXE.

In Makawao, you can go Mediterranean at **Casanova Italian Restaurant & Deli**, a stylish bistro that serves Italian-style seafood and pasta dishes. For something faster, cheaper and more casual, you can try the adjacent deli. The restaurant and the deli are open seven days a week. ~ 1188 Makawao Avenue; 572-0220. MODERATE TO DELUXE.

HIDDEN ►

Or head across the street to **Polli's Mexican Restaurant**. This sombreros-on-the-wall-and-oilcloth-on-the-tables eatery offers a full selection of Mexican dishes. A local gathering place popular

FIVE-STAR GENERAL STORE

Upcountry's contribution to the culinary revolution that has been sweeping Hawaii the past few years is **Haliimaile General Store**. A former plantation store that has been converted into a chic gathering place, it puts a creative spin on American cuisine and serves roast duckling, fresh island fish and beef from the Big Island. Dinner only on Saturday and Sunday. ~ 900 Haliimaile Road, Haliimaile; 572-2666. DELUXE.

with residents throughout Maui's Upcountry region, Polli's has become an institution over the years. It will inevitably be crowded with natives dining on tacos, burritos, tamales and tostadas. ~ 1202 Makawao Avenue, Makawao; 572-7808. BUDGET TO MODERATE.

On the lower slope of Haleakala, **Kula Lodge Restaurant** enjoys a panoramic view of the island. Through picture windows you can gaze out on a landscape that rolls for miles to the sea. The exposed-beam ceiling and stone fireplace lend a homey feel, as do the homemade pastries. Specialties include rack of lamb, pasta dishes and vegetarian entrées. ~ Haleakala Highway, Kula; 878-1535. MODERATE TO DELUXE.

GROCERIES

Along the Haleakala Highway there's a **Foodland**, open from 5 a.m. to midnight. ~ Pukalani Terrace Center; 572-0674.

You can also count on **Down to Earth Natural Foods** for health foods and New Age supplies. Open from 8 a.m. to 8 p.m. ~ 1169 Makawao Avenue, Makawao; 572-1488.

SHOPPING

Baldwin Avenue in the western-style town of Makawao has developed over the years into a prime arts-and-crafts center. Housed in the falsefront stores that line the street you'll find galleries galore and a few boutiques besides.

The Courtyard at 3620 Baldwin Avenue is an attractive wood-frame mall that contains **Hot Island Glass**, with a museum-quality collection of handblown glass pieces. ~ 572-4527. Also here is **Viewpoints Gallery**, which puts many of the higher-priced Lahaina galleries to shame. ~ 572-5979.

Gecko Trading Company is a small shop that features contemporary fashions at reasonable prices. ~ 3621 Baldwin Avenue; 572-0249.

The kids will love **Maui Child Toys & Books** for the puppets, art supplies, wooden toys and music tapes. ~ 3643 Baldwin Avenue, Makawao; 572-2765.

Check out **Goodie's** for the gift items: crystal mobiles, locally made jewelry, picture frames. There are also women's fashions by local designers. ~ 3633 Baldwin Avenue, Makawao; 572-0288.

On the outskirts of Makawao, the 1917 Mediterranean-style Baldwin mansion is home to the **Hui Noeau Visual Arts Center**. ◄ HIDDEN Here you can view rotating educational exhibits, purchase works by Maui artists or take the plunge yourself at one of the regular workshops on painting, printmaking, pottery, sculpture and much, much more. ~ 2841 Baldwin Avenue; 572-6560.

In the Kula Lodge complex, the **Curtis Wilson Cost Gallery** sells prints, limited editions and originals by Curtis Wilson Cost. The emphasis is on local landscapes and ocean scenery. ~ Haleakala Highway; 878-6544.

Proteas of Hawaii is a good place to find Maui's signature plant. They also sell orchids. ~ 210 Mauna Place, Kula; 878-2533.

NIGHTLIFE   There are live bands on the weekends and disco music several week-nights at **Casanova Italian Restaurant**. One of Upcountry's only nightspots, it features a range of live acts—from local Mauian to internationally known. There's a drag show every Thursday night. Cover. ~ 1188 Makawao Avenue, Makawao; 572-0220.

BEACHES & PARKS   **POLIPOLI SPRING STATE RECREATION AREA** 🏃 Located at 6200-foot elevation on the slopes of Haleakala, this densely forested area is an ideal mountain retreat. Monterey and sugi pine, eucalyptus and Monterey cypress grow in stately profusion; not far from the campground there's a grove of redwoods. From Polipoli's ethereal heights you can look out over Central and West Maui, as well as the islands of Lanai, Molokai and Kahoolawe. Miles of trails, some leading up to the volcano summit, crisscross the park. Polipoli has a picnic area, restrooms and running water. ~ From Kahului, take Haleakala Highway (Route 37) through Pukalani and past Waiakoa to Route 377. Turn left on 377 and follow it a short distance to the road marked for Polipoli. About half of this ten-mile road to the park is paved. The second half of the track is extremely rough and often muddy. It is advisable to take a four-wheel-drive vehicle.

▲ There is meadow-style camping (a state permit is required) for up to 20 people; the cabin houses up to ten people and rents on a sliding scale from $10 single and $14 double up to $50 for ten people. The spacious cabin (three bedrooms) is sparsely furnished and lacks electricity. It does have a wood heating stove, gas cooking stove, gas lanterns, kitchen utensils and bedding. It can be rented from the Division of State Parks. It's recommended to bring in drinking water.

KEOKEA PARK is a pleasant picnic spot on Route 37 in Keokea. There's a rolling lawn with picnic tables and restrooms.

▼▼▼▼▼▼▼▼▼▼▼▼▼▼▼▼
Haleakala National Park

It seems only fitting that the approach to the summit of Haleakala is along one of the world's fastest-climbing roads. From Kahului to the summit rim—a distance of 40 miles along Routes 37, 377 and 378—the macadam road rises from sea level to over 10,000 feet, and the silence is broken only by the sound of ears popping from the ascent.

At the volcano summit, 10,023-feet in elevation, you look out over an awesome expanse—seven miles long, over two miles wide, 21 miles around. This dormant volcano, which last erupted around 1790, is the central feature of a 28,665-acre national park that extends all the way through the Kipahulu Valley to the sea. The crater

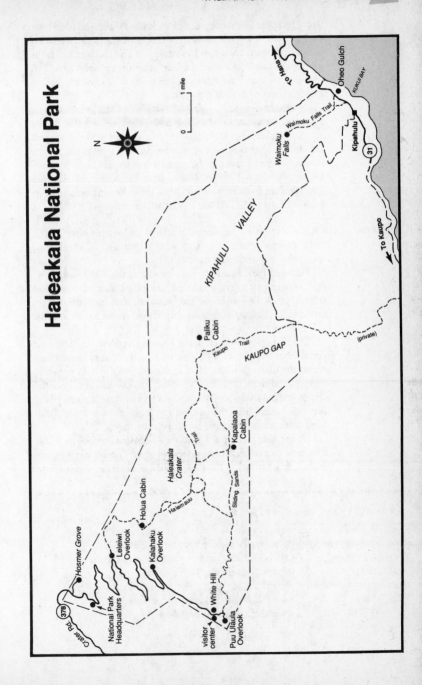

floor, 3000 feet below the rim, is a multihued wasteland filled with cinder cones, lava flows and mini-craters. It's a legendary place, with a mythic tradition that's as vital as its geologic history. It was from Haleakala ("House of the Sun") that the demigod Maui lassoed the sun and slowed its track across the sky to give his mother more daylight to dry her tapa cloth.

In the afternoon, the volcano's colors are most vivid, but during the morning the crater is more likely to be free of clouds. Before going up Haleakala, call 871-5054 for a weather report. Then you can decide what time of day will be best for your explorations. Remember that it takes an hour-and-a half to two hours to reach the summit from Kahului, longer from the Kaanapali–Kapalua area. Be sure to bring warm clothes since the temperature drop from sea level to 10,000 feet can be 30° or more.

SIGHTS

On the way up to the summit you'll pass **Hosmer Grove** (6800-feet), a picnic area and campground surrounded by eucalyptus, spruce, juniper and cedar trees.

National Park Headquarters, located at the 7030-foot elevation, contains an information desk and maps, and makes a good starting point. Be sure to see the Hawaiian state bird, the nene, a rare species of Hawaiian goose, that likes to rest in a pond nearby. ~ 572-9306.

The first crater view comes at **Leleiwi Overlook**, an 8800-foot perch from where you'll be able to see all the way from Hana across the island to Kihei. Here at sunset, under correct meteorological conditions, you can see your shadow projected on the clouds and haloed by a rainbow. To experience this "Specter of the Brocken," stand atop the volcano rim looking toward the cloud-filled crater with the setting sun at your back.

Up the hill, a side road leads to **Kalahaku Overlook**, a 9324-foot aerie that offers a unique view of several cinder cones within the volcano. Just below the parking lot are numerous **silverswords**.

LATE SLEEPERS, TAKE NOTE

One of Maui's favorite rituals is a predawn trip to the top of Haleakala to watch the sun rise. Unfortunately, the weather can be foggy and cold. Besides that, getting up early is probably the last thing you want to do on vacation. If so, consider the alternative: Sleep late, take your time getting to the top and arrive in time for sunset. But, then again, you'll miss a dazzling, almost religious experience. In any case, call 871-5054 to check on the weather before making the trip up!

Related to sunflowers, these spike-leaved plants grow only on Maui and the Big Island. They remain low bristling plants for 20 years or more before blooming into a flowering stalk. Each plant blossoms once, sometime between May and November, and then dies.

The best view of the wilderness area is farther up the road at the **Haleakala Visitors Center,** 9745-feet elevation, where you'll find an information desk, as well as a series of exhibits about the volcano. From this vantage point you can gaze out toward Koolau Gap to the north and Kaupo Gap to the south. Several peaks located along the volcano loom out of the clouds; cinder cones, including 600-foot Puu o Maui, rise up from the crater floor.

From the visitors center a short trail heads up to **White Hill.** Composed of andesite lava and named for its characteristic light color, this mound is dotted with stone windbreaks once used as sleeping places by Hawaiians who periodically visited the summit of Haleakala.

It's a short drive to the summit at **Puu Ulaula Overlook.** From the plate-glass lookout you can view the Big Island, Molokai, Lanai, West Maui and wilderness area itself. On an extremely clear day this 360° panorama may even include a view of Oahu, 130 miles away.

Perched high above atmospheric haze and the lights of civilization, Haleakala is also an excellent spot for stargazing. If you can continue to the end of Skyline Drive, past the **Haleakala Observatory,** you'll see that it is also an important center for satellite tracking and television communications.

While the views along the volcano rim are awesome, the best way to see Haleakala is from the inside looking out. With 36 miles of hiking trails, two campsites and three cabins, the wilderness provides a tremendous opportunity for explorers. Within the belly of this monstrous volcano, you'll see such geologic features as cinder cones, lava tubes and spatter vents. The Hawaiians marked their passing with stone altars, shelters and adze quarries. You may also spy the rare nene (a Hawaiian relative of the Canada goose), as well as chukar partridges and pheasants.

The **volcano floor** is a unique environment, one of constant change and unpredictable weather. Rainfall varies from 12 inches annually in the southwestern corner to 200 inches at Paliku. Temperatures, usually hovering between 55° and 75° during daylight, may fall below freezing at night. Campers should come prepared with warm clothing and sleeping gear, a tent, poncho, lantern and stove (no open fires are permitted). Don't forget the sunblock, as the elevation on the bottom averages 6700 feet and the ultraviolet radiation is intense.

◀ HIDDEN

Within the wilderness area you can explore three main trails. **Sliding Sands Trail,** a steep cinder and ash path, begins near the

Haleakala Visitors Center. It descends from the rim along the south wall to Kapalaoa cabin, then on to Paliku cabin. In the course of this ten-mile trek, the trail drops over 3000 feet. From Paliku, the **Kaupo Trail** leaves the crater through Kaupo Gap and descends to the tiny town of Kaupo, eight miles away on Maui's southeast coast. **Halemauu Trail** (8 miles) begins from the road three-and-a-half miles beyond National Park Headquarters and descends 1400 feet to the crater floor. It passes Holua cabin and eventually joins Sliding Sands Trail near the Paliku cabin.

CAMPING   There are campgrounds at **Holua** and **Paliku** that require a permit from National Park Headquarters. Permits are given out on a first-come, first-served basis (not available in advance), so plan accordingly. Camping is limited to two days at one site and three days total at both. The campgrounds have pit toilets and running water. There is also a 12-person cabin at each campsite and at **Kapalaoa**. Equipped with wood stoves, pit toilets, cooking utensils and mattresses, these primitive facilities are extremely popular. So popular, in fact, that guests are chosen by a monthly lottery three months in advance. ~ For more information, write Haleakala National Park, P.O. Box 369, Makawao, Maui, HI 96768, or call 572-9306.

▼▼▼▼▼▼▼▼▼▼▼▼▼▼

Outdoor Adventures

The opportunities for adventuring on the Valley Isle are numerous and the conditions for several activities are outstanding. Whale watching, for example, is top-notch on Maui as humpbacks return each year to the waters off Lahaina to give birth. For cyclists, there are thrilling rides down the slopes of Haleakala and challenging courses on Hana's curving coast. Maui is also home to several of the world's premier windsurfing spots including Hookipa Beach on the island's north shore.

DIVING   Maui offers a wide variety of snorkeling and diving opportunities ranging from Black Rock off Kaanapali to Honolua Bay not to mention Olowalu, Ahihi–Kinau Reserve and Ulua Beach. While most of the dive operators are located near the island's south coast resorts, there are also good diving and snorkeling opportunities on the north shore at Paia's Baldwin Beach Park, as well as Hana's Waianapanapa State Park. From Maui it's also easy to reach neighboring destinations such as the Molokini Crater Marine Preserve and reefs off Lanai.

MOLOKINI   Molokini, a crescent-shaped crater off Maui's southern coast, offers one of the island's great snorkeling adventures. Every day dozens of boatloads of people pull up to dive the remarkably clear waters. Visibility typically ranges between 80 and 150 feet, conditions so clear you can spot fish before even entering the water. During winter months, you're also likely to see the humpback whales cavorting nearby.

Makena Boat Partners operates the 46-foot *Kai Kanani,* which departs from Makena Beach, and goes closer to the largely submerged volcano than other touring vessels. ~ 879-7218. Other companies operating excursions include **Lahaina Divers** at 143 Dickenson Street, Lahaina ~ 667-7496 and **Maui Classic Charters** at 1215 South Kihei Road, Kihei ~ 879-8188. You can also sail to the islet on the **Silent Lady,** a 64-foot whaling schooner. Most tours include snorkeling equipment, food and drinks in the price of admission. ~ Maalaea Harbor; 242-6499.

LAHAINA   **Extended Horizons** offers trips to Lanai for divers of varying abilities, and snorkelers can come along. ~ Mala Wharf, Lahaina; 667-0611.

Ocean Riders Adventure Rafting specializes in all-day snorkeling trips to Lanai. ~ Mala Wharf, Lahaina; 661-3586.

Lahaina Divers Inc. is another well-liked dive operator. ~ 143 Dickenson Street, Lahaina; 667-7496.

KIHEI-WAILEA AREA   **Bill's Scuba Shop Underwater Habitat** runs scuba and snorkeling trips off Wailea Point, Holoa Point and Molokini Crater. Certification classes and night dives are available. ~ 36 Keala Place, Kihei; 879-3483.

Molokini Divers features scuba and snorkeling trips to this popular islet. Visibility of 150 feet makes this marine preserve a favorite place to splash down. ~ Kihei Boat Harbor, Kihei; 879-0055.

Another recommended tour operator that also rents equipment is **Maui Dive Shop** ~ Azeka Place Shopping Center, South Kihei Road, Kihei, 879-3388; and Kihei Town Center, South Kihei Road, Kihei, 879-1919.

Well-known by underwater photographers, **Mike Severns Diving** runs trips for certified divers to Molokini and Makena. His dives focus on the southwest rift of Haleakala, a fascinating place to study marine life. Led by informative biologists, these trips are an excellent way to see Maui's hidden marine life. ~ Kihei Boat Ramp, Kihei; 879-6596.

Maui Sun Divers provides all gear and offers everything from beginner trips to certification classes to night dives. ~ Kihei; 879-3337.

Interested in learning underwater photography? Sign on with **Ed Robinson's Diving Adventures.** A prominent oceanic photographer, Robinson leads excursions aboard the *Seadiver II* and *Manakai* to the Lanai Cathedrals, Molokini and other favored dive sites. ~ Kihei; 879-3584.

SURFING & WIND-SURFING

If you must go down to the sea again, why not do it on a board. Popular spots include Honolua Bay on the northwest coast, Hookipa Beach near Paia and Kanaha Beach Park in the Kahului area, as well as Napili Bay and Maalaea on the south coast. You can also take beginner lessons in the Lahaina area.

LAHAINA   A good place to start is **Maui Surfing School**. Andrea Thomas and her staff offer small classes and free board rental, and guarantee you'll be able to surf after one lesson. ~ Adjacent to Lahaina Harbor; 875-0625.

KAANAPALI–KAPALUA AREA   The **Kaanapali Windsurfing School** offers surfing and windsurfing lessons on the adjacent beach. Ninety-minute windsurfing lessons come with a guarantee of success. Four-person surfing classes are also offered, weather permitting. Rentals are available. ~ Whalers Village, Kaanapali; 667-1964.

KAHULUI–WAILUKU AREA   **Mistral High Wind Center** is a full-service windsurfing school that can even plan complete windsurfing holidays. ~ 261 Dairy Road, Kahului; 871-7753.

Similar opportunities await at **Windsurfing West**. Here the lessons include video replay (instant feedback) at the water's edge and are guaranteed to have you up and sailing in no time. ~ 415 Dairy Road, Kahului; 871-8733.

Thanks to a convenient radio communication system, instructors at the **Court Larnard Windsurfing School** at the Maui Windsurfing Company remain in constant contact with their students. Lessons are at Kanaha Beach Park, which has a protected area ideal for beginners. Safe, onshore winds blow you back toward the beach. Rentals are also available here. ~ 520 Keolani Place, Kahului; 877-4816.

You can buy windsurfing gear at **Lightning Bolt**, the oldest surf shop on Maui. ~ 55 Kaahumanu Avenue, Kahului; 877-3484.

FISHING

The deep blue sea around Maui can be nirvana for sportfishing enthusiasts. Choose between party boats, diesel cruisers and yachts custom-designed for trolling. All outfits provide equipment and bait. Just bring your own food and drinks and you're in business. If it's not too rough, your skipper may head for the productive game fishing waters between Maui and the Big Island. If conditions are choppy, you're more likely to fish the leeward side of the island or off neighboring Lanai.

There is also good fishing from the shore in many places. For information on the best spots, ask at local fishing stores, or try the following beaches: Hoaloha Park, Launiupoko State Wayside Park, Honokowai Beach Park, D. T. Fleming Park, Honokohau Beach, Keawakapu Beach, Poolenalena Beach Park, Black Sands Beach, Little Beach and Waianapanapa State Park.

LAHAINA   Ideal for groups up to four, **Robalo-One** is a stable 23-foot vessel that hits speeds up to 40 miles per hour in pursuit of game fish. You'll catch snapper, wrasse, barracuda or jack crevalle on half-day trips. ~ Lahaina Harbor; 661-0480.

Lucky Strike Charters fishes for marlin, mahimahi, wahoo and tuna with light and medium tackle. Light-tackle bottom fishing is also available. ~ Lahaina Harbor; 661-4606.

Islander II and **Hinatea** are matching sportfishing boats offering identical trips into coastal waters. On half- and full-day trips you'll fish for marlin, tuna, mahimahi, wahoo and shark. ~ Lahaina Harbor; 667-7548.

KIHEI-WAILEA AREA   In the Kihei area, contact **Carol Ann Charters** for half- and full-day fishing trips great for catching marlin, tuna, mahimahi and *ono*. ~ Maalaea Harbor; 877-2181.

Rascal Charters fishes for ahi, *ono*, mahimahi and marlin. Half- and full-day trips aboard a 31-foot vessel include game and bottom fishing. ~ Maalaea Harbor; 874-8633.

SAILING & WHALE WATCHING

From mid-December until the middle of May, it is prime whale-watching season on Maui. Humpback whales, measuring about 40 feet and weighing over 40 tons, migrate as many as 4000 miles from their summer home in Alaska. On the journey south, they consume tons of krill and tiny fish, then fast while in Hawaii. It is in the waters off Maui that they give birth to their young, babies that can weigh as much as three tons and gain up to 100 pounds a day.

Eager to protect the whales who winter in these waters, local officials have forced power craft to keep their distance from these cetaceans. But these restrictions are not so severe as to unduly interfere with the many sailing vessels that offer whale-watching opportunities off the Maui coast. You can also enjoy dive trips or pure performance rides on these beautiful vessels.

A prime area for whale watching lies along Honoapiilani Highway between Maalaea Bay and Lahaina, particularly at McGregor Point. So while you're visiting Maui, always keep an eye peeled seaward for vaporous spume and a rolling hump. The place you're standing might suddenly become an ideal crow's-nest.

About 2000 of the world's 10,000 humpbacks make the annual migration to Maui's southwestern coast each year. Today they are an endangered species, protected by federal law from whalers. Several local organizations study these leviathans and serve as excellent information sources.

The **Pacific Whale Foundation** issues daily reports over local radio stations during whale season. This same organization conducts "eco-adventure cruises," the profits from which help fund their whale protection projects. They have snorkeling tours to

Molokini and whale-watching cruises, both led by marine natural-
ists. Most interesting is their dolphin adventure, where you snorkel
Lanai's untouched coral reefs and see spinner and bottlenose dolphins in one of the island's many hidden coves. ~ 101 North Kihei
Road, Kihei; 879-8860. Whale hotline: 800-942-5311.

LAHAINA   Trilogy specializes in sailing adventures. They also offer
six-person whale-watching trips aboard a 41-foot sloop, as well as
snorkeling excursions, sunset trips and joysailing. Special trips include Molokai and Lanai. ~ Lahaina Harbor; 661-4743.

Scotch Mist Sailing Charters offers half-day snorkeling trips to
Lanai, as well as trips to the coral gardens of west Maui. Whale
watching and champagne sunset sails are also available. ~ Lahaina
Harbor; 661-0386.

First Class runs snorkeling, performance and sunset sailing
trips. ~ Lahaina Harbor; 667-7733.

Windjammer Cruises has a 70-foot, three-masted schooner ideal
for sunset dinner sails. You can dine on island cuisine, listen to live
Polynesian entertainment and take in the views of Kahoolawe,
Molokai and Lanai. ~ 505 Front Street, Lahaina; 661-8600.

Or, for a more intimate experience, try the six-passenger **Cind-
erella**, a 50-foot yacht. ~ Maalaea Harbor; 242-2779.

Trilogy Excursions receives high praise from repeat clients who
climb aboard the 50-foot catamaran for excursions to Lanai. Once
on the nearby island, they can swim and snorkel Hulopoe Bay
Marine Reserve, enjoy a Hawaiian barbecue and tour Lanai City.
~ 180 Lahainaluna Road, Lahaina; 661-4743.

Island Marine Activities offers whale-spotting cruises from
mid-December to May. ~ 113 Prison Street, Lahaina; 661-8397.

KAANAPALI–KAPALUA AREA   Kapalua Kai is a popular catamaran offering picnic-and-snorkeling and sunset sails. It sails Maui's
most scenic waters and features whale-watching excursions in winter months. ~ Kaanapali; 667-5980.

PARA-SAILING & HANG GLIDING

Lahaina and Kaanapali Beach are perfect places to become airborne. Wonderful views of Maui's west side and neighboring
Molokai add to the fun. The typical parasailing trip includes 30 to
45 minutes shuttling out and back to the launch point and eight to
ten minutes in the air.

Parasail Kaanapali riders rise as high as 900 feet. ~ Mala Wharf;
669-6555. UFO Parasailing lets you ascend up to 800 feet and, if
you wish, fly with a companion. ~ Whalers Village, Kaanapali;
661-7836. For hang gliding from some of the most beautiful spots
on the island, try **Hang Gliding Maui** ~ Makawao; 572-6557.

KAYAKING

A sport that's growing in popularity, kayaking is an exciting way
to explore the waters.

KAANAPALI–KAPALUA AREA Kayaks are available from **Kaanapali Windsurfing School** ~ Whalers Village, Kaanapali; 667-1964.

KAHULUI–WAILUKU AREA In Central Maui, **Maui Sea Kayaking** offers day trips to Maui and Lanai and full-moon trips to Molokini. Or they'll lead you on an overnight "romance" retreat, for which a guide will arrange a seaside campsite that is off-the-beaten-track and inaccessible by car. In the morning, the guide will return to prepare your breakfast and lead the way back to civilization. They also lead surfers to beaches good for surfing. ~ Puunene; 572-6299.

KIHEI–WAILEA AREA A place to learn this adventure sport is **Kelii's Kayak Tours**. Guided tours include the Makena-La Perouse area on Maui's south shore, a north shore tour exploring the Honolua Bay/Honokohau area and a sunset excursion along Papawai Point. Along the way you might spot dolphins, flying fish or whales. ~ 158 Lanakila Place, Kihei; 874-7652.

Kayak rentals and tours can also be arranged through **South Pacific Kayaks**. Their guided trips include snorkeling, and you're likely to see whales, sea turtles and dolphins. ~ 2439 South Kihei Road, Kihei; 875-4848.

Rafting trips are the adventurous way to enjoy the Maui coast. Easily combined with dive and whale-watching trips, these sturdy craft are a great way to reach hidden coves and beaches.

RAFTING

LAHAINA **Hawaiian Rafting Adventures** operates half- and full-day trips to Lanai. ~ 1223 Front Street, Lahaina; 661-7333. Whale-watching trips are great fun in the winter months.

Ocean Riders Adventure Rafting will take you out to Lanai and, weather permitting, Molokai, for a glorious day of snorkeling. All trips are aboard rigid-hull inflatable boats. ~ Mala Wharf, Lahaina; 661-3586.

✔ **CHECK THESE OUT—UNIQUE OUTDOOR ADVENTURES**

- Snorkel at **Ahihi-Kinau Natural Area Reserve** amid two dozen types of technicolor coral and 100 species of equally dazzling fish. *page 264*
- Bike down the 10,000-foot slopes of a volcanic crater with **Cruiser Bob's Haleakala Downhill** and arrive at sea level in time for breakfast. *page 317*
- Hike the **King's Highway**, an ancient Hawaiian trail along the beach that traverses the black domain of a 1790 lava flow. *page 318*
- Follow the **Hana-Waianapapa Coastal Trail** to a pair of sea caves that legend tells were once the hiding place of a Hawaiian princess. *page 318*

Another company offering tours is **Captain Steve's Rafting Excursions**, which heads out regularly in search of tropical fish, dolphins and exotic birdlife. One trip not to miss circumnavigates Lanai. ~ Mala Wharf, Lahaina; 667-5565.

KIHEI–WAILEA AREA   **Blue Water Rafting** offers both rafting and snorkeling trips to Molokini. ~ Kihei Boat Ramp, Kihei; 879-7238.

**RIDING
STABLES**

Maui's volcanic landscape, beaches and sculptured valleys are choice sites for equestrian excursions. A variety of rides are available across the island—from the shoreline of Hana to the slopes of Haleakala, you can count on seeing wildlife, lava fields and those famous Maui sunsets.

KIHEI–WAILEA AREA   **Makena Stables** leads trail rides across the scenic 20,000-acre Ulupalakua Ranch on the south slope of Haleakala. Mountain trails cross a 200-year-old lava flow. Choose among three-hour, four-hour and all day rides, including one to the Tedeschi winery. ~ 7299 South Makena Road, Makena; 879-0244.

HANA HIGHWAY   **Oheo Stables** offers three-hour outings up the backside of Haleakala. Trips ascend through a tropical rainforest and include views of waterfalls and the Kipahulu Valley. Highlights include the view from Pipiwai lookout above Oheo Gulch. ~ Hana Highway, one mile south of National Park Headquarters at Pools of Ohea; 667-2222.

UPCOUNTRY AND HALEKALA   Hit the trail on Maui's north shore with **Adventures on Horseback** and you'll ride along 300-foot cliffs, see lush rainforests and take a break to swim in waterfall-fed pools. ~ Makawao; 242-7445.

At **Thompson Ranch and Riding Stables** ride through pastureland on short day and sunset trips that offer views of the other islands. With special arrangements the full-day Haleakala ride enters the volcano at 10,000 feet. ~ Thompson Road, Kula; 878-1910.

For tours of Haleakala National Park, contact **Pony Express Tours**, which leads half- and full-day horseback trips through the wilderness area. ~ 667-2200. On the weekends **Charlie's Trail Rides and Pack Trips** provides overnight horseback trips from Kaupo through Haleakala. ~ 248-8209.

GOLF

With more than a dozen public and private courses, Maui is golf heaven. Choices on the Valley Isle range from country club links to inexpensive community courses. Also, several resorts offer a choice of championship courses ideal for golfers looking for a change of pace. These are open to the public for a hefty fee.

KAANAPALI–KAPALUA AREA   The **Kaanapali Golf Courses** are among the island's finest. The championship par-71 North Course, designed by golf course architect Robert Trent Jones Sr., has a slight incline. The easier South Course is intersected by Maui's popular sugar cane train. ~ Kaanapali Beach Resort, Kaanapali; 661-3691.

With three courses, the **Kapalua Golf Club** is one of the best places to golf on Maui. For a real challenge, try the par-73 Plantation Course, built in the heart of pineapple country. The oceanfront Bay Course was created by Arnold Palmer himself. The Village Course ascends into the foothills. ~ 300 Kapalua Drive, Kapalua; 669-8044.

KIHEI–WAILEA AREA   The **Wailea Golf Club,** located in the heart of the Wailea Resort complex, offers three courses, all with ocean views. The 18-hole "blue course" heads uphill along the slopes of Haleakala. The more challenging "emerald course" has slightly more difficult greens. The "gold course" is the longest and most challenging, with 93 bunkers. There are two clubhouses on the premises. ~ 100 Wailea Golf Club Drive; 879-2966.

Located next to the Maui Prince Resort, **Makena Golf Course** has two 18-hole courses. Designed by Robert Trent Jones Jr., the "North" and "South" courses are intended to blend into the natural Hawaiian landscape while offering high-challenge golf. Rolling terrain and beautiful views of the neighbor islands make these links a treat. ~ 5415 Makena Alanui, Wailea; 879-3344.

KAHULUI–WAILUKU AREA   **Waiehu Municipal Golf Course** is the island's only publicly owned course. With a front nine on the shoreline and a challenging back nine along the mountains, this course offers plenty of variety. Other amenities include a driving range and practice green. ~ Kahekili Highway, Waiehu; 243-7400.

Sandalwood is one of Maui's newest courses. Somewhat hilly, this par-72 course was designed by Nelson Wright. Three holes have lakes or ponds. There's a restaurant and pro shop on the premises, as well as a practice range, a chipping green and three putting greens. ~ 2500 Honoapiilani Highway, Wailuku; 242-7090.

In the same area, the private **Grand Waikapu Valley Country Club** is an 18-hole gem offering great ocean views. Water features abound on this course. ~ 244-7090.

HANA HIGHWAY   The **Maui Country Club** is a relatively easy nine-hole course open to the public on Mondays. ~ 48 Nonohe Place, Paia; 877-7893.

UPCOUNTRY AND HALEAKALA   The upcountry **Pukalani Country Club,** on the slopes of Haleakala, is an 18-hole public course. Bring a jacket or sweater because these links can get cool or windy. Boasting the highest elevation of all Maui's courses, this one is a sleeper (with great views). ~ 360 Pukalani Street; 572-1314.

If you're an avid tennis fan, or just in the mood to whack a few balls, you're in luck. Public tennis courts are easily found through-   **TENNIS** out the island. Almost all are lighted and convenient to major resort destinations.

LAHAINA   In the Lahaina area, you'll enjoy the courts at the **Lahaina Civic Center** ~ 1840 Honoapiilani Highway; or at **Malu-ulu-olele Park** on Front and Shaw streets.

KAANAPALI–KAPALUA AREA   There are several resorts in the area that open their courts to the public. One is the **Hyatt Regency Maui** ~ 200 Nohea Kai Drive, Kaanapali; 661-1234. Another is the **Maui Marriott** ~ 100 Nohea Kai Drive, Kaanapali; 667-1200.

The **Kapalua Tennis Garden** offers ten hard courts. ~ 100 Kapalua Drive, Kapalua; 669-5677.

KIHEI–WAILEA AREA   There are public courts at **Kalama Park** on Kihei Road and **Maui Sunset Condominiums** on Waipulani Road. **Makena Resort Tennis Club** is a favorite resort that lets the public use their courts. ~ Makena Resort, 5400 Makena Alanui, Makena; 879-8777. **Wailea Tennis Club** has eleven hard courts, three of which have lights. ~ 131 Wailea Iki Place, Wailea; 879-1958;

KAHULUI–WAILUKU AREA   In the Kahului area, try the courts at the **Kahului Community Center** on Onehee and Uhu streets and the **Maui Community College** on Kaahumanu and Wakea avenues. In Wailuku, try **Wailuku War Memorial** at 1580 Kaahumanu Avenue, or the public courts at Wells and Market streets.

HANA HIGHWAY   In the Hana area try the **Hana Ball Park**.

UPCOUNTRY AND HALEAKALA   Popular Upcountry courts are found at the **Eddie Tam Memorial Center** in Makawao and the **Pukalani Community Center** in Pukalani.

For general information, call the County Department of Parks and Recreation at 243-7389.

BIKING

If you've ever wanted to zip down a mountainside or go off-road in volcanic highlands, you've come to the right place. While Maui is best known for its downhill cycling trips, there are also many other challenging adventures. For example, you can enjoy the remote route from Hana to Ulupalakua or head from Kapalua to Wailuku via Kahakuloa.

Chris' Bike Adventures runs such intriguing trips as the Haleakala Wine Trek, a tour of the mountain's remote backside and a trip along the island's hidden northwest coast, complete with off-road biking. Unlike other bike tours, this company lets riders bicycle at their own pace. Half- and full-day trips include gourmet lunch. ~ Kula; 871-2453.

At **Maui Downhill**, you'll enjoy sunrise day-trips and mid-morning runs on Haleakala. The sunrise run is a beautiful 38-mile trip from the crater to sea level. Other, less strenuous trails also offer great views of the mountain, ranchlands and verdant forests. ~ 199 Dairy Road, Kahului; 871-2155.

Similar trips are offered by **Cruiser Bob's Haleakala Downhill.** Equipment includes full-face helmets, windbreaker pants and custom megabrakes. ~ 99 Hana Highway, Paia; 579-8444.

Another company operating Haleakala downhill bike tours is **Maui Mountain Cruisers,** which serves breakfast or lunch on morning or midday rides. ~ 296 Alamaha, Kahului; 871-6014.

For those of you who prefer to go it alone, the **Bike Shop** has a store in Kahului that both rents and sells bikes and accessories, and also does repair work. ~ 111 Hana Highway; 877-5848.

HIKING

Many people complain that Maui is overdeveloped. The wall-to-wall condominiums lining the Kaanapali and Kihei beachfront can be pretty depressing to the outdoors lover. But happily there is a way to escape. Hike right out of it.

The Valley Isle has many fine trails that lead through Hana's rainforest, Haleakala's magnificent valley, up to West Maui's peaks and across the south shore's arid lava flows. Any of them will carry you far from the madding crowd. It's quite simple on Maui to trade the tourist enclaves for virgin mountains, untrammeled beaches and eerie volcanic terrain. One note: A number of trails pass preserved cultural or historical sites. Please do not disturb these in any way. For more information, contact the Division of Forestry and Wildlife, Na Ala Hele Trails and Access Program. ~ 54 South High Street, Room 101, Wailuku, HI 96793; 243-5352.

You might want to obtain hiking maps; they are available from **Hawaii Geographic Maps & Books.** ~ P.O. Box 1698, Honolulu, HI 96806; 538-3952.

If you're uncomfortable about exploring solo, you might consider an organized tour. The **National Park Service** provides information to hikers interested in exploring Haleakala or other sections of the island. What follows is a basic guide to most of Maui's major trails. ~ Haleakala National Park, P.O. Box 369, Makawao, Maui, HI 96768; 572-9306.

In Maui's Upcountry, you may spot axis deer, Hawaiian owls and pheasants.

KAHULUI–WAILUKU AREA The main hiking trails in this Central Maui region lie in Iao Valley, Kahului and along Kakekili Highway (Route 340).

Iao Stream Trail (1 mile) leads from the Iao Valley State Monument parking lot for half a mile along the stream. The second half of the trek involves wading through the stream or hopping across the shoreline rocks. But your efforts will be rewarded with some excellent swimming holes en route. You might want to plan your time so you can relax and swim.

Not far from Kahului Airport on Route 360, birders will be delighted to find a trail meandering through the **Kanaha Pond Wildlife Sanctuary**. This jaunt follows two loop roads, each one mile long, and passes the natural habitat of the rare Hawaiian stilt and the Hawaiian coot. The trails in the Kanaha Pond area are closed during bird-breeding season (April–August). Permits are necessary from the State Division of Forestry. ~ 243-5352.

Northwest of Kahului, along the Kahekili Highway, are two trails well worth exploring, the **Waihee Ridge Trail** and **Kahakuloa Valley Trail**.

Waihee Ridge Trail (3 miles) begins just below Maluhia Boy Scout Camp outside the town of Waihee. The trail passes through a guava thicket and scrub forest and climbs 1500 feet en route to a peak overlooking West and Central Maui. The trail summit is equipped with a picnic table rest stop.

KIHEI–WAILEA AREA **King's Highway Coastal Trail** (5.5 miles) follows an ancient Hawaiian route over the 1790 lava flow and is considered a desert region. The trail begins near La Perouse Bay at the end of the rugged road that connects La Perouse Bay with Makena Beach and Wailea. It heads inland through groves of *kiawe* trees, then skirts the coast and finally leads to Kanaloa Point. From this point the trail continues across private land. Because segments of the trail pass through the Ahihi-Kinau Natural Reserve, which has stricter regulations, call Na Ala Hele Trails and Access Program for more information. ~ 243-5352.

HANA HIGHWAY **Hana-Waianapanapa Coastal Trail** (3 miles), part of the ancient King's Highway, skirts the coastline between Waianapanapa State Park and Hana Bay. Exercise extreme caution near the rocky shoreline and cliffs. The trail passes a *heiau*, sea arch, blowhole and numerous caves while winding through lush stands of *hala* trees.

Waimoku Falls Trail (2 miles) leads from the bridge at Oheo Gulch up to Waimoku Falls. On the way, it goes by four pools and traverses a bamboo forest. (Mosquito repellent advised.) Contact Haleakala National Park Headquarters for information on this trail.

UPCOUNTRY The main trails in Maui's beautiful Upcountry lie on Haleakala's southern slopes. They branch out from Polipoli Spring State Recreation Area through the Kula and Kahikinui Forest Reserves.

Redwood Trail (1.7 miles) descends from Polipoli's 6200-foot elevation through impressive stands of redwoods to the ranger's cabin at 5300 feet. There is a dilapidated public shelter in the old CCC camp at trail's end. A four-wheel drive is required to reach the trailhead.

Plum Trail (2.3 miles) begins at the CCC camp and climbs gently south to Haleakala Ridge Trail. The route passes plum trees as well as stands of ash, redwood and sugi pine. There are shelters at both ends of the trail.

Tie Trail (0.5 mile) descends 500 feet through cedar, ash and sugi pine groves to link Redwood and Plum Trails. There is a shelter at the Redwood junction.

Polipoli Trail (0.6 mile) cuts through cypress, cedars and pines en route from Polipoli Campground to Haleakala Ridge Trail.

> If you're planning to explore Haleakala volcano, be sure to bring cold-weather gear; temperatures are much lower than at sea level and the summit occasionally receives snow.

Boundary Trail (4.4 miles) begins at the cattle guard marking the Kula Forest Reserve boundary along the road to Polipoli. It crosses numerous gulches planted in cedar, eucalyptus and pine. The trail terminates at the ranger's cabin.

Waiohuli Trail (1.4 miles) descends 800 feet from Polipoli Road to join Boundary Trail. Along the way it passes young pine and grasslands, then drops down through groves of cedar, redwood and ash. There is a shelter at the Boundary Trail junction.

Skyline Road (6.5 miles) begins at 9750 feet, near the top of Haleakala's southwest rift, and descends more than 3000 feet to the top of Haleakala Ridge Trail. The trail passes a rugged, treeless area resembling the moon's surface. Then it drops below timberline at 8600 feet and eventually into dense scrub. The unobstructed views of Maui and the neighboring islands are awesome. Bring your own water.

Haleakala Ridge Trail (1.6 miles) starts from Skyline Trail's terminus at 6550 feet and descends along Haleakala's southwest rift to 5600 feet. There are spectacular views in all directions and a shelter at trail's end.

CAMPING

Though extremely popular with adventurers, Maui has very few official campsites. The laws restricting camping here are more strictly enforced than on other islands. The emphasis on this boom island favors condominiums and resort hotels rather than outdoor living, but you can still escape the concrete congestion at several parks and unofficial campsites (including one of the most spectacular tenting areas in all Hawaii—Haleakala Wilderness Area).

Camping at **county parks** requires a permit. These are issued for a maximum of three nights at each campsite, and cost $3 per person per night, children 50¢. Permits can be obtained at War Memorial Gym adjacent to Baldwin High School, Route 32, Wailuku, or by writing the Department of Parks and Recreation Permit Department, 1580 Kaahumanu Avenue, Wailuku, Maui, HI 96793; 243-7389.

State park permits are free and allow camping for five days. They can be obtained at the Division of State Parks in the State Building, High Street, Wailuku, or by writing the Division of State Parks. ~ 54 South High Street, Room 101, Wailuku, Maui, HI 96793; 243-5354. You can also rent cabins at Wainapanapa and Polipoli state parks through this office.

For weather forecasts on Maui, call 877-5111; marine conditions, 877-3477.

If you plan on camping in the Haleakala Wilderness Area, you must obtain a permit on the day you are camping. You can do so at Haleakala National Park headquarters, located on the way to the valley. These permits are allocated on a first-come, first-served basis.

Remember, rainfall is heavy along the northeast shore around Hana, but infrequent on the south coast. Also, Haleakala gets quite cold; you'll need heavy clothing and sleeping gear.

It is best to bring along your own camping gear, but in a pinch check **Maui Expeditions**, which sells and rents supplies. ~ Kihei Commercial Center, 300 Ohukai, Kihei; 875-7470. **Maui Sporting Goods** has a large selection of gear for sale. ~ 92 North Market Street, Wailuku; 244-0011. **Gaspro Inc.** sells a limited amount of camping equipment. ~ 365 Hanakai Street, Kahului; 877-0056.

Transportation

Three airports serve Maui—Kahului Airport, Kapalua-West Maui Airport and Hana Airport.

AIR

The **Kahului Airport** is the main landing facility and should be your destination if you're staying in the Central Maui region or on the southeast coast in the Kihei–Wailea area. United Airlines, Delta Air Lines and a couple of charter companies offer nonstop service from the mainland. American Airlines stops in Honolulu en route.

If you land at the Kahului Airport, you will arrive at a bustling airport that has been expanded. I never realized how popular Maui was until I first pushed through the mobs of new arrivals here. In addition to the masses, you'll find a coffee shop and lounge, newsstand, gift shop, lei stand, baggage service and information booth (872-3893).

Kapalua-West Maui Airport serves the Lahaina–Kaanapali region. Aloha Island Air, Mahalo Air and Trans Air all fly into the facility.

Hana Airport, really only a short landing strip and a one-room terminal, sits near the ocean in Maui's lush northeastern corner. Aloha Island Air and Air Molokai land in this isolated community. And don't expect very much ground transportation waiting for you. There is no bus service here, though there is a car rental agency.

One of the few ferry services in Hawaii is provided by **Sea Link of Hawaii**. Their 118-foot *Maui Princess* provides trips daily between Maui and Molokai. ~ 533-6899.

Another ferry, **Expeditions** operates out of Maui and links Lahaina with Manele Bay on Lanai. There are five boats per day in each direction. The 45-minute trip provides a unique way to travel between the islands. ~ P.O. Box 10, Lahaina, HI 96767; 661-3756.

If, like most visitors to Maui, you arrive at the airport in Kahului, you certainly won't want for car rental agencies. There are quite a few with booths right at the airport. A number of others are located around town.

In Kahului, the airport car-rental agencies are as follows: **Andres Rent A Car** (877-5378), **Avis Rent A Car** (871-7575, 800-331-1212), **Budget Rent A Car** (871-8811, 800-527-0700), **Dollar Rent A Car** (877-2731, 800-800-4000), **Hertz Rent A Car** (877-5167, 800-654-3131) and **National Interrent** (871-8851, 800-227-7368).

The rental agencies outside the airport include several companies that rent older model cars at very competitive rates. Two of these are **Word of Mouth Rent A Used Car** (877-2436, 800-533-5929) and VIP **Car Rentals** (877-2054, 800-367-6080).

If you find yourself in the Lahaina–Kaanapali area wanting to rent a car, try **Avis Rent A Car** (661-4588, 800-331-1212), **Budget Rent A Car** (661-8721, 800-527-0700), **Dollar Rent A Car** (667-2651, 800-800-4000), **Hertz Rent A Car** (661-3195, 800-654-3131) or **National Interrent** (667-9737, 800-227-7368). Among these agencies, Dollar is located at the Kapalua West Maui Airport, and Budget and Hertz are near the airport.

Dollar Rent A Car is the sole company in Hana. ~ 248-8237, 800-800-4000

Kihei is served by **Avis Rent A Car** (879-1980, 800-654-3131) and **Kihei Rent A Car** (879-7257).

There are several companies on the island of Maui that rent four-wheel-drive vehicles. Some outfits offering jeeps are **Adventures Rent A Jeep** (190 Papa Place, Kahului; 877-6626, 800-701-5337) and **Budget Rent A Car** (871-8811, 661-8721, 800-527-0700).

A & B Moped Rental rents mopeds by the hour, day or week. These vehicles provide an exhilarating and economical way to explore the area. Though they are not intended for long trips or busy roadways, they're ideal for short jaunts to the beach. ~ 3481 Lower Honoapiilani Road, Honokowai; 669-0027.

PUBLIC TRANSIT

There is almost no general transportation on Maui and the little that is provided lies concentrated in one small sector of the island. The **Lahaina Express** (661-8748) travels between Lahaina and Kaanapali. Picking up the baton in Kaanapali, the **Kaanapali Trolley** runs through this popular resort area. ~ 667-7411. **Akina Bus Service** operates buses in the town of Lahaina. ~ 879-2828.

Speedy Shuttle (875-8070) offers transportation from Kahului Airport to resorts on the island. (It's recommended that you call at least a day in advance, though last-minute pickups are available.) **Alii's Coach** (879-4853) provides transportation throughout the island, including to airports.

AERIAL TOURS

Much of Maui's best scenery is reached via serpentine roads or steep mountain drives. While the views are stunning, the best way to get a bird's-eye view is from the air. Helicopters, fixed-wing aircraft and gliders all make it easy to see the volcanic uplands, waterfall splashed cliffs and dreamy back-country beaches.

There's also a west Maui/Molokai flight highlighting the tallest waterfall in the state, Molokai's Kahiwa. **Hawaii Helicopters** offers tours ranging from 30 minutes to five hours. The longer tours stop in Hana for 45 minutes to three hours, offering a chance to explore this verdant area's beaches and waterfalls via van. ~ Kahului Heliport; 877-3900.

At **American Pacific Air** you can choose between a 45-minute tour of West Maui or a one-hour-and-40-minute circle tour of the entire island aboard four- and six-seater Cessnas. ~ Kahului Airport; 871-8115.

For aerobatic flights and scenic tours in an open cockpit aircraft, try **Biplane Barnstormers**. Trips range from 20 minutes to an hour and 40 minutes and reach a wide variety of destinations around the island. A special 30-minute aerobatic flight, guaranteed to knock your socks off, includes barrel rolls, loops and four-leaf clovers. ~ 878-2860.

▼▼▼▼▼▼▼▼▼▼▼▼▼▼▼▼▼▼▼▼

Addresses & Phone Numbers

MAUI ISLAND

County Department of Parks and Recreation ~ Wailuku; 243-7230; permits, 243-7389

Division of State Parks ~ Wailuku; 984-8109

Haleakala National Park Headquarters ~ 572-7749, 572-9306

State Department of Land and Natural Resources ~ 984-8100

Weather Report ~ 877-5111 for entire island; 871-5054 for recreational areas; 572-7749 for Haleakala National Park

LAHAINA

Ambulance ~ 911

Barber Shop ~ For Shear, 724 Luakini Street; 667-2866

Books ~ Waldenbooks, Lahaina Cannery Mall; 667-6172

Fire Department ~ 911

Fishing Supplies ~ Lahaina Fishing Supply & Marine Hardware, Lahaina Shopping Center; 661-8348

Hardware ~ Maui Home Supply, 1087 Limahana Street; 661-4025

Library ~ Wharf Street; 662-3066

Liquor ~ Nagasako Super Market, Lahaina Shopping Center; 661-0985

Pharmacy ~ Lahaina Pharmacy, Lahaina Shopping Center; 661-3119

Photo Supply ~ Fox Photo One Hour Lab, 139 Lahainaluna Road; 667-6255

Police Department ~ 911

Post Office ~ 1760 Honoapiilani Highway; 667-6611

KIHEI–WAILEA

Ambulance ~ 911

Fire Department ~ 911

Police Department ~ 911

KAHULUI–WAILUKU

Ambulance ~ 911

Barber Shop ~ Kahului Barber Shop, First Kahului Shopping Center, Kaahumanu Avenue; 871-4221

Books ~ Waldenbooks, Maui Mall Shopping Center, Kaahumanu Avenue; 877-0181

Fire Department ~ 911

Fishing Supplies ~ New Maui Fishing Supply, 1823 Wells Street, Wailuku; 244-3449

Hardware ~ Maui Home Supply, 400 South Hana Highway, Kahului; 877-0011

Hospital ~ Maui Memorial Hospital, 221 Mahalani Street, Wailuku; 244-9056

Laundromat ~ W & F Washerette, 125 South Wakea Avenue, Kahului; 877-0353

Library ~ 251 High Street, Wailuku; 243-5566

Liquor ~ Party Pantry, 261 Dairy Road, Kahului; 871-7690

Pharmacy ~ Longs Drugs, Maui Mall, Kaahumanu Avenue; 877-0041

Photo Supply ~ Roy's Photo Video, Maui Mall, Kaahumanu Avenue; 871-4311

Police Department ~ 911

Post Office ~ 250 Imikala Street, Wailuku; 244-4815

HANA
Ambulance ~ 911
Fire Department ~ 911
Police Department ~ 911

SEVEN

Lanai

Eight miles from Maui, across the historic whaling anchorage at Lahaina Roads, lies the pear-shaped island of Lanai. The word *lanai*, usually meaning "porch," is more appropriately translated as "swelling" on this humpbacked isle. In profile the island, formed by an extinct volcano, resembles the humpback whales that frequent its waters. It rises in a curved ridge from the south, then gradually tapers to the north. The east side is cut by deep gulches, while the west is bounded by spectacular sea cliffs rising 1500 to 2000 feet. Lanaihale, the island's tallest peak, stands 3370 feet above sea level.

First discovered by Captain Cook's men in 1779, Lanai was long avoided by mariners, who feared its reef-shrouded shores and saw little future in the dry, barren landscape. You can still see testaments to their fear in the rotting hulks that lie off Shipwreck Beach.

Ancient Hawaiians believed Lanai was inhabited only by evil spirits until Kaululaau, son of the great Maui chief Kakaalaneo, killed the spirits. Kaululaau, a Hawaiian-style juvenile delinquent who chopped down fruit trees with the gay abandon of young George Washington, had been exiled for such destructive behavior to Lanai by his father. After the wild youth redeemed himself by making the island safe from malevolent spirits, Lanai was settled by Hawaiians and controlled by powerful Maui chiefs.

Most archaeologists doubt that the native population, which lived from taro cultivation and fishing along the eastern shore, ever exceeded 2500. Even periods of peak population were punctuated by long intervals when the island was all but deserted. Lying in Maui's wind shadow, Lanai's rainfall ranges from 40 inches along its northeast face to a meager 12 inches annually in the barren southwest corner.

Like Molokai, its neighbor to the north, Lanai for centuries was a satellite of Maui. (Even today it is part of Maui County.) Then in 1778 it was overwhelmed by the forces of Kalaniopuu, the king of the Big Island. Later in the century, an even more powerful monarch, Kamehameha the Great, set up a summer residence along the south coast in Kaunolu.

During the 19th century, Lanai was a ranchers' island with large sections of flat range land given over to grazing. Missionaries became active saving souls and securing property in 1835 and by the 1860s one of their number had gained control of Lanai's better acreage. This was Walter Murray Gibson, a Mormon maverick whose life story reads like a sleazy novel. Despite being excommunicated by the Mormon church, Gibson went on to become a formidable figure in Hawaiian politics.

Gibson was not the only man with a dream for Lanai. George Munro, a New Zealand naturalist, came to the island in 1911 as manager of a plantation complex that originally tried to grow sugar on the island and then turned to cattle raising. While his herds grazed the island's tablelands, Munro worked in the rugged highlands. He extended the native forest, planting countless trees to capture moisture and protect eroded hillsides. He restored areas ravaged by feral goats and imported the stately Norfolk pines that still lend a mountain ambience to Lanai City. And, most important, Munro introduced an ecological awareness that hopefully will continue to pervade this enchanting island.

The land that Gibson and Munro oversaw changed hands several times until James Dole in 1922. Dole, descended from missionaries, was possessed of a more earthly vision than his forebears. Pineapples. He converted the island to pineapple cultivation, built Lanai City, and changed the face of Lanai forever.

Filipinos, now about 50 percent of the island's population, were imported to work the fields. Until a few years ago they were bent to their labors all over Lanai, wearing goggles and gloves to protect against the sharp spines that bristle from the low-lying plants. Pineapples are cultivated through plastic sheets to conserve precious water and harvesting is done by hand. Up until the early 1990s, you could see hundreds of acres covered in plastic. Downtown Lanai would roll up the streets at 9 p.m., but the lights would burn bright in the pineapple fields as crews worked through the night loading the hefty fruits onto conveyor belts.

That was yesterday, back when Lanai retained something of an ambiguous reputation. Most tourists, hearing that Lanai was nothing but pineapples and possessed only 20 miles of paved roads and a single ten-room hotel, left the place to the antelopes and wild goats.

Now, however, the sleeping midget is beginning to awaken. You still rent your car in an old gas station with scuffed floors and deer trophies on the wall. And there are still only three paved roads on the island. But nothing else here will ever be the same.

Stores are being renovated, old plantation homes are receiving fresh coats of paint, and new housing developments are going up. Castle & Cooke, the conglomerate that now owns the island, has poured $350 million into the place, building two resorts and transforming little Lanai into luxurious Lanai. The Manele Bay Hotel, a 250-room oceanfront extravaganza, opened in 1991 just one year after the christening of the Lodge at Koele, a rustic but refined 102-room resort situated along Lanai's forested mountain slopes.

Meanwhile the island's pineapple cultivation is declining precipitously from a peak of about 18,000 acres to a period in the near future when it will total a mere 200 acres, sufficient to supply island needs and give visitors a glimpse at what life was like "back when." Fields are being converted to alfalfa and oats; cattle raising is being reintroduced; and the island's Filipino and Japanese population is quitting the plantation and going to work for the tourist industry.

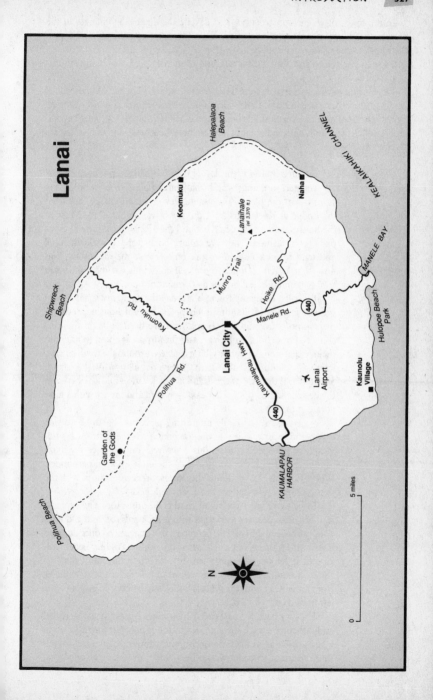

Lanai

Shipwreck Beach

Halepalaoa Beach

Keomuku

Naha

Lanaihale
(el 3,370 ft.)

Munro Trail

Keomuku Rd.

Hoike Rd.

Manele Rd.

KEALAIKAHIKI CHANNEL

MANELE BAY

440

Lanai City

Polihua Rd.

Kaumalapau Hwy.

Hulopoe Beach Park

Kaunolu Village

Lanai Airport

440

Garden of the Gods

Polihua Beach

KAUMALAPAU HARBOR

N

0   5 miles

In the midst of all the construction, and despite the disturbing changes in the lifestyle of the local people, this lovely little isle retains its charm. Even now only a fraction of Lanai's 140 square miles is developed. The rest of the island is covered with a network of jeep and hiking trails guaranteed to keep the heartiest adventurer happy.

Here is an entire island that fits the description "hidden Hawaii." Almost all of Lanai's 2400 citizens live in rustic Lanai City at the island's center and most tourists are concentrated here or along a single beach at the Manele Bay Resort. Just beyond these clusters lie mountains, ranchlands and remote beaches—untouched realms ripe for exploration.

▼▼▼▼▼▼▼▼
Lanai City

Situated at 1645 feet, **Lanai City** is a trim community of corrugated-roof houses and small garden plots. Tourist brochures present the place as a quaint New England village, but until the Lodge at Koele was built the town was rather drab. Most of the houses were constructed around the 1920s in traditional company-town fashion. They are square boxes topped with tin roofs and tend to look alike. Norfolk pines break the monotony, and now that Lanai is much more self-conscious, many homes are freshly painted in a rainbow assortment of hues.

It is still a company town, but today the company is harvesting tourists instead of planting pineapples. Several housing developments and condominium complexes have been built on the outskirts to house hotel employees and the airport is about to undergo major expansion. With everything centered around the town square, Lanai City embraces almost the entire population of the island. Situated at the center of the island at an elevation midway between the beach and the mountain peaks, it is cool and breezy with a temperate climate.

Nevertheless, the really interesting places on Lanai lie outside town, and most require driving or hiking over jeep trails. It's advisable to get specific directions wherever you go, since the maze of pineapple roads can confuse even the most intrepid pathfinder. Where possible, I've included directions; otherwise, check with the jeep rental shop in Lanai City or at the hotels.

To be extra safe, ask about road conditions, too. The slightest rain can turn a dusty jeep road into a slick surface, and a downpour can transmogrify it into an impassable quagmire. I once dumped a jeep into a three-foot ditch when the trail to Polihua Beach collapsed. It had been raining steadily for three days and the soft shoulder couldn't support the weight of a vehicle. I was 11 miles from Lanai City with the wheels hopelessly embedded and an hour left until dark.

The way back led past pretty menacing country, heavily eroded and difficult to track through. Rain clouds brought the night on in a rush. I gathered up my poncho and canteen, convinced myself that the worst to come would be a cold and wet night outdoors, and began trekking back to civilization. Fortunately, after five miserable hours I made it. But the entire incident could have been avoided if I had first checked road conditions and had allowed at least several hours of daylight for my return.

This shouldn't discourage you, though. With the proper precautions, exploring Lanai can be a unique experience, challenging but safe. To make things easy, I'll start with a journey to the island's northeastern shore, part of which is over a paved road. Then I'll continue clockwise around the island.

LODGING

Prior to the 1990s the only inn on the entire island was the **Hotel Lanai**, a modest mountain retreat. Set 1600 feet above sea level and surrounded by Norfolk pines, it offers clean, medium-sized rooms equipped with private baths. The lodge was built in the '20s, as was most of Lanai City, but was refurbished several years ago when it passed to new management. It features a restaurant and lounge, and is a local gathering place. A lot of folks hang out in the lobby here, making for a warm, friendly atmosphere, and the staff is congenial. Choose between small standard rooms, medium-sized accommodations, and rooms with lanais. There are only ten units in this U-shaped hostelry, so reservations can be troublesome if even a dozen of tourists or locals descend on the island. It's advisable to arrange transportation with the hotel at the time of making reservations. ~ P.O. Box 520, Lanai City, HI 96763; 565-7211, 800-321-4666, fax 565-4713. DELUXE.

The **Lodge at Koele**, a fashionable 102-room hideaway, is a study in style and decorum. The most noteworthy feature is the lobby, a vaulted-ceiling affair faced on either end with a stone fireplace that rises to the roofline. Etched-glass skylights extend the length of the room, illuminating the "great hall." The Victorian guest rooms are done with four-poster beds, lacquer boxes, statuettes and decorative plates. To make sure you remember that even

LANAI EXPERIENCES

- Stay at the **Hotel Lanai**, a 1920s-era retreat that until a few years ago was the only hotel on the entire island. *page 329*
- Search for glass fishing balls and nautilus shells on a strand named for the rusting hulls offshore—**Shipwreck Beach**. *page 332*
- Follow the **Munro Trail** to the top of Lanai for a crow's nest view of Oahu, Maui, Molokai and Hawaii. *page 334*
- Look but don't jump from **Kahekili's Leap**, where ancient Hawaiian warriors once plunged from a cliff. *page 338*
- Hike through the **Garden of the Gods**, whose eroded landscape makes it Hawaii's answer to the Dakota Badlands. *page 338*

here amid the Norfolk pines you are still in Hawaii, an overhead fan beats the air in languid motions.

Backdropped by mountains and surrounded by miles of pineapple fields, the emphasis at the Lodge is on staying put. There are cloisters lined with wicker chairs, a croquet court, a swimming pool and two jacuzzis that look out on field and forest, and a congenial staff to take care of every request. ~ P.O. Box 774, Lanai City, HI 96763; 565-7300, 800-321-4666, fax 565-3868. ULTRA-DELUXE.

DINING

The **Hotel Lanai** offers wholesome meals at modest prices. The dinner menu features an assortment of steak, seafood and other platters, plus sandwiches and burgers. Decorated with island photographs along the knotty pine walls, this is a cozy place to share a meal. You can strike up a conversation with a local resident, sit back and enjoy the mountain air or bask in the glow of the restaurant's two fireplaces. Watch the hours, though, or you'll get shut out. Continental breakfast is served only from 7 to 9:30 a.m., and dinner from 5:30 to 9 p.m. ~ Lanai City; 565-7211. MODERATE TO DELUXE.

If the hotel restaurant is closed, Lanai City has two alternatives. The first is **S. T. Property**, a luncheonette that serves breakfast, lunch and dinner. ~ 711 Lanai Avenue; 565-6537. BUDGET.

HIDDEN ►

Your second alternative, the **Blue Ginger Café**, rests in an old plantation house and serves three solid meals a day. Simple drawings of tropical fish adorn the place and the red paint on the cement floor has worn away almost completely. But the white walls shine and the dinners are served piping hot. Breakfasts and plate lunches are pretty standard, but the evening meal is sophisticated enough to include sirloin steak, *saimin*, shrimp Cantonese and lemon chicken. ~ 409 7th Street; 565-6363. MODERATE.

◆◆

SWEET DREAMS

You can discover for yourself whether **Dreams Come True on Lanai**. That's what Michael and Susan Hunter, two local jewelry makers, claim can happen when you stay in the six-bedroom house they transformed into one of the island's only bed and breakfasts. Set in Lanai City and surrounded by fruit trees and flowering gardens, the house is decorated with hand-carved screens and furniture that the owners transported from Sri Lanka and Bali. There's a large living room for guests as well as a selection of single and double rooms, some with canopied four-poster beds. ~ 547 12th Street, Lanai City; 565-7065, 800-566-6961. MODERATE.

Left: A Native Hawaiian weaves baskets at Kawakiu Beach on Molokai.

Below left: The Big Island is home to numerous anthurium farms.

Below right: A silversword in Haleakala Crater on Maui. Each plant blooms once and then dies.

The northeast coast of Kauai is dotted with secluded beaches.

On Lanai, isolation is the engine of ingenuity. Confronted with all that land and so few people, The Lodge at Koele transformed sections of the island into an organic garden, hog farm and cattle ranch. After adding a master chef, they had the ingredients for two gourmet restaurants that would be the pride not only of tiny Lanai but any island. Meals in The Terrace and The Formal Dining Room (jackets are required) are as enticing as the hotel's sumptuous surroundings.

The Terrace serves breakfast, lunch and dinner in a more casual atmosphere. Here the day begins with sweet rice waffles and *lilikoi*-coconut chutney, breakfast bread pudding, or bacon and eggs fresh from the farm. By evening the chef progresses to steamed seafood gyoza, and oven-braised lamb shank with herbed polenta, as well as vegetarian specialties. ~ 565-7300. DELUXE.

The Formal Dining Room serves dinner only; feast on roasted rack of lamb or Lanai venison loin with mashed sweet potatoes. Both restaurants overlook the back of the lodge grounds, with views of the fishpond, fountain and orchid house. ~ 565-7300. ULTRA-DELUXE.

GROCERIES

For standard food needs, try **Richard's Shopping Center**. This "shopping center" is really only a small grocery store with a dry goods department. Richard's is open Monday through Saturday from 8:30 a.m. to noon and from 1:30 to 6:30 p.m. ~ 8th Street; 565-6047.

If, by some strange circumstance, you can't find what you're seeking here, head down the street to **Pine Isle Market**. Open daily from 8 a.m. to noon and 1:30 to 7 p.m. Closed Sunday. ~ 565-6488.

SHOPPING

Granted, it doesn't have much competition (in fact it doesn't have any competition), but **Heart of Lanai Art Gallery** in Lanai City would be remarkable regardless of where it was located. Many of the paintings and sculptures were done by local artists and depict the plantation culture that was once Lanai's lifeblood but is now fast becoming its legacy. Closed Sunday. ~ 363 7th Street; 565-6678.

Otherwise, you will have to seek out the gift shop at The **Lodge at Koele** (565-7300) or the **Hotel Lanai** (565-7211).

NIGHTLIFE

Visitors find this a great spot to get the sleep they missed in Lahaina or Honolulu. If rest isn't a problem, Lanai may be a good place to catch up on your reading or letter writing. One thing is certain—once the sun goes down, there'll be little to distract you. You can have a drink while listening to local gossip at the **Hotel Lanai** (565-7211) or while mixing with the gentry at **The Lodge at**

Koele (565-7300), where the lounge possesses a kind of gentlemen's library atmosphere with an etched-glass-and-hardwood interior. But on an average evening, even these night owl's nests will be closed by 10 o'clock. In addition to its plush lounge, The Lodge at Koele features hula dancers on weekends at lunchtime or other live entertainment in the lobby (The Grand Hall) at night.

▼▼▼▼▼▼▼▼▼▼▼▼▼▼▼
Northeast—Shipwreck Beach and Naha

From Lanai City, Route 430 (Keomuku Road) winds north through hot, arid country. The scrub growth and red soil in this barren area resemble a bleak southwestern landscape, but the sweeping views of Maui and Molokai could be found only in Hawaii.

By the way, those stones piled atop one another along the road are neither an expression of ancient Hawaiian culture nor proof of the latest UFO landing. They were placed there by imaginative hikers. Each one is an *ahu*, representative of a local tradition in which columns of three or so stones are built to help ensure good luck.

SIGHTS

Near the end of the macadam road you can turn left onto a dirt road. This track leads past colonies of intermittently inhabited squatters' shacks, many built from the hulks of vessels grounded on nearby **Shipwreck Beach**. The coral reef paralleling the beach has been a nemesis to sailors since whaling days. The rusting remains of a barge and a 1950s-era oil tanker still bear witness to the navigational hazards along this coast. Needless to say, this is one of the best areas in Hawaii for beachcombing. Look in particular for the Japanese glass fishing floats that are carried here on currents all the way from Asia.

HIDDEN ►

At the end of the dirt road, a path marked with white paint leads to clusters of ancient **petroglyphs** depicting simple island scenes. Those interested in extensively exploring the coast can hike all the way from Shipwreck eight miles west to Polihua Beach along jeep trails and shoreline.

Back on the main road (continuing straight ahead as if you had never made that left turn that led to Shipwreck Beach) you will discover that the macadam gives way to a dirt road that leads along the northeast shore for 12 teeth-clicking miles. It was along this now-deserted coast that the ancient Hawaiian population lived. Numbering perhaps 2000 in pre-Western times, they fished the coast and cultivated taro.

The ghost town of **Keomuku**, marked by a ramshackle church that is being refurbished, lies six miles down the road. It's another mile and a half to **Kahea Heiau**, a holy place that many claim is the reason Keomuku was deserted. It seems that stones from this temple were used to build the nearby Maunalei Sugar Company plantation despite warnings against disturbing the sacred rocks. So when the plantation failed in 1901 after its sweet water mysteriously turned brackish, the Hawaiians had a heavenly explanation. It was shortly after this incident that most of the rest of Lanai's populace moved up to Lanai City, leaving only spirits along the coast.

When James Dole bought Lanai in 1922, he paid $1.1 million for the entire island.

Club Lanai, the waterfront complex that caters to day visitors from Maui, is located along the beach nearby. One way to spend just a day on Lanai is to catch a round-trip catamaran ride from Lahaina with this outfit. You'll land at a seven-acre visitor park along a sandy beach on the island's eastern shore. This private facility provides a dining area and bar as well as an array of equipment for beach and water sports. Guests snorkel on a coral reef, learn Hawaiian arts and crafts, and stroll along the strand. They do not, however, get an opportunity to tour around the island. Meals are provided. All you do is show up at Pier 4 in Lahaina Harbor at 6:45 a.m. to board a catamaran that returns you to Lahaina around 3:30 p.m. ~ 871-1144.

Several miles farther, past numerous salt-and-pepper-colored beaches, the road ends at the old Hawaiian village of **Naha**. Today nothing remains of this once prosperous colony.

SHIPWRECK BEACH 🏊 🛶 This strand is actually a string of small sandy patches that stretches for eight miles along the north coast, all the way to Polihua Beach. The glass fishing balls, driftwood and occasional nautilus shells on the beach make this a beachcomber's paradise. The remains of misguided ships that gave the beach its name also add to the allure. It's often windy. You can swim here but the water is shallow and you must beware of sharp coral—a protecting reef is 200 yards offshore. Snorkeling is not advised because of sharks. There's good diving for lobsters, but again, be cautious! You'll find good fishing for *ulua*, *papio* and octopus in the area between the squatters' houses and the petroglyphs. There are no established facilities at the beach. ~ Ten miles north of Lanai City. Head north on Route 430 (Keomuku Road) and turn left at the end of the paved road. See the "Northeast—Shipwreck Beach and Naha" section above for more details.

BEACHES & PARKS

HALEPALAOA BEACH AND NAHA BEACH 🏊 🛶 A string of salt-and-pepper-colored sand beaches lies along the 12-mile dirt road to Naha. While most are unattractive and crowded with shoals, they do offer great views of Molokai, Maui and Kahoolawe. The Naha road winds in and out along the seafront, with numerous access roads leading to the shore. The prettiest strand is Halepalaoa Beach, a mile-long white-sand corridor partially bordered by sand dunes. Club Lanai, a day-trip center for visitors from Maui, is located here. These are swimming beaches; most are well-protected by shoals, but the waters are shallow. Snorkeling is a possibility here but beware of currents. You can also fish here. Several beaches, including Naha, have small picnic areas ~ Take Route 430 north from Lanai City and continue on after it turns southward and becomes a dirt road. The dirt road extends for about 12 miles, ending at Naha; Halepalaoa Beach is about seven miles out along the dirt road.

Munro Trail

HIDDEN ▶

Named for New Zealand naturalist George Munro, this seven-mile jeep trail climbs through rainforest and stands of conifers en route to **Lanaihale**, the highest point on Lanai. From this 3370-foot perch you can see every major Hawaiian island except Kauai.

On the way to Lanaihale, about two miles up the trail, you'll pass **Hookio Gulch**. The ridge beyond is carved with a defense work of protective notches made by warriors who tried futilely to defend Lanai against invaders from Hawaii in 1778.

A footpath leads to an overlook above 2000-foot deep **Hauola Gulch**, Lanai's deepest canyon. Here you may see axis deer clinging to the sharp rockfaces, seeming to defy gravity as they pick their way along the heights.

This knife-edge ridge, little more than 100 feet wide in places, is studded with ironwood and eucalyptus trees, as well as the stately Norfolk pines that New Zealand naturalist George Munro personally planted along the heights. From this aerie the slopes fall away to reveal the twin humps of Maui. The Big Island rests far below you, anchored in open ocean. The sea itself is a flat, shimmering expanse.

From Lanaihale you can either turn around or continue and descend through open fields to Hoike Road, which connects with Route 440. The Munro Trail begins in Koele off Route 430 (Keomuku Road) about a mile north of Lanai City. Be sure to check road conditions and try to go early in the morning before clouds gather along the ridgetop. While it's rough going at times, the trail affords such magnificent views from its windswept heights that it simply must not be ignored by the adventurous sightseer.

Southeast—Manele Bay

HIDDEN ▶

Heading south from Lanai City on Route 440 (Manele Road), you'll be traveling through the Palawai Basin, the caldera of the extinct volcano that formed the island. This was also the heart of Lanai's once extensive pineapple plantation.

The explorer can detour off the main highway to the **Luahiwa petroglyphs**. Finding them requires obtaining explicit directions, then driving through a field, and finally climbing a short distance up a steep bluff. But the Luahiwa petroglyphs—portraying human figures, deer, paddles and turtles—are among the finest rock carvings in Hawaii and are definitely worth the search. As you approach each cluster of boulders, you'll see pictographic stories begin to unfold. One in particular depicts a large outrigger canoe, sails unfurled, being loaded Noah-style with livestock. Preparing, perhaps, for the ancient migration north to the Hawaiian Islands? To locate the petroglyphs, head south from Lanai City on Route 440. Turn left at the first dirt road. Follow the lower road as it curves along the bottom of the hillside. After passing below a water-tank and pipeline, the road forks and you follow the left fork. The road goes into a horseshoe curve; when you come out of the curve there will be black boulders on the hillside above you to the left. Spread across a few acres, they contain the petroglyphs.

Covered in scrub vegetation along much of its surface, Lanai still supports several rare endemic bird species as well as axis deer, mouflon sheep and pronghorn antelope.

The main road leads through agricultural fields and winds down to the twin bays at **Manele Small Boat Harbor** and **Hulopoe Bay**, which together comprise a marine life conservation area. Just offshore from the cinder cone that separates these two harbors is a sea stack, **Puu Pehe**, known not only for its beauty but its legends as well. Puu Pehe was a lovely Maui girl kidnapped by a Lanai warrior who kept her hidden in a sea cave. One day when he went off in search of water, a huge sea wave swept the girl to her death. Stricken with grief and remorse, the young warrior buried her on top of the rock island and then jumped to his death from its heights.

The small-boat harbor at Manele, rimmed by lava cliffs along the far shore, contains ruins of ancient Hawaiian houses. You'll also see an old wooden chute protruding from the rocks, a loading platform used years ago to lead cattle onto ships. Today this rock-rimmed anchorage is a mooring place for fishing boats and yachts. Hulopoe offers the island's finest beach, a crescent of white sand with gentle waves, crystalline waters and a fine park facility. You'll find the stone ruins of an ancient Hawaiian home and canoe house at the north end of the beach. Just above the beach, on the grounds in front of the plush Manele Bay Hotel, stands the remains of an *ahu* or traditional Hawaiian shrine.

LODGING

While The Lodge at Koele is situated at 1600-feet elevation in Lanai City, eight miles from the ocean, Lanai's other fashionable new resort, the **Manele Bay Hotel** is a traditional beachfront resort. Set on a bluff overlooking the best beach on the island, it is a 250-room extravaganza designed along both Asian and Mediterranean lines and surrounded by artistically planted gardens. Elegance here is in no way subdued: It speaks from the stone floors and white columns, the dark-paneled library and the recessed ceilings. The two-tiered lobby combines art deco windows with traditional Hawaiian murals; the lower level is a terrace with glass doors that open onto ocean views.

Guest accommodations look out either on the beach or the grounds, which are sculpted into five different theme gardens—Japanese, Bromeliad, Hawaiian, Chinese and Cosmopolitan. Each room is spacious, done in pastel hues and decorated with Asian armoires and color sketches of Hawaiian flora. The four-poster beds are accented with quilts and upholstered throw pillows. Add a four-leaf clover-shaped pool, six tennis courts, spa and workout room and you will realize that sleepy little Lanai is never going to be the same again. ~ 1 Manele Bay Drive; 565-7700, 800-321-4666, fax 565-3868. ULTRA-DELUXE.

DINING

Outside Lanai City the dining choices, a grand total of three, are concentrated at the Manele Bay Hotel. Here, ladies and gentlemen, lunch is served at the **Pool Grille** on a bougainvillea-covered terrace. Set poolside just above the beach, this patio dining facility features island salads, including a seasonal fruit offering. There is also a standard assortment of sandwiches, as well as grilled mahi-mahi on *nori* bread and other specialties. Lunch only. ~ 565-7700. MODERATE.

This spacious resort offers more formal dining in the **Hulopoe Court Restaurant**, a high-ceiling dining room with glass doors that open onto a veranda overlooking the ocean. Island murals adorn the walls and pineapple motif chandeliers dominate the room. The decor blends Asian and Polynesian styles and the menu features Hawaiian regional cuisine. Breakfast and dinner only. ~ 565-7700. DELUXE.

Sweeping views of Hulopoe Bay star at the **Ihilani Dining Room**. The menu features French-Mediterranean cuisine and specializes in duck, lamb and fresh fish dishes. The service is formal, and the wine list extensive. Dinner only. ~ 565-7700. ULTRA-DELUXE.

NIGHTLIFE

Down along Hulopoe Beach at the Manele Bay Hotel, the **Hale Ahe Ahe Lounge** combines several different settings, each equally inviting. The lounge itself has dark textured walls, a hardwood bar and a clubby ambience. It features piano or contemporary Hawaiian music nightly. Out on the terrace you can settle into a comfortable armchair or lean against the rail and enjoy the ocean view. The adjacent Holokai Room is a game room complete with backgammon board and an air of relaxed elegance. ~ 565-2000.

BEACHES & PARKS

HULOPOE BEACH PARK Lanai's finest beach also possesses the island's only fully developed park. Set in a half-moon inlet and fringed with *kiawe* trees, this white-sand beach is an excellent spot for all sorts of recreation. It is also the site of the

250-room Manele Bay Hotel, which rests on a bluff about 50 yards above the waterfront. Part of a marine life conservation area, Hulopoe has a lava terrace with outstanding tidepools along its eastern point. There is also a wading area for children at this end of the park. If you continue a short distance along this eastern shoreline you'll also encounter **Puu Pehe Cove**, a small beach with abundant marine life that is excellent for swimming and snorkeling. Little wonder that Hulopoe is the island's favorite picnic spot. It's also recommended for surfing and fishing. Prime catches are threadfin, *ulua*, and bonefish. This is the most accessible surf-casting beach on the island. There are permanent restrooms and showers. ~ Take Route 440 (Manele Road) south from Lanai City for eight miles.

▲ This is it—the only campground on the island! There are six campsites at the far end of the beach. Expect to pay a $5 registration fee plus a charge of $5 per camper per day. Permits are issued by the Lanai Company. ~ P.O. Box 310, Lanai City, Lanai, HI 96763; 565-8200.

MANELE BAY Primarily a small-boat harbor, this cliff-fringed inlet is populated by sailboats from across the Pacific. Carouse with the crews, walk along the jetty or scramble up the rocks for a knockout view of Haleakala on Maui. It's a very good place for swimming since the harbor is well protected, but you need to be wary of boat traffic. Because Manele Bay is part of a marine preserve the snorkeling is notable and the fishing is limited. Only pole fishing is allowed—no nets. There's a park for picnicking, and just around the corner at Hulopoe Beach are facilities for camping, swimming and other sports. ~ Located Route 440 south of Lanai City.

Southwest—Kaumalapau Harbor & Kaunolu

A southwesterly course along Route 440 (Kaumalapau Highway) will carry you steadily downhill for about six miles to **Kaumalapau Harbor**. This busy little harbor was built by pineapple interests and used primarily to ship the fruit on barges to Honolulu. During the heyday of Lanai's pineapple industry, more than a million pineapples a day were loaded onto waiting ships. On either side of Kaumalapau, you can see the *pali*, which rises straight up as high as 1000 feet, protecting Lanai's southwestern flank. These lofty sea cliffs are an ideal vantage point for watching the sunset.

The most interesting point along this route involves a detour near the airport and a journey down a *very* rugged jeep trail to **Kaunolu Village**. A summer retreat of Kamehameha the Great and now a national historic landmark, this ancient fishing community still contains the ruins of more than 80 houses as well as stone shel-

◄ HIDDEN

ters, petroglyphs and graves. Pick your way through it carefully, lest you step on a ghost. Kamehameha's house, once perched on the eastern ridge, looked across to **Halulu Heiau** on the west side of Kaunolu Bay. Commanding a dominant view of the entire region, these rocky remains are bounded on three sides by cliffs that vault 1000 feet from the ocean.

From nearby **Kahekili's Leap,** warriors proved their courage by plunging more than 60 feet into the water below. If they cleared a 15-foot outcropping and survived the free fall into 12 feet of water, they were deemed noble soldiers worthy of their great king.

Just offshore from this daredevil launching pad lies **Shark Island,** a rock formation that bears an uncanny resemblance to a shark fin. Could it be that warriors skilled enough to survive Kahekili's Leap had then to confront the malevolent spirit of a shark?

▼▼▼▼▼▼▼▼▼
Northwest— Polihua Beach

HIDDEN ►

From Lanai City, a graded pineapple road that disintegrates into an ungraded dirt track leads about seven miles to the **Garden of the Gods.** This heavily eroded area resembles the Dakota Badlands and features multihued boulders that change color dramatically during sunrise and sunset. A fantasy land of stone, the Garden of the Gods is planted with ancient lava flows tortured by the elements into as many suggestive shapes as the imagination can conjure. The colors here vibrate with psychedelic intensity and the rocks loom up around you as though they were the gods themselves—hard, cold, dark beings possessed of untold power and otherworldly beauty.

Past this surreal and sacred spot, Polihua Trail, a rugged jeep road, descends several miles to the ocean. **Polihua Beach,** stretching more than a mile and a half, is the longest and widest white-sand beach on the island. Once a prime nesting beach for green sea turtles, it is an excellent spot to watch whales as they pass close by the shoreline

BEACHES & PARKS

HIDDEN ►

POLIHUA BEACH 🏊 🚶 ⛵ A wide white-sand beach situated along Lanai's northwest shore, this isolated strand, with a stunning view of Molokai, rivals Kauai's trackless beaches. Swimming is allowed here but exercise caution—strong winds and currents prevail throughout this region. The water here is sometimes muddy but when it's clear, and when the Fish and Game Division declares it "in season," you can dive for lobsters. According to local anglers, this is the best spot on the island for fishing. Common catches include *papio*, *ulua*, bonefish, threadfin and red snapper. There are no facilities here. ~ It's about 11 miles from Lanai City through pineapple fields and the Garden of the Gods. The last half of the drive is over a rugged jeep trail. For specific directions and road conditions, check with the jeep rental garages.

With so much virgin territory, Lanai should be ideal for camping. But here, as on the other islands, landowners restrict outdoors lovers. The villain is the outfit that manages the island. It permits island residents to camp where they like, but herds visitors into one area on the south coast. This campsite, at Hulopoe Beach, has facilities for six sites. Once filled to capacity, no other camping is permitted on the entire island! So make reservations early.

Outdoor Adventures

CAMPING

DIVING

Although there are no establishments on the island that rent scuba or snorkeling gear, a number of outfitters that operate out of Maui provide everything you'll need (including refreshments) to test the waters off Lanai. One area—Cathedrals—is considered the best dive site in Hawaii. Expect to float among Hawaiian green turtles, butterfly fish, black sturgeons and eels.

Trilogy conducts most dives at the Molokini Crater Marine Preserve. ~ Lahaina Harbor; 661-4743.

Scotch Mist Sailing Charters offers half-day snorkeling trips to Turtle Reef. ~ Lahaina Harbor; 661-0386.

Club Lanai also takes its divers and snorkelers out to Turtle Reef. ~ Lahaina Harbor; 871-0626.

Catering to all levels of experience, **Dive Maui** explores over 20 locations, including the Cathedrals. ~ 900 Front Street, Lahaina; 667-2080.

GOLF

The premier course on the island is one designed by Greg Norman and Ted Robinson, **The Experience at Koele**. ~ 565-7300.

The nine-hole **Cavendish Golf Course**, also in Lanai City, is open to the public as well. ~ No phone.

Or try **Challenge at Manele**, a newly opened 18-hole golf course at the Manele Bay Hotel. ~ 565-7700.

TENNIS

Call the County Department of Parks and Recreation for information on the public courts in Lanai City. ~ 565-7878.

Courts are available at **The Lodge at Koele** ~ Lanai City; 565-7300; and the **Manele Bay Hotel** ~ near Hulopoe Beach; 565-7700.

RIDING STABLES

The Lodge at Koele offers horseback riding and equestrian tours. Choose between five rides that take you on various trails around the lodge. The Koele Ride is an hour-long leisurely walking ride that follows a wooded trail and gives riders stunning views of Maui, Molokai and Lanai City. ~ 565-7300.

BIKING

Given the lack of paved roads, bicycle use is somewhat restricted on Lanai. There are a few nice rides from Lanai City, but all are steep in places and pass over pockmarked sections of road. One goes south eight miles to Manele Bay and the beach at Hulopoe, another diverts west to busy little Kaumalapau Harbor, and the last heads north 14 miles to Shipwreck Beach.

Lanai City Service Inc. is a good place to obtain information concerning Lanai roads. ~ 565-7227.

HIKING

Hikers on Lanai are granted much greater freedom than campers. Jeep trails and access roads are open to the public; the only restriction is that hikers cannot camp along trails. Since most of the trails lead either to beaches or points of interest, you'll find them described in the regional sightseeing and "Beaches & Parks" sections above.

In addition to these listings, there are two other trails to consider. The **Ancient Graveyard Trail** (.5 mile) winds to a picturesque graveyard that has been used since ancient times.

The **Koloiki Ridge Trail** (5 miles) leads through forest lands and the Cathedral of Pines (a group of pines resembling a gothic church) to a ridge that runs between Naio Gulch and Maunalei Valley. This moderately difficult hike provides views of Molokai and Maui.

▼▼▼▼▼▼▼▼▼▼ Transportation

AIR

Planes to Lanai land at **Lanai Airport** amid an endless maze of tilled fields four miles from downtown Lanai City. This tiny landing strip, slated for major expansion, currently has a small gift shop and a courtesy telephone for car rentals (you'll be picked up in a shuttle). There are no lockers or public transportation. A few rooms house airline offices. Hawaiian Airlines offers jet service to the islands; Aloha Island Air flies propeller-driven planes and features competitive rates. ~ 565-6757.

If you're staying at any of the island hotels, they will provide transportation into town, as will any of the island's car rental agencies if you're renting a vehicle from them.

BOAT

A ferry service called **Expeditions** operates out of Maui and links Lahaina with Manele Bay on Lanai. There are five boats per day in each direction. The 45-minute crossing provides a unique way to arrive on the island. ~ P.O. Box 10, Lahaina, HI 96767; 661-3756.

CAR & JEEP RENTALS

Lanai City Service Inc., which is affiliated with Dollar Rent A Car, rents automatic compact cars with free mileage. But renting a car on Lanai is like carrying water wings to the desert: there's simply nowhere to go. Rental cars are restricted to pavement, while most of Lanai's roads are jeep trails: four-wheel drive is the only way to fly. ~ 1036 Lanai Avenue; 565-7227.

The first time I visited the island of Lanai, I rented a vintage 1942 jeep. The vehicle had bad brakes, no emergency brake, malfunctioning windshield wipers and no seat belts. It was, however, equipped with an efficient shock absorber—me. Today, Lanai City Services Inc., described above, rents new and reliable jeeps. (Be aware that the rental car collision insurance provided by most credit cards does not cover jeeps.)

BOAT TOURS

There are boat tours of Lanai offered by Maui-based outfits, **Club Lanai** (871-0626) and **Trilogy** (661-4743).

HITCHING

Officially, it's illegal, but actually it's common. The folks in these parts are pretty friendly, so rides are easy to get. The trick lies in finding someone who's going as far as you are—like all the way out to Shipwreck Beach or out to the Garden of the Gods.

▼▼▼▼▼▼▼▼▼▼▼▼▼▼▼▼▼▼▼▼▼

Addresses & Phone Numbers

LANAI ISLAND
Camping Permits ~ Lanai Company, Lanai City; 565-7233
Weather ~ 565-6033

LANAI CITY
Ambulance ~ 911
Fire Department ~ 911
Hospital ~ Lanai Community Hospital, 628 7th Street; 565-6411
Laundromat ~ 7th Street next to Heart of Lanai Art Gallery; 565-6678
Library ~ Fraser Avenue; 565-6996
Police Department ~ 312 8th Street; 911
Post Office ~ 731 Lanai Avenue; 565-6517

EIGHT

Molokai

Between the bustling islands of Oahu and Maui lies an isle which in shape resembles Manhattan, but which in spirit and rhythm is far more than an ocean away from the smog-shrouded shores of the Big Apple. Molokai, Hawaii's fifth-largest island, is thirty-eight miles long and ten miles wide. The slender isle was created by three volcanoes that mark its present geographic regions: one at West End where the arid Mauna Loa tableland rises to 1381 feet, another at East End where a rugged mountain range along the north coast is topped by 4970-foot Mount Kamakou, and the third, a geologic afterthought, which created the low, flat Kalaupapa Peninsula.

Considering that the island measures a modest 260 square miles, its geographic diversity is amazing. Arriving at Hoolehua Airport near the island's center, travelers feel as though they have touched down somewhere in the American Midwest. Red dust, dry heat and curving prairie surround the small landing strip and extend to the west end of Molokai. This natural pastureland gives way in the southcentral region to low-lying, relatively swampy ground and brown-sand beaches with murky water.

The prettiest strands lie along the western shore, where Papohaku Beach forms one of the largest white-sand beaches in the state, and at the east end around Halawa Valley, a region of heavy rainfall and lush tropic vegetation. To the north is the vaunted pali, which rises in a vertical wall 2000 feet from the surf, creating the tallest sea cliffs in the world. Here, too, is an awesome succession of sharp, narrow valleys cloaked in green moss.

Kaunakakai, a sleepy port town on the south shore, is the island's hub. From here a road runs to the eastern and western coasts. Kalaupapa and the northern *pali* are accessible overland only by mule and hiking trails.

Even in a region of islands, Molokai has always been something of a backwater. To the early Hawaiians it appeared desiccated and inhospitable and they named it *molo*, "barren," *kai*, "sea." The rich Halawa Valley was settled in the 7th century and the island developed a haunting reputation for sorcery and mystical occurrences. In ancient times it was also called *pule-oo*, or "powerful prayer," and was revered for the potency of its priests.

When Captain James Cook "discovered" the island in November 1778, he found it bleak and inhospitable. Not until 1786 did a Western navigator, Captain George Dixon, bother to land. When Kamehameha the Great took it in 1795, he was actually en route to the much grander prize of Oahu. His war canoes are said to have loomed along four miles of shoreline when he attacked the island at Paku-hiwa Battleground and slaughtered the island's outnumbered defenders.

The next wave of invaders arrived in 1832 when Protestant missionaries introduced the Polynesians to the marvels of Christianity. Around 1850 a German immigrant named Rudolph Meyer arrived in Molokai, married a Hawaiian chieftess, and began a reign as manager of the Molokai Ranch that lasted for almost a half-century.

Leprosy struck the Hawaiian Islands during the 19th century, and wind-plagued Kalaupapa Peninsula became the living hell to which the disease's victims were exiled. Beginning in 1866, lepers were torn from their families and literally cast to their fates along this stark shore. Here Father Damien de Veuster, a Belgian priest, the Martyr of Molokai, came to live, work and eventually die among the afflicted.

For years Molokai was labeled "The Lonely Isle" or "The Forgotten Isle." By 1910 a population that once totaled 10,000 had decreased to one-tenth the size. Then in 1921, Polynesians began settling homesteads under the Hawaiian Homes Act, which granted a 40-acre homestead to anyone with over 50 percent Hawaiian ancestry. Molokai eventually became "The Friendly Isle," with the largest proportion of native Hawaiians anywhere in the world (except for the island of Niihau, which is closed to outsiders). With them they brought a legacy from old Hawaii, the spirit of aloha, which still lives on this marvelous island. Young Hawaiians, sometimes hostile on the more crowded islands, are often outgoing and generous here. And of all the islands, Molokai offers you the best opportunity to "go native" by staying with a Hawaiian family.

During the 1920s, while Hawaiians were being granted the hardscrabble land that had not already been bought up on the island, Libby (which later sold out to Dole) and Del Monte began producing pineapples across the richer stretches of the island. The company towns of Maunaloa and Kualapuu sprang up and Molokai's rolling prairies became covered with fields of spike-topped fruits. Over the years competition from Asia became increasingly intense, forcing Dole to shut its operation in 1975 and Del Monte to pull out in 1982.

As elsewhere in Hawaii, the economic powers realized that if they couldn't grow crops they had better cultivate tourists. During the 1970s thousands of acres along the island's western end were allocated for resort and residential development and the sprawling Kaluakoi Resort was built. While this hotel and condominium complex has only been marginally successful, a master plan for future development, bitterly opposed by native Hawaiians and environmentalists, is still in the works. In 1996, vandals destroyed five miles of water pipes on Molokai Ranch, which had earlier closed access to several beaches and evicted a number of former plantation workers from their homes.

Today the island's population numbers about 7000. It still does not possess a single traffic light or elevator and the weak economy has saved it from the ravages of development that plagued the rest of Hawaii during the 1980s. Change is coming, but like everything on Molokai, it is arriving slowly. Time still remains to see Hawaii as it once was and to experience the trackless beaches, vaulting seacliffs, sweeping ranchlands and forested mountains that led ancient Hawaiians to believe in the mystical powers of Molokai.

Kaunakakai to East End

You don't need a scorecard, or even a map for that matter, to keep track of the sightseeing possibilities on Molokai. Across its brief expanse, the Friendly Isle offers several rewards to the curious, none of which are difficult to find.

First of course is the falsefront town of Kaunakakai, a commercial hub that more resembles a way station on the road to Dodge City. From here a simple two-lane road, Route 450 (Kamehameha V Highway), threads its way along the southern shore in search of the Halawa Valley at the far east end of the island.

SIGHTS

It is only too appropriate that **Kaunakakai** gained its greatest fame from someone who never existed. Known for a song written about "The Cock-eyed Mayor of Kaunakakai," the town has in fact had only one mayor—whether he was cock-eyed, no one will say. This somnolent village, with its falsefront buildings and tiny civic center, is administered from Maui. Poor but proud, it possesses a population of fewer than 3000, and has a main drag (Ala Malama Street) that extends a grand total of three blocks but still represents the hub of Molokai.

Nearby is the **wharf**, extending seaward almost a half-mile and offering a mooring place for a few fishing boats, charter outfits, and private sailboats. A good place to gaze out on the island of Lanai, it is also an ideal vantage from which to take in the velvet green slopes that rise toward the ridgeline of Molokai.

Close to the pier landing rest the rocky remains of **Kamehameha V's Summer Home**, where Hawaii's king luxuriated during the late-19th century.

From Kaunakakai to Halawa Valley, a narrow macadam road leads past almost 30 miles of seascapes and historic sites. Route 450 runs straight along the south shore for about 20 miles, presenting views across the Kalohi and Pailolo channels to Lanai and Maui. Then the road snakes upward and curves inland before descending again into Halawa Valley.

Due to the calm, shallow waters along the southeastern shoreline, this area once supported one of the greatest concentrations of fishponds in Hawaii. Numbering as many as five dozen during the pre-Western period, these ancient aquaculture structures were built of lava and coral by commoners to raise fish for Hawaiian royalty. Small fish were trapped within these stone pens, fattened and eventually harvested. You will see the rebuilt remains of several as you

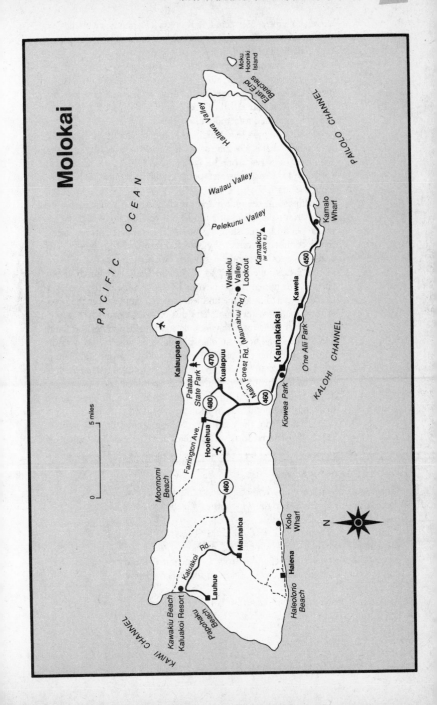

Molokai

PACIFIC OCEAN

KAIWI CHANNEL

Moku Hooniki Island

Halawa Valley

Wailau Valley

Pelekunu Valley

East End Beaches

PAILOLO CHANNEL

Kamalo Wharf

Waikolu Valley Lookout

Kamakou (el 4,970 ft.)

450

Kawela

Kaunakakai

One Alii Park

KALOHI CHANNEL

Main Forest Rd. (Maunahui Rd.)

460

Kiowea Park

Kalaupapa

Palaau State Park

470

Kualapuu

480

Farrington Ave.

Moomomi Beach

Hoolehua

460

Kaluakoi Rd.

Maunaloa

Kolo Wharf

Halena

Haleolono Beach

Kaluakoi Resort

Kawakiu Beach

Papohaku Beach

Lauhue

N

0   5 miles

drive along the coast, including **Kalokoeli Fishpond**, two miles east of Kaunakakai, **Keawanui Fishpond**, about 12 miles east of town, and **Ualapue Fishpond**, a mile farther east.

About five miles from town lies Kawela, once an ancient city of refuge, now known as the place where two battles were fought at **Pakuhiwa Battleground**. In his drive to become Hawaii's first monarch, Kamehameha the Great launched a canoe flotilla that reportedly extended four miles along this shore.

This is also the site of **Kakahaia National Wildlife Refuge**, a 42-acre habitat that is a nesting area for a dozen species of coastal and sea birds. Centered around Kakahaia Beach Park, the preserve includes a 15-acre freshwater pond that rests immediately inland from the coast.

Just past the ten-mile marker (indicating that you are ten miles east of Kaunakakai), a dirt road leads to **Kamalo Wharf**, an old pineapple and cattle shipping point. This natural harbor, once a major commercial center (by Molokai standards!), is now a gathering place for occasional fishermen and boats.

It's a half-mile farther to **St. Joseph Catholic Church**, a tiny chapel built by Father Damien in 1876. A statue of the bespectacled priest, clad in a cape and leaning on a cane, graces the property. A small cemetery completes this placid tableau.

A monument (past the 11-mile marker) designates the **Smith and Bronte Landing**, an inhospitable spot where two aviators crash-landed after completing the first civilian transpacific flight in 1927. The 25-hour flight from California, scheduled to land in Honolulu, ended abruptly when the plane ran out of gas. (An opening in the trees past the 12-mile marker reveals the aforementioned Keawanui Fishpond, one of Molokai's largest.)

Set back from the road in a clearing framed by mountains is **Our Lady of Seven Sorrows Catholic Church**, located 14 miles east

MOLOKAI EXPERIENCES

- Ride a mule down the world's highest seacliffs along a harrowing succession of switchbacks to the windblasted **Kalaupapa Peninsula**. *page 360*

- Cruise to Maui aboard the 118-foot **Maui Princess** while watching the waters for dolphins and humpback whales. *page 363*

- Try the Molokai honey, bread and pastries at **Kanemitsu's Bakery** then step out onto the main street of a town that has no traffic lights. *page 347*

- Wander the beach in **Halawa Valley** and explore a luxurious agricultural region inhabited by Hawaiians for 1300 years. *page 351* of Kaunakakai. Originally built by Father Damien in 1874 and reconstructed almost a century later, it's a pretty chapel surrounded by coconut trees and flanked by a small cemetery.

One of the largest temples in the islands, **Iliiliopae Heiau**, rests ◄ *HIDDEN*
hidden in the underbrush on private land just inland from the highway. Measuring about 100 yards in length and 30 yards in width, it was once a center of sorcery and human sacrifice that today consists of a stone platform and adjoining terraces. This is also the trailhead for the Wailau Valley Trail. According to legend, the *heiau*'s stones were all transported from this distant valley and assembled in a single night. ~ 15 miles east of Kaunakakai; for permission and directions, call Pearl Petro at 558-8113.

The best way to visit this ancient site is on the **Molokai Wagon Ride**, a horse-drawn tour conducted by several delightful local fellows. ~ Located at Mapulehu Mango Grove, 15 miles east of Kaunakakai; 558-8380.

The Molokai Wagon Ride also visits the nearby **Mapulehu Mango Grove**, a stand of 2500 fruit trees that were planted during the 1930s and now represent one of the largest such groves in the world. The wagon ride winds up at a picturesque beach where guests enjoy a Molokai-style lunch on the beach complete with coconut husking and Hawaiian net throwing.

At the **Mapulehu Glass House** you can tour a somewhat overgrown funky old garden. Spanning ten acres and centered around a greenhouse, it features flowering ginger and other exotic plants as well as poorly tended patches. ~ 15 miles east of Kaunakakai, marked by a flagpole and mailbox number 800; 558-8160.

The ruins of the island's first **sugar mill** stand near Route 450's 20-mile marker. All that remains of this early factory, which burned down about a century ago, is a solitary stack.

Just beyond the 20-mile marker is Kumimi Beach, which presents your first view of **Moku Hooniki Island** as well as other-worldly vistas of Maui.

The road now begins a sinuous course along a string of pearl-white beaches, then climbs above a rocky coastline. As you curve upward into Molokai's tropical heights, the roadside flora becomes increasingly colorful and dense. First you encounter the open pastures and rolling ranchland of 14,000-acre **Puu o Hoku Ranch**, then dive into the tropical foliage of Molokai's windblown northeast coast.

As the road winds high above **Halawa Valley** it offers several ◄ *HIDDEN*
vista points from which to view this V-shaped canyon bounded by green walls. Directly below, tropical greenery gives way to white surf and then aquamarine ocean. A river bisects this luxuriant region. At the far end, surrounded by sheer walls, two waterfalls—Hipuapua and Moaula—spill down the mountainside. Obviously East End has withheld its most spectacular scenery until the last.

Archaeologists believe that Molokai's first settlement was established here, possibly as early as the 7th century. The ancient Hawaiians terraced the surrounding slopes, planting taro and living off the largesse of the sea.

In 1946 (and again in 1957) a tidal wave swept through the valley, leveling buildings and leaving salt deposits that destroyed the agricultural industry. Today you can drive down into the valley, where you'll find a park, a lovely curve of sandy beach, freshwater Halawa Stream, an old church and several other structures. A hiking trail leads to 250-foot Moaula Falls and 500-foot Hipuapua Falls, which lie to the interior of this awesomely beautiful vale. (Please note, however, that at last report this trail had been closed by the landowner and was not open to the public.)

LODGING   Polynesian architecture is the theme at **Hotel Molokai**. Set on a small unappealing beach two miles east of Kaunakakai, this hotel charges a moderate price for a very tiny room with twin beds. I found spotty mirrors, bumpy rugs, shared lanai and a tacky interior of shingled (yes, shingled) walls. All that's okay in a low-rent hostelry, but why pay more for less? Actually, you're probably paying for what's outside: a shrub-rimmed lawn with coconut trees, and along the shore a pool and thatch pavilions. Amid all this splendor you'll find a cluster of brown-shingle buildings with elegantly curved Polynesian roofs and plate-glass windows reflecting the view. These are the deluxe rooms; they have wood paneling, high-beamed ceilings and a much more appealing atmosphere. ~ Kamehameha V Highway; 553-5347, 800-423-6656, fax 553-5047. MODERATE TO DELUXE.

If privacy is what you're after, you'll love **Kamalo Plantation Bed & Breakfast**. Set on five acres of orchards and tropical gardens, the inn features a large secluded cottage in the middle of the grounds and two guest rooms in the open, airy house. Screen windows let in the tropical smell of the flowering trees, and each room has a private lanai. Breakfast consists of homemade bread and fresh fruit from the orchard. ~ HCO1 Box 300, Kaunakakai, HI 96748; phone/fax 558-8236. MODERATE.

OVIEDO'S LUNCH COUNTER

If you're into Filipino fare, try **Oviedo's Lunch Counter**. This mom-and-pop restaurant serves up spicy steaming dishes at low prices. You'll find plank board walls surrounding a few plastic chairs and yellow formica tables. The steam-tray cuisine includes chicken papaya, pig's feet, turkey tail adobo and mango beans. Open for lunch and early dinner. ~ 553-5014. BUDGET.

If you're traveling with several folks or want kitchen facilities, there are also condominiums: **Molokai Shores** and **Wavecrest Resort**. Both offer oceanfront accommodations with full kitchen, lanai and color TV. Each is a series of low-slung buildings that forms a U-shaped configuration around a landscaped lawn extending to the beach. Within the grounds are palm trees, a swimming pool, shuffleboard and barbecue areas. Of the two, Wavecrest (rates from $109), 12 miles east of Kaunakakai, is the better bargain; in addition to a few extra features including tennis courts and a dishwasher, the rates are slightly lower than those at Molokai Shores (rates from $125), just one mile east of Kaunakakai. ~ **Molokai Shores:** 553-5954, 800-535-0085, fax 800-633-5085. **Wavecrest Resort:** 558-8103, 800-535-0085, fax 558-8206.

CONDOS

A gourmet will starve on Molokai, but someone looking for a square meal at fair prices should depart well-fed. The budget restaurants are clustered along Ala Malama Street in Kaunakakai.

DINING

Kanemitsu's Bakery serves tasty meals at appetizing prices. A local institution, it's a simple café with molded seats, formica tables and an interesting folk art mural presenting a map of Molokai. The lunch special varies but the price is low whether you are dining on pork chops, beef teriyaki, breaded mahimahi or fried chicken. Kanemitsu's is a favorite with the breakfast crowd, which is drawn in by the bakery as well as a menu of omelettes, hot cakes and egg dishes served with Portuguese sausage or that island favorite, Spam. No dinner. Closed Tuesday. ~ 553-5855. BUDGET.

◀ *HIDDEN*

Outpost Natural Foods has a takeout counter at the back of its tiny health food store. Here you can fuel up with delicious sandwiches, salads and smoothies that are both nutritious and inexpensive. There are also burritos and daily specials. Open for lunch only. Closed Saturday. ~ 70 Makaena Street; 553-3377. BUDGET.

The nearest Molokai approaches to a supermarket is **Misaki's**, a medium-sized grocery store on Kaunakakai's main drag, Ala Malama Street. The prices are higher and the selection smaller here than at the chain markets, so it's wise to bring a few provisions from the larger islands. Open 8:30 a.m. to 8:30 p.m., Sunday 9 a.m. to noon. ~ 553-5505.

GROCERIES

Outpost Natural Foods, down the street and around the corner from Misaki's, offers a friendly atmosphere as well as juices, herbs, dried fruit, fresh local produce and other health food items. Closed Saturday. ~ 70 Makaena Street; 553-3377.

Try **Kanemitsu's Bakery** for delicious Molokai honey, bread and pastries. ~ 553-5855.

On the East End, **Wavecrest Resort**, 12 miles out, has a "general store" with a very limited supply of groceries (primarily canned goods) and a hearty stock of liquor.

SHOPPING

You needn't worry about falling into the shop-till-you-drop syndrome on Molokai. Long before you have even begun to think about being tired you will have visited every store on the island. Shopping is still an adventure here, since the few stores operating are all owned by local people and provide a window into life on Molokai.

Ala Malama Street, Kaunakakai's main street, offers a modest row of shops. **Molokai Island Creations** specializes in clothing, jewelry, glassware and gift items made by Molokai artists. ~ 553-5926.

Imports Gift Shop features casual wear, cultured and mabe pearls, and Hawaiian heirloom jewelry. Closed Sunday. ~ Ala Malama Street; 553-5734.

For beachwear you can try **Molokai Surf**. Closed Sunday. ~ Ala Malama Street; 553-5093.

Molokai Fish & Dive, "home of the 'original' Molokai T-shirt designs," features its signature clothing and souvenirs as well as beach items and sporting equipment. ~ Kaunakakai; 553-5926.

The Kahua Center (Wharf Road) has a couple interesting stores. **Dudoit Imports** (no phone) features local arts and crafts, antiques and jewelry, and **Lorenzo's Gallery of Fine Art and Molokai Treasures** (553-3748) has a beautiful collection of paintings by local artists. Closed weekends.

BEACHES & PARKS

O'NE ALII PARK 🏊 🤽 🎣 ⛱️ This spacious park features a large grass-covered field and coconut grove plus a narrow beach with an excellent view of Lanai. A reef far offshore makes this area very shallow and affords ample protection. It's excellent for children. Snorkeling, though, is only mediocre. As for surfing, all the action is far out on the reef and it's rarely any good. Surf-casting isn't bad here but it's even better farther to the east. The most common catches are *manini*, red and white goatfish, parrotfish, *papio*, *ulua*, milkfish and mullet. The facilities here include a picnic area, restrooms, showers and electricity at the pavilion. ~ Four miles east of Kaunakakai on Route 450.

▲ Mainly tent camping; no hookups. Very popular and therefore sometimes crowded and noisy. County permit required.

KAKAHAIA BEACH PARK 🏊 🤽 🎣 ⛱️ This is a long, narrow park wedged tightly between the road and the ocean. Near a national wildlife refuge, Kakahaia is an important nesting area for native and migratory birds. Picnicking, swimming, snorkeling, surfing and fishing are much the same as at O'ne Alii Park. Day use only. ~ Six miles east of Kaunakakai on Route 450.

PUKOO BEACH 🏊 ⛱️ This crescent-shaped strand is mirrored by another curving beach just to the west. Maui lies directly across the channel and there are also marvelous views of Lanai. With a shallow, rocky bottom, this beach provides only mediocre swimming. However, it's very popular with anglers. There are no facilities. ~ The old Neighborhood Store 'n' Snack Bar (now closed), located on Route 450 near the 15-mile marker, is your landmark. Just past here, traveling east, turn into the second driveway on the right. This access road leads a short distance to the beach.

KUMIMI BEACH, POHAKULOA POINT AND OTHER EAST END BEACHES Beginning near the 18-mile marker on Route 450, and extending for about four miles, lies this string of small sandy beaches. These are among the island's loveliest, featuring white sands and spectacular views of the islands of Maui and Lanai. The swimming is very good, but beware of heavy currents and high surf. Plentiful coral makes for great snorkeling and good lobster diving. There are numerous surfing breaks throughout this area. Pohakuloa Point (or Rock Point), located eight-tenths of a mile past the 20-mile marker, is one of Molokai's top surfing spots. These are also good beaches for surfing. Barracuda are sometimes caught in the deeper regions. Also bonefish, mountain bass, threadfin, *manini*, red and white goatfish, *ulua*, *papio*, parrotfish, milkfish, and mullet. There is a small market near the 15-mile marker. ~ These pocket beaches are located along Route 450 between the 18- and 22-mile markers.

HALAWA BEACH PARK Set in lush Halawa Valley, one of Molokai's most splendid areas, the park is tucked neatly between mountains and sea on a grassy plot dotted with coconut palms and ironwood trees. Cliffs, waterfalls, two pocket beaches—altogether a heavenly spot, though sometimes rainy and almost always windy. This is a very good place to swim because it is partially protected by the bay. But exercise caution anyway. Snorkeling is good, though the water is sometimes murky. It's one of the very best spots on the island for surfing. Fishing is also notable; the reefs studding this area make it a prime locale for many of the species caught along East End Beaches. The park is a bit weatherbeaten and overgrown and although there are a picnic area and restrooms, the running water must be boiled or treated chemically. ~ Thirty miles east of Kaunakakai on Route 450.

▲ Not permitted in the park, but people camp on the other side of Halawa Stream on property owned by Puu o Hoku Ranch. You will have to park and carry your gear to where you want to camp.

Kaunakakai to West End

Generally, if you are not pointed east on Molokai, you are headed westerly. The thoroughfare that carries you across the prairie-like plains of west Molokai is Route 460, also called the Maunaloa Highway, another two-lane track. Along the way you can venture off in search of the plantation town of Kualapuu and the vista point overlooking Kalaupapa, but eventually you will arrive at road's end out in the woodframe town of Maunaloa. From this red-dust municipality it's a short jaunt to Papohaku Beach, Molokai's western shore.

SIGHTS

Just a mile west of the cock-eyed town of Kaunakakai on Route 460 is the **Kapuaiwa Grove**, planted in the 1860s by Kamehameha V. This magnificent stand of coconut palms, once 1000 in number, consists of particularly tall trees. The grove creates the sensation of being in a tropical dream sequence, with hundreds of palm trees flashing green and yellow fronds and extending to the lip of the ocean. Some appear to stand in columns, but others have bent so far to the wind they have fallen out of formation.

Strung like rosary beads opposite the grove are seven tiny churches. This **Church Row** includes Protestant, Mormon, Jehovah's Witness and several other denominations. Like sentinels protecting the island from the devil, they too are gathered in rows. The most intriguing are the oldest, tiny woodframe structures with modest steeples. These one-room chapels lack worldly frills like stained glass and are furnished with creaky wooden pews that seat a few dozen parishioners. Stop by and inquire about services; visitors are always welcome.

A side trip along Route 470 leads past the tinroof town of **Kualapuu**. Filled with modest plantation houses, it harkens back to an earlier era when Molokai cultivated pineapples rather than tourists. Today its claim to fame is a 1.4 million gallon reservoir that is reportedly the largest rubber-lined water tank in the world.

Farther up Route 470, Kalai is home to the R. W. Meyer Sugar Mill, which is the highlight of the new **Molokai Museum and Cultural Center**. There is an 1878 steam-generated operation that has been restored in sparkling fashion. The mule-driven cane crusher, copper clarifiers and dependable old steam engine are ready and waiting for Molokai to return to its old ways. There are also well-presented displays and heirlooms of the German immigrant family that owned the mill, as well as native Molokai artifacts. Admission. ~ Route 470, Kalai; 567-6436.

Route 470 ends at the **Kalaupapa Lookout**. Here cliffs as green as Ireland fall away in dizzying fashion to reveal a softly sloping tableland 1600 feet below, the Kalaupapa Peninsula. Fringed by white-sand beaches, this geologic afterthought extends more than two miles out from the foot of the *pali*. A lighthouse and landing strip occupy the point of the peninsula. Nearer the cliffs, a cluster of houses comprises the famous leper colony; while neighboring Kauhako Crater, a nicely rounded circle far below you, represents a vestige of the volcano that created this appendage. Ringed by rock and water, protected by the tallest sea cliffs in the world, Kalaupapa Peninsula is a magnificent sight indeed.

A short hike from the lookout, **Phallic Rock** protrudes obscenely from the ground amid an ironwood stand as thick as pubic hair. This geologic formation, so realistic it almost seems sculpted, was said to represent the Hawaiian fertility god, who was turned to stone when his wife caught him admiring a beautiful young girl. Legend says that a woman offering gifts and spending the night here will return home pregnant.

According to legend, Molokai was the child of the god Wakea and his mistress Hina, whose cave still lies along the southeastern edge of the island.

Route 480 will take you into the town of Hoolehua, where you'll find **Purdy's Natural Macadamia Nut Farm.** Located right behind the island's only high school, this small grove of 70-year-old macadamia nut trees is open to the public for free tours and tastings. The owner will explain the growing cycles of the trees and demonstrate harvesting and cooking techniques. Visitors can taste the raw product and also sample the nut after it's been naturally roasted, a process that cuts down greatly on the fat and calories found in nuts sold in stores. ~ Lihipali Avenue, Hoolehua; 567-6601.

Route 460 continues over dry rolling plains toward Molokai's West End. This arid plateau, windswept and covered by deep red, iron-rich soil, was once planted in pineapple. Today Molokai Ranch, which still owns much of the region, has turned to hay cultivation to feed cattle.

If nothing else, the West End is rich in myth and history. As Hawaiian storytellers recount, the region around Maunaloa, the volcano that formed this side of the island, was once a cultural focus of the Polynesians. It was here that the hula originated; from the slopes of Maunaloa the goddess Laka spread knowledge of the sensuous dance to all the other islands.

Like the pineapple industry itself, Route 460 ends in **Maunaloa.** With the departure of Dole's operations in 1975, this company town assumed the dusty, falsefront visage of the Wild West after the mines petered out and the saloons shut down. In true revival spirit, however, local craftspeople and artists have converted a few buildings into shops and galleries. Besides these more recent additions to the rustic landscape, the old post office remains and there is a classic general store. Framed by Norfolk pines and filled with 1920s-era tinroof plantation houses, Maunaloa itself is a classic.

Perhaps the island's most unexpected and exotic feature is the nearby **Molokai Ranch Wildlife Conservation Park.** Part of Molokai Ranch's sprawling 52,000-acre spread, this 350-acre game preserve is roamed by about 80 African and Asian animals. Barbary sheep, eland, Indian blackbuck, rhea, wild turkeys, zebra, crown crane, giraffe and oryx are among the species that have transformed Molokai's West End into a kind of "Little Africa." Tours feature a "giraffe picnic" where you can feed and pet the curious critters. Horseback riding is also available. The Malihini Rodeo happens every Wednesday and Friday, and any adventurous soul 16 years or older can learn rodeo skills from Hawaiian cowboys. Admission. ~ P.O. Box 259, Maunaloa, HI 96770; 552-2741.

Molokai's West End was once a rich adze quarry. The rock, vital to a Stone Age society, was fashioned into tools that were in turn used to create weapons, canoes, bowls and other necessities.

Any tour of West End should of course finish at the west end. **Papohaku Beach,** a sparkling three-mile long swath of white sand, would be a fitting finale to any tour. Reached by taking Kaluakoi Road from Route 460 and driving through the rolling hills of sprawling Kaluakoi Resort, Papohaku is one of the largest beaches in the state. During World War II troops practiced shore landings along this coast. But today you will have the beach and surrounding sand dunes almost entirely to yourself.

HIDDEN ► **MOLOKAI'S OUTBACK** For a splendid tour of Molokai's mountainous interior, take a drive or hike on the Main Forest Road (located four miles west of Kaunakakai). This bumpy dirt road requires four-wheel-drive vehicles along its ten-mile-length.

Deer, quail, pheasant, doves and chukkar partridge populate the route. Numerous secondary roads and trails lead to the very edge of the mammoth Molokai Forest Reserve, through which the main road passes. These side roads offer excellent possibilities for adventurous hikers.

After nine miles, the main road passes **Lua Moku Iliahi,** known to the English-speaking world as the **Sandalwood Measuring Pit.** This depression, dug into the earth to match the hull size of an old sailing vessel, was used by 19th-century Hawaiians to gauge the amount of sandalwood needed to fill a ship. It's another mile to **Waikolu Picnic Grove,** a heavily wooded retreat ideal for lunching or camping. Here you'll find picnic facilities and an outhouse. (State permit required to camp.) Across the road, **Waikolu Valley Lookout** perches above Waikolu Valley, which descends precipitously 3000 feet to the sea.

Here you can also explore **Kamakou Preserve,** a 2774-acre sanctuary managed by The Nature Conservancy. Home to more than 200 plants that live only in Hawaii, the preserve is a lush rainforest from which Molokai draws most of its water supply. There are several forest birds, including the *apapane* and *amakihi*. For information on visiting the reserve or to check the condition of the Main Forest Road (which may be closed in wet weather), call 553-5236.

To reach the Main Forest Road, take Route 460 west from Kaunakakai. There is a white bridge a little more than three-and-a-half miles from town, just before the four-mile marker. Take a right on the dirt road right before the bridge and you're on the Main Forest Road.

On the west end of Molokai, far from the madding crowd, you'll find a 6700-acre master-planned complex, the Kaluakoi Resort. Divided into four different parts, this is Molokai's premier resting spot, offering both seclusion and comfort set near a luxurious three-mile-long beach. Here you'll find the essence of plush living: wasp-waisted pool, tennis courts, golf course, a view of Oahu across the channel and an oceanfront lounge and restaurant.

CONDOS

The 103-rooms of the **Kaluakoi Hotel and Golf Club** are located in a two-story building and have all the necessities: lanai, color TV, tile bathroom, overhead fan, rattan furniture. These start at $95 a night. For an ultra-deluxe price tag, you can buy a piece of that ocean view in a studio unit with a kitchenette. ~ Kaluakoi Resort, Kepuhi Beach Road; 552-2555, 800-777-1700, fax 552-2821.

Kaluakoi Villas offers spacious cottages that feature full kitchens, as well as condo-like units that include kitchenettes. All accommodations feature TVs and VCRs, rattan furniture and ceiling fans. Cottages start at $120. ~ Kaluakoi Resort, Kepuhi Beach Road; 552-2721, 800-525-1470, fax 552-2201.

Ke Nani Kai, a 120-unit condominium located within Kaluakoi Resort, has one- and two-bedroom units starting at $95 per night. From December through March there's a four-night minimum. The complex includes a pool, tennis courts and an outdoor party area with barbecues. ~ Kaluakoi Resort, Kepuhi Beach Road; 552-2761, 800-888-2791, fax 552-0045.

Nearby **Paniolo Hale**, has 31 units starting at $95 per night. These also include all the amenities and access to a pool, barbecue area and paddle tennis. ~ Kaluakoi Resort, Kepuhi Beach Road; 552-2731, 800-367-2984, fax 552-2288.

Everyone has heard of fast food but what about slow food? **Kualapuu Cook House** bills itself as the international headquarters for a "slow food chain." Set in an old plantation house, it serves *saimin*, chili and hamburgers. If you want to get serious about it, there is chicken stir-fry, teriyaki plate and mahimahi—even New York steak. The pies are homemade and the place is bright with local color. Closed Sunday. ~ Route 480, Kualapuu; 567-6185. BUDGET TO MODERATE.

DINING

◀ HIDDEN

Out in Maunaloa, there's a gathering spot called **Jojo's Café**. Its menu includes a variety of ethnic and all-American dishes. At lunch, sandwiches are available; for dinner, you'll find an array of fresh fish and curries. Like many of the mom-and-pop businesses on Molokai, it is located in a tinroof plantation house. You can expect old plantation photos, an antique bar and booths, homespun decor and an easy friendly atmosphere. Closed Sunday. ~ Maunaloa; 552-2803. BUDGET TO MODERATE.

The aforementioned Kaluakoi Hotel, on the island's far west end, has a pennysaver **snack bar** with sandwiches. That's just light artillery to back up the hotel's big gun, the **Ohia Lodge**, Molokai's finest restaurant. This multilevel, handsomely appointed establishment (high-beamed ceiling, rattan furnishings) looks out on the distant lights of Oahu. You can order from an extensive surf-and-turf menu that includes orange-glazed almond chicken, medallions of mahimahi, tenderloin of beef with bordelaise sauce and roast breast of duck. Seeking a place to splurge? Well, this is it. Breakfast and dinner. ~ 552-2555. DELUXE.

GROCERIES Out West End way, **Maunaloa General Store**, in Maunaloa a few miles away from Kaluakoi Resort, has a limited stock of grocery items. Open 9 a.m. to 7 p.m. except Sunday (10 a.m. to 2 p.m.). ~ 552-2868.

SHOPPING Over on Molokai's West End in the red-dust town of Maunaloa you'll stumble upon two great shops that share the same building and the same telephone. **Big Wind Kite Factory** has an astonishing assortment of high flyers. There are diamond kites, dancer kites, windsocks and rainbow tail kites. You can even pick up flags and banners here. At **The Plantation Gallery** there are aloha shirts, batik sarongs, tribal art, shell necklaces and other original pieces by over 30 Molokai craftspeople. They also have the largest collection of books about Hawaii and Hawaiian culture on the island. ~ 552-2364.

There are also a few shops at **Kaluakoi Hotel** down the road in the Kaluakoi Resort complex. One of them is the **Laughing Gecko**, a boutique offering antiques, artwork, and a variety of local handicrafts such as *lauhala* mats and *koa* bracelets. ~ 552-2320.

NIGHTLIFE To step out in style, head west to Kaluakoi Hotel's **Ohia Lounge**. The rattan furnishings, carpets, overhead fans and marvelous view of Honolulu, not to mention the band on the weekends, make it *the* place. ~ 552-2555.

BEACHES & PARKS **KIOWEA PARK** Watch for falling coconuts in the beautiful Kapuaiwa Grove, which is the centerpiece of this beach park. Towering palm trees extend almost to the water, leaving little space for a beach. The swimming here is only okay; the water is well-protected by a distant reef, but the bottom is shallow and rocky, and the water is muddy. This also makes for mediocre snorkeling. Common fish catches include mullet, *manini*, parrotfish, milkfish, and *papio*, plus red, white, and striped goatfish; crabbing is good in the evening. (This park is generally restricted to homesteaders, but if you stop for a picnic you may be allowed by the locals to stay.) A nice place to visit, but I wouldn't want to fall asleep in the shade of a coconut tree. Facilities include picnic area, restrooms and pavilion. ~ Located one mile west of Kaunakakai on Route 460.

▲ Camping is usually restricted to homesteaders. If the park is vacant however, the Hawaiian Homelands Department in Hoolehua will issue permits for $5; hours are Monday through Friday from 7:45 a.m. to 4:30 p.m. ~ 567-6104.

PALAAU STATE PARK Set in a densely forested area, this 233-acre park is ideal for a mountain sojourn. Several short trails lead to petroglyphs, a startling phallic rock, and the awesome Kalaupapa Lookout. The trail down to Kalaupapa Peninsula is also nearby. There are picnic area, restrooms and pavilion. ~ Take Route 460 six miles west from Kaunakakai, then follow Route 470 (Kalae Highway) about six more miles to the end of the road.

▲ State permit required. Tent camping only.

MOOMOMI BEACH 🏖 🐚 ⚓ 🚶 A small, remote beach studded with rocks and frequented only by local people—what more could you ask? While Moomomi is a small pocket beach, many people use the name to refer to a three-mile length of coastline that extends west from the pocket beach and includes two other strands, Kawaaloa Beach and Keonelele Beach. Moomomi offers good swimming, but use caution because the bottom is rocky and the beach is only partially protected. The snorkeling is very good along reefs and rocks. As for surfing, there are fair breaks at the mouth of the inlet. There's good surf-casting from the rocky headland to the west. Keonelele Beach forms the coastal border of the Moomomi Dunes, a unique series of massive sand dunes that extend as far as four miles inland, covering Molokai's northwestern corner. Also known as the Desert Strip, this unique ecosystem is overseen by the Nature Conservancy (553-5236), which can provide information and tours. The preserve protects five endangered plant species and is a habitat for the endangered Hawaiian green sea turtle. You'll find no facilities at the park. ~ Take Route 460 west from Kaunakakai to Hoolehua. Go right on Route 481 (Puupeelua Avenue), then left on Farrington Avenue. Farrington starts as a paved road, then turns to dirt. After 2.2 miles of dirt track, the road forks. Take the right fork and follow it a half-mile to the beach. A four-wheel drive vehicle may be required.

◄ HIDDEN

▲ Camping on a grassy plot elevated from the beach is allowed on weekends. Obtain permit and keys at Molokai Ranch.

HALENA AND OTHER SOUTH COAST BEACHES 🏖 🐚 ⚓ 🚶 Don't tell anyone, but there's a dirt road running several miles along a string of trackless beaches on the south shore. (Note, however, that at last report this road was closed to the public.) The first

◄ HIDDEN

one, **Halena,** is a very funky ghost camp complete with a dozen weatherbeaten shacks and a few primitive facilities. To the west lies **Haleolono Beach,** with its pleasant bay and lagoon. To the east is **Kolo Wharf** (an abandoned pier collapsing into the sea), plus numerous fishponds, coconut groves and small sand beaches. This is an excellent area to explore, camp, hike, fish (bass, threadfin, inenui, red goatfish) and commune with hidden Hawaii. The swimming is also good if you don't mind muddy water. It's wise to boil or chemically treat the water. Note: You need the permission of Molokai Ranch to get to these beaches. ~ Take Route 460 to Maunaloa. As you first enter town (before the road curves into the main section), you'll see houses on the left and a dirt road extending perpendicularly to the right.

Now, to get to Halena, take a right at the fork, then a quick left (there are signs posted), then drive a few hundred yards to the end. The shore is nearby; simply walk west along the beach several hundred yards to the shacks.

To get to Haleolono Beach, walk about a mile west along the beach from Halena.

To get to Kolo Wharf and the other beaches, go straight where the road forks. Kolo is two miles east over an equally rugged road. Sand beaches, coconut groves and fishponds extend for another six miles past Kolo. Then the road turns inland, improving considerably, and continues for seven miles more until it meets the main road two miles west of Kaunakakai.

For current information about road access contact Molokai Ranch. ~ 552-2767. At last report, the roads in this region were closed to the public.

HIDDEN ► **KAWAKUI BEACH** 🏊 🎣 ⛱ This idyllic spot is my favorite Molokai campground. Here a small inlet, tucked away in Molokai's northwest corner, is edged by a beautiful beach with a sandy bottom. Nearby is a shady grove of *kiawe* trees, fringed by the rocky coastline. On a clear night you can see the lights of Oahu across Kaiwi Channel. This is a very good place to swim because the inlet offers some protection, but exercise caution. Snorkeling is good in summer near the rocks when the surf is low. People fish here for mountain bass, threadfin, inenui and red goatfish. There are no facilities here. Try Kaunakakai. ~ Take Route 460 west from Kaunakakai for about 12 miles. Then take a right onto the dirt road that leads downhill. Follow this bumpy dirt road about seven miles to the beach. The road forks a few hundred yards before the ocean. Take the right fork to Kawakui; the left fork leads to a series of white-sand beaches offering excellent possibilities for exploring and swimming.

▲ That shady grove is a perfect site to pitch a tent.

PAPOHAKU BEACH This splendid beach extends for three miles along Molokai's west coast; it's an excellent place to explore, collect puka shells, or just lie back and enjoy the view of Oahu. Backed by *kiawe* trees and low sand dunes, Papohaku is the largest beach on the island, averaging 100 yards in width. Swimming is excellent, but use caution. There's not much rock or coral here so the snorkeling is only mediocre. You'll find good breaks for surfing when the wind isn't blowing from the shore. Use caution, especially in the winter months. The beach is also popular with bodysurfers. The fishing is good, usually for mountain bass, threadfin, *inenui* and red goatfish. There are picnic areas, restrooms and showers; the Kaluakoi Hotel, with snack bar and restaurant, is about a half-mile away. ~ Take Route 460 for about 14 miles from Kaunakakai. Turn right onto the road to the Kaluakoi Resort. Continue past the hotel (don't turn onto the hotel road) and down the hill. Follow this macadam track, Kaluakoi Road, as it parallels the beach. Side roads from Kaluakoi Road and Pohakuloa Road (an adjoining thoroughfare) lead to Papohaku and other beaches.

▲ Tent only. County permit required.

The ultimate Molokai experience is the pilgrimage to the Kalaupapa leper colony along the rugged north shore of the island. Isolated on a 12-square-mile lava tongue that protrudes from the north shore, this sacred and historic site can be reached only by foot, mule or plane.

▼▼▼▼▼▼▼▼
Kalaupapa

Here about 68 victims of Hansen's Disease live in solitude. Doctors have controlled the affliction since 1946 with sulfone drugs, and all the patients are free to leave. But many are 60 to 90 years old, and have lived on this windswept peninsula most of their lives.

The story of the remaining residents goes back to 1866 when the Hawaiian government began exiling lepers to this lonely spot on Molokai's rain-plagued north coast. In those days Kalaupapa was a fishing village, and lepers were segregated in the **old settlement** at Kalawao on the windy eastern side of the peninsula. The place was treeless and barren—a wasteland haunted by slow death. Lepers were shipped along the coast and pushed overboard. Abandoned with insufficient provisions and no shelter, they struggled against both the elements and disease.

SIGHTS

◄ HIDDEN

To this lawless realm came Joseph Damien de Veuster, Father Damien. The Catholic priest, arriving in 1873, brought a spirit and energy that gave the colony new life. He built a church, attended to the afflicted and died of leprosy 16 years later. Perhaps it is the spirit of this "Martyr of Molokai" that even today marks the indescribable quality of Kalaupapa. There is something unique and inspiring about the place, something you will have to discover yourself.

To visit Kalaupapa, you can fly, hike or ride muleback; there are no roads leading to this remote destination. Once there you must take a guided tour; no independent exploring is permitted. And no children under 16 are allowed. Flights and hiking tours are organized by **Damien Tours** (567-6171) and **Molokai Mule Ride** (567-6088). For flight information, check **Aloha Island Air** (567-6115), **Molokai Shuttle** (567-6847) or **Paragon Air** (244-3356) from Maui.

As far as I'm concerned, the mule ride is the only way to go. The Molokai Mule Ride conducts tours daily, weather permitting. You saddle up near the Kalaupapa Lookout and descend a 1664-foot precipice. Kalaupapa unfolds below you as you switchback through lush vegetation on a three-mile-long trail. The ride? Exhilarating, frightening, but safe. And the views are otherworldly.

On the tour you will learn that Kalaupapa has been designated a national historical park. Among the points of interest within this refuge are numerous windblasted structures, a volcanic crater and several monuments. You'll also visit Saint Philomena Church, built by Father Damien in the 1870s, and Kalawao Park, an exotically beautiful spot on the lush eastern side of the peninsula.

Definitely visit Kalaupapa. Fly in and you'll undergo an unforgettable experience; hike and it will become a pilgrimage.

▼▼▼▼▼▼▼▼▼▼▼▼▼▼

Outdoor Adventures

CAMPING

With so little development and such an expanse of untouched land, Molokai would seem a haven for campers. Unfortunately, large segments of the island are owned by Molokai Ranch and other private interests; with the exception of a few beaches on Molokai Ranch property, these tracts are closed off behind locked gates.

There are a few parks for camping. A county permit is required for Papohaku Beach and O'ne Alii Park. Permits are $3 per person a day (50 cents for children) and are obtained at the County Parks and Recreation office in Kaunakakai. Hours are 8 a.m. to 4 p.m., Monday through Friday, so get your permit in advance. ~ 553-3204.

Permits for Kiowea Park, when available, are issued by the Hawaiian Homelands Department in Hoolehua. The fee is $5 per night at Kiowea for a group of any size. ~ 567-6104.

◆◆

HOT OFF THE PRESS! OUTDOOR ADVENTURE

As this book went to press, the **Molokai Ranch Wildlife Conservation Park** announced a new lodging and recreational program. It includes tent camping (complete with running water, lights and oceanview lanai) hiking, kayaking and mountain biking adventures. ~ Molokai Ranch Outfitters Center, P.O. Box 259, Maunaloa, HI 96770; 552-2681, 800-254-8871, fax 552-2773.

Camping at Palaau State Park is free but requires a permit from the Department of Land and Natural Resources (243-5354) on Maui, or from the park ranger (567-6083).

Molokai Fish & Dive sells camping gear. ~ Kaunakakai; 553-5926. For camping-gear rentals go to **Fun Hogs Hawaii**. ~ Kaluakoi Hotel and Golf Club; 552-2555.

DIVING

If you're not traveling with gear, the following outfitters can rent you snorkeling equipment. Several provide snorkeling trips to prime spots around the island, and you might check with them regarding other activities such as scuba diving, kayaking and sailing. The best place for snorkeling on Molokai is at the 20-mile marker on the east side of the island. Here you're likely to see sturgeon, trumpetfish and a few green turtles.

Check out **Molokai Fish & Dive** for masks, fins and snorkels. ~ Kaunakakai; 553-5926. **Bill Kapuni's Snorkeland Dive Adventure** rents snorkel equipment and is the only dive outfitter on the island. He leads dives to spots where it's not uncommon to see tiger sharks, hammerhead sharks and countless green turtles. He also teaches PADI classes. ~ 553-9867. **Molokai Action Adventures** offers snorkeling expeditions and leads kayaking trips. ~ Kaunakakai; 558-8184. **Fun Hogs Hawaii** offers kayaking, snorkeling and catamaran excursions. ~ Kaluakoi Hotel and Golf Club; 552-2555.

SAILING

Providing Molokai's only sailing adventure, Molokai Charters operates **Satan's Doll**, a 42-foot sloop that is docked on the wharf in Kaunakakai. Step aboard for sunset cruises, whale-watching tours and snorkeling excursions to Lanai. ~ 553-5852.

FISHING

Depending on the weather, deep-sea fishing charters will take you to various spots that are within ten to twenty miles of Molokai. Here you're likely to catch mahimahi, tuna, marlin and *ono*.

Contact **Alyce C Commercial and Sport Fishing** (558-8377), **Shon-A-Lei II** (553-5242) or **Molokai Action Adventures** (558-8184), all in Kaunakakai.

RIDING STABLES

Molokai Wagon Ride sponsors wagon and saddle tours to scenic and historic sites at Mapulehu on eastern Molokai; this outfit also rents horses with guides. ~ 558-8380. **Molokai Ranch** offers a two-hour horseback ride to a secluded beach on the west end where you stop to kayak, swim and snorkel before heading back. ~ 552-2741.

BIKING

Traffic is light and slow-moving, making Molokai an ideal place for two-wheeling adventurers. The roads are generally good, with some potholes out East End near Halawa Valley. The terrain is mostly flat or gently rolling, with a few steep ascents. Winds are strong and sometimes make for tough going. For mountain bike rentals and excursions, contact **Fun Hogs Hawaii**. ~ Kaluakoi Hotel and Golf Club; 552-2555.

HIKING

Molokai features some splendid country and numerous areas that seem prime for hiking, but few trails have been built or maintained and most private land is off-limits to visitors. Some excellent hiking possibilities, but no official trails, are offered along the beaches described above. Palaau State Park also has several short jaunts to points of interest.

The only lengthy treks lead to the island's rugged north coast. Four valleys—Halawa, Wailau, Pelekunu and Waikolu—cut through the sheer cliffs guarding this windswept shore.

The **Pelekunu Trail** begins several hundred yards beyond the Waikolu Valley Lookout (see the section on "Molokai's Outback"). It is unmaintained and extremely difficult. Traversing Nature Conservancy property, the trail leads to a lookout point and then drops into the valley.

The **Wailau Trail** is another very difficult trail; it takes about 12 hours and passes through some muddy rainforest regions. The trailhead is off Route 450 about 15 miles east of Kaunakakai. The trail extends across nearly the entire island from south to north. Dangers include deep mud and wild boar. To hike it, you must obtain permission from Pearl Petro. Send a self-addressed stamped envelope. ~ P.O. Box 25, Kaunakakai, HI 96748; 558-8113.

The **Kalaupapa Trail** is the easiest and best-maintained trail descending the north *pali*. A trail description is given in the "Kalaupapa" section in this chapter. To hike here you must obtain permission and pay $30 for a mandatory tour of the leper colony. Call Damien Tours for permission and information. ~ 567-6171.

The only valley accessible by car is Halawa. The **Halawa Valley Trail** (which at last report was closed to the public), one of Molokai's prettiest hikes, extends for two miles from the mouth of the valley to the base of Moaula Falls. This 250-foot cascade tumbles down a sheer cliff to a cold mountain pool perfect for swimming. Hipuapua Falls, a sister cascade just a third of a mile north, shoots 500 feet down the *pali*.

The trail is marked near the end of Route 450 a short distance from the beach. There is a parking area, and the attendant will give you information concerning the status of public access to the trail.

▼▼▼▼▼▼▼▼▼▼

Transportation

AIR

When your plane touches down at **Molokai Airport**, you'll realize what a one-canoe island you're visiting. There's a snack bar and adjoining lounge, which seem to open and close all day, plus a few car rental and airline offices. It's seven miles to the main town of Kaunakakai. There's no public transportation available. However, shuttle service can be arranged through some of the hotels, and taxis are available.

The airport is served by several airlines: Hawaiian Airlines carries passengers in turbo prop planes. Aloha Island Air and Molokai Shuttle fly small prop planes and are the most exciting way to reach Molokai. To fly direct from Honolulu to Kalaupapa, try Aloha Island Air, which can always be relied upon for friendly service.

BOAT

If you'd prefer to arrive by boat, Sea Link of Hawaii provides round-trip service from Maui aboard the 118-foot **Maui Princess**. The one-and-a-half-hour cruise provides a unique opportunity to travel between the islands by sea. ~ 553-5736.

CAR RENTALS

The existing companies are: **Dollar Rent A Car** (567-6156, 800-800-4000 from the mainland, 800-342-7398 in Hawaii) and **Budget Rent A Car** (567-6877, 800-451-3600).

JEEP RENTALS

Budget Rent A Car rents jeeps, but requires that you drive them only on paved roads! ~ 567-6877, 800-451-3600. (Be aware that the rental car collision insurance provided by most credit cards does not cover jeeps.)

▼▼▼▼▼▼▼▼▼▼▼▼▼▼▼▼▼▼▼▼▼▼▼▼
Addresses & Phone Numbers

MOLOKAI ISLAND
County Parks and Recreation ~ Kaunakakai; 553-3204
Hawaiian Homelands Department ~ Hoolehua; 567-6104
Weather ~ 552-2477

KAUNAKAKAI
Ambulance ~ 911
Fire Department ~ 911
Library ~ Ala Malama Street; 553-5483
Liquor ~ Molokai Wine and Spirits, Ala Malama Street; 553-5009
Pharmacy and Photo Supply ~ Molokai Drugs, behind the Post
    Office on Ala Malama Street; 553-5790
Police Department ~ 553-5355 or 911
Post Office ~ 120 Ala Malama Street; 553-5845

NINE

Kauai

Seventy miles northwest of Oahu, across a storm-wracked channel that long protected against invaders, lies Kauai. If ever an island deserved to be called a jewel of the sea, this "Garden Isle" is the one. Across Kauai's brief 33-mile expanse lies a spectacular and wildly varied landscape.

Along the north shore is the Hanalei Valley, a lush patchwork of tropical agriculture, and the rugged Na Pali Coast with cliffs rising 2700 feet above the boiling surf. Spanning 14 miles of pristine coastline, the narrow valleys and sheer walls of Na Pali are so impenetrable that a road entirely encircling the island has never been built. Here, among razor-edged spires and flower-choked gorges, the producers of the movie *South Pacific* found their Bali Hai. To the east flows the fabled Wailua River, a sacred area to Hawaiians that today supports a sizable population in the blue-collar towns of Wailua and Kapaa.

Along the south coast stretch the matchless beaches of Poipu, with white sands and an emerald sea that seem drawn from a South Seas vision. It was here in November 1982 that Hurricane Iwa, packing 110-mile-an-hour winds and carrying devastating tidal waves, overwhelmed the island. Ironically, it was also this area that sustained some of the most severe damage when Hurricane Iniki struck in September 1992.

The tourist enclave of Poipu gives way to rustic Hanapepe, an agricultural town asleep since the turn of the century, and Waimea, where in 1778 Captain James Cook became the first Westerner to tread Hawaiian soil. In Kauai's arid southwestern corner, where palm trees surrender to cactus plants, snow-white beaches sweep for miles along Barking Sands and Polihale.

In the island's center, Mount Waialeale rises 5148 feet (Mount Kawaikini at 5243 feet is the island's tallest peak) to trap a continuous stream of dark-bellied clouds that spill more than 450 inches of rain annually, making this gloomy peak the wettest spot on earth and creating the headwaters for the richest river system in all Hawaii—the Hanapepe, Hanalei, Wailua and Waimea rivers. Also draining Waialeale is the Alakai Swamp, a wilderness bog that covers 30 square miles of the island's interior. Yet to the west, just a thunderstorm away, lies a barren landscape seemingly borrowed from Arizona and featuring the 2857-foot-deep Waimea Canyon, the Grand Canyon of the Pacific.

From Lihue, Kauai's largest and most important city, Route 50 (Kaumualii Highway) travels to the south while Route 56 (Kuhio Highway) heads along the north shore. Another highway climbs past Waimea Canyon into the mountainous interior.

Papayas, taro and bananas grow in lush profusion along these roads, and marijuana is grown deep in the hills and narrow valleys, but sugar is still Kauai's most significant crop. Tourism has overtaken agriculture in the Kauai economy and is becoming increasingly vital to the island's 56,000 population. The tourist industry grew steadily until the 1992 hurricane, and the ominous construction of condos in Poipu and Princeville threatened to turn Kauai into the Maui of the 1990s. But Iniki slowed the pace considerably and seriously damaged an economy that is suffering in other areas as well.

Particularly disconcerting is the decline of the sugar industry, which is intensifying demands to replace agricultural income with tourist dollars. But the Garden Isle still offers hidden beaches and remote valleys to any traveler possessing a native's sensibility. And even though sugar is in retreat, some cane fields are still evident across most of the island. A few years ago, Kauai provided a window on 19th-century life, when sugar was king. Deep-green stalks covered the landscape in every direction, edging from the lip of the ocean to the foot of the mountains. But two major hurricanes and a waning industry have led to many cane fields being left fallow or converted to coffee, sunflowers and corn.

Nevertheless, island sugar mills are still redolent with the cloyingly sweet smell of cane, and mammoth cane trucks, sugar stalks protruding like bristles from a wild boar, continue to charge down dusty roads. Depending on the phase of the growing cycle, visitors pass fields crowded with mature cane, tall as Midwest corn, or deep-red earth planted with rows of seedlings. In the evening, when harvested cane is set afire, black smoke billows from deep within the fields.

Historically, Kauai is Hawaii's premier island—the first to be created geologically and the first "discovered" by white men. It was here that Madame Pele, goddess of volcanoes, initially tried to make her home. Perhaps because of the island's moist, tropical climate, she failed to find a place dry enough to start her fire and left in frustration for the islands to the southeast.

Formed by a single volcano that became extinct about six million years ago, Kauai is believed by some anthropologists to be the original island populated by Polynesians. After Captain Cook arrived in 1778, explorers continued to visit the island periodically. Ten years later, settlers began to arrive, and in 1820 the first missionaries landed in the company of Prince George, son of Kauai's King Kaumualii. By 1835, the Koloa sugar plantation was founded, becoming the first successful sugar mill in Hawaii.

Kauai was the site not only of the original but the anomalous, as well. In 1817, George Scheffer, a Prussian adventurer representing Czar Nicholas of Russia, built a fort in Waimea. He soon lost the support of both the Czar and Kauai's King Kaumualii, but left as his legacy the stone ruins of Russia's imperialist effort.

Kauai was the only island not conquered by Kamehameha the Great when he established the Hawaiian kingdom. Thwarted twice in his attempts to land an attack force—once in 1796 when high seas prevented an invasion from Oahu and again in 1802 when his battle-ready army was suddenly ravaged by disease—he finally won over Kaumualii by diplomacy in 1810.

But Kauai's most fascinating history is told by mythmakers recounting tales of the *Menehunes*, the Hobbits of the Pacific. These miniature forest people labored like giants to create awesome structures. Mysterious ruins such as the Menehune Fishpond outside Lihue reputedly date back before the Polynesians and are attributed by the mythically inclined to an earlier, unknown race. Supernaturally strong and very industrious, the *Menehunes* worked only at night, completing each project by dawn or else leaving it forever unfinished. Several times they made so much noise in their strenuous laboring that they frightened birds as far away as Oahu.

They were a merry, gentle people with ugly red faces and big eyes set beneath long eyebrows. Two to three feet tall, each practiced a trade in which he was a master. They inhabited caves, hollow logs and banana-leaf huts, and eventually grew to a population of 500,000 adults.

Some say the *Menehunes* came from the lost continent of Mu, which stretched across Polynesia to Fiji before it was swallowed by floods. Where they finally traveled to is less certain. After the Polynesians settled Kauai, the *Menehune* king, concerned that his people were intermarrying with an alien race, ordered the *Menehunes* to leave the island. But many, unwilling to depart so luxurious a home, hid in the forests. There, near hiking trails and remote campsites, you may see them even today.

▼▼▼▼▼▼▼▼▼
Lihue Area

Unappealing in appearance, Lihue sits at the crossroads between the tropical regions of the north and the sunsplashed beaches to the south. So a visit to Lihue is inevitable. Commercial and civic center of the island, the town is an odd amalgam of contemporary Hawaii and traditional plantation life. The sugar mill at the edge of town, with its aging conveyor belts and twin smoke stacks, is still a vital element in the landscape. A portion of the 11,000 population continues to live in woodframe plantation houses, and cane fields surround the town. But the airport here is an international landing strip that has grown considerably during the past two decades and Lihue possesses Kauai's main port, Nawiliwili Harbor. Lihue also boasts the island's largest concentration of restaurants and shopping centers.

SIGHTS   Among the attractions you will find is the **Kauai Museum**, a two-building complex rich in Hawaiiana. This is a prime spot to learn about the history, culture and natural history of the island. The main building focuses on Hawaiian heritage with its displays of feather leis and ancient calabashes. In the adjacent exhibition, Kauai's natural history unfolds and 19th-century plantation life is revealed in a collection of old photographs. Closed Sunday. Admission. ~ 4428 Rice Street, Lihue; 245-6931.

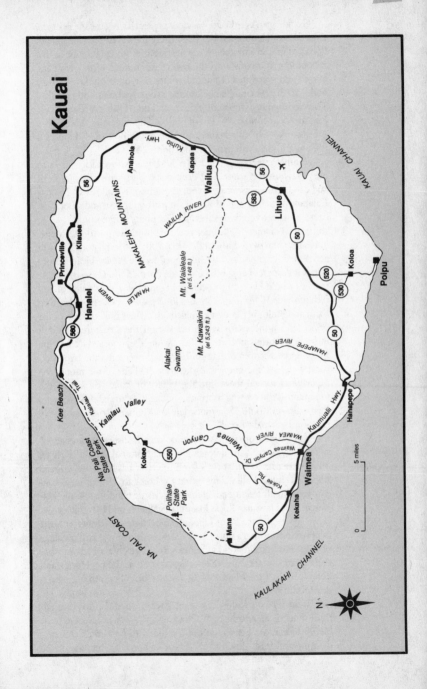

Providing an even wider window on Kauai's sugar-cane heritage, **Grove Farm Homestead** is a beautifully preserved 80-acre spread. Founded in 1864 by the son of missionaries, the plantation is like an outdoor museum with the main house, farm office, workers' homes and a private cottage still intact. Surrounding these tinroof buildings are banana patches, grape arbors, gardens and pastures. Two-hour guided tours of this fascinating facility are available (usually on Monday, Wednesday and Thursday) by reservation. Admission. ~ Call in advance or write to P.O. Box 1631, Lihue, HI 96766, and they will provide directions; 245-3202.

Another interesting side trip from Lihue is down Rice Street to busy **Nawiliwili Harbor**. This deep-water port, with its cruise ships and cargo vessels, is a major transit point for island sugar. Nearby **Kalapaki Beach** is one of Kauai's most popular strands, both because of its proximity to Lihue and its pretty white sands.

From Nawiliwili Harbor, you can continue on to the **Mene-hune** (or **Alakoko**) **Fishpond**. This 900-foot-long pond, spread across a valley floor and backdropped by the Hoary Head Mountain Range, dates back well before the Polynesians. Or so the myth-makers would like you to believe. Legend has it that a line of lep-rechaun-like *Menehunes* 25 miles long passed rocks from hand to hand and built the pond in a single night. Their only request of the prince and princess for whom they built the structure was that these two mortals not watch them while they worked. When the *Menehunes* discovered that curiosity had overcome the two, who were watching the midget workers by the light of the moon, the *Menehunes* turned them into the pillars of stone you see on the mountainside above the fishpond. ~ Take Rice Street to Nawiliwili, then right on Route 58, a quick left on Niumalu Road and finally right on Hulemalu Road.

HIDDEN ►

Also visible from the vista overlooking the fishpond, and accessible to kayakers, is the adjoining **Huleia National Wildlife Refuge**, a 238-acre preserve that rises from the river basin up the wooded slopes of Huleia Valley. This estuary is home to 31 bird species including four different endangered species of waterbirds—the Hawaiian stilt, Hawaiian duck, Hawaiian gallinule and Hawaiian coot.

A short distance from Lihue, Kuhio Highway (Route 56), the main road to Kauai's north shore, descends into the rustic village of **Kapaia**. Sagging wood structures and a gulch choked with banana plants mark this valley. On the right, **Lihue Hongwanji Temple**, one of the island's oldest, smiles from beneath a modern-day facelift.

To the left, off Kuhio Highway, Maalo Road threads through three miles of sugar cane to **Wailua Falls**. These twin cascades tumble 80 feet into a heavenly pool fringed with *hala* trees. A steep, difficult trail leads down to the luxurious pool at the base of the falls; or if you're not that ambitious, a more easily accessible pool lies just a couple hundred yards past the falls.

Follow Kuhio Highway and you'll arrive in **Hanamaulu**, an old plantation town where falsefront stores and tinroof houses line the roadway.

Or you can head a mile-and-a-half southwest from Lihue on Kaumualii Highway (Route 50) to **Kilohana** for a view of the luxurious side of island life. This 16,000-square-foot Tudor mansion was once home to the Wilcoxes, one of the island's most prominent families. Today, the 1935 house serves as a center for arts-and-crafts shops and museum displays, and the 35 surrounding acres

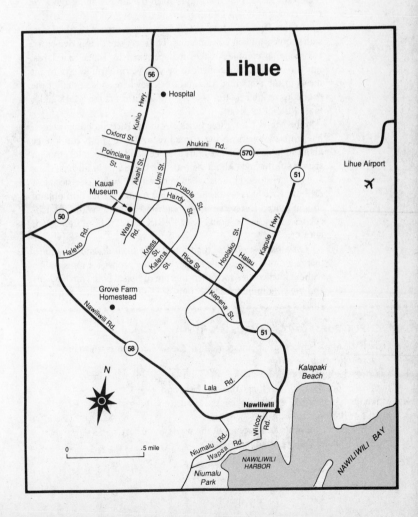

are devoted to a re-creation of traditional plantation life. Wander down the "coral path" and you'll pass a tropical garden and a succession of corrugated-roof houses. Papaya, banana and avocado trees line the route and roosters crow in the distance. Directly behind the plantation grounds, fields of sugar cane roll to the foothills of the mountains. Carriages pulled by Clydesdales tour the grounds and wagon tours lead out into the cane fields. ~ Kaumualii Highway; 245-5608.

LODGING   If you are in search of budget-priced lodging facilities, there are few places in all Hawaii as inviting as Lihue. Three low-cost establishments are located just two miles from the airport and a block or two from downtown Lihue.

At the **Tip Top Motel** you'll find trim rooms with tile floors, stall showers and air conditioning. The sheer size of this two-story, two-building complex makes it impersonal by Kauai standards, but I found the management to be very warm. You'll have to eat meals in the adjoining restaurant or elsewhere, since none of the rooms have kitchenettes. ~ 3173 Akahi Street, Lihue; 245-2333, fax 246-8988. BUDGET.

The **Motel Lani**, three blocks from the Rice Shopping Center, has ten cozy rooms facing a small patio where guests can lounge about in lawn chairs. The units are clean and comfortable, though sparsely furnished. About half are air conditioned; all have fans and refrigerators. This place has a noisy lobby (with television) just off busy Rice Street. Rooms with kitchenettes are hard to obtain, so you'll need to reserve these in advance. Rooms without kitchenettes are easier to book. ~ 4240 Rice Street, Lihue; 245-2965. BUDGET.

On a back street less than a half-mile from downtown Lihue, there's a motel called **Hale Lihue**. Here the proprietor rents rooms without kitchenettes and others that are equipped both with kitchens and air conditioning. The rooms are simply furnished and well-

✔ **CHECK THESE OUT—UNIQUE SIGHTS**

- Gaze back into 19th-century plantation life at **Grove Farm Homestead**, an 80-acre outdoor museum. *page 368*
- Discover the myth of the *Menehunes*, a Hobbit-like people who single-handedly built the 900-foot-long **Alakoko Fishpond**. *page 368*
- Make the beach speak, while enjoying the coral reefs and surfing breaks at **Barking Sands**. *pages 388, 396*
- View one of the most beautiful scenes in the world (no exaggeration!) at **Hanalei Valley Lookout**. *page 412*

kept. There's a lobby with television plus a tiny garden in the front yard. ~ 2931 Kalena Street, Lihue; 245-2751. BUDGET.

Conveniently situated across the street from Nawiliwili Park is the **Garden Island Inn**. You'll find it near the corner of Waapa Road and Wilcox Road, a short stroll from Kalapaki Beach. Each room is light and airy with comfortable furnishings, attractive appointments and overhead fans. You'll hear occasional noise from passing trucks and planes. Children are welcome, and several of the large rooms are sufficiently spacious for families. All of the fully equipped units have refrigerators, wet bars and microwave ovens. The grounds are trimly landscaped and highlighted by a koi pond in which several dozen carp flash their colors. ~ 3445 Wilcox Road, Lihue; 245-7227, 800-648-0154. MODERATE.

Colony's Banyan Harbor Resort, a collection of woodframe buildings across a busy street from Nawiliwili Harbor, has one- and two-bedroom condominiums with ocean and garden views. Most of the 148 units here are leased by the month, but a handful rent by the night. ~ 3411 Wilcox Road, Lihue; 245-7333, 800-422-6926, fax 246-4776. MODERATE TO DELUXE.

DINING

◄ HIDDEN

For the money, the best breakfast spot on the island is **Ma's Family**. This nondescript café makes up in clientele what it lacks in physical beauty. Early in the morning the place is crowded with locals on their way to the cane fields. In the world of breakfasts, this is the bargain basement. Or if you want to go Hawaiian at lunch, order a *laulau*, poi and *lomi* salmon dish. No dinner. ~ 4277 Halenani Street, Lihue; 245-3142. BUDGET.

What Ma's is to breakfast, **Hamura Saimin** is to lunch and dinner. It's just around the corner, so you're liable to see the same faces lining Hamura's curving counter. When I ate there the place was packed. I had the *"saimin* special," a combination of noodles, won tons, eggs, meat, onion, vegetables and fish cake in a delicious broth. ~ 2956 Kress Street, Lihue; 245-3271. BUDGET.

Yokozuna Ramen serves delicious lunches and dinners. Ramen, miso soup and various Japanese dishes are among the offerings. ~ Kuhio Highway, across from McDonald's; 246-1008. BUDGET.

Want to go Japanese? Try **Restaurant Kiibo**. The place used to be just a noodle house, but a remodeling job has changed the interior into a contemporary-style restaurant with a tatami room. The cuisine has also evolved. Today, you'll find the menu filled with yakitori, tempura and tofu dishes, as well as sushi and sashimi. ~ 2991 Umi Street, Lihue; 245-2650. MODERATE.

The **Lihue Barbeque Inn** offers Asian dishes as well as all-American meals. Breakfasts at this comfortable establishment are pretty standard; the lunch menu includes salads, soups, sandwiches, hamburgers and a daily special that often features teriyaki and curry dishes; at dinner, there's steak, lobster, shrimp tempura and scampi. Closed Sunday. ~ 2982 Kress Street, Lihue; 245-2921. MODERATE.

A favorite among tourists is the **Tip Top Café and Bakery**. Visitors can take their pick from any in a succession of booths in this large and impersonal eatery. Breakfasts are inexpensive (and the macadamia nut pancakes are delicious). Lunch entrées are not very imaginative and have received negative reviews from readers. The well-known bakery serves macadamia nut cookies, the house specialty. No dinner. Closed Monday. ~ 3173 Akahi Street, Lihue; 245-2333. BUDGET.

For good food at modest prices, Lihue is a prime spot. This is the center of most island business, so it contains numerous restaurants that cater largely to local folks.

If you're in Nawiliwili, check out **The Beach Hut**. They offer a full breakfast menu; for lunch and dinner, there are hamburgers, sandwiches and salads. Order at the window and dine upstairs on a deck overlooking the water. ~ 3474 Rice Street, Nawiliwili; 246-6330. BUDGET.

Nearby and ever popular, the **Kauai Chop Suey** features an ample Cantonese menu. Closed Monday. ~ 3501 Rice Street, Nawiliwili; 245-8790. MODERATE.

The Pacific Ocean Plaza promises several good restaurants, including **Café Portofino**, a bright and attractive Italian restaurant with a partial ocean view. Comfortably furnished and nicely decorated, it features several pasta dishes as well as house specialties like stuffed calamari, scampi, eggplant parmigiana and sautéed rabbit. There's also an espresso bar. ~ 3501 Rice Street, Nawiliwili; 245-2121. MODERATE TO DELUXE.

J. J.'s Broiler is widely known for its "Slavonic steak," a tenderloin that's broiled, then sliced thin and basted with a wine, butter and garlic sauce. This family-style eatery offers standard steak dishes, seafood platters and a salad bar, and enjoys a waterfront location overlooking Kalapaki Beach. With its windswept terrace and open-air dining room, it has a sunny Southern California ambience. ~ 3416 Rice Street, Nawiliwili; 246-4422. DELUXE.

If it's atmosphere and a taste of the Orient you're after, reserve a tea room at the **Hanamaulu Café**. My favorite is the garden room overlooking a rock-bound pond filled with carp. Lunch and dinner are the same here, with an excellent selection of Japanese and Chinese dishes. There's also a sushi bar at night. Children's portions are available. Closed Monday. ~ Kuhio Highway, Hanamaulu; 245-2511. MODERATE.

Take a plantation manor, add a flowering garden, and you have the setting for **Gaylord's**. Elevating patio dining to a high art, this alfresco restaurant looks out on the spacious lawns and spreading trees of Kilohana plantation. The menu features fresh island fish, shrimp, duck with juniper berry sauce and barbecued baby back ribs, in addition to exotic daily specials. A rare combination of Old

and percolate up into the sand. Both are excellent for sunbathing and swimming. Snorkeling is very good, and bodysurfers frequent Running Waters Beach. Since both beaches are pretty close to civilization, I don't recommend camping at either beach. There are no facilities here. ~ Take the road leading through the Marriott Kauai property in Nawiliwili. Follow this road to the golf course clubhouse. Park and walk across the golf course in a direction several degrees to the right of the lighthouse. The smaller beach can be reached by walking from Running Water Beach toward the lighthouse for about three-tenths of a mile.

HANAMAULU BEACH PARK 🏊 ⚓ Here's an idyllic park nestled in Hanamaulu Bay and crowded with ironwood and coconut trees. The beach is a narrow corridor of sand at the head of Hanamaulu Bay. The bay is well-protected, affording excellent swimming, but the water is usually murky so there is not much snorkeling. I found this a great place for picnicking and shell collecting. Anglers can expect to hook bonefish, mullet and big-eyed scad. A picnic area, restrooms, showers and a playground are some of the facilities here; it's one mile to the restaurants and the small market in Hanamaulu. ~ Take Kuhio Highway to Hanamaulu, then turn down the road leading to the bay.

▲ Needles from the ironwood trees make a natural bed at this lovely site. Tent and trailer camping; county permit required.

All during the 1980s and early 1990s, the Poipu Beach region represented the fastest-growing tourist destination on Kauai. With the construction of new condominiums and the opening of the Hyatt Regency Kauai in 1991, it was one of the most popular spots in the entire state. However, Hurricane Iniki slowed the pace of development, and has significantly diminished Poipu's previous pattern of steady growth. Some of the hotels along the beach are still closed for reconstruction after Hurricane Iniki: The Sheraton Kauai, for example, isn't scheduled to reopen until late 1997.

▼▼▼▼▼▼▼▼▼
Poipu Area

What you will find in this warm, dry, sunny southeastern corner is a prime example of everyone's favorite combination—the old and the new. The traditional comes in the form of Koloa town, site of Hawaii's first successful sugar mill, a 19th-century plantation town that has been refurbished in tropical colors. For the modern, you need look only a couple miles down the road to Poipu, a series of scalloped beaches that has become action central for real estate developers.

Anchoring these enclaves to the east is Puuhi Mount, scene of the last volcanic eruption on Kauai. To the north rises the Hoary Head Range, a wall of wooded mountains that divides the district from the Huleia Valley and Lihue. Everywhere else you'll find fields lying fallow or acres that are still planted with sugar.

Without doubt, you'll want to drive out from Lihue along Kaumualii Highway (Route 50) to explore the south coast. Along the way, if you possess a Rorschach-test imagination, you'll see **Queen Victoria's Profile** etched in the Hoary Head Range. (Need a helping eye? Watch for the Hawaii Visitors Bureau sign on the side of the highway.)

When you turn south toward Poipu on Maluhia Road (Route 520), you won't need a road sign to find what locals refer to as **Tree Tunnel**, an arcade of towering swamp mahogany trees that forms a shadowy tunnel en route to the timeworn town of **Koloa**. The remains of the original sugar plantation stand in an unassuming pile on the right side of the road as you enter town; a plaque near this old chimney commemorates the birth of Hawaii's sugar industry, a business that dominated life in the islands throughout most of the 19th century. A sugar mill continues to operate just outside town and Koloa still consists primarily of company-town houses and humble churches surrounded by fields of sugar cane. But the main street was gentrified during the 1980s as tropical-colored paints were added to the old woodframe and falsefront town center. The tiny **Koloa History Center**, located in the freshly refurbished Old Koloa Town Mall, provides a brief introduction to the history of the area in the form of artifacts from the old plantation days. ~ Koloa Road, Koloa.

If a one-word association test were applied to **Poipu**, the word would be "beach." There really is no town here, just a skein of hotels, condominiums and stores built along a series of white-sand beaches. Nevertheless, this is Kauai's premier playground, a sunsoaked realm that promises good weather and good times. Scene of devastating damage during the 1982 Hurricane Iwa and 1992 Hurricane Iniki, Poipu continues to emerge phoenix-like from every natural setback. Today, many of the resort facilities have been entirely rebuilt, though several hotels still remain in ruins.

While civilization has encroached to the very side of the sea, nature continues to display some of its gentle wonders along the colorful reefs and pearly sands. Most remarkable of all is **Spouting Horn** (end of Lawai Road), an underwater lava tube with an opening along the shore. Surf crashing through the tube dramatically transforms this blowhole into a miniature Old Faithful. Try to time your visit with the high tide when the spumes from Spouting Horn reach their greatest heights. The mournful sounds issuing from the blowhole are said to be the plaintive cries of a legendary lizard or *moo*. It seems that he was returning from another island where he had been told of the death of his two sisters. Blinded by tears he missed his landing and was swept into the blowhole. (You should also look around at this intriguing coastline, which is covered by coral outcroppings and tidepools and is the location of several archaeological sites.)

One place for people wanting to rough it or to establish a base camp is **Kahili Mountain Park,** run by the Seventh Day Adventist Church. Facing the Hoary Head Range and backdropped by Kahili Mountain, this 197-acre domain offers an easy compromise between hoteling and camping. The one- and two-bedroom cabins come equipped with lanai and private bathroom, plus a funky kitchenette. Cooking utensils and bed linens are provided. Furnishings seem a bit spartan: The floors are uncarpeted and the sole decoration is the surrounding mountains. Thank God for nature. At this rustic resort you can rope-swing into the swimming pond or hike the nearby trails. The facilities include cabinettes with shared baths as well as the cabins. Both types of facilities should be reserved several months in advance. ~ Write to Kahili Mountain Park, P.O. Box 298, Koloa, Kauai, HI 96756. The park is three miles from Koloa town and about one mile off Kaumualii Highway; 742-9921. BUDGET.

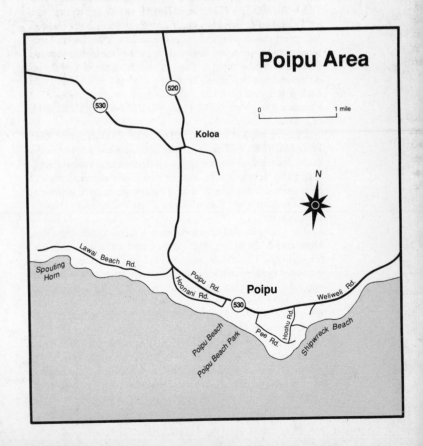

HIDDEN ▶   Once upon a time the island's best vacation spot was the **Garden Isle Cottages**. That was before the 1982 hurricane flattened the complex's beachfront cottages. Still, there are some pretty one- and two-bedroom cottages left, all located on a small bluff overlooking the ocean. These hideaways are decorated with artistic flair: Oil paintings and woven pieces adorn the walls, the furnishings are rattan and the kitchens are modern. Overlooking Poipu Beach from the rim of a volcano are two additional units with 360-degree ocean and mountain views. Moderate to deluxe for the studios and one-bedrooms, ultra-deluxe for the two-bedroom cottages. There is usually a two-night minimum stay. ~ 2666 Puuholo Road, Koloa; 742-6717, 800-742-6711. MODERATE TO ULTRA-DELUXE.

Similarly, **Koloa Landing Cottages** in Poipu offers a studio, a one-bedroom unit, and three cottages, one of which sleeps up to six. These are attractive facilities with kitchens. With a garden setting and family atmosphere, they evoke a comfortable sense of familiarity. Three-night minimum. ~ 2704-B Hoonani Road, Poipu; 742-1470, 800-779-8773, fax 332-9584. MODERATE TO DELUXE.

Poipu Bed & Breakfast Inn is a lovely woodframe house with four guest rooms. The decor is dominated by white wicker furniture and merry-go-round horses (there's one in the living room and in three of the bedrooms). You can also expect wall-to-wall carpeting and overhead fans. There are small porches in front and back plus a yard complete with garden and mango tree. ~ 2720 Hoonani Road, Poipu; 742-1146, 800-227-6478, fax 742-6843. DELUXE TO ULTRA-DELUXE.

Another bed and breakfast run by the same people is the **Ocean Front Inn**. This five-bedroom house sits across the street from the ocean. It's trimly decorated and has a large front porch and backyard patio. Several rooms have private lanais and jacuzzis, and each room comes equipped with a microwave and refrigerator. ~ 2650 Hoonani Road, Poipu; 742-1146, fax 742-6843. DELUXE TO ULTRA-DELUXE.

For a place located right on the water, there's **Gloria's Spouting Horn Bed & Breakfast**. Rebuilt since Hurricane Iniki, this custom-designed beachhouse features three oceanfront guest rooms decorated in American oak and English walnut antiques. Open and airy, Gloria's is a place where you can relax on the lanai that sits just above the waves, lie in a hammock or go surfing outside your front door. ~ 4464 Lawai Beach Road, Poipu; phone/fax 742-6995. ULTRA-DELUXE.

It would be an elastic stretch of the imagination to call the **Hyatt Regency Kauai** a hidden destination. This *is*, after all, a Hyatt Regency—with over 600 guest rooms, two pools, five restaurants, five lounges and several acres of manmade lagoons. But before this luxury resort was built, the beach on which it sits was one of the great hidden locales on Kauai. Shipwreck Beach is still a magnificent crescent of white sand, and the Hyatt Regency Kauai, back-dropped by cane fields and deep-green mountains, enjoys some of the seclusion for which Shipwreck was renowned. With its wood-paneled lobby, atrium garden and plush guest rooms, it is one of the prettiest hotels in Hawaii. ~ 1571 Poipu Road, Poipu; 742-1234, fax 742-6229. ULTRA-DELUXE.

One of the most unique condos around is **Poipu Crater Resort**. Located just 600 yards from the beach, it's also one of the best deals. This entire 30-unit facility rests in the caldera of an extinct volcano. The accommodations are contained in attractive woodframe houses; all are two-bedroom condos and rent for about $100, depending on length of stay. Pool, tennis courts, sauna, barbecue. ~ Hoohu Road, Poipu; 742-7400, 800-367-8020, fax 742-9121.

CONDOS

◀ *HIDDEN*

Poipu Kai Resort consists of a succession of separate buildings spread around a spacious lawn. There are six pools and nine tennis courts on the property plus a restaurant, jacuzzi and barbecues. It's across the street from Brennecke Beach. One-bedroom condos start at around $125 ($110 from April 1 to December 21). ~ 2827 Poipu Road, Poipu; 742-7400, 800-367-8020, fax 742-9121.

Poipu Shores is a small (39 unit) complex right on the ocean with a swimming pool so close to the water the waves seem poised to break across it. One-bedroom units start at $170 ($150 off-season). ~ 1775 Pee Road, Poipu; 742-7700.

At **Sunset Kahili Condominiums** one-bedroom apartments are $90 to $100 double; two bedrooms will run $120 to $130 for one to four people. Some units have ocean views. Three-night minimum. ~ 1763 Pee Road, Poipu; 742-1691, 800-827-6478, fax 742-6058.

Poipu Kapili, neatly situated a short stroll from Poipu Beach, has one- and two-bedroom oceanview condos from $150. It's a 60-

✦✦

✔ **CHECK THESE OUT—UNIQUE LODGING**

- *Budget:* Light the wood-burning stove, survey the surrounding forest and settle in at 5000-foot high **Kokee Lodge Cabins**. *page 389*
- *Moderate:* Sleep in a yurt and while away the days in a hammock and jacuzzi at the secluded **Keapana Center Bed and Breakfast**. *page 402*
- *Deluxe:* Relax in your own house on a bluff overlooking the ocean at **Garden Isle Cottages**. *page 378*
- *Ultra-deluxe:* Roost on a clifftop near a white-sand beach, checker-board valley and misty mountains at **Princeville Resort**. *page 414*

Budget: under $50 Moderate: $50–$90 Deluxe: $90–$120 Ultra-deluxe: over $120

unit complex with pool and tennis courts. ~ 2221 Kapili Road, Poipu; 742-6449, 800-443-7714, fax 742-9162.

Out on the road to Spouting Horn, **Lawai Beach Resort**, a large complex located across the street from the ocean, has one-bedroom units starting at $235 ($210 off-season). Two-bedroom units start at $300 ($290 off-season). There are three pools plus tennis courts and spas. ~ 5017 Lawai Road, Koloa; 742-9581, fax 742-7981.

At nearby **Kuhio Shores**, one-bedroom apartments are $89 for one to four people; two bedrooms, two baths, cost $99 for one to six people. On the shore, but lacking a beach. There's a one-week minimum. ~ 5050 Lawai Road, Poipu; 742-6120, 800-325-6423, fax 245-9337.

The best way to shop for value and location among Poipu condos is to contact one of the local rental agencies. They include **Poipu Beach Resort Association** at 2240 Hoonani Road in Koloa (742-7444, fax 742-7887), **Grantham Resorts** at 2721 Poipu Road in Poipu (742-7220, 800-325-5701, fax 742-9001) and **R & R Realty & Rentals, Inc.** at 1661 Pee Road in Poipu (742-7555, 800-367-8022, fax 742-1559). Talk to these agencies at length. Ask them about the best deals they have to offer in the season you're going. If interested, you can also ask about packages that include rental cars.

DINING

"Snack bar" comes closer to describing the low-priced dining facilities here than "restaurant." This lovely beach area hosts no full-sized budget restaurants. In Koloa town, two miles from Poipu, there's the **Kauai Kitchens**, a snack bar next to the Big Save Market. No dinner. ~ Koloa Road, Koloa; 742-1712. BUDGET.

Also in Koloa, you might consider **Koloa Broiler**. Nothing fancy; it's a bright, airy café with a broil-your-own kitchen and adjoining bar. There's steak, beef kabob, mahimahi, chicken, fresh island fish, barbecue baby-back pork ribs and hamburger to choose from. Of course, the quality of the food depends on your own culinary abilities; this could prove to be Kauai's best (or worst) restaurant. The one thing you can bank on is that this family-style establishment will transform dining from a spectator sport to a way of meeting fellow chefs. ~ 5412 Koloa Road, Koloa; 742-9122. MODERATE.

A CONDO WITH SOUL

A particularly well-known destination, **Kiahuna Plantation** is a 35-acre beachfront spread. This complex of resort condominiums is landscaped with lily ponds, lagoon and a spectacular cactus garden. The units are housed in attractive plantation-style structures, which dot the resort's rolling lawns. ~ 2253 Poipu Road, Poipu; 742-6411, 800-462-6262, fax 742-9051. ULTRA-DELUXE.

The Japanese are represented in tiny Koloa town by **Taisho Restaurant,** a simple and appealing dining spot. There are two small dining areas, decorated in traditional Asian fashion, and a full Japanese menu. Dinner only. ~ 5470 Koloa Road, Koloa; 742-1838. MODERATE.

Budget-priced cafés in Poipu are rare as unicorns. The best place to look for a quick, inexpensive meal is in the Poipu Shopping Village on Poipu Road. Here you'll find takeout stands dispensing sub sandwiches and other nutritious items. The **La Griglia Italian Grill** offers patio dining and a complete menu. Entrées include manicotti, eggplant parmesan, spinach lasagna and angelhair pasta with puttanesca sauce. They also serve pizza, hamburgers and a half-dozen different salads. ~ 2360 Kiahuna Plantation Drive, Koloa; 742-2147. BUDGET.

Also in the Poipu shopping Village is **Keoki's Paradise,** a beautiful patio-style restaurant centered around a tropical garden and pond. They feature a steak-and-seafood menu. The setting alone makes it worth a visit. ~ 2360 Kiahuna Drive, Koloa; 742-7534. MODERATE TO DELUXE.

Overlooking Poipu Beach is **Brennecke's Beach Broiler.** Downstairs at this two-level dining spot you'll find a budget-priced deli serving sandwiches. The upper deck is occupied by an open-air restaurant that serves appetizers and lunch from noon to 4 p.m. daily, then stokes the *kiawe* broiler for dinner selections that include fresh fish dishes, steak, chicken and seafood kabob. There's also pasta. ~ Hoone Road, Koloa; 742-7588. MODERATE TO DELUXE.

Two of Hawaii's most famous chefs have restaurants in Poipu. Jean-Marie Josselin, who cut his culinary teeth on A Pacific Café in Kapaa, opened **Beach House Restaurant,** an oceanfront dining room on the road to Spouting Horn. This is Hawaii regional cuisine with a tip of the toque to the Mediterranean. Start with steamed clams in sherry roasted garlic broth or calamari tapas. Main courses include wild mushroom penne with shrimp and mussels, braised lamb shank with gnocchi and sea scallops fettuccine. Dinner only. ~ 5022 Lawai Road, Koloa; 742-1424. DELUXE.

It seems like everywhere you go in Hawaii these days, Roy Yamaguchi has a restaurant. On Kauai it is **Roy's Poipu Bar & Grill,** an informal dining room with the kitchen behind a glass partition. The menu is a Pacific Rim sampler, a mix of Hawaiian and Asian dishes. You can order ginger-seared mahimahi, hibachi-style salmon, *kiawe*-grilled ribeye steak or an *imu*-baked pizza. Or at least that's what was on the ever-changing menu last time I was in. In any case, it's hard to go wrong. Dinner only. ~ Poipu Shopping Village, 2360 Kiahuna Plantation Drive, Koloa; 742-5000. DELUXE.

The House of Seafood is situated among a cluster of condominiums and overlooks a set of tennis courts. That should tell you something about this traditional, white-tablecloth dining room.

And even more about the surf-and-turf cuisine. We're talking filet mignon and lobster, filet mignon and fish, filet mignon and scampi, filet mignon and crab legs. Or, if combinations are not your cup of tea, there's steak dijon, medallions cognac, coquilles St. Jacques and bouillabaisse. Dinner only. ~ 1941 Poipu Road, Poipu; 742-6433. DELUXE TO ULTRA-DELUXE.

The Hyatt Regency Kauai, located at 1571 Poipu Road in Poipu (742-1234), is home to three recommended restaurants. The signature restaurant here is **Dondero's**, a fashionable Italian dining spot. Here you can begin with carpaccio or *prosciutto con melone*, progress to minestrone or a pomodoro salad, then get serious with a list of entrées that includes cioppino, shrimp wrapped in pancetta, veal scallopine, sautéed scallops and lamb chops. Each week a different region of Italy is reflected in the menu's changing specialties. Festive and original, it's a solid choice for a special meal. Dinner only. ULTRA-DELUXE.

Somewhat less expensive is the Hyatt Regency's **Ilima Terrace**, where you can dine beside a koi pond and listen to the tumble of waterfalls. The decor is plantation style and the menu ranges from barbecue to prime rib to island seafood. Informal in atmosphere, this open-air dining room serves sandwiches and light fare as well as more expensive entrées and buffet spreads. ~ MODERATE TO DELUXE.

The Hyatt Regency's most imaginative restaurant is without doubt **Tidepools**. The theme is grass-shack Polynesia, with each of the several dining rooms resembling a classic *hale*. Set in a quiet lagoon and graced with classic Hawaiian sunsets, it's a great place to dine. The offerings are a mix of fresh island fish, lamb and beef, as well as Japanese dishes like sukiyaki. ~ ULTRA-DELUXE.

GROCERIES   There's a **Big Save Market** which includes a dry goods section and is definitely the place to shop on the way to Poipu Beach. ~ Koloa Road, Koloa; 742-1614.

BARTERING OVER THE BLOWHOLE

My favorite shopping spot around Poipu has always been at the **Spouting Horn**. Here, next to the parking lot that serves visitors to the blowhole, local merchants set up tables to sell their wares. You're liable to find coral and puka shell necklaces, trident shell trumpets, rare Niihau shell necklaces and some marvelous mother-of-pearl pieces. You are free to barter, of course, though the prices are pretty good to begin with. If you're interested in jewelry, and want to meet local artisans, this is an intriguing spot. ~ End of Lawai Road, Poipu.

Also popular with local shoppers is **Sueoka Store**, a classic old grocery store right in the center of town. ~ Koloa Road, Koloa; 742-1611.

If you're already soaking up the sun at Poipu, you have two grocery options. **Brennecke's Mini-Deli** is conveniently situated across the street from Poipu Beach Park. This mom-and-pop business has liquor, cold drinks and a limited selection of groceries. ~ Hoone Road, Poipu; 742-1582.

To increase your choices and decrease your food bill, head up Poipu Road to **Kukuiula Store**. This market has prices nearly competitive with Big Save. ~ Poipu and Lawai roads, Poipu; 742-1601.

SHOPPING

On the way to Poipu, the former plantation town of Koloa supports a cluster of shops as well as a miniature mall. Several clothing stores line Koloa Road. The mall, called **Old Koloa Town** (even though it was totally overhauled in the 1980s), houses a string of small jewelry stores, a T-shirt shop and a photo studio. ~ Koloa Road, Koloa.

Bougainvilla has hand-painted clothing and collectible jewelry. ~ 5492 Koloa Road, Koloa; 742-9232.

The original store in Hanapepe proved so popular that **Kauai Fine Arts** opened another shop in Koloa. While I prefer the first store, this one also has a fascinating collection of antique maps and rare artwork. Either one definitely merits a visit. ~ 5424 Koloa Road, Koloa; 742-7608.

Poipu Shopping Village on Poipu Road is a sprawling complex which, before the 1992 hurricane, was dotted with upscale shops. As the mall steadily recovers, there are a few stores to choose from, including several galleries and boutiques, as well as a sundries shop.

You can also venture down to the **Hyatt Regency Kauai**. It's a spectacular property, well worth touring, and also offers a half-dozen sleek shops. ~ 1571 Poipu Road, Poipu; 742-1234.

NIGHTLIFE

To catch a local crowd, head down to **Brennecke's Beach Broiler**. There's no music, but the crowds are young and the views otherworldly. ~ Hoone Road, Koloa; 742-7588.

Keoki's Paradise in Poipu Shopping Village features contemporary Hawaiian music every Thursday through Saturday night. You can sit outdoors in a garden setting and enjoy the sounds. ~ 2360 Kiahuna Plantation Drive, Koloa; 742-7543.

The Hyatt Regency Kauai, the lavish resort on Shipwreck Beach, hosts several top nightspots. My favorite is **Stevenson's Library**, a stately wood-paneled lounge that evokes a sense of colonial-era Polynesia. For a drink in the open air by the beach, try the **Tidepools Lounge**. For dancing, check out **Kuhio's**. A deejay spins Top-40 tunes on Friday and Saturday nights.

BEACHES & PARKS

POIPU BEACH AND WAIOHAI BEACH 🏊 🏄 🛶 Extending along the main hotel area in Poipu are two adjacent white-sand beaches crowded with visitors. Popular with sunbathers, swimmers and water-sport aficionados, both are protected by a series of off-shore reefs. At Poipu Beach there is good surfing for beginners near the beach, for intermediate surfers about 100 yards offshore and for expert surfers about a half-mile out at "First Break." This beach is also popular with windsurfers. Waiohai Beach has an offshore break near the reef known as "Waiohai." There's fishing from the nearby rocks (the beach area is usually crowded). There is full range of facilities in the hotels that line both strands. ~ Along Poipu Road near the Waiohai hotel.

POIPU BEACH PARK 🏊 🎣 🛶 This has got to be one of the loveliest little parks around. There's a well-kept lawn for pic-nickers and finicky sunbathers, a crescent-shaped beach with pro-tecting reef and the sunny skies of Poipu. Swimming is excellent, and the entire area has some of the best diving on the island. An offshore sandbar makes for good bodysurfing. Bonefish, rockfish and *papio* are common catches; there's also good spearfishing on the nearby reefs. You'll find a picnic area, restrooms, showers, playground and lifeguards. Market and restaurants are situated across the street. ~ On Hoone Road in Poipu.

SHIPWRECK BEACH 🏊 🎣 🛶 Back in the 1980s (remember way back then?), this was one of the greatest of Kauai's hidden beaches. Then condominiums began crawling along the coast and eventually the Hyatt Regency Kauai was built right on the beach. Today, it's a sandy but rock-studded beach, quite beautiful but bor-dered by a major resort. Swimming is good when the surf is low. This is also an outstanding bodysurfing and windsurfing area (the best spot is at the east end of the beach). Fishing is good from nearby Makawehi Point. There is a full host of (expensive) facili-ties at the hotel. Otherwise, it's a mile to markets and restaurants around Poipu Beach. ~ From the Poipu Beach area, follow Poipu Road east and simply look for the Hyatt Regency Kauai, which borders the beach.

HIDDEN ► **MAHAULEPU BEACH** 🏊 🎣 🛶 If you've come to Hawaii seeking that South Seas dream, head out to these lovely strands. Mahaulepu is a dreamy corridor of white sand winding for two miles along a reef-protected shoreline and including several strands and pocket beaches. In addition to being incredibly beautiful and ripe with potential for outdoor sports, Mahaulepu is important sci-entifically. Remains of extinct birds have been found here; flocks of seabirds inhabit the area; and petroglyphs have been discovered along the shoreline. If that's not enough, the beach boasts 100-foot-high sand dunes. There are well-protected sections of beach where you can swim. Snorkeling and surfing are also good at this beach. There are rocky areas along this stretch where you can fish. The beach has no facilities. ~ From the Poipu Beach area, follow Poipu Road east past the Hyatt Regency Kauai at Shipwreck Beach. Beyond Shipwreck, the pavement ends and the thoroughfare becomes a cane road. Continue on the main cane road (which is like a dirt road continuation of Poipu Road). Follow this road for about two miles (even when it curves toward the mountains and away from the ocean). Numerous minor cane roads will intersect from the right and left: ignore them. Finally, you will come to a crossroads with a major cane road (along which a line of telephone poles runs). Turn right and follow this road for about a mile (you'll pass a quarry off in the distance to the right), then watch on the right for roads leading to the beach. You will encounter a guard shack at the turnoff where you are required to sign a waiver to continue onto the property. The beach entrance is closed from 6:30 p.m. to 7:30 a.m.

▼▼▼▼▼▼▼▼▼▼
Waimea Area

The Western world's relationship with Hawaii, a tumultuous affair dating back more than two centuries, began in southwest Kauai when Captain James Cook set anchor at Waimea Bay. Cook landed on the leeward side of the island, a hot, dry expanse rimmed by white-sand beaches and dominated to the interior by Waimea Canyon, the "Grand Canyon of the Pacific."

Like the district surrounding Poipu, this is sugar-cane country. Several small harbors dot the coast and the population is concentrated in company towns consisting of old plantation cottages and falsefront stores.

SIGHTS

One of the first plantation towns you'll encounter driving west on Kaumualii Highway (Route 50) is Kalaheo. Here, a left on Papalina Road will lead a mile up to **Kukuiolono Park**, a lightly visited Japanese garden complete with stone bridge, ornamental pool and florid landscaping. Take a stroll through this peaceful retreat and you'll also enjoy a stunning view that sweeps across a patchwork of cane fields to the sea.

Back on the main road, nearby **Olu Pua Gardens and Plantation** features an international assortment of plant life cultivated in patterns that represent different themes. There's a hibiscus garden, a palm garden, *kau kau* garden (a section devoted to edible plants) and a tropically luxurious "jungle garden." After paying a hefty entrance fee, you are led through this former plantation estate by a tour guide. Admission. ~ Kaumualii Highway, Kalaheo; 332-8182.

En route from one tinroof town to the next, you'll pass the **Hanapepe Valley Lookout**, which offers a view of native plant life dramatically set in a gorge ringed by eroded cliffs.

HIDDEN ►

Be sure to take the nearby fork into **Hanapepe**, a vintage village complete with wooden sidewalks and weather-beaten storefronts. During the 1924 sugar strike, 16 workers were killed here by police. Even today, the independent spirit of those martyrs pervades this proud little town. For a sense of Hanapepe during the plantation days, drive out Awawa Road. Precipitous red lava cliffs rim the roadside, while rickety cottages and intricately tilled fields carpet the valley below.

Russian Fort Elizabeth State Historical Park, just outside Waimea near the mouth of the Waimea River, is now just a rubble heap. Historically, it represents a fruitless attempt by a maverick adventurer working for a Russian trading company to gain a foothold in the islands in 1817. Designed in the shape of a six-pointed star, the original fort bristled with guns and had walls 30 feet thick.

An earlier event, Captain James Cook's 1778 "discovery" of Hawaii, is commemorated with a lava monolith near his landing place in Waimea. Watch for roadside markers to **Cook's Monument**. ~ On the road to Lucy Wright Park.

Cook was not the only outsider to assume a role in Waimea's history. It seems that those industrious leprechauns who built the fishpond outside Lihue were also at work here constructing the **Menehune Ditch**. This waterway, built with hand-hewn stones in a fashion unfamiliar to the Polynesians, has long puzzled archaeologists. ~ Outside town on Menehune Road.

HIDDEN ►

You'll pass the town of Kekeha, home of a sugar mill and a colony of plantation houses, before arriving at the next stop on Kaumualii Highway's scenic itinerary—**Barking Sands Airfield**. Actually, it's not the airfield but the sands that belong on your itinerary. These lofty sand dunes, among the largest on the island, make a woofing sound when ground underfoot. This, according to scientists, is due to tiny cavities in each grain of sand that cause them to resonate when rubbed together. (Similar sands are found in Egypt's Sinai Desert, the Gobi Desert of Mongolia and in Saudi Arabia.) If you have trouble making the sound, remember what one local wag told me: The hills actually got their name from tourists becoming "dog-tired" after futilely trying to elicit a growl from the mute sand. (Since the beach here at Major's Bay is on a military reservation, call 335-4221 to make sure the facility is open.) There are also guided tours of the adjacent **Pacific Missile Range Facility**, an important launch area for military and meteorological rockets and the site of periodic war games. Tours are given the first and third Wednesday of each month. Reservations for the tours should be made a week or two in advance; call 335-4278 for more information.

Having made a fool of yourself trying to get sand to bark, continue on past the dilapidated town of Mana (along a graded dirt road for the last five miles) to the endless sands of **Polihale State**

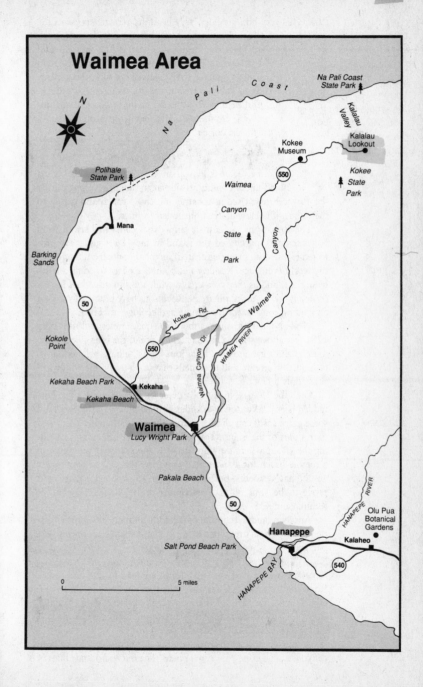

Waimea Area

Na Pali Coast

Na Pali Coast
State Park

Kalalau
Valley

Kalalau
Lookout

Kokee
Museum

550

Kokee
State
Park

Polihale
State Park

Waimea

Canyon

State

Park

Mana

Barking
Sands

50

Kokole
Point

550

Kokee   Rd.

Waimea   Canyon

Dr.

WAIMEA RIVER

Kekaha Beach Park

Kekaha

Kekaha Beach

Waimea
Lucy Wright Park

Pakala Beach

50

HANAPEPE   RIVER

Olu Pua
Botanical
Gardens

Hanapepe

Kalaheo

Salt Pond Beach Park

540

0   5 miles

HANAPEPE BAY

Park. This very hot, very dry, very beautiful retreat represents the last stretch of a 15-mile-long sand beach, one of the longest in the state, that begins way back in Kekaha. The sand marathon ends at the foot of the Na Pali cliffs, in an area sacred to the Hawaiians. Here the ancients built **Polihale Heiau**, a temple whose ruins remain. And here the road ends, further passage made impossible by the sea cliffs that wrap around Kauai's northwest corner.

A swinging footbridge crosses the Waimea River at the Menehune Ditch. Swaying with every step you take, the wood-and-wire span is a rather unsettling way of crossing the river.

The desert-like beach of Polihale provides an excellent view of **Niihau**, Hawaii's westernmost inhabited island. About 250 native Hawaiians live on this privately owned island under conditions similar to those prevailing during the 19th century. Used as a cattle and sheep ranch and closed to the public, it is Hawaii's last unspoiled frontier.

The Robinsons, a Scottish family that came to Hawaii from New Zealand, purchased the island in the 1860s and have protected (some critics say segregated) its inhabitants from the rest of the world ever since. Residents of Niihau are free to come and go from the island as they please, and while the situation does have a company-town aura about it, the Robinsons have historically shown an abiding concern for the people and ecology of Hawaii.

While Niihau measures a mere 73 square miles and rises only 1281 feet above sea level at its highest point, the island lays claim to rich fishing grounds and is famous for its Niihau shell necklaces, fashioned from rare and tiny shells that wash up on the windward shore only a few times a year.

Until the 1980s, Niihau fully deserved its nickname, "The Forbidden Island." But today outsiders with a sense of adventure (and some extra cash) can climb aboard a **Niihau Helicopter** flight and tour a part of the island. You'll fly over most of the island, avoiding the village where the population is concentrated, and land on a remote beach for a short hike along the shore. You won't meet any Niihau residents, but you will have an experience that could prove to be your ultimate encounter with "hidden Hawaii." ~ Kaumakani; 335-3500.

HIDDEN ►

Another candidate in the contest for ultimate adventure—one that is free, doesn't require a helicopter and always lies open to exploration—is **Waimea Canyon**. Touring the "Grand Canyon of the Pacific" involves a side trip from either the town of Waimea or Kekaha. Waimea Canyon Drive leads from the former and Kokee Road climbs from the latter; they join about halfway up the mountain. For an overview of the entire region, go up along Waimea Canyon Drive, since it hugs the canyon rim and provides the best views, then follow Kokee Road down.

As the paved road snakes along the side of this 2857-foot-deep canyon, a staggering panorama opens. The red and orange hues of a barren southwestern landscape are splashed with tropic greens and yellows. Far below, the Waimea River, which carved this ten-mile-long chasm, cuts a sinuous course. Several vista points provide crow's-nest views of the territory, including one (Poohinahina Overlook at 3500-feet elevation) that provides views of the canyon to the east and Niihau in the west.

The road continues deep into Kauai's cool interior before arriving at **Kokee State Park**. Here you'll find a restaurant, cabins and the **Kokee Museum**, a small display space devoted to the flora, fauna and natural history of the area. This intriguing exhibit also features collections of shells and Hawaiian artifacts. ~ 335-5871.

It's a short drive onward and upward to the **Kalalau Lookout** where Kauai's other face is reflected in knife-edged cliffs and overgrown gorges that drop to the sea 4000 feet below. Another nearby overlook gazes out across the Alakai Swamp to Mount Waialeale. (Because of cloud cover in the valley, it's best to arrive at the overlook before 10 a.m. or after 4 p.m.) One more spectacular scene along the way, one more reason to bring you back to this magnificent island.

Accommodations on Kauai's southwest side include beachside cottages in Waimea and ethereal facilities in Kokee State Park.

LODGING

Waimea Plantation Cottages is one of the most alluring and secluded facilities on the entire island. Here in a spectacular coconut grove, fronting a salt-and-pepper beach, is a cluster of rustic 1920s-era plantation cottages. Each has been carefully restored and many are furnished with period pieces. These one, two and multibedroom houses have full kitchens. Maid service is every fourth day. Like the rest of the complex, the swimming pool follows the style of an earlier era (most visitors swim here since the offshore waters are usually murky). The place is a little gem out on Kauai's remote westside. ~ Kaumualii Highway, Waimea; 338-1625, 800-992-4632, fax 338-2338. DELUXE TO ULTRA-DELUXE.

◀ HIDDEN

Nestled in secluded woods between Waimea Canyon and the Kalalau Valley Lookout are the **Kokee Lodge Cabins**. Each of the 12 mountain cabins, varying in size from one large room to two-bedroom complexes, comes with complete kitchen, wood-burning stove and rustic furnishings. These cedar cabins, 5000 feet above sea level, are a mountaineer's dream. With forest and hiking trails all around, Kokee is ideal for the adventurer. It gets chilly, so bring a jacket or sweater. And try to make reservations for the cabins in advance; this place is popular! If you can't make future plans, you'll have to call and hope for a cancellation or last-minute reservation. Some cabins sleep as many as seven people. ~ 335-6061. BUDGET.

Traveling west toward Waimea Canyon and Barking Sands, you'll find the watering places decrease as rapidly as the rainfall. Most

DINING

restaurants en route are cafés and takeout stands. If you're on a budget, you're in luck; if you're looking for an exclusive, elegant establishment, you'll find slim pickings out Waimea way.

At the **Kalaheo Steak House** you'll step into a comfortable wood-paneled dining room. Pull up a chair, rest your elbows on the table (it's permitted) and choose among sirloin, filet mignon, scampi, Cornish hens and several other appealing entrées. Dinner only. ~ 4444 Papalina Road, Kalaheo; 332-9780. MODERATE.

HIDDEN ►   **Camp House Grill** is a trim little café with an island-style lunch and dinner menu. Favored by nearby residents, they serve *huli huli* chicken and pork ribs. ~ Kaumualii Highway, Kalaheo; 332-9755. BUDGET TO MODERATE.

The best restaurant along this highway is Hanapepe's **Green Garden Restaurant**. Dining is indoors, but the tropical plants convey a genuine garden feeling. At breakfast you can enjoy eggs and hot cakes along with a steaming cup of coffee. The lunch menu features a broad selection of meat, seafood and Asian platters, all priced comfortably. And for dinner, the deliciously varied menu ranges from pork chow mein to rock lobster tail. I particularly enjoyed the seafood special, a platter of mahimahi, shrimp, oysters and scallops. Children's portions are available. Closed Tuesday. ~ Kaumualii Highway, Hanapepe; 335-5422. MODERATE.

If you'd prefer to go ethnic, there's **Sinaloa**, a brightly colored taqueria, sporting overhead fans, tile counter and a kind of pastel rainbow atmosphere. The menu covers the spectrum of south-of-the-border dishes. ~ 1-3959 Kaumualii Highway, Hanapepe; 335-0006. BUDGET TO MODERATE.

"Gourmet vegetarian Italian" is the way they describe the food at **Hanapepe Bookstore Cafe**. Every Thursday, Friday and Saturday night you'll find them preparing such entrées as marinated eggplant lasagna, pasta primavera with portabello mushrooms or marinara dishes made with locally grown produce. They're also

✔ CHECK THESE OUT—UNIQUE DINING

- *Budget:* Try the oxtail soup or dine on shrimp tempura and Korean chicken wings at **The Saimin Stand**. *page 390*
- *Moderate:* Sit out on the garden patio or in a dining room filled with nautical gear at **Kapaa Fish & Chowder House**. *page 403*
- *Deluxe:* Don't miss **A Pacific Café**, where the cuisine is "Hawaii regional," the prices are reasonable and the food is otherworldly. *page 402*
- *Ultra-deluxe:* Step into **Tidepools** and enjoy classic Polynesian surroundings plus a menu of fresh island fish and Japanese favorites. *page 381*

Budget: under $8 Moderate: $8–$16 Deluxe: $16–$24 Ultra-deluxe: over $24

open for breakfast and lunch Tuesday through Saturday. That's when you can stop by for a Caesar salad, a "healthnut sandwich," pasta specials, garden burgers or baked frittata. ~ 3830 Hanapepe Road, Hanapepe; 335-5011. MODERATE TO DELUXE.

Da Imu Hut Café has Hawaiian dishes, *saimin*, fried chicken, teriyaki chicken, fried noodles and hamburgers at 1950s prices. It's not much on looks, but it fills the belly. ~ Hanapepe Road, Hanapepe; 335-0200. BUDGET.

In Waimea, there's **Yumi's**, a short-order restaurant with a rotating menu. They serve breakfast and lunch. Closed Sunday. ~ 9691 Kaumualii Highway, Waimea; 338-1731. BUDGET.

Steaks, naturally, are the order of the day at **Wranglers Steakhouse**. Here guests can choose to take their meals outside or indoors in a rustic dining room. Hardwood floors and galvanized awnings contribute to the Western feel, as do the old wagon and wooden horse. Also on the menu are sandwiches, hamburgers and Mexican food. No lunch on Saturday; Sunday brunch. ~ 9852 Kaumualii Highway, Waimea; 338-1218. MODERATE.

The only real sit-down establishment past Waimea is **Toi's Thai Kitchen**. The lunch and dinner menu consists primarily of Thai food, but hamburgers, fried chicken and mahimahi are also served. Dining is on a patio and the menu includes satays, curries and several ginger-sauce dishes. ~ Eleele Shopping Center, 178 Hanapepe Bay; 335-3111. MODERATE.

Waimea Canyon Plaza may be little more than a fork on the road up to the mountain, but it houses **The Saimin Stand**, one *da kine* place. In addition to the obvious dish (or bowl, rather), they have bento, fried noodles, shrimp tempura, Hawaiian plate, Korean chicken wings and even oxtail soup. That's not mentioning the daily specials at this local favorite. ~ Kekaha and Kokee roads, Kekaha; 337-1428. BUDGET.

◄ HIDDEN

When you're up in the heights above Waimea Canyon you'll be mighty glad to discover **Kokee Lodge** in remote Kokee State Park. From the dining room of this homey hideaway, you can gaze out at the surrounding forest; or step over to the lounge with its lava rock fireplace and *koa* bar. The restaurant offers a buffet line with breakfast and lunch items. For breakfast try the pastries, muffins or cornbread, and for lunch choose from soups, sandwiches and salads. ~ 335-6061. MODERATE.

GROCERIES

There are two **Big Save Markets** along Kaumualii Highway. Traveling west from Lihue, the first is in the Eleele Shopping Center. ~ 335-3127. The second is in the center of Waimea. ~ 338-1621. Also along the highway is the **Menehune Food Mart**, a convenience store in Kalaheo. ~ 332-7349. For groceries past Waimea, try the **Menehune Food Mart** on Kekaha Road in Kekaha. ~ 337-1335.

SHOPPING

Hanapepe, a turn-of-the-century town with a falsefront main street, is steadily developing into an art center. **The Village Gallery** showcases the work of several local artists, including some evocative and imaginative pieces. ~ 3890 Hanapepe Road, Hanapepe; 335-0340.

Lele Aka Studio Gallery is dedicated to the futuristic portraits of a single artist. ~ 3876 Hanapepe Road, Hanapepe; 335-5267.

Similarly, the **Dawn M. Traina Gallery** has silkscreens of early Hawaiian scenes created by the store's namesake. ~ 3840-B Hanapepe Road, Hanapepe; 335-3993.

The fashions of **Cane Field Clothing** include classic early-20th-century dresses. They also have an assortment of hats, purses and body lotions in this charming shop. ~ 3878 Hanapepe Road, Hanapepe; 335-3191.

HIDDEN ►

This is also the home of **Kauai Fine Arts**, a singular gallery with an outstanding collection of antique maps and prints. With a varnished pine interior that creates a captain's cabin atmosphere, this is one of my favorite Kauai shops. ~ 3848 Hanapepe Road, Hanapepe; 335-3778.

You can buy a hand-painted coconut (the kind you mail home) at **Giorgio's Gallery**. Better yet, consider one of Giorgio's tropical oil paintings or hand-painted surfboards. Or one of his brother's sculptures. ~ 1-3437 Kaumualii Highway, Hanapepe; 335-3949.

Collectibles & Fine Junque has an amazing collection of glassware, aloha shirts, dolls and old bottles. It's a good place to pick up antiques or knickknacks. ~ 9821 Kaumualii Highway, Waimea; 338-9855.

BEACHES & PARKS

SALT POND BEACH PARK A pretty, crescent-shaped beach with a protecting reef and numerous coconut trees, this park is very popular with locals and may be crowded and noisy on weekends. It's a good place to collect shells, though. The road leading to the park passes salt ponds that date back hundreds of years and are still used today to evaporate sea water and produce salt. Swimming is good in this well-protected area. Snorkeling is fair and there is diving near rocks and along the offshore reef. For

RED DIRT SHIRTS

Head up to Kalaheo and you'll discover **Paradise Sportswear**, home of the "original Red Dirt shirt." Made with dyes from the iron-rich soil of Kauai, these T-shirts have become a cottage industry with workers all over the island dyeing them. If your shirt starts fading, don't worry— just roll it in the dirt or wash it with mud and it will look like new again! ~ Kaumualii Highway, Kalaheo; 335-5670.

surfing, there's a shore break by the mouth of the Hanapepe River nearby in Port Allen. Sandy and shallow with small waves, this area is safe for beginners. There are left and right slides. Along the outer harbor edge near Port Allen Airport runway there are summer breaks, for good surfers only, which involve climbing down a rocky shoreline. At Salt Pond there are occasional summer breaks (left and right slides) requiring a long paddle out. This is also a very popular windsurfing area. Rockfish and mullet are the most common catches here. Facilities include a picnic area, restrooms and showers. Markets and restaurants are a mile away in Hanapepe. ~ Take Kaumualii Highway to Hanapepe. Turn onto Route 543 and follow it to the end.

▲ There's a grassy area near the beach for tent camping; a county permit is required.

PAKALA BEACH 🏊 🤿 🏄 ⛵ This long narrow ribbon of sand is bounded by trees and set in perfectly lush surroundings. ◄ HIDDEN
Surfers will probably be the only other people around. They may come out of the water long enough to watch the spectacular sunsets with you and to tell you of the fabled summer waves that reach heights of 10 to 12 feet. If this book were rating beaches by the star system, Pakala Beach would deserve a constellation. When the surf is low it's a good place to swim. You can also snorkel along the reef. This is one of Hawaii's top summer surfing spots. The incredibly long walls that form along a wide shallow reef allow you to hang ten seemingly forever. Hence the nickname for these breaks— "Infinity." The one drawback: It's a long paddle out. Fishing is good from the rock outcropping off to the left. There are no facilities here; markets and restaurants are two miles away in Waimea. ~ Along Kaumualii Highway near the 21-mile marker (two miles east of Waimea) you'll see a concrete bridge crossing Aakukui stream with the name "Aakukui" chiseled in the cement. Go through the gate just below the bridge and follow the well-worn path a few hundred yards to the beach.

▲ Not recommended; the area behind the beach is strictly private.

LUCY WRIGHT PARK 🏊 🏄 ⛵ This five-acre park at the Waimea River mouth is popular with locals and therefore sometimes a little crowded. Despite a sandy beach, the park is not as appealing as others nearby: The water is often murky from cane field spillage. If you're in need of a campground you might stop here, otherwise, I don't recommend the park. Swimming is fair, unless the water is muddy. Surfing varies from small breaks for beginners to extremely long walls that build four different breaks and is best near the river mouth. There's a left slide. In Waimea Bay, there are parrotfish, red goatfish, squirrelfish, *papio*, bonefish, big-eyed scad and threadfin.

You can also fish from the pier a few hundred feet west of the park. Facilities include a picnic area, restrooms, showers and playground. Markets and snack bars are in Waimea. ~ Located in Waimea.

▲ Tent camping only. County permit required.

KEKAHA BEACH 🏃 This narrow beach parallels Kaumualii Highway for several miles along the eastern edge of Kekaha. Although close to the highway, the lovely white strand offers some marvelous picnic spots, but the rough surf and powerful currents make swimming dangerous. There are many surfing spots along this strip; the foremost, called "Davidson's," lies off Oomano Point.

KEKAHA BEACH PARK 🏊 🏃 ⛵ Set on a beautiful ribbon of sand, this 20-acre park is a great place to kick back, picnic and catch the sun setting over the island of Niihau. Swimming is good when surf is down; otherwise it can be dangerous. For surfers, immediately west of the park are several breaks, including "Inters" (near Kaumualii Highway and Akialoa Street) and "First Ditch" and "Second Ditch," located in front of two drainage ditches. Anglers try for threadfin. There are picnic facilities and restrooms; restaurants and markets are nearby in Kekaha. ~ On Kaumualii Highway in Kekaha.

HIDDEN ▶ **KOKOLE POINT** 🏊 🏃 ⛵ Out by an old landing strip/drag strip, a local dump and a rifle range, there is a wide sandy beach that stretches forever and offers unofficial camping and outrageous sunsets. Fishermen, joggers and beachcombers love the place, but those who hold it nearest their hearts are surfers. The breaks here go by such names as "Rifle Range," "Targets," and "Whispering Sands." Currents and high surf usually make swimming unadvisable. However, fishing is good. There are no facilities. ~ Take the road that leads off Kaumualii Highway one mile west of Kekaha (there's a sign directing traffic to the dump). Follow any of the dirt roads in as far as possible. These will lead either to the dump or to a nearby landing strip. Walk the last three-tenths of a mile to the beach.

▲ Local people pitch their tents here regularly.

BARKING SANDS 🏊 🤿 🏃 🏄 ⛵ The military installation at Major's Bay is bounded by very wide beaches that extend for miles. You'll see the Barking Sands dunes and magnificent sunsets and get some of the best views of Niihau anywhere on Kauai. The weather is hot and dry here: a great place to get thoroughly baked, but beware of sunburns. The Pacific Missile Range Facility is located here, and the area is sometimes used for war games. These beaches are usually open on weekends, holidays and nighttime hours only, and are sometimes closed for maneuvers. Swimming is good, but exercise caution. The coral reefs make for good snorkeling. Major's Bay is an excellent surfing spot with both summer and winter breaks. Other breaks include "Rockets" near the rocket launch pad,

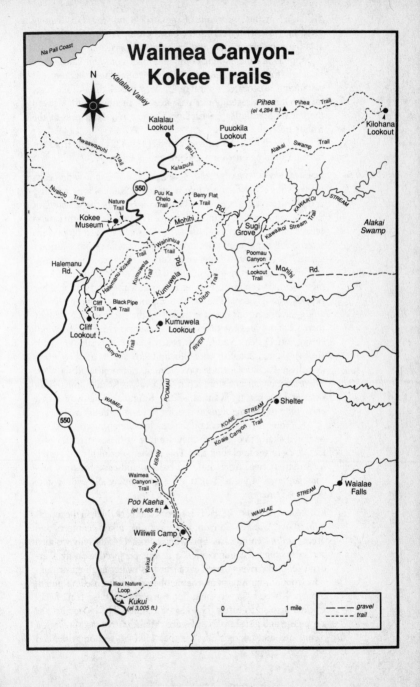

Waimea Canyon-
Kokee Trails

Na Pali Coast

Kalalau Valley

N

Pihea
(el 4,284 ft.)▲   Pihea   Trail

Kilohana
Lookout

Kalalau
Lookout

Puuokila
Lookout

Alakai   Swamp   Trail

Awaawapuhi   Trail

Kalapuhi
Trail

Nualolo   Trail

550

Puu Ka
Ohelo
Trail ▲

Berry Flat
▲ Trail

Rd.

KAWAIKOI   STREAM

Alakai
Swamp

Nature
Trail

Kokee
Museum

Mohihi

Sugi
Grove

Kawaikoi Stream Trail

Waininua   Trail

Poomau
Canyon

Halemanu
Rd.

Halemanu-Kokee   Trail

Kumuwela   Trail

Kumuwela   Rd.

Kumuwela   Trail

Lookout
Trail

Mohihi   Rd.

Cliff
Trail

Black Pipe
▲ Trail

Ditch   Trail

Cliff
Lookout

Kumuwela
Lookout ●

Canyon   Trail

RIVER

WAIMEA

POOMAU

Shelter ●

KOAIE   STREAM

Koaie Canyon   Trail

RIVER

Waialae
Falls ●

Waimea
Canyon ▶
Trail

STREAM

WAIALAE

Poo Kaeha ▲
(el 1,485 ft.)

Wiliwili Camp ●

Kukui   Trail

Iliau Nature
Loop

Kukui ▲
(el 3,005 ft.)

0   1 mile

— — — gravel
········· trail

"Kinkini" at the south end of the airfield runway and "Family Housing" just offshore from the base housing facility. Windsurfers also frequent Major's Bay and "Kinkini." A particularly good fishing spot is around Nohili Point; the most common catches are bonefish, threadfin and *ulua*. There are no facilities; markets and restaurants are located several miles away in Kekaha. ~ Take Kaumualii Highway several miles past Kekaha, then watch for signs to the Pacific Missile Range Facility. You can request a pass at the front gate.

▲ Check with the security guards (335-4221) at the front entrance. Camping only on weekends and holidays.

HIDDEN ▶ **POLIHALE STATE PARK** This 300-foot-wide beach blankets the coast for over two miles along Kauai's west end and is the United States' westernmost park. It borders the sea cliffs of the Na Pali Coast, covering 138 acres. The hot, dry weather is excellent for sunbathing, and prime for burning, so load up on sunscreen. You might even want to bring an umbrella or other form of shade. The afternoons bring great sunsets. This park has magnificent mountain surroundings: Niihau looms in the distance. Swimming is good in summer, but dangerous in winter and during other periods of high surf. The safest swimming is at Queen's Pond, along the beachfront near the middle of the park. Surfing is okay; there's a shore break with left and right slides. There's good windsurfing off Queen's Pond. This beach is also especially great for shell collecting. Bonefish, threadfin and *ulua* are the most common game fish. Facilities include a picnic area, restrooms and showers. There's a convenience store ten miles away in Kekaha; for restaurants and markets try Waimea. ~ Take Kaumualii Highway until it ends, then follow the signs along dirt roads for about five miles.

▲ You can pitch a tent on the beach under a star-crowded sky, or find a shady tree (though they are rare in these parts) for protection against the blazing sun. This is a wonderful place to camp for a day or two. After that, the barren landscape becomes tiresome and monotonous. Tent and trailer camping allowed. A state permit is required.

KOKEE STATE PARK This spectacular park, high in the mountains above Waimea Canyon, is a mecca for hikers, campers and other outdoor enthusiasts. Sprawling across 4345 heavily wooded acres, this rugged country offers a unique perspective on the Garden Isle. In the rivers there's excellent freshwater angling for rainbow trout during August and September; a state license is required, though. Kokee has everything but a grocery store, so come well-stocked or plan to eat at the lodge restaurant. The lodge also has a museum and gift shop. Nearby are cabins, restrooms, showers, a picnic area and hiking trails. See the "Hiking" section at the end of this chapter for trail descriptions. ~ Take Kaumualii Highway to Waimea, then pick up Waimea Canyon Drive from Waimea or Kokee Road from Kekaha. They eventually join and lead about 15 miles up to the park.

▲ An area at the north end of the park has been allocated for tent camping. There are also several wilderness camps along the hiking trails. A state permit is required for nonwilderness camping.

If Lihue is the commercial center of Kauai, **Wailua** is the cultural heart of the island. Here along the Wailua River, the only navigable river in Hawaii, the *alii* built *heiaus* and perpetuated their princely lines.

Wailua–Kapaa Area

There are broad surfing beaches here as well as cascades and grottoes up along the Wailua River. The Hawaiian nobility added fishponds and coconut groves to these natural features and forbade commoners from entering their domain.

> What attracted Hawaiian royalty to Kauai's east coast was the weather along this windward shore, cooler in the summer than the baking sands of Poipu but not so moist as the tropical rainforests to the north.

The oral tradition they handed down tells of a Tahitian holy man named Puna, one of the first Polynesians to arrive in Hawaii, who chose this sacred spot to live. Other legends recount the lost tribe of Mu, a pre-Polynesian people, dwarfish and cruel, who inhabited caves far up the Wailua River.

Developed as a resort destination before Poipu and Princeville, this area has nevertheless avoided the overdevelopment that plagues other parts of the island. Wailua and **Kapaa**, while hosting a string of oceanfront condominiums, remain working-class towns, maintaining a contemporary version of the cultural pride of the ancient *alii*.

SIGHTS

Lydgate Park, situated at the confluence of the Wailua River and the ocean, bears the rocky remains of the **Hauola Place of Refuge**. Here *kapu* breakers under sentence of death could flee; once inside its perimeter, their crimes were absolved. A stone retaining wall also marks the ancient **Hikina Heiau**. ~ Kuhio Highway, Wailua.

On the other side of the highway you can step from the sacred to the profane. Billing itself as "Kauai's best-kept secret," **Smith's Tropical Paradise** is actually the island's biggest tourist trap. Covering 30 riverside acres is a series of gardens and mock Pacific villages in the form of a tropical theme park. There are hibiscus, bamboo and Japanese gardens as well as re-creations of life in Polynesia, the Philippines and elsewhere. On Monday, Wednesday and Friday evenings, they stage a luau and show. Admission. ~ 174 Wailua Road, Wailua; 821-6895.

Fittingly, the adjacent marina is the departure point for boat trips up the Wailua River to **Fern Grotto**. The scenery along the way is magnificent as you pass along a tropical riverfront that is luxuriously overgrown. The grotto itself is a 40-foot cavern draped with feathery ferns, a place so beautiful and romantic that many people choose to be married here. But the boat ride is one of the most cloyingly commercial experiences in Hawaii, a 20-minute voyage during which you are crowded together with legions of tourists and led in chants by a narrator with an amplifier. Admission. ~ 821-6892.

Past Coco Palms Resort (which is still closed due to Hurricane Iniki), the road courses through Kauai's most historic region, the domain of ancient Hawaiian royalty. Watch for Hawaii Visitors Bureau signs pointing out the **Holo-Holo-Ku Heiau**, one of the oldest temples on the island, a place where human sacrifices were performed. A short distance uphill, you'll find a small but interesting Japanese cemetery. Ironically, this is also the site of **Pohaku-Ho-o-Hanau**, a sacred spot where royal women came to give birth.

As you continue up Route 580, the lush Wailua Valley opens to view. On the left along the hilltop rest the rocky remains of **Poliahu Heiau**. A short path leads down to the **Bell Stone**, which resounded when struck with a rock, loudly signaling the birth of royal infants. All these places, vital to Hawaiian myth, were located along the old King's Highway, a sacred thoroughfare used only by island rulers.

HIDDEN ►

For some vivid **mountain scenery**, continue on Route 580 past **Opaekaa Falls**. The road passes through **Wailua Homesteads**, a ranch and farm region filled with fruit orchards and macadamia nut trees. It ends at **Keahua Forestry Arboretum**, where hiking trails wind through groves of painted gum trees. The adjoining state forest climbs all the way to Waialeale, providing unique views of the world's wettest place.

As the road dips down into Kapaa, you'll be passing from one Hawaiian era to another. This 19th-century town, with its false-front stores and second-story balconies, is home to everyday folks. This is where the local plumber, carpenter and fisherman live. The population is Japanese, Hawaiian, Caucasian, Filipino and Chinese. They reside in small plantation houses and attend the local churches that dot the surrounding countryside.

In its northerly course between Wailua and Kapaa, Kuhio Highway (Route 56) passes the **Coconut Marketplace** with its sprawling shopping mall and grove of royal palm trees.

Follow the highway and you'll arrive at a curving ribbon of sand known as Kealia Beach. Across the road, in various states of disrepair, are a local school, store and post office. These clapboard buildings represent in its entirety the tiny town of **Kealia**.

HIDDEN ►

From Kealia, the Kuhio Highway climbs and turns inland through sugar cane fields and continues through the town of **Anahola**, a small Hawaiian homestead settlement. Beyond this tiny

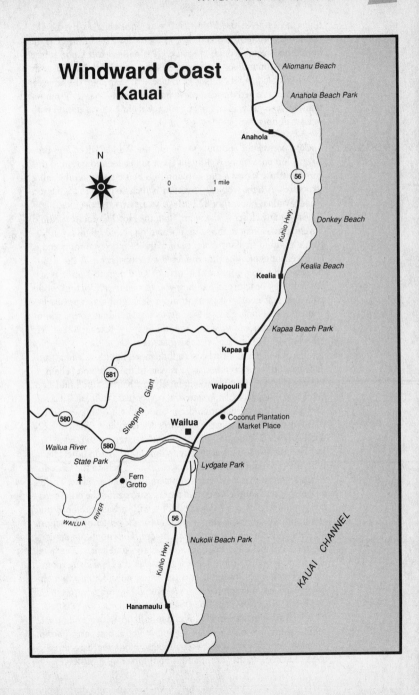

Windward Coast
Kauai

Aliomanu Beach

Anahola Beach Park

Anahola

56

Donkey Beach

Kealia Beach

Kealia

Kapaa Beach Park

Kapaa

Waipouli

581

Sleeping Giant

580

580

Wailua

Coconut Plantation Market Place

Wailua River State Park

Lydgate Park

Fern Grotto

WAILUA RIVER

56

Nukolii Beach Park

Kuhio Hwy.

Kuhio Hwy.

KAUAI CHANNEL

Hanamaulu

N

0   1 mile

town, a "Hole in the Mountain" was once chiseled by the elements. According to legend, it was formed when an angry giant hurled his spear through the rock. This natural formation in the **Anahola Mountains**, a major sightseeing point of interest, was clearly visible from the highway. But several years ago, the same elements that created the feature partially closed it. Today, the mountains are a single wall of angling rock and clinging vegetation with one small opening.

LODGING   Tucked between a coconut grove and the Wailua River, the **Fern Grotto Inn** enjoys one of Kauai's most idyllic locations. Amid this garden setting stands a classic plantation house and several smaller structures. A light tropical breakfast is included. ~ 4561 Kuamoo Road, Wailua; phone/fax 822-2560. MODERATE TO DELUXE.

To get any closer to the water than the **Hotel Coral Reef**, you'd have to pitch a tent in the sand. Located on Kuhio Highway in Kapaa, it's within strolling distance of markets and restaurants and is an excellent choice for the wanderer without wheels. A floral garden leads out to a comfortable strip of sand next to Kapaa Beach Park. In this beachfront building you can enjoy a touch of wood paneling, soft beds, refrigerator and a delightful seascape just beyond those sliding glass doors. A second building offers rooms with fans and ocean views. ~ Kuhio Highway, Kapaa; 822-4481, 800-843-4659, fax 822-7705. MODERATE.

The **Kauai Sands Hotel** costs a little more, but it's still a bargain. This beachfront accommodation is part of the only hotel chain in the world owned by a Hawaiian family, the Kimis. You'll find a relaxed and spacious lobby, restaurant, two pools, a well-tended lawn, carpeting, lanai, imaginative decor and a touch of Hawaiiana. ~ 420 Papaloa Road near the Coconut Marketplace, Wailua; 822-4951, 800-367-7000, fax 822-0978. MODERATE TO DELUXE.

The nearby **Kauai Beach Boy**, a link in the Aston hotel chain, is another extremely appealing place. Located behind the Coconut Marketplace, it's popular with swimmers and shoppers alike. There's a pool, bar and shuffleboard and tennis courts amid the hotel's central grounds, plus a windswept lobby with adjoining shops and restaurant. For pleasant surroundings near the center of the action, it's definitely among the area's top choices. The rooms are air conditioned and include televisions, refrigerators and lanais. The hotel also features one-bedroom suites with kitchenettes and living rooms. The decor is quite tasteful, and the rates, considering what the hotel provides, are reasonable. ~ 484 Kuhio Highway, Kapaa; 822-3441, 800-922-7866, fax 822-0843. DELUXE TO ULTRA-DELUXE.

The **Kauai International Hostel** has both dormitory and private rooms at low prices. Facilities, as you might expect, are spartan. There's a scruffy yard with two buildings; guests share a television room, kitchen, washer-dryer and a pool table. Like hostels every-

where, it's a good deal for the dollar. ~ 4532 Lehua Street, Kapaa;
823-6142. BUDGET.

Keapana Center Bed and Breakfast, set in the mountains out-   ◄ *HIDDEN*
side Kapaa, is a lush three-acre complex offering a restful environment and otherworldly views. This hilltop bed and breakfast provides a unique escape that somehow seems perfectly suited to the
slow rhythms of Kauai. There's also a separate yurt, situated away
from the main building and equipped with a small outdoor bathroom and kitchen (breakfast not included). From the center, you
can hike the surrounding mountains, drive to a nearby beach or
relax in the jacuzzi or on the windswept lanai with its hammock
and inviting armchairs. A rare retreat. Two-day minimum for the
rooms; five-day minimum for the yurt. ~ 5620 Keapana Road;
822-7968, 800-822-7968. BUDGET TO MODERATE.

GAY LODGING   With panoramic views of the Wailua River Canyon and a location deep within the canyon near waterfalls, **Aloha
Kauai** has four rooms decorated in a tropical '50s style. Turn on
the ceiling fans and relax on the rattan furniture,
take a dip in the pool on the patio or get up early   From Kapaa, there's an
for a full-course breakfast. ~ 156 Lihau Street, Ka-   excellent view of the
paa; 822-6966, 800-262-4652. MODERATE.   **Sleeping Giant**, a re-

The "straight-friendly" **Hale Kahawai Bed & Break-** cumbent figure natu-
fast, also overlooking the Wailua River gorge, offers two rally hewn out of
rooms and a studio with kitchenette. There's a golden   the nearby moun-
bamboo patch and a small waterfall in the koi pond—not tain range.
to mention a hot tub and a natural waterfall across the
street. Homemade breads and fresh juices are served for
breakfast in the dining lounge or on the lanai. ~ 185 Kahawai
Place, Kapaa; 822-1031, fax 823-8220. MODERATE TO DELUXE.

There are four comfortable, airy guest rooms at the gay-friendly,
clothing-optional bed and breakfast **Mohala Ke Ola**. It's situated
right across the river from Opaekaa Falls and offers grand views
of Mount Waialeale. Pool; jacuzzi; continental breakfast on the deck.
~ 5663 Ohelo Road, Kapaa; phone/fax 823-6398, 888-465-2824.
MODERATE TO DELUXE.

Looking like it has been lifted straight out of the Japanese
countryside, **Mahina Kai** has a Japanese garden and teahouse to
match. The three rooms and two-bedroom apartment of this bed
and breakfast are fitted with kimono quilts and shoji screen doors;
the apartment includes a full kitchen. There's an indoor pond and
a pool as well as an ocean view from this two-acre property. ~ 4933
Aliomanu Road, Anahola; 822-9451, 800-337-1134. DELUXE TO
ULTRA-DELUXE.

Wailua Bay View offers one-bedroom apartments, $110 for up to   **CONDOS**
four people; three-night minimum stay. Ocean view. ~ 320 Papaloa
Road, Kapaa; 822-3651, 800-767-4707, fax 245-8115.

Studio apartments at **Kapaa Sands Resort** are $80 single or double, $90 for an oceanfront unit. Two-bedroom apartments, $104 (one to four people); $115 for an oceanfront location. ~ 380 Papaloa Road, Kapaa; 822-4901, 800-222-4901, fax 822-1556.

Mokihana of Kauai has studio apartments that run $65 single or double. These units are supplied with a hotplate and small refrigerator. Oceanfront units start at $75. ~ 796 Kuhio Highway, Kapaa; 822-3971, fax 822-7387.

Kauai Kailani features two-bedroom apartments, $65 for up to four people; $7.50 for each extra person. This offers a lot of square footage for the money, but there's one catch—reservations are difficult to obtain and should be made a year in advance. Three-night minimum. ~ 856 Kuhio Highway, Kapaa; 822-3391, fax 822-7387.

DINING

Antique Japanese screens set the theme at **Restaurant Kintaro**, where you can dine at the sushi bar or enjoy *teppanyaki*-style cooking. If you decide on the latter, choose between filet mignon, shrimp, scallops, steak teriyaki or oysters sautéed with olive oil. They also prepare traditional tempura and yakitori dinners as well as *yose nabe* (Japanese bouillabaisse). Closed Sunday. ~ 4-370 Kuhio Highway, Wailua; 822-3341. DELUXE.

There are short-order stands galore at the Coconut Marketplace. **Paradise Chicken-N-Ribs** delivers what its name promises. ~ 822-2505. **Taco Dude** sells tacos and burritos. ~ 822-1919. **Auntie Sophie's Grill** features good old American food like hot dogs and hamburgers. ~ 823-0833. The **Fish Hut** lives up to its name. ~ 822-1712. You'll never guess what they serve at **Aloha Kauai Pizza**. ~ 822-4511. Any time from early morning until 8 or 9 p.m., several of these stands will be open. An interesting way to dine here is by going from one to the next, nibbling small portions along the way. ~ Kuhio Highway, Wailua. BUDGET.

Hidden (but certainly not hiding) in the wings at Coconut Marketplace is **Buzz's Steak & Lobster**. Dim lighting, potted palms, tropical paintings, overhead fans—all these spell Polynesia. There is a surf-and-broiler menu. ~ Kuhio Highway, Wailua; 822-0041. DELUXE.

The **Waipouli Delicatessen and Restaurant** is a small Japanese-style luncheonette serving Asian and American food and owned by a delightful Asian woman. It's open for breakfast daily and for dinner on the weekends and for takeout from 2:30 to 7 p.m. daily except Tuesday. ~ Kuhio Highway, Waipouli; 822-9311. BUDGET.

It's beef, beef and beef at **The Bull Shed**. We're talking about prime rib, beef kebab, top sirloin, garlic tenderloin and teriyaki steak. All this in a captain's-chair-and-fish-trophy restaurant that's so close to the surf your feet feel wet. Speaking of surf, they also serve lobster, broiled shrimp, Alaskan king crab and fresh fish.

Dinner only. ~ 796 Kuhio Highway, Kapaa; 822-3791. MODERATE
TO DELUXE.

For a light, healthful meal, you can cross the street to **Papaya's
Natural Foods**. This takeout counter with outdoor tables has pasta,
pizza, sandwiches, vegetable stir-fry, grilled fish and salads. For
dinner try the create-your-own fish special. Closed Sunday. ~ Kauai
Village Shopping Center, 4-831 Kuhio Highway, Kapaa; 823-0191.
BUDGET.

The best restaurant on the island, **A Pacific Café** serves beautifully presented Hawaii regional cuisine. The accent is on fresh-
ness, with an open-kitchen design and a menu that changes daily.
The restaurant ranks high among local critics, who rave about the
opakapaka with orange saffron sauce, swordfish with ratatouille,
curry lobster, grilled ahi with eggplant and wok-seared sirloin. The
decor is a simple mix of Asian and Hawaiian with paintings by
local artists adorning the walls. Dinner only. ~ Kauai Village Shopping Center, 4-138 Kuhio Highway, Kapaa; 822-0013. DELUXE.

Up Kapaa way on Kuhio Highway in the center of town, there's
a restaurant known to Mexican food aficionados for miles around.
Norberto's El Café draws a hungry crowd of young locals for din-   ◄ HIDDEN
ner. The owners raise a lot of their own beef and vegetables, and
they serve monstrous portions. If you're not hungry, order à la
carte. If you are, choose from a solid menu ranging from enchiladas (including Hawaiian taro-leaf enchiladas) to burritos to chile
rellenos. Children's portions are available and all meals can be converted to cater to vegetarians. Definitely worth ◆◆◆◆◆◆◆◆◆◆◆◆◆◆◆◆◆◆◆◆◆◆◆
checking out. Closed Sunday. ~ Kuhio Highway,   *Kalua* pig, *lomi* salmon
Kapaa; 822-3362. MODERATE.   and poi highlight the
The local crowds attest to the quality and value   Hawaiian menu at the
at **Kapaa Bakery & Espresso Bar**. Serving breakfast   **Aloha Diner**. ~ Wai-
and lunch only, this tiny place offers delicious waffles,   pouli Complex, 971-F
bagels and smoothies in the morning. Later in the day   Kuhio Highway,
there are soups and salads as well as bagel sandwiches   Waipouli; 822-3851.
with hummus, smoked turkey breast and other special   BUDGET.
treats. ~ 1384 Kuhio Highway, Kapaa; 823-6008. BUDGET
TO MODERATE.

One of the loveliest dining spots hereabouts is **Kapaa Fish &
Chowder House**. These creative restaurateurs have converted a
warehouse into a collection of cozy rooms. Each is trimly decorated, comfortably furnished and adorned with nautical items and
an assortment of potted plants; the back room is a garden patio.
They serve stir-fry fish dishes, shellfish, tiger prawns, calamari,
rack of lamb, New York steak and chicken. ~ 4-1639 Kuhio Highway, Kapaa; 822-7488. MODERATE TO DELUXE.

Given the popular bar scene, the grill half of **Side Out Bar &
Grill** seems like an afterthought. But this is a great place to chow

down on Cajun and all-American cuisine. There's a *pupu* menu at the bar, a selection of sandwiches and a list of entrées that includes prime rib à la bayou and mardi gras chicken. ~ 4-1330 Kuhio Highway, Kapaa; 822-7330. BUDGET.

GROCERIES   There are two major grocery stores in the Wailua–Kapaa area. Try **Foodland** in the Waipouli Town Center. ~ Waipouli; 822-7271. Or shop at **Safeway**. ~ Kauai Village Shopping Center, Kapaa; 822-2464. There's a **Big Save Market** at the Kapaa Shopping Center. ~ 1105-F Kuhio Highway; 822-4971.

Café Espresso, located at the Coconut Marketplace, has a good selection of coffees and teas as well as delicious almond-poppyseed cake. There's also an espresso bar and an assortment of soups, sandwiches and baked goods here. ~ Kuhio Highway, Wailua; 822-9421.

Some of the best hamburgers on the island are found at **Duane's Ono Char Burger**. ~ Kuhio Highway, Anahola; 822-9181. BUDGET.

Ambrose's Kapuna Natural Foods, conveniently located on Kuhio Highway, is a recommended shopping place for health food aficionados. At this store you can find fresh local produce in season, as well as other natural food items. ~ 770 Kuhio Highway, Waipouli; 822-7112.

Ara's Sakana-Ya Fish House has a wide variety of fresh fish and seafood, as well as island *poke*. ~ 3-4301 Kuhio Highway, Suite 102, Hananaulu; 245-1707.

To the north is the **Whaler's General Store**. This well-stocked market is the largest store between Kapaa and Princeville. ~ Kuhio Highway, Anahola; 822-5818.

SHOPPING   One of the top shopping spots on Kauai is the **Coconut Marketplace**. This theme mall consists of wooden stores designed to resemble little plantation houses. For decor you'll find the pipes, valves, gears and waterwheels characteristic of every tropical plantation. This is a good place for clothing, curios, jewelry, toys, Asian imports, T-shirts, luggage, plus leather goods, betters and bests. If you don't want to buy, you can always browse or have a snack at the many short-order stands here. In any case, it's worth a walk through. ~ Kuhio Highway, Wailua.

Two galleries within the Marketplace are worthy of note. **Island Images** (822-3636) features premier Hawaiian artwork by artists such as George Sumner, Jan Parker, Pegge Hopper, Roy Tabora and Randy Puckett. Fine art prints, limited edition lithographs and *raku* pottery can be purchased at Island Images. Also consider **Ship Store Galleries** (822-7758), which highlights an eclectic group of artists. **Indo-Pacific Trading Company** (822-5709), also in the Coconut Marketplace, has classic aloha shirts ("silkies"), carved ceremonial pieces from the Pacific, handworked jewelry and a sleek collection of custom-made furniture.

Kauai Village Shopping Center, a multi-store complex in the center of Kapaa, is another of Kauai's shopping destinations. Anchored by a grocery store, it features a string of small shops. **Kahn Fine Arts at Kauai Village** (822-4277) has original sculptures, paintings and lithographs by Hawaiian artists. There's a **Waldenbooks** (822-7749) in this complex that sells an array of local titles as well as national bestsellers. **Mangos for Men** (822-7655), nearby in the same mall, has aloha shirts galore. ~ Kuhio Highway, Kapaa.

Talk about unusual, **Island Hemp & Cotton** specializes in things made from the evil weed. There's a very attractive line of women's clothing here, not to mention soap, paper, body lotion and even coffee filters, all fabricated from hemp. ~ 1373 Kuhio Highway, Kapaa; 821-0225.

Tin Can Mailman specializes in new and used as well as rare books, particularly Pacific Rim titles. It is also rich in stamps, maps and botanical prints. ~ 1353 Kuhio Highway, Kapaa; 822-3009.

Also stop by **Nightengayles** up the street. Here you'll find specialty clothing, art pieces and handwrought jewelry. ~ 1312 Kuhio Highway, Kapaa; 822-3729.

Gilligans, at the Outrigger Kauai Beach Hotel, is a chic video disco with big crowds, a big screen and a pink marble bar. Every Thursday night the club hosts the Kauai Comedy Club. ~ 4331 Kauai Beach Drive, Wailua; 245-1955.

NIGHTLIFE

Also check out the **Jolly Roger**. It's a karaoke bar with a lively crowd. ~ Coconut Marketplace, Kuhio Highway, Wailua; 822-3451.

The **Side Out Bar & Grill** always seems to have something happening. Whether it's Monday Night Football (at four in the afternoon!) or the contemporary and Hawaiian soloists who perform Wednesday through Sunday, there's guaranteed to be a scene. ~ 4-1330 Kuhio Highway, Kapaa; 822-7330.

Charlie's Place, another popular East Shore spot, has live entertainment several nights a week, usually Thursday through Saturday. There's often a soloist playing Hawaiian music. ~ 4-1421 Kuhio Highway, Kapaa; 822-3955.

Rocco's rocks every Friday and Saturday night. After an evening of quiet dinner music, this Italian restaurant cranks things up with a rock-and-roll band after 10 p.m. ~ New Pacific House, 4504 Kukui Street #5, Kapaa; 822-4422.

NUKOLII BEACH PARK 🏊 🎣 🚶 🚤 Located adjacent to the Outrigger Kauai Hilton Hotel, this is a long narrow strand with a shallow bottom. From the park, the beach extends for several miles all the way to Lydgate Park in Wailua. One of the island's prettiest beaches, it provides an opportunity to use the park facilities or to escape to more secluded sections (adjacent to Wailua Golf Course). A dirt road parallels the beach north of the park for about a

BEACHES & PARKS

◀ HIDDEN

half-mile, but if you seek seclusion, just start hiking farther north along the shore. You'll find places galore for water sports. Swimming is good in well-protected and shallow waters. Snorkeling is good among reefs and there are good surf breaks on the shallow reef at "Graveyards." Fishing is best near reefs. A small market and restaurants are in Hanamaulu. ~ At the end of Kauai Beach Drive. To reach the more secluded sections, go north from Lihue on Kuhio Highway and take a right onto the road that runs along the southern end of the Wailua Golf Course. This paved road rapidly becomes a dirt strip studded with potholes. Driving slowly, proceed a quarter-mile, then take the first left turn. It's another quarter-mile to the beach; when the road forks, take either branch.

▲ There are many spots for unofficial camping along the beach.

LYDGATE PARK 🏊 🤿 🪑 🚶 The awesome ironwood grove and long stretches of rugged coastline make this one of Kauai's loveliest parks. Near the Wailua River, it is also one of the most popular. Two large lava pools, one perfect for kids and the other protecting swimmers and snorkelers, make it a great place to spend the day. Swimming is very good. Surfers must take a long paddle out to breaks off the mouth of Wailua River. There's a right slide. This park is also popular with windsurfers. *Ulua* is the most common catch. There is a picnic area, showers and restrooms. Wailua's restaurants, markets and sightseeing attractions are all close. ~ From Kuhio Highway, turn toward the beach at Leho Drive, the road just south of the Wailua River.

KAPAA BEACH PARK 🏊 🚶 While it sports an attractive little beach, this 15-acre facility doesn't measure up to its neighbors. Located a block from the highway as the road passes through central Kapaa, the park is flanked by ramshackle houses and a local playing field. The area sports a picnic area and restrooms. Swimming and fishing are only fair, but there is good squidding and torchfishing. ~ Located a block from Kuhio Highway, Kapaa.

KEALIA BEACH 🏊 🪑 🚶 This strand is one of those neighbors that makes Kapaa Beach the pimply kid next door: It's a wide, magnificent beach curving for about a half-mile along Kuhio Highway. The swimming is good, but requires caution. Good surfing and bodysurfing can be found at the north end of the beach. Fish here for *papio*, threadfin and *ulua*. There are no facilities but the one-store town of Kealia is just across the road. ~ On Kuhio Highway, Kealia.

▲ Unofficial camping at the north end of the beach.

HIDDEN ►   **DONKEY BEACH OR KUMU BEACH** 🏊 🪑 🚶 This broad, curving beach is flanked by a grassy meadow and towering ironwoods. Favored as a hideaway and nude beach by locals, it's a gem that should not be overlooked. Also note that the two-mile stretch from here north to Anahola is lined by low sea cliffs that open onto at least four pocket beaches. This entire area is popular with beachcombers, who sometimes find hand-blown Japanese glass fishing balls. (Several other hidden beaches are strung anonymously along cane roads paralleling the coast from Kealia to Anahola. Watch for them as you travel through this area.) Swimmers take care: Currents here can be treacherous and the nearest lifeguard is a world away. Right off Donkey Beach there is good surfing and bodysurfing. Just north of the beach is "14 Crack," a popular left slide break. This is a popular spot for pole-fishing and throw-netting. There are no facilities here. ~ Follow Kuhio Highway north from Kealia. At the 11-mile marker the road begins to climb slowly, then descends. At the end of the descent, just before the 12-mile marker, there is a cane road on the right. Take this road; bear right and watch for Donkey's Beach on the left within a half-mile. (Since the road is presently chained, you'll have to hike in from Kuhio Highway.)

> **Wailua River State Park,** near Lydgate Park, features sacred historic sites and breathtaking views of river and mountains.

▲ Unofficial camping is common.

ANAHOLA BEACH PARK ◄ HIDDEN A slender ribbon of sand curves along windswept Anahola Bay. At the south end, guarded by ironwood trees, lies this pretty little park. Very popular with neighborhood residents, this is a prime beachcombing spot where you may find Japanese glass fishing balls. There is a protecting reef here; but as elsewhere, use caution swimming because of the strong currents. Snorkeling is good behind the reef. Surfers have a long paddle out to summer and winter breaks along the reef (left and right slides). There is a break called "Unreals" offshore from the old landing. This is also a popular bodysurfing beach. There's good torchfishing for lobsters, and anglers often catch *papio*, rudderfish, *ulua*, threadfin, bonefish and big-eyed scad. Facilities include a picnic area, restrooms and showers. It's less than a mile to the market and snack bar in Anahola. ~ Turn onto Anahola Road from Kuhio Highway in Anahola; follow it three-quarters of a mile, then turn onto a dirt road that forks left to the beach.

▲ You can pitch a tent on the grassy area near the beach; county permit required.

ALIOMANU BEACH ◄ HIDDEN On the far side of Anahola Bay, separated from the park by a lagoon, sits another sandy beach. Shady ironwood trees, several roadside houses and a picnic table dot this area, which is a favorite among locals. What makes Aliomanu particularly popular is the offshore reef, one of Kauai's longest and widest fringing reefs. This is an excellent area for gathering edible seaweed. Swimming is fairly safe in the lagoon but use caution seaside. Local residents spear octopus and go torchfishing here. It is a mile to the market and snack bar in Anahola. ~ Turn off Kuhio Highway onto Aliomanu Road just past Anahola.

▲ There is unofficial camping along the beach.

▼▼▼▼▼▼▼▼▼
North Shore

It is no accident that when it came time to choose a location for Bali Hai, the producers of *South Pacific* ended their search on the North Shore of Kauai. The most beautiful place in Hawaii, indeed one of the prettiest places on earth, this 30-mile stretch of lace-white surf and emerald-green mountains became Hollywood's version of paradise.

While the scenery is so spectacular as to seem mythic, there is nothing insubstantial about the North Shore. The tiny villages that dot the waterfront are populated by people with a strong sense of defending their environment. With development concentrated in the resort complex of Princeville, Hanalei remains a tiny town of taro fields and one-lane bridges. The village of Kilauea is still a sanctuary for a vast population of waterfowl and attempts to widen the North Shore's lone road have been fought with religious intensity.

SIGHTS

Backdropping this thin line of civilization is the **Na Pali Coast**. Here, sharp sea cliffs vault thousands of feet from the ocean, silver waterfalls streaming along their fluted surfaces. There are pocket beaches ringed by menacing rock formations and long, wide strands as inviting as a warm tub.

The North Shore is wet and tropical, drawing enough precipitation to dampen the enthusiasm of many tourists. It is suited for travelers who don't mind a little rain on their parade if it carries with it rainbows and seabirds and a touch of magic in the air.

Your civic introduction to this realm comes in **Kilauea**, a former sugar town with a cluster of stores and a couple noteworthy churches. The cottages that once housed plantation workers are freshly painted and decorated with flowering gardens and the place possesses an air of humble well-being.

HIDDEN ►

But as everywhere along the North Shore, humankind is a bit player in the natural drama being presented here. To take in that scene, you need venture no farther than **Kilauea National Wildlife Refuge**. Here on Kilauea Point, a lofty peninsula that falls away into precipitous rockfaces, you'll have the same bird's-eye view of the Na Pali Coast as the boobies, tropicbirds, albatrosses and frigate birds, some of which nest in the cliffs. As you stand along this lonely point, gazing into the trees and along the cliffs, birds—graceful, sleek, exotic birds—swarm like bees. A vital rookery, the preserve is also home to Hawaiian monk seals and green turtles, as well as occasional whales and dolphins. Closed weekends. ~ End of Kilauea Road, Kilauea; 828-1413.

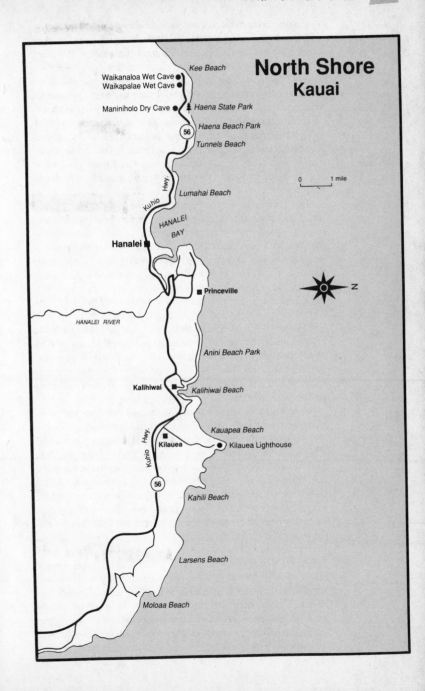

Kee Beach

Waikanaloa Wet Cave ●
Waikapalae Wet Cave ●

Maniniholo Dry Cave ●   🌲 Haena State Park

North Shore
Kauai

56 Haena Beach Park

Tunnels Beach

Kuhio Hwy.

Lumahai Beach

0   1 mile

HANALEI
BAY

Hanalei ■

■ **Princeville**

HANALEI RIVER

Anini Beach Park

Kalihiwai ■

Kalihiwai Beach

Kuhio Hwy.

Kauapea Beach

■
Kilauea   ● Kilauea Lighthouse

56

Kahili Beach

Larsens Beach

Moloaa Beach

Z

Counterpoint to this natural pageant is the **Kilauea Lighthouse**, a 52-foot-high beacon built in 1913 that bears the world's largest clamshell-shaped lens. Capable of casting its light almost 100 miles, it is the first sign of land seen by mariners venturing east from Asia. This old lighthouse, now replaced by a more modern beacon, sits on the northernmost point of Kauai. People gather at the point for interpretive talks of the bird life and natural history of the region.

Civilization stakes its claim once again at **Princeville**, a 11,000-acre planned resort community that combines private homes, condominiums and the elegant Princeville Hotel. Set along a luxurious plateau with scintillating views of the Na Pali Coast, it is a tastefully designed complex complete with golf courses and acres of open space.

Past Princeville, the road opens onto the **Hanalei Valley Lookout,** a vista point that transcends prose with its beauty. Below you spreads a patchwork of tropical vegetation, fields of broad-leafed taro that have been cultivated for over 1200 years. This green carpet, swaying and shimmering along the valley floor, is cut by the thin silver band of the Hanalei River. Framing this scene, as though a higher power had painted the entire tableau, are deep-green cliffs, fluted and sharp, that rise 3500 feet from the tilled fields.

These taro patches and surrounding wetlands comprise the 917-acre **Hanalei National Wildlife Refuge,** home to the Hawaiian duck, Hawaiian stilt, the Hawaiian moorhen and the Hawaiian coot, all of which are endangered. For a close-up version of this panorama, turn left onto Ohiki Road near the old bridge at the bottom of the hill. It will lead you back several eras to a region of terraced fields and simple homesteads.

HIDDEN ▶ In town, a combination of ramshackle buildings, dramatic mountain views and curving beaches creates a mystique that can only be described in a single word—**Hanalei**. It makes you wonder if heaven, in fact, is built of clapboard. The town is little more than a string of woodframe bungalows and falsefront stores lining the main road (the *only* road). On one side a half-moon bay, rimmed with white sand, curves out in two directions. Behind the town the *pali*, those awesome cliffs that fluctuate between dream and reality in the focus of the mind, form a frontier between Hanalei and the rest of the world.

It's almost superfluous that the **Waioli Mission House**, built in 1836, provides glimpses of a bygone era: The entire town seems a reflection of its former self. But this one-time home of Abner and Lucy Wilcox, missionaries from New England, extends a special invitation to step back into the 19th century. A small but stately house, shiplap in design with a second-story lanai, it sits amid palm and *hala* trees on a broad lawn. The rooms look undisturbed since the days when the Wilcoxes prayed and proselytized. The china rests in the cupboard and an old rocker sits in one room while the canopied bed and cradle still occupy a bedroom. The walls are decorated with paintings of the Wilcox family and knickknacks from their era are scattered about the entire house. Guided tours are led Tuesday, Thursday and Saturday. The house has been closed for repairs needed after Hurricane Iniki struck, and is scheduled to reopen in late 1997. ~ 245-3202.

> All along the North Shore, numerous side roads lead from Kuhio Highway through fields and meadows to **hidden beaches**.

The road winds on from Hanalei past single-lane bridges and overgrown villages. The air seems moister and the real world more distant as you pass **Lumahai Beach,** a sandy scimitar where Mitzi Gaynor vowed to "wash that man right out of my hair" in the 1957 movie *South Pacific*. ~ Off Kuhio Highway about five miles west of Hanalei.

Several caves along this route were created eons ago when this entire area was underwater. The first is **Maniniholo Dry Cave,** which geologists claim is a lava tube but which legend insists was created by *Menehunes*. The **Waikapalae** and **Waikanaloa Wet Caves** nearby are said to be the work of Pele, the Hawaiian fire goddess, who sought fire in the earth but discovered only water.

The legendary gives way to the cinematic once more at **Kee Beach,** a lovely strand with protecting reef that was used to film some of the torrid love scenes in *The Thorn Birds*. This is the end of the road, beyond which the fabled Kalalau Trail winds along the Na Pali Coast.

The North Shore is short on bargains, but at **Hanalei Inn** there are eight studio units, five with kitchens. They are attractive, well-maintained rooms with outdoor barbecues, hardwood floors, local art on the walls and fresh flowers. There's also a tiny budget-priced room for unfinicky backpackers looking for a place to crash for the night; it sleeps two. This intimate inn sits amid a garden 100 yards from the beach. ~ Kuhio Highway, Hanalei; 826-9333. BUDGET TO MODERATE.

LODGING

At the YMCA's beachfront **Camp Naue**, there are dormitory accommodations in bunkhouses. Bring your own bedding. There is also an adjacent area for camping and a private cabin (sleeps up to six people) with private kitchen and bath. Reservations can only be made for large groups or for the cabin; otherwise, it is on a first-come, first-served basis. ~ Write to P.O. Box 1786, Lihue, Kauai, HI 96766. The camp is located off Kuhio Highway, Haena; 246-9090. BUDGET.

Hanalei Bay Resort, spectacularly perched on a hillside overlooking the coastline, provides full vacation facilities. Outstanding for the price, the 22-acre property, which descends to a beach, contains a restaurant, lounge, tennis courts and a spacious swimming pool. The guest rooms are located in multiplex cabanas dotted around the grounds; some include kitchens. ~ 5380 Honoiki Road, Princeville; 826-6522, 800-827-4427, fax 826-6680. DELUXE TO ULTRA-DELUXE.

The North Shore's premier resting place is a clifftop roost called the **Princeville Resort**. Situated on a point and sporting one of the best views this side of paradise, it's a 252-room complex decorated in European style with a large touch of Hawaiiana. The hotel rises above a white-sand beach and features several restaurants and shops as well as a pool and jacuzzi. Trimmed in gold plating and marble, this is a concierge-and-doorman resort long on service. ~ Princeville; 826-9644, 800-826-4400, fax 826-1166. ULTRA-DELUXE.

Shakti Gawain, popular New Age teacher and author of *Creative Visualization*, has converted part of her Kilauea home, **Kai Mana**, into a bed and breakfast. The house sits on five acres along a bluff overlooking Kauapea Beach. There are four rooms and a cottage, each simple and pleasant in decor with tile baths, wall-to-wall carpeting and a tropical motif. Guests have access to a lanai, kitchenette, lounge area, tennis court and a washer-dryer. A steep trail leads down to the beach, one of the prettiest on Kauai. Here several times during the year, Shakti Gawain personally conducts weeklong "intensives," which include group sessions, voice dialogues, healing massages and meditation classes. ~ P.O. Box 612, Kilauea, HI 96754; 828-1280, 800-837-1782, fax 828-6670. DELUXE.

CONDOS

In the Princeville resort complex, a few miles east of Hanalei, are several condos: **The Cliffs at Princeville** has condominiums from $155. ~ 826-6219, 800-367-8024, fax 826-2140. The **Pali Ke Kua** offers one- and two-bedroom apartments for $159 and up. ~ 826-9066, fax 826-4159. **Kaeo Kai** has studios from $130. ~ 826-6549, fax 826-6715. These are modern, fully equipped units with all the amenities. There is a swimming pool on each property.

Hanalei Colony Resort is the only oceanfront condo complex and the most highly recommended. Two-bedroom apartments, $110 single or double; $130 ocean view; $185 oceanfront. ~ Kuhio Highway, Hanalei; 826-6235, 800-628-3004, fax 826-9893.

For information on other condominiums, as well as cottages and houses, and to learn where the best deals are available during any particular time, check with **Hanalei Aloha Rental Management**. You can also browse (virtually) through every one of their properties on the World Wide Web at www.hanalei-vacations.com. ~ P.O. Box 1109, Hanalei, HI 96714; 826-7288, 826-7280.

DINING

If you'd simply like a pizza, the little town of Kilauea contains **Pau Hana Pizza**, a combination kitchen and bakery that cooks up some delicious pies. ~ Kong Lung Center, Lighthouse Road, Kilauea; 828-2020. MODERATE.

taurant offers many of the same fish found on the menu to take home and cook yourself; it's open 11 a.m. to 6 p.m. ~ 5-5016 Kuhio Highway, Hanalei; 826-6113. DELUXE.

At **Charo's** you'll discover the best of two worlds—oceanfront dining and good food. Owned by the renowned entertainer Charo, this breezy establishment sits in a secluded corner of Kauai. With tile floor, colorful furnishings and bamboo decor, it's a great spot for drinking and dining. The dinner menu features fresh fish, steak, chicken and shrimp dishes. At lunch there are sandwiches and fish platters. ~ Adjacent to Hanalei Colony Resort on Kuhio Highway, five miles west of Hanalei; 826-6422. DELUXE.

GROCERIES

The best place on the North Shore is **Foodland**. It's very well stocked and open from 6 a.m. to 11 p.m. ~ Princeville Shopping Center, off Kuhio Highway; 826-9880.

Hanalei supports one large grocery store on Kuhio Highway, **Big Save**. ~ Ching Young Village, Hanalei; 826-6652.

About four miles west of Hanalei, **Wainiha General Store** has a small assortment of food items. ~ 826-6251. Along with **Mr. Sandwich** nearby, it's your last chance for provisions before reaching the end of the road at Haena. ~ 826-4579.

Hanalei Natural Foods has organic and health-related items. ~ Ching Young Village, Kuhio Highway, Hanalei; 826-6990.

Banana Joe's Tropical Fruit Farm has ripe, delicious fruits as well as smoothies, fruit salads and dried fruit. They can also arrange farm tours. ~ 5-2719 Kuhio Highway, Kilauea; 828-1092.

SHOPPING

Kong Lung Co. in Kilauea has a marvelous assortment of Pacific and Asian treasures as well as a selection of Hawaiian books. Don't miss this one. ~ Kilauea Lighthouse Road; 828-1822.

Princeville is the closest you will come to a shopping center on the North Shore. The **Princeville Shopping Center** features a cluster of shops that represents the area's prime spot for window browsers. ~ Off Kuhio Highway; 826-3040.

Hanalei's **Ching Young Village** is a small shopping mall that contains a variety store, clothing shops and several other outlets. ~ Kuhio Highway, Hanalei.

Across the street you'll find the **Hanalei Center**, which houses several shops in the Old Hanalei School Building. ~ Kuhio Highway, Hanalei; 826-7222.

Kai Kane is an attractively decorated shop featuring fashions of their own design. It's a great place to shop for alohawear. ~ 5-5016 Kuhio Highway, Hanalei; 826-5594.

Yellowfish Trading Company has a marvelous collection of antiques and Hawaiian collectibles. ~ Hanalei Center, Kuhio Highway; 826-1227.

Ola's showcases the work of over 100 craftspeople from Hawaii and the mainland. ~ Off Kuhio Highway, next to Hanalei Dolphin Restaurant; 826-6937.

On the Road To Hanalei has tapa cloth, woodcarvings, jewelry, quilts and other locally and globally fashioned craft items. ~ Located next to Ching Young Village, Kuhio Highway, Hanalei; 826-7360.

Just out of town as you head toward Kee Beach is **Last Chance**, the "last store on the North Shore," selling hiking, surfing, fishing, hunting and camping supplies. ~ 826-4579.

If you're interested in homemade goods, you'll find a few more stores in other small towns along the North Shore.

NIGHTLIFE   In all the world there are few entertainment spots with as grand a view as the Princeville Hotel's **Living Room Bar**. Overlooking Hanalei Bay and the Na Pali Coast, it also features a singer and pianist playing standards and contemporary music nightly. ~ Princeville; 826-9644.

At nearby Hanalei Bay Resort's **Happy Talk Lounge**, you can enjoy the views of Hanalei Bay and relax with either Hawaiian music or jazz Tuesday through Sunday. ~ 5380 Honoiki Road, Princeville; 826-6522.

For a tropical drink amid a tropical setting, place your order at **Tahiti Nui Restaurant**. ~ 5-5134 Kuhio Highway, Hanalei; 826-6277. Or try the **Hanalei Dolphin Restaurant**. ~ Trader Building, Hanalei; 826-6113.

The **Hanalei Gourmet** has a guitarist/vocalist every night. ~ 5-5161 Kuhio Highway, Hanalei; 826-2524.

BEACHES & PARKS

HIDDEN ►   **MOLOAA BEACH** 🏊 🤿 ⚓ Nestled in Moloaa Bay, a small inlet surrounded by rolling hills, Moloaa Beach is relatively secluded, though there are a few homes nearby. A meandering stream divides the beach into two strands. You'll see horses grazing on the nearby bluff, and a coral reef shadowing the shore. There is good beachcombing at the west end of the strand. Swim with caution. Snorkeling and fishing are good, as is lobster diving. There are no facilities. ~ Take Koolau Road where it branches off Kuhio Highway near the 16-mile marker. Go one-and-three-tenths miles, then turn onto Moloaa Road. Follow this to the end. All roads are paved.

HIDDEN ►   **LARSENS BEACH** 🏊 🤿 ⚓ This narrow, sandy beach extends seemingly forever through a very secluded area. Rolling hills, covered with small trees and scrub, rim the strand. A protecting reef provides excellent swimming and snorkeling. Glass fishing balls and other collectibles wash ashore regularly, making this a prime beachcombing spot. It is also very popular for seaweed gathering and throw-netting. There are also good fishing spots. There are no facilities here. ~ It's hard to get to, but more than worth it when you arrive. Take Koolau Road as it branches off Kuhio Highway near the 16-mile marker. Go two-and-one-half miles to a cane road on the right, which switches back in the opposite direction. Get on this road, then take an immediate left onto another dirt road (lined on either side with barbed wire). Don't let the fences scare you— this is a public right of way. Follow it a mile to the end. Hike through the gate and down the road. This leads a half-mile down to the beach, which is on your left. (There is also an access road from Koolau Road that is located one-and-one-fifth miles from the intersection of Koolau Road and Kuhio Highway.)

▲ This is a splendid place to set up an unofficial camp.

KAHILI BEACH 🏊 🏄 🛶 Tucked away in Kilauea Bay, this   ◀ HIDDEN
beach is bordered by tree-covered hills and a rock quarry. It's a lovely, semi-secluded spot with a lagoon that represents one of Hawaii's most pristine estuaries. Kahili is also a prime beachcombing spot. For a spectacular view of windswept cliffs, follow the short quarry road that climbs steeply from the parking area. Swimming is good when the sea is calm. The favorite surf break is "Rock Quarry," located offshore from the stream. Fishing is rewarding, and the reef at the east end of the beach is also a favored net-throwing spot. There are no facilities. ~ Take Kilauea Road from its beginning for seven-tenths mile toward the lighthouse in Kilauea. You'll pass through town; on the outskirts of town, before the road veers up toward the lighthouse, turn right onto the narrow dirt road. This road leads one-and-one-half miles to the beach.

▲ Unofficial camping.

KAUAPEA BEACH OR SECRET BEACH 🏊 Inaccessibility means   ◀ HIDDEN
seclusion along this hidden strand. Ideal for birdwatching, swimming and unofficial camping, this half-mile-long beach lies just below Kilauea Lighthouse. Very wide and extremely beautiful, it is popular with nudists and adventurers alike. No facilities spoil this hideaway. ~ The beach can be seen from Kilauea Lighthouse, but getting there is another matter. From Kuhio Highway just west of Kilauea turn onto Kalihiwai Road (be sure to get on the eastern section of Kalihiwai Road, near Banana Joe's Tropical Fruit Farm). The road immediately curves left; go right onto the first dirt road; proceed three-tenths mile to a parking lot; from here follow the fenceline down into a ravine to the beach.

▲ An excellent spot for unofficial camping.

KALIHIWAI BEACH 🏊 🏄 🛶 Bounded by sheer rock wall on   ◀ HIDDEN
one side and a rolling green hill on the other, this semi-secluded beach is crowded with ironwood trees. Behind the ironwoods, the Kalihiwai River has created a large, shallow lagoon across which stretches the skeleton of a bridge, a last grim relic of the devastating 1946 tidal wave. "Kalihiwai" is one of the top surfing breaks on the North Shore. It's also popular for bodysurfing. Swimmers

should exercise caution. Bonefish and threadfin are the most common catches. This is also a popular spot for surround-netting of akule. Facilities are limited to picnic tables. Market and restaurants are about a mile away in Kilauea. ~ Take heed—there are two Kalihiwai Roads branching off Kuhio Highway between Kilauea and Kalihiwai. (The washed-out bridge once connected them.) Take the one closest to Lihue. This bumpy macadam road leads a short distance directly to the beach.

▲ Unofficial camping under the ironwoods.

ANINI BEACH PARK 🏊 🎣 🏄 ⛵ 🛶 Here a grass-covered park fronts a narrow ribbon of sand, while a protecting reef parallels the beach 200 yards offshore. I thought this an ideal place for kids: The ocean is glass smooth and the beachcombing is excellent. As a result, it's very popular and sometimes crowded. Swimming is excellent and very safe. Snorkeling is also topnotch. Surfers' note: There are winter breaks on very shallow reef (left and right slides). This is also a very popular windsurfing site. Bonefish, *papio* and *ulua* are regularly caught here. People also torchfish, throw-net, spear octopus and harvest seaweed at Anini. Facilities include a picnic area, restrooms and a shower. A market and restaurants are located about two miles away in Kilauea; the Princeville shopping complex is eight miles distant. ~ Between Kilauea and Hanalei, turn off Kuhio Highway onto the second Kalihiwai Road (the one farthest from Lihue, on the Hanalei side of the Kalihiwai River). Then take Anini Road to the beach.

▲ Pleasant, but lacks privacy. A county permit is required. Tent camping only.

PRINCEVILLE BEACHES 🏊 🎣 🏄 There are three beaches directly below the plateau on which the Princeville resort complex rests. The most popular is *Puu Poa Beach*, a long and wide strand located next to the Princeville Hotel and reached through the hotel. It offers good swimming and easy access to the hotel's (expensive) facilities but is often crowded. The other two are pocket beaches. *Sealodge Beach*, reached via a right of way near unit two of the Sealodge condominium, is a white-sand beach backdropped by cliffs. Offshore is a surfing break called "Little Grass Shacks." *Pali Ke Kua Beach* consists of two mirror-image beaches, one below Pali Ke Kua condos and the other below Puu Poa. They are both good spots for swimming and snorkeling and feature a surf break called "Hideaways."

HANALEI BAY BEACHES 🏊 🏄 🛶 ⛴ A sandy, horseshoe-shaped strip of sand curves the full length of Hanalei Bay. Along this two-mile strand there are four beach parks. *Black Pot Beach Park*, a local gathering place, lies at the eastern end of the bay and is bounded on one side by the Hanalei River and on the other by

Hidden Beaches and Cane Roads

Strung like jewels along Kauai's shore lies a series of hidden beaches that are known only to local people. Among these are some of the loveliest beaches on the entire island, removed from tourist areas, uninhabited, some lacking so much as a footprint. For the wanderer, they are an uncharted domain, and to the camper they can be a secret retreat.

Over a dozen of these hideaways are described in the accompanying sections on Kauai's beaches. Some are located right alongside public thoroughfares; others require long hikes down little-used footpaths. Most can be reached only by private cane roads. These graded dirt roads are owned by sugar plantations and marked with menacing "No Trespassing" signs. Officially, the public is not permitted, and few tourists ever travel along them. But local people use cane roads all the time.

They do so with the greatest courtesy and discretion, realizing that they are treading on private property. They watch cautiously for approaching cane trucks, and yield to plantation traffic. Most important, they respect the awesome beauty of these areas by leaving the beaches as they found them. As one Hawaiian explained to me, the golden rule for visitors is this: "If you want to go native, act like one!"

I certainly recommend that you go native, and I can't think of a better place to do so than one of Kauai's secluded beaches.

a 300-foot-long pier (Hanalei Landing). With showers and life-guard facilities available, it is very popular with watersport enthusiasts of all stripes—swimmers, surfers, bodysurfers, windsurfers, kayakers and anglers. It is located at the eastern end of Weke Road. *Hanalei Pavilion Beach Park*, located along Weke Road between Pilikoa and Aku roads, is a favorite picnic spot. *Waioli Beach Park*, a small facility set in an ironwood grove, is situated near the center of the half-moon-shaped bay. It can be reached from the end of either Hee or Amaama roads. *Waikoko Beach* is a slender strand paralleled by a shallow reef. Popular with families who come here to swim and snorkel, it lies along Kuhio Highway on the western side of the bay.

Anini Road snakes along the shoreline for several miles on either side of Anini Beach Park. Numerous dirt roads lead a short distance off the road to secluded beaches. These offer the same natural features as the park, plus privacy.

There are three major surf breaks here. "Impossible" breaks require a long paddle out from the pier; right slide. "Pine Tree" breaks, off Waioli Beach Park, are in the center of the bay. "Waikoko" breaks are on the shallow reef along the western side of the bay. All are winter breaks. Surfing in Hanalei is serious business, so be careful. Early morning and late afternoon are the best surfing times. The bay is also a popular bodysurfing area. Fish for squirrelfish, rockfish, red bigeye, *oama*, big-eyed scad, *ulua* and *papio*. There is crabbing off Hanalei Landing pier. All beaches have picnic areas, restrooms and marvelous ocean and mountain views. ~ In Hanalei just off Kuhio Highway.

▲ Tent camping permitted on weekends and holidays at Black Pot Beach Park only. A county permit is required.

LUMAHAI BEACH 🏊🚶 Many people know this strand as the Nurse's Beach in the movie *South Pacific*. Snuggled in a cove and surrounded by lush green hills, Lumahai extends for three-fourths of a mile. With white sand against black lava, it's a particularly pretty spot. Swim only when the sea is very calm and exercise extreme caution. You can try for *papio* and *ulua*. There are no facilities. ~ Watch for a vista point near the five-mile marker on Kuhio Highway. From here, a crooked footpath leads to the beach.

TUNNELS BEACH AND OTHER HAENA BEACHES 🏊 ⛵ 🏄 🎣
There are beach access roads all along Kuhio Highway near Haena. Taking any of these dirt roads will shortly lead you to secluded strands. Most popular of all is "Tunnels," a sandy beach with a great offshore reef. One of Kauai's best spots for water sports, this is where many of the boats headed along the Na Pali Coast are launched. According to divers, the name "Tunnels" derives from the underwater arches and tunnels in the reef; but surfers claim it's from the perfect tunnel-shaped waves. Windsurfers consider this one of the

best sites on Kauai. You'll also find swimmers, snorkelers, sunbathers and beachcombers here. Kepuhi Point is one of the best fishing spots on the North Shore; Tunnels attracts fishermen with nets and poles. There are no facilities here. ~ These beaches are located along Kuhio Highway near Wainiha Bay and Kepuhi Point. Tunnels is two-fifths mile east of Maniniholo Dry Cave.

HAENA BEACH PARK 🚶 🚿 This grassy park, bounded by the sea on one side and a sheer lava cliff on the other, is right across the street from Maniniholo Dry Cave. It's very popular with young folks and provides good opportunities for beachcombing. There are very strong ocean currents here, which make swimming impossible. Surfing "Cannon's" breaks on a shallow reef in front of Maniniholo Dry Cave is for experts only (right slide). There is excellent surfcasting and torchfishing for red bigeye, squirrelfish, *papio* and *ulua*. Cardinal fish are sometimes caught on the reef at low tide during the full moon. A picnic area, restrooms and a shower are the facilities here. Markets and restaurants are a few miles away in Hanalei. ~ Kuhio Highway five miles west of Hanalei.

▲ It's an attractive campground, sometimes crowded, open to both tents and trailers, and requiring a county permit. There is also camping nearby at the YMCA's Camp Naue (246-9090).

HAENA STATE PARK AND KEE BEACH 🏊 🏄 🚶 🚿 At the end of Kuhio Highway, where the Kalalau trail begins, 66-acre Haena State Park encompasses a long stretch of white sand, with Kee Beach at its western end. This reef-shrouded beach is one of the most popular on the North Shore. When the surf is gentle, swimming is superb and there's often a lifeguard. At such times, this is one of the best snorkeling beaches on Kauai, with its coral reef brilliantly colored and crowded with tropical fish. There are also 4000-year-old sea caves to explore. The Haena shoreline is also one of the island's best shelling beaches. Surfing is good at "Cannons" and "Bobo's" breaks. This is also a prime windsurfing area. There is good fishing along the reef. There are restrooms and showers. ~ At the end of Kuhio Highway.

▼▼▼▼▼▼▼▼▼▼▼▼

Outdoor Adventures

CAMPING

To visit Kauai without enjoying at least one camping trip is to miss a splendid opportunity. This lovely isle is dotted with county and state parks that feature ideal locations and complete facilities. There are also many hidden beaches where unofficial camping is common.

Camping at **county parks** requires a permit. These are issued for seven days. You are allowed to camp seven consecutive days at one county park and a total of 60 days at all county parks. Permits cost $3 per person per night; children under 18 are free. Permits can be obtained weekdays at the Division of Parks and Recreation.

You can also buy permits from a ranger at the campsite for $5 per person per night. ~ 4444 Rice Street, Suite 150, Lihue; 241-6660.

State park permits are free. They allow camping five consecutive days at each park, and should be requested at least one month in advance for winter, six months to a year in advance for summer reservations. These permits are issued by the Department of Land and Natural Resources. ~ 3060 Eiwa Street, Lihue, HI 96766; 241-3444.

The State Division of Forestry also maintains camping areas in the **forest reserves**. These are free; permits are available at the State Division of Forestry. ~ 3060 Eiwa Street, Room 306, Lihue, HI 96766; 241-3433. Camping is limited at each site, and there's a four-night maximum on the Kukui Trail campsites near Waimea Canyon and a three-night limit at the Sugi Grove and Kawalkoi sites in the rainforest area at the top of Waimea Canyon.

Surfing on Kauai means summer breaks in the south and winter breaks in the north.

Camping elsewhere on the island is officially prohibited but actually quite common. Local folks use discretion in selecting hidden beaches for camping, and so can you. By the way, an extra effort should be made to keep these areas clean. One of the best suggestions I've ever heard is to leave your campsite cleaner than when you arrived.

Rainfall is much heavier along the North Shore than along the south coast, but be prepared for showers anywhere. The Kokee area gets chilly, so pack accordingly. And remember, boil or chemically treat all water from Kauai's streams. Water from some of these streams can cause dysentery, and none of the waterways are certified safe by the Health Department.

If you arrive on Kauai without camping equipment, go to **Pedal 'n Paddle** where you can rent all you'll need. ~ Ching Young Village, Hanalei; 826-9069. Or shop at **Last Chance**, which sells hiking and camping supplies. ~ Kuhio Highway, Wainiha; 826-4579.

DIVING

The Garden Isle offers snorkeling and scuba opportunities at such spots as Haena Beach, Tunnels Beach, Moloaa and Koloa Landing. In the Poipu area, Koloa Landing has a number of green sea turtles in its midst and is mainly for experienced snorkelers. The beach in front of Lawai Beach Resort is another popular spot for snorkelers. Brennecke's Beach was wiped out by Hurricane Iniki but is being restored. Even if you have your own equipment, it's a good idea to stop by one of the local dive shops to pick up a map, as well as advice on local conditions. To familiarize yourself with the region's treasures you may want to begin with a group tour. **Snorkel Bob's Kauai** rents snorkeling equipment returnable at branches on all the other islands. The shop puts together a tip sheet of the best current snorkel spots (factoring in the weather, tides and so forth). ~ 4480 Ahukini Road, Lihue; 245-9433. Scuba lessons and rentals are available at **Bay Island Water Sports Inc.** ~ Princeville Hotel, Princeville; 826-7509. **Seasport Divers** rents snorkeling and scuba equipment and offers lessons, tours, and day and night dives. ~ 2827 Poipu Road, Poipu; 742-9303. **The Exploration Company** rents snorkel gear. ~ Waimea; 335-9909. **Fathom Five Divers** rents diving and snorkeling equipment. ~ Poipu Road, Koloa; 742-6991. Another good possibility for snorkeling rentals is **Hanalei Surf Company.** ~ 5-5161 Kuhio Highway, Hanalei; 826-9000. **Pedal 'n Paddle** has snorkels, masks and fins as well as boats for rent. ~ Ching Young Village, Hanalei; 826-9069.

Conditions at the Poipu beaches are are usually gentler than on the other side of the island. But if you're qualified, you might want to take on challenging North Shore beaches like Hanalei. Keep in mind that conditions can be extremely dangerous during the winter months. Don't try this area unless you're an expert. **Progressive Expressions** rents surfboards. ~ 5428 Koloa Road, Koloa; 742-6041. Surfing champing Margo Oberg offers surfing lessons at **Nukaumoi Beach and Surf Center** on Poipu Beach. ~ Next to Brennecke's Beach Broiler, Poipu; 742-8019. Surfboards, boogie boards or sales are also at **Hanalei Surf Company.** ~ 5-5161 Kuhio Highway, Hanalei; 826-9000. There are rentals and beginner-to-expert windsurfing lessons are at **Windsurf Kauai.** ~ Hanalei; 828-6838. For rentals and lessons in Anini Beach call **Anini Beach Windsurfing.** ~ 826-9463. In Wailua the **Kauai Water Ski and Surf Company** rents surfboards. ~ 4-356 Kuhio Highway, Wailua; 822-3574.

SURFING & WIND-SURFING

Both saltwater and freshwater fishing opportunities make Kauai popular with anglers. Intriguing possibilities include overnight adventures off the Niihau coast, fishing for giant tuna and marlin. Keep a sharp eye out on your trip and you may spot spinner dolphins or breaching whales along the way.

FISHING

    Sea Lure Fishing Charters provides everything you need to fish for marlin, ahi, *ono* and *aku* on Kauai's south and east coasts. The four-hour charter accommodates up to six people. ~ Nawiliwili Harbor, Lihue; 808-822-5963. **Sport Fishing Kauai** cruises offshore in search of a similar catch. ~ Kukuiula Harbor and Port Allen; 742-7013. Head inland to fish for bass on Kauai's reservoirs with **Cast and Catch Freshwater Bass Guides.** ~ Koloa; 332-9707. **Fishing For Fun** takes groups of four on cruises to the leeward side of Niihau for nocturnal bait fishing. After spending the night aboard the 32-foot-long *Dankat*, you'll head to Lehua Island and across the Kaulakahi Channel to the Barking Sands area for the ultimate 24-hour fishing experience. Passengers are encouraged to bring snorkeling equipment. ~ Nawiliwili Harbor; 822-3899.

BOAT TOURS

The trade winds ensure excellent sailing in Kauai waters. From a catamaran trip along the southern shore to a thrilling trip along the rugged Na Pali Coast, these waters are ideal for cruising. Many of the cruises stop at isolated beaches and also offer excellent snorkeling opportunities. **True Blue Charters** rents sailboats and runs skippered cruises off the island's east coast. ~ Kalapaki Beach, Lihue; 246-6333.

For south coast sailing tours on the 55-foot-long *Spirit of Kauai* catamaran, weigh anchor with **Captain Andy's Sailing Adventures**. Along the way, you may spot humpback whales or giant green sea turtles. Sunset and moonlight sails are among the intriguing possibilities. ~ Kukuiula Harbor; 822-7833. **Paradise River Rentals** leads tours and rents Boston Whalers, Porta-Boats and kayaks, ideal for exploring rivers and wildlife refuges. ~ Kilohana Plantation, one mile west of Lihue on Route 50, 245-9580; and 4-1105 Kuhio Highway, Kapaa, 823-2628, 800-662-6287. **Blue Water Sailing** runs four-hour snorkel sails in the open ocean. Sunset sails are also available. ~ Hanalei Bay from May to September; Port Allen Boat Harbor, October to April; 828-1142.

The safest swimming along the North Shore is in the summer when the surf is relatively low.

Captain Zodiac offers rafting expeditions along the Na Pali Coast. Two- to five-hour trips include visits to sea caves, beautiful reefs and an ancient fishing village. Backpacker drop-offs and sunrise and sunset cruises, are offered in summer, while whale watching along the north shore in the winter months is also featured. ~ Hanalei; 826-9371, 800-422-7824. **Na Pali Adventures** also serves the Na Pali Coast with motor-powered catamarans. Snorkeling equipment is provided on these narrated tours of historic Kauai, while from January through early April the focus is on whale watching. ~ Hanalei; 826-6804, 800-659-6804. Zodiac and catamaran tours of the Na Pali Coast are also offered by **Hanalei Sea Tours**. ~ Hanalei; 826-7254, 800-733-7997.

KAYAKING

Kayaking is one of Kauai's fastest growing water sports. And why not. Choose from verdant river valleys or, if you like, go down to the sea again. **Island Adventures** paddles up the Huleia River to a picturesque wildlife refuge. ~ Lihue; 245-9662. **Outfitters Kauai** goes around Spouting Horn in Poipu where you'll paddle past a lava tube. You can also bring your snorkel gear along, as there will be time to explore. ~ 2827-A Poipu Road, Poipu Beach; 742-9667. **Kayak Kauai Outfitters** rents kayaks and runs and snorkel trips. They also sponsor river tours of waterfalls on the Wailua River, as well as day and overnight tours of the Na Pali Coast. More experienced kayakers can explore sea caves along the Na Pali Coast. This trip includes a lunch break at the ruins of an ancient Hawaiian fishing village. ~ Kapaa, 822-9179; Hanalei, 826-9844, 800-437-

3507. **Luana of Hawaii** kayaks up the Hanalei River in glass-bottom craft twice daily at 9:30 a.m. and 1:30 p.m. Extra added attractions on these guided trips include waterfalls and mountain scenery. ~ Ching Young Village, Hanalei; 826-9195. If you want to go out on your own, you can rent a kayak from **Kauai Water Ski and Surf Company**. ~ 4-356 Kuhio Highway, Wailua; 822-3574.

If you've ever wondered what it feels like to waterski through paradise, why not head for the town of Wailua. The serene Wailua River is the perfect place to glide through verdant canyons graced by waterfalls. You can practice your slalom technique, try out a pair of trick skis or enjoy yourself on the hydroslide.

WATER-SKIING

Kauai Water Ski and Surf Company offers trips for intermediate to advanced waterskiers. Hot doggers will want to try out the competition slalom course. ~ 4-356 Kuhio Highway, Wailua; 822-3574.

From scenic coastal trail rides to journeys up the Hanalei Valley, Kauai is an equestrian's delight. Colorful Waimea Canyon offers another intriguing possibility.

RIDING STABLES

In the Poipu area, try **CJM Country Stables**. Possibilities include two-hour rides along the south shore to Mahaulepu and Haupu beaches. They also offer a three-hour "breakfast ride" departing at 8:30 a.m. and covering some of the best beaches in the Poipu area. You may be tempted to return later on foot to explore these hidden spots. (No rides on Sunday.) ~ At the end of Poipu Road; 742-6096.

Garden Island Ranch offers rides in the Waimea Canyon region, including the canyon rim. A best bet here is the sunset beach ride. ~ Kaumualii Highway, Waimea; 338-0052. In the Hanalei area, contact **Princeville Ranch Stables** for four-hour picnic rides to waterfalls (includes a moderately strenuous hike), as well as 90-minute country rides to stunning viewpoints overlooking Hanalei Valley. The ranch also leads a two-and-a-half-hour cattle drive every Wednesday morning. ~ Kuhio Highway, Princeville; 826-6777.

Some of the best golfing in Hawaii is found on the Garden Isle. In addition to outstanding resort courses at Princeville, the Marriott Kauai and the Hyatt Regency Kauai, you can enjoy several excellent public courses. Beautifully situated with dramatic ocean and mountain backdrops, all of these links will make your game a pleasure.

GOLF

Kiele Course and the **Kauai Lagoons Course**, both created by Jack Nicklaus, are two of the island's best-known golfing spots. ~ Both are located at the Marriott Kauai, Nawiliwili; 241-6000, 800-634-6400. Next door to the Hyatt Regency Kauai is the demanding 18-hole **Poipu Bay Resort Golf Course**. ~ 2250 Ainako

Street, Koloa; 742-8711. On the south side of the island, **Kukuio-lono Golf Course** is also popular. ~ Kalaheo; 332-9151. If your idea of a public golf course is long lines and boring terrain, head for the **Wailua Golf Course**. ~ Wailua; 241-6666. The golfing public is well served here and the low green fees make this beauty a best buy. With 27 holes, the **Princeville Makai Golf Course** was designed by Robert Trent Jones. ~ Princeville; 826-3580. It is complemented by the demanding 18-hole **Prince** course next door. There's also a driving range to help sharpen your skills. ~ Princeville; 826-5000.

TENNIS

With a variety of public and resort courses available, it's a good idea to include a racket in your carry-on luggage. The **County Department of Parks and Recreation** is your best source of information on public courts. ~ 241-6670. You'll find public courts in Lihue (Hardy Street), Koloa (Maluhia Road), Waimea (Kaumuali Road) and Kekaha (Elepaio Road). In Wailua you'll find courts at Wailua Homestead (Kamalu Road) and Wailua Houselots (corner of Lanikila and Nonou streets). Also consider Kapaa Aray Park in Kapaa.

BIKING

There are no bikeways on Kauai and most roads have very narrow shoulders, but the Garden Isle is still the most popular island for bicycling. Roads are good, and except for the steep 20-mile climb along Waimea Canyon, the terrain is either flat or gently rolling. The spectacular scenery and network of public parks make this a cyclist's dream.

Bike Rentals   In Poipu, head for **Outfitters Kauai**. ~ 2827-A Poipu Road; 742-9667. **Bicycle John** rents mountain bikes by the day and by the week, and is a full-service sales and repair shop as well. ~ 3142 Kuhio Highway, Lihue; 245-7579. In Hanalei, try **Pedal 'n Paddle**. ~ Ching Young Village; 826-9069.

Bike Repairs   **Bicycles Kauai** can supply you with needed parts and take care of any emergency repairs. They are also a full-service sales and rental shop, and lead two- to five-hour tours of Waimea Canyon and other Kauai destinations. ~ 1379 Kuhio Highway, Kapaa; 822-3315.

Guided Tours   **Kayak Kauai Outfitters** has two morning and afternoon trips. Out of Hanalei, they offer a historical tour of Hanalei town and end the ride with a stop at the beach. Or you can pedal out to Donkey Beach along a cane *hau* road, which affords sweeping views of the ocean and mountains. From the Kapaa location, tours lead through mountain terrain along the Sleeping Giant Trail to the Keahua Arboretum. ~ Hanalei, 826-9844, 800-437-3507; Kapaa, 822-9179.

HIKING

Hiking is among the finest, and certainly least expensive, ways of touring the Garden Isle. Kauai's trails are concentrated in the Na

Pali Coast and Waimea Canyon–Kokee regions, with a few others near the Wailua River. Most are well maintained and carefully charted. For further information, contact the State Department of Land and Natural Resources. ~ 241-3444.

WAILUA RIVER While none of these hikes actually follow the Wailua, all begin near Route 580, which parallels the river.

Nonou Mountain Trail—East Side (1.8 miles long) begins off Haleilio Road at the parking lot in the Wailua Houselots and climbs 1250 feet to the Sleeping Giant's head at Mount Nonou summit.

Nonou Mountain Trail—West Side (1.5 miles) begins off Route 581 and ascends 1000 feet to join the East Side trail.

Keahua Arboretum Trail (0.5 mile) begins two miles past the University of Hawaii Wailua Experiment Station on Route 580. This nature trail is lined with native and foreign plants.

Kuilau Ridge Trail (2.1 miles) begins on Route 580 near the Keahua Arboretum. This scenic hike goes past several vista points and picnic areas.

WAIMEA CANYON–KOKEE Kokee State Park has about 45 miles of hiking trails through rugged, beautiful country. Along the mountain paths listed here, you'll discover some of the finest hiking in all Hawaii.

Alakai Swamp Trail (3.5 miles) passes through bogs and scrub rainforests to the Kilohana Lookout above Hanalei Bay. This very muddy trail begins off Mohihi (Camp 10) Road.

Awaawapuhi Trail (3.3 miles) starts on Route 550 midway between Kokee Museum and Kalalau Lookout. It leads through a forest to a vista at 2500-feet elevation that overlooks sheer cliffs and the ocean. The trail then connects with Nualolo Trail for an eight-and-a-half-mile loop.

Berry Flat Trail (1 mile) and **Puu Ka Ohelo Trail** (0.3 mile) combine off Mohihi (Camp 10) Road to form a loop that passes

---

✔ CHECK THESE OUT—UNIQUE OUTDOOR ADVENTURES

- Hike a 15-mile-long beach that resembles the Saudi Arabian desert and ends at a sacred temple in **Polihale State Park**. *page 387*
- **Kayak** up the Huleia River to a remote wildlife refuge or paddle out on the ocean past a dramatic blowhole. *page 425*
- Climb up into **Waimea Canyon**, the "Grand Canyon of the Pacific," and choose from among 45 miles of hiking trails. *page 429*
- Join **Captain Zodiac** on a rafting expedition along the Na Pali Coast past sea caves and luxurious valleys. *page 425*

an interesting assortment of trees, including California redwood, *ohia*, *sugi* pine and *koa*.

Black Pipe Trail (0.4 mile) links Canyon Trail with Halemanu Road. It follows a cliff past stands of the rare *iliau* plant, a relative of Maui's famous silversword.

Canyon Trail (1.4 miles) forks off Cliff Trail and follows Waimea Canyon's northern rim to a vista sweeping down the canyon to the sea.

Cliff Trail (0.1 mile) begins at the end of the right fork of Halemanu Road and offers an easy hike to a viewpoint above Waimea Canyon.

Ditch Trail (1.5 miles) runs from Mohihi Road at one end to Waininiua Road at the other. It's a rugged trail with spectacular views of forest areas and the Poomau River.

Halemanu-Kokee Trail (1.2 miles) sets out from the old ranger station. Birdwatchers should especially enjoy this easy jaunt.

Iliau Nature Loop (0.3 mile) starts along Route 550 on a short course past 20 local plant species, including the *iliau*, endemic only to the Garden Isle. This trail offers good views of both Waimea Canyon and Waialae Falls.

Kalapuhi Trail (1.7 miles) begins at Route 550 en route to a plum grove. The plums are in season every other year. In a good year, you can enjoy both plums and a fine hike; other years, you'll have to settle for the latter.

Kawaikoi Stream Trail (1.8 miles), a loop trail, starts on Mohihi (Camp 10) Road across from Sugi Grove and follows near the stream through a manmade forest.

Koaie Canyon Trail (3 miles) branches off the Waimea Canyon trail near Poo Kaeha. It crosses the Waimea River and passes ancient terraces and rock walls en route to Lonomea camp, a wilderness campsite. Here you'll find a shelter and a stream chock-full of swimming holes.

Kukui Trail (2.5 miles) leads from Route 550 near Puu Kukui and descends 2000 feet to the Waimea River. You'll encounter switchbacks along the west side of Waimea Canyon; the trail ends at Wiliwili Camp, a wilderness campsite. You must register at the trailhead.

Kumuwela Trail (0.8 mile) begins off Mohihi (Camp 10) Road and passes through a fern-choked gulch.

Nature Trail (0.1 mile) begins behind the Kokee Museum and passes through a *koa* forest.

Nualolo Trail (3.8 miles) starts near Park headquarters. Along the way you'll be able to see Nualolo Valley on the Na Pali Coast.

Pihea Trail (3.8 miles) offers excellent views of Kalalau Valley and the Alakai Swamp. Pihea also features a variety of birds and plant life. This trail begins at Puuokila Lookout.

Hiking Kalalau

Kauai's premier hike, one of the finest treks in all the islands, follows an 11-mile trail along the rugged Na Pali Coast. This ancient Hawaiian trail to Kalalau Valley descends into dense rainforests and climbs along windswept cliffs. Streams and mountain pools along the path provide refreshing swimming holes. Wild orchids, guavas, *kukui* nuts, mangoes and mountain apples grow in abundance.

The trail begins near Kee Beach at the end of Kuhio Highway. After a strenuous two-mile course the trail drops into Hanakapiai Valley. From here, two side trails—the **Hanakapiai Valley Loop Trail** (1.3 miles) and its extension, the **Hanakapiai Falls Trail** (2 miles)—climb through the valley and up to Hanakapiai Falls, respectively. Fringed by cliffs and possessing a marvelous sand beach, Hanakapiai makes an excellent rest point or final destination.

If you bypass the side trails and continue along the Kalalau Trail, you'll find that as it climbs out of Hanakapiai Valley, it becomes slightly rougher. Sharp grass presses close to the path as it leads through thick foliage, then along precipitous cliff faces. Four miles from Hanakapiai Valley, the trail arrives at Hanakoa Valley. There are several shacks and campsites here as well as a steep one-third-mile trail that goes up to Hanakoa Falls.

The final trek to Kalalau, the most difficult section of the trail, passes scenery so spectacular as to seem unreal. Knife-point peaks, illuminated by shafts of sunlight, rise thousands of feet. Frigate birds hang poised against the trade winds. Wisps of cloud fringe the cliffs. The silence is ominous, almost tangible. A foot from the trail, the ledge falls away into another sheer wall, which plummets a thousand feet and more to the surf below.

The narrow, serpentine trail then winds down to Kalalau Valley. A well-fed stream rumbles through this two-mile-wide vale. If you must use the water here, be sure to boil or otherwise purify it. Farther along, a white-sand beach sweeps past a series of caves to the far end of the valley. You may want to stop awhile and explore the caves, but if you swim here or at Hanakapiai, exercise extreme caution. The undertow and riptides are wicked.

Kalalau has many fine campsites near the beach, but firewood is scarce and cutting trees is *kapu*, so you'd best bring a campstove. Camping at Hanakapiai, Hanakoa or Kalalau will necessitate a state permit. Anyone hiking beyond Hanakapiai also needs a permit. These are available from the State Parks office. ~ 3060 Eiwa Street, Lihue; 241-3444.

Poomau Canyon Lookout Trail (0.3 mile) heads through a stand of Japanese *sugi* trees and a native rainforest. It begins from Mohihi (Camp 10) Road and ends at a vista overlooking Poomau and Waimea Canyons.

Waimea Canyon Trail (8 miles) can be reached from the Kukui Trail. It follows the Waimea River through the center of the canyon.

Waininiua Trail (0.4 mile) leads from the unpaved Kumuwela Road through a forest where ginger grows.

▼▼▼▼▼▼▼▼▼▼▼▼▼
Transportation

AIR

Visiting Kauai means flying to the jetport near Lihue or the landing strip near Princeville. Unless you're staying on the north shore, it is more convenient to fly to the more centrally located Lihue Airport. ~ 246-1448. Aloha Airlines, Mahalo Airlines and Hawaiian Airlines operate here; Aloha Island Air flies in and out of Princeville.

The Lihue Airport has a restaurant, cocktail lounge, lockers, newsstand and flower shop. What you won't find are buses, far more useful to most travelers than cocktails and flowers. Transportation (it's two miles into town) requires reserving a seat on a shuttle, renting a car, hailing a cab, hitching or hoofing. Cabs generally charge about $4 to Lihue. At Princeville Airport, it's either walk or rent a vehicle.

CAR RENTALS

Across the street from the terminal at Lihue Airport you'll find a series of booths containing car rental firms. These include Alamo Rent A Car (246-0645, 800-327-9633), Avis Rent A Car (245-3512, 800-331-1212), Budget Rent A Car (245-9031, 800-527-0700), Dollar Rent A Car (245-3651, 800-800-4000), Hertz Rent A Car (245-3356, 800-654-3131) and National Interrent (245-5636, 800-227-7368).

At Princeville Airport the two choices are Avis Rent A Car (826-9773, 800-331-1212) or Hertz Rent A Car (826-7455, 800-654-3131). There are also rental companies located in resort areas like Poipu and Wailua. One of these is Westside U-Drive (332-8644) in Poipu.

JEEP RENTALS

Budget Rent A Car has four-wheel-drives. However, most Kauai roads, including cane roads, are accessible by car so you probably won't need a jeep. ~ Lihue Airport; 245-9031, 800-527-0700.

Kauai Mountain Tours has full-day, off-road four-wheel-drive tours into the mountains of Kokee State Park around Waimea Canyon. ~ 245-7224.

PUBLIC TRANSIT

Kauai Bus is a shuttle that travels between Lihue and Hanalei six times a day from 6:45 a.m. to 6 p.m. It stops at about a dozen places, including the major shopping centers. ~ 241-6410.

HITCHING & WALKING

Hitching is permitted on Kauai provided you stay off the paved portion of the road. Like everywhere else, luck hitchhiking varies here. In the summer, there will be many extended thumbs along the road, particularly in the Hanalei area. The folks who pick up strangers are usually fellow tourists or local haoles.

Walking on the highways is permitted against the flow of traffic and well off the roadways, but I encountered no problem walking with traffic while thumbing.

AERIAL TOURS

Whether you choose a whirlybird's-eye view from a helicopter or prefer the serenity of a glider, aerial sightseeing is one of Kauai's great thrills. From simple flyovers to thrilling acrobatic flights, you'll gain a unique perspective on the island's canyons and rainforests, hidden beaches and tropical retreats. Try flying with **Island Helicopters**. ~ Lihue Airport; 245-8588, 800-829-5999. Or call **Ohana Helicopter Tours**. ~ Lihue Airport; 245-3996, 800-222-6989. **Hawaii Helicopters** features unique glimpses of scenic treasures like Waialeale, the Na Pali Coast and Waimea Canyon. If you want an airplane tour, **Fly Kauai** will take you on a one-hour ride over the most beautiful parts of the island or on a three-island tour featuring Lehua and Niihau. ~ Lihue Airport; 246-9123. **Niihau Helicopters** specializes in trips to the Forbidden Isle. ~ Kaumakani; 335-3500.

▼▼▼▼▼▼▼▼▼▼▼▼▼▼▼▼▼▼▼▼▼

Addresses & Phone Numbers

KAUAI ISLAND

County Department of Parks and Recreation ~ 241-6660

Department of Land and Natural Resources ~ 3060 Eiwa Street, Lihue; 241-3444

Kauai Visitors Bureau ~ 3016 Umi Street, Lihue; 245-3971

Weather ~ 245-6001

Kauai Hotline (for a vacation planner) ~ 800-262-1400

LIHUE

Ambulance ~ 911

Barber Shop ~ Ikeda Barber Shop, 4446 Hardy Street; 245-4983

Fire Department ~ 911

Fishing Supplies ~ Lihue Fishing Supply, 2985 Kalena Street; 245-4930

Hardware ~ Ace Hardware, 4444 Rice Street; 245-4091

Hospital ~ Wilcox Memorial, 3420 Kuhio Highway; 245-1100

Library ~ 4344 Hardy Street; 241-3222

Liquor ~ City Liquor, 4347-B Rice Street; 245-3733

Pharmacy ~ Longs Drug Store, Kukui Grove Center, Kaumualii Highway; 245-7771

Photo Supply ~ Don's Camera and Fine Jewelry Center, 4286 Rice Street; 245-6581

Police Department ~ 3060 Umi Street; 241-6711 or 911 for emergencies

Post Office ~ 4441 Rice Street; 246-0793

POIPU AREA

Ambulance ~ 911

Fire Department ~ 911

Laundromat ~ Beside Big Save Market, Koloa Road, Koloa

Police Department ~ 911

WAIMEA AREA

Ambulance ~ 911

Fire Department ~ 911

Laundromat ~ Menehune Center Laundromat, 9887 Waimea Road, Waimea

Police Department ~ 338-1831 or 911 for emergencies

WAILUA AREA

Ambulance ~ 911

Fire Department ~ 911

Laundromat ~ Kapaa Laundry Center, Kapaa Shopping Center, Kapaa; 822-3113

Police Department ~ 911

NORTH SHORE

Ambulance ~ 911

Fire Department ~ 911

Police Department ~ 826-6214 or 911 for emergencies

Recommended Reading

The Beaches of Oahu, by John R.K. Clark. University of Hawaii Press, 1977. This book, and companion volumes that cover the other islands, provides excellent background information on all the beaches.

Hawaii, by James Michener. Bantam Books, 1978. This lengthy historic novel skillfully blends fact and fiction, dramatically tracing the entire course of Hawaiian history.

Hawaii Pono, by Lawrence H. Fuchs. Harcourt Brace Jovanovich, 1961. A brilliant sociological study of 20th-century Hawaii which vividly portrays the islands' ethnic groups.

Hawaii: The Sugar-Coated Fortress, by Francine Du Plessix Gray. Random House, 1972. A hard-hitting analysis of modern-day Hawaii which details the tragic effect Western civilization has had on the Hawaiian people.

Hawaiian Antiquities, by David Malo. Bishop Museum Press, 1971. Written by a Hawaiian scholar in the nineteenth century, this study contains a wealth of information on pre-European Hawaiian culture.

Hawaiian Hiking Trails, by Craig Chisholm. Fernglen Press, 1986. The best single-volume hiking guide available, this handbook provides excellent descriptions of Hawaii's most popular treks.

The Legends and Myths of Hawaii, by David Kalakaua. Charles E. Tuttle Company, 1972. Written by Hawaii's last king, this fascinating collection includes fables of the great chiefs and priests who once ruled the islands.

Polynesian Researches: Hawaii, by William Ellis. Charles E. Tuttle Company, 1969. This missionary's journal originally appeared in the 1820s. Despite some tedious sermonizing, it poignantly portrays Hawaii at a historic crossroads and graphically describes volcanoes and other natural phenomena on the big island.

Shoal of Time, by Gavan Daws. University Press of Hawaii, 1974. The finest history written on Hawaii, this volume is not only informative but entertaining as well.

Shore Fishing in Hawaii, by Edward Y. Hosaka. Petroglyph Press, n.d. This how-to guide is filled with handy tips on surf-casting, fabricating your own equipment and identifying Hawaii's fish species.

Lodging Index

Dining Index

Index

Abbreviations used for island names are (H) Hawaii, (K) Kauai, (L) Lanai, (M) Maui, (Mo) Molokai and (Oa) Oahu.

Roads – *at scales larger than 1:3 million*

Motorway/Highway

Other Main Road

– *at scales smaller than 1:3 million*

Principal Road: Motorway/Highway

Other Main road

Main Railway

Towns & Cities

☐ Population > 5,000,000

☐ 1–5,000,000

○ 500,000–1,000,000

○ < 500,000

☐ **Paris** National Capital

✈ Airport

International Boundary

International Boundary – not defined or in dispute

Internal Boundary

River

Canal

Marsh or Swamp

Relief

▲ 1510 Peak (meters)

5,000 meters (16,405 feet)
4,000 (13,124)
3,000 (9,843)
2,000 (6,562)
1,000 (3,281)
500 (1,641)
200 (656)
100 (328)
0

Land below sea level

Note:
The 0–100 contour layer
appears only at scales
larger than 1:3 million

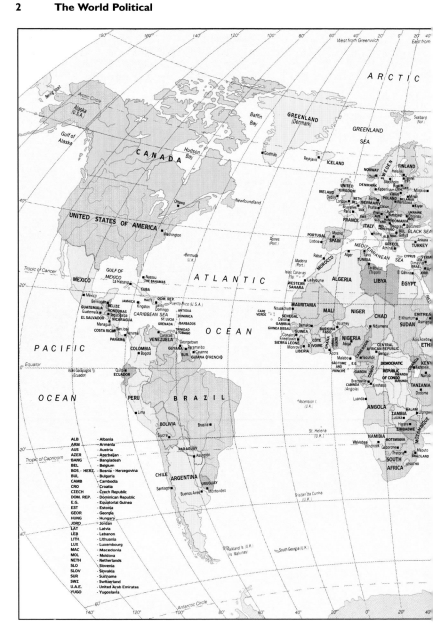

ALB - Albania
ARM - Armenia
AUS - Austria
AZER - Azerbaijan
BANG - Bangladesh
BEL - Belgium
BOS. - HERZ. - Bosnia - Herzegovina
BUL - Bulgaria
CAMB - Cambodia
CRO - Croatia
CZECH - Czech Republic
DOM. REP. - Dominican Republic
E.G. - Equatorial Guinea
EST - Estonia
GEOR - Georgia
HUNG - Hungary
JORD - Jordan
LAT - Latvia
LEB - Lebanon
LITH - Lithuania
LUX - Luxembourg
MAC - Macedonia
MOL - Moldova
NETH - Netherlands
SLO - Slovenia
SLOV - Slovakia
SUR - Suriname
SWZ - Switzerland
U.A.E. - United Arab Emirates
YUGO - Yugoslavia

Scale 1:11800 000

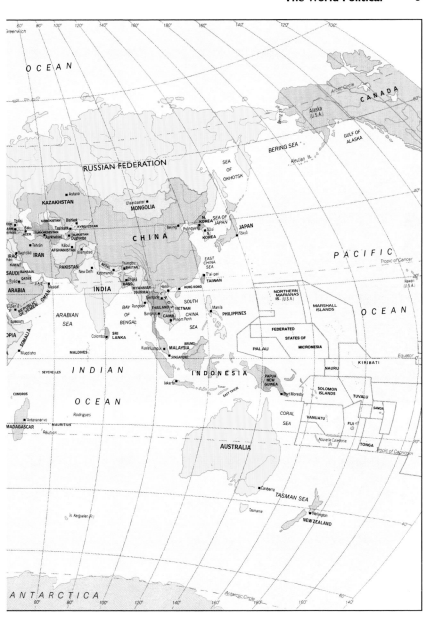

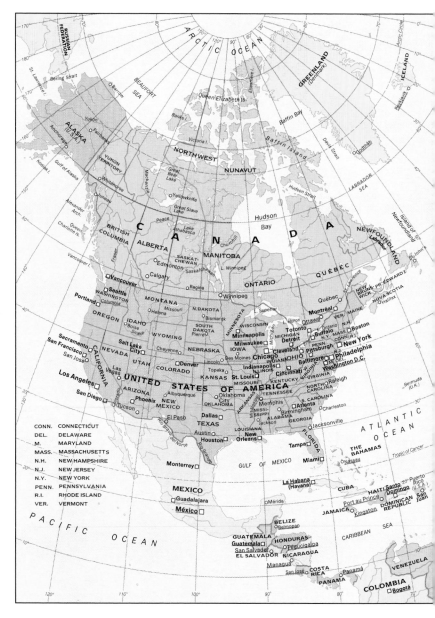

CONN. CONNECTICUT
DEL. DELAWARE
M. MARYLAND
MASS. MASSACHUSETTS
N.H. NEW HAMPSHIRE
N.J. NEW JERSEY
N.Y. NEW YORK
PENN. PENNSYLVANIA
R.I. RHODE ISLAND
VER. VERMONT

0   500   1000   1500 km

0   250   500   750   1000 miles

Scale 1:57 400 000

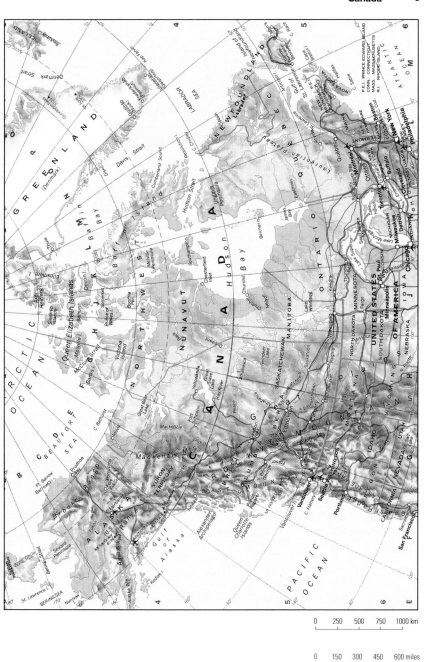

0   250   500   750   1000 km

0   150   300   450   600 miles

Scale 1:41 400 000

HAWAIIAN ISLANDS
1:10 000 000
0   100 miles
0   200 km

ALASKA
1:40 000 000
0   400 miles
0   800 km

0   250   500   750   1000 km

0   200   400   600 miles

Scale 1:27 600 000

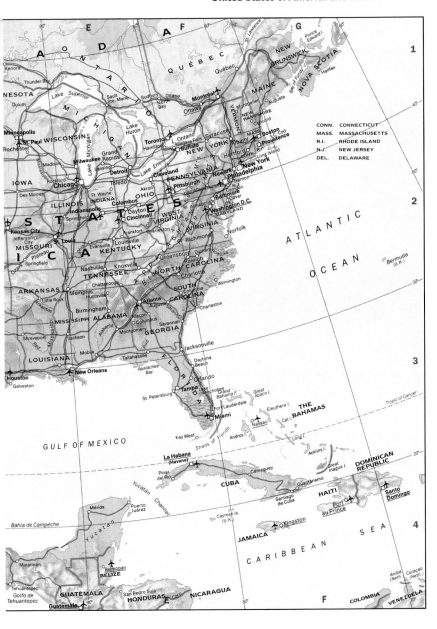

CONN.	CONNECTICUT
MASS.	MASSACHUSETTS
R.I.	RHODE ISLAND
N.J.	NEW JERSEY
DEL.	DELAWARE

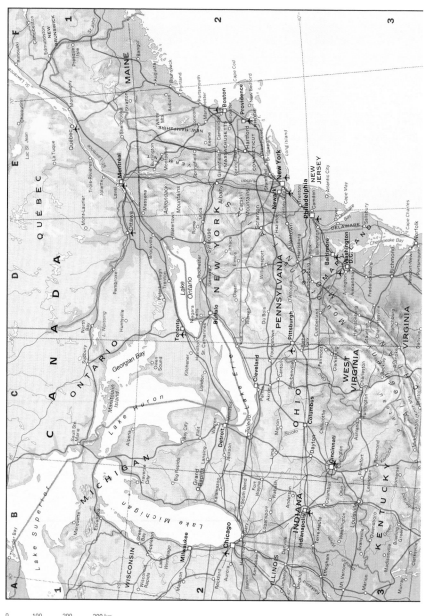

0   100   200   300 km

0   100   200 miles

Scale 1:11 800 000

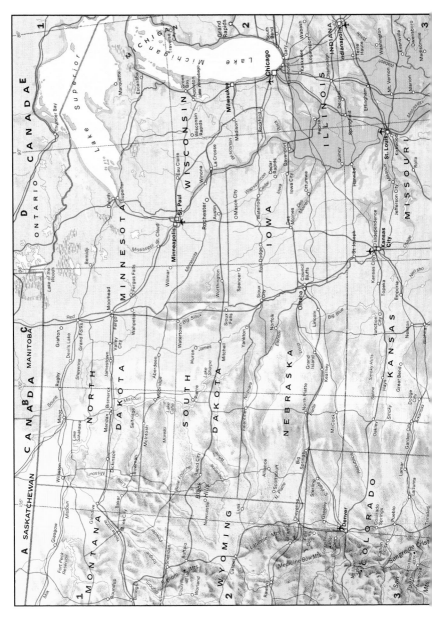

0   100   200   300 km

0   100   200 miles

Scale 1:11 800 000

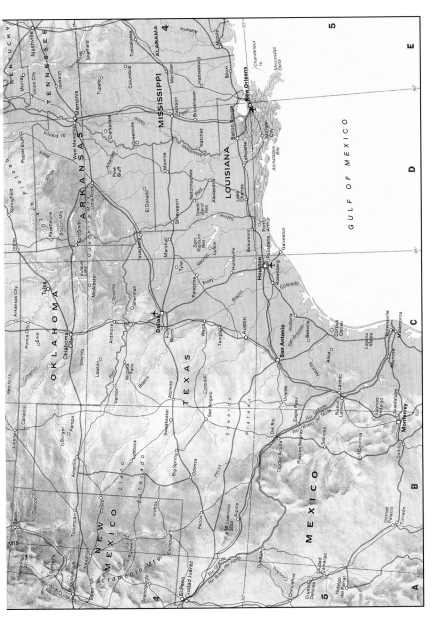

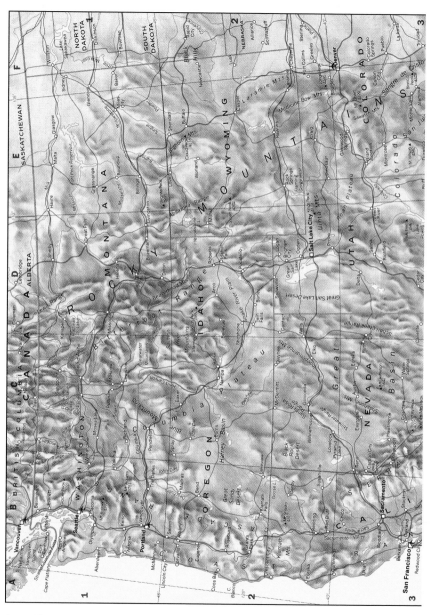

Scale 1:11 800 000

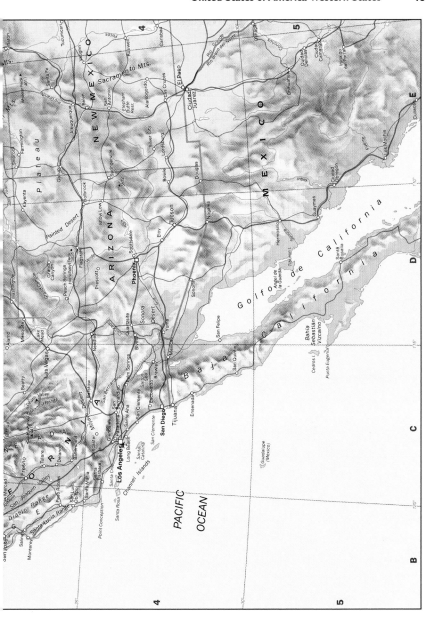

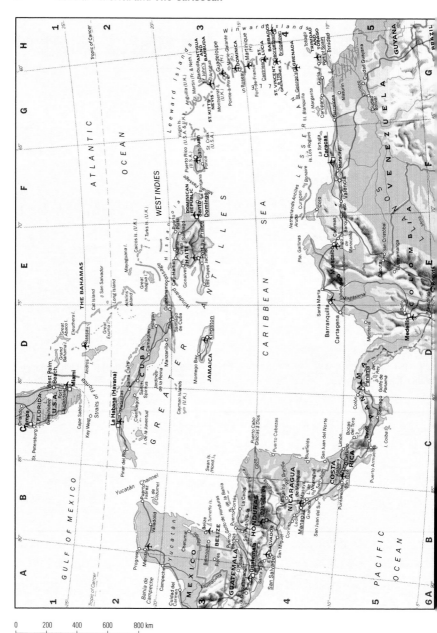

0   200   400   600   800 km

0   250   500 miles

Scale 1:23 500 000

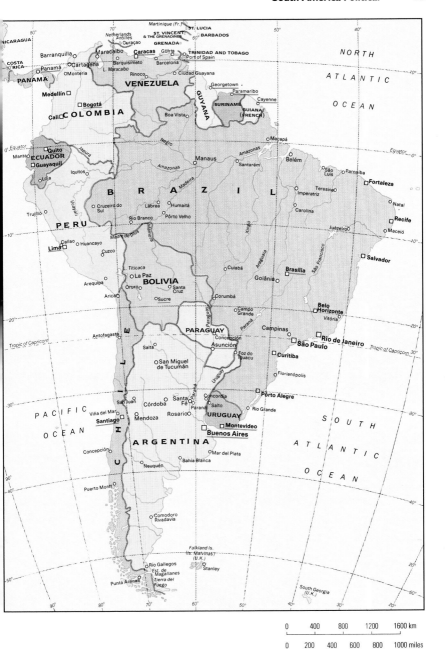

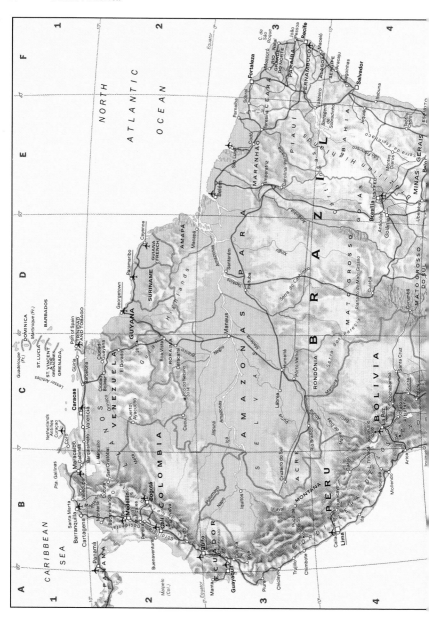

| 0 | 200 | 400 | 600 | 800 | 1000 km |

| 0 | 150 | 300 | 450 | 600 miles |

Scale 1:35 200 000

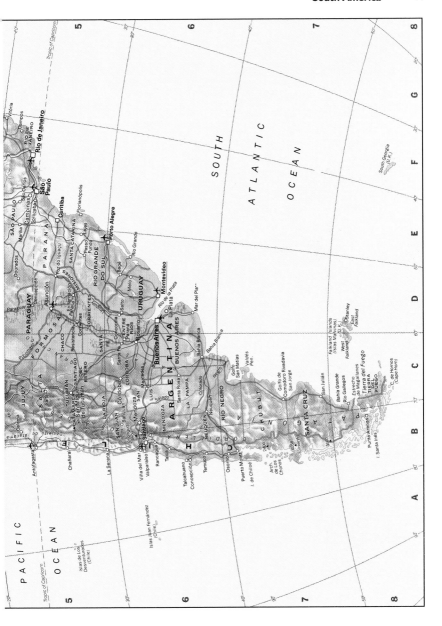

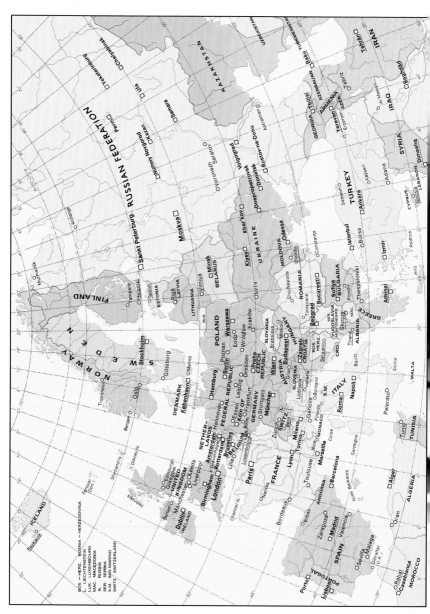

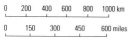

| 0 | 200 | 400 | 600 | 800 | 1000 km |

| 0 | 150 | 300 | 450 | 600 miles |

Scale 1:35 200 000

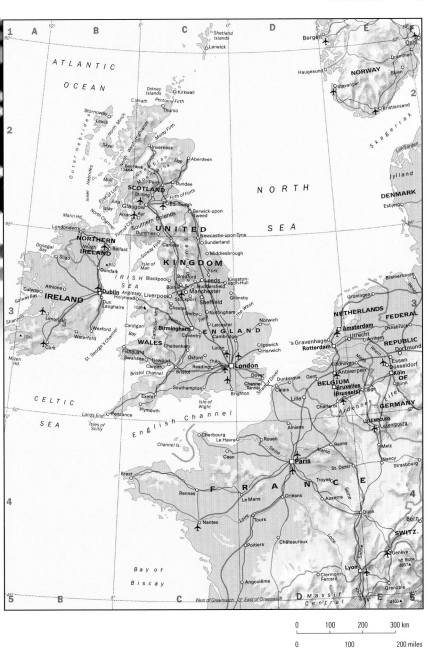

0   100   200   300 km

0   100   200 miles

Scale 1:11 000 000

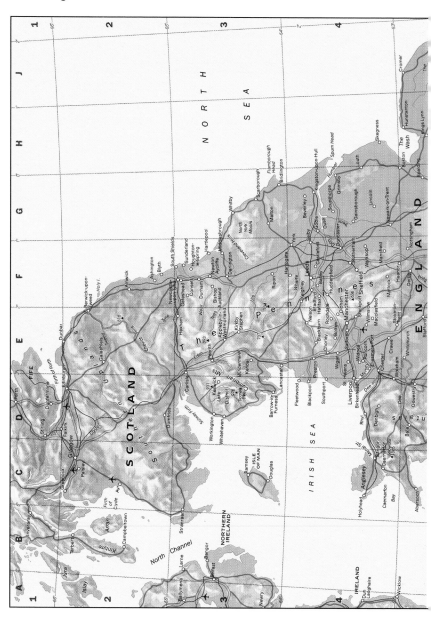

Scale 1:3 600 000

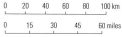

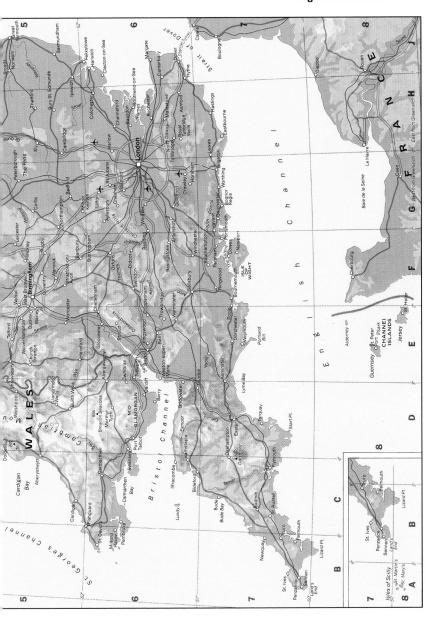

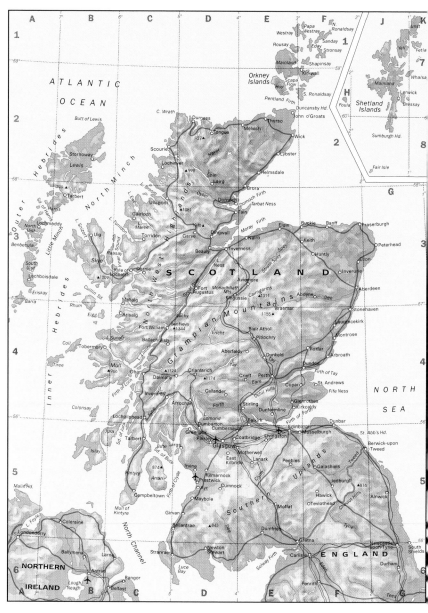

Scale 1:3 600 000

0   20   40   60   80   100 km

0   15   30   45   60 miles

Scale 1:3 600 000

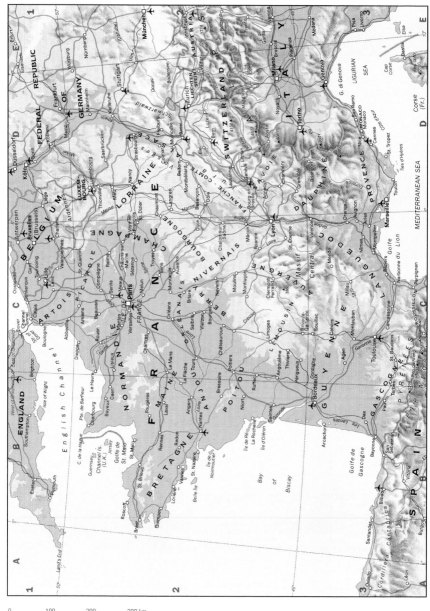

0   100   200   300 km

0   100   200 miles

Scale 1:9 000 000

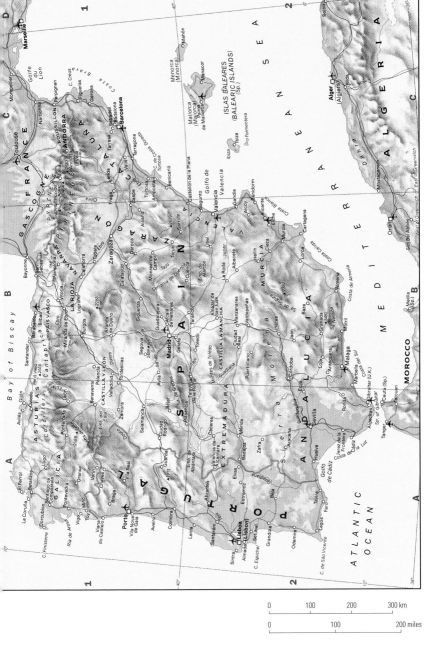

Scale 1:9 000 000

Scale 1:9 000 000

0   100   200   300 km

0   100   200 miles

Scale 1:9 000 000

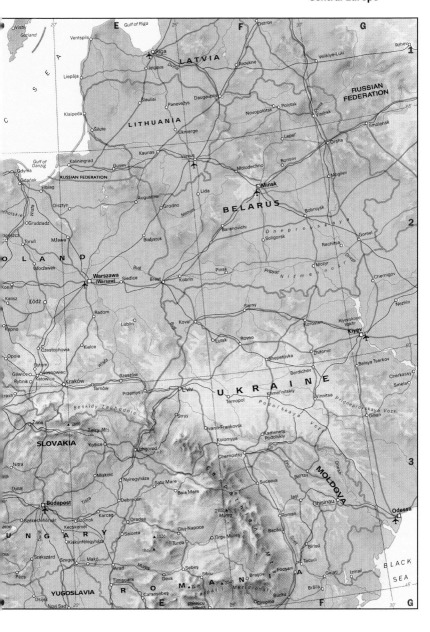

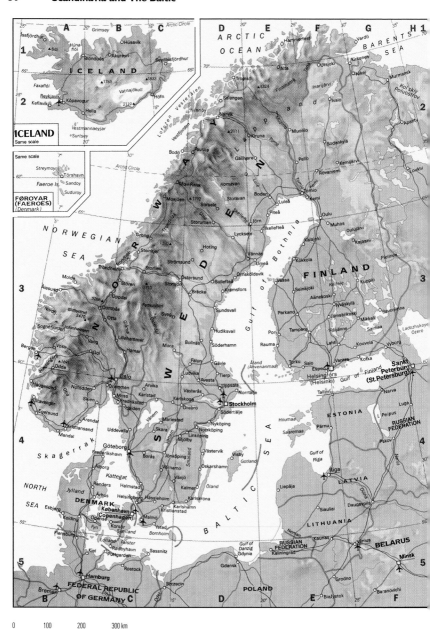

Scale 1:13 200 000

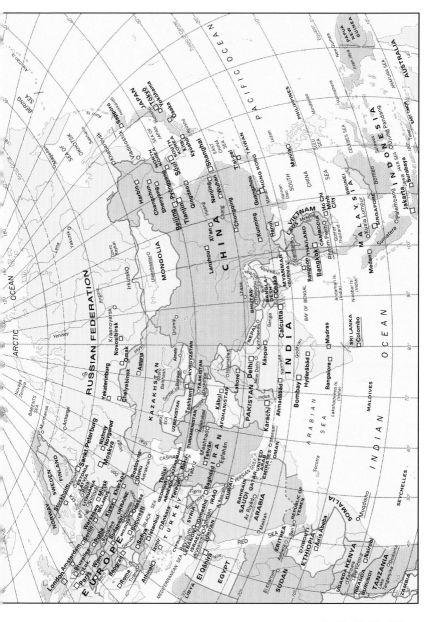

0 400 800 1200 1600 km

0 200 400 600 800 1000 miles

Scale 1:84 000 000

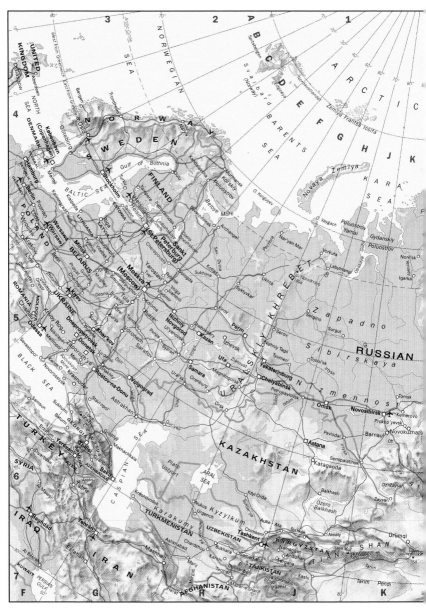

0   200   400   600   800   1000 km

0   150   300   450   600 miles

Scale 1: 37 200 000

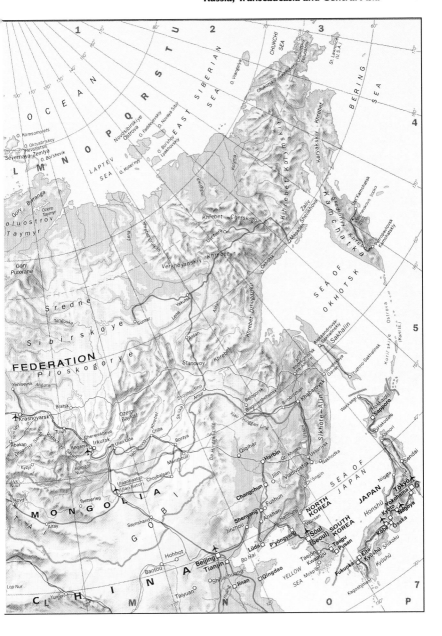

ARCTIC OCEAN

O. Komsomolets

O. Oktyabr'skoy
Revolyutsii
Severnaya Zemlya

O. Bol'shevik

Gory Byrranga

Ozero
Taymyr

p-oluostrov
Taymyr

Gory
Putorana

Sredne

Sibirskoye

Ploskogorye

FEDERATION

Yeniseysk   Angara

Krasnoyarsk

Bratsk

Abakan   Sayan
Zapadnyy   Sayan
Kyzyl

Ozero
Baykal

Irkutsk

Ms.
Nuur

Hövsgöl
Nuur

Ulaanbaatar   Choybalsan

Ulan Bator

Hovd   Tsetserleg

M O N G O L I A

Altay

Saynshand

G O B I

Hohhot

Baotou   Beijing

C H I N A   Tianjin

Lop Nur

Yumen

Taiyuan

Shijiazhuang

Jinan

Bo Hai

Qingdao

YELLOW
SEA

LAPTEV
SEA

O. Kotel'nyy

Novosibirskiye
Ostrova   O. Faddeyevskiy   O. Novaya Sibir'

O. Bol'shoy
Lyakhovskiy

EAST
SIBERIAN
SEA

CHUKCHI
SEA

Ostrov
Vrangelya

Chukotskiy

St. Lawrence I.
U.S.A.

BERING
SEA

Kolyma

Khrebet Cherskogo

Ust'Nera

Verkhoyanskiy   Khrebet

Khrebet Dzhugdzhur

Yakutsk

Lena

Aldan

Stanovoy   Khrebet

Tunguska

Suntar

Oka

Tuluy

Cheremkhovo
Angarsk   Ulan Ude   Chita

Borzya

Manzhouli

Jinzhou

Baotou

Khrebet Koryakskiy

Koryakskiy   Khrebet

Zaliv
Shelikhova

Magadan

Okhotsk

SEA OF
OKHOTSK

Kamchatka

Sredinnyy Khrebet

Ust'-Kamchatsk

Petropavlovsk-
Kamchatskiy

Ostrova
(Kuril Is.)

Kuril'skiye

Aleksandrovsk-
Sakhalinskiy

Sakhalin

Yuzhno-Sakhalinsk

Wakkanai

Hokkaido

Sapporo

Hakodate

Aomori

Sendai

Niigata

JAPAN

Honshū   TOKYO
Yokohama
Kyoto   Kawasaki
Kobe   Osaka   Nagoya
Kita-
Kyūshū   Shikoku
Fukuoka

Kyūshū

Kagoshima

SEA OF
JAPAN

Vladivostok

Nakhodka

Ussuriysk

Sikhote-Alin

Khabarovsk

Amur

Komsomol'sk-
na-Amure

Sovetskaya
Gavan'

Belogorsk

Blagoveshchensk

Svobodnyy

Birobidzhan

Xiao Hinggan Ling

Qiqihar

Da Hinggan Ling

Or Khuara

Harbin

Jilin

Changchun   Fushun

Shenyang   Anshan

Sŏngjin

NORTH
KOREA

Hamhŭng

Wŏnsan

P'yŏngyang

SOUTH
KOREA

(Seoul) SŎUL

Taejŏn   Taegu   Pusan

Kwangju

Mokpo

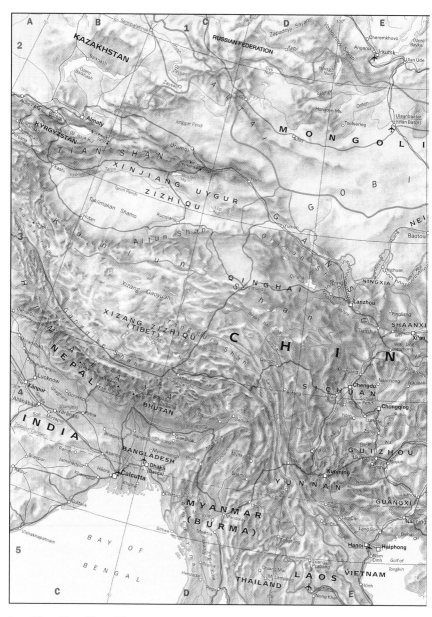

0   200   400   600   800 km

0   100   200   300   400   500 miles

Scale 1: 26 900 000

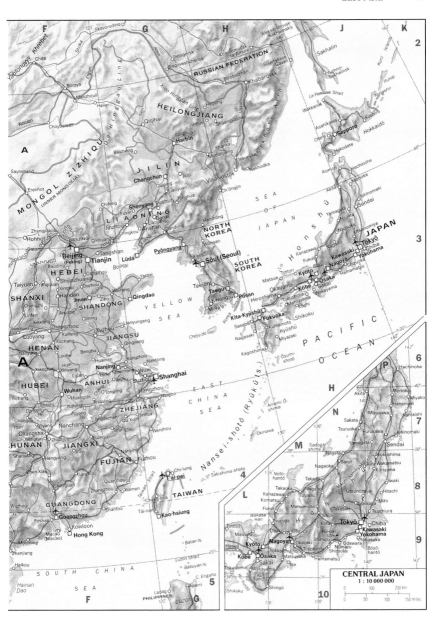

CENTRAL JAPAN
1 : 10 000 000

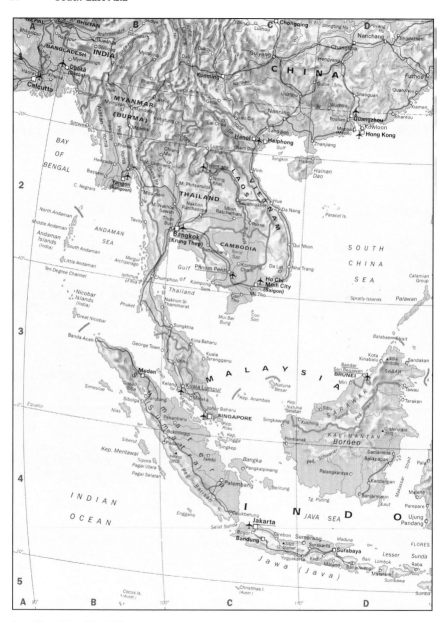

| 0 | 200 | 400 | 600 | 800 km |

| 0 | 100 | 200 | 300 | 400 | 500 miles |

Scale 1: 29 000 000

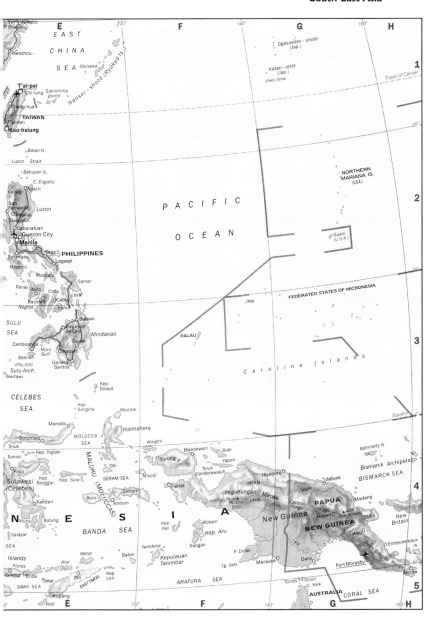

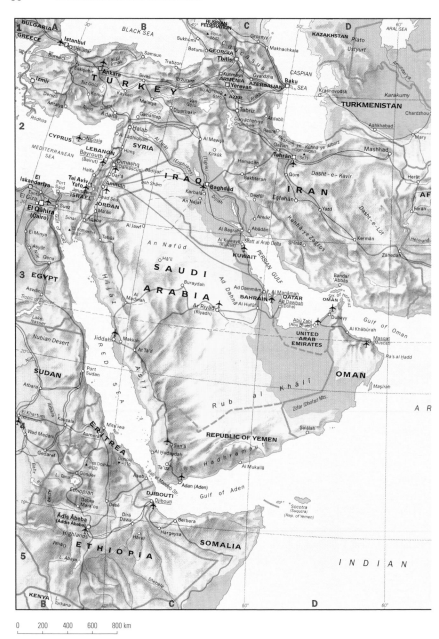

Scale 1: 29 000 000

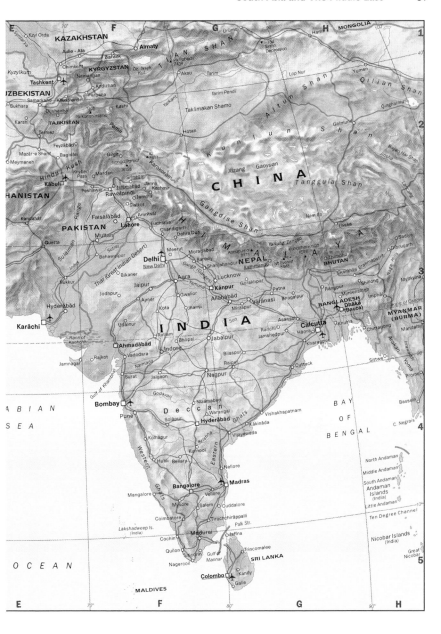

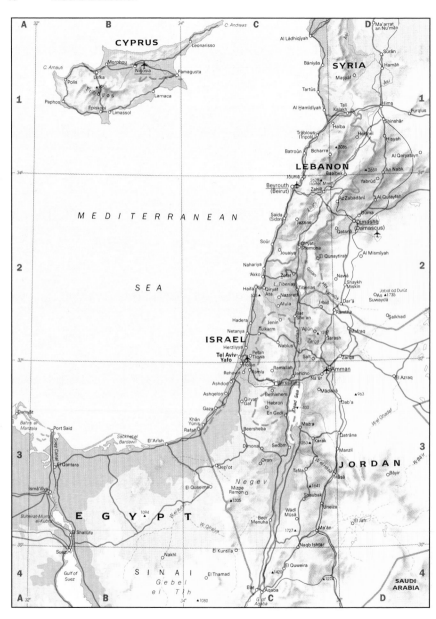

Scale 1: 4 500 000

0   25   50   75   100 km

0   15   30   45   60 miles

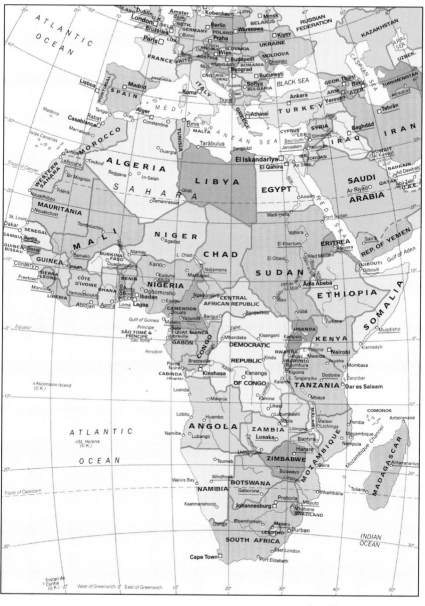

0   400   800   1200   1600 km

0   250   500   750   1000 miles

Scale 1: 66 200 000

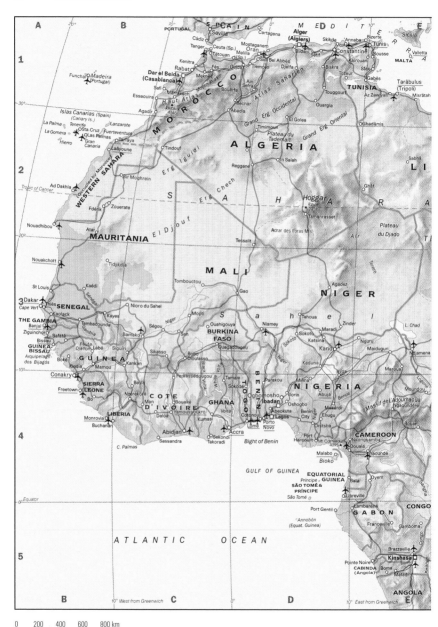

0   200   400   600   800 km

0   100   200   300   400   500 miles

Scale 1: 32 400 000

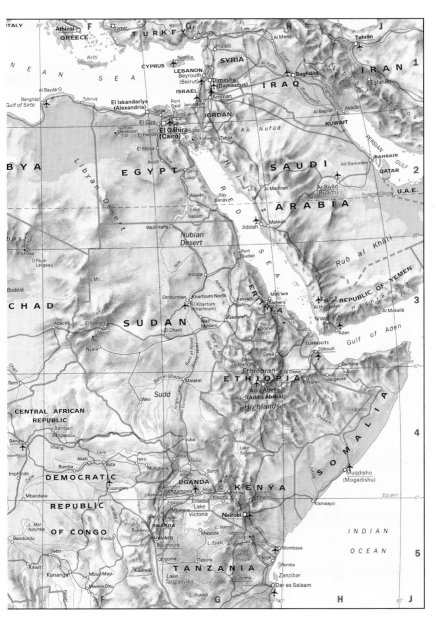

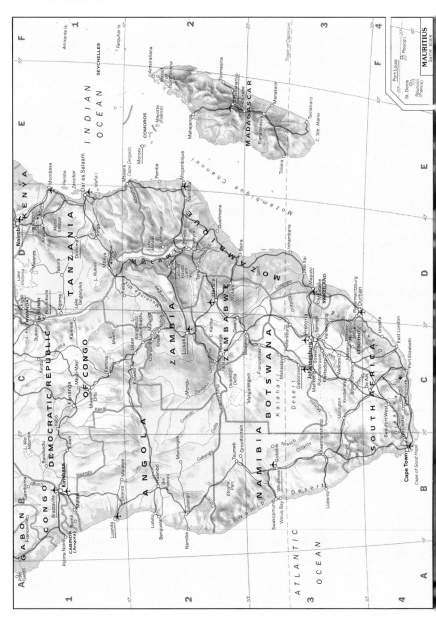

0   200   400   600   800 km

0   100   200   300   400   500 miles

Scale 1: 32 400 000

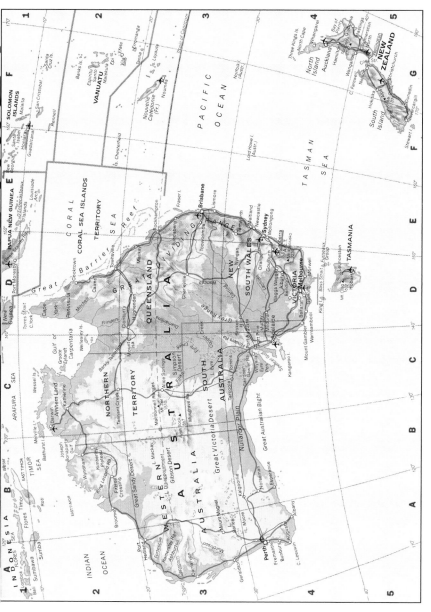

Scale 1 : 40 000 000

| 0 | 200 | 400 | 600 | 800 | 1000 km |
| 0 | 200 | 400 | | 600 miles |

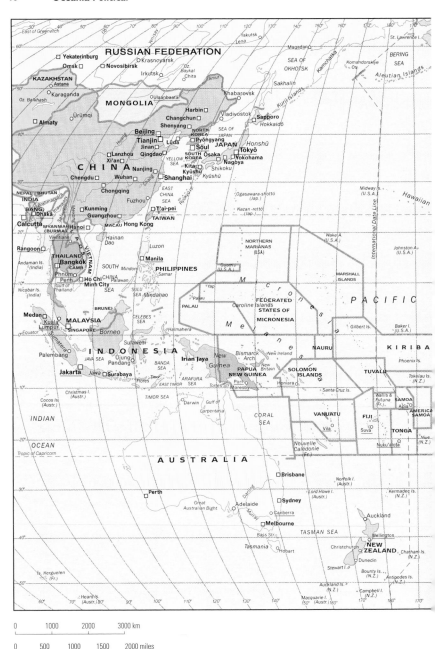

0   1000   2000   3000 km

0   500   1000   1500   2000 miles

Scale 1: 99 300 000

HIDDEN GUIDES

Adventure travel or a relaxing vacation?—"Hidden" guidebooks are the only travel books in the business to provide detailed information on both. Aimed at environmentally aware travelers, our motto is "Adventure Travel Plus." These books combine details on unique hotels, restaurants and sightseeing with information on camping, sports and hiking for the outdoor enthusiast.

THE NEW KEY GUIDES

Based on the concept of ecotourism, The New Key Guides are dedicated to the preservation of Central America's rare and endangered species, architecture and archaeology. Filled with helpful tips, they give travelers everything they need to know about these exotic destinations.

ULTIMATE FAMILY GUIDES

These innovative guides present the best and most unique features of a family destination. Quality is the keynote. In addition to thoroughly covering each destination, they feature short articles and one-line "teasers" that are both fun and informative.

Order Form

Ulysses Press books are available at bookstores everywhere. If any of the following titles are unavailable at your local bookstore, ask the bookseller to order them. Or you can order them directly from Ulysses Press (P.O. Box 3440, Berkeley, CA 94703; 510-601-8301, 800-377-2542).

HIDDEN GUIDEBOOKS

____ Hidden Boston and Cape Cod, $9.95

____ Hidden Carolinas, $15.95

____ Hidden Coast of California, $15.95

____ Hidden Colorado, $13.95

____ Hidden Florida, $15.95

____ Hidden Florida Keys and Everglades, $9.95

____ Hidden Hawaii, $16.95

____ Hidden Idaho, $13.95

____ Hidden Maui, $12.95

____ Hidden Montana, $12.95

____ Hidden New England, $16.95

____ Hidden Oregon, $12.95

____ Hidden Pacific Northwest, $16.95

____ Hidden Rockies, $16.95

____ Hidden San Francisco and Northern California, $15.95

____ Hidden Southern California, $15.95

____ Hidden Southwest, $16.95

____ Hidden Tahiti $15.95

____ Hidden Wyoming $12.95

THE NEW KEY GUIDEBOOKS

____ The New Key to Belize, $14.95

____ The New Key to Cancún and the Yucatán, $13.95

____ The New Key to Costa Rica, $15.95

____ The New Key to Ecuador and the Galápagos, $15.95

____ The New Key to Guatemala, $14.95

ULTIMATE FAMILY GUIDEBOOKS

____ Disneyland and Beyond, $12.95

____ Disney World and Beyond, $12.95

Mark the book(s) you're ordering and enter the total cost here ➾ ☐

California residents add 8% sales tax here ➾ ☐

Shipping, check box for your preferred method and enter cost here ➾ ☐

☐ Book Rate   **FREE! FREE! FREE!**

☐ Priority Mail $3.00 First book, $1.00/each additional book

☐ UPS 2-Day Air $7.00 First book, $1.00/each additional book

☐

Billing, enter total amount due here and check method of payment ➾

☐ Check   ☐ Money Order

☐ VISA/MasterCard _____ Exp. Date _____

Name _____Phone _____

Address _____

_____

City _____ State _____ Zip _____

MONEY-BACK GUARANTEE ON DIRECT ORDERS PLACED THROUGH ULYSSES PRESS.

ABOUT THE AUTHOR

RAY RIEGERT is the author of eight travel books, including *Hidden San Francisco & Northern California*. His most popular work, *Hidden Hawaii*, won the coveted Lowell Thomas Travel Journalism Award for Best Guidebook as well a similar award from the Hawaii Visitors Bureau. In addition to his role as publisher of Ulysses Press, he has written for the *Chicago Tribune*, *Saturday Evening Post*, *San Francisco Examiner & Chronicle* and *Travel & Leisure*. A member of the Society of American Travel Writers, he lives in the San Francisco Bay area with his wife, co-publisher Leslie Henriques, and their son Keith and daughter Alice.

ABOUT THE PHOTOGRAPHER

BOB HOLMES, born in England, launched his U.S. photography career in 1976 when Ansel Adams asked him to come work in the United States. His photographs have appeared in most of the major travel magazines including *National Geographic*, *Geo*, *Islands* and *Travel & Leisure*. In addition to his magazine credits, he has 15 books in print including The Thomas Cook Guides to California, Boston & New England, and Hawaii, as well as Fodor's *Essential California*. He lives in Mill Valley, California with his wife and two daughters.